Ancient Libraries

Edited by
JASON KÖNIG
KATERINA OIKONOMOPOULOU
GREG WOOLF

CAMBRIDGE
UNIVERSITY PRESS

CAMBRIDGE
UNIVERSITY PRESS

University Printing House, Cambridge CB2 8BS, United Kingdom

Cambridge University Press is part of the University of Cambridge.

It furthers the University's mission by disseminating knowledge in the pursuit of education, learning and research at the highest international levels of excellence.

www.cambridge.org
Information on this title: www.cambridge.org/9781316628843

© Cambridge University Press 2013

This publication is in copyright. Subject to statutory exception and to the provisions of relevant collective licensing agreements, no reproduction of any part may take place without the written permission of Cambridge University Press.

First published 2013
4th printing 2014
First paperback edition 2016

A catalogue record for this publication is available from the British Library

Library of Congress Cataloguing in Publication data
Ancient libraries / edited by Jason König, Katerina Oikonomopoulou, Greg Woolf.
   pages cm
Includes bibliographical references and index.
ISBN 978-1-107-01256-1
1. Libraries – History – To 400.   I. König, Jason.   II. Oikonomopoulou, Aikaterini, 1977–
III. Woolf, Greg.
Z722.A53   2013
002.093 – dc23   2012032869

ISBN 978-1-107-01256-1 Hardback
ISBN 978-1-316-62884-3 Paperback

Cambridge University Press has no responsibility for the persistence or accuracy of URLs for external or third-party internet websites referred to in this publication, and does not guarantee that any content on such websites is, or will remain, accurate or appropriate.

Ancient Libraries

The circulation of books was the motor of classical civilisation. But books were both expensive and rare, and so libraries – private and public, royal and civic – played key roles in articulating intellectual life. This collection, written by an international team of scholars, presents a fundamental reassessment of how ancient libraries came into being, how they were organised and how they were used. Drawing on papyrology and archaeology, and on accounts written by those who read and wrote in them, it presents new research on reading cultures, on book collecting and on the origins of monumental library buildings. Many of the traditional stories told about ancient libraries are challenged. Few were really enormous, none was designed as a research centre and occasional conflagrations do not explain the loss of most ancient texts. But the central place of libraries in Greco-Roman culture emerges more clearly than ever.

JASON KÖNIG is Senior Lecturer in Greek at the University of St Andrews. He works broadly on the Greek literature and culture of the Roman Empire. He is author of *Athletics and Literature in the Roman Empire* (2005) and *Saints and Symposiasts: The Literature of Food and the Symposium in Greco-Roman and Early Christian Culture* (2012), and editor, jointly with Tim Whitmarsh, of *Ordering Knowledge in the Roman Empire* (2007).

KATERINA OIKONOMOPOULOU is a postdoctoral research fellow for the programme 'Medicine of the Mind, Philosophy of the Body – Discourses of Health and Well-Being in the Ancient World' at the Humboldt-Universität zu Berlin. She is co-editor, with Frieda Klotz, of *The Philosopher's Banquet: Plutarch's 'Table Talk' in the Intellectual Culture of the Roman Empire* (2011).

GREG WOOLF is Professor of Ancient History at the University of St Andrews. His books include *Becoming Roman: The Origins of Provincial Civilization in Gaul* (1998); *Et tu Brute: The Murder of Julius Caesar and Political Assassination* (2006); *Tales of the Barbarians: Ethnography and Empire in the Roman West* (2011); and *Rome: An Empire's Story* (2012). He has also edited volumes on literacy, on the city of Rome and on Roman religion, and has published widely on ancient history and Roman archaeology.

Contents

List of figures [*page* viii]
Notes on contributors [xi]
Acknowledgments [xviii]
List of abbreviations [xix]

Introduction: approaching the ancient library [1]
GREG WOOLF

PART I CONTEXTS

1 Libraries in ancient Egypt [23]
KIM RYHOLT

2 Reading the libraries of Assyria and Babylonia [38]
ELEANOR ROBSON

3 Fragments of a history of ancient libraries [57]
CHRISTIAN JACOB

PART II HELLENISTIC AND ROMAN REPUBLICAN LIBRARIES

4 Men and books in fourth-century BC Athens [85]
PASQUALE MASSIMO PINTO

5 From text to text: the impact of the Alexandrian library on the work of Hellenistic poets [96]
ANNETTE HARDER

6 Where was the royal library of Pergamum? An institution found and lost again [109]
GAËLLE COQUEUGNIOT

7 Priests, patrons, and playwrights: libraries in Rome before 168 BC [124]
MICHAEL AFFLECK

8　Libraries in a Greek working life: Dionysius of Halicarnassus, a case study in Rome　[137]
DANIEL HOGG

9　Libraries and intellectual debate in the late Republic: the case of the Aristotelian corpus　[152]
FABIO TUTRONE

10　Ashes to ashes? The library of Alexandria after 48 BC　[167]
MYRTO HATZIMICHALI

11　The non-Philodemus book collection in the Villa of the Papyri　[183]
GEORGE W. HOUSTON

12　"Beware of promising your library to anyone": assembling a private library at Rome　[209]
T. KEITH DIX

PART III　LIBRARIES OF THE ROMAN EMPIRE

13　Libraries for the Caesars　[237]
EWEN BOWIE

14　Roman libraries as public buildings in the cities of the Empire　[261]
MATTHEW NICHOLLS

15　Flavian libraries in the city of Rome　[277]
PIER LUIGI TUCCI

16　Archives, books and sacred space in Rome　[312]
RICHARD NEUDECKER

17　Visual supplementation and metonymy in the Roman public library　[332]
DAVID PETRAIN

18　Libraries and reading culture in the High Empire　[347]
WILLIAM A. JOHNSON

19　Myth and history: Galen and the Alexandrian library　[364]
MICHAEL W. HANDIS

20 Libraries and *paideia* in the Second Sophistic: Plutarch and Galen   [377]
ALEXEI V. ZADOROJNYI

21 The professional and his books: special libraries in the ancient world   [401]
VICTOR M. MARTÍNEZ AND MEGAN FINN SENSENEY

Bibliography   [418]
General index   [463]
Index locorum   [474]

List of figures

6.1 The acropolis of Pergamum [G. Coqueugniot after Halfmann 2004 fig. 2]. [*page* 111]
6.2 The sanctuary of Athena Polias [from Bohn 1885 pl. 1]. [112]
6.3 The rooms behind the northern *stoa* – plan [from Bohn 1885 pl. 3]. [112]
6.4 The great hall – section and plan of remains [from Bohn 1885 pl. 33]. [113]
6.5 The Pergamene copy of Phidias' Athena [from Winter 1908 pl. 8]. [114]
6.6 Reconstruction of the great hall as a book repository [from Götze 1937]. [115]
6.7 Reconstruction of the great hall as a banqueting room [drawing by Wulfhild Aulmann for Strocka 2000 fig. 5]. [118]
14.1 The façade of the library of Celsus at Ephesus [reconstruction by M. Nicholls]. [268]
14.2 The library of Rogatianus at Timgad viewed from the street [reconstruction by M. Nicholls]. [271]
15.1 The plan of the *Templum Pacis* according to the investigations of I. Gismondi (in 1941–6), G. Gatti (in 1959) and Bianchi-Meneghini (in 2007). Respectively published in Lugli (1946) tav. 5; Gatti (1960) 219; Meneghini, Santangeli Valenzani (2007) 5 (adapted)]. [279]
15.2 Flavian and Severan brickwork (inside the monastery) and squared-stone masonry of the rear wall of the *Templum Pacis* (towards the Basilica of Maxentius). On the right, imprint of the Flavian (two lowermost courses) and Severan blocks (I–XXI and cornice) of the rear wall of the *Templum Pacis* on the buttress of the Basilica of Maxentius [photos: author]. [280]
15.3 The wall with niches – the one on the left is original – incorporated into the monastery of SS. Cosma e Damiano [photos and drawing: author]. [282]
15.4 The corner of the hall towards the Via Sacra in a drawing by B. Peruzzi (Uffizi, Arch. 383, adapted from Bartoli, A. [1914–22] vol. II.

List of figures   ix

fig. 216. In the box, the rear wall of the *Templum Pacis* along the Clivus ad Carinas (elevation adapted from B. M. Apollonj Ghetti, "Nuove considerazioni sulla basilica romana dei SS. Cosma e Damiano", *Rivista di Archeologia Cristiana* 50 (1974) fig. 28); B. Peruzzi's drawings (Uffizi, Arch. 382–3) from Bartoli, A. [1914–22] vol. II, figs 215–16 [photos: author]. [284]

15.5 Plans (at the same scale) of the library of the *Templum Pacis* – the arrows indicate the entrances (above, right) and the Flavian library of Apollo (below) [drawing: author]. Apollo's library from Iacopi (2007) 13 and Iacopi, Tedone (2005/2006) tav. 2; the lost fragment 20b of the Marble Plan from Carettoni, Colini, Cozza, Gatti (1960) *La pianta marmorea di Roma antica*, pl. XXII. [287]

15.6 The area involved in the fire of AD 192, from the *Templum Pacis* (above) to the Palatine hill (below) [drawing: author]. [294]

16.1 Rome's imperial fora. Reconstructed view by Inklink, from Meneghini (2007) fig.16. [313]

16.2 Rome, Forum of Trajan. Reconstructed view by Inklink, from Meneghini (2007) fig. 93. [315]

16.3 Rome, location of the *Atrium Libertatis*, from Coarelli (1999b) fig. 6. [319]

16.4 Rome, the sacred area and libraries of Palatine Apollo, from Rodríguez Almeida (1981) pl. 14. [321]

16.5 Rome, *Templum Pacis*, from Colini (1937) pl. 3. [324]

16.6 Rome, library and map room of *Templum Pacis*, from Castagnoli and Cozza (1956–8) fig. 15. [325]

16.7 Portrait of Chrysippos from the area of the *Bibliotheca Pacis*, after Papini (2005) fig. 3. [325]

16.8 Rome, *Templum Pacis*. Reconstructed view by Inklink, from Meneghini (2007) fig. 54. [327]

16.9 Pergamum, library in the *Asklepieion* with statue of Hadrian, from Ziegenaus and De Luca (1968) pl. 68 and Wegner (1956) pl.14b. [330]

18.1 Forum of Trajan. James Packer's reconstruction of the SW library. Packer 1997, vol. I, fig. 78. [348]

18.2 (a) Sterling Memorial Library. (b) Biblioteca Angelica, Rome. [349]

Notes on contributors

MICHAEL AFFLECK is a PhD student in Classics at the University of Queensland, investigating the development of Roman libraries in the late Republic and early Empire, particularly as reflected in the use made of libraries, both public and private, by Roman writers, taking Pliny the Elder as the main example. He is also a librarian with 15 years' experience in academic and other libraries.

EWEN BOWIE was Praelector in Classics at Corpus Christi College, Oxford, from 1965 to 2007, and successively University Lecturer, Reader, and Professor of Classical Languages and Literature in the University of Oxford. He is now an Emeritus Fellow of Corpus Christi College. He has published articles on early Greek elegiac, iambic, and lyric poetry; on Aristophanes; on Hellenistic poetry; and on many aspects of Greek literature and culture in the context of the Roman Empire from the first century BC to the third century AD, including Plutarch and the Greek novels. He recently edited (jointly with Jas Elsner) a collection of papers on *Philostratus* (Cambridge, 2009) and (jointly with Lucia Athanassaki) a collection of papers entitled *Archaic and Classical Choral Song* (2011). He is currently completing a commentary on Longus' *Daphnis and Chloe* for Cambridge University Press.

GAËLLE COQUEUGNIOT is a researcher at the Institut de recherche sur l'architecture antique, Lyon. She taught at the Université Lyon II and at University College, London. Her research primarily concerns the administration and architecture of the Hellenistic Aegean, through the study of ancient archives and administrative centres. She is also assistant director of the excavations at the Graeco-Roman site of Dura-Europos (Syria). Her publications include several articles on the organization of Graeco-Roman archives and libraries, and on the agora and sanctuaries of Dura-Europos. She is also the editor with P. Leriche and S. de Pontbriand of *Europos-Doura Varia 1* (2012).

T. KEITH DIX is Associate Professor in the Department of Classics at the University of Georgia. He has published articles on ancient libraries and literacy, Virgil, Ovid, Aristophanes, Athenian history, and epigraphy. He is the author with Carl Anderson of 'Beware the Ides of March: Rome in 44 BCE', a classroom game (in development) in the Reacting to the Past pedagogy.

MICHAEL W. HANDIS is Associate Professor and Associate Librarian for Collection Management at the Mina Rees Library, The Graduate and University Center, City University of New York. His research interests include ancient and Byzantine history, ancient libraries, and political history. He has articles published in the *WESS Newsletter* (2009) and *Collection Building* (2007), and entries in *Milestone Documents in American History* (2008); the *Scribner Encyclopedia of American Lives* (2005); and the *Encyclopedia of Lesbian, Gay, Bisexual and Transgender History in America* (2004). In 2011, he delivered a paper to the Library Association of the City University of New York on his research in ancient libraries. He is currently on sabbatical researching the library of Pantainos in Athens, Greece.

ANNETTE HARDER is Professor of Ancient Greek Language and Literature at the University of Groningen in the Netherlands. She has written on Greek tragedy and published a number of mythographic papyri, but her main field of interest is Hellenistic poetry. She has published various articles on this subject, organises the biennial Groningen Workshops on Hellenistic Poetry, and has edited several volumes of the series *Hellenistica Groningana*. She has also published a Dutch translation of a selection of Callimachus' poetry and an edition with introduction and commentary of Callimachus' *Aetia*.

MYRTO HATZIMICHALI is Lecturer in Classics at the University of Cambridge. Her research interests centre on intellectual and cultural history, especially on the ways in which literary and philosophical texts were transmitted, received, and professionally studied in the Hellenistic and early Imperial periods. She is the author of *Potamo of Alexandria and the Emergence of Eclecticism in Late Hellenistic Philosophy* (Cambridge, 2011), and has contributed chapters to volumes on the philosopher Antiochus of Ascalon and on Hellenistic poetry, as well as to the forthcoming *Encyclopaedism from Antiquity to the Renaissance* (eds. König and Woolf).

DANIEL HOGG is Head of Classics at Cranleigh School, Surrey. His main research interests lie in Greek and Roman historiography of the late Republic and early Empire. He wrote his D.Phil. dissertation on the relationship between speech and action in the *Antiquitates Romanae* of Dionysius of Halicarnassus. He has published variously on Dionysius, on aspects of early Roman history, and on the intellectual history of the ancient world. He completed his D.Phil. at the University of Oxford in 2009, and has held teaching and postdoctoral research positions at Oxford, St Andrews and Ludwig-Maximilians-Universität, Munich.

GEORGE W. HOUSTON is Professor of Classics Emeritus at the University of North Carolina at Chapel Hill. His research interests include Latin literature, Latin epigraphy, Roman technology, and libraries and book collections in the Roman world. He has published extensively on ancient libraries, including papers on the personnel of public libraries (*TAPA* 2002), public libraries in the city of Rome (*MEFRA* 2006; with T. Keith Dix), and book collections in Egypt (in *Ancient Literacies*, edited by W. Johnson and H. Parker, 2009). He is currently at work on a book-length study of the contents and management of book collections in the Roman world.

CHRISTIAN JACOB is Directeur de recherche at the CNRS and Directeur d'études at the Ecole des hautes études en sciences sociales, Paris. His main research area is scholarly practices and traditions in the ancient world. Among other topics, he focused on Alexandrian literary and scientific culture, on Athenaeus of Naucratis, and on Greek geography and cartography. He is also interested in comparatism and interdisciplinary approaches to the history of knowledge and literate cultures and has edited various collections of essays on the history of libraries, on textual canonicity, and scholarship. His main current project is the *Lieux de savoir* series (two volumes already published, 2007 and 2011).

WILLIAM A. JOHNSON, Professor of Classical Studies at Duke University, works broadly in the cultural history of Greece and Rome. He has lectured and published on Plato, Hesiod, Herodotus, Cicero, Pliny (both Elder and Younger), Gellius, Lucian, and on a variety of topics relating to books and readers, both ancient and modern. Recent work has focused on establishing deep contextualization for specific ancient reading communities, with particular attention to the relationship between literary texts and social structure. His books include *Readers and Reading Culture in the High Empire, a Study of Elite Reading Communities* (2010), *Ancient Literacies* (with Holt Parker, 2009), and *Bookrolls and Scribes in Oxyrhynchus* (Toronto, 2004). Forthcoming are two edited volumes: *The Essential Herodotus and Thucydides* and (with Daniel Richter) *The Oxford Handbook to the Second Sophistic.*

JASON KÖNIG is Senior Lecturer in Greek at the University of St Andrews. His publications include *Athletics and Literature in the Roman Empire* (Cambridge, 2005), *Ordering Knowledge in the Roman Empire* (Cambridge, 2007) (jointly edited with Tim Whitmarsh), and *Greek Literature in the Roman*

Empire (2010). His most recent book is *Saints and Symposiasts: The Literature of Food and the Symposium in Greco-Roman and Early-Christian Culture* (Cambridge, 2012).

VICTOR M. MARTÍNEZ is a postdoctoral scholar in the Department of Classics at the University of North Carolina at Chapel Hill. He was awarded his doctorate in Art History from the University of Illinois at Urbana-Champaign in 2009. His research concerns the reception of Greek myth and images in pre-Roman Italy and intersections between pottery and the Roman economy. His publications include 'Terracotta sculpture and objects' in *Palatine East Excavations*, vol. II (forthcoming) and 'Western Roman Amphorae' in *Palatine East Excavations*, vol. III (in preparation). His current book project is tentatively entitled, *Networks of Intoxication: the Case of Late Roman Wines from Italy, ca. 250–700 CE*, which takes a network approach to understanding the ceramic evidence for the Italian wine industry during the declining years of the Roman Empire.

RICHARD NEUDECKER is Researcher at the Deutsches Archäologisches Institut in Rome and teaches Classical Archaeology at the Ludwig-Maximilians-Universität of Munich. His publications on *Die Skulpturenausstattung römischer Villen in Italien* (1988) and *Die Pracht der Latrine. Zum Wandel öffentlicher Bedürfnisanstalten in der kaiserzeitlichen Stadt* (1994) fall within a wider research interest in the cultural history of Roman Imperial times; with Paul Zanker he edited *Lebenswelten. Bilder und Räume in der römischen Stadt der Kaiserzeit* (2005).

MATTHEW NICHOLLS is Lecturer in the Department of Classics at the University of Reading. His research concerns cultural, intellectual, and architectural history at Rome and in the provinces of the Empire. He is particularly interested in ancient public libraries, on which he is writing a book, and has published numerous articles on the subject. These include pieces in the *Journal of Roman Studies* (2011) and *Greece & Rome* (2010) on the implications for library history of the newly discovered *Peri Alupias* of Galen. He is also interested in digital architectural modelling as a way of exploring ancient cities and buildings.

KATERINA OIKONOMOPOULOU is Lecturer (elect) in Classics at the University of Patras, Greece. She completed a D.Phil. in Classics at the University of Oxford, and from 2007 to 2010 she was Postdoctoral Research Fellow for the Leverhulme project 'Science and Empire in the Roman World' at the University of St Andrews. She is currently a postdoctoral research fellow at the Humboldt-Universität zu Berlin. Her publications include *The*

Philosopher's Banquet: Plutarch's Table Talk *in the Intellectual Culture of the Roman Empire* (co-edited with Frieda Klotz, 2011).

DAVID PETRAIN is Assistant Professor of Classical Studies at Vanderbilt University. His research focuses on interactions between Greek and Roman literary traditions, and on cross-fertilizations between the communicative strategies of verbal and visual art. His publications have treated Roman elegy, Hellenistic epigram, and the narrative structures of visual storytelling in the ancient world. He is the co-editor, with Jan Kwapisz and Mikolaj Szymanski, of *The Muse at Play: Riddles and Wordplay in Greek and Latin Poetry* (2012). His monograph, *Homer in Stone: The* Tabulae Iliacae *in their Roman Context*, is forthcoming from Cambridge University Press.

PASQUALE MASSIMO PINTO is Researcher and Lecturer in Classical Philology at the University of Bari, Italy. His research interests concern the Athenian culture of the fourth century BC, the Attic orators (textual and biographical tradition), papyrology, and the history of classical studies. He is the author of *Per la storia del testo di Isocrate* (2003) and *Medea Norsa – Harold Idris Bell. Carteggio 1926–1949* (2005). His latest publications include: 'P. Kellis III Gr. 95 and Evagoras I', *ZPE* (2009); 'Monumenti d'autore e storie di testi', *Philologus* (2010); and 'Constantinos Simonidis in the Gennadius Library', *The New Griffon* (2011). He is one of the editors of a new edition of Isocrates (forthcoming).

ELEANOR ROBSON is Reader in Ancient Middle Eastern Science at the University of Cambridge and the British Institute for the Study of Iraq's Chair of Council. Her research focuses on the socio-political contexts of intellectual activity in ancient Mesopotamia and the online edition of cuneiform texts. She has published widely on topics from Babylonian mathematics to Sumerian literature to the ethics of postwar cultural heritage. She is the author of *Mathematics in Ancient Iraq: A Social History* (2008, winner of the History of Science Society's Pfizer Prize, 2011), co-editor with Karen Radner of *The Oxford Handbook of Cuneiform Culture* (2011), and director of the AHRC-funded research project, 'The Geography of Knowledge in Assyria and Babylonia, 700–200 BC' (2007–12). With Steve Tinney and Niek Veldhuis, she runs the Open Richly Annotated Cuneiform Corpus (oracc.org).

KIM RYHOLT is Associate Professor of Egyptology at the University of Copenhagen. He is the director of the Center for Canon and Identity Formation (University of Copenhagen Programme of Excellence) and the Papyrus Carlsberg Collection. His research interests include political history, propaganda, literature, and libraries. He has published extensively on literature in the demotic script and the Tebtunis temple library, including several monographs. He is currently editing (with G. Barjamovic) and contributing to a volume entitled *Libraries before Alexandria*, which presents an historical account of libraries in Egypt, Mesopotamia and Anatolia from *c.* 2600 BC to AD 300.

MEGAN FINN SENSENEY earned her Master of Science in Library and Information Science in 2008 and is currently pursuing a Certificate of Advanced Study in Digital Libraries at the Graduate School of Library and Information Science at the University of Illinois at Urbana-Champaign, where she also serves as Project Coordinator for Research Services. Her research interests include library history, special collections, and digital humanities. She has previously published an article on the topic of ancient libraries in the *International Journal of the Book*, entitled 'The Book as Performance: Written Works, Theater, and Repositories in Classical Antiquity' (2010).

PIER LUIGI TUCCI is Assistant Professor of Roman Art and Architecture in the Department of History of Art, Johns Hopkins University. He has also held posts at the Scuola Normale Superiore of Pisa, the Istituto Italiano per gli Studi Filosofici in Naples, and Royal Holloway, University of London and Exeter University in the UK. His research interests cross the boundaries between Classics and archaeology and include Late Antiquity, the Middle Ages, and the Renaissance. He has published several papers on various ancient monuments in Rome, as well as on Renaissance architecture and antiquarianism – he is the author of *Laurentius Manlius. La riscoperta dell'antica Roma, la nuova Roma di Sisto IV* (2001). He is currently finishing a book on the *Templum Pacis* and working on the final publication of his research on the Capitoline Hill.

FABIO TUTRONE is a Research Fellow in Latin literature at the University of Palermo (Italy), where he also obtained his PhD in Greek and Latin Philology and Culture in 2009. He works on different themes related to ancient literature, science, and philosophy, but in particular the study of animal representations and man–animal relationships in Roman culture. He has published several papers on Lucretius and his cultural background, as well as on literary topics of ethical and anthropological interest (education, violence, technical knowledge, and man's relationship to nature). His contributions include a major book on animals in Latin literature, *Filosofi e animali in Roma antica. Modelli di animalità e umanità in Lucrezio e Seneca* (2012).

GREG WOOLF is Professor of Ancient History at the University of St Andrews. His research concerns the cultural history of the Roman Empire. He has published on literacy, on monumentality, on the ancient economy, and most recently on religious history. His books include *Becoming Roman: the origins of provincial civilization in Gaul* (1998) and *Tales of the Barbarians: ethnography and imperialism in the Roman West* (2011). He is also the editor with Alan Bowman of *Literacy and Power in the Ancient* World (1994); with Catharine Edwards of *Rome the Cosmopolis* (2003); and with Jason König of *Encyclopaedism from Antiquity to the Renaissance* (forthcoming) which derives from the same project as this volume.

ALEXEI V. ZADOROJNYI studied Classics in Moscow and in Oxford; he received his PhD from the University of Exeter in 1999. He is currently Senior Lecturer in Classics at the University of Liverpool. His research interests include intellectual history under the Empire, Greco-Roman literary criticism, intertextuality, and paratextual 'writtenness'; to date he has been exploring these themes mainly, but not exclusively, through Plutarch. He is co-editing (with Fran Titchener) the *Cambridge Companion to Plutarch*.

Acknowledgments

From the first organisation of the Ancient Libraries Conference, held at the University of St Andrews in September 2008, through the editing of this book, we have become very conscious of how many scholars have been thinking about ancient libraries for much longer than we have. We are grateful too for the contributions of all the participants, but perhaps it is not invidious to single out for special thanks Keith Dix, George Houston, Christian Jacob, William Johnson, and Matthew Nicholls who have been generous with advice and tolerant of our meanderings around the stacks that are so familiar to them. We are also very glad to acknowledge the support of our colleagues in the School of Classics at St Andrews, in particular of Joseph Howley, then studying with us and now at Columbia University, and of Margaret Goudie who organised the original conference with the same cheerful efficiency she has organised so many others. The staff of the University Library at St Andrews, of the Sackler and Bodleian Libraries in Oxford, and of the Joint Library of the Hellenic and Roman Societies have been a constant support. Michael Sharp and his colleagues at the Press have helped us transform a conversation into a book. We close with gratitude to the Leverhulme Trust, the generosity of which has made all this possible.

List of abbreviations

ANRW	Temporini, H. and W. Haase (eds.) (1972–) *Aufstieg und Niedergang der Römischen Welt*, 88 vols. to date. Berlin and New York.
BNP	Cancik, H., H. Schneider and M. Landfester (eds.) (1996–) *Brill's New Pauly: Encyclopaedia of the Ancient World* (English transl. managing editors: C. F. Salazar and F. G. Gentry), 20 vols. Leiden.
CAD	Gelb, J. *et al.* (eds.) (1956–) *The Assyrian Dictionary of the Oriental Institute of the University of Chicago*, 20 vols. to date. Chicago, IL. Downloadable from http://oi.uchicago.edu/research/pubs/catalog/cad/.
CAG	*Commentaria in Aristotelem Graeca* (1882–1902). Berlin.
CAH	Edwards, I. E. S. *et al.* (eds.) (1970–2000) *The Cambridge Ancient History*, 14 vols. Cambridge.
CIG	Boeckhuis, A. (1827–77) *Corpus Inscriptionum Graecarum*, 4 vols. Berlin.
CIL	*Corpus Inscriptionum Latinarum* (1896–). Berlin.
CMG	*Corpus Medicorum Graecorum* (1915–). Leipzig and Berlin.
DNP	Cancik, H. and H. Schneider (eds.) (1996–) *Der Neue Pauly*, 20 vols. Stuttgart and Weimar.
FIRA	Riccobono, S. (1941) *Fontes Iuris Romanae Antejustiniani*, 3 vols. Florence.
IG	*Inscriptiones Graecae* (1913–) 2nd edn. Berlin.
IGR	Cagnat, R. *et al.* (1906–28) *Inscriptiones Graecae ad res Romanas pertinentes*. Paris.
IK Smyrna	Petzl, G. (1982–7) *Die Inschriften von Smyrna* (Inschriften griechischer Städte aus Kleinasien 23), 2 vols. Bonn.
ILS	Dessau, H. (1892–1916) *Inscriptiones Latinae Selectae*, 5 vols. Berlin.
IvE	H. Wankel, R. Merkelbach, *et al.* (eds.) (1979–84) *Inschriften von Ephesos*, 8 vols. Bonn.
IvP	Fränkel, M. (1890–5) *Inschriften von Pergamon*, 2 vols. Berlin.

List of abbreviations

Kühn	Kühn, G. C. (ed.) (1821–33) *Galeni Opera Omnia*. Leipzig.
LIMC	Fondation pour le Lexicon Iconographicum Mythologiae Classicae (ed.) (1981–99) *Lexicon Iconographicum Mythologiae Classicae*, 8 vols. Zurich-Munich.
LTUR	Steinby, E.M. (ed.) (1993–2000) *Lexicon Topographicum Urbis Romae*. Rome.
NSA	*Notizie degli scavi di antichità*.
OGIS	W. Dittenberg (ed.) (1905) *Orientis Graeci Inscriptiones Selectae*. Leipzig.
ORF	Malcovati, H. (1976–9) *Oratorum Romanorum Fragmenta* 4th edn., 2 vols. Milan.
PIR	Groag, E. *et al.* (eds.) (1933–) *Prosopographia Imperii Romani*, 2nd edn. Berlin.
RAC	F. J. Dölger *et al.* (eds.) (1950–) *Reallexicon für Antike und Christentum*, 24 vols. to date. Stuttgart.
RE	A. Pauly and H. Wissowa (eds.) (1839–80) *Paulys Realencyclopädie der classischen Altertumswissenschaft*, 84 vols. Stuttgart.
RlA	M. P. Streck *et al.* (eds.) (1932–) *Reallexikon der Assyriologie und Vorderasiatischen Archäologie*, 12 vols. to date. Berlin.
SAA	S. Parpola *et al.* (eds.) (1987–) *The State Archives of Assyria*, 18 vols. to date, Helsinki. Online at *http://oracc.org/saao*.
SEG	*Supplementum Epigraphicum Graecum* (1923–). Leiden.
TLL	*Thesaurus Linguae Latinae* (1900–). Leipzig.

Journal abbreviations not in *L'année philologique*:

RendLinc	*Rendiconti della Reale Accademia dei Lincei*.
SL&I	*Studi Latini e Italiani*.

Papyrological collections are cited according to the abbreviations listed in *The Checklist of Editions of Greek, Latin, Demotic and Coptic Papyri, Ostraka and Tablets* edited by John F. Oates, Oakville, CT; Oxford: Oxbow for American Society of Papyrologists, 5th edn. 2001.

Where the names of ancient authors and the titles of books are abbreviated in the notes, it is according to the conventions listed in the *Oxford Classical Dictionary*.

Introduction

Approaching the ancient library

GREG WOOLF

Histories of ancient libraries

'Bibliotheca' takes its name from the Greek, for *biblion* is translated 'of books' and *thēkē* is a storeroom.[1]

That definition of *bibliotheca* – the most common Latin term for library – is taken from the *Etymologies* of Isidore, Bishop of Seville, a 'vastly important conduit for classical antiquity into the medieval world'.[2] Composed in the first decades of the seventh century AD, by which time most of the Iberian peninsula had been part of the Visigothic kingdom for nearly two centuries, the *Etymologies* themselves were both the last Latin encyclopaedic work of antiquity and one of the foundations of mediaeval scholarship. Like the *Natural History* of Pliny the Elder and Solinus' *Collection of Memorable Things*, Isidore's compendium preserved and passed on a small part of Greek and Roman knowledge, once the great libraries of antiquity were gone. Unlike them, the fruits of Isidore's miscellenistic research were subordinated to a thoroughly Christian reordering of knowledge.

The research from which this book derives was conducted as part of a project sponsored by the Leverhulme Trust on *Science and Empire in the Roman World*. One of the objectives of that project was to examine the institutional and intellectual frameworks of knowledge production under the Empire, and the means by which that knowledge was organised and transmitted through space and time. A companion volume on pre-modern encyclopaedisms considers grand projects of synthesis and organisation at the level of the book.[3] This volume considers the corresponding physical institution, the ancient library. As the example of Isidore shows, these discussions are in practice closely interwoven.[4]

Isidore offers us not only a definition of library – if one which we will need to refine – but also the only history of libraries that has survived

---

[1] Isid. *Etym*. 6.3.1.   [2] Henderson 2007a: 151. For expansion of the theme, Henderson 2007b.
[3] König and Woolf forthcoming b. The project was also conceived as a successor to König and Whitmarsh 2007.
[4] On encyclopaedism and libraries, see also Too 2010: 116–26, König and Woolf forthcoming a.

from antiquity. Yet Greek and Roman libraries were almost a thousand years old by his day, and there had been earlier reflections on the theme, reflections on which Isidore drew, if mostly indirectly. It is possible to trace a series of ancient attempts to write a history of libraries. Modern accounts of the phenomenon, based largely on the same snippets of information, have tended to reproduce the ancient narrative perhaps more than has been realised or admitted.

The first such account about which we know anything was a three-book work entitled *de Bibliothecis* composed by Varro in the last century BC. It is often mentioned along with the story that he was commissioned by the dictator Caesar to organise the first public libraries of Rome.[5] At the very least both Varro's work and Caesar's project attest a growing sense in the late Republic of the centrality of libraries for both the history of books and for contemporary reading cultures. Varro's history of libraries is quite likely the main source for the Elder Pliny's account of writing materials, composed in the middle of the first century AD but which describes nothing after the time of Caesar. Pliny's theme is the rivalry between the Hellenistic kings of Alexandria and Pergamum which led to the invention of parchment as an alternative to papyrus.[6] Another, shorter version of this narrative had already been related by Vitruvius.[7] Varro's researches may also lie behind a chapter of Aulus Gellius' mid-second-century AD *Attic Nights* which summarises the story that the tyrant Pisistratus created the first-ever library in Athens; that it was stolen by the Persian king Xerxes; and was then returned by Seleucus Nicanor. Gellius too tells the story of how the Ptolemies accumulated books in Alexandria, and how many of them were destroyed during Caesar's Alexandrian War.[8] Anecdotes of collection, theft and destruction are – as Christian Jacob points out in his contribution to this collection – repeated motifs in ancient writing about libraries. Most recur in modern histories too.

Isidore's history of libraries makes use of the same anecdotes but incorporates them into a new, Christianised master narrative. Book six of the *Etymologies* is entitled 'Books and Ecclesiastical Offices'. Its first two long chapters deal with the Old and New Testaments; and then there is the chapter on libraries. After the definition with which this chapter began comes the story of how Esdra the Scribe was inspired to restore and systematise the Old Testament after the Chaldeans had burned the Law, and the texts of other works had become corrupted by the Gentiles. There follow the

---

[5] e.g. Fedeli 1988: 49, Casson 2001: 79. More tentatively Rawson 1985: 51.
[6] Plin. *HN* 13.68–70. Varro is cited, but the precise work is not specified.
[7] Vitr. 6 Praef. 4.   [8] Gell. 7.17.

stories of Pisistratus, Xerxes and Seleucus, just as in Gellius; then the great competition between kings and cities to amass books and translate them into Greek, culminating in the creation of the library of Alexandria. Isidore is interested in the translations of the scriptures into Greek and Latin: in chapter four the divinely inspired translation of the Hebrew scriptures into the Greek Septuagint is set in the library of Alexandria. The fifth chapter provides an account of the creation of the first libraries at Rome through plunder and accumulation: Aemilius Paullus and Lucullus who brought Hellenistic libraries back to Rome are followed by Caesar and Pollio who set out to create the first 'public' ones in the city. Then in chapter six we come to the creation of the first Christian libraries, pride of place being given to the library created at Caesarea by Pamphilus, based on the collections of Origen, which would provide the crucial resource for Eusebius' scholarship.[9] There follows chapter seven on who had written the most books – *apud Graecos... Romae... apud nos* – (among the Greeks, at Rome, and among us [the Christians that is]). His answers were Varro in Latin, Didymus in Greek[10] and among the Christians Origen, Jerome and Augustine. Isidore continues with accounts of different kinds of books, of book production and thence, via calendars, into sacred offices. Considerable work has gone into stitching together the classical and the biblical, and the Greek, the Roman and the Christian. The anecdotes giving each library a founding genius remain, and have been supplemented with new ones drawn from the Old Testament and the lives of the Fathers.

Perhaps the most vivid example is provided by Isidore's account of translators in chapter four of book six of the *Etymologies*. Following the claim at the end of chapter three that the library of Alexandria contained 70,000 books, he tells the story of Ptolemy asking Eleazar the priest to provide seventy translators to render the scriptures of the Old Testament, which he had in the library of Alexandria, from Hebrew into Greek. Each scholar sat in a separate cell and each produced a complete and identical version, that which we call the Septuagint. A longer version of this legend, in which a key role is also played by Demetrius of Phaleron, a pupil of Theophrastus and so in the Aristotelian tradition, is provided in the *Letter of Aristeas*, a Hellenistic work of uncertain authorship and date but which was used by Philo and Josephus.[11] Isidore then adds the names of three other Hebrew to Greek translations, those of Aquila, Symmachus and Theodotion, and mentions the anonymous Fifth Edition. He then discusses the Christian

---

[9] On which now Grafton and Williams 2006.   [10] See Hatzimichali (this volume).
[11] Bagnall 2002: 349–50 for a recent discussion of this problematic source.

editions produced by Origen and ends by celebrating Jerome's expertise in all three languages and his creation of the Latin Bible, more or less what we know as the Vulgate. From Alexandria to Caesarea the story of libraries reveals a clear pattern. Isidore has woven together all these stories into a history of divine inspiration in the world.[12] God was in the Library.

Modern historians of ancient libraries have struggled to tell a different story.[13] For the total amount of testimony is rather small. Platthy gathered 182 *testimonia* relating to Greek libraries.[14] No similar collection exists for Roman libraries, and in fact there is surprisingly little mention in the literature of the period of buildings that were clearly central to much literary production.[15] Many of the chapters in this collection necessarily return to careful re-interpretation of the same few key passages. An indication of the scarcity of testimony is that the recent discovery of Galen's *On the Avoidance of Grief* has dramatically increased our knowledge.[16] We do, of course, possess some additional evidence from outside the literary tradition. Epigraphy helps understand the management of the imperial libraries.[17] A handful of inscriptions and one letter of Pliny record municipal library building in the West.[18] To this we can add rare and precious papyrological documentation.[19] Finally, archaeological data help us visualise ancient libraries. But this evidence too must be used with more caution than hitherto. It looks increasingly likely that there were no monumental libraries before the early imperial period. Even then, libraries acquired no distinctive architectural form, and so are difficult to identify without epigraphical support.[20] Much recent research has been concerned with establishing the physical organisation of the monumental libraries of the Roman period, and the implications for their use.[21]

---

[12] The theme is expanded in the chapters contributed by Andrew Merrills and Elizabeth Keen to König and Woolf forthcoming b.
[13] Jacob (this volume).   [14] Platthy 1968.
[15] Johnson (this volume) on the rare and limited mention of libraries within literary texts of the early Empire.
[16] Boudon-Millot *et al.* 2010, discussed in many chapters of this book, among them those of Johnson, Neudecker, Tucci and Zadorojnyi. For a clear account of its significance for library studies, see Nicholls 2011.
[17] Dix 1994, Dix and Houston 2006, Bowie (this volume).
[18] On Comum, Plin. *Ep.* 1.8 with *CIL* 5.5262 discussed in Dix 1996. For municipal libraries more generally, see Cagnat 1906, Fedeli 1988: 51–4, Casson 2001: 109–23 (with the comments of Houston 2001) and Nicholls (this volume).
[19] Houston 2007, 2009 and (this volume).
[20] For a cautionary tale, see Coqueugniot (this volume).
[21] Discussions in the contributions to this volume of Neudecker, Nicholls, Petrain and Tucci. The issue is also the subject of the first third of Perrin 2010.

Approaching the ancient library 5

On the basis of this material, a number of histories of the ancient library have been written, each telling broadly similar stories of the gradual emergence of institutions that have seemed familiar to many scholars.[22] This collection does not seek to replace those works, but it does aim to challenge them, and on more than just the particulars. William Johnson writes of a 'revisionist view of Roman public libraries' and Christian Jacob advocates the deconstruction of 'the synthetic surveys, the continuous narrative of the history of ancient libraries'. This is the work we are currently engaged on. Very few pieces of the available testimony and material evidence are not interrogated in the pages that follow. No single programme unites the two dozen or so scholars who have contributed, most of whom gathered in St Andrews at a conference held in September 2008. But we share a willingness to press the evidence harder; to be more open to alternative and less familiar reconstructions of ancient libraries; and to set the slender testimony in some wider contexts. Among the contexts deployed to this end in this volume are perspectives from wider non-Greek and Roman literacies;[23] reading cultures that are unlike our own;[24] and comparative approaches.[25]

Alien libraries

Our goal, in other words, is to understand that centrality of libraries remarked on by Varro and his successors, but to do so within cultural scholarly practices quite different to our own.

To take a simple example, our notion of public libraries is profoundly misleading if applied to antiquity because of the close connections between modern public libraries and ideals of universal literacy, of widening access to knowledge, and state and municipal promotion of education.[26] Making libraries public at the end of the Roman Republic was, by contrast, just another aspect of the opening up of aristocratic cultures of exclusion, and described in the same language as the opening up of aristocratic gardens to the people of Rome, or the creation of sculpture galleries in the porticoes of the city for the display of Greek art works and especially depictions of

---

[22] Cavallo 1988, Blanck 1992, Casson 2001, Höpfner 2002f. We have learned much from the essays gathered in Perrin 2010.
[23] Robson (this volume), Ryholt (this volume). Compare Savaş *et al.* 2003.
[24] Johnson (this volume) drawing on Johnson 2010 and also on Johnson and Parker 2009.
[25] Jacob 1998, Martínez and Senseney (this volume).
[26] On which, see the chapters by Nicholls and Neudecker (this volume).

Greek myth. Collections of books had until then been housed in specialised rooms within grand rural residences, which excavations of the Villa of the Papyri at Herculaneum and descriptions of Lucullus' library allow us to imagine as decorated with busts of philosophers, and connected to secluded porticoes and gardens.[27] Vitruvius in his manual on architecture discussed libraries alongside private picture galleries (*pinacothecae*), elegant private rooms (*cubicula*) and dining rooms (*triclinia*), in other words the most secluded and exclusive portions of the aristocratic house. That no Latin word was coined for either picture gallery or library marks their enduring exclusivity within the elaborate geography of Roman culture.[28] Making libraries public was about making the people of the city of Rome feel like aristocrats, not about emancipating the upwardly mobile or educating the masses.

Equally, when we think about the knowledge production associated with ancient libraries we need to put aside Enlightenment notions of scholarly enterprise independent of political or religious affiliation. Ancient libraries were often housed in temples, and they were closely connected with the display of the power and reputation of their founders. *Bibliothecae* displayed one kind of treasure, just as *pinacothecae* displayed another. Both books and paintings were most often acquired by war, or else purchased and reproduced at great cost. Either means of acquisition signalled the power and status of their founders. Much of the mythologising of the library of Alexandria, considered in several contributions to this volume, evidently contributed to building the reputation of the Ptolemies as successors to the Pharoahs and rivals to other Macedonian kings.[29] Even municipal libraries were closely attached to the names of the benefactors who created them. At Ephesus, the sophist Celsus was buried in his foundation, just as the emperor Trajan's remains had been placed just a few years earlier at the base of the column that rose between the Ulpian libraries attached to the vast forum he had built at the heart of Rome from the spoils of the Dacian Wars. Ancient libraries were created by political and military power, and there is no sign that they powered the development of any kind of intellectual activity independent of it. The librarians of Alexandria and Rome alike were royal or imperial

---

[27] For vivid evocations of the Villa of the Papyri, see Sider 2005 and Zarmakoupi 2010. On visual elements within the ancient library, see Petrain (this volume). On Lucullus' library, Dix 2000.

[28] Vitr. 6.4.1 discusses all these rooms as component parts of a grand house grouped around its main halls. On the co-ordination of 'Greek' and 'Latin' rooms within aristocratic houses, see Wallace-Hadrill 2008: 190–6.

[29] Among others, the essays of Jacob, Handis and Zadorojnyi. See also Bagnall 2002 for a devastating debunking.

appointments.[30] Most of those we know to have used these libraries were drawn from the ruling elites of the Empire. It is no surprise that ancient libraries did not spin off academies, like those founded in European nations from the seventeenth century on, nor foster the creation of anything like a modern intelligentsia that might stand back from the higher echelons of state and society alike.

Modern preconceptions of the function and organisation of libraries, then, can easily obstruct investigations of their ancient analogues. Yet we need a common starting point even for a different and fragmentary history, and Isidore's etymological definition – that libraries are storehouses for books – is not quite sufficient. After all that would allow bookshops and warehouses containing books to qualify, and (depending on how we defined 'book') also accumulations of legal material, contracts and private letters.

Implicit in the notion of *bibliotheca* is the principle of *selection*: a library is not an indiscriminate collection of books. That selection depends partly on content, and partly on the kind of use envisaged for the future. Robson in her contribution offers a further pragmatic distinction between *archives*, that contain 'legal, epistolary, and administrative records', and *libraries* that contain deliberate collections of scholarly and literary works. We may extend this dichotomy based on contents to a distinction in use. Both archives and libraries store books which have been selected with future readers in mind. The creators of both archives and libraries envisage the possibility that what is stored there may be accessed and used by others. Often posterity is imagined as a new version of the present: scribes write with scribes in mind, government officials for their successors, scholars for colleagues yet unborn and astrologer-priests painstakingly record their observations of the heavens for the benefit of future priests. Archives store information that scribes and their masters might, in some imaginable future scenario, wish to recover. On Augustus's death he left a brief account of the numbers and deployment of the troops, of the financial reserves and of monies owed.[31] It is possible to imagine his successor, the imperial freedmen and perhaps others wishing to access this material either to recover information about the past or plan for the future. A letter of Trajan claims that he had consulted the *commentarii* of earlier emperors (in vain) to look for a general ruling on how to deal with foundlings raised as slaves.[32] Documents of these kinds were the material of archives. But the books stored in the Palatine and Ulpian libraries were

[30] Houston 2002. Hatzimichali, Bowie this volume.   [31] Suet. *Aug.* 101.
[32] Plin. *Ep.* 10.66. On imperial archives, Posner 1972, Culham 1989, Gros 2001b, Moatti 2003. In all periods it is easier to document the creation of archives than their effective use.

different because they were designed for different kinds of readers who would not consult them simply for information.

What distinguishes libraries from other bookstores, then, is the identity of their imagined future readers, and the uses they can be imagined making of treasure houses of literature, scientific writings and the like. This takes us back at once to the question of reading cultures and scholarly practices.

The essays gathered in this volume offer a series of vignettes of reading communities clustered around the precious collections of literary works that formed ancient libraries. One snapshot is provided by the intensive use of a small number of texts by Aristotle and his successors in the teaching of philosophy.[33] Then there are the successive stages of philological enquiry carried out at Alexandria, practices that not only generated better texts of the classics of the new canon, but also secondary texts, commentaries, systematic works on grammar and the like.[34] The domestication of such practices at Rome in the late Republic offers another snapshot, with large collections being mined for historical data among other things.[35] At later stages Plutarch and Gellius, Athenaeus and Galen and a few others offer tantalising images of the use of libraries as places for the very erudite to hunt down either very rare texts, or else more reliable versions of commonly copied ones.[36] How about the smaller municipal libraries? Pliny does not say why he created a library at Comum, but at the same time he created a foundation to support children there, and on another occasion contributed to the cost of a teacher in the town.[37] Should we imagine this local library connected more with educational than scholarly activity?

Our histories of the ancient library also need to leave space for serendipity. Collections of books inspire uses other than those for which they were created. Who knows what the Ptolemies thought would be the consequence of their book collecting: a better title to Hellenism for Macedonians ruling Egyptians? A better text of Homer? The pleasure of winning in an arbitrary competition played among kings? But they could not have envisaged the effects of their activities on either scholarship or poetics. Half a millennium later Pamphilus created a library of Christian texts at Caesarea in support of a sort of Christian philosophical school, which would promote Origen's controversial application of philological techniques to scripture. His pupils

---

[33] Pinto this volume.   [34] For example, the chapters of Harder and Hatzmichali this volume.
[35] Tutrone and Hogg, this volume.
[36] Johnson and Zadorojnyi in this volume. See also Jacob 2000 and Wilkins 2007 on Athenaeus, and on Galen Nutton 2009, Nicholls 2011.
[37] Plin. *Ep.* 1.8 on the library foundation and the alimentary scheme, 4.13 on the provision for a *praeceptor*'s salary.

included the Cappadocian Fathers and Jerome, but the library also allowed Eusebius to generate innovative fusions of Christian and classical literary genres in Greek, rather as Isidore would do later in Latin. The consequences of book collection are unpredictable.

Most difficult of all is the question of how these libraries were organised. The earliest collections were probably so small that a simple ordering by author was probably sufficient. For the larger collections several principles have been suggested. One way to imagine the choice offered the first librarians is to ask what pre-existing ordering principles might have been applied to the classification of books. The oldest was by author, not necessarily alphabetised of course: it was as common for ancients as it is for us to use the name of the author as shorthand for a text or group of texts ('I have been reading Homer', 'Varro argues somewhere that', 'From Aristotle we learn' and so on). Then there was the ordering of literary works implicit in the educational curricula, an ordering that in part corresponded to our map of ancient genres – tragedians together, then writers of comedy and so on. Finally there were the various philosophical orderings of the world, like that implicit in Pliny's *Natural History*,[38] or indeed today in the library of the Warburg Institute in London, which following a plan devised by its founder groups books on four floors devoted to the themes of image, word, orientation and action. How a library is ordered has clear implications for the way it may be used, especially in an age before analytical catalogues. Yet even the more basic principles – such as whether Roman libraries often, sometimes or always physically separated Greek from Latin texts – are matters of debate.[39] And there is no reason to think that all ancient libraries followed the same principles of organisation.

Libraries and literatures

The first texts that can be reasonably regarded as books appeared in the Bronze Age of the Near East, and the first collections of books are attested in the temples and palaces of third millennium Mesopotamia, and Syria and second millennium Anatolia and Egypt.[40] Libraries in this sense were

---

[38] For recent characterisations of Pliny's cosmology and its relation to the organization of the *Natural History*, see Beagon 1992: 26–33, Doody 2010: 23–30 and König and Woolf forthcoming a.
[39] Nicholls 2010a.
[40] Casson 2001: 1–16 for a short account. The greater durability of cuneiform tablets relative to papyrus probably explains why Egyptian collections are first attested later than Mesopotamian ones.

widespread in the Near East in the last millennium BC well before the development of alphabetic scripts. The care invested in amassing the huge collections, like those of the Hittite kings at Hattusas and of Assurbanipal at Nineveh, suggests libraries were already central to these cultures.[41] Epic poetry, religious texts and royal decrees and letters featured in all these contexts, alongside administrative documents of various kinds. The various scripts used were complex and difficult to learn, and probably very few who were not scribes could read them. But 'scribal literacy' only refers to a restricted number of writers and readers, and many other members of those societies used these texts in other ways. Modern notions of literature privilege reading above other ways of consuming texts. Around the reading cultures of antiquity we should envisage wider communities of listeners, enjoying retellings of the Epic of Gilgamesh in Mesopotamia or the legends that grew up around the figure of Imhotep in Egypt. Even after the spread of alphabetic scripts, the situation did not change radically. The library of Pisistratus is certainly a myth, but if anyone had compiled collections of Greek texts in the archaic period they would have consisted entirely of verse, almost all of it written for oral performance on public occasions. Even the first Latin 'literature' consisted of plays and hymns, despite the fact that it was composed in a Mediterranean intellectual universe dominated by the Hellenistic amalgam of scholarship and poetics.

The contributions to this volume by Robson and Ryholt make clear there was no sharp break in either the Egyptian or cuneiform traditions before Roman antiquity. Ryholt discusses the presence in the temple library of Roman Tebtunis of texts written in demotic, hieratic and hieroglyphic Egyptian, and also in Greek. Many of the literary texts found in the temple libraries of Seleucid Mesopotamia and Roman Egypt were very ancient indeed. By the first millennium BC the technology of books was broadly similar, cuneiform tablets apart. Papyrus scrolls remained the dominant medium until late antiquity, but were always supplemented by texts written on parchment or linen, with shorter less permanent notes on pottery ostraka or wooden tablets and monumental writing on stone and occasionally bronze. Alongside the older traditions, however, there were now newer literatures, many of them written in the family of alphabetic scripts descended from that devised in Phoenicia around the start of the last millennium BC. Robson describes the rise of Aramaic and its relatives in the Near East. Through the mediation of Phoenicians and Greeks, versions of the alphabet spread throughout the Mediterranean world and were widely

---

[41] On Hattusas, Savaş *et al.* 2003, on Nineveh, Robson this volume.

imitated and adapted as far afield as Spain, Gaul and southern Britain. Only a few of these societies used the script to create anything we might consider books, and fewer amassed collections we might call libraries.

It is easy to forget the chronological and geographical proximity of all these different traditions and literatures across the ancient Mediterranean and Near East. The centrepiece of the library of the Villa of the Papyri at Herculaneum was the Epicurean philosophical writings of Philodemus who lived there as an honoured guest of his Roman patron in the middle of the last century BC.[42] The library he created, supplemented by other texts,[43] was still apparently valued and in use when Vesuvius buried the entire town in mud in AD 79. Philodemus had been brought up, however, in the city of Gadara in present day Jordan, just a hundred miles or so from where the Qumran community was, during exactly the same period, creating the collection which we call the Dead Sea Scrolls.[44] The Qumran library included portions of the Hebrew Bible, of its Samaritan variant and also of the Septuagint, the Greek translation mentioned by Isidore, along with idiosyncratic sacred texts and rules in Hebrew and in Aramaic. Writing technology, scripts, even one of the languages was shared between the library of Philodemus and that of the Qumran community, yet the vast differences in genre, in notions of authority and in tradition give us no hesitation in assigning the two to such different literary traditions that the two libraries might have been assembled on different continents or planets! Such juxtapositions were not unusual. Egyptian temples like that at Tebtunis often operated in close proximity to nome capitals where the children of the metropolite class, among others, were drilled in Homer and the Greek classics. Or consider the larger cities of the Mediterranean world. Greek was the main language of the Jewish diaspora in that region, so in any large city such as Alexandria, Rome, Ephesus and Carthage we might expect there to be communities using Greek versions of the Hebrew Bible in close proximity to others listening to sophists and reading Homer. Or again consider the great number of languages that have been recovered on documents from the relatively minor city of Dura Europus on the Euphrates: these included Greek, Latin, Palmyrene, Syriac, Hebrew, Middle Persian, Parthian and Safaitic.

To be sure, some of these languages and literatures were more closely connected than others. Educated westerners certainly claimed familiarity with Greek as well as Latin, and a number of Greek writers could certainly

---

[42] Gigante 1995 for a short account. See also, Sider 2005.   [43] Houston, this volume.
[44] For an introduction, see the special issue of *Near Eastern Archaeology* (2000) 63 (3) 'Qumran and the Dead Sea Scrolls: Discoveries, Debates, the Scrolls and the Bible'.

read Latin fluently and in the case of some – Plutarch probably, Dio Cassius and Arrian certainly – must have been able to speak it fluently too. Perhaps such bilingualism was also common among the senior priests of Roman Egypt. Paul read Hebrew, wrote in Greek and presumably spoke Aramaic fluently. Equally there were works of cultural and literal translation. The Septuagint has been mentioned already. Josephus in the preface to his Greek account of the Jewish War describes it as a translation of an account he had already written in Aramaic for the diaspora communities outside the Empire. Plutarch's essay *On Isis and Osiris* probably drew on some Egyptian original, if perhaps not directly. Philo's philosophical writing represents the creation of new genres of Jewish literature not only in Greek but also based on Greek models. Manetho, Berossus and Philo of Byblos all produced histories in Greek based on non-Greek written traditions.[45]

Yet in spite of this high-profile traffic between them, these traditions remained effectively parallel until late antiquity. Despite the many potential mediators and actual bilinguals, the mainstream literary traditions – from Latin historiography to the Mishnah – developed in effective ignorance of each other, fascinated by the classical, canonical and authoritative works in their own tradition, oblivious to what was being created around them. Only the Greek and Latin traditions exercised major mutual influence during the early imperial period. In modern jargon, the ancient Mediterranean and the Near East was more like a salad bowl than a melting pot. Only with the coming of Christianity were enterprises like those of Eusebius of Caesarea, Jerome and much later Isidore of Seville undertaken which set about creating a unitary sense of the past and a single set of literary authorities.[46]

What kept these parallel literatures apart? Not a language barrier, clearly, nor distance nor the inaccessibility of texts. The only plausible explanation is in terms of reading communities, as defined by William Johnson.[47] Each community formed collective judgments about what was and what was not worth reading and worth citing. It had its own notions of authority – scripture in the Jewish sense was not the same as canonicity as it had developed in Alexandria. Each reading community was also characterised by a reading culture that set parameters on how to read and use books, and on what sorts of books were appropriate for particular kinds of critical engagement. Plotinus was allegedly horrified when Origen turned the tools of classical philology on barbarian scriptures, and many Christians also found his results deeply problematic. The notion of a textual

[45] Dillery 2007. [46] Momigliano 1975, and in particular relation to historiography 1963, 1990.
[47] Johnson 2010.

community was originally framed to describe something on a rather smaller scale, such as a mediaeval monastery the life of which was focused on the exegesis, contemplation, copying or criticism of a small body of texts.[48] Precise ancient analogues might include Aristotle's Academy and the Qumran community. But if the idea was extended a little we could envisage those particularly engaged in producing and reading or hearing Latin literature during the early Empire as constituting a form of dispersed and larger textual community, one sufficiently predictable for an author to know the difference between an obvious allusion and an obscure one, and between daring stylistic innovation and what would be universally decried as a solecism. Communities of this kind set the rules. Tacitus could easily have consulted either the Septuagint or Josephus' *Antiquities* before composing the first chapters of book five of the *Histories* if he had wanted to. His choice not to do so was fixed by the expectations of the community for whom he wrote. And a key way in which the views of each reading (and listening) community were expressed was in the contents of their libraries.

Libraries and the history of the book

Most of the essays gathered in this volume are concerned with the place of libraries in the reading cultures of classical antiquity. The libraries of Assyrian and Persian emperors, those of the many Jewish communities of the diaspora, the first collections of Syriac texts and the development of Christian libraries in tandem with Christian literatures are fascinating, but must be left for others to explore.

The history of libraries in the Mediterranean world begins in the classical period. The Linear B tablets piled up in the Mycenaean palaces of southern Greece and Crete are certainly archives in Robson's sense rather than libraries. Alphabetic writing was put to many uses in archaic Greece and Italy, but few books were produced and even into the classical period oral culture and performance dominated public life.[49] The literacies that emerged first in Greek cities, and then in societies influenced by them, are not easy to characterise in a single term, but they were certainly not 'restricted', 'scribal' or 'hieratic'.[50] By the beginning of the fifth century BC, illustrations of papyrus rolls begin to appear on pottery. The first prose

---

[48] Stock 1983, applied to early Christianity by Lane Fox (1994).
[49] Thomas 1989, 1992; Goldhill and Osborne 1999.
[50] On ancient literacies, see Harris 1989; Bowman and Woolf 1994; Woolf 2000 and Johnson and Parker 2009, with a valuable bibliographical essay.

texts were created soon after.[51] During the fourth century a debate emerged over the rival claims of oral and written authority.[52] Numbers of books were not the only key variable. The specific social context of the classical city state was naturally also influential, fostering the emergence of wealthy classes some of whose members chose to engage in intellectual pursuits. This is the development that Robson singles out as a key difference between the way classical and ancient Mesopotamian societies used writing.[53] Even if much critical and philosophical activity was conducted orally, it revolved around books. The first reading (and listening) communities had appeared.

Several contributors to this volume return to the rich if problematic testimony about Aristotle's library and its afterlife.[54] But perhaps the most important datum to emerge from it is the essentially private nature of book collecting in the classical city. Private collections of books recur throughout antiquity.[55] It is likely that private libraries of this sort remained by far the commonest kind of library beyond the fall of the western Empire. Next to appear were libraries housed in temples and in *gymnasia*. Last of all came that tiny number created by kings and emperors to which most of the literary testimony is devoted.

It requires a conscious effort to remember that eye-catching projects like the creation of the library of Alexandria or the Palatine library of Augustus were developed against the background of a developing book trade, operating alongside and in complex relationship with the reciprocal lending and sharing of books among the wealthier members of reading communities.[56] A very great part of the production and circulation of books must have taken place within the mansions of the propertied classes whose literary tastes could be serviced by skilled slaves. This must certainly have been the case for the private special libraries required and amassed by doctors, jurists and professionals.[57] Perhaps the book trade was more important for the upwardly mobile consumers of school texts.

Despite the relatively large amount of ancient testimony devoted to the Great Library of Alexandria, and the rival collections built up by the Attalid kings of Pergamum and the Antigonids of Macedonia, we do not know for certain what triggered this bibliographical arms race. Should we see it as the combination of the established tradition of Macedonian royal patronage of scholars and poets with new resources? Or were Hellenistic kings adopting

---

[51] Cavallo 1975, Blanck 1992.   [52] Detienne 1988, Pinto, this volume.
[53] Robson, this volume.   [54] Especially Jacob, Tutrone, Zadorojnyi.
[55] Dix this volume for the late Republican version. Affleck this volume on temple libraries.
[56] Kleberg 1975, Tutrone, Dix, this volume   [57] Martínez and Senseney, this volume.

a Near Eastern royal idiom, rather as they did when they created hunting reserves for themselves? Nor do we know who the kings expected to use their great libraries. Were they conceived of simply as treasure houses? Were the first librarians skilled curators of collections that were never intended to be widely accessible? Finally we need to find space in this picture for municipal libraries. The libraries of Carthage that the Romans dispersed after their conquest of the city were perhaps the first great collections of books not associated with a king. But what was contained within them and who had access? Another early collection of books from the second century BC is known only from the painted *dipinti* that listed authors in the collection on the wall of what may have been a *gymnasium* or was just a private house in the Sicilian city of Tauromenium.[58]

It is easier to discuss the impact of the creation of great libraries on the wider production and circulation of books. The new Galen text suggests the imperial libraries might be thought of as repositories of better quality texts. If so, they *might* have been used as a brake on textual drift. How far this was actually done is very unclear. Links are made in Augustan poetry between the creation of the Palatine library and the establishment of a new and better Latin canon, and Ovid professes himself keen that his poetry should be lodged there.[59] But there is a poor correlation between the canon Horace wished for in the *Letter to Augustus* and what has survived from classical antiquity.[60] Perhaps the needs of the schools and the tastes of private book collectors were in the end more influential in determining the evolving shape of Latin and Greek literatures than the contents or accession policies of ancient public libraries?

On the other hand the creation of monumental libraries represented a powerful endorsement of the cult of learning and of book culture more generally. If at first this move was intended to associate the emperors with the tastes and values of influential sections of the Roman elite, the fact that monumental libraries were then created in Italian and provincial towns shows the wider impact of imperial sponsorship of literature. Further stimuli would come in the form of imperial chairs in major cities, the patronage of orators and the addition of literary competitions to the festival cycle in the capital. All these innovations were widely imitated. The emperors did not invent the notion of an educated imperial elite but they promoted it: library building was one means at their disposal to make their sponsorship of the arts visible.

---

[58] Manganaro 1976; Battistoni 2006. We are grateful to Jonathon Prag for information and discussion.
[59] Ov. *Trist.* 3.1.   [60] Hor. *Ep.*2.1.

The other story always told in this connection is that of the loss of books at the end of antiquity. Varro, by the look of it, already ended his account *de Bibliothecis* with collateral damage caused to books during Caesar's war in Alexandria. Any loss was clearly not fatal to scholarship in the city.[61] The fate of the Great Library has aroused a great deal of recent attention, partly in response to the work of Luciano Canfora and the creation of the new *Bibliotheca Alexandrina*.[62] The new Galen manuscript also puts blazing libraries on the agenda, this time in Rome. Ancients were shocked by these conflagrations because so much symbolic capital had been invested in vast collections of books. The long term consequences, it is now widely agreed, were less significant. Disagreement exists over how important great libraries were as opposed to private collections in the transmission of manuscripts:[63] probably the answer differs from one kind of text to another.

What most needs to be explained is not occasional cataclysmic losses of ancient manuscripts – which in any case had a limited life – so much as the shifts in the criteria that determined which texts were recopied and which not, both in general and at the point when papyrus rolls were replaced by codices. No text could survive more than a few centuries unless the papyrus rolls on which at least one version was written down were copied out again. Long and esoteric works of prose probably never existed in many copies, and so their chances of survival were in general less than school texts like Virgil's *Aeneid*. The shift from scrolls to codices was another gauntlet that each text had to run. Finally we need to take account of the new priorities of Christian scholars on whom survival through the early Middle Ages depended. The story of the transmisson of Latin literature is a sobering one. It seems likely that most of what had been written survived in AD 500 and rich editions were still being produced for private collections in the late fifth century, yet between 550 and 750 almost no non-Christian manuscripts were recopied, so that when the scholars of the Carolingian renaissance began collecting and copying classical books (most of which had probably survived in private collections in Italy) a great part of Latin literature was gone forever.[64] If those general processes are clear, it is not always easy to pick out the factors that influenced the survival or loss of particular texts. By what set of parallel chances did Pliny's *Natural History*

---

[61] Hatzimichali this volume, von Staden 2004.
[62] Canfora 1986a. See more recently, El-Abbadi 1992, Empereur 2003, El-Abbadi and Fathallah 2008.
[63] Bagnall 2002: 359–60 challenging the claim of Canfora 1989 that large libraries were relatively insignificant in the transmission of texts.
[64] Reynolds and Wilson 1974: 70–90, Reynolds 1983: xiii–xxx.

survive when Ennius' *Annales* did not? The latter had been phenomenally popular in the late Republic, and survived for centuries longer, at least in a few copies available to grammarians. (And perhaps philosophers too, since there may have been a copy of book six in the Villa of the Papyri.[65]) The *Natural History* by contrast is exactly the sort of text we might expect to be most at risk from attrition. Yet all but a few hundred lines of Ennius have been lost, and Pliny's work somehow survived until the tastes and needs of the Middle Ages made it phenomenally popular. Luck and deliberate choice both played a part in the loss of one and the survival of the other.

How important were libraries in these processes? At Constantinople the tradition of creating and developing imperial libraries remained unbroken, if more energetically in some periods than others. Nearly 300 works of classical scholarship were summarised by the ninth-century Patriarch Photius in his *Bibliothēkē*. During the eighth century the Abbasid Caliphate sponsored a great campaign of translation which, among other things, created Arabic versions of the mass of philosophical, scientific and technical prose available in Greek (or in Syriac or Pahlavi translation) and stored them in a court library, the *bayt al-hikma*. Some of the originals must have survived in the municipal libraries of the former eastern Roman provinces, some were consulted in Constantinople.[66] The situation in the west was different. There is little evidence of anything resembling a library north of the Alps between the sixth and the mid-eighth centuries. The 'classical holdings' of the greatest monastic libraries that appeared during the Carolingian renaissance, libraries like those of St Gall and Lorsch, may have depended ultimately on a small number of exemplars surviving in private aristocratic collections and school collections rather than on the relics of great western libraries.[67] The history of the book is a complex one marked by periods of gradual loss alternating with energetic episodes of copying, dissemination and accumulation. The creation and destruction of ancient libraries has a place in that story, but it does not supply the central narrative.

Libraries and knowledge

Both we and the ancients make great metaphorical play with the idea of a library.[68] Several particularly compendious ancient texts were entitled

---

[65] Houston, this volume.   [66] Gutas 1998.
[67] On the resurgence of library culture and its connections with copying of classical texts, McKitterick 1989:166–210. On Carolingian classicism, Innes 1997, especially at 279–82.
[68] Jacob 2000, Too 2000, 2010.

Bibliothēkē and it was a common conceit to imagine particularly learned individuals as holding a library in their heads. Modern scholars often write of 'Galen's library' or 'Aristotle's library' meaning those books he had read, knew well or might refer to, or else use 'library' to refer to the scholarly universe of the day, its capaciousness, its resistance to enquiry and its organisation.[69] Our concern in this volume has been more concrete, with the actual institution of the library, not because those other issues are not important to us – quite the reverse – but because the force of a metaphor only emerges from a full understanding of the literal sense of the term.

Let us close this introduction by asking what place libraries – in the widest possible sense – had in the knowledge culture of antiquity? Scholars in the humanities today sometimes refer to libraries as 'our laboratories' meaning the comprehensive and expertly curated collections of books and electronic resources that are the essential resources needed for conducting research. We have already suggested that modern analogies of this kind be treated with caution, and that it is anachronistic to imagine either the Alexandrine Mouseion or the many libraries of imperial Rome as imperial research centres. Smaller collections were certainly linked to education, but most private collections reflect the social and recreational activities of those who owned them. The kinds of knowledge created were specific to the tastes and interests of the elite.

All the same, some of the contributions to this volume suggest a range of unintentional consequences of the accumulation of books, consequences which had the potential to transform the knowledge landscape.

Already by the early third century BC scholars in Alexandria had begun to compare variants in manuscripts with the aim of establishing a better 'text' than any surviving manuscript exemplified.[70] Perhaps this is a likely side-effect of accumulating multiple copies of the same work, and perhaps the task of sorting out correct readings seemed at first an easy piece of house-keeping. But critical philology clearly developed a momentum of its own, generating new questions as well as new methods.[71]

A second possibility enabled by large collections of texts was systematic comparison not of divergent texts but of discrepant accounts. Historiography offers just one way to track this process. Herodotus and Thucydides certainly had earlier books in their sights when they created their own, even if the contemporary debates over written and oral authority obscure this slightly. But the activity of Timaeus and Polybius seems different in

---

[69] e.g. Wilkins 2007.   [70] Harder, this volume.   [71] Hatzimichali, this volume.

kind, and much closer to modern library based research. When Cato set out to gather material to write the *Origines*, he was not able to simply compare and adjudicate between two or more rival accounts – as might a Diodorus or a Dionysius – but he had to comb a mass of written source material for data that might be extracted and reorganised. Historians needed libraries because their source material was diverse and because prose texts were rarely as widely available as verse. The greatest libraries were certainly not designed to facilitate this activity, but as Diodorus makes clear, it was impossible without access to them.[72] What was true of historical enquiry was certainly true of any other kind of research that required the consultation of rare texts. Medicine is a case in point, and perhaps we should add mathematics, astronomy, geography and those other sciences characteristic of the Hellenistic and early Roman period.

A third effect will have been the way that concentrations of books create concentrations of scholars. Cicero described how Lucullus' library became a gathering place for Greek scholars in Rome.[73] How far similar effects characterised the imperial libraries is less clear: this was clearly not a preferred locale for elite self-representation, compared to the public spaces of the city or the most private quarters of suburban villae.[74] But there is plentiful anecdotal evidence for the temporary migration of scholars to Rome and Athens in the early imperial period, and it would be odd if no scholarly communities crystallised around, for instance, the library of Hadrian in Athens.

Ancient libraries, we may wish to conclude, were products of habits of book use deeply embedded in the social and political worlds of ancient elites. The circulation of books among private libraries was just one strand in the dense exchange networks that connected the powerful. The municipal libraries they built in their home towns were another way to legitimate their leadership by an easy conversion of economic into cultural capital. Kings and emperors joined in because they followed the cultural lead of elites, and because they had the resources to outdo them. We should not expect ancient libraries to generate radical new ideas or technologies that might transform the societies in which they were located. The gulf between ancient libraries and either today's research hubs or the products of the Scientific Revolution and the Enlightenment is profound.

That said, the contributors to this volume have illustrated a wide range of unintentional consequences of the creation of libraries. The simple

---

[72] Diod. Sic. 1.4.2–5.   [73] Dix 2000 commenting on Plut. *Luc.* 42.1–2.
[74] Johnson, this volume.

accumulation of books led to new habits of reading and then of criticism and analysis, and perhaps too to new vistas of the field of enquiry and certainly to new ideals of erudition. Around the books gathered in libraries emerged new communities of readers with characters of their own, and among them perhaps the first individuals we can term scholars, as well as scholarly.

Much of the new knowledge that these scholars produced was not deemed sufficiently useful by their many successors to survive. But a number of works – and fields of knowledge – were created that are difficult to imagine emerging from any other institutional context. Books rotted away and a few were destroyed in fires and other accidents. But the survival of some of the texts generated by library culture was of real cultural significance. Gellius' *Attic Nights* and Pliny's *Natural History* found unlikely homes in the hearts of Carolingian monks, mathematical and medical treatises helped kick-start Islamic science, and a great treasure trove of Greek literature was amassed in Byzantium with major consequences for the European Renaissance. Perhaps just as important was the transmission – through great compendious and encyclopaedic works like Pliny's *Natural History*, Isidore's *Etymologies* and Jerome's *Chronicon* and *De Viris Illustribus* – of a vision of the world of knowledge that had briefly been physically housed in the greatest libraries of classical antiquity. The new worlds of knowledge and new libraries that began to be constructed in the eighth and ninth centuries owed a good deal to those classical precursors, and so do we.

PART I

Contexts

1 | Libraries in ancient Egypt

KIM RYHOLT

The library of Alexandria

Ancient Egypt is well known as the country which housed the most famous library of antiquity, the library of Alexandria. The details surrounding the foundation of this institution remain unclear. The idea may have originated with Ptolemy I, but the available sources indicate that actual construction did not take place until the reign of Ptolemy II and the credit is perhaps entirely his.[1]

Much is known about the wide range of scholarly activities and groundbreaking achievements of the library of Alexandria. But the possibility that any aspect of contemporary *Egyptian* culture may have played a part in the decision to create this institution has been given little if any serious consideration. The inspiration for its creation is usually sought in the Greek world and there alone.[2] There is, however, very limited evidence of institutional libraries in the Greek world before the Hellenistic era. By contrast, Egypt had a millennia-long tradition of temple libraries, and one that is well documented. At least a part of the activities for which the library in Alexandria would become famous, had long been the stock in trade of these libraries. This tradition is largely unknown outside a relatively small group of Egyptological specialists because it has received limited attention and general studies are not readily accessible. Yet substantial source material is available. In marked contrast to the situation with Greek and Roman libraries, for which we rely almost exclusively on secondary literary sources and the architecture of monumental buildings, the Egyptian material largely consists of contemporary and primary evidence in the form of actual writings from the libraries along with the titles and biographical statements of the people associated with them. The possibility that the large-scale, systematic collections of religious, scientific and historical writings kept at the temple libraries may have played a part in inspiring the creation of the library of Alexandria should, in my opinion, be given serious consideration.

[1] Cf. Bagnall 2002: 348–51. [2] An exception is Shubert 1993.

It is, in this relation, important to keep in mind that Egypt in general had become a source of much inspiration to the Greek world after Psammetichus I, in the mid-seventh century, allowed large numbers of Greeks to settle in Egypt and Naucratis was founded. In the wake of the Greeks becoming familiar with Egypt and its culture, numerous scholars are said to have travelled there to study. This was centuries before the foundation of the library of Alexandria. And, according to our sources, the object of their journeys was precisely those cities that housed the greatest temples and temple libraries. These journeys would prove anything but futile. Above all, the Greeks soon learned the art of writing on papyrus. This made it possible to commit to writing works like those of Homer and Hesiod, some time between the eighth and the sixth centuries BC. Without the development of written culture which followed in the fifth century there could have been no library of Alexandria. The Greeks also learned the mathematical decimal system from the Egyptians and the calendrical system based on the solar year, to mention just two other fundamental borrowings.

In addition to the rich testimony to intellectual interaction between Greek and Egyptian cultures in the centuries preceding the creation of the library of Alexandria, I would like to draw attention to a further source which seems to me of crucial importance. This so-called Satrap Stela is an inscription set up by Ptolemy I when he was still just the viceroy of Egypt on behalf of the king of Macedon and had not yet assumed the titles of kingship.[3] The text relates how Ptolemy returned to Egypt from the conquered Persians a number of divine images and, what is especially interesting in connection with the present paper, the writings from the Egyptian temple libraries. This achievement is mentioned foremost in the text, even before the announcement of the decision to relocate the royal residence from Memphis to Alexandria.

The Satrap Stela provides direct testimony that the ambitious Ptolemy realised the importance of maintaining and preserving that wisdom which Greeks, throughout the centuries, had travelled to Egypt in order to familiarise themselves with. Had these texts not been considered of utmost importance, they would hardly have been mentioned so prominently by Ptolemy. Evidently the Persians had also taken an interest in these texts. If they had merely wished to deprive the Egyptians of these writings, in which their ancient culture and science was codified, they would surely just

---

[3] A recent translation is Ritner in Simpson 2003: 392–7.

have set them ablaze, rather than to try and carry them off wholesale to Persia.

Libraries in ancient Egypt

What in fact constitutes a temple library? Although an actual temple library was discovered more than 75 years ago and there are likely remains from other temple libraries or priestly communities in various collections, these have received only a minimal amount of attention.[4] Until the 1990s hardly any of the material had been published and to date most of the relevant material still remains to be studied and made available. Earlier studies of Egyptian temple libraries have therefore focused on more indirect source material.[5]

The earliest textual references to libraries date back to the Fourth Dynasty (*c.* 2550 BC). They consist of titles of officials associated with buildings containing what is described as 'sacred writings', which indicate that we are dealing with religious or other cultic texts, rather than administrative documents. One vast category of material which must surely have been kept in some form of libraries are the liturgical texts known collectively as the Pyramid Texts. The corpus so far attested amounts to about 300 pages in a modern English edition.[6] These early indirect attestations of libraries are contemporary with two other important developments in relation to the history of writing in Egypt; the emergence of biographical texts inscribed on the walls of the tombs of officials, and the first statues depicting officials in the scribal pose. While no literary papyri survive from this period, the extensive use of papyri in the administration is documented by the remains of four archives from the late third millennium which have been found at royal mortuary temples. In one case the archival architecture was still partially preserved and this single archive was large enough to have accommodated several thousand papyri.[7]

A substantial number of literary papyri are preserved from the Middle Kingdom and Second Intermediate Period (sc. the first half of the second millennium), but only a single library with a known archaeological context

---

[4] See in more detail Ryholt forthcoming a. A general survey of Egyptian literature from the Late Period and Greco-Roman Egypt may be found in Ryholt 2010.
[5] The most comprehensive study of Egyptian libraries to date is Burkard 1980, cf. also Assmann 2001. A series of new studies on Egyptian libraries will be published by Parkinson forthcoming, Hagen forthcoming, and Ryholt forthcoming a.
[6] Faulkner 1969, Allen 2005.   [7] Ryholt forthcoming b.

survives. This is a small collection of twenty-three papyri found *in situ* within a box in a tomb at Thebes. The archaeological context and the fact that most of the texts were magical or medico-magical indicates that we are dealing with a private professional library pertaining to some form of magical practitioner.[8] It further contained some poetical literature, including the *Tale of Sinuhe* and the *Tale of the Eloquent Peasant*.

More importantly, it is also from the time of the Middle Kingdom that we have the first references to scribes and texts associated with the so-called 'House of Life'.[9] This institution has often been thought to represent a kind of academy, but it is never directly associated with teaching. It is, however, not until the Late Period (*c*. 664 BC onwards) that we have more substantial information on the activities of this institution. At this point in time, the House of Life can be shown to be intimately linked to the cult of Osiris who played a central and dominating role in Egyptian religion.[10] Accordingly, the institution was associated with wisdom and even arcane knowledge and one of its primary activities was the study and composition of the religious and magical texts that allowed the maintenance of the cult all over Egypt.

The Tebtunis temple library

The only large-scale temple library preserved to us from ancient Egypt is the Tebtunis temple library which will be the focus of the remaining part of this chapter.[11] The library was found *in situ* and seems to have been abandoned in the early third century AD. It thus represents one of the latest collections of ancient Egyptian literature. It may nonetheless be considered largely representative of earlier libraries since a significant number of the texts it contained are already attested in much older versions.

Tebtunis is the southernmost settlement in the Fayum Oasis which is located south of Cairo, immediately to the west of the Nile. During the Hellenistic Period and well into the second century AD, the Fayum was a very prosperous part of Egypt. The archaeological remains at Tebtunis are particularly well preserved since the settlement is located in the dry desert climate outside the edge of present-day cultivation. The site itself is considerable, covering about 120 acres. It includes a large town-area with private

---

[8] Quack 2006a: 72–7.   [9] Gardiner 1938.   [10] Ryholt forthcoming (a).
[11] A general survey of the Tebtunis temple library and its contents may be found in Ryholt 2005 (cf. now Ryholt 2012 for literary papyri) and more detailed surveys of the religious texts in von Lieven 2005 and Quack 2006b.

houses, a main temple, several smaller chapels, a large processional street or dromos, baths and several cemeteries. The main temple was dedicated to Soknebtunis, a form of the crocodile god Sobek whose name simply means 'Sobek, Lord of Tebtunis'. It is to this temple that the library here discussed belonged.

The modern excavation history of the temple library is a very complex affair, many details of which are still not entirely clear.[12] The earliest known batches of material were discovered during an English expedition in 1899 and a German one in 1902, but the bulk of the material was only excavated by local Egyptian villagers in 1930 and by an Italian expedition in 1931. The papyri discovered by the English are now in Oxford and Berkeley, those by the Germans in Berlin, and those by the Italians in Florence. The most substantial part, which was found by the local villagers, ended up on the antiquities market. As a result groups of papyri were dispersed between many institutions and individuals: the lion's share was acquired by Copenhagen.

No official report on the excavation of the papyri and their archaeological context were ever published by any of the three official expeditions. However, according to the scant information available, the papyri excavated by the Italian mission were found in two adjoining cellars, i.e. two subterranean rooms. These were located in relation to one of the houses built against the inside of the temenos wall which surrounded the temple and less than twenty metres from the sanctuary itself. The exact location of the house remains disputed[13] and we have no detailed description of the cellars. For this reason important questions remain open: How large were the cellars? Did they contain niches or shelves or evidence of containers such as baskets, boxes or jars? Which papyri were found where? Were any other types of objects found with the papyri? Were papyri kept here during, or only after, the period of the temple's use?

Because of the uncertainty as to the precise location of the building under which the two cellars were located, it also remains uncertain what it looked like, but none of the preserved architecture in the row of buildings against the temenos wall is particularly imposing. There is nothing to indicate that Egyptian temple libraries were ever constructed as prestigious monuments as far as architecture is concerned. It is extremely unlikely that any of

---

[12] The excavation history is discussed in detail by Ryholt forthcoming c.
[13] Cf. Rondot 2004: 31. Prof. Claudio Gallazzi (pers. com.) kindly informs me that records available to him suggest that the house was located at another location within the same general area.

them would have resembled the Roman period libraries preserved in Rome, Athens, Ephesus and Timgad which were built as large-scale monuments by emperors and wealthy Roman citizens.[14]

Let us proceed to the date, size and contents of the Tebtunis temple library. The material spans the first and second centuries AD. There are indications that the bulk of the material might have been written between 100–150 AD. The latest dated papyri are from the early third century AD. The size of the library is more difficult to estimate owing to its very poor state of preservation. The papyri have been reduced to tens of thousands of smaller fragments. For this reason work on individual texts is immensely time-consuming; most of them remain to be studied in detail and published. A tally based on my study of the fragments in the different collections indicates that they represent around 400 texts.

For the present purpose, the texts may conveniently be divided into three major groups: cultic, scientific and narrative. The cultic texts, by which I mean texts related to the cult at the temple and its priesthood, represent about 60 per cent of the total holdings. The remaining texts from the library are made up of roughly equal amounts of scientific texts and historical narratives. In addition to this material, there is a small number of wisdom texts which are not easily attributed to any of the three above-mentioned groups.

It is also necessary to add a comment on the use of scripts. The temple library includes material written in four different scripts. The majority of texts, about two thirds, are written in demotic. This had originally been the script used for administration and other everyday purposes, but over time its use expanded so as to include scientific and narrative literature. After the Roman conquest of Egypt its use gradually became restricted demographically to the priestly communities. Within the temple library, the majority of the scientific texts and all the historical narratives are written in demotic. The cultic texts are mostly written in hieratic which was used for most of the remaining third of the library. This script was exclusively used by priests in the Hellenistic and Roman periods. Finally, there are a limited number of texts written in the hieroglyphic script, several of which were intended for the very purpose of learning this script, and a few further texts written in Greek. The latter are nearly all scientific (medical and astrological) in nature. There is almost no evidence of Greek poetic literature within the temple library, but numerous copies of various Greek authors – not least

---

[14] See conveniently Casson 2001.

the works of Homer – have been found in the private houses of the priests, and it is clear that they were familiar with such material.

The cultic literature[15]

I will begin the presentation of selected texts from the temple library with the cultic material. Two of the most fundamental texts within this category are the Daily Temple Ritual and the Offering Ritual. The Daily Temple Ritual provides step-by-step instructions concerning the basic ritual which was performed every day in every temple in Egypt. There may have been minor variations from temple to temple, but on the whole the ritual was the same. The earliest manuals on the daily ritual are preserved in three papyri from the tenth century BC and relate specifically to the cults of Amun and Mut at Thebes, while a series of reliefs at the temple of Seti I (*c.* 1300 BC) at Abydos furnish us with the most complete set of pictorial representations of the acts that were performed during the ritual. Regular offerings also formed a central part of the cult and are similarly described in the Offering Ritual which has not survived from earlier periods.

In addition to the rituals that were performed on a daily basis, the temple library includes manuals relating to rituals carried out during festivals that were celebrated only on specific dates during the year. An example is provided by a manual relating to the Bastet festival which was a kind of New Year celebration. One of the fundamental Egyptian myths, known as *the Myth of the Sun's Eye*, relates how the sun-god had once grown weary of man and decided to let his daughter eradicate all of mankind.[16] His daughter changed herself into Sakhmet, a ferocious lioness, and started a wholesale slaughter. The sun-god soon changed his mind, but his daughter had grown fond of human blood and refused to stop. Fortunately a priest from Heliopolis came up with the idea of brewing a large amount of beer and mixing this with red ochre so that it would resemble blood. Sakhmet drank the beer and, according to plan, grew drunk, suffered a hangover and gave up her enterprise, and so mankind was saved. In celebration of this event, the Egyptians held a nationwide annual celebration, the 'Feast of Drunkenness', in honour of Bastet at New Year's day. The festival is also described by Herodotus (2.59–60).

---

[15] For a more detailed description of the contents of the Tebtunis temple library and fuller references, see Ryholt 2005, 2010. The latter contribution also provides a general survey of the surviving literature of Late Period and Greco-Roman Egypt.
[16] One version is translated by Wente in Simpson 2003: 289–98.

The amount of magical literature in the temple library is much smaller than one would expect to find during earlier periods. However, by the time of the Roman occupation of Egypt there were severe restrictions on the use of magic, and in 199 AD, during the reign of Septimius Severus, an official decree declared that the practice of magic was punishable by death.[17] These sanctions seem mainly to have been put in place to avoid the potential dangers of malicious magic, and it is therefore significant that the temple library does not seem to include any magical spells to gain influence over the feelings and health of others. Such spells had been very common in earlier times and are still attested in a single Theban archive of demotic texts of slightly later date than our temple library. The few magical texts from the temple library mainly concern the protection for pharaoh. They were, in other words, used for the priests who assumed the role of pharaoh in carrying out the cult.

The cultic material also includes a large number of manuals or reference works containing what may be termed 'priestly knowledge'. Such reference works already existed in earlier times, but the number and the scope of their contents seems to have expanded during the Late Period. Through these manuals, the priests sought to classify and explain their entire surrounding world. The themes include the ideal temple and its priesthood, the gods and their mythology, the characteristics of each geographical division of Egypt, the universe, time and space, and so forth. Several of the manuals survive in multiple copies within the Tebtunis temple library and are also attested elsewhere in Egypt. It seems reasonable to assume that these would have been present in more or less every temple.

Four of the most important manuals – to judge from the number of surviving copies – are the so-called Book of the Temple, the Mythological Manual, the Priestly Manual and the Book of Nut. These were all written in the hieratic script, except in the case of the Book of Nut where there is also a hieroglyphic version. With somewhere in the order of twenty copies within the Tebtunis temple library alone, the Book of the Temple is by far the best attested manual of priestly knowledge. It consists of two parts. The first is a treatise on the ideal temple, which provides a detailed description of all important elements of the temple and their significance. The other is a treatise on the temple personnel, which provides a description of all relevant temple occupations, including the role and training

---

[17] Cf. Ritner 1995: 3,355–6, on official Roman hostility towards Egyptian magic.

of specific priests. The Priestly Manual contains a concise description of each geographical division of the country according to a fixed structure which provides information about the name of the main deity, the main temple, the title of the high priest, the sacred lake, the sacred tree, the sacred mound, etc. In contrast to these lists, the Mythological Manual provides narrative accounts of numerous myths about local gods throughout Egypt.

I would like to go into slightly more detail about the fourth manual whose original title reads 'The Plan of the Movement of the Stars'. This manual is more commonly referred to as the Book of Nut because the older hieroglyphic versions are dominated by a large image of the Goddess Nut who personifies the sky. As the original title implies, this was a treatise on the sky and the heavenly bodies. Knowledge of these matters was essential for the priests, partly because of rituals associated with certain celestial events, and partly because an understanding of astronomy was fundamental to the art of astrological divination (on which see below). But the aspect of this composition to which I would particularly like to draw attention is not its contents, but the light it sheds on textual transmission. The Book of Nut is first attested in the underground temple built by Seti I at Abydos (c. 1300 BC), some 1500 years before the copies of the text found in the temple library. Curiously, at a time of such wealth and might as the early Nineteenth Dynasty, it was apparently not possible for the people put in charge of the construction of the underground temple of Seti I at Abydos to gain access to an intact copy of the Book of Nut. The copy at their disposal was damaged and in the text, as copied onto the walls of his temple, blank spaces were left to indicate where words or passages were damaged or illegible. This is noteworthy since it might be taken as an indication that the text was an even older composition which had suffered during its transmission. Another interesting circumstance is the fact that the Tebtunis temple library contained different versions of the text. One contains the same blank spaces as the text used by King Seti I, while the same passages appear to be intact in another. The question which presents itself is: why was the damaged version kept if an undamaged version was available? The answer is presumably that the scribes were in doubt whether the undamaged version was original or whether the intact passages in question were later restorations; it might therefore have been considered better to be on the safe side and retain both versions. The text also shines light on another aspect of textual criticism. Ancient Egyptian priests, like the later scholars at the library of Alexandria, sometimes encountered passages in older texts which they felt required comment for one reason or another.[18] In the case of the Book of Nut, the scribes evidently sought to distinguish clearly between the original text and the later commentaries. In doing so, they took advantage of the fact that they had two scripts at their disposal and retained the original text in hieratic while the commentaries were added in demotic.

The temple library also included a number of texts relating to the classical Egyptian language. The Egyptians continued to compose and copy certain types of texts in this stage of the language until the large-scale closing of temples which began during the third century AD. To this end they not only compiled lists of archaic words, but even copied out entire ancient texts which they considered to represent fine examples of the classical stage of their language. A good example is provided by a series of hieroglyphic inscriptions copied from tombs at Assiut and preserved in two papyri. The actual tombs, some of which are still preserved, date to the Middle Kingdom (*c.* 2000–1800 BC) and were about two millennia old by the time these two papyrus copies were made.

Another noteworthy text is an exceptionally large onomasticon known as *The Great Tebtunis Onomasticon*. This text is interesting not just for its contents, but also for the lemmata that were later added. It was originally written in the hieratic script and one or more later scribes transcribed specific words into the demotic and Coptic scripts above the line. This is one of the oldest Coptic texts that we have and it is an invaluable source for the pronunciation of Egyptian, which was normally written without indication of the vowels, in the Roman era. I will not go into the rich contents of the onomasticon, but I would like to draw attention to one section which contains a list of old verbs of action. What makes this list noteworthy is the fact that it was excerpted from none other than the historical inscriptions of Ramesses III (*c.* 1175 BC) which are still preserved in the temple of Medinet Habu at Thebes. It is therefore clear that this lengthy inscription had been carefully studied and that a list of archaic words was then entered into a compilation which was circulated throughout the country. Texts such as these shed light on another aspect of literary scholarship that also formed an important subject of study at the library of Alexandria, that is, lexicography. Many old texts, not least the works of Homer, contained rare and archaic words. In Egypt lexical lists belong to a tradition that extended beyond the second millennium BC.[19]

---

[18] The phenomenon of commentaries in relation to Egyptian literature is discussed by von Lieven 2007: 263–7.
[19] Osing 2001.

The scientific literature

The second group of material I should like to present is the scientific literature. The temple library includes at least a dozen medical papyri, most written in demotic but three in Greek. The presence of this material is not surprising; healing and medicine were intimately associated with temples and the House of Life more or less as far back as our sources take us. An example of the very prominent role of medicine and medical studies at the temple libraries is provided by two biographical inscriptions set up by court physicians in the sixth century BC, both of whom relate how they were placed in charge of restoring the House of Life at the great temples of Abydos and Sais.[20] One of the texts dates to the time when Egypt had become part of the Persian empire. The court physician tells that the Persian king Darius I ordered that he should rebuild the House of Life because he, the king, understood the importance of the Egyptian medical art. About a century later Herodotus (2.84) speaks very enthusiastically about the Egyptian art of healing, above all because of the high level of specialisation which to him apparently was out of the ordinary. A more direct indication of Greek interest in Egyptian medical expertise is provided by the fact that certain aspects of it can be traced in the later Greek medical traditions, including the Hippocratic corpus.[21]

Divination, the art of predicting the future on the basis of various types of omina, seems to have played a much more important role at the temples than has hitherto been assumed.[22] There are far more manuals relating to divination than medicine, around sixty in total, but it should be noted that the average divination text is likely to have been considerably shorter than medical treatises. The divination texts from the temple library may be divided into two main groups: divination based on the position of the heavenly bodies, i.e. astrology, and divination based on the interpretation of dreams.

The astrological texts, which are by far the most numerous, can be subdivided into two groups. One group concerns predictions about the country as a whole. These predictions are based on the observation of the annual rise of Sirius (Egyptian Sothis) and the constellation in which this star appears. The rise of the star coincided with the beginning of the inundation – the rise of the Nile – and marked the beginning of the year. Since it was the level of the inundation which largely determined the extent of the yearly

---

[20] Posener 1936: 1–26, Gardiner 1938: 165.   [21] Ritner 2000, cf. also Harris 1971.
[22] A general survey of divination in ancient Egypt may be found in von Lieven 1999.

agricultural produce and the wealth of the state, it is not surprising that the *Sothis omina* should come to be associated with the well-being of the country as a whole. In fact one of the common statements in the Sothis texts is 'the Nile will be in balance this year' or sometimes the opposite. Other predictions include statements such as 'a small rebellion will take place in Egypt' or 'a ruler will die'. It still remains uncertain exactly what was done with these predictions once they had been established.

The second group of astrological texts are personal, i.e. predictions about the future of individuals. These texts provide an interesting social study since they, indirectly, inform us about the everyday worries of their intended users, just as modern horoscopes do. And the concerns are very much the same. The topics in question include career, wealth, health, friends, relationships, marriage and children.

The books on dream interpretation are closely related to those on personal astrology since they concern individuals and provide the same type of predictions. These texts are divided into sections which systematically explore specific themes, e.g. dreams about certain types of objects or actions.

The narrative literature

The third major category of texts comprises narrative literature. When I first began to make the inventory of the texts from the temple library, I was surprised at the scope of this material. Over the years it has become evident that it has a clear common denominator: all the narrative literature concerns historical characters or characters that were perceived as historical. At the same time it is clear from the actual contents of the narratives that we are largely dealing with historical fiction. It would, however, be a grave misunderstanding to see the narratives as mere entertainment. It was precisely this type of narrative material that was widely exploited by classical authors in their accounts of Egyptian history. This is well illustrated by the works of authors like Herodotus and Diodorus, to mention just a few, as well as the *Aigyptiaka* composed by the Egyptian priest Manetho in the early third century BC. In a few fortuitous instances, the Egyptian versions of specific stories told by these authors have even been identified among the holdings of temple libraries. An example is the Pheros Story mentioned below.

These circumstances indicate that the narrative material found at the temple libraries was deliberately selected and kept as some form of record about Egypt's past. It is surely no coincidence that the majority of texts concern the greatest kings and sages from the past. Many texts celebrate a glorious past where Egypt defeats and humiliates those same foreign people – Assyrians, Kushites, Persians – who, in the historical reality, had invaded and occupied the country. Such texts exemplify how major national traumas were manipulated in fiction, and the material offers a valuable insight into a kind of native Egyptian history that was based on a vague historical memory, but largely invented.

The largest group of related narratives, more than twenty papyri in all, concern Prince Inaros of Athribis (Inaros I) who became famous for his rebellion against the Assyrians during their brief occupation of Egypt in the seventh century BC. It is noteworthy that the relatively short encounter with the Assyrians caused the greatest trauma in later historical memory, at least to judge from the surviving literary material from the Tebtunis temple library and elsewhere.[23] The accounts of the exploits of Inaros and his allies expanded over the centuries and by the Roman period they had developed into a whole story cycle – the Inaros stories – which in several respects resembles the Arthurian stories. Just as independent stories would develop around several of the characters associated with King Arthur, such as Sir Lancelot, so we find independent stories about several of Inaros' allies. Several of these stories take place after the death of Inaros. We also find fantastic elements such as a battle with a sorceress who leads the Assyrian army on behalf of King Esarhaddon. In one of the dramatic episodes she turns herself into a gigantic griffin through magic and nearly slays the entire Egyptian army before Inaros kills her and saves the day.

The Inaros stories were apparently not sufficient to fulfill the need for Egyptian redemption in relation to the Assyrians; the hated Assyrians were represented as a people who had been humiliated by the Egyptians since the earliest history. Thus in another lengthy narrative we find King Djoser and his chancellor Imhotep also managing to defeat and humiliate the Assyrians – once again fighting a woman who leads the Assyrian army on behalf of a frightened king.[24] Since Djoser and Imhotep lived in the middle of the third millennium BC, this is a gross anachronism. The story about Djoser and Imhotep is also interesting for other reasons. Imhotep was the first known historical individual to become deified and he was venerated as the greatest sage in later times. Very little is known about the historical person except what may be inferred from a single contemporary inscription which records his name and titles and which indicates he served as one of

---

[23] The Assyrian invasion of Egypt in Egyptian literary tradition is discussed in Ryholt 2004.
[24] A detailed description of the story may now be found in Ryholt 2009.

the most senior officials of King Netjerkhet. This king would later be known as Djoser and became renowned for the construction of the first pyramid tomb, the famous Step Pyramid. The narrative is divided into a series of episodes which also mention the birth of Djoser, the royal tomb and the family of Imhotep.

A final narrative I would like to single out is the Petese Stories.[25] This is a compilation of seventy short stories about the virtues and vices of women. In several respects we are here dealing with a text of outstanding literary importance. According to Greek literary tradition, its alleged author, Petese, a prophet from the ancient city of Heliopolis, was Plato's Egyptian instructor in the art of astrology. Moreover, the introduction to the text states that the numerous stories were compiled on the prophet's behalf as a literary testament by which he would be remembered for posterity. The inspiration apparently came from a personal experience by Petese. According to another text, the prophet had once deciphered a more than two-millennia-old text which had been discovered in the temple of Heliopolis and which no-one else could read. This text was written by none other than Imhotep himself, the greatest sage of all in Egyptian tradition. And, just as the memory of Imhotep lived on through his writings, Petese also sought to gain immortality in this manner. The Petese Stories are cited by title in two other contemporary Egyptian literary texts, and they would therefore seem to have been well known and widely circulated. Even more remarkable is the fact that one of the stories included in this compilation was heard by Herodotus when he visited Egypt some six hundred years earlier and incorporated into his *Histories* in a Greek adaptation, i.e. the Pheros Story (Hdt. 2.111).

Conclusions

My purpose in this chapter has been two-fold: first to present some examples of the library tradition in ancient Egypt; and second to demonstrate how this tradition is relevant to our understanding of the cultural environment of the country in which the library of Alexandria was founded.

It is not my contention that the library of Alexandria was merely a Greek version of an Egyptian temple library or to belittle its achievements. It is indisputable that there are very significant differences. Above all, the library of Alexandria was vastly larger and much better funded than any Egyptian

---

[25] See Ryholt 2006: 1–19 for an outline of its contents and literary importance.

library is likely to have been and the Egyptian temple libraries were anything but public.

On the contrary, there are indications that these libraries zealously protected their writings which were frequently described as 'secret' throughout the three millennia which our sources cover. The primary reason for restricting access to the literature may well have been to protect it from abuse and to retain its potency. Knowledge was power, and it is obvious how magic or knowledge about the future gained through divination might be misused. There may also have been an element of protection of special expertise when literature, such as the medical type, was not made readily available to outsiders. Some temples enjoyed a high regard in relation to medical expertise and became important centres for pilgrimage, and they may well have wished to protect that status. The secretive attitude of the temple libraries was still in effect when Greek scholars began to seek out Egypt as a source of wisdom. It is, for instance, recounted how frustratingly difficult it was for visitors such as Pythagoras, Plato and Eudoxus to get the priests to share their wisdom (Strabo, *Geography* 17.1.29; Porphyry, *Life of Pythagoras* 7–8). Whether this is a historical fact in relation to the three named individuals is less important than the fact that such a statement exemplifies a general opinion that Egyptians did not readily impart their knowledge.

So, although scholarly activities such as textual criticism, commentary and lexicography, as well as studies in sciences such as medicine, were undertaken at the Egyptian temple libraries long before the creation of the library of Alexandria became famous in these areas, it is hardly likely that they could ever have achieved the same impact. However this may be, the present paper will hopefully provide some idea of the wealth of information to be gained from the Egyptian temple libraries.

2 | Reading the libraries of Assyria and Babylonia

ELEANOR ROBSON

Many ancient collections of scholarly writings on cuneiform tablets have been excavated from palaces, temples and private houses of second- and first-millennium Mesopotamia.[1] Assyriologists usually refer to these collections as 'libraries', but there has been little debate about how this label shapes our assumptions about their functions and meanings in Assyrian and Babylonian society. The classic model of a cuneiform library is Assurbanipal's library in the seventh-century BC Assyrian capital, Nineveh: a royal collection forged through inheritance, coercion and creative innovation in order to support royal decision-making. But that model can be tested against data from other excavated assemblages of scholarly writings from family dwellings and institutional buildings, before and after the end of indigenous rule in the sixth century BC. Both textual and architectural evidence can be used to explore questions of library formation, use and sponsorship within cuneiform culture of the first millennium BC.

Cuneiform literacies

In the region of the Tigris and Euphrates rivers, writing has been used in urban contexts since the late fourth millennium BC.[2] Clay tablets and other

---

[1] This chapter grows out of two research projects which I co-direct. *The Geography of Knowledge in Assyria and Babylonia, 700–200 BC: A Diachronic Comparison of Four Scholarly Libraries* (http://oracc.org/cams/gkab), funded by the UK Arts and Humanities Research Council and co-directed by Steve Tinney, edits and studies the tablets from Ezida, Huzirina, Reš discussed here and a family house from late Achaemenid-early Hellenistic Uruk. The manuscripts are published online in transliteration, English translation and glossaries as part of *The Corpus of Ancient Mesopotamian Scholarship* (http://oracc.org/cams/gkab). *Knowledge and Power in the Neo-Assyrian Empire* (http://oracc.org/saao/knpp), funded by the UK Higher Education Academy and co-directed by Karen Radner, presents and discusses the Neo-Assyrian court scholars' correspondence with the king in seventh-century Nineveh; the letters, queries and reports themselves form part of *The State Archives of Assyria Online* (http://oracc.org/saao). I am very grateful to both Karen and Steve as well as to other project members past and present – Marie Besnier, Philippe Clancier, Graham Cunningham, Ruth Horry, Phil Jones, Fran Reynolds, Kathryn Stevens and Greta Van Buylaere – as well as various friends, students and collaborators too numerous to mention.

[2] For a wide-ranging introduction to cuneiform culture, see Radner and Robson 2011.

inscribed artefacts survive in vast quantities, often in good archaeological context. As they were manufactured to fit the size of the text they would carry, tablets range in size from a USB stick or smaller to a laptop computer but are typically the size of a mobile phone or a little larger. The wedge-shaped cuneiform script, with a repertoire of 600 or more graphemes, was as visually and structurally complex as modern Chinese or Japanese and thus primarily the preserve of professional scribes and the urban elite. The first language to be recorded in cuneiform was Sumerian, a linguistic isolate that probably died out as a vernacular some time around 2000 BC but which continued to thrive in learned and liturgical contexts for a further two millennia. From at least the mid-third millennium, cuneiform was also used to write the Semitic language Akkadian – from the same linguistic family as Arabic and Hebrew – often in close association with Sumerian. Nowadays we divide Akkadian into two main dialects written (and spoken) in different parts of the region: Assyrian, in the area centred on Nineveh around modern-day Mosul in northern Iraq; and Babylonian, including the literary and scholarly Standard Babylonian, south of modern-day Baghdad.

From the eighth century BC Aramaic, another Semitic language, migrated eastwards from the Mediterranean coast. It increasingly supplanted Akkadian as the regional vernacular, not least because it offered much easier access to literacy through its grapheme set of just 22 letters. Nebuchadnezzar's deportation of the Judaeans to Babylon in 587 BC also brought Hebrew into the mix, shortly followed by (Indo-European) Old Persian through Cyrus the Great's conquest of Babylonia in 539 BC – an event that marks the end of indigenous rule in Mesopotamia. Greek came with Alexander the Great in 330 BC, if not before. None of these alphabetic incomers instantly supplanted cuneiform culture, which clung on, in increasingly restricted contexts, until the first century AD. However, the relatively perishable writing media of the alphabetic scripts – papyrus, leather, waxed wooden writing boards – means that cuneiform clay tablets overwhelmingly dominate the archaeological and textual record. We must constantly remind ourselves that in the first millennium BC cuneiform culture was a minority culture in Assyria and Babylonia, in close and often subservient interaction with other literacies.

The overwhelming majority of surviving cuneiform tablets document the upkeep of large institutions and wealthy families: their income, expenditure and legal rights. However, a significant minority comprise the byproducts of becoming literate, numerate and learned: from elementary writing exercises and calculations to excerpts from the great works of Sumerian and Akkadian literature and scholarship. Scribal and scholarly training depended heavily on memorisation, so that writing was often simply a means of learning by heart and written exercises essentially ephemeral byproducts of that process. Gradually the emphasis shifted, however, from the transmission of knowledge through memory and recitation (with concomitant textual flexibility) towards an increasing dependence on copying out manuscripts (and careful recording of sources) in the first millennium BC. A parallel tradition of editorial work, commentary-writing and recording the oral traditions around texts also developed at the same time. So far as we know, all of those engaged in such literary and scholarly activities made their livelihoods from this knowledge, whether through royal patronage, priestly employment, or solicitation of private clients for performance of ritual. As far as we can tell, there was no wealthy, leisured class for whom intellectual activities were optional, if challenging, pastimes.[3]

Dozens of collections of literary and scholarly tablets have been excavated, from family homes, temples and palaces, but they have rarely been studied holistically.[4] Rather, while archaeologists have published their architecture in excavation reports, Assyriologists have mined them for manuscripts of individual compositions. The resulting publications are usually standard editions that draw on manuscripts from a multiplicity of archaeological findspots regardless of date, place or context and which emphasise homogeneity at the expense of variation. Perhaps for that very reason, there is an assumption that all cuneiform libraries were essentially similar: they contained the same sorts of texts on carefully copied manuscripts whose contents changed little over the centuries.[5] However, as well as the apparently standard works (many of which are rather less than standardised on closer inspection of their manuscript sources), from mythology to omens to ritual, first-millennium BC cuneiform libraries typically also held commentaries on those works,[6] whether freshly composed or themselves copies of traditional material, as well as new compositions which build on the intellectual tradition.

It is not immediately obvious whether 'library' is necessarily the right word for all such archaeological assemblages of scholarly tablets. Modern definitions of libraries, deriving ultimately from ancient Greek ideas, typically entail statements such as, 'A place set apart to contain books

---

[3] This aspect of ancient Mesopotamian society, so striking to Classicists, goes largely unremarked in Assyriological circles.
[4] du Toit 1998 already makes this point.
[5] The classic formulation of this stance is Oppenheim 1960; slightly revised as 1977 [1964]: 13–23.
[6] For a major new study of commentaries in cuneiform scholarship, see Frahm 2011b.

for reading, study, or reference'.[7] However, Assyriologists tend to define libraries not in terms of their ancient functions but in relation to their disposition when excavated. That is, archaeological assemblages of scholarly, literary tablets are typically labelled as 'libraries', in opposition to assemblages of legal, epistolary and administrative records, known as archives (even if excavation often produces admixtures of the two in the same findspots).[8]

In order to reconcile the Assyriological definition of the cuneiform 'library' with the more usual ones, we must confront two serious questions: first, whether cuneiform tablets can ever be considered as books, and if so under what circumstances; and second, what the functions of such collections of tablets were. I have argued for a positive response to the first question elsewhere;[9] this chapter is an attempt at a partial answer to the second. There was certainly a native concept of library, albeit more restricted than in other ancient cultures: sporadically attested from the seventh to the second centuries BC, the word *gerkinakku* describes a room – usually in a temple – in which scholarly tablets were deposited, and the contents of that collection.[10] For present purposes this is what we shall take 'library' to mean.

What did cuneiform libraries contain? Who created, supported and used them? Where were they housed? How were they formed, maintained and abandoned? And why did they exist at all? I shall not attempt to give exhaustive answers, but aim to provide some fruitful ways forward by comparing four scholarly tablet collections from the first millennium BC, at least three of which were themselves described as *gerginakku* in antiquity.

Assurbanipal's library at Nineveh

The one cuneiform library that is well known outside the tiny world of Assyriology is Assurbanipal's library at Nineveh. From their heartland on the northern Tigris, the Assyrians had ruled much of the Middle East since the early first millennium BC. By the time Assurbanipal (669–c. 630) came to power, the capital city, Nineveh, hosted a splendid array of palaces and

---

[7] OED online (2010) sv. 'library'; cf. Canfora 1989: 77–8.
[8] For instance, in the standard reference work on ancient Near Eastern libraries and archives, Pedersén 1998: 2–3.
[9] In Robson 2007a I make the case that scholarly tablets of the first millennium BC can in some senses be seen as books because (amongst other reasons) their contents were transmitted as much by copying as by memory.
[10] *CAD* G: 86–7.

temples, funded and furnished through plunder and tribute. The citadel of Nineveh, also known by the Ottoman Turkish name Kuyunjik, was amongst the first Assyrian cities to be rediscovered in the nineteenth century. It was dug by Austen Henry Layard and others in 1847–55, well before the advent of recorded, stratigraphic archaeology, yielding around 30,000 tablets and fragments. This first large discovery of cuneiform texts made its way to the British Museum, where it is still housed today. A combination of excavators' notes and textual evidence from the tablets themselves suggests that there may have been four royal libraries on the royal citadel, as well as a substantial archive: in the Southwest Palace, built for King Sennacherib (704–681) in the early seventh century; in the North Palace, constructed for his grandson Assurbanipal; and in the nearby temples of Nabû, god of wisdom, and the great goddess Ištar, both now largely destroyed.[11] All but the last contained tablets bearing colophons showing that they were written or collected on Assurbanipal's behalf.[12]

The meagre archaeological data is further complicated by the fact that the whole citadel was looted and burned during the Babylonian and Median sack of Nineveh in 612 BC. Nevertheless, museological evidence puts the total number of surviving library tablets (that is, excluding archival records) in seventh-century Nineveh at at least 20,000 plus several thousand further waxed writing boards. They were acquired through a number of means. The large majority were the result of indigenous copying and recall, editing and composing, and inheritance.[13] But about 3,500 – over 17 per cent – arrived in Nineveh through forced acquisition in Babylonia (then a rebellious province of the Assyrian empire) or by the capture of Babylonian scholars themselves, who were put to writing out tablets in fetters.[14] They

---

[11] Reade 1986. Reade 1998–2011 gives an excellent survey of the likely findspots of tablets in the British Museum's Kuyunjik collection.

[12] In Assyriological parlance, colophons are inscriptions added to a tablet after the main text has been finished, containing information about the circumstances of production. This ancient metadata may include any or all of: the name of the work, a description of the exemplar from which it was copied, the name and ancestry of the copyist/and or owner of the tablet, the location and date, and sometimes injunctions against loss or theft. Hunger 1968 is the standard reference work on cuneiform colophons, now much in need of revision though still immensely valuable. Hunger 1968 nos. 317–39 are his editions of the Assurbanipal colophons.

[13] The letters *SAA* 10: 177, 240 and 255, from various court scholars to King Esarhaddon, all report on – or complain about – the complexities of collecting, collating and editing old tablets.

[14] The inventories *SAA* 7: 49–56 enumerate the scholarly contents of a large number of confiscated tablets and writing boards entering the libraries of Nineveh in 648 BC, most or all of which were formerly owned by named individuals, mostly Babylonians. *SAA* 11: 156 lists the enforced copying labour of nearly thirty scribes, at least some of whom are also Babylonian. See Parpola 1983 for a detailed account.

can be identified today by their use of Babylonian sign-forms and spelling habits.[15]

The vast quantity, and often fragmentary state, of the Nineveh tablets means there is still no comprehensive overview of the libraries' contents.[16] Meanwhile, two overlapping subsets of the corpus have been categorised by genre. Nearly three-fifths of the identified works on tablets written in Babylonian script concern divination, especially celestial omens.[17] Hymns, incantations and rituals comprise a further third of the Babylonian tablets from Nineveh, while the majority of the remaining tenth are medical recipes. Genres such as word lists, mathematics, myths and epics represent a tiny fraction of the whole. Similarly about 800 learned commentaries survive from the Assyrian royal library, of which nearly a half concern extispicy (divination from the entrails of sacrificed animals), just under a third deal with celestial omens and about a seventh treat word lists.[18] Even if neither the Babylonian texts nor the commentaries are fully representative samples of the collection as a whole, together they suggest that pre-horoscopic astrology, sacrificial divination and the performance of ritual dominated the libraries' holdings.

Although there had been an Assyrian royal tradition of tablet collecting since the late second millennium BC, in which most kings participated, there are good reasons to associate the libraries of Nineveh particularly closely with Assurbanipal. Most members of the Assyrian royal family had some training in cuneiform writing, but Assurbanipal himself was especially literate and cultured.[19] As a boy he had trained for the priesthood as he was not (yet) a direct heir to the throne.[20] But his father Esarhaddon was unexpectedly nominated crown prince in 694 BC, ahead of his older brother, and became king in 681.[21] He in turn named Assurbanipal as his heir after the untimely death of one of the latter's older brothers in 672.[22] Esarhaddon then appointed his chief scribe and astrologer, Balasî, to act as Assurbanipal's tutor.[23] It has even been suggested that some of the hundreds of tablets written in Assurbanipal's name were actually inscribed by him in the final stages of his training and, in the traditional manner, deposited

---

[15] See Fincke 2004.
[16] The British Museum's ongoing Ashurbanipal Library Project, with the aid of funding from the Andrew Mellon Foundation, has begun a systematic online catalogue and image database of the Kuyunjik Collection, with the long-term aim of providing as much documentation as possible (www.britishmuseum.org/research/research_projects/ashurbanipal_library_phase_1.aspx).
[17] Fincke 2004. [18] Frahm 2004. [19] Zamazálova 2011; Frahm 2011a.
[20] Villard 1997. [21] Porter and Radner 1998: 146. [22] Weissert and Radner 1998.
[23] In the letter SAA 10: 39, written in the summer of 671 BC, Balasî thanks Esarhaddon for the appointment.

ina gerginakki bīt Nabu ša qereb Ninua 'in the *gerginakku* of Nabû's temple which is in the middle of Nineveh' as offerings to the god of wisdom.[24] In his official inscriptions he made much of this divinely bestowed wisdom, most famously and lengthily in a passage from the inscription now known as L4 (lines 10–18):

Marduk, the sage of the gods, gave me wide understanding and broad perceptions as a gift.

Nabû, the scribe of the universe, bestowed on me the acquisition of all his wisdom as a present.

Ninurta and Nergal gave me physical fitness, manhood and unparalleled strength. I learnt the lore of the wise sage Adapa, the hidden secret, the whole of the scribal craft.

I can discern celestial and terrestrial portents and deliberate in the assembly of the experts.

I am able to discuss the series 'If the liver is a mirror image of the sky' with capable scholars.

I can solve convoluted reciprocals and calculations that do not come out evenly.

I have read cunningly written text in Sumerian, dark Akkadian, the interpretation of which is difficult.

I have examined stone inscriptions from before the flood, which are sealed, stopped up, mixed up.[25]

The 'capable scholars' referred to here constituted the entourage of experts, supported by a patronage system of land grants and royal gifts, who served the Assyrian court and aided the king in his decision-making.[26] An undated roster from Assurbanipal's reign shows that there could be up to forty in attendance at any one time, including Syro-Anatolian augurs and Egyptian scribes and dream interpreters.[27] Some 1,350 extant scholarly letters, divinatory queries and astrological reports to Esarhaddon and Assurbanipal provide extraordinarily rich insights into the workings of Assyrian court scholarship.[28] Assyrian and Babylonian diviners, exorcists, astrologers, physicians and lamenters all cited scholarly writings in their

---

[24] Livingstone 2007: 113; Hunger 1968: nos. 327–8, 338–9.
[25] Translated by Livingstone 2007: 100.
[26] On patronage, see Westbrook 2005; on Assyrian royal decision-making, see Radner 2011.
[27] The roster is *SAA* 7: 1; see Radner 2009 on foreign scholars at the Assyrian court.
[28] The scholarly correspondence is published in *SAA* 4; 8; 10; see http://oracc.org/saao/knpp (note 1) for a wide-ranging introduction to the politics of scholarship at the Neo-Assyrian court.

correspondence with the king, albeit some with more regularity than others.[29] We do not know whether they all had access to the royal library, were citing from their personal collections, or were quoting from memory. But an astrologer named Akkullanu seems to have managed some literary production in the royal library, overseeing several other scholars from various disciplines and reporting regularly to Assurbanipal on editorial matters.[30]

Nineveh, then, provides the standard image of the Mesopotamian 'library' found in many popular accounts of library history: an enormous royal collection, acquired by fair means or foul, whose primary function was to provide large datasets of omens to aid royal decision-making and rituals to ensure continued divine support for the crown. But how generalisable is this picture? Over forty assemblages of scholarly tablets from first-millennium Assyria and Babylonia have been excavated to date.[31] We shall compare Nineveh with three of them.

Ezida, another Assyrian royal library

Assurbanipal's library is not the only Assyrian royal tablet collection to have been discovered. Ancient Kalhu (modern Nimrud), some 30 kilometres south of Nineveh on the Tigris, had served as the Assyrian capital in the ninth to eighth centuries and remained a royal city until its destruction in 614 BC. In 1949–63 a team led by Max Mallowan for the British School of Archaeology in Iraq ran a substantial excavation on its citadel.[32] In 1955–7, a few hundred metres south of the palace, they unearthed a temple dedicated to Nabû, the god of wisdom, and his divine consort Tašmetu, which, like its counterpart in Nineveh, went by the Sumerian name Ezida (Sumerian 'True/loyal House'). In a small room opposite the main shrine was a deposit of some 250 fragmentary scholarly tablets, the remains of an originally much more substantial *gerkinakku*.[33]

---

[29] See Villard 1998 on literary quotations in scholarly letters; Robson 2011a and Veldhuis 2010 on quotations from omen collections.
[30] Akkullanu's letters on royal library matters are published as *SAA* 10: 101–3.
[31] Pedersén 1998: 275–80.
[32] The final excavation report is Mallowan 1966; Oates and Oates 2001 give a very useful and detailed account of the ancient city; Curtis *et al.* 2008 present the results of recent research.
[33] The primary publication of the Ezida tablets – comprising a catalogue and scale drawings of each – is Wiseman and Black 1996; Black 2008 gives an accessible overview of the corpus; an online edition is in progress at http://oracc.org/cams/gkab?ezida.

Although these meagre remnants comprise an assemblage that is literally a hundredth of the size of Assurbanipal's library at Nineveh, their make-up is remarkably similar. The genres best represented in Ezida are hymns, incantations and rituals (some 40%) and omens (27%), followed by word lists (15%) and medical recipes (7%). These are exactly those genres best attested in the commentaries and Babylonian-script tablets of Kuyunjik.

Further, although only about thirty tablets (about 12%) preserve any trace of a colophon, almost all of them give vital information about the men who worked there. An *āšipu* ('exorcist') named Banunu repeatedly exhorts readers, *gerginakka lā taparrar ikkil Ea šar Apsu* 'Do not disperse the library! Taboo of the god Ea, king of the Apsu!'[34] Banunu is also attested in Nineveh, as one of the overseers of the captive Babylonian scholars described above.[35] Most of the remaining colophons name scribes and scholars from just two well-connected families, which traced their ancestry to Assyrian court scholars of the early first millennium BC.[36] While the descendants of the *āšip šarri* ('royal exorcist') Issaran-šumu-ukin dominated the library in the ninth and eighth centuries, by the 720s they had been replaced by the family of Gabbu-ilani-ereš, who had been King Assurnaṣirpal's chief scholar. His seventh-century descendants are well known from the library tablets and royal correspondence of Nineveh. They include Nabû-zuqup-kena, the most prominent royal scholar in the days of kings Sargon II (721–705) and Sennacherib (704–670), and his sons Adad-šumu-uṣur and Nabû-zeu-lešir, King Esarhaddon's chief exorcist and chief scribe respectively. It is therefore reasonable to conclude that Ezida was a royal library very similar in function and personnel to, if much smaller than, Assurbanipal's library in Nineveh.

Interestingly, Nabû-zuqup-kena's many scholarly tablets were all apparently discovered in Nineveh. Yet fully two-thirds of his colophons explicitly state that the tablet was written at Kalhu,[37] thereby highlighting the vexed question of mobility of tablets, scholars and indeed whole libraries (although it is possible that there was nineteenth-century confusion or carelessness over findspots). For there is good evidence that the whole institution of Ezida moved, or perhaps bifurcated, not once but twice in the course of Neo-Assyrian history as the royal court moved from Kalhu to Sargon's short-lived capital Dur-Šarruken and thence to Nineveh under Sennacherib.[38] The building itself was replicated, with minor alterations,

---

[34] Wiseman and Black 1996: nos. 116, 188; see http://oracc.org/cams/gkab?gerginakku. Ea was the crafty god of the fresh spring waters under the earth (the Apsu, from which the English word 'abyss' descends via Greek).

[35] See note 14.   [36] The details are presented in Robson forthcoming.

[37] Hunger 1968: nos. 293–4, 297, 305; Baker and Pearce 2001.

[38] Robson and Stevens forthcoming.

on each move, and its staff and tablet holdings transported and/or duplicated. Assyrian temples of the god Nabû all have essentially the same layout, with double shrines (one each for Nabû and Tašmetu) and adjacent throne rooms — not only in the royal cities of Kalhu, Assur and Dur-Šarruken but also in western provincial towns such as Guzana and Hadatu.[39] It is thus highly likely that the now-vanished Ezida of Nineveh, to which the young Assurbanipal offered his tablets, also followed this pattern.

Although the half-built city of Dur-Šarruken was definitively abandoned on Sargon's unpropitious death in battle, Kalhu was never entirely eclipsed by Nineveh. It remained an important royal centre and its Ezida continued to acquire new holdings, as demonstrated by the colophons of Esarhaddon-era royal scholars mentioned above. It also continued to attract pious donations of personnel and land right through the seventh century BC.[40]

The close relationship between Neo-Assyrian kingship, deity and scholarship is elegantly realised in the architecture of the Kalhu Ezida. The temple, which is — as already mentioned — on the royal citadel just a short walk from the principal palace, is entered via a monumental gateway that features colossal beneficent spirits in typical Assyrian style. But whereas most temples and palaces famously feature monumental winged bulls, Ezida's entrance is flanked by giant fish-men, originally covered in gold leaf,[41] who represented the primordial sages who brought wisdom and civilisation to humankind in deep antiquity. Off the temple's first courtyard, which was surrounded by primarily utilitarian offices, are two further courts. A large courtyard to the south gave access to the twin shrines of Nabû and Tašmetu, whose larger-than-life statues could gaze directly on the scholars at work in and around the tablet store immediately opposite. And to the west, a smaller courtyard led on to a small-scale throne room and miniature versions of the twin shrines, so that the king could visit with appropriate ritual and protocol. Contemporary records and letters show that this area of the temple was known as the '*akītu* suite', which was set aside for an annual 'sacred marriage' ritual between Nabû and Tašmetu, lasting several days and presided over by the king or the mayor of Kalhu on his behalf.[42] This was not identical to the well-known Babylonian new-year *akītu*, in which Nabû also played a central role,[43] but served a similar function in renewing kingship and fertility as spring reached its peak.

---

[39] Turner 1968.
[40] The legal records *SAA* 12: 95–8 record private votive donations of personnel and land to the Ezida temple in Kalhu, the latest dated to 621 BC.
[41] Oates and Oates 2001: 111.   [42] See Postgate 1974; Oates and Oates 2001: 119–23.
[43] On the Babylonian *akītu* festival, see Bidmead 2002.

In sum, we should probably understand the temples of Nabû in Kalhu and Nineveh as branches of the same institutional network, providing divinely legitimated advice to the Neo-Assyrian throne. It just so happens that the fabric of the Kalhu Ezida has survived much more intact than its Nineveh counterpart, even if its tablets have not fared as well as the famous (but somewhat misnamed) Assurbanipal's library.

Huzirina, a school collection in provincial Assyria

We turn now to a third archaeological assemblage of scholarly tablets from seventh-century Assyria, far from the pomp and intrigue of the royal court. Huzirina (modern Sultantepe) was a small town some 400 kilometres west of Nineveh and about 20 kilometres north of Harran. A long-lived merchant city, provincial capital and cult centre of the moon god Sin, Harran (Akkadian 'Road' or 'Journey') was located at the crossroads of two vital overland trade routes: east–west from the Assyrian heartland to Aleppo and the northeastern corner of the Mediterranean; and north–south down the Balikh river from Anatolia to the Euphrates and Babylonia.[44] After the fall of Nineveh in 612 BC, it briefly became the Assyrian capital as the empire regrouped and tried to fight back against the invading Medes and Babylonians. So Huzirina was not completely cut off from the intellectual currents of the empire, but neither was it at the centre of its scholarly activity.

The site of Sultantepe was investigated briefly in 1951–2 by an Anglo-Turkish team led by Seton Lloyd and Nuri Gökçe for the British Institute of Archaeology in Ankara.[45] Owing to some 7 metres of post-Assyrian strata above the seventh-century levels, the excavation was limited to a series of trenches around the edges of the high central acropolis. It turned out that an artificial brick platform had been made after levelling the old summit, in order to construct a monumental public building on it – almost certainly a temple, perhaps to the moon god of Harran or to the goddess Ištar – and associated smaller structures. Amongst them was a courtyard house with a small domestic altar made of rubble and plaster built against its outer wall, close to the front entrance. On top of the altar, the excavators found a pile of nearly 400 scholarly tablets,[46] surrounded and protected by

---

[44] Lloyd and Brice 1951: 80–1.
[45] Preliminary reports are Lloyd and Gökçe 1953; Lloyd 1954. No final excavation report was ever written.
[46] The tablets were catalogued and published as scale drawings by Gurney and Finkelstein 1957; Gurney and Hulin 1964; an online edition is in progress at http://oracc.org/cams/gkab huzirina.

a semi-circle of empty storage jars and covered with a heap of stone and pottery vessels.[47] The whole of the surrounding area was covered in smashed household goods and even a decapitated skull, leading the archaeologists to posit that the tablets had been hurriedly secreted over the shrine for protection as the Babylonians and Medes threatened Harran and its environs in 610 BC.

The composition of the cached tablet collection differs markedly in some respects from that of the contemporary Assyrian royal libraries. As in the Ezida temple, hymns, incantations and rituals dominate (45% of the corpus), but omens comprise just 7% of the extant tablets. Medical recipes (11%) and word lists (7%) survive in somewhat similar proportions to Kalhu, but the most noticeable difference is the relatively large percentage of literary works (15%). Over fifty manuscripts of many of the great Akkadian classics – including *The Epic of Creation, Gilgamesh, Anzu, Nergal and Ereshkigal* and *The Poem of the Righteous Sufferer* – were found here, compared to just a handful in Kalhu. However, where the tablets from the royal cities are generally, as one might expect, elegantly executed in a clear hand and good orthography, the Huzirina tablets tend to poor spelling and sometimes incomprehensible script.[48]

The scribes attested in the Huzirina colophons are particularly revealing of the collection's function.[49] Best attested are members of the Nur-Šamaš family, who – it is reasonable to assume – probably lived in the immediately adjacent house. The paterfamilias was one Qurdi-Nergal, priest of the gods Zababa and Baba of Erbil, Harran and Huzirina, who is named as a *šamallû ṣehru* 'junior apprentice scribe' in a tablet dating to 701 BC. His son Mušallim-Baba appears in colophons, as well as one Ninurta-[. . .], perhaps Qurdi-Nergal's great-grandson, in 619 BC.[50] We know nothing about how Qurdi-Nergal and his family made their living, although two fragmentary royal land grants from seventh-century Huzirina exempt cultic personnel from certain taxes and provide the temple(s) with regular offerings.[51]

Several unrelated men also wrote tablets *ana tāmarti Qurdi-Nergal* 'for Qurdi-Nergal's viewing', including one Nabu-ah-iddin and his pupil Nabu-rehtu-uṣur. Using identical wording to the *āšipu* Banunu in Kalhu, the latter warns against the dispersal of the *gerginakku* as a taboo of the god Ea, in the colophon to a literary work copied in 701 BC.[52] A further fifteen

---

[47] Lloyd and Gökçe 1953: 37.   [48] Gurney 1952: 26.
[49] The colophons were first edited by Hunger 1968: nos. 351–408; for a more thorough discussion, see Robson forthcoming.
[50] See Gurney 1997 for a family tree.   [51] They are *SAA* 12: 24; 48.
[52] http://oracc.org/cams/gkab?P338355.

šamallû (seḫrūtu) '(junior) apprentice scribes' are named in the Huzirina cache. Particularly noteworthy are Šum-tabni-uṣur, son of a royal doctor; Nabu-ibni, son of an Assyrian scribe; Mutaqqin-Aššur, son of a scribe of the city of Assur; Nabu-šumu-iškun, son of the *turtānu*'s senior scribe; and Bel-le'i-..., son of the *turtānu*'s scribe. The *turtānu* was the most senior of Assyria's military officials who, not coincidentally, also governed the province immediately to the north of Harran.[53] Conspicuously, none of these young men hailed from the royal cities of Kalhu, Dur-Šarruken or Nineveh.

In this light, it is tempting to posit the Huzirina tablet collection as the remains of a scribal school, run by Qurdi-Nergal and his descendants, for the sons of provincial officials and the like. The tablets were produced, as was traditional, by copying or dictation, by youths in their late teens or early twenties in the final stages of training, for their older teachers.[54] The quality of the manuscripts, the rather backwater location and the social status of the apprentices collectively suggest that this was not an establishment of the highest educational standing – they would have been in the royal cities of the heartland – but certainly had aspirations and pretensions to cultural roundedness. As its students were not preparing to access the inner circle of the royal court, they had no great need for omens. But as they were probably destined for positions in the middle ranks of imperial governance, they were given a thorough grounding in the classics of their culture as well as in standard works of healing, prayer and penitence.

Reš, a city temple in Hellenistic Uruk

The Huzirina-Kalhu comparison shows that the composition and function of cuneiform libraries depended on socio-political circumstances: in the seventh century BC the collections of royal institutions differed quite dramatically from those in private priestly households. We shall now consider a fourth and final assemblage of scholarly tablets, from a city in second-century BC Babylonia, to test the impact of Persian and Seleucid rule on native intellectual culture.

The city of Uruk was ancient, august and enormous, even by Mesopotamian standards. It was here, in the late fourth millennium BC, that the world's first writing had been developed for managing temple assets.[55]

---

[53] Radner 2006: 59.
[54] See Robson 2008: 227–60 and Maul 2010 for such patterns of apprenticeship in later Babylonia and Neo-Assyrian Assur respectively.
[55] An authoritative and engaging introductory account is Nissen, Damerow and Englund 1993.

By the early third millennium it had grown to 5.5 square kilometres – about twice the size of Athens at its greatest extent and half the size of imperial Rome three millennia later.[56] By the late third millennium it had become known as the home of the legendary king Gilgamesh, a reputation which it retained even in the Seleucid period.[57] Uruk was still a thriving urban centre in the late first millennium BC and, along with Babylon itself, one of the last bastions of cuneiform culture in the face of increasing Hellenisation.

The Deutsche Orient-Gesellschaft conducted several long series of excavations at Uruk over much of the twentieth century. Their primary focus was the enormous temple complex at the centre of the city which in the Seleucid period comprised two ziggurats and three gigantic temples: Reš, dedicated to the sky-god Anu-Zeus, and Eanna and Irigal (or Ešgal), both dedicated to Ištar-Venus.[58] In the winter of 1959–60 the team uncovered some 140 tablets and fragments in a small paved room adjacent to the southeastern gate of Reš, off one of its dozen courtyards.[59] This area of the temple had already been excavated once in 1912–13 and had also been thoroughly covered in looting pits, so that it is impossible to determine its exact function.

It is highly likely that at least 170 illicitly excavated tablets from Seleucid Uruk, which entered European and north American collections in the first decades of the twentieth century, also come from this findspot,[60] not least because many of the names and dates tally with those on the formally recovered tablets. However, no direct joins between the two groups of tablets have yet been made. In what follows we thus distinguish between 'Reš' tablets, formally excavated in the temple, and 'Uruk' tablets, which on internal evidence are highly likely to have been looted from the same locus.

The Reš tablets date from SE (Seleucid Era) 15–150 (297–162 BC), although the temple itself was not completed until 251 BC.[61] Some tablets must, then, have been moved here from other places, including perhaps the Eanna temple. For amongst the illicitly excavated tablets is one with a colophon that ends, *ummānu ša šuma lā ušannû u ina gerginakki išakkanu Ištar hadîš lippalissu ša ultu Eanna ušeṣṣû aggiš Ištar lišteddiš* 'The scholar

---

[56] Nissen 1988: 71–2.
[57] On the role of Uruk in *The Epic of Gilgamesh*, see George 2003: 91–137.
[58] For their architectural history, see Downey 1988: 17–35; Kose 1998: 93–242, 257–76.
[59] The tablets were catalogued and published as scale drawings by van Dijk and Mayer 1980 and were discussed most recently by Clancier 2009: 86–90, 99–101, 406–9; an online edition is in progress at http://oracc.org/cams/gkab?resh.
[60] van Dijk and Mayer 1980: 13; for a list and an online edition in progress, see http://oracc.org/cams/gkab?illicitly.
[61] Downey 2003: 188. The Seleucid Era (SE) was deemed to have begun on New Year's Day (signalled by the first new moon after the spring equinox) in 311 BC, Seleucus I Nicator's first regnal year in Babylonia.

who does not change a line and deposits (it) in the library: may the goddess Ištar look joyfully on him! He who removes it from the Eanna temple: may Ištar keep pursuing him angrily!'[62]

About sixty of the Reš tablets are unidentifiable fragments and another thirty are legal and administrative records. Of the remaining fifty manuscripts, twenty-three (46%) are hymns, incantations and rituals and eighteen (36%) are omens. So far, so much like earlier libraries. But if we factor in the extra 170 Uruk scholarly tablets that are likely to have come from the same findspot, we find a very different picture: 115 (51%) of the new total contain mathematical astronomy – a genre invented since the fall of native rule – fifty-one (23%) contain hymns, incantations and rituals, and thirty-seven (16%) bear omens.

The shift in interests is explicable once we look at the composers and copyists of the texts. In Seleucid Babylonia (as in Neo-Assyrian Kalhu and elsewhere), families identified themselves with eponymous ancestors.[63] The ancestral names attested more than once in the Reš tablets are Ahi'utu, Ekur-zakir and Sin-leqi-unninni.[64] The Uruk scholarly tablets were written exclusively by men from those same three families, plus that of Hunzû, and even by the same individuals as are found in the Reš corpus.

For instance, amongst the Reš tablets is a prayer to be offered as a bull is sacrificed in order to make the skin of a ritual kettle-drum from its hide. Its colophon, which dates the tablet to 176 BC, reads:

A *šu'illakku*-prayer of the prize bull of the temple-workshop.

Tablet of Anu-aba-uter, son of Anu-belšunu, descendant of Sin-leqi-unninni. Hand of Anu-balassu-iqbi, son of Nidintu-Anu, son of Anu-belšunu, descendant of Sin-leqi-unninni, Urukean. Uruk, the 21st day of Ululu (month VI), year 1 hundred 36, Seleucus was king.[65]

And a list of ancient royal sages, written eleven years later, ends:

[Tablet] of Anu-belšunu, son of Nidintu-Anu, descendant of Sin-leqi-unninni, lamentation priest of Anu and Antu, Urukean. (Written with) his own hand. Uruk, the 10th day of Ayyaru (month II), year 1 hundred 47, Antiochus was king. He who fears Anu shall not carry it off.[66]

---

[62] Hunger 1968: no 106; to appear online as http://oracc.org/cams/gkab?P363709.
[63] See Brinkman 2006 for the origins of this practice.
[64] Ahi'utu: three times, all in archival records; Ekur-zakir: three times: once in a scholarly colophon and twice in archival records, and Sin-leqi-unninni: five times in scholarly colophons and once in a legal record; see van Dijk and Mayer 1980: 26–9.
[65] van Dijk and Mayer 1980: no. 6; online edition at http://oracc.org/cams/gkab?P363270.
[66] van Dijk and Mayer 1980: no. 89; online edition at http://oracc.org/cams/gkab?P363353.

Three generations of the Sin-leqi-unninni family – descendants of the fabled editor of *Gilgamesh*[67] – are attested here: in the first colophon we have the paterfamilias Anu-belšunu the elder and his two sons Nidintu-Anu (named after his grandfather and thus the eldest son)[68] and Anu-aba-uter. Nidintu-Anu's sons Anu-belšunu the younger and Anu-balassu-iqbi wrote the second and first tablets respectively.

Four of these five men are also attested on legal and scholarly tablets excavated illicitly from Uruk.[69] Anu-belšunu the elder may have been born in SE 63 (249 BC) if we are to believe a horoscope written in his name.[70] He was intellectually and economically active from SE 83 at the latest to at least SE 123 (229–189 BC). As a young man he copied scholarly tablets – mostly omens, rituals and mathematical astronomy – for his father Nidintu-Anu and (yet another) Anu-belšunu of the Ahi'utu family and then trained three of his own sons. Nidintu-Anu the younger copied out a lamentation to the god Ellil for Anu-belšunu in SE 108 (204 BC) while Anu-aba-uter wrote a building ritual, some astrological medicine and a great deal of mathematical astronomy for him and for Šamaš-eṭir of the Ekur-zakir family between SE 112 and SE 121 (200–191 BC). Anu-belšunu the younger is not attested outside the Reš corpus but his younger brother Anu-balassu-iqbi was trained by uncle Anu-aba-uter in laments and mathematical astronomy from SE 130 to SE 136 (182–176 BC).

How are we to make sense of the apparently antithetical combination of lamentation and ritual and mathematical astronomy written by these men? All were known by the title of '*kalû* (lamentation priest) of Anu and Antu', the all-important deities whose sanctuaries were at the heart of Reš. The role of the Seleucid *kalû*, just as it had been in Neo-Assyrian times, was to soothe and placate the gods through ritual performance of lamentation in times of disturbance and distress: during repairs to the gods' sanctuaries for instance, or at times of solar and lunar eclipse. A vast and intricate body of *kalûtu* – *kalûs'* laments and rituals – survives from Seleucid Uruk, much of it anonymous but significant numbers from the Sin-leqi-unninni men's hands.[71] As the legal documents from Reš and elsewhere in Uruk show, the *kalûs* and other priests supported themselves through prebends – rights to shares in the temple's offerings income – and through the management of agricultural and urban land. Royal support for the temple was sporadic at best.

---

[67] On Sin-leqi-unninni see George 2003: 28–33.   [68] On such naming practices, see Baker 2002.
[69] Discussed in more detail by Robson 2008: 240–60.
[70] Edited by Beaulieu and Rochberg 1996.
[71] Many of the laments are edited by Cohen 1988 and the rituals by Linssen 2004. For tablets by and for the Sin-leqi-unninni family, see http://oracc.org/cams/gkab?sin-leqi-unninni.

However, Anu-aba-uter and his mentor Šamaš-eṭir of the Ekur-zakir family – who later became chief priest of Reš – also took the archaic title 'scribe of *Enūma Anu Ellil*'. In Neo-Assyrian times this term had designated men such as crown prince Assurbanipal's tutor Balasî, who made qualitative observations of the night sky and interpreted them through omens from the great handbook *Enūma Anu Ellil*. The gradual mathematisation of the night sky had begun in eighth-century Babylon, with systematic observation of lunar eclipses. By the Seleucid period, only lip service was paid to celestial omens, as zodiacal schemas and increasingly sophisticated predictive models took over. This intellectual shift is clearly visible in the Uruk tablets.[72] In the late third century, Anu-belšunu the elder's generation still copied *Enūma Anu Ellil* and made short-term predictions based on simple periodicities. By the early second century – in Anu-aba-uter's generation – we find short-term predictions alongside the mature mathematical astronomy now known by historians as Systems A and B, but no celestial omens. Another twenty years later, Anu-balassu-iqbi and his contemporaries only used Systems A and B.

For the *kalûs* of Uruk, then, astronomy was a specialised branch of their discipline. We might imagine that, as faith in the old belief systems declined in the course of the early Hellenistic period, the priesthood needed to maintain a strong worshipper base in order to protect their social standing as well as their economic support system. Much of their allure rested on the impressive public chanting of elaborate lamentations, accompanied by the beating of kettle-drums, to placate the upset gods during solar and lunar eclipses. In this light, we can see the ever-increasing mathematisation of their predictive methods as a means of ensuring the continued accuracy of ritual timings – and as a conspicuous display of intellectual endeavour that was currently beyond Greek competence.[73] Sadly, the project failed within a few generations. Anu-balassu-iqbi is the last known astronomer-*kalû* of Uruk, while Reš itself was destroyed by fire in 124 BC, shortly after the Parthian conquest, and never rebuilt.[74]

Conclusions: the four libraries compared

As Yun Lee Too reminds us, 'the words "ancient library" [may not] always refer to the same thing where different people of antiquity are concerned'.[75] She worries that 'the [modern] scholarly emphasis on the

---

[72] On the evolution of celestial scholarship in Seleucid Uruk, see Robson 2007b.
[73] As argued by Bowen 2002.   [74] Downey 2003: 189.   [75] Too 2010: 4.

Alexandrian library that constructs this institution as *the* ancient library suggests that "ancient library" might indeed be a static entity'. A similar privileging of Assurbanipal's library at Nineveh permeates the perceptions of cuneiform libraries of the ancient Middle East. However, this brief survey has shown how various the contents and functions of such collections actually were.

The scholarly tablets of the Kalhu Ezida not surprisingly provide the closest match to the Nineveh library. In this Assyrian royal temple, active throughout the eighth and seventh centuries BC, royal advisors worked in kin-based groups, supported by direct and institutional patronage from the king. Here, as in Nineveh, the emphasis was on omens, incantations and ritual to provide divinely authorised guidance to the crown. As part of a network of such institutions, the Kalhu Ezida was partially emptied of its tablets as the capital moved, first to the short-lived new city of Dur-Šarruken and later to Nineveh; yet it continued to function and was destroyed only at the end of the empire in *c.* 614 BC.

The cache of tablets found outside a domestic dwelling at Huzirina, not far from the western Assyrian city of Harran, provides a contemporary contrast. It seems to have belonged to a priestly family, active *c.* 718–610 BC, who educated the sons of local officials – but conspicuously no young men from royal cities – and perhaps also had income through royal and private endowments to the temple with which they were associated. Here the emphasis was on incantations, (non-royal) ritual, medicine and literature – the last two genres noticeably more prominent than the royal library. The collection was hidden away for safe-keeping as invaders attacked the rump of the Assyrian empire, and never returned for.

Finally, the remains of a much-looted tablet room in Reš, the main city temple of Uruk in Seleucid Babylonia, contained the professional and legal records of a few priestly families, especially over the period *c.* 220–170 BC. The descendants of Ekur-zakir and Sin-leqi-unninni served as lamentation priests and astronomers of the god Anu, supported by prebendary income and land holdings. Their scholarly writings accumulated, as the tablets of Huzirina had, through young men copying and composing for older mentors. But in Reš the tight focus on astronomy, lamentations and ritual was closely aligned to the *kalûs'* professional interests, rather as the contents of the Ezida had been. As the men of Reš had no royal patronage, however indirect, they set their own priorities and agendas, responding very differently to the divine world than the Assyrians had. Because they depended ultimately on continued offerings from worshippers, their income and prestige withered with the loss of indigenous culture and finally failed in the mid-second century BC.

This sketch of the libraries of Assyria and Babylonia marks the beginning of a large-scale research endeavour, not its final outcome. I have briefly surveyed just four of the forty or more excavated assemblages of scholarly tablets from the region, and based my analysis of them on corpora that we are still in the process of editing. It is likely that future research will necessitate substantial revisions and improvements to the picture painted here.

However, it is already clear that, in contrast to many libraries of the classical world, cuneiform 'libraries' apparently had no public face or function. There were certainly no dedicated library buildings. While tablet collections could be housed in monumentally large urban temples such as Ezida or Reš, which stood literally and metaphorically at the heart of Assyrian and Babylonian cities, it is highly unlikely that any but the scholarly personnel who created and used them had any notion of their existence. There is little or no evidence (yet) of librarians, catalogues or other finding aids,[76] absences which further hint at very restricted user (and production) communities.

On the other hand, we can already see that, while cuneiform 'libraries' had much in common, they were neither static nor universally similar. Collections accrued as much through educational copying and composition by younger men for older mentors as by acquisition or by other means. Their scale, composition and function depended heavily on the particular needs and interests of the institutions and individuals, both patrons and scholars, who used them. Once royal patronage disappeared with the end of indigenous rule, scholarly communities had to rely exclusively on religious and private support. New genres of writing, such as personal horoscopes, astrological medicine and mathematical astronomy, reflect the effort put in to attracting and retaining new clientele.[77] The model of the cuneiform *gerginakku* was robust and flexible enough to support both tradition and innovation for several hundred years after the loss of political engagement with native intellectual culture.

---

[76] The records from Nineveh mentioned above (note 14) should be understood as booty rosters, not acquisition lists; and we should be wary of labelling Akkullanu, Banunu or any of their colleagues as 'librarians' (notes 13, 30).

[77] On personal horoscopes, see Rochberg 1998; on astrological medicine, Heessel 2008; on mathematical astronomy, Steele 2008: 39–66.

3 | Fragments of a history of ancient libraries

CHRISTIAN JACOB

Introduction

In our contemporary western world, libraries are undoubtedly icons of culture and scholarship as well as places of learning and literate entertainment. This status depends on several assumptions. First, despite the development of digital libraries and databases, printed books and journals are still considered as the medium and the archive *par excellence* of knowledge, whatever the discipline. Second, the number of books available exceeds the buying and reading abilities of any one individual, and has done at least since the Renaissance; it makes sense to select a part of them, and to collect them in places where they may function as a shared resource for a community of users more or less sharply defined. Books from public libraries can be browsed and read without being owned. Third, libraries are archives of old books that are still considered useful and worth preserving, whether for their historical value, for the knowledge they convey, or for their meaning. Through their architectural organization, their interior arrangement and that of their holdings, libraries may be considered as material embodiments of a particular model of cultural memory and of the transmission of knowledge. Old books are not necessarily outdated, they are steps in intellectual genealogies and they can still play an active part in the process of learning. Fourth, collections of books mirror a certain idea and organization of knowledge, memory, and culture, either universal and encyclopedic, or selective and focused on a particular discipline or literary genre. Finally, despite the differences of scales and purposes, a national library, a university or public library, and a private library share some basic features, such as rooms, or at least furnitures and shelves where books are stored according to various ordering principles, allowing them to be kept, retrieved, and eventually read.

When investigating the history of libraries – whether in the west or in other cultural realms – our familiarity with these institutions and their functions can be a cause of anachronism. That in turn may lead us to emphasize technical aspects, such as architecture, catalogues, book collections, staff, and readers, without questioning the cultural specificity of libraries and their potentially different nature, purpose, and status in past societies. The fragmentary and often indirect evidence on which we have to rely may make it impossible to answer many questions about the organization of ancient libraries. These may include questions about the way books were ordered, the extent to which they were accessible to readers, the rules of behaviour in these places, and the range of operations one was allowed or supposed to perform with books, such as reading, copying excerpts or a whole text, or commenting on them and discussing them with friends.

Indeed, as historians and philologists, we should question both the physical and conceptual nature of ancient Greek and Roman libraries. Our investigation depends not only on the testimony that has reached us, but also the absence of information or the silence of our sources about particular aspects of these institutions. We should try to locate ancient libraries in their political, social, and cultural frame, and to consider them as historical artefacts shaped by manifold variables. As far as extant sources allow it, we should investigate the nature, purpose, meaning, and uses of ancient libraries by situating them at the crossroads between histories of architecture and of literacy, studies of books as material objects and in terms of textual transmission, and at the intersection of social and political processes. Libraries need to be understood in relation to the creation of literatures designed to be read rather than to be performed orally. Put otherwise, they need to be understood against the background of the emergence of readers, whether scholars, students, writers, or *amateurs* of literature.

When did the first libraries appear in the classical world? Or rather from which point and according to which criteria can we legitimately use the word "library?" Does the owner of a few books have a "library?" Is he aware that he possesses a "library" and would he use that word? Is a *biblion thēkē* linked to a particular physical arrangement of material? Is a *capsa* containing a few book-rolls a library? Does a library need shelves, either open shelves or shelves within a cupboard? Or should the term library be reserved to denote a dedicated room within a building, or indeed an entire building devoted to books? And is a building a library if it is only a storage place for books? Or must it also be a reading room or a space devoted to other uses, such as social meetings, lectures, and teaching? Are private and public libraries the same thing? If so, what are the social rules and borders distinguishing those allowed to enter the place from those who are not?

It is, to be sure, impossible to answer such crucial questions in a general way. Classical Athens, the Hellenistic kingdoms, Rome during the Republic or under imperial rule, and the provincial cities of the Roman Empire offer a range of contrasting situations. Although literary testimony, inscriptions, and sometimes archaeological remains allow us today to identify some places and buildings as libraries, it is far more difficult to reconstruct ancient ideas of the library and their historical evolution. The literary sources that have survived do not provide us with a global picture, but rather depict a variety of local situations, viewed from a range of standpoints. In this chapter, I would like to propose an approach deconstructing the synthetic surveys, the continuous narrative of the history of ancient libraries. Instead, I shall put the emphasis on just a few fragments, a few pieces of testimony and I shall comment upon them, as snapshots of local situations, to be interpreted for themselves, each according to its own logic and agenda. Such a focus on primary sources is a first and much needed step for future work. Jenö Platthy's *Sources on the earliest Greek Libraries* was a groundbreaking book.[1] What is needed today, however, is a revised and augmented edition, accompanied by a commentary on all the pieces of testimony contained within it. Naturally these pieces of testimony do not provide us with transparent and objective information. They were shaped by strategies of cultural representation. They demand to be read, questioned, and interpreted.

FRAGMENT 1. Xenophon, *Memorabilia*, 4, 2

Τοῖς δὲ νομίζουσι παιδείας τε τῆς ἀρίστης τετυχηκέναι καὶ μέγα φρονοῦσιν ἐπὶ σοφίᾳ ὡς προσεφέρετο νῦν διηγήσομαι. καταμαθὼν γὰρ Εὐθύδημον τὸν καλὸν γράμματα πολλὰ συνειλεγμένον ποιητῶν τε καὶ σοφιστῶν τῶν εὐδοκιμωτάτων καὶ ἐκ τούτων ἤδη τε νομίζοντα διαφέρειν τῶν ἡλικιωτῶν ἐν σοφίᾳ καὶ μεγάλας ἐλπίδας ἔχοντα πάντων διοίσειν τῷ δύνασθαι λέγειν τε καὶ πράττειν, (...)

Εἰπέ μοι, ἔφη, ὦ Εὐθύδημε, τῷ ὄντι, ὥσπερ ἐγὼ ἀκούω, πολλὰ γράμματα συνῆχας τῶν λεγομένων σοφῶν ἀνδρῶν γεγονέναι; καὶ ὁ Εὐθύδημος, Νὴ τὸν Δί', ἔφη, ὦ Σώκρατες· καὶ ἔτι γε συνάγω, ἕως ἂν κτήσωμαι ὡς ἂν δύνωμαι πλεῖστα.

(...) Τί δὲ δὴ βουλόμενος ἀγαθὸς γενέσθαι, ἔφη, ὦ Εὐθύδημε, συλλέγεις τὰ γράμματα; ἐπεὶ δὲ διεσιώπησεν ὁ Εὐθύδημος σκοπῶν ὅ τι ἀποκρίναιτο, πάλιν ὁ Σωκράτης, Ἆρα μὴ ἰατρός; ἔφη· πολλὰ γὰρ καὶ ἰατρῶν ἐστι συγγράμματα. καὶ ὁ Εὐθύδημος, Μὰ Δί', ἔφη, οὐκ ἔγωγε. Ἀλλὰ μὴ ἀρχιτέκτων βούλει γενέσθαι;

γνωμονικοῦ γὰρ ἀνδρὸς καὶ τοῦτο δεῖ. Οὔκουν ἔγωγ', ἔφη. Ἀλλὰ μὴ γεωμέτρης ἐπιθυμεῖς, ἔφη, γενέσθαι ἀγαθός, ὥσπερ ὁ Θεόδωρος; Οὐδὲ γεωμέτρης, ἔφη. Ἀλλὰ μὴ ἀστρολόγος, ἔφη, βούλει γενέσθαι; ὡς δὲ καὶ τοῦτο ἠρνεῖτο, Ἀλλὰ μὴ ῥαψῳδός; ἔφη· καὶ γὰρ τὰ Ὁμήρου σέ φασιν ἔπη πάντα κεκτῆσθαι. Μὰ Δί' οὐκ ἔγωγ', ἔφη· τοὺς γάρ τοι ῥαψῳδοὺς οἶδα τὰ μὲν ἔπη ἀκριβοῦντας, αὐτοὺς δὲ πάνυ ἠλιθίους ὄντας. (...)

---

[1] Platthy 1968.

I will now show his method of dealing with those who thought they had received the best education, and prided themselves on wisdom. He was informed that Euthydemus, the handsome, had formed a large collection of the works of celebrated poets and professors, and therefore supposed himself to be a prodigy of wisdom for his age, and was confident of surpassing all competitors in power of speech and action.

(…)

"Tell me, Euthydemus, am I rightly informed that you have a large collection of books written by the wise men of the past, as they are called?"

"By Zeus, yes, Socrates," answered he, "and I am still adding to it, to make it as complete as possible."

(…)

"Tell me, Euthydemus, what kind of goodness do you want to get by collecting these books?"

And as Euthydemus was silent, considering what answer to give,

"Possibly you want to be a doctor?" he guessed: "Medical treatises alone make a large collection."

"Oh no, not at all."

"But perhaps you wish to be an architect? One needs a well-stored mind for that too."

"No, indeed I don't."

"Well, perhaps you want to be a good mathematician, like Theodorus?"

"No, not that either."

"Well, perhaps you want to be an astronomer?"

And as he again said no, "Perhaps a rhapsodist, then? They tell me you have a complete copy of Homer."

"Oh no, not at all; for your rhapsodists, I know, are consummate as reciters, but they are very silly fellows themselves." (translation O. J. Todd, The Loeb Classical Library)

The dialogue between Socrates and the young Euthydemus, contained in book four of Xenophon's *Memorabilia*, offers fascinating testimony to some of the ways in which books were regarded in fifth and fourth century BC Athens. Socrates, who challenges the sophists' claims to knowledge, sets a trap for a young Athenian who believes in the educative power of books. In order to be relevant and meaningful to Xenophon's audience, this episode presumably alludes to what must have been common concerns among those ambitious young men who were most eager to get a high social position in the city. Euthydemus considers books as tools with which to get the upper hand over his fellow students. Learning is not considered in terms of self-enrichment, but as a competitive process, through which one strives to be the best and to reach the top position.

The sophists were accustomed to teaching through lectures and oral performances, displaying their rhetorical and intellectual skills as well as their polymathic knowledge. They were travelling teachers or visiting professors, staying for short periods of time in those Greek cities where audiences and students could be met. Socrates, by contrast, was a resident master: his activity was located in various locations around the city of Athens. His main task was to deconstruct the illusory knowledge taught by the sophists and to lead his followers along a path where truth was both a goal to attain and a means of self discovery. To these two forms of learning, Euthydemus prefers, or rather adds, a third one, the use of books. There is an element of arrogance in this choice: Euthydemus does not want to receive lessons from anyone, or at least he does not want to give the appearance of doing so. Books are discreet teachers and they protect self-esteem.

What about finding books and collecting them together? Euthydemus is represented as the proud owner of a set of material objects, each of which has a value and a price. Their value and their purpose lies less in the papyrus medium employed in their manufacture, than in the text written on them. Books can be bought, or else one can copy a text oneself from one book-roll to another: the copyist is, so to speak, the publisher of the text. Before they can be read, book-rolls need to be handled appropriately, as fragile objects that should be kept safe in a box or a chest. The reader needs to learn how to roll and unroll them without tearing the papyrus fibers. It was possible to add a tag or a few words at the beginning or at the end of the roll, to identify the author and the title of the work. If books were to disclose the text and the knowledge they contained, they had to be read or listened to. A reader needed to be trained in the difficult skill of following texts written in *scriptio continua*, without accents and punctuation marks. His eyes should move ahead of his voice along the written lines of each column, murmuring or reading aloud the text: using one's voice was helpful to divide words and sentences and to catch their meaning. Reading aloud also provided a text with its correct melody and prosody: as Dionysius Thrax, a later grammarian, put it, one does not read tragedy, elegiac poetry, comedy or prose in the same way, all with the same tone. Being a book collector implied the intellectual ability to understand the scope and meaning of a given text, and also to make sense of the juxtaposition of different texts in a collection, of the analogies, and of the differences organizing them, of the way they presupposed, completed or excluded one another. A book collector should find his own bearings on the map of written literature and knowledge.

Reading a book might be a slow learning process. The teacher's voice was replaced by that of the reader. The reader might glance through a text written on a book-roll, or might read it again and again, or read it aloud and memorize it, or browse forwards or backwards. The reader could take all the time he needed to understand a text and to appropriate its content, unlike the audience of the sophists' virtuoso performances, where the listeners had to grasp what they could on the spot. Instead of attending their public lectures, Euthydemus chose to read books written by the most famous sophists and poets, those with a reputation for learning. Wisdom and knowledge were deemed to be fixed and stored in written texts.

One could believe in the power of books and be content with reading and studying a single book, one in which universal knowledge and wisdom were supposed to be encompassed. Such was the case in cultures of the holy and revealed book. Books of that sort provided readers with absolute truth and ultimate knowledge, but also the anguish of interpretation from literal meaning to the hidden contents. Through this style of hermeneutics, texts might be made to answer all the questions one could ask, even questions with which they were not originally concerned.

But Euthydemus chose to acquire as many books as possible. For him, a man's knowledge seems to have been proportionate to the number of books he possessed. Such a collecting process could be endless. Knowledge embedded in books could be accumulated like gold or silver. Socrates ironically praises Euthydemus for trying to make capital out of his knowledge. The young man has no doubt that knowledge can be transmitted via books, from the writer to his readers and that this knowledge will remain unchanged, no matter how often the text is read. He does not question the medium of writing that encodes the writer's words and thought.

During his dialogue with Euthydemus, Socrates slowly undermines the over-confident manner in which the young man relies on books as a medium of knowledge, and as a secret training for a successful political career. Through a series of questions, he makes Euthydemus aware that his personal library is useless and is not an infallible key to success. Socrates does admit that books might be useful for learning technical skills and arts, such as medicine, architecture, geometry or astronomy, and that possessing

Homer's complete works is required for someone who wishes to become a rhapsode capable of performing recitations of Homer's poems. This is an interesting insight into the use and the representation of books in early fourth-century Athens. Books might be a medium for learning those *technai*, which depended on the acquisition of specific skills and experience, and on principles that can be expressed in a systematic way through writing. Significantly enough, rhetoric is not mentioned by Socrates, although sophists such as Gorgias did in fact write handbooks devoted to this art. However, Socrates' argumentation forces Euthydemus to admit that simply buying as many books as possible is useless training for those who wish to become future political leaders, or even wise citizens. Euthydemus loses his illusions, and has to admit: "I think I should better shut up, because I have a good chance of knowing nothing at all." At least, he has understood that talking with Socrates was more valuable than owning a personal library. According to Xenophon, he became one of the philosopher's closest followers, modeling his own life on that of his master. Socrates for his part stopped harassing him and taught him the simplest and clearest notions of the few things he considered worth knowing and honourable to practice.

It is indeed ironic that we read about this episode in a written text, and that Xenophon's book was intended to perpetuate the oral teaching of Socrates.

FRAGMENT 2. Athenaeus, *Deipnosophistae*, V, 36–7, 203e

περὶ δὲ βιβλίων πλήθους καὶ βιβλιοθηκῶν κατασκευῆς καὶ τῆς εἰς τὸ Μουσεῖον συναγωγῆς τί δεῖ καὶ λέγειν, πᾶσι τούτων ὄντων κατὰ μνήμην;

And concerning the number of books, the arrangement of the libraries, and the collection in the Mouseion, why need I even speak, since they are in all men's memories. (translation Charles Burton Gulick, The Loeb Classical Library)

FRAGMENT 3. Strabo, *Geography*, 17, 1, 8

τῶν δὲ βασιλείων μέρος ἐστὶ καὶ τὸ Μουσεῖον, ἔχον περίπατον καὶ ἐξέδραν καὶ οἶκον μέγαν ἐν ᾧ τὸ συσσίτιον τῶν μετεχόντων τοῦ Μουσείου φιλολόγων ἀνδρῶν. ἔστι δὲ τῇ συνόδῳ ταύτῃ καὶ χρήματα κοινὰ καὶ ἱερεὺς ὁ ἐπὶ τῷ Μουσείῳ τεταγμένος τότε μὲν ὑπὸ τῶν βασιλέων νῦν δ' ὑπὸ Καίσαρος.

The Museum is also a part of the royal palaces; it has a public walk, an Exedra with seats, and a large house, in which is the common mess-hall of the men of learning who share the Museum. This group of men not only hold property in common, but also have a priest in charge of the Museum, who formerly was appointed by the kings, but is now appointed by Caesar. (translation Horace Leonard Jones, The Loeb Classical Library)

Athenaeus provides us with long excerpts from Callixeinos' treatise *On Alexandria*.[2] However, after the famous description of the Dionysiac procession organized by Ptolemy II Philadelphus (V, 196b–203d) and before discussing the ships constructed by Ptolemy Philopator (V, 203e–206d), we find this very frustrating statement about the Alexandrian library: "why need I even speak, since they are in all men's memories."

In the elitist scholarly games of Athenaeus' characters, there was no need to provide reminders of what everyone knew. But Athenaeus' modern readers have lost a unique occasion to get precious, first-hand information about the Alexandrian library, its material organization, and its link to the Mouseion. As expert book collectors, fond of lexical and antiquarian problems, Larensis' guests belong to an extended Alexandrian tradition, while Athenaeus of Naucratis personifies the expertise in librarianship inherited from his Hellenistic predecessors. Although the Alexandrian library belongs to memory, nothing suggests that it had vanished at the time of Athenaeus. It is significant he does not allude to the tradition of the burning of the library, during the Alexandrian war of Julius Caesar. From Athenaeus' statement, one can just infer that the peak of the library's splendor was linked with Ptolemy Philadelphus.

Athenaeus uses the plural form of the noun *bibliothēkē*. Does he hint at the two libraries of Alexandria, located in the Mouseion and in the Serapeum, or at the material set-up where the book-rolls were stored, that is the bookshelves? As Luciano Canfora stressed, *bibliothēkē* does not mean the library as a building, but the storage furniture where books were kept.[3] The plural form *bibliothēkai* is understandable in such a context. *Kataskeuē* refers to the material arrangement of these storage devices. The word *sunagōgē* refers to the collection of books in the Mouseion. The Alexandrian library was not a building, but a collection of book-rolls stored in the Mouseion complex. In Athenaeus' allusive sentence, the number of books, the arrangement of the *bibliothēkai* and the *sunagōgē* in the Mouseion are considered as different and complementary features that distinguished the Alexandrian library. The noun *sunagōgē* refers to a collection of objects more than to the assembly of scholars.

In his description of the Ptolemies' palatial area in Alexandria, Strabo mentions the Mouseion, but not the library. Should it be interpreted as a proof of the destruction of the library, for which Caesar's army would be

---

[2] Rice 1983.   [3] Canfora 1986b: 91, 95, 147.

responsible, according to a rich literary tradition? Strabo was in Egypt in 25/24 BC. He does not allude to the burning of the library. On the other hand, his *Geography* attests a deep familiarity with Alexandrian scholarship, with the grammatical and philological tradition of Homer's critics as with the works of Eratosthenes. Could Strabo be aware of the burning of the Mouseion's library without relating it? Or does his short description of the Mouseion imply *a silentio* that the library survived Caesar's war, since it was not an independent building, but a collection of books stored in the Mouseion, perhaps in rooms opening on a portico?[4]

It is hard not to notice the silence of extant Greek and Roman sources on the material organization of the library of the Mouseion, on its *kataskeuē*, according to Athenaeus' word, on its staff (beyond the list of the chief librarians), on the way book-rolls were stored, and on the activity of scholars themselves. Most of the tradition on the Alexandrian library focuses on the legend of its foundation linked with the translation of the Septuagint, or on its destruction during Caesar's war.[5] As far as I know, we have very few explicit allusions by Hellenistic writers to their actual use of the book collection of the Mouseion. An exception could be Strabo, quoting Hipparchus about the link between Eratosthenes' revision of old geographical maps and the huge collection of books he could rely on (II.1.5 C 69): it is however a general and an abstract statement. More elaborate is Vitruvius' tale about the appointment of Aristophanes of Byzantium as librarian in Alexandria, after he had displayed his memory skills and his first-hand knowledge of the collection of books (he is able to retrieve the precise book-rolls he needs for proving plagiarism) (*De Architectura*, VII, Praef. 4–7). This fascinating testimony, however, written at the end of the last century BC, tells us more about the Roman conception of reading and libraries than about the collection of books in third century BC Alexandria.[6]

Hellenistic scholars and writers were deeply reliant on written sources, on books from the past and so on the use of libraries. From literary hermeneutics to polymathic compilations and to poetical mimesis, modern readers can grasp just a part of the intellectual and creative processes underlying texts and fragments inherited from the golden age of ancient libraries. Most of the time, however, libraries form an abstract background to the process of composition, an implicit horizon. Under the Roman Empire, by contrast, libraries were sometimes vividly described, as monumental buildings and

---

[4] Canfora 1986b: 210; Empereur 2003: 181.
[5] On the *Letter of Aristeas* and its rich tradition, see Canfora 1996.   [6] Jacob 2010.

as places for scholarly and social activities, as Aulus Gellius' *Noctes Atticae* testify.

This evolution suggests perhaps a change of focus on libraries, considered not only as collections of book-rolls, but also as public buildings, and as political foundations in Rome and in cities of the Empire.

FRAGMENT 4. Strabo, *Geography*, 13, 1, 54

Ἐκ δὲ τῆς Σκήψεως οἵ τε Σωκρατικοὶ γεγόνασιν Ἔραστος καὶ Κορίσκος καὶ ὁ τοῦ Κορίσκου υἱὸς Νηλεύς, ἀνὴρ καὶ Ἀριστοτέλους ἠκροαμένος καὶ Θεοφράστου, διαδεδεγμένος δὲ τὴν βιβλιοθήκην τοῦ Θεοφράστου, ἐν ᾗ ἦν καὶ ἡ τοῦ Ἀριστοτέλους· ὁ γοῦν Ἀριστοτέλης τὴν ἑαυτοῦ Θεοφράστῳ παρέδωκεν, ᾧπερ καὶ τὴν σχολὴν ἀπέλιπε, πρῶτος ὧν ἴσμεν συναγαγὼν βιβλία καὶ διδάξας τοὺς ἐν Αἰγύπτῳ βασιλέας βιβλιοθήκης σύνταξιν. Θεόφραστος δὲ Νηλεῖ παρέδωκεν· ὁ δ᾽ εἰς Σκῆψιν κομίσας τοῖς μετ᾽ αὐτὸν παρέδωκεν, ἰδιώταις ἀνθρώποις, οἳ κατάκλειστα εἶχον τὰ βιβλία οὐδ᾽ ἐπιμελῶς κείμενα· ἐπειδὴ δὲ ᾔσθοντο τὴν σπουδὴν τῶν Ἀτταλικῶν βασιλέων ὑφ᾽ οἷς ἦν ἡ πόλις, ζητούντων βιβλία εἰς τὴν κατασκευὴν τῆς ἐν Περγάμῳ βιβλιοθήκης, κατὰ γῆς ἔκρυψαν ἐν διώρυγί τινι· ὑπὸ δὲ νοτίας καὶ σητῶν κακωθέντα ὀψέ ποτε ἀπέδοντο οἱ ἀπὸ τοῦ γένους Ἀπελλικῶντι τῷ Τηίῳ πολλῶν ἀργυρίων τά τε Ἀριστοτέλους καὶ τὰ τοῦ Θεοφράστου βιβλία. ἦν δὲ ὁ Ἀπελλικῶν φιλόβιβλος μᾶλλον ἢ φιλόσοφος·

διὸ καὶ ζητῶν ἐπανόρθωσιν τῶν διαβρωμάτων εἰς ἀντίγραφα καινὰ μετήνεγκε τὴν γραφὴν ἀναπληρῶν οὐκ εὖ, καὶ ἐξέδωκεν ἁμαρτάδων πλήρη τὰ βιβλία. Συνέβη δὲ τοῖς ἐκ τῶν περιπάτων τοῖς μὲν πάλαι τοῖς μετὰ Θεόφραστον οὐκ ἔχουσιν ὅλως τὰ βιβλία πλὴν ὀλίγων, καὶ μάλιστα τῶν ἐξωτερικῶν, μηδὲν ἔχειν φιλοσοφεῖν πραγματικῶς, ἀλλὰ θέσεις ληκυθίζειν· τοῖς δ᾽ ὕστερον, ἀφ᾽ οὗ τὰ βιβλία ταῦτα προῆλθεν, ἄμεινον μὲν ἐκείνων φιλοσοφεῖν καὶ ἀριστοτελίζειν, ἀναγκάζεσθαι μέντοι τὰ πολλὰ εἰκότα λέγειν διὰ τὸ πλῆθος τῶν ἁμαρτιῶν. πολὺ δὲ εἰς τοῦτο καὶ ἡ Ῥώμη προσελάβετο· εὐθὺς γὰρ μετὰ τὴν Ἀπελλικῶντος τελευτὴν Σύλλας ᾖρε τὴν Ἀπελλικῶντος βιβλιοθήκην ὁ τὰς Ἀθήνας ἑλών, δεῦρο δὲ κομισθεῖσαν Τυραννίων τε ὁ γραμματικὸς διεχειρίσατο φιλαριστοτέλης ὤν, θεραπεύσας τὸν ἐπὶ τῆς βιβλιοθήκης, καὶ βιβλιοπῶλαί τινες γραφεῦσι φαύλοις χρώμενοι καὶ οὐκ ἀντιβάλλοντες, ὅπερ καὶ ἐπὶ τῶν ἄλλων συμβαίνει τῶν εἰς πρᾶσιν γραφομένων βιβλίων καὶ ἐνθάδε καὶ ἐν Ἀλεξανδρείᾳ. περὶ μὲν οὖν τούτων ἀπόχρη.

From Scepsis came the Socratic philosophers Erastus and Coriscus and Neleus the son of Coriscus, this last a man who not only was a pupil of Aristotle and Theophrastus, but also inherited the library of Theophrastus, which included that of Aristotle. At any rate, Aristotle bequeathed his own library to Theophrastus, to whom he also left his school; and he is the first man, so far as I know, to have collected books and to have taught the kings in Egypt how to arrange a library. Theophrastus bequeathed it to Neleus; and Neleus took it to Scepsis and bequeathed it to his heirs, ordinary people, who kept the books locked up and not even carefully stored.

But when they heard how zealously the Attalid kings to whom the city was subject were searching for books to build up the library in Pergamum, they hid their books underground in a kind of trench. But much later, when the books had been damaged by moisture and moths, their descendants sold them to Apellicon of Teos for a large sum of money, both the books of Aristotle and those of Theophrastus. But Apellicon was a bibliophile rather than a philosopher; and therefore, seeking a restoration of the parts that had been eaten through, he made new copies of the text, filling up the gaps incorrectly, and published the books full of errors. The result was that the earlier school of Peripatetics who came after Theophrastus had no books at all, with the exception of only a few, mostly exoteric works, and were therefore able to philosophize about nothing in a practical way, but only to talk bombast about commonplace propositions, whereas the later school, from the time the books in question appeared, though better able to philosophize and Aristotelize, were forced to call most of their statements probabilities, because of the large number of errors. Rome also contributed much to this; for, immediately after the death of Apellicon, Sulla, who had captured Athens, carried off Apellicon's library to Rome, where Tyrannion the grammarian, who was fond of Aristotle, got it in his hands by paying court to the librarian, as did also certain booksellers who used bad copyists and would not collate the texts – a thing that also takes place in the case of the other books that are copied for selling, both here and at Alexandria. However, this is enough about these men. (translation Horace Leonard Jones, The Loeb Classical Library)

Strabo provides us with the oldest testimony about the fate of Aristotle's library. His account deserves a careful examination, even if one should be reminded that Strabo wrote his *Geography* more than 300 years after Aristotle's death. He relied on intermediary sources and he also mirrors an evolution in the conception of books, texts, and libraries. This is the main point I would like to stress in my commentary on this fragment.

First, one should notice the alternate use of *bibliothēkē/biblia*. The word *bibliothēkē* appears only as a singular noun. It obviously means a collection of books, not a room or a building. I am not even sure it implies a specific storage device such as boxes or a chest. A *bibliothēkē* can be transmitted as a material belonging, be moved, carried away, buried, excavated: it is a collection of books, a set of book-rolls. Interestingly enough, a *bibliothēkē* may include another *bibliothēkē*, that is the *bibliothēkē* of someone else. Theophrastus' *bibliothēkē* includes Aristotle's *bibliothēkē*: although the two collections of books are put together, it is still possible to make a distinction between them. A *bibliothēkē* is a set of book-rolls collected by an owner whose identity matters in order to understand its content and its selection principles. This ownership or provenance remains noticeable and relevant even after the owner's death.

The verbs διαδεδεγμένος, παρέδωκεν, and κομίσας, the expressions κατάκλειστα εἶχον, κατὰ γῆς ἔκρυψαν ἐν διώρυγί τινι, οὐδ᾽ ἐπιμελῶς κείμενα describe the various hazards to which this set of objects was exposed; book-rolls might be carried away or kept in a hiding place and they might be severely damaged according to the storage conditions. When Sulla took hold of Apellicon's *bibliothēkē* in Athens and brought it to Rome, he obviously seized books, not shelves or a building.

A closer reading of Strabo's narrative reveals an interesting evolution of the meaning and of the status of this *bibliothēkē* and of the books it encompassed. Strabo provides us with a form of cultural genealogy of the concept of library itself, of its nature, of its uses. The first stage was a collection of books belonging to Aristotle himself, a private possession he bequeathed to his successor as the head of the Peripatos, Theophrastus. Strabo does not describe the content of this collection or its uses. He focuses on its legal status. Belonging to Aristotle, the collection is also linked to the Peripatos community, where fellows and students shared a life devoted to intellectual investigation, to philosophy, science, and polymathy. In 323 BC, after Alexander's death, Aristotle left Athens and fled to Stagira. Theophrastus remained in Athens and he became the scholarch of the Peripatos until his death. His will is quoted by Diogenes Laertius.[7] Its main purpose was to make sure that the school would survive his death. He gave detailed instructions on the various developments and improvements to be made to the school's buildings, as well as provisions for the future of the community. Some clauses relate to Theophrastus' own belongings and estates. It is interesting to stress the context surrounding the legacy of books to Neleus:

The estate at Stagira belonging to me, I give to Callinus. All the books, I give to Neleus. The garden and the walk and all the houses adjoining the garden, I give to such of my friends herein named as may wish to study and practice philosophy there in common...[8]

Theophrastus does not allude to a *bibliothēkē*, but to books, to *all* the books, that is Aristotle's books and his own. The buildings, the garden, and the future of the school were entrusted collectively to a group of senior fellows. The books, as Theophrastus' personal property, were given to Neleus, who was a senior member of the group. Theophrastus' intent was probably to entrust someone reliable with the care of books and not to leave it as a collective belonging. As one of Aristotle's surviving students, Neleus

---

[7] Diog. Laert. 5. 51–7.
[8] Diog. Laert. 5.52. Translation R. D. Hicks, Loeb Classical Library, slightly modified.

was possibly expected to be the next scholarch of the school.[9] Literally interpreted, Theophrastus' will gave up all the books to Neleus. It did not anticipate that Neleus might leave the community.

Strabo's story begins after Theophrastus' death. Neleus of Scepsis inherited the *bibliothēkē* that included the collection of Aristotle. The latter was the core of Theophrastus' *bibliothēkē*: the two collections remained discernible, and book-rolls were still linked with their previous owner. The stages of the *bibliothēkē*'s development were considered worth remembering and preserving. Perhaps such a cumulative process was intended to be pursued when the collection of books would be bequeathed again to the next scholarch.[10] Neleus of Scepsis, who inherited Theophrastus' books, was perhaps expected to get this position, but instead the Peripatos community chose Strato of Lampsachus as its leader.[11] Neleus was not willing to remain as simply one member of the community, *inter pares*. It seems there was no legal way to dispossess Neleus of the *bibliothēkē* he had inherited from Theophrastus, nor to prevent him from carrying it away when he decided to return to his homeland. The *bibliothēkē* was no longer a shared resource, the written memory of a community of learning, but a private belonging. Such a dreadful event had not been anticipated by Aristotle and Theophrastus.

In this first Athenian episode of the story of Aristotle's library, according to Strabo, we should stress the ambiguous status of the *bibliothēkē*, open to conflicting interpretations. It was a set of material objects, *biblia*, a personal belonging. As such, Theophrastus transmitted them to the heir he chose. But at the same time, the library was a resource shared among a community of learning, who used the book-rolls without owning them. They were a tool for philosophers and scholars who needed such a written archive in order to learn, to think, and to expand knowledge. The archive was to be enriched by the new books written, copied or bought by the new scholarch. Such an utopia relied on the assumption that no legal or institutional obstacle would stand in the way of the transmission of the collection from its current owner to his successor.

Episode two of Strabo's story takes place in Scepsis, a city in Mysia. Neleus is back home. Considering Theophrastus' *bibliothēkē* to be his own possession, he felt entitled to take it away. Nothing suggests Neleus tried

---

[9] See Canfora 1986b: 35–6.
[10] See Canfora 1986b: 198, who mentions as a possibility the direct and personal transmission of books from one scholarch to another one.
[11] As Canfora, 1986b: p. 37, rightly stresses, Strato's connection with Ptolemy Lagos and with Ptolemy Philadelphus was certainly a trump card in the competition for the scholarch's position.

to found a new philosophical school in Scepsis, to create a Mysian clone of the Peripatos. The books were bequeathed to Neleus' heirs, probably relatives, and not to an intellectual successor without any familial link. Neleus' heirs were not philosophers or scholars, but ἰδιῶται ἄνθρωποι. For them, Aristotle's and Theophrastus' books were useless and meaningless, they were just papyrus rolls and they were ignorant of even their correct handling and conservation. However, they were aware of the value of the collection and they kept the book-rolls in a safe place, as a part of the family's inheritance. In Scepsis, the status of Neleus' book-rolls changed in a twofold way. First, they became valuable objects, not for their intellectual content, but for their origin and their previous history. As such they could be coveted by book collectors and eventually be carried away and merged into the royal library created by the Attalids in Pergamum. Anyone aware of the events in the Peripatos knew that the house of Neleus' heirs was likely the place where one could get hold of the precious collection of books. In order to avoid such a dispossession, these books had to be protected and hidden. Neleus' family considered these books a long-term investment that could turn to good account. Second, the books are presented by Strabo as fragile and destructible objects, threatened by insects and humidity. The emphasis is placed on their materiality, as rolls of papyrus sheets that could rot or be pierced by tiny holes.

In episode three, Neleus' descendants sold Aristotle's and Theophrastus' books for a huge price to Apellicon of Teos.[12] The books were at that time badly damaged. Their status changed again. Apellicon was not interested in this collection for its philosophical content and value, but because it was a set of rare and unique books, whose origin and history could be tracked. He was a *philobiblos*, not a *philosophos*. From Neleus to Apellicon, the shifting interest in Aristotle's and Theophrastus' books reveals a change of focus as well as an evolution of the two libraries' status and purpose. These books were the core of a shared scholarly resource in the Peripatos and at the same time the private possession of its scholarch. They were then reduced to becoming the private belongings of Neleus' heirs, deprived of their intellectual and social function. In the Scepsis cache, they were just material objects to be stored. Meanwhile a new kind of library emerged. The state library of the Attalid kings was a response to the Alexandrian library. Collecting books was now a political issue, a way to claim a continuity from and a control over the Hellenic tradition. The Pergamum library tried to

---

[12] Strabo's account is confirmed by Athenaeus, *Deipnosophists*, V, 214d–e, relying on Poseidonius: Apellicon is described as familiar with the philosophy of the Peripatos. Thanks to his fortune, he was able to buy and to merge whole libraries, and Aristotle's library was one of them.

compete with the supremacy of the Mouseion of Alexandria in gathering together as many books as possible, in finding rare texts and editions. The involvement of Apellicon, in the beginning of the last century BC, shows that such an interest was shared by wealthy collectors. Apellicon is a *philobiblos*, because he is less interested by the content of texts to be studied and read, than by rare books themselves, whose value relies on their provenance and their uniqueness.

In episode four, Apellicon decided to make copies of the texts written on the damaged book-rolls. While copying them onto a brand new papyrus book-roll, he tried to make corrections and to fill the blanks created by insects and moisture. The written text was clearly considered as independent of its material medium, as a continuous sequence of letters forming words, sentences, and discourse. The copying of texts from old book-rolls to new ones entails the loss of the prestige vested in those unique material objects that could be traced back to Aristotle and Theophrastus themselves. But such a copy is the only way to save a text when its material medium is corrupted. The shift of focus from the book-roll to writing emphasizes a particular property of texts. Through the process of copy and reproduction, texts may keep their power, their meaning, and eventually their literal form. Such a postulate seems obvious, but it relies on cultural assumptions that are not. The dissociation of a text from its medium, as well as from a specific writing or language, presupposes the autonomy of the text as an intellectual object. In such a cultural frame, different copies of a text, whether produced by hand or a printing press, may be considered as similar and equivalent. One can get a copy of a text even if one is not the owner of the original book. Other factors, however, introduce differences, such as the quality of handwriting and of the text's edition, as well as the copyist's fame and expertise. In the handwritten transmission of texts, as well as in early print culture, it was impossible to achieve a perfect equivalence between a text and its copies. Unintentional errors and omissions and deliberate changes and corrections generated differences and variants. Cultural and intellectual criteria define the threshold at which these differences and variants are noticed and considered as annoying, or even as unacceptable. As Strabo laments, the text itself of Neleus' books, and not only their original medium, was severely corrupted by the copyist. Apellicon released copies (ἐξέδωκεν) of the texts he inopportunely revised (ἐπανόρθωσιν). The verb *ekdidōmi* and the noun *ekdosis* refer to the decision of a writer to make his text public, that is to let copies circulate.[13] Apellicon behaved like the scholars from Alexandria

---

[13] Van Groningen 1963: 1–17.

and Pergamum who "published" revised editions of classical literature. As an intermediary between the writer and his readers, the "corrector" (*diorthōtēs*) claims the authority to revise the transmitted text. Unfortunately, his revised copies of the Peripatetic books were scattered with errors.

We have seen that Strabo did not give any clue as to the nature of the book collection Neleus carried away, except that it was composed of the "libraries" of Aristotle and of Theophrastus. In the Apellicon episode, however, it is implicit, but obvious that the copyists reproduced the works of Aristotle and perhaps those of Theophrastus too. According to Diogenes Laertius, Theophrastus bequeathed *all* the books to Neleus. This comprehensive collection included works by Aristotle and Theophrastus as well as other texts from a wide range of authors, in various fields, such as literature, rhetoric, philosophy, and the sciences. This was a key resource for the polymathic, scientific, and philosophical activities of the school. Books had provided Aristotle and his students with a mine of information, of primary sources, of historical materials, and of previous answers to lasting philosophical questions. Strabo makes no reference to this part of the Peripatos library, because his main interest (and that of the source he relies on) is in the fate of Aristotle's own writings, their misfortunes, and in the role played by Tyrannion in their recovery. We will see below (see fragment 7) that another ancient source completes Strabo's account and sheds some light on the fate of this second part of Aristotle's library.

Strabo emphasized the impact of the reappearance of these texts on the Peripatos.[14] After Neleus' departure, the philosophical school missed its most precious resource, the "esoteric" writings of Aristotle himself, that is treatises intended for the insiders, for the members of the philosophical community. Very few books remained, mainly exoteric ones, that is texts intended for public lectures. Two points are striking in Strabo's testimony. First, the members of the school did not have their own copies of Aristotle's esoteric treatises: these treatises were unique copies and they were kept in the scholarch's library. As a result, once the collection was carried away from Athens, there was no "back-up" available. Second, esoteric treatises were used as a way of extending Aristotle's teaching beyond his own lifetime. After Neleus' departure, the core of Aristotelian doctrine relied on oral tradition, on exoteric treatises, and on texts written by Aristotle's and Theophrastus' successors. When the members of the Peripatos eventually recovered a part of their lost library, through Apellicon's edition of Aristotelian treatises,

---

[14] Strabo's version of the fate of Aristotle's library raised many doubts and questions among the historians of the Peripatos. It is beyond the scope of this chapter to unfold the thread of the controversy. As a few landmarks in this debate, see Düring 1950, Moraux 1951, Grayeff 1956.

they were able to revive Aristotle's original teaching. But they faced a new challenge. The corruption of texts caused a corruption of doctrine, and some textual errors involved conceptual approximations.

The fifth and last episode of Strabo's account of the Aristotle library takes place in Rome. After Apellicon's death, Sulla, the new master of Athens (86 BC), seized his library and brought it to Rome. Apellicon's bibliophile collection, among other rare books, included the original and damaged book-rolls bought from Neleus' heirs.[15] This is a new step in the history of this particular collection and of ancient libraries in general. Books were now a part of the war booty Roman generals brought back home. Libraries from Greek rulers or collectors adorned the *villae* of the victorious generals. These collections played a major part in the importation of the Greek cultural tradition, of its literature, and of scholarship. They were an important material medium of Hellenism. State libraries in Hellenistic kingdoms had been a dynamic factor in the development of civic and private libraries. Although differing in scale, these different kinds of libraries reflected the same estimation of books as an archive of culture, knowledge, and literature. The libraries of Alexandria and Pergamum were at the origin of a new scholarly field: bibliography and expertise in Greek books. Their catalogues provided *literati* with a map of Greek literature. Their universal scope was completed by practical manuals intended for beginners in the art of book-collecting.[16]

Organizing a library and taking care of old Greek books were now recognized as technical tasks that should be entrusted to specialists. Sulla hired one of them to be in charge of his library. The librarian was the key person who must be seduced or corrupted by anyone who wished to have access to rare books or to make copies of them. Strabo and Plutarch document the activity of scholars and professional scribes in the background of Sulla's library. On the one hand, Tyrannion the grammarian played a key part in a new edition of Aristotle's texts. Apellicon was a φιλόβιβλος, Tyrannion is a φιλαριστοτέλης: he is less interested in the rarity of the physical books and in their famous origin than in the philosophical content of the texts they contained, in Aristotle's doctrine. On the other hand, book-sellers hired incompetent scribes to produce copies for sale, without proper philological care, without even comparing the copies with the original text to check their accuracy (οὐκ ἀντιβάλλοντες). Strabo's emphasis on

---

[15] Plut. *Sull.* 26.1–3, follows and completes Strabo's version.
[16] For example, Artemon of Cassandreia, quoted by Ath. 12. 515d–e and XV 694a. On Herennius Philo and Telephus of Pergamum, see *RE* XV 653–4 (Gudeman, 1912) and *RE* XIX 369–71 (Wendel, 1934).

Tyrannion's role in the recovery of Aristotle's texts is meaningful. Tyrannion was a Greek freedman, a grammarian familiar with Aristotelian philosophy, and a personal friend of Atticus and Cicero. Strabo was one of Tyrannion's students in Rome, in 44 BC. It is most likely that Strabo's information on the fate of Aristotle's books was provided by Tyrannion himself.[17] According to Plutarch,[18] however, Tyrannion was a link rather than an end in the chain of transmission of Aristotle's texts. He entrusted his own copies of the precious texts to Aristonicus of Rhodes who played a major part in the cataloguing and the further editing of Aristotle's texts.

Strabo's account of the fate of Aristotle's library is a major testimony. Its importance is not restricted to the history of the Peripatos and the transmission of Aristotelian philosophy. It also touches on the history of books and libraries, on their conceptual genealogy. From episode one to episode five, one can unwind a fascinating thread. At one end, there is Aristotle, a philosopher who writes texts and collects books. As material possessions which are also a shared intellectual resource, these books had a particular legal status. They could be transmitted through a will. At the other end, there are readers, accustomed to buy copies of old Greek texts in book-shops and there are also professionals in charge of books. Those professionals included librarians, scribes, grammarians, philosophers, and specialists in book conservation, in the copying and correction of texts, and of their interpretation. Along this thread, books travelled through geographical space, from Athens to Scepsis, from Scepsis back to Athens, from Athens to Rome. Their value and meaning changed accordingly, with shifts from the material medium to the written text, from the written text to the philosophical doctrine. In fourth century BC Athens, Aristotle's treatises were unique copies kept in the scholarch's private library: they were the core of Aristotle's philosophical work in progress and the most up-to-date archive of his thought. Exoteric writings, written for a wider and external readership, were just popular philosophical texts. At the time of Tyrannion and Strabo, the manuscripts of Aristotle's writings were considered a precious and unique archive that could renew philosophical studies and perpetuate the teaching of the founder of the Peripatos.

FRAGMENT 5. Strabo, *Geography*, 13, 1, 54

ὁ γοῦν Ἀριστοτέλης τὴν ἑαυτοῦ Θεοφράστῳ παρέδωκεν, ᾧπε καὶ τὴν σχολὴν ἀπέλιπε, πρῶτος ὧν ἴσμεν συναγαγὼν βιβλία καὶ διδάξας τοὺς ἐν Αἰγύπτῳ βασιλέας βιβλιοθήκης σύνταξιν.

---

[17] See Canfora 1986b: 189. [18] Plut. *Sull.* 26. 2.

At any rate, Aristotle bequeathed his own library to Theophrastus, to whom he also left his school; and he is the first man, so far as I know, to have collected books and to have taught the kings in Egypt how to arrange a library. (translation Horace Leonard Jones, The Loeb Classical Library)

In Strabo's account of the fate of Aristotle's library that I have just discussed, there is a sentence that deserves a specific commentary. Aristotle is said to be the first who gathered a collection of books and to have taught the kings in Egypt the way to organize a library.[19] Strabo does not mean that Aristotle himself was the founder and the supervisor of the Alexandrian library, but that the Peripatos' library was a model, an inspiration for Ptolemy Lagos and for his son Ptolemy Philadelphus. Two eminent members of Aristotle's school, Demetrius of Phaleron and Strato of Lampsachus, played a major part in this process as intellectual advisers of the kings. Demetrius of Phaleron is a key figure in the legend of the foundation of the Alexandrian library. Strato of Lampsacus was the preceptor of Ptolemy Philadelphus, and he succeeded Theophrastus as scholarch of the Peripatos. The influence of the Athenian Peripatos on the concept and the polymathic program of the Museum is very clear.

I would like to stress two points in Strabo's sentence. First, he alludes to books acquired and gathered by Aristotle from various origins, not to his own writings. As we have seen, the next steps of Strabo's story focus on Aristotle's works and their fate, from Scepsis to Rome, and not on his collection of literary, philosophical, and scholarly books. Second, Strabo draws a distinction between a collection of books and a βιβλιοθήκη: what characterizes a library is its σύνταξις, the way it orders and organizes the collected books. The organization of a library is not a random disposition of book-rolls on the shelves. It relies on a classification, on a predefined pattern, on an intellectual and *a priori* scheme.

Unfortunately, we have few clues about the way Aristotle organized his collection of books. Did it mirror a general organization of knowledge or the organization of the world to be known? Was it organized according to literary genres? What was the practical side of this organization? How did the intellectual scheme of the library concretely organize the storage space provided for the book-rolls? The necessity of a σύνταξις results from the increasing number of books collected. As an organizing principle, it allows any book to be stored in its correct place within an encompassing order. As a convention, it could be shared by a community of users. Beside his own writings, Aristotle's library gathered a wide range of literary, philosophical,

---

[19] For an overall discussion of this tradition, see Canfora 1999: 167–75.

and scholarly books, to be a unique resource that provided the members of the Peripatos with a mass of primary evidence, of *doxai*, of texts of the past that could be used in the intellectual activities of the school.

A library should be ruled by some organizing principles, making possible the dispatch of new books into such or such category. The σύνταξις is the best way to keep control of an expanding collection. It provides the library's users with an overall scheme, where general divisions can lead to a particular book. Such a general order is the main difference between a collection and a library. Aristotle taught the Ptolemies the complex art of organizing a collection of books, that is the creation of a global order where any new book could find its proper place and meaning.

FRAGMENT 6. Suda, Lexicon, s.v. Callimachus

Πίνακες τῶν ἐν πάσῃ παιδείᾳ διαλαμψάντων, καὶ ὧν συνέγραψαν, ἐν βιβλίοις κ' καὶ ρ'

Tables of those who distinguished themselves in all the fields of culture, and of their writings, in 120 book-rolls.

The remaining fragments of Callimachus' *Pinakes* are unfortunately too scarce and too allusive to allow us to grasp a full idea of their content and purpose.[20] The main problem concerns the relationship of these *Pinakes* to the Alexandrian library. Should they be considered as a catalogue of the library? The word "catalogue" is perhaps misleading because it suggests what a modern library catalogue should be, either a card index or printed volumes or an online database, organized according to the alphabetic order of authors, or titles, sometimes by key words, and providing the call number necessary to find the books on the shelves. Today, a library catalogue has a practical purpose: it is a reference tool to be used by readers within the library itself.

One should stress that the title of Callimachus' work does not allude to the Alexandrian library. On the other hand, it is obvious that this work is connected to the library. What is the nature of this connection? Callimachus does not belong to the first generation of Alexandrian scholars who worked in the Museum and were in charge of the first steps of the organization of the collection. That generation included Zenodotus, Lycophron, and Alexander, who, according to Tzetzes, were in charge of Homeric epics, comedies, and tragedies. Callimachus is not mentioned among the head librarians of the collection. But he was likely commissioned to be the supervisor of a huge task: writing down the list of all the authors who played a pre-eminent part

---

[20] Pfeiffer 1949, fragm. 429–53.

in *paideia*, and a list of their works. At the time of Ptolemy II Philadelphus, the growth of the book collection had clearly made necessary some form of inventory. Through its universal and polymathic ambition, the library was assimilated to the whole of culture, to *paideia*. The *Pinakes* were at the same time an inventory and a map of this written world. It was possible for the first time to make use of an ordered inventory of Greek literature, classified by literary genre and disciplines, with an alphabetical list of writers and a catalogue of their works, supplemented by additional metadata such as the number of book-rolls or lines, or the incipit of the text.

The Suda provides us with the title and the number of book-rolls of Callimachus' work. In order to have the comprehensive map of written culture, one had to be sure that no *volumen* was missing. Unfortunately, ancient tradition has not preserved the total number of texts and authors listed by Callimachus. Using the *Pinakes* required some expertise and some prior knowledge of their general organization. Did the divisions of the *Pinakes* mirror the physical distribution of book-rolls on the shelves of the Museum? We can suppose they did. In the absence of a call-number system, specific texts could be likely accessed through the spot they occupied on this map of Greek written tradition, through the literary genre or the scholarly field they belonged to. Were the *Pinakes* organized according to the scheme of Aristotle's library, to its *suntaxis* ? It is impossible to answer such a question. The best we can say is that Callimachus' work may well have mirrored the organization of the Alexandrian library.

The extant fragments suggest another striking feature. Callimachus did not make an inventory of books, but of authors and of their works. This means his *Pinakes*' purpose went beyond the actual collection of the Alexandrian library. It was authoritative enough to become a reference work for anyone interested in books, or contemplating making a new collection, whether for a private library or a city library. This reference work was transmitted beyond Alexandria and survived the Ptolemaic period to become an authoritative source for anyone concerned about the authenticity or authorship of a particular text or the number of the book-rolls composing it. In the second century AD, Athenaeus testifies that Callimachus' *Pinakes* (along with their equivalent at the Pergamum library) remained a must-read for any serious amateur of old Greek books. The *Pinakes* were, so to say, a portable Alexandrian library, reduced to an endless list of author names and of titles. If we should draw an analogy, the equivalent of Callimachus' work today would be the Library of Congress online catalogue or Worldcat.org, that is a resource that allows any reader in the world to identify or authenticate a book from its ISBN, from its author name, or from a part of its title. For librarians, book-sellers or book-collectors, for scholars in the

Hellenistic and Graeco-Roman world, Callimachus' *Pinakes* might fulfil an analogous function.

As an inventory of the extant Greek literature, relying on the books collected in the Alexandrian library, Callimachus' endeavor faced an impossible challenge. The map matched the territory, and the bibliography of the library for only a short span of time. *Addenda* and *corrigenda* were soon needed. Aristophanes of Byzantium was in charge of this update.[21] The Pergamum librarians produced their own reference bibliography.

FRAGMENT 7. Athenaeus, *Deipnosophists*, I, 4

ἦν δέ, φησί, καὶ βιβλίων κτῆσις αὐτῷ ἀρχαίων Ἑλληνικῶν τοσαύτη ὡς ὑπερβάλλειν πάντας τοὺς ἐπὶ συναγωγῇ τεθαυμασμένους, Πολυκράτην τε τὸν Σάμιον καὶ Πεισίστρατον τὸν Ἀθηναίων τυραννήσαντα Εὐκλείδην τε τὸν καὶ αὐτὸν Ἀθηναῖον καὶ Νικοκράτην τὸν Κύπριον ἔτι τε τοὺς Περγάμου βασιλέας Εὐριπίδην τε τὸν ποιητὴν Ἀριστοτέλην τε τὸν φιλόσοφον <καὶ Θεόφραστον> καὶ τὸν τὰ τούτων διατηρήσαντα βιβλία Νηλέα· παρ' οὗ πάντα, φησί, πριάμενος ὁ ἡμεδαπὸς βασιλεὺς Πτολεμαῖος, Φιλάδελφος δὲ ἐπίκλην, μετὰ τῶν Ἀθήνηθεν καὶ τῶν ἀπὸ Ῥόδου εἰς τὴν καλὴν Ἀλεξάνδρειαν μετήγαγε.

Athenaeus says that he owned so many ancient Greek books that he surpassed all who have been celebrated for their large libraries, including Polycrates of Samos, Peisistratus the tyrant of Athens, Eucleides, likewise an Athenian, Nicocrates of Cyprus, the kings of Pergamum, Euripides the poet, Aristotle the philosopher, Theophrastus, and Neleus, who preserved the books of the two last named. From Neleus, he says, our King Ptolemy, surnamed Philadelphus, purchased them all and transferred them with those which he had procured at Athens and at Rhodes to his beautiful capital, Alexandria. (transl. Charles Burton Gulick)

Larensis is the wealthy Roman host of the learned banquets staged by Athenaeus of Naucratis. These few words about his library belong to the beginning of book 1 of the *Deipnosophists*, a section known only in an abridged form, the *Epitome*. However, the words ὁ ἡμεδαπὸς βασιλεὺς Πτολεμαῖος, "our king Ptolemaeus," suggest that a part at least of the sentence could be a literal quotation of Athenaeus. The size and importance of Larensis' book collection are emphasized within a general scheme of the history of Greek libraries. A few other sources partly mirror its general logic, such as Aulus Gellius and Isidore of Seville.[22]

Athenaeus' version of the history of ancient libraries does not start with a *prōtos heuretēs*, with a founder. Its underlying principle is the continuous

---

[21] Fragments 368–9, Slater 1986. See also Slater 1976: 234–41.
[22] Gell. 7.17, 1–3; Isid. *Etym.* VI, 3.

growth of book collections. Libraries are linked to individuals who gathered them and to their location. According to Athenaeus (and his source), books were widespread and numerous enough to allow Polycrates and Pisistratus to gather impressive collections.

One might distinguish three different categories of libraries. First there are the libraries of rulers: the tyrants of Samos, Athens and Cyprus, the kings of Pergamum, and Ptolemy II Philadelphus. Second there are the private libraries of writers, of which Euripides is the only example produced here. Third there are the libraries of the Peripatetic philosophers: Aristotle, Theophrastus, and Neleus. These three threads converge on Alexandria, since Ptolemy Philadelphus bought books from Athens, Rhodes, and from the Peripatetic school. Athenaeus seems to contradict Strabo's version of the transmission of the Peripatos library and he contradicts himself too, since he alludes elsewhere to the purchase by Apellicon of Aristotle's books.[23] Could such an expert in old Greek books and in all the fields of Hellenistic scholarship be so mistaken or inconsistent? The only way to reconcile Strabo's testimony and that of Athenaeus, and the two contradictory traditions provided by Athenaeus himself, is to admit that "the books of Aristotle" may refer to two different collections: the books written by Aristotle himself, that is his esoteric treatises, and the books purchased and acquired by Aristotle, that is his "research library", with texts from various authors. One could imagine that Neleus was approached by envoys of Ptolemy, eager to buy "the books of Aristotle" for the Museum library and that he sold them the second part of "Aristotle's library", literary, historical, philosophical, and scientific texts from various origins.[24] Such a collection, however, was not worthless: it provided the scholars of the Museum with a precious resource of books and perhaps also helped disseminate to Alexandria the *syntaxis* (organization) of the Peripatos library as well as its intellectual project.

In Athenaeus' genealogy of libraries, Larensis' collection in Rome marks the temporary term of this history of ancient libraries. Oddly enough, one important step is missing: the Roman public libraries, founded by a series of emperors beginning with Augustus. The imperial libraries are like the invisible standpoint from which Athenaeus' history of ancient libraries is constructed. They define a paradigm in which the library is linked with political power. The ruler's prestige is expressed in his sponsorship of arts and sciences, and in the symbolic mastery of culture and tradition represented by great collections of books. Influenced by the Alexandrian model, Caesar

---

[23] Ath. 5. 214d–e.
[24] This interpretation was proposed by Moraux 1973: p. 13, n. 29 and was developed by Canfora 1986b: 35–9, 189–98 and 1999: 51–3.

seems to have planned to create a library in Rome. Varro was commissioned to draw up some preliminary plans. The need to imagine a corresponding *Greek* political paradigm perhaps explains why the origin of public libraries is located in Athens under the rule of Pisistratus, in a period where there were neither the books nor the readers for such an institution.

However, Larensis is not a tyrant, nor a philosopher, nor a Hellenistic ruler, nor a Roman emperor. He is a member of the imperial administration and elite. He is also an educated and wealthy book-collector. Last but not least, he is a very generous host for the deipnosophists' club, and the way Athenaeus grants him a pre-eminent position at the end of the history of Greek libraries is a form of praise as well as a dedication of his work. The Roman Larensis is depicted as the true heir of the famous Greek book-collectors from the past. His private library bears comparison with those of Alexandria, Pergamum, and Athens. His house is at once the Peripatos and the Alexandrian Mouseion, a place where scholars and literati share the intellectual and social pleasures of symposia, reviving the tradition of table talks, *zētēseis*, and *problēmata*.

A final point should be stressed. From Pisistratus in Athens to Larensis in Rome, Athenaeus' history of ancient libraries is ruled by a recurring pattern: the *translatio librorum*, the transfer of books. The first step is Neleus' departure from Athens with Aristotle's and Theophrastus' books. The second step is the massive purchase of books from Athens and Rhodes by Ptolemy, and their transfer to Alexandria. The third step is the development of a collection of ancient Greek books in Larensis' house in Rome. The fourth and last step is the transfer of Larensis' library into Athenaeus' text, through the countless quotations scattered over the deipnosophists' table talks. During this process, the meaning and the status of book collections changed. One could imagine that the tyrants of Athens and Cyprus gathered such books as were available at that time – lyric poetry and epic were likely at the core of such collections. The Peripatos library included the writings of Aristotle and his successors as well as older texts from the sixth and fifth centuries BC. The Pergamese and Alexandrian libraries were clearly devoted to gathering as many books as possible from the Greek past. They also contributed to the production of new scholarly literature, and these new texts were merged into the patrimonial collections. Larensis' library, at the end of the second century AD, specialized in "ancient Greek books." Time is a key factor. At that time, collecting old Greek books was an antiquarian hobby, and it required particular intellectual and critical skills as well as wealth to satisfy such a passion. Athenaeus, through hundreds of excerpts and bibliographical references, tried to sublimate the material library of Larensis into a library condensed into the format of a book, ruled by the aesthetics of variety, by the pleasures of curiosity, by the fun of pedantic games, and by the unique training of readers who bring back to life old texts, old words, old songs, old facets of the Greek cultural and social experience.[25]

Conclusion

A history of ancient libraries could be written on the basis of archaeological remains, where they are available, and occasionally on the morsels of positive information to be drawn from literary testimony. I have chosen to follow another path: reading and understanding each source for its own inner logic, trying to establish in each case its purpose, what it reveals, and what it hides. Beyond their literal meaning, beyond their informative content, these testimonies provide us with a cultural and historical view on the representation of libraries, of books, and of texts in the ancient world. As an alternative to a positivist reading of these fragments, I have tried to experiment with deciphering and interpreting this testimony according to its own categories and the rhetorical and social purposes of the texts from which I have excerpted them. My approach relies on a few chosen passages. It should be indeed extended to the whole corpus of evidence about libraries in the ancient world. But the goal should be the same: using this evidence in order to unfold a conceptual, social, and political genealogy of the library. Each piece of testimony should come under scrutiny, again and again. Nothing should be taken for granted. The cultural representations that underlie the literal meaning of the words concerned should be revealed.

[25] See Jacob 2000; 2001.

PART II

Hellenistic and Roman Republican libraries

4 Men and books in fourth-century BC Athens

PASQUALE MASSIMO PINTO

The cultural background

Between the last quarter of the fifth and the beginning of the fourth century BC a major change appears to have taken place in Athenian culture. Despite differences of opinion over specific problems, today scholars tend to agree that the textual and archaeological evidence together allows us to reconstruct an age in which literacy became more widespread and a "book culture" gradually gained ground.[1] We may observe the spread of a new cultural medium, the book, in the life of the *polis* and also infer that this change took place not only in everyday life but also in people's minds. The papyrus roll, introduced into Greece from Egypt during the preceding centuries, proved to be an effective medium for preserving writing and an easy and versatile means of written communication. It was employed to preserve regulations governing the lives of citizens of the *polis*; to circulate political programmes and cultural polemics; to advertise a victory won in the law courts through publication of the successful speech; and as an aid to study and entertainment both for individuals and for groups of listeners and readers.[2] In addition, there is another aspect which must be taken into consideration when dealing with Greek written culture of this period, namely the development of the genres of prose. By the fourth century, prose had partly replaced poetry and drama as a means of communicating social and political values and ideas.[3]

It is against the background of these developments that this chapter deals with the emerging practice of preserving and collecting books, and

---

[1] The 1952 paper of Eric Turner, *Athenian Books in the Fifth and Fourth Centuries B.C.*, can still serve as a valid point of departure for those who want to carry on research on this subject. For studies in this line, cf. Kenyon 1932: 19–24; Davison 1962; Knox 1985: 1–16; Harris 1989: 65–115; Thomas 1992, 2009; Blanck 2008: 156–9.

[2] The works of fourth-century authors have been variously investigated, especially with reference to the relationships between orality and writing or between writing and performance: see, for instance – besides the much-debated Havelock 1963 – Dover 1968; Gastaldi 1981; Usener 1994; Thomas 2003.

[3] See Norden 1898, especially at 79–121. For a recent study, cf. Wallace 1995; for the role of Isocrates in this change, see Nicolai 2004b.

on their use for a variety of intellectual purposes. It will do so through the discussion of selected testimony drawn mainly from Athenian prose writers of the fourth century. Their works contain significant clues to understanding how a private library was imagined in this period, what kind of books were considered worth collecting, and how these collections were designed to be employed.

Personal and practical libraries

Libraries in fourth century Athens were either small collections of books available only to the owner, his family, and friends, or else personal collections that made up the core of larger libraries, such as those in higher schools, that were open to students and assistants. The libraries of the Platonic *Academy* or of the Aristotelian *Peripatos* were in their own way private and closed institutions. There were no public libraries in fourth-century Athens, in the sense that no collection of books had been put together on the initiative of the state. The belief that Pisistratus established a library in Athens as early as the sixth century has no foundation in fact. The story seems to have originated from a misunderstanding of his role in the collection and division of the Homeric *corpus*.[4] Given that the library was confined to the private sphere of existence, the most likely place to find a book was in private homes, where books might be kept for a variety of reasons, even as a kind of family "relic."[5] Such were, for instance, the manuscripts of Solon preserved in the house of Critias at the end of the fifth century according to the story told by Plato in the homonymous dialogue.[6] Those writings, γράμματα as Plato says, which Solon had partly translated from the Egyptian, had been the source of information about the most ancient history of the world for that refined writer and politician (113b: διαμεμελέτηταί τε ὑπ' ἐμοῦ παιδὸς ὄντος, "and I studied them when I was a boy" – Critias there admits). The story also casts some light on the role of

---

[4] Cf. Gell. 7.17.1–2 and the other testimonies collected by Platthy 1968: 97–110. Cf. also Pfeiffer 1968: 25. Pasquali 1930: 942 wondered what an Athenian library could have contained in the time before the Persian Wars apart from some epic poems. For a brief overview on libraries in the Greek and Roman world, see now Otranto 2010.

[5] There is also evidence that for a long time some books were considered worthy of being preserved in temples or sanctuaries, which were the only places from which their knowledge was to be obtained. Such was the case of the book which Heraclitus left in the temple of Artemis, according to Diog. Laert. 9.5–6, cf. Cambiano 1988: 70–1; Nicolai 2000: 224 and Perilli 2007: 41–4.

[6] Pl. *Criti.* 113a–b cf. Nesselrath 2006: 246–7.

important Athenian families in the first stages of the transmission of ancient texts.[7]

A book could also be regarded as a personal treasure with a strong autobiographical significance, a possession to be enjoyed with friends sharing the same (in this case, philosophical) interests. This emerges from another lively page of Plato set some time after the death of Socrates. The prologue of the *Theaetetus* takes us outside Athens, to the *agora* of Megara, where the philosopher Euclides and his friend Terpsion come across each other and recall the former's past meetings with Socrates.[8] Of course, the "dramatic" setting of Plato's dialogue is, as usual, fictitious, but it arguably reflects actual practices of his time. Soon we are taken from the *agora* to a more private place, as Euclides invites Terpsion to his house and their conversation turns to the reading, or rather to the hearing of a book read aloud by a young slave. It is worth dwelling briefly on this. The text read by the slave was written in a kind of a home-made book, since it was put together by Euclides himself at different times and contained the transcriptions of Socrates' conversations with other people (including Theaetetus) as told to Euclides by Socrates himself, that is to say the dialogue that a modern reader finds immediately after the prologue.[9] Euclides' book was the end product of a long process of drafting, expansion, and revision: the final copy was recorded on a papyrus roll. He was rightly proud to show the results of these efforts to his friend, as the deictic adjective τουτί suggests (*Tht.* 143b: τὸ μὲν δὲ βιβλίον, ὦ Τερψίων, τουτί, "here is the book, Terpsion"). This prologue also contains useful information about the way an ancient author worked. Euclides is portrayed as having reconstructed the text of Socrates' conversations as a direct dialogue, that is without connectives like "he said," "he answered" and the like.[10]

---

[7] Cf. Canfora 1988: 6 and Loraux 1989: 253–4.
[8] Pl. *Tht.* 142a–143c. On the "dramatic" date of the dialogue (after 369) cf. Diès 1950: 120–1.
[9] This is not the only reference in Plato to the "construction" of a book. Portraits of authors "assembling" their books can be found, for instance, in *Phdr.* 278d–e and in *Menex.* 236a–b where Aspasia is described as "gluing together" (συγκολλῶσα) a funeral oration. See also Nieddu 2003: 77–8 and 81, Pébarthe 2006: 76–7; Labriola 2010.
[10] This indeed looks like a literary device through which Plato himself describes for his readers his own way of working. On the passage, cf. also Small 1997: 203–4; Cambiano 2007: 107–8. A controversial list of ancient book collectors known centuries later to Athenaeus included a Euclides of Athens among others such as Polycrates of Samos, Pisistratus, Nicocrates of Cyprus, the kings of Pergamum, Euripides, Aristotle, Theophrastus, and Neleus (Ath. 1.3a). Modern interpreters identify this Euclides with the Athenian archon of 403/2 BC. Nevertheless, one may wonder whether the Megarian philosopher, who studied in Athens, should not be taken into consideration as an alternative candidate on the evidence of this passage. On this list, cf. the paper of Christian Jacob in the present volume.

The literature of the fourth century has handed down to us even more detailed representations of libraries. Alexis, in his comedy entitled *Linos*, put on the stage what we may call a professional library, the collection of books that belonged to a teacher. In a well known fragment of the play preserved by Athenaeus, Alexis described Linos, the mythical teacher of Heracles,[11] asking his pupil to choose a book from a selection.[12] This collection included, as expected, mostly poets: Orpheus, Hesiod, tragedies, Choerilus, Homer, Epicharmus, but also "prose works of various kinds" (συγγράμματα παντοδαπά), and even a book on cookery by a Simos (Ὀψαρτυσία), which the perpetually hungry Heracles chooses without hesitation. Some of these works were part of the traditional repertory of a teacher. But what is interesting here is the fact that this catalogue was considered a plausible one for Alexis' audience. Still more interesting for us is the way in which the physical space of this small library is imagined. If the books were actually shown on the stage, they were probably presented as standing in at least one container for papyrus rolls, a cylindrical leather case for example, with their titles written on the *verso*, i.e. on the outside of the papyrus rolls.[13] In any case, Linos invites Heracles to get closer to a particular spot on the stage, to choose a book from there (βιβλίον ἐντεῦθεν ὅ τι βούλει προσελθὼν γὰρ λαβέ) and, after taking his time to decipher the titles carefully (ἔπειτ' ἀναγνώσει πάνυ γε διασκοπῶν ἀπὸ τῶν ἐπιγραμμάτων ἀτρέμα τε καὶ σχολῇ), to show the book to him (and of course to the audience). Certainly, Linos' library sounds impressive if compared with the anecdote in which Plutarch tells us of a teacher, whom Alcibiades once met in the last quarter of the fifth century, who did not even possess a copy of Homer.[14]

Small technical libraries too, used for different trades, certainly circulated at the time. In the *Aegineticus*, one of the surviving court speeches of Isocrates, a book-collection used for mantic art is mentioned (τὰς βίβλους τὰς περὶ τῆς μαντικῆς). It belonged to a man called Polimenaetus and

---

[11] Lively pictures on vases displaying Heracles at the school of Linos are collected in Beck 1975 pl. 5, nos. 26–8, and 6 no. 29; cf. also *LIMC* IV.1 1988: 833–4, *LIMC* IV.2 1988: 557–8 nos. 1,666–73. A scene of Linos using a book to teach Musaeus is reproduced in Beck 1975 pl. 6, no. 30 and *LIMC* IV.2 1992: 147.

[12] Ath. 4.164a–d = Alexis, fr. 140 K.-A. However, there are scholars who think that the scene was set in front of a bookstall in the market, cf. Caroli 2010: 117, n. 17.

[13] Otherwise we could imagine the book-rolls lying on the shelves of a cupboard or of a niche. It appears less probable that the titles were written by that time on thin strips of papyrus or leather hanging from one end of the roll. For comments on the passage, see Birt 1882: 446; Platthy 1968: 115–17 test. 44; Nesselrath 1990: 227–8 and n. 138; Arnott 1996: 409–11; Del Corso 2003: 19; Caroli 2007: 20–2.

[14] Plut. *Alc.* 7.1.

was bequeathed after his death to one of his friends, who in turn devoted himself to this profession and earned a considerable amount of money as a result.[15] As far as the activity of Isocrates himself as a logographer is concerned, Aristotle (quoted by Dionysius of Halicarnassus) stated that bundles of Isocrates' court speeches were to be found on sale in Athens. Leaving aside the debate on Isocrates and his attempt to cover up his past as a logographer, this is of course useful information concerning what could be found on Athenian bookstalls in the fourth century and about the uncontrolled circulation of court speeches. What is interesting again is that such a "library," made up of book-rolls falsely inscribed with Isocrates' name by the sellers, was available to people who might be seeking speeches of this kind for their own personal legal needs.[16]

Food for thought: books for intellectual purposes

Let us now turn our attention to the use of books by learned men. There is evidence for a strong interest in purchasing and gathering books for intellectual purposes. The type of intellectual who collected books is well represented, at the end of the fifth century, by Euripides and it is known that Aristophanes teased him about this in the *Frogs*, an extremely remarkable document about the cultural life of Athens at the turn of the two centuries. There Euripides is blamed for putting Aeschylus' art on a diet of beets tossed with a juice of "chatterings filtered from books" (στωμυλμάτων ἀπὸ βιβλίων) and further we see Euripides and his entire family team getting on Dionysius' scales "holding books" (ξυλλαβὼν τὰ βιβλία).[17]

Ancient anecdotes also emphasize the enthusiasm that learned men had for buying books, even at a very high price. A group of testimonies concern Plato's expensive purchase of a treatise of the Pythagorean Philolaus.[18] Others refer to his passion for the *Mimes* of Sophron and the poems of Antimachus.[19] Aristotle, in turn, was credited with paying three Attic talents for some books of Speusippus.[20] The libraries of the institutions which

---

[15] Isoc. *Aeg.* 5. Cf. Wilamowitz-Moellendorff 1889: 123 n. 1; Platthy 1968: 144 test.106; Nieddu 1984: 259 and n. 180; Dillery 2005: 222.
[16] Dion. Hal. *Isoc.* 18 = Arist. fr. 128 Gigon. See Dover 1968: 25–6. On the problems relevant to the court speeches of Isocrates, cf. Whitehead 2004.
[17] Ar. *Ran.* 943 and 1409. Evidence on Euripides and books is collected in Kannicht 2004: 73–4, test. 49–50b. See also Nieddu 1984: 254–5; Dover 1993: 34–5.
[18] Gell. 3.17 = Timon, fr. 54 Di Marco; Diog. Laert. 3.9 = Satyrus, fr. 16 Müller; Diog. Laert. 8.85 = Hermippus, fr. 69 Bollansée; Diog. Laert. 8.84.
[19] Diog. Laert. 3.18 and Procl. *In Ti.* 90.21–4 Diehl.
[20] Gell. 3.17 = Düring 1957: 337 test. 42b.

Plato and Aristotle created, the Academy and the Lyceum, appear to have grown up around the personal libraries of the two philosophers.[21] Even if intended for the use of the schools, they continued to be regarded as personal property. This is especially clear for Aristotle who bequeathed his library to his successor Theophrastus, as we understand from Strabo's *testimonium* on the fate of Aristotle's library.[22]

Around the middle of the century Xenophon in his *Memorabilia* portrays Socrates conversing with a young man, Euthydemus, who was very keen on collecting books. "Tell me, Euthydemus, am I rightly informed that you have a large collection of books (πολλὰ γράμματα) written by the wise men of the past?" – Socrates asks him. And Euthydemus admits to the insistent philosopher that he has gathered books and that he goes on gathering them with great care (καὶ ἔτι γε συνάγω, ἕως ἂν κτήσωμαι ὡς ἂν δύνωμαι πλεῖστα, "and I will collect them until I get as many as possible").[23] Socrates then lists a series of professions which could profit by a collection of books (thus confirming for us the circulation of such technical libraries): doctor, architect, mathematician, astronomer, and even rhapsodist (since he knows that Euthydemus' library included also "all the verses [i.e. books] of Homer"). But of course in Socrates' view none of these books could lead to virtue. This scene, set at the end of the fifth century, was probably imagined by Xenophon in response to the book-collecting practices of his own day. It displays the first profile of a conscious book-collector and shows that by this time it was considered appropriate to use books as a means of learning practical or professional skills.[24]

Testimony to the use of private libraries for scholarly practices can also be found in contemporary literature. A series of passages suggests that recourse to books had gradually become usual in intellectual *milieux*, since these scenes all concern the search and selection of material for cultural purposes. The most significant passage comes, once again, from Xenophon's *Memorabilia*. Socrates and a group of pupils and collaborators are engaged in unrolling papyrus rolls (ἀνελίττων), reading texts (διέρχομαι) and extracting (ἐκλεγόμεθα) and copying the most interesting passages from the works of ancient authors preserved in books (τοὺς θησαυροὺς τῶν πάλαι σοφῶν

---

[21] For anecdotes on the library of Plato cf. Platthy 1968: 121–4, test. 54–61, and Swift Riginos 1976: 165–79. Several passages in Plato's works refer to the use of books as usual practice, cf. e.g. Del Corso 2003: 12. On the library of Aristotle, cf. Platthy 1968: 124–9 test. 64–74 and Düring 1957: 337–8 test. 42a–d. On research and writing in the Lyceum, cf. Vegetti 1992 and Cambiano 1988: 78–81.
[22] Strabo 13.1.54–55, also discussed by Jacob, this volume, as is the next passage discussed.
[23] Xen. *Mem.* 4.2.8. Cf. Platthy 1968: 130 test. 77; Cavallo 1988: 29; Perilli 2007: 37–8.
[24] Morgan 1999: 54.

ἀνδρῶν οὓς ἐκεῖνοι κατέλιπον ἐν βιβλίοις γράψαντες).[25] It is not easy to say whether this reflects the habits of Socrates or rather a way of working more familiar to Xenophon himself. But it is nonetheless remarkable, especially for the words used. The content of these books is regarded as a θησαυρός, a treasure, and the idea that writing in books is the means by which such treasures are preserved is emphasized.[26] The practice of reading books and making extracts from them was also treated as a common one by Alcidamas, a strong critic of written culture, in his pamphlet *On those who write speeches*. He begins by stating that even people lacking any culture whatsoever might easily compose speeches, by simply resorting to the written works of past authors and selecting ideas from different sources (καὶ παραθέμενον τὰ τῶν προγεγονότων συγγράμματα πολλαχόθεν εἰς ταὐτὸν ἐνθυμήματα συναγεῖραι).[27] This method of working was not unknown to Plato who refers in the *Laws* to those who extract sections and entire passages from every kind of author to create new texts (οἱ δὲ ἐκ πάντων κεφάλαια ἐκλέξαντες καὶ τινας ὅλας ῥήσεις εἰς ταὐτὸν συναγαγόντες).[28] Isocrates too appears to allude to this practice in the *Ad Nicoclem* where, while dealing with the *inventio* of arguments by those who devote themselves to paraenetic speeches, he states that the one who is able to collect (ἀθροῖσαι) the greatest number of ideas and precepts scattered (διεσπαρμένων) in the thoughts of the ancient authors (ἐν ταῖς τῶν ἄλλων διανοίαις) and to re-edit them in a more accurate form, this one shall be regarded as "the most accomplished in composing speeches" (χαριέστατον). Isocrates repeats this idea further on, where he criticizes the fact that most people would not show any interest "if one were to make a collection of what we call maxims from the works of the leading poets" (εἴ τις ἐκλέξειε τῶν προεχόντων ποιητῶν τὰς καλουμένας γνώμας).[29] Finally, references to this way of working also occur in Aristotle ("we ought to make extracts from written works", ἐκλέγειν ἐκ τῶν γεγραμμένων).[30]

---

[25] Xen. *Mem.* 1.6.14. The scene is anticipated (*Mem.* 1.2.56) by Policrates' criticism that Socrates "selected" (ἐκλεγόμενον) from poets passages which could be useful in justifying his illicit behavior. See now Bandini and Dorion 2000: 165–6.

[26] In Xenophon's *Memorabilia* books are called θησαυροί only here and in 4.2.9 (where Euthydemus' library is mentioned), cf. Gigon 1953: 163, Bandini and Dorion 2000: 165.

[27] Alcidamas, *Soph.* 4. For a well documented treatment of the subject, cf. Mariss 2002: 115–16.

[28] Pl. *Leg.* 811a. On the passage and its relation to the issue of the origin of anthologies, cf. Ford 2002: 194–7, and the critical remarks by Nicolai 2004a: 195–7. Also the selection of passages for teaching required a book collection: on teaching anthologies and book circulation, see now Del Corso 2005: 17–20.

[29] See Isoc. *Ad Nic.* 41 and 44. On the first passage, cf. Nicolai 2004b: 28–9.

[30] Arist. *Top.* 105b. Evidence on this practice for a later period is collected by Dorandi 2000b: 27–50.

Collating books

The most impressive instance of excerpting in the fourth century comes from an author, Isocrates, who held his own works in great esteem and made them into a sort of reference "library" for his own use.[31] The self-quotations from previous works that he included in his *Antidosis* actually form an annotated anthology from his former books: there is no parallel in the literature of this age. The case is highly remarkable not only for the study of ancient literary composition but also for the history of ancient criticism and for the history of Isocrates' text. The large quantity of texts inserted in the new work required Isocrates and his collaborators to single out and find the chosen sections in the author's library, that is to say in the book-rolls containing the final version of the works from which he had decided to make extracts.

These examples lead us to consider in brief also the evidence provided by the way in which fourth-century books are structured. Explicit quotations, references, and allusions to texts of other authors proliferate in prose texts of this time and clearly point to the use of books in the compositional process. Among Aristotle's works, a treatise like the *Rhetoric*, to give just one example, required a preliminary collection of extracts from works of other authors, since it is unlikely that all the quotations with which the work is full were made solely from memory.[32] These notes were subsequently inserted in the relevant places as the draft of Aristotle's course on rhetoric took its shape, a process which implies the availability of books for teacher and pupils. For this reason, quotations, and long quotations in particular, allow us a glimpse into the "workshop" of ancient authors. Such is the case of the long quotation from the Ὧραι (*Seasons*) of Prodicus, the famous tale of Heracles at the crossroads, inserted by Xenophon in his *Memorabilia*, and which is presented as a mnemonic *tour de force* of Socrates (ὅσα ἐγὼ μέμνημαι, "as far as I remember", he says before his performance).[33] Quotations from poetry are also widespread in Attic oratory. The speeches that Aeschines and Demosthenes published after the political trials in which they faced each other (Aeschines' *Against Timarchus, On the embassy* and *Against Ctesiphon*;

---

[31] For the large self-quotations in the *Antidosis* (*Paneg.* 51–99 = *Antid.* 59; *Pac.* 25–56 and 132–45 = *Antid.* 65; *Ad Nic.* 14–39 = *Antid.* 72; *C. soph.* 14–18 = *Antid.* 195; plus *Nic.* 5–9 = *Antid.* 253–7), cf. Pinto 2003: 107–42 and Nicolai 2004b.

[32] On this aspect, cf. Knox 1985: 13. For Aristotle's way of working, cf. Düring 1954: 69 and n. 2 and Düring 1957: 368–9.

[33] Xen. *Mem.* 2.1.21–34 = Prodic. fr. 2 D.-K. Cf. Gigon 1956: 60–2. Prodicus' book is known and mentioned by Plato as well (*Symp.* 177b). On its circulation, cf. Nieddu 1984: 250. For a recent analysis of the quotation in Xenophon, cf. Sansone 2004.

Demosthenes' *On the embassy* and *On the crown*) include a great number of verses inserted throughout the argumentation. In the revised versions of these texts made to be circulated at the end of the trials those verses are read, by means of a fictitious device already employed by Isocrates in his *Antidosis*, by a γραμματεύς, a secretary of the court. Of course, a few verses from Homer or Hesiod or from a tragedy might be quoted by heart during the actual debates. But it is more difficult to imagine Demosthenes reciting or reading (or making someone else read) in the court sixteen lines from Sophocles' *Antigone* or thirty-nine lines from an elegy of Solon.[34] The same must be true for the fifty-five lines from Euripides' *Erechtheus* or the thirty-two lines from Tyrtaeus that we read in Lycurgus.[35]

The Athenian authors took part in the life of the *polis* from different points of view. The book was a suitable medium for them to circulate ideas as well as cultural and political programmes. For the same reason they read each other's works. This is explicitly stated by Isocrates, for instance, at the beginning of his *Busiris*, referring to one of his opponents, Polycrates, where he says that he has read some of the works composed by Polycrates (τῶν δὲ λόγων τινάς, ὧν γέγραφας, αὐτὸς ἀνεγνωκώς).[36] Therefore polemics, one of the main features of the literature of the century, affected different fields of intellectual production (philosophy, rhetoric, historiography, oratory) and can be traced in particular in the works of the great cultural protagonists of the age, including Xenophon, Isocrates, Plato, Aristotle, and Demosthenes. These polemics are rarely explicit; usually they are in the form of more or less recognizable allusions or parodies. More than a century ago Gustav Teichmüller attempted to produce a survey of the cultural quarrels of the century;[37] even the volumes of Werner Jaeger's *Paideia* are still useful for the reconstruction of this tangled network of intellectual relationships; and scholarship goes back periodically to single cases. I will recall here just a single instance. An anecdote dating back to ancient biographical traditions (*qui de Xenophontis Platonisque vita et moribus pleraque omnia exquisitissime scripsere*) and collected in the second century AD by Aulus Gellius reported that as soon as the first two books of Plato's *Republic* were put into circulation, Xenophon started composing the *Cyropedia*, a work on

---

[34] Dem. *De falsa leg.* 247 = Soph. *Ant.* 175–90, *De falsa leg.* 255 = Solon, *Eleg.* 4 West².
[35] Lyc. *Leoc.* 100 = Eur. fr. 360 Kannicht, *Leoc.* 107 = Tyrtaeus, *Eleg.* 6–7 Prato. A brief survey of passages and bibliography in Pinto 2003: 7–8 and nn. 6–8. On the significance of the large quotations from poetry in Lycurgus' *Against Leocrates*, cf. Nicolai 2004a: 192–4.
[36] Isoc. *Bus.* 1. Cf. Livingstone 2001: 93–4. For recent studies focussing on Xenophon, see Danzig 2003, 2005. On the practice of discussing philosophical books, see Cambiano 2007.
[37] Teichmüller 1881–4.

a different form of government, the monarchic system.[38] A fictitious story, probably, but one which tells us much about the effect of reading a newly published book in the period we are observing.

All these passages imply that reading books, selecting sections, and copying them out was considered a prerequisite for the accomplishment of a new literary product. In this way, we can occasionally glimpse the ancient author working with books, possibly with the support of others, even if we know very little of the specific dynamics. It is clear from Isocrates' *Panathenaicus*, for example, that he was surrounded by assistants and pupils who not only used to analyze and discuss the works of their teacher but also took an active part in the composition of his speeches.[39] It is probably not excessive to imagine something similar happening in the case of other important Athenian *entourages*.

Towards a new idea of the library

We do not know if there was a library in the school of Isocrates: there is scanty information about where this institution was located, a late source placing it near the Lyceum.[40] But the scholarly practices mentioned above and the different professions that Isocrates' former pupils reputedly practised (as rhetoricians, politicians, generals, poets, dramatists, historians, antiquarians etc.) all speak in favor of the existence of a diversified collection of books.[41] It is also possible to connect the school of Isocrates to the establishment of a library outside Athens thanks to evidence that until now has not been fully appreciated. Nymphis, a historian from Heraclea in Pontus, who lived in the third century BC, recorded that Clearchus, who had been a pupil of Isocrates for four years, was the first among the local dynasts to establish a library in his time (βιβλιοθήκην μέντοι κατασκευάσαι πρὸ τῶν ἄλλων οὓς ἡ τυραννὶς ἀπέδειξεν ὀνομάζεσθαι). This fragment has been preserved by the Byzantine scholar Photius in his so-called *Bibliotheca* and by good fortune can be combined with the information we have about the ties of Clearchus to the school of Isocrates, from Isocrates' letter to Clearchus' son Timotheus. This evidence reveals the existence of a library

---

[38] Gell. 14.3.3: *Xenophon inclito illi operi Platonos, quod de optimo statu reipublicae civitatisque administrandae scriptum est, lectis ex eo duobus fere libris, qui primi in volgus exierant, opposuit contra conscripsitque diversum regiae administrationis genus, quod Παιδείας Κύρου inscriptum est.* Cf. Danzig 2003.
[39] Isoc. *Panath.* 200–68. Commentary in Roth 2003: 216–60.
[40] Anon. *Vita Isocr.* in Mathieu and Brémond 1928, xxxvi ll. 116–17.
[41] An attempt to outline a library of Isocrates is in Pinto 2006.

in a Greek colony on the Black Sea before the middle of the fourth century (Clearchus was murdered around 353/2). It ascribes its foundation to a man who had received his higher education in Athens, at the school of an influential teacher who was well aware of the importance of books.[42] Something similar, if on a rather different scale, was accomplished at the end of the century by Demetrius of Phalerum, philosopher and politician, a pupil of Aristotle and Theophrastus, who became the counsellor of Ptolemy I and is credited by some ancient sources with conceiving the project of establishing a library in Alexandria.[43] His example connects the experiences and practices of Athenian learned men of the fourth century directly with the foundation of the greatest library of the ancient world. It is conveniently recalled at the end of this survey.

---

[42] See Phot. *Bibl.* chap. 224, 222b 25–7 Bekker, quoting Memnon (*FGrHist* 434 fr. 1), who ultimately drew on Nymphis, and Isocr. *Epist.* VII. Cf. Pasquali 1930: 942; Platthy 1968: 158 test. 134; Trampedach 1994: 85.

[43] This is probably the meaning of what we read in Strabo 13.1.54: "Aristotle [...] was the first, as far as we know, to collect books and to teach the kings of Egypt how to put a library together." Cf. Pfeiffer 1968: 98–104; Jacob 1996: 48 and 52; Canfora 1999.

5 | From text to text

The impact of the Alexandrian library on the work of Hellenistic poets

ANNETTE HARDER

Introduction

The subject of this chapter is the impact of the Alexandrian library on the work of some Hellenistic poets, who lived and worked at Alexandria in the third century BC and whose poetry is well known for its scholarly and learned character.

The famous library at Alexandria was founded as part of Ptolemaic cultural politics, which stimulated art and scholarship and tried to keep alive the Greek tradition in the new context of Alexandria in the third century BC. The library aimed at collecting as much of Greek literature as possible and must have been a prestigious and important institution.[1] The fact that the position of librarian was coupled with that of the tutor of the Ptolemaic princes suggests that its status was very high indeed. Some of the librarians, such as Eratosthenes and Apollonius Rhodius, were also poets, and another poet, Callimachus, though not a librarian, was involved in the library because he made a descriptive 'catalogue' of its possessions, the so-called *Pinakes*.[2]

Given the apparent prestige and importance of the library, it is striking that, as far as we can judge by the evidence, none of the Hellenistic poets refers to it explicitly.[3] One may wonder whether this reticence is in any way compensated for by implicit references to the library in the same poets' poetry and, if so, in what way the poets show their use of it, and what this may tell us about the role attributed to the library in Alexandria in the third century BC.[4] In this chapter I will address these questions and focus on

---

[1] See on the library in general e.g. Fraser 1972: 1.320–35; Bagnall 2002; and for briefer, but useful surveys Gutzwiller 2007: 19–23; Stephens 2010: 54–6.
[2] See e.g. Pfeiffer 1968: 126–34; Fraser 1972: 452–4; Blum 1991.
[3] In this respect it is interesting to compare the paper of Alexei Zadorojnyi in this volume, where the 'low-key presence' of libraries at the time of the Second Sophistic is discussed.
[4] Although much has been written about the Alexandrian library (see n.1) and on the learned character of Alexandrian poetry, the connection between the two can still be explored in a more systematic way, with which I hope to make a start in this chapter. Good recent introductions to Hellenistic poetry with ample references to its scholarly character and with further bibliography can be found in e.g. Fantuzzi and Hunter 2004; Gutzwiller 2007; Clauss and Cuypers 2010a.

the work of two poets whose connection with the library is indisputable because of external evidence, i.e. Callimachus and Apollonius Rhodius. I will investigate how Callimachus' *Aetia*, a work about the 'causes' or 'origins' of various rituals and related matters, and Apollonius Rhodius' *Argonautica*, about the expedition of Jason and his Argonauts to Colchis in search of the Golden Fleece, show traces of wide reading and seem to attribute a specific role to the Alexandrian library. I will look at three aspects of their work: I will briefly discuss the reflection of philological research in their poetry and their involvement with the literary tradition in general, and then focus on the antiquarian contents of their poetry in the field of myth, history and geography.[5]

Philology

One potential impact of the library may be the way in which philological knowledge or discussion finds its way into the texts of Callimachus and Apollonius, and is reflected particularly in their vocabulary. Often we find these authors using rare poetic or dialect words, or else words known from Homer of which the sense is disputed. Sometimes the text also recalls passages in Homer where the actual text is disputed and may thus reflect the work of scholars working on the edition of the Homeric text.

As this aspect of the work of both authors is well documented in commentaries, books and articles, I refrain from giving many examples here and refer only to Callimachus fr. 67.1–14,[6] as a typical instance:

> Αὐτὸς Ἔρως ἐδίδαξεν Ἀκόντιον, ὅππότε καλῆι
>   ἤιθετο Κυδίππηι παῖς ἐπὶ παρθενικῆι,
> τέχνην – οὐ γὰρ ὅγ' ἔσκε πολύκροτος – ὄφρα λέγο[
>   τοῦτο διὰ ζωῆς οὔνομα κουρίδιον.
> ἦ γάρ, ἄναξ, ὁ μὲν ἦλθεν Ἰουλίδος, ἡ δ' ἀπὸ Νάξου,   5
>   Κύνθιε, τὴν Δήλωι σὴν ἐπὶ βουφονίην,
> αἷμα τὸ μὲν γενεῆς Εὐξαντίδος, ἡ δὲ Προμήθ[ου,
>   καλοὶ νησάων ἀστέρες ἀμφότεροι.
> πολλαὶ Κυδίππην ὀλ[ί]γην ἔτι μητέρες υἱοῖς

---

[5] Sometimes the authors also show traces of scientific knowledge, as in *Aet.* fr. 75.12–14, where Callimachus reacts to views on epilepsy and sides with Hippocrates in rejecting the notion that this was a sacred disease. In this respect, however, it seems less easy to establish whether the knowledge is found in the library or rather derived from a kind of ongoing scientific discourse in the contemporary society.

[6] The fragments are numbered as in Harder 2012.

ἑδνῆστιν κεραῶν ἤιτεον ἀντὶ βοῶν· 10
κείνης ο[ὐ]χ ἑτέρη γὰρ ἐπὶ λασίοιο γέροντος
  Σιληνοῦ νοτίην ἵκετο πιδυλίδα
ἠοῖ εἰδομένη μάλιον ῥέθος οὐδ' Ἀριήδης
  ἐς χ]λορὸν εὐδούσης ἁβρὸν ἔθηκε πόδα

Eros himself taught Acontius, when the boy burned
  with love for the girl Cydippe,
his tricks – for he was not very cunning –, in order that . . .
  all through his life . . . that lawful name.
For, lord, he came from Iulis, she from Naxos, 5
  Cynthian, to your sacrifice of oxen at Delos,
offspring, one of them of the family of Euxantius, the other of
  Promethus,
    both beautiful stars on their islands.
Many mothers asked Cydippe when she was still small
  as a bride for their sons paid for with horned oxen, 10
for no other girl went to the watery spring of hairy old
  Silenus with a face that looked more like the dawn
than hers nor did such a girl put down her delicate feet
  in the dance for the sleeping Ariadne

This fragment is from the beginning of the love story of Acontius and Cydippe in *Aetia* 3 and, while introducing the young lovers, contains a large number of learned elements. Thus, e.g. in fr. 67.3 Callimachus states that Acontius was not πολύκροτος ('clever, cunning') and thereby refers to *Od.*1.1 ἄνδρα... πολύτροπον ('a versatile, cunning man'), where the adjective appears as a variant indicating Odysseus (although we cannot be certain that this variant was already known to Callimachus);[7] in 10 the word ἑδνῆστιν ('bride'), about Cydippe as a bride to be paid for, is found only here and seems to have been formed as a contrast with the rare Homeric ἀνάεδνος (of brides 'for whom one does not pay'); in 13 we read μάλιον ('more'), a rare Ionic form for μᾶλλον ('more'), and then ῥέθος, a noun which is found only in the plural in Homer (where it may mean 'limbs' or 'nostrils') and in the singular, meaning 'face', seems to be Aeolic, and Ἀριήδης, a Cretan form of the name of Ariadne, which Zenodotus wanted to read in *Il.*18.592.

It is clear that for this kind of vocabulary the library, with its large numbers of varying texts of Homer, works by other poets and glossaries, provided not only the ideal basis, but was in fact also necessary. Although one could

---

[7] For details on this as well as on the other issues discussed in this passage, see the commentary of Harder 2012.

imagine that poets were alluding to passages from Homer which they knew by heart and that readers would pick up these allusions because of their own knowledge of Homer, it seems hard to conceive that such specific knowledge as the presence of textual variants or the occurrence and interpretation of obscure dialect forms did not depend on books in the library. In this respect it must be significant that we find general allusions to Homer also in earlier Greek poetry, but that this very detailed kind of reference is typical of the Hellenistic and later periods.[8]

The literary tradition

The *Aetia* and the *Argonautica* are both very much part of the Greek literary tradition and this in itself may also be regarded as a sign of the library's influence. Because they refer to many different literary genres, both works remind the reader of the variety of literary texts which were part of that tradition and could be found in the library.

Apollonius positions himself in the narrative epic tradition of Homer and reminds his readers of Homer all the time, e.g. by means of allusions to specific passages, reworkings of typical Homeric scenes or his treatment of Homeric similes. Apart from this, he also refers his readers to the genre of Greek tragedy by his treatment of the love of Medea for Jason. On this scale the theme of romantic love appears in epic for the first time in the *Argonautica*; it owes a great deal in particular to the plays of Euripides on the subject of female love and, of course, to his *Medea*.[9] Now, both Homer and Euripides were mainstream authors and may well have been familiar to a Greek audience without the help of the Alexandrian library. It is therefore more significant that on a smaller scale also other genres are evoked, such as Pindar's epinicians at the end of book 4, which recalls Pindar's fourth *Pythian Ode*, and, through the songs of Orpheus, the various genres of didactic epic, hymn, epinician and *epithalamium*,[10] which were probably collected in the library.

In a similar way Callimachus in his *Aetia* places himself in the tradition of the didactic poetry of Hesiod (who in his *Theogony* related the origins of the

---

[8] See on this kind of allusion also e.g. Gutzwiller 2007: 169–70, who, however, does not explicitly relate it to the presence of the library.

[9] For an extensive discussion of Apollonius' debt to tragedy, see Schmakeit 2003; on Apollonius and epic, see e.g. Knight 1995.

[10] I owe this observation to J. Klooster, who drew attention to the generic variety of Orpheus' songs in a paper entitled 'Orpheus and the Hymnic Origins of Poetry in the *Argonautica* of Apollonius' (given at Groningen on 2 June 2006).

Greek gods). But he also plays with a range of other literary genres, alluding to Homer, writing a Pindaric epinician in elegiacs in his *Victoria Berenices* (fr. 54–60j) and shaping some of his poems, such as the *Coma Berenices* (fr. 110), or the poem about the tomb of Simonides (fr. 64), like extended epigrams. In the case of the *Coma Berenices* the model is a votive epigram, since the lock dedicated to the gods by Berenice II tells about its fate. The fragment about Simonides offers a variation on a funeral epigram in which the dead poet tells about the destruction of his tomb and prays for revenge. On a smaller scale Callimachus also evokes other genres. Thus he recalls the conclusion of a hymn at the end of the story of the Charites at Paros, where these goddesses are addressed with a hymnic farewell and a request for lasting fame (fr. 7.13–14). In the *Coma Berenices* he reminds his readers of the *epithalamium* by means of a range of allusions, such as, for instance, the description of Berenice's locks mourning the separation of their sister lock in fr. 110.51. In the prologue to the *Aetia* he employs allusions to reference a great range of the Greek literary tradition: he evokes various kinds of epic and elegy, referring to specific authors such as Philitas and Mimnermus (and perhaps Antimachus), and also works such as Aristophanes' *Frogs*, Pindar's *Paeans*, Plato's *Ion* and a choral ode from Euripides' *Heracles Furens*.[11]

All this suggests a broad familiarity with the literary tradition and an awareness of literary genres that may be hard to imagine without the help of the library. It also shows that both authors shared a tendency to rework and revitalise the older genres in a new context.

Myth, history and geography

Both Callimachus and Apollonius also give evidence of great knowledge in the fields of myth, history and geography, a knowledge which suggests wide reading on these topics in works they may well have found in the library. In contrast with their treatment of philological issues and their reception of the literary tradition, where the readers seem to be expected to discover the references and allusions themselves, here we often have fairly clear and explicit markers of sources, particularly in Callimachus, but to a certain extent also in Apollonius.

On the whole, the local character of many of the stories in the *Aetia* suggests local histories were used as source material even when they are

---

[11] For further discussion and details, see Harder 1998 and 2002.

not mentioned. But on several occasions we find explicit indications of sources.[12] In fr. 75.53–77 Callimachus states that he has found the love story of Acontius and Cydippe, which he has just told, in the Cean history of Xenomedes of Ceos. He then goes on to summarise this prose history in some twenty lines of elegiac couplets, telling how the island was first inhabited by the Corycian nymphs from Mount Parnassus, then by other people, who finally gave it its name 'Ceos', and by the Telchines, who were destroyed by the gods because of their impious behaviour. After their destruction, the island was repopulated by the descendants of the only survivors, Macelo and Dexithea, and its four towns were founded. It is easy to imagine that the work of Xenomedes was preserved in the Alexandrian library and that Callimachus consulted it for this part of the *Aetia*. However, he did not just use the work as a source, but in addition he compressed it into a small piece of poetry, selecting from it what he thought fit to tell, and thus presented it to his readers in a new form. At the same time this may perhaps have inspired his readers to go and look up the original work of Xenomedes for themselves.

Elsewhere, at the end of the story of Melicertes, we find another brief source-indication in fr. 92.2–3:

Λε]ανδρίδες εἴ τι παλαιαὶ
φθ[έγγ]ονται[ ]υφαν ἱστορίαι

if the old Leandrian stories have something to tell ...

Here Callimachus probably refers to the work of Leandrius of Miletus, whose *Milesiaca* (presumably a local history of Miletus) again could easily have been stored in the library. In fr. 103 Callimachus refers to a *kurbis*, a pillar with an inscription, as a kind of source for the story of Androgeos, who appeared as the 'Hero of the Stern' in Phaleron. This source indication is less easy to interpret in terms of the library. Could one perhaps assume that the text on the *kurbis* was at some stage transcribed by a local historian into his work?[13]

Sometimes we also find indications of a dispute in which several views were given, as in the question about the parents of the Graces. In *Scholia Florentina* 30–5 (Pfeiffer 1, p.13) we read that the narrator, i.e. 'the young

---

[12] See in general Krevans 2004: 178–81.
[13] Elsewhere the ancient scholia mention Callimachus' sources, as in the *Scholia Florentina* on the story of the Charites at Paros (fr. 3–7), where they mention the *Argolica* by Hagias and Dercylus and Aristotle's *Parian Politeia*. Here we cannot know whether these sources were also mentioned by Callimachus, or were just added by the scholia. In any case here too it is easily conceivable that Callimachus consulted these works in the library.

Callimachus' who, in a dream, is asking the Muses on Mount Helicon about the aetiology of various Greek rituals, has heard from Clio that the Graces are daughters of Dionysus and the Naxian nymph Coronis, after he himself had mentioned that some people said they were daughters of Hera and Zeus, whereas others said that they were daughters of Eurynome and Zeus (cf. fr. 6), and a third group said that they were daughters of Euanthe and Zeus. Here Callimachus creates an impression of a scholar-poet confronted with several conflicting traditions, which could well be preserved in works in the library, and trying to find his way among them. The idea that the Muses must provide the final answer suggests a play with the notions of the modern, but confusing luxury of an extensive library and the reliability of the Muses as a time-honoured source of knowledge.

Apart from these more or less explicit references to sources, there are also other hints about the consultation of sources, which may even involve suggesting that the reader goes to read the sources for himself if he wants to know more. Thus in fr. 43.28–83 on the foundations of Sicilian cities there is repeated emphasis on the knowledge of 'the young Callimachus' who tells the Muses about the foundations of all the Sicilian cities before he finally formulates his question about the unusual founder cult at Zancle. We find verbs such as φήσω ('I will tell of...') (fr. 43.42), ἔχω...ἐνισπε[ῖν ('I am able to tell of...') (fr. 43.52) and οἶδα ('I know...') (fr. 43.46 and 50). All this knowledge may be derived from authors such as Thucydides and Timaeus, who wrote about Sicily at some length, and/or from local histories of Sicily.[14] As Callimachus' descriptions of the various towns and their foundations are very brief and often somewhat cryptic (such as, e.g., fr. 43.48–9 'I know of Cretan Minoa, where the daughters of Cocalus poured boiling water on the son of Europa'), the passage seems to invite the readers to go and read these works for themselves. Again, as in the case of the parents of the Graces, the emphasis on the scholar-poet's own knowledge is neatly balanced by the question to the Muses, who at the end of Callimachus' long catalogue of foundation stories must explain the ritual performed for the founder of Zancle.

An even more explicit invitation to further reading is found in SH 264.1 from the *Victoria Berenices*, a poem celebrating a victory of Berenice II in the chariot races at Nemea which stood at the beginning of *Aetia* 3: αὐτὸς ἐπιφράσσαιτο, τάμοι δ' ἄπο μῆκος ἀοιδῆι ('let him find out for himself and cut short the length of the song'). Here, apparently, the reader is asked to go and find out about the story of Heracles killing the Nemean lion,

---

[14] See e.g. Fraser 1972, 1.766; Fabian 1992: 171 and 182–3; Pearson 1987: 54.

which Callimachus seems to have left out or treated only cursorily in his story about Heracles spending the night before this event with the poor farmer Molorcus in his cottage and watching Molorcus' battle against an invasion of mice. Perhaps for many readers in the third century BC the story of Heracles killing the Nemean lion was sufficiently well known, so that there was no need to consult further sources. Still, one could argue that Callimachus plays with the notion of people going to read in the library the many texts that told this famous story, so that he as a modern and innovative poet does not need to tell it once again. Thus the *Aetia* as a product of the well stocked library of Alexandria also seems to send its readers back to that same library again in order to profit even more from it.

In the *Argonautica* too we find many antiquarian details, such as *aitia*, i.e. rituals and monuments founded by the Argonauts on their travels, or all kinds of mythographical or geographical information, which the poet may well have found in the histories of local authors. In fact the scholia in several instances refer the reader to such works. It is, however, less easy to form a picture of Apollonius' sources than in the case of the *Aetia*, because of the epic presentation, which is less personal than that of Callimachus and tends to have a narrator who is less 'visible'. Even so, there is a considerable number of small references to other authorities for a certain statement, such as 'they say . . . ' or 'they call . . . '. Although we do find this kind of reference also in earlier authors who had no access to the Alexandrian library, such as Homer, Pindar and Euripides,[15] there seems to be a deliberate contrast with Homer. There the so-called φασί-utterances are generally part of the character-text and rarely of the narrator-text,[16] whereas in the *Argonautica* they are all part of the narrator-text, as in e.g. *Argon.* 1.23–7 about Orpheus' parents, Calliope and Oeagrus, and about the way he is charming rocks and rivers with his song, 1.238 about the name of Magnesian Pagasae, or 1.941 about an island called Mount of Bears. This suggests that Apollonius wanted to emphasise the dependence of the human narrator on the reports of others. Taken together, these references could create an impression of a well documented epic and of an author who is dependent on the tradition and may well have been busy consulting numerous sources in the library.

---

[15] For references, see Harder 2012 on Callim. *Aet.* fr. 75.4.
[16] See de Jong 1987: 48 and 237–8. On the distinction between narrator-text (i.e. the text of the narrator who is telling his readers about the events) and character-text (i.e. the dialogues and speeches of the characters in the story, which are quoted in direct discourse), see de Jong 1987 in general.

In many, though not all, of these cases the scholia in fact refer the reader to authors and texts which may well have been among Apollonius' sources in the library. Thus we read in the scholia on *Argon.* 1.23–25a:

Ἡρόδωρος (*FGrH* 31 F 42) δύο εἶναι Ὀρφεῖς φησιν, ὧν τὸν ἕτερον συμπλεῦσαι τοῖς Ἀργοναύταις. Φερεκύδης ἐν τῇ ϛ´ (*FGrH* 3 F 26) Φιλάμμωνά φησι καὶ οὐκ Ὀρφέα συμπεπλευκέναι. ἔστι δέ, ὡς Ἀσκληπιάδης (*FGrH* 12 F 6c), Ἀπόλλωνος καὶ Καλλιόπης· ἔνιοι δὲ ἀπὸ Οἰάγρου καὶ Πολυμνίας.

Herodorus says that there are two Orpheuses, one of whom sailed with the Argonauts. Pherecydes in book 6 says that Philammon, not Orpheus has sailed with them. According to Asclepiades he is a son of Apollo and Calliope, according to others of Oeagrus and Polymnia.

When one collects all the relevant instances a picture emerges which includes a considerable number of authors. It should be noted, though, that the scholia also mention later authors such as Apollodorus of Athens, Demetrius of Scepsis or Strabo, as in e.g. the scholia on *Argon.* 1.238:

Παγασαί· ἀκρωτήριον Μαγνησίας· ὠνομάσθη δὲ ἀπὸ τοῦ ἐκεῖ πεπῆχθαι τὴν Ἀργώ. ὁ δὲ Σκήψιος (fr. 52 Gaede) ἀπὸ τοῦ πηγαῖς περιρρέεσθαι τοὺς τόπους.

Pagasae: a headland of Magnesia; it was thus called because the Argo was built there. But Demetrius of Scepsis states that it was because the area was surrounded by springs.

This must mean that the scholiasts collected evidence and parallels from various periods and did not necessarily aim at giving the *sources* of Apollonius. Still, one may assume, particularly when Apollonius takes sides in a much debated issue or offers very specific details of a local nature, that he consulted the earlier sources mentioned by the scholia. The list thus established includes a variety of prose-authors, such as Herodotus, Timaeus, Timagetus, Pherecydes, Ephorus, Xenophon, Asclepiades, and local historians such as Neanthes and Deilochus (about Cyzicus); Herodorus, Nymphis and Promathidas (about Heracleia); and Nymphodorus (about peoples along the coast of the Black Sea).[17] As Delage remarks, the scholia 'montrent chez Apollonios des lectures nombreuses et une prédilection pour les prosateurs et pour les chroniques locales peu connues'.[18] Once, in *Argon.* 4.1381–92, the story (about the Argonauts carrying the Argo through the desert during twelve days and nights) is attributed to the Muses and the narrator says that he is retelling it. As in the *Aetia* passages discussed above, the contrast with

---

[17] See also Delage 1930: 277–81. For some other passages, see e.g. the scholia on Ap. Rhod. *Argon.* 2.297, 854; 4.990.
[18] Delage 1930: 281.

the other hints at sources makes one wonder about the intentions behind this reference to the Muses. Here it seems to be to underline the unusual and almost unbelievable achievement of the Argonauts, which seems to stand out even more because of the suggestion that a more than human authority must be adduced.

As in the *Aetia* we also find passages where something is rather emphatically *not* told in the *Argonautica*. In *Argon*. 1.648–9 Apollonius asks why he should tell at length about Aethalides, who after his death was destined to live sometimes on earth and sometimes below the earth and could find no forgetfulness. The scholia tell us that according to Pherecydes this was a gift from Hermes and that the Pythagoreans say that, through a number of reincarnations, Aethalides eventually became Pythagoras. Apollonius' refusal to speak at length about these things may inspire the readers to further reading, as in Callimachus' more explicit *SH* 264. In a similar way Apollonius in *Argon*. 1.919–21 stops speaking about the island of Electra (i.e. Samothrace), because it is not lawful to sing about the mysteries of its gods. Again the scholia refer to several sources, such as Hellanicus and Aristotle, which may well have been available to Apollonius, as well as to his readers. In *Argon*. 1.1220 Apollonius decides to tell nothing more about Heracles and the Dryopians, and the scholia refer to Archilochus, Pherecydes and Callimachus (who treated the story in *Aetia* fr. 24–5). In *Argon*. 4.247–52 Apollonius adopts a respectful silence about sacrifices for Hecate and adds that the altar built by the Argonauts is still there in his own time. The scholia refer to Nymphis, who probably in the first half of the third century BC wrote a work on Heracleia, in which he stated that there was a sanctuary of Hecate in Paphlagonia, founded by Medea. In all four cases the scholia give us an indication of Apollonius' sources and hints of possible further reading for his readers. As in the *Aetia* it is precisely by *not* telling something that Apollonius seems to make the library, where the reader may go and find the information the poet is holding back, into a kind of living presence in his work.

An interesting aspect of the accumulation of knowledge is also that it seems to lead to discussion and controversies. We already saw this kind of thing in Callimachus' discussion about the parents of the Graces. There are other passages too where both Callimachus and Apollonius get involved in discussions, for example in debating the return journey of the Argonauts, of which there were several versions involving different routes, or the location of death of Medea's brother Apsyrtus. In both cases we have evidence of the views of Callimachus and Apollonius and also some material to relate their views to the older literary and mythographic tradition.

Thus in Callimachus' *Aetia* the Argonauts return to Greece along the same route as they came, i.e. through the Bosporus (fr. 9), as in Sophocles (*Scythae* F 547) and Euripides (*Med.* 431–3 and 1263–4, where this is implicit in the chorus's addressing of Medea as someone who passed through the Symplegades), as well as in the fifth-century historian Herodorus (*FgrH* 31 F 10). In the *Argonautica* they follow the Ister (as instructed by Argus in *Argon.* 4.282–93) and from there go on into the Adriatic Sea, and the scholia on 4.303–6b refer to Timagetus, who may have been Apollonius' source for this version. In other sources the Argonauts took yet another route and went through the Phasis. We find this route with some variations as to details in Hesiod (fr. 241), Pindar (Pi. *P.*4.24–7), Antimachus (fr. 76 M) and Hecataeus (*FgrH* 1 F 18).

Similarly, in Callimachus' *Aetia* (fr. 8) Apsyrtus is killed by Medea at home in Colchis, as in Sophocles (*Colchides* F 343 I and II) and Euripides (*Med.*1334), whereas in *Argon.* 4.452–81 Medea lets Jason kill Apsyrtus on the island of Artemis on the Argonauts' homeward journey, after trapping him herself. As in the case of the return journey, Callimachus and Apollonius do not only differ from each other, but both poets also differ from Pherecydes (*FgrH* 3 F 32), where Medea kills Apsyrtus during the flight on the Argo, strewing parts of him on the sea in order to delay the Colchians.

In both cases we get the impression of a mixed tradition, well documented in the library. It seems that Callimachus and Apollonius, by means of alluding to each other's work in various ways, made sure that their readers knew that they had chosen different versions. Because of these passages (to which many other examples could be added) it seems clear that the contents of the work of Callimachus and Apollonius owe a great deal to the library and are hardly conceivable without access to the large amount of literature which was collected there.[19]

Conclusions

We may infer that the reading of Callimachus and Apollonius was very wide indeed and covered a large range of subjects from the fields of philology, the

---

[19] The impact of the library is also fairly obvious in the contents of other works, e.g. in Lycophron's *Alexandra* or in didactic poetry, where prose sources must have been frequently consulted, as in Aratus *Phaenomena*. In fact, the availability of so much material in the library may to a certain extent account for the increasing popularity of the genre of didactic poetry in the Hellenistic period, because poets *could* now find a great deal of accumulated knowledge in prose texts which they could 'transfer' to poetry.

literary tradition, myth, history and geography. We see unmistakable traces of this reading in form, language, contents and in the treatment of genre in their poetry.

We also see that the poets did much more than simply read and transmit the information gathered in the library. In fact they were able to handle the large amounts of information which were available in a very creative manner, and made use of it as a tool for shaping their own kinds of poetry. They recycled the large amounts of prose and poetry of earlier generations and transformed the old texts into new texts. By thus producing their own original poetry, they showed the vitality of the tradition and the importance of preserving it in an institution such as the Alexandrian library.

Two aspects of the way in which both poets worked with the material in the library seem particularly striking.

In the first place, in Callimachus' *Aetia* we find a number of rituals which are of a local nature, relating to places far from Alexandria to which neither Callimachus[20] nor many of his readers would be likely to travel; indeed some of these rituals may already have been obsolete in Callimachus' own day. In the *Argonautica* too we must probably take the 'even now' in many aetiological passages with a grain of salt, particularly considering the fact that the expedition of the Argonauts was part of the very distant past before the Trojan War. This suggests that both authors created a view of the present world filled with rituals and monuments, which for themselves and their audience existed to a large extent only in books, and in many cases had possibly come into existence only when local communities invented their own pasts, and local authors had written them down. Thanks to the library of Alexandria, Callimachus and Apollonius could create such a bookish world in which the Greek past seemed to live on for ever. This sense of a bookish world may have been enhanced by the poets' language, which as we saw owed a great deal to older poetic genres and reflected philological research on these genres, and by the form of their poems, which also frequently recalled the older literary genres found in the library.

In the second place, the poets seem to refer their readers back to the library. The *Aetia* and *Argonautica* are products of the library, but the relevance of the library does not stop there. Readers are invited to think about the different points of view in scholarly discussions or to complete the picture with other information, for which they in their turn must consult the library. Thus the poets who have created their works thanks to the library also seem to guarantee an ongoing interest and readership for the library

---

[20] Cf. perhaps *Aet.* fr. 178.27–34, where the narrator appears as someone who has not travelled and consults a fellow guest at a symposium from the island of Icus.

and thus emphasise its importance as an institution central to the cultural life of Alexandria.

Two main reasons for this central role of the library can be supposed, both applicable at the same time. The fairly new institution of the library with which Callimachus and Apollonius were closely involved must have been a stimulus in its own right. The large amount of texts and knowledge which was available on this scale for the first time in history must have fed an appetite for acquiring knowledge and an eagerness for making as much use of it as possible. Thus the engagement with the library seems to be a natural response to the vast increase of available material. On the other hand we must bear in mind that the library was very much part of Ptolemaic cultural politics. Using the material in the library and reminding the reader obliquely and subtly of the new Ptolemaic context for poetry was therefore an ideologically charged gesture and would be just what was expected of the poets working in Alexandria in the environment of the Ptolemaic court.

The fact that this involvement with the library was conveyed to readers without ever mentioning the library explicitly is an issue that still demands further investigation. It could be that the poets played with the notion of still upholding the old conventions of the oral transmission of poetry and knowledge, contrasting it with the modern way of acquiring information through the library. If so, they would at the same time be undermining the notion of orality by the bookish character of their work and questioning the importance of the library by the pretence of orality. The result would be an interesting kind of tension, fitting in well with the self-conscious poetry of the Hellenistic poets, who wrote in a period of gradual transition between different ways of storing and transmitting scholarly knowledge.[21]

---

[21] I wish to thank the editors and their anonymous readers for their comments on an earlier version of this chapter, which I have gladly made use of.

6 | Where was the royal library of Pergamum?

An institution found and lost again

GAËLLE COQUEUGNIOT[*]

Numerous literary *testimonia*,[1] both Greek and Latin, have evoked the greatness of the Hellenistic library of Pergamum and its rivalry with the Ptolemaic library of Alexandria. According to Strabo,[2] this institution was founded by King Eumenes II in the first decades of the second century BC, but we can probably trace it back to the end of the previous century and the reign of Attalus I. Soon, the Attalid library entered into a competition over knowledge with the Great Library of Alexandria, founded over a century before. Many stories and legends were transmitted about this rivalry over scholars and literary works. The most renowned is probably the legend of the invention of parchment,[3] whose Attalid origin is remembered in many languages: περγαμένα in Greek, *membrana Pergami* in Latin, *Pergament* in German, *pergamino* in Spanish, etc. More than the anecdotes concerning rivalry in the purchase of rare books, the competition between the two royal courts of Alexandria and Pergamum is most emphasised in the philological rivalry between the scholars attached to the two libraries.[4] It is visible for example in the contrasting research of the Pergamene scholar Crates of Mallos and the Alexandrian Aristarchos on Homer and Hesiod.[5] While the Alexandrian scholars termed themselves *grammatikoi*, Crates and his Pergamene colleagues preferred to be referred to as *kritikoi*.

Though less famous than its Egyptian rival, the royal library of Pergamum has been widely discussed in modern works on literacy, on the transmission of knowledge and on library studies. Most of all, it acquired a central position in the scholarship on ancient libraries after the discovery, in the

---

[*] I wish to thank the conference organisers Prof. G. Woolf, Dr K. Oikonomopoulou and Dr J. König, and all the attendants of the conference for their enriching discussions and comments; I also thank Dr J. Baird and Dr R. van Bremen for their useful comments on this chapter. All opinions and mistakes remain my own. I also want to acknowledge the Institut de recherche sur l'architecture antique (CNRS-Université Lyon-Lumière) for their financial support to attend this conference.

[1] For a convenient gathering of the *testimonia* (both literary and epigraphic), see Platthy 1968: 160–5.
[2] Strabo 13.1.54.   [3] This legend is known from Varro, in Plin. *HN*. 13.70.
[4] For a short presentation on the scholars attached to the Attalid court, see Radt 1999: 277–9.
[5] Nagy 1998: 213–28.

late nineteenth century, of ruins associated with this institution, the only recognised archaeological remains of a Hellenistic library.

This chapter focuses on the remains that have been linked to the royal library of Pergamum. It examines the architectural and material features concerned, the possible organisation of the building and ultimately – and most significantly – it raises the question of the identification of the remains as the Attalid library.

The discovery of the royal Attalid library of Pergamum

In the 1880s, German archaeologists were undertaking extensive excavations on the acropolis of Pergamum (Figure 6.1), the capital city of the Attalid kingdom. A large architectural complex in the south-west corner of this acropolis was discovered and rapidly identified as the sanctuary of *Athena Polias*, the city's main deity (Figure 6.2).[6] It consisted of a large terrace on which a temple was erected and enclosed, on the northern and eastern sides, by a double-storey colonnade. A monumental entrance opened through the eastern colonnade.[7] Like many of the Pergamene colonnades, the northern *stoa* stands against the cliff. On the ground floor it consists of a single double-row of columns, while on the upper floor it opened out into four rooms built directly on the rock (Figures 6.3 and 6.4). The three westernmost of these rooms were razed to the ground, and nothing much can be said of their original setting. However, in the eastern room, which was much larger than the three others, several architectural elements were preserved and have, since their discovery, been the basis of numerous reconstructions and analyses.

The archaeologists who discovered the sanctuary proposed that the four rooms behind the northern *stoa* be identified as the great royal library of Pergamum often mentioned by the ancient writers.[8] This identification was reinforced by comparisons with other buildings and texts referring to ancient libraries in the Greco-Roman world and by several artefacts and details that the archaeologists have associated with the complex. Among the data used as evidence, we can mention the statues of Athena inspired by Attic fifth century works that were found in the northern *stoa*, and the statue bases of ancient writers and historians discovered in and around the sanctuary. These artefacts have been presented in detail in early

---

[6] Bohn 1885.
[7] It has been reconstructed in one of the halls in the Pergamonmuseum of Berlin.
[8] Conze 1884; Bohn 1885: 56–72.

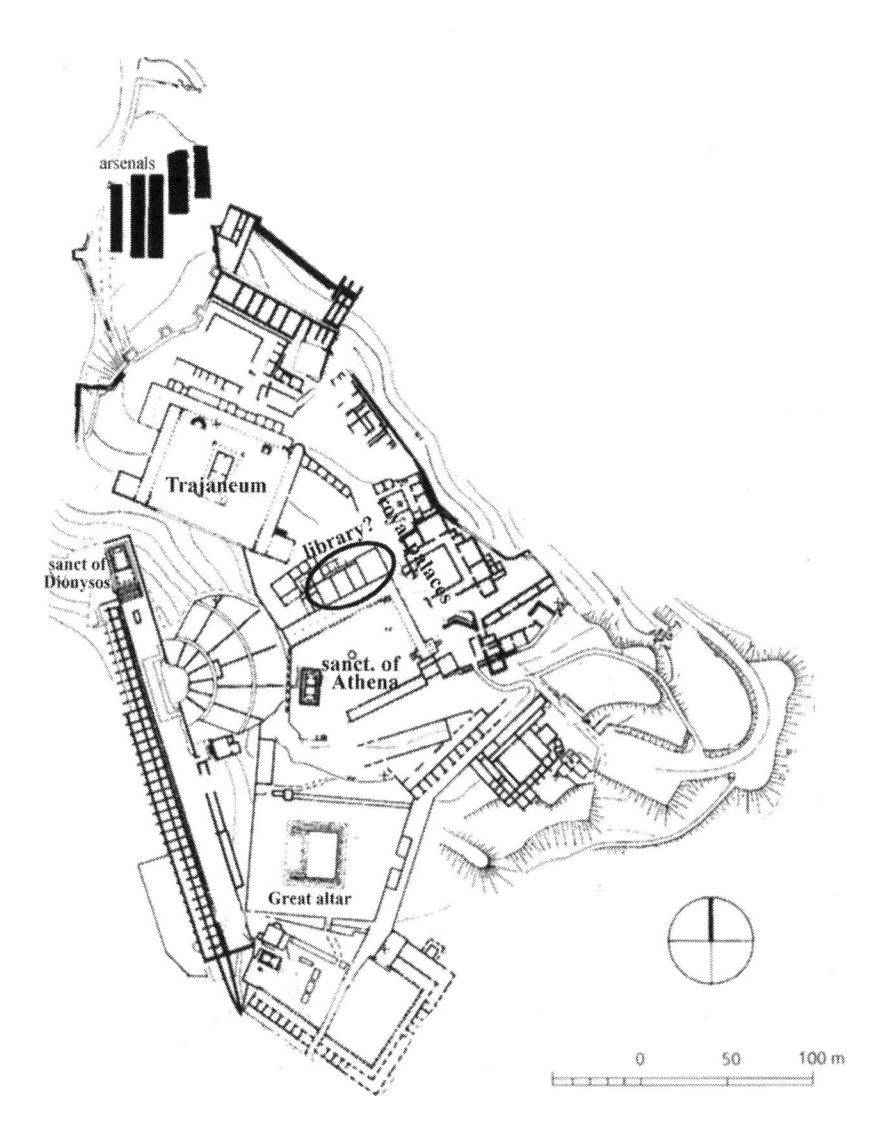

Figure 6.1 The acropolis of Pergamum

publications, and will be discussed later. Most of all however, it is the architectural characteristics of the largest eastern room (the so-called 'great hall') that led to the identification.

The north-eastern hall: arrangement and function

This large room – 13.53 metres wide and 16.85 metres deep – is the best preserved part of the sanctuary of Athena. It is situated in the north-eastern

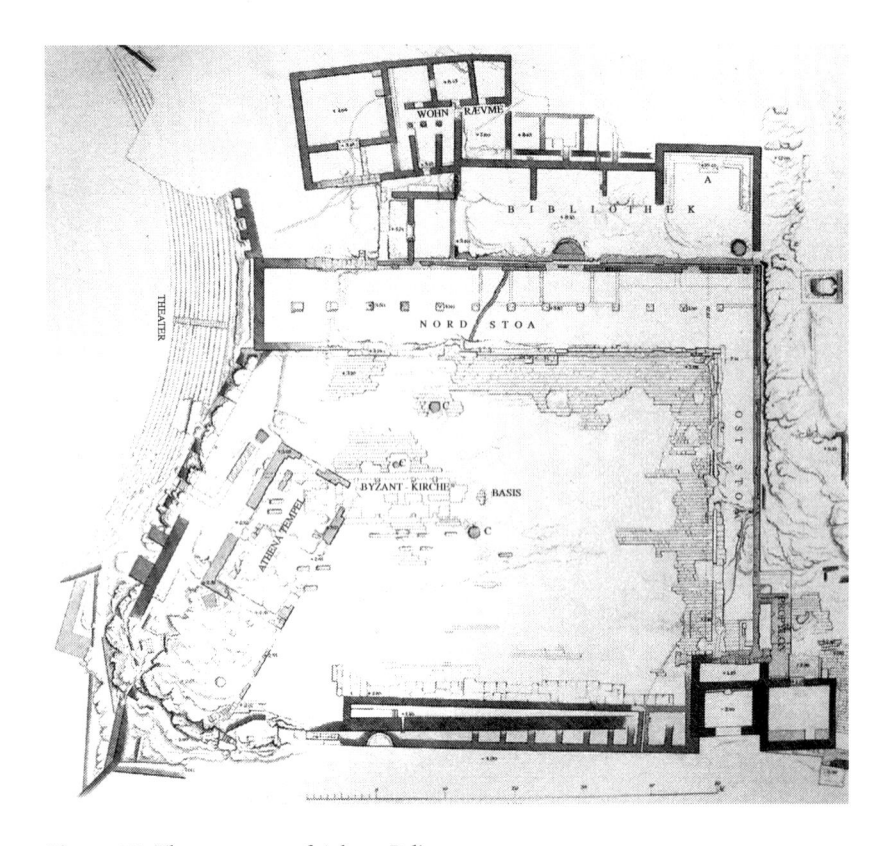

Figure 6.2 The sanctuary of *Athena Polias*

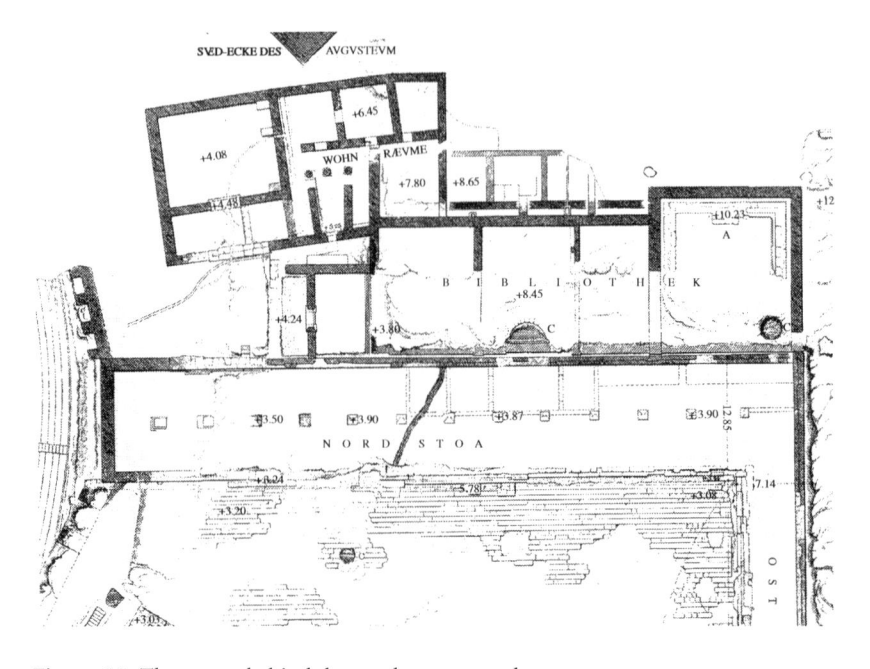

Figure 6.3 The rooms behind the northern *stoa* – plan

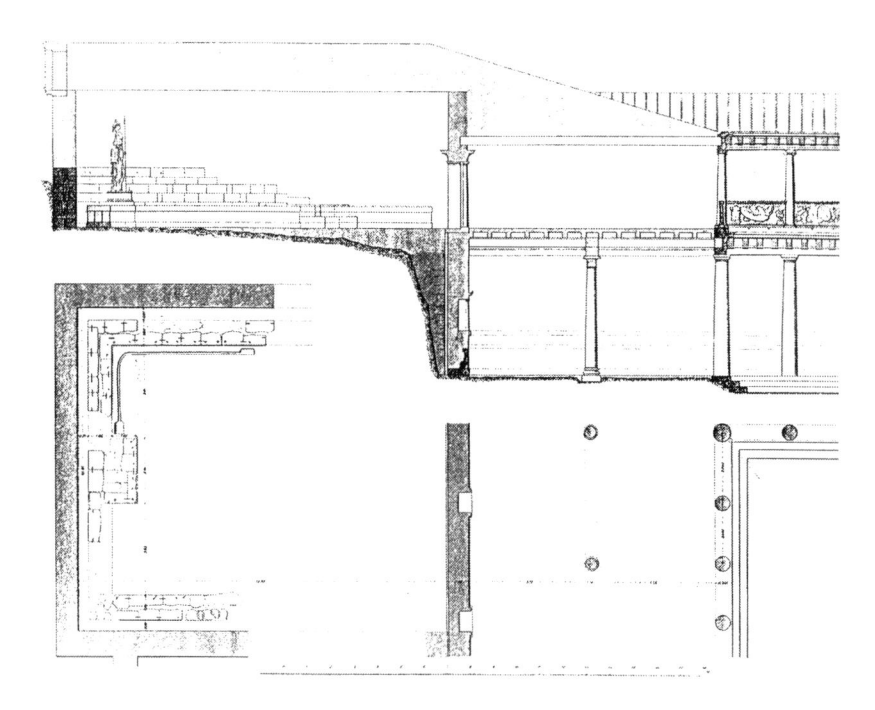

Figure 6.4 The great hall – section and plan of remains

corner of the *stoa*, on the upper storey. Its walls of trachyte-stone are preserved up to 2.20 metres high. In the walls, quadrangular holes are disposed every 1.05 metres, about 2 metres above ground; two other holes, 0.95 metres above the ground, have been found in the middle of the back wall.

A small podium, 1.05 metres wide and about 0.90 metres high, stood 0.50 metres from the rear and side walls. It was originally covered by fine stone slabs, whose remains were unearthed in the proximity of the foundations. In the middle of the rear, north side of the room, this podium was enlarged to take the shape of a base 2.10 metres wide and 2.75 metres long. It is most probably on this base that stood the colossal statue of Athena discovered in the remains of the *stoa*. This statue, over three metres in height and made in the second century BC in Pentelic marble, was a copy of the famous chryselephantine *Athena Parthenos* of Phidias (Figure 6.5).[9]

Other features identified in this room, but often overlooked in later descriptions, are a drain carved in the rock along the eastern side of the

---

[9] Winter 1908: 33–46 (no. 24).

Figure 6.5: The Pergamene copy of Phidias' Athena

podium and a cistern in the south-east corner. Finally, the hall and the neighbouring rooms were paved with mosaics.

The first publication on the sanctuary of *Athena Polias* and its different structures was written by the architect R. Bohn in 1885 as the second volume of the series *Altertümer von Pergamon*.[10] In this volume, he described the various features of the sanctuary's *stoa* and identified the four rooms behind its upper level as the great royal library of the Attalids. The director of the German expedition, A. Conze, had already presented this identification the previous year in an article dedicated to the library.[11] This identification was based on several details, especially the statue of Athena, which they compared to the often-mentioned statues of Minerva that usually adorned

[10] Bohn 1885. [11] Conze 1884.

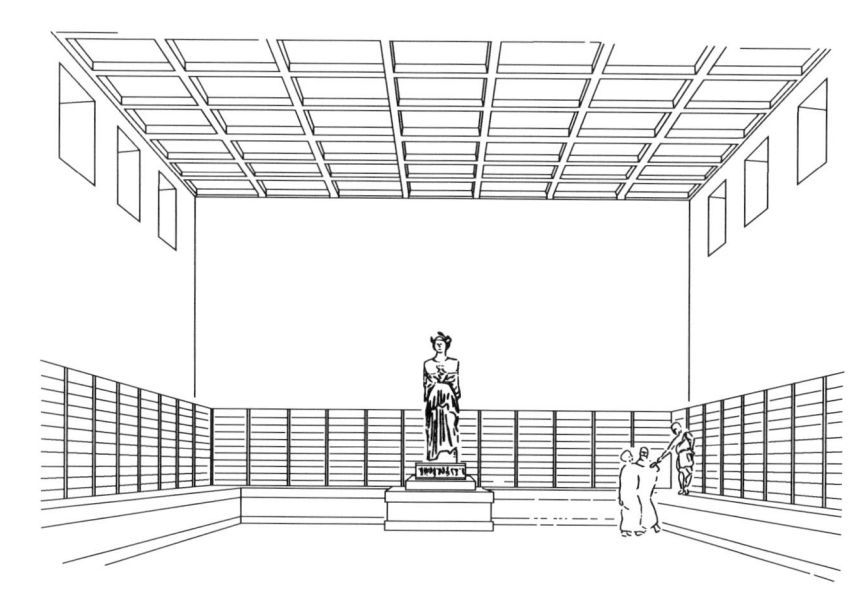

Figure 6.6 Reconstruction of the great hall as a book repository

Roman libraries.[12] Moreover, the podium and the holes in the walls of the great hall were thought to belong to a system of bookshelves similar to that discovered in the shops of the Athenian *stoa* of Attalos. The great hall of the sanctuary of Athena was on this basis taken to be an ἀποθήκη βιβλίων, a *book depository*.[13] R. Bohn proposed to reconstruct wooden bookshelves on the podium that were attached to the walls with long metal strips, the space between this construction and the walls preserving the rolls from humidity and moisture. In this restitution of the royal library, book-stacks were reconstructed in the three eastern rooms, and the *stoa*'s upper level was used for reading, discussing and wandering.

This reconstruction was largely accepted by the scholarly community and was reproduced without much question in the following century. The only variations proposed by subsequent scholars concern Bohn's reconstruction of the bookshelves in the great hall, which ignored certain archaeological data such as the slabs from the podium and some of the holes in the walls. B. Götze proposed in the 1930s another arrangement with bookshelves backed up against the walls and fronted by the podium (Figure 6.6), mimicking the

---

[12] Juv. *Sat* 3.219.
[13] The argumentation behind this identification is the same – word for word – in the two publications; cf. especially Conze 1884: 1,260–2 and Bohn 1885: 68–9.

podium and niches of the Roman library of Celsus in Ephesus, discovered in the 1900s.[14]

More recently, W. Höpfner has proposed a new reconstruction of the great hall of the library. His reasoning was that the fragility and the cost of the book-rolls required better protection than that provided by simple open bookshelves.[15] To accommodate the rolls, he proposed to reconstruct wooden cupboards, both in the podium of the great hall and in wooden podia in the three additional rooms of the northern *stoa*, while admitting that such a restitution was not really based on solid material data.[16] According to him, the most precious volumes of the collection were deposited in the great hall in elaborate cupboards and niches with Doric and Ionic entablatures. Two such niches were found in the debris of the *stoa* during the nineteenth-century excavation and were originally thought to have decorated the back wall of the *stoa*'s ground level. The new restitution places them in the southern wall of the great hall, with wooden copies standing on the podium along the hall's three other sides. Following critics of this new restitution, W. Höpfner proposed small modifications – for example, the cupboards are now supposed to be marble instead of wood – and an attractive illustration was included in his recent book on ancient libraries.[17] In the holes in the walls were clamps from which a gutter seems to have hung, draining the rainwater that came in through large windows in the upper part of the walls.

Overall, very few scholars challenged the identification of the rooms located behind the northern *stoa* of the sanctuary of *Athena Polias* with the royal Attalid library, although the restitution of the great hall as a stackroom was challenged several times. The first to question this restitution, a decade after the discovery of the sanctuary, was K. Dziatzko, a specialist in the history of libraries.[18] While not discussing the attribution of these rooms to the library complex, he particularly criticised Bohn's restitution of bookshelves, on the grounds that it did not take all archaeological data into account. Instead, he proposed an alternative reconstruction for the hall, as a reception hall and a banquet room.[19] In particular, the podium was according to him a large base for statues, while the holes in the walls indicate that a sculpted frieze once adorned them. Finally, the drain and the cistern carved in the bedrock could be explained by the use of this hall as

---

[14] Götze 1937: 228–36. [15] Höpfner 1996: 32.
[16] In Höpfner 1996: 34, he admits that his restitution of wooden cupboards on podia in the three small rooms especially is *freilich nur Spekulation*.
[17] Höpfner 2002a. [18] Dziatzko 1896, especially 39–44. [19] *Ibid.*, 45–6.

a banquet room with movable wooden couches, following the tradition of the *oikos* in the Alexandrian Museum.

The next scholar who questioned the bookshelves' reconstruction was Ch. Callmer in a long paper on ancient libraries.[20] He also preferred to see the great hall as a ceremonial hall with statues and sculptures. It is actually this reconstruction, in which the great hall is compared to the great *oikos* of the Alexandrian library[21] and the books themselves were stocked in the three smaller rooms, that most subsequent scholars adopted until the 1990s.[22]

In the 1990s, a series of papers put the question of the library of Pergamum and its physical arrangement at the centre of new debates. While W. Höpfner proposed his reconstruction with cupboards, H. Wolter von dem Knesebeck and M. Strocka preferred to assign auxiliary honorific functions to the great hall. The former[23] accepted the restitution of statues on the podium, but proposed that from the holes in the walls were hung large wooden, marble or bronze plaques inscribed with the catalogue of the Pergamene library, like the catalogues discovered in Rhodes and Tauromenion. The latter[24] favoured the identification of the great hall as a banquet room, with a stucco cornice on the wall, couches on the podium and a drain to easily wash the mosaic floor (Figure 6.7). This banquet hall would have been used by the scholars attached to the royal library.

Despite some criticisms and alternative reconstructions of the great hall's arrangements and function, the identification of the four rooms opening into the upper-floor of the sanctuary's *stoa* as the royal library of Pergamum had not been seriously challenged until the last twenty years. Two contributions however have lately voiced doubts about this identification, although they have been largely ignored by the scholarly community. The first doubts were expressed by L. L. Johnson in a PhD on ancient libraries,[25] defended in the 1980s at Brown University, that remains unpublished. Her argument focused on the primary location of the so-called library, in a *stoa* of the sanctuary of Athena. The location of these rooms inside the sanctuary was, in her view, sufficient to explain most of the archaeological data found in or around them. Her conclusion was that they should be identified with storerooms for offerings to the titular goddess, not with the physical setting for the Attalid library. In 1995, H. Mielsch came independently to the same conclusion, preferring to compare the *stoa*, its backrooms and the sanctuary's esplanade to a museum (in the modern sense of the word) in the

---

[20] Callmer 1944: 149–52.   [21] As described in Strabo 17.2.8 C, 793–4.
[22] See, for example, Strocka 1981: 303–4 and Blanck 1992: 186.
[23] Wolter von dem Knesebeck 1995: 48–52.   [24] Strocka 2000: 158–65, Radt 2003.
[25] Johnson 1984: 47–60.

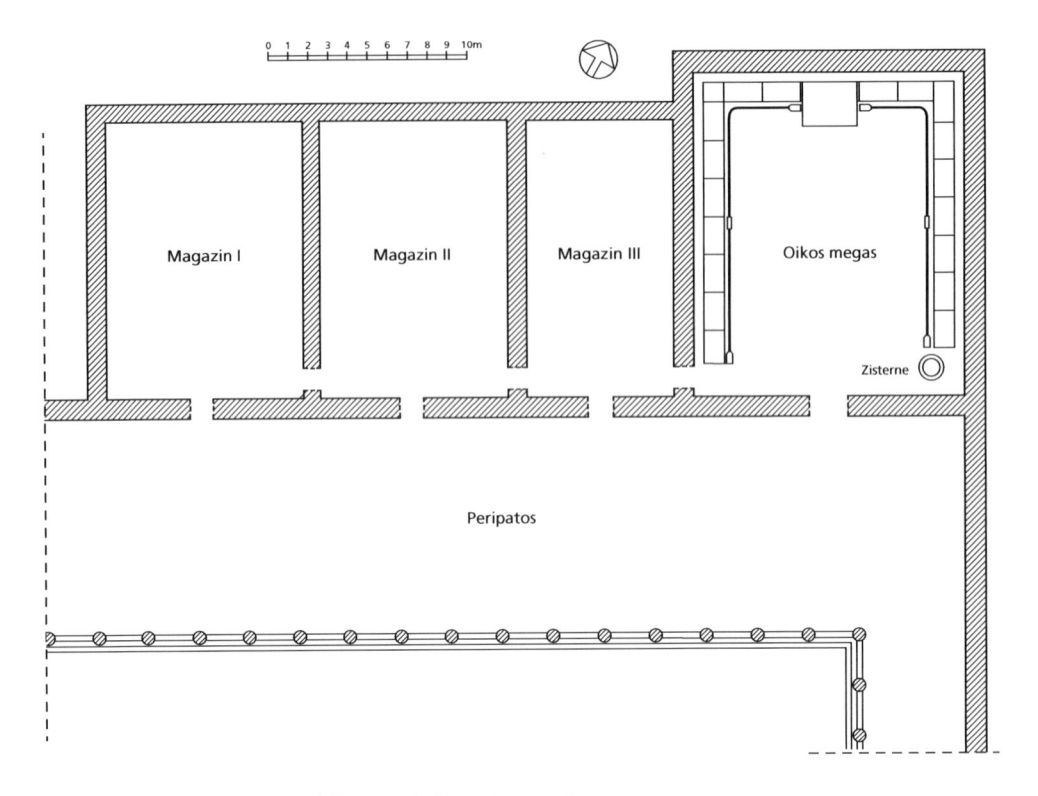

Figure 6.7 Reconstruction of the great hall as a banqueting room

making, exhibiting imported statues and works of art inspired by classical Athenian sculpture.[26]

The basis of the identification of the library

Given the doubts raised about the identification of the Attalid library with the *stoa* of the sanctuary of Athena, it is necessary to take a closer look at the material and textual data used as a basis for this identification. We have already seen that much of the argumentation behind A. Conze's and R. Bohn's identification concerns the architectural setting of the great hall. Other archaeological and textual *testimonia* were also used, mostly as a means to strengthen the identification, but without much detail given.

As the various reconstructions proposed since its excavation attest, the original setting of the great hall remains the object of much speculation,

[26] Mielsch 1995: 772–9.

and can therefore hardly serve as a basis for such an identification. This is even truer as the various reconstructions of bookshelves or cupboards seem rather random, and have largely been refuted in the last century. The other reconstructions of the hall proposed by various scholars, although they appear plausible in the archaeological and historic context, cannot on their own support its alleged relationship with the royal library.

If it was indeed used as a banquet room, as suggested by the mosaic floor, drain and cistern, the reference to the Alexandrian *oikos* is only a feeble link with such an intellectual institution. First of all, the importance of the *oikos* for shared meals between scholars of the Alexandrian Museum – and therefore its link to the Ptolemaic library that was also part of this Museum – is known only from scanty and late literary *testimonia*, the most significant being the short description provided by Strabo in the Augustan period. We should remember that none of these *testimonia* provides us with a precise description of the physical settings related to the Museum, the library and the *oikos*, and any comparison remains therefore haphazard. Moreover, even if the Attalid library is said to have been the greatest rival of the Alexandrian library, it does not mean that the kings of Pergamum chose to copy its architectural design or organisation. Last but not least, banqueting rooms are by no means exclusive to intellectual institutions of this type. Actually, *hestiatoria* are extremely common features in Greek sanctuaries, where sacred meals regularly took place.[27] The use of the great hall as a banquet room is therefore more readily connected to such cultic meals in honour of Athena than to a library and a hypothetical 'museum'.

The other alternative reconstruction proposed for the great hall is that of a repository of offerings, an exhibition room for statues and other works of art dedicated to Athena. The primary argument for such a reconstruction is the location of the hall, behind one of the colonnades of the goddess' sanctuary. As a room belonging to this sanctuary, it was naturally dedicated, with its contents, to the titular deity. The podium found in the room could indeed have been used as a base for statues. However, we should note that no evidence – either literary or material – has ever been given for the existence of collections of art associated with a library in Hellenistic times. The earliest attested connection between a public library and a display of statues and sculptures appears more than three centuries later in the libraries of imperial Rome, where statues adorned the porticoes and rooms linked to libraries.

In short, the main component of the so-called royal library of Pergamum, and the principal piece of evidence for its location in the sanctuary of Athena,

---

[27] Roux 1975, among others.

does not point towards this identification. The most probable functions of the great hall are indeed in correlation with the location of the hall within the main sanctuary of the city.

With this alleged evidence in favour of a library complex no longer acceptable, the reconstruction of the three side rooms, which were levelled to the ground, and the function of the *stoa* appear quite baseless. The side rooms were often considered as stack rooms for the library's collections, but it is equally possible to propose restitutions of these rooms as repositories for offerings, banquet rooms or 'annex rooms' of the sanctuary. Finally, there is no reason to consider that the existence of the *stoa* itself is linked with the existence of a library in its back rooms. Though literary and epigraphic *testimonia* for other Greek and Roman libraries seem often to place a colonnade in library complexes,[28] such colonnades were a common feature of the ancient public landscape, and can be found in association with many buildings in civic, economic and religious centres.[29]

Because it was directly associated with the physical settings of the great hall, the inventors of the library and subsequent scholars also used the colossal statue of Athena found in the foot of the great hall as an argument for the identification of the library. As already stated above, this statue, over 3 metres high, is a copy inspired by Phidias' *Athena Parthenos* (Figure 6.5). This statue was originally placed in the central part of the great hall's podium, directly in the axis of the entrance. It is almost complete, with the exception of the arms, but the remains of the base show the goddess was holding a spear on her right side.[30] However, there is no evidence of the object held in her left hand, which is therefore the subject of some conjecture. In a recent reconstruction, Athena is depicted with an owl, symbol of wisdom particularly fitting for an intellectual institution's protector.[31] However, it is also possible – and at least as fitting in the context – to reconstruct a statue more closely related to its original model that was holding a winged victory. Phidias' statue was indeed a depiction of the victorious Athena, clad in armour, holding spear and shield, and presenting a Victory, a *Nike*.[32] The Pergamene copy also portrays an armour-clad goddess holding a spear; it would be only logical to complete the group with a small *Nike* held in the left hand, especially since we are reminded that, in Pergamum, the goddess was often revered as *Nikephoros*, 'holder of victory'.[33] The reference to the military role of Athena and her position as protector of the city and the Attalid dynasty appears also in the reliefs of the *stoa*'s parapet, depicting owls,

---

[28] Höpfner 2002a: 41. [29] Coulton 1976. [30] Winter 1908: 33–46.
[31] Höpfner 2002a fig. 59. [32] Lehmann-Hartleben 1932. [33] Johnson 1984: 57–9.

trophies and other military images, and in several dedicatory inscriptions to *Athena Nikephoros* found in or near the sanctuary. On the basis of these indications, as well as the proximity of the sanctuary to the theatre and the athletic structures in the lower terrace, M. Kohl has recently proposed to equate the long-searched-for *Nikephorion* of Pergamum with the sanctuary of *Athena Polias*.[34]

The statue from the great hall does not need to relate to a cultural institution and is no justification for the identification of the library, as the *stoa* was already naturally dedicated to the goddess, guardian of the city and tutelary protector of the Attalid dynasty. The choice of Phidias' *Athena Parthenos* as a model for this monumental statue and its material – Pentelic marble – demonstrates the admiration of the Attalid rulers for fifth-century Athenian art. Similar admiration and inspiration is also demonstrated by several other sculptures found in the sanctuary[35] and by the Attalids' euergetism at Athens.

Support for the identification of these rooms as a library was also sought in the discovery in the area of the sanctuary of Athena of six inscribed bases that originally held statues of ancient writers and historians. These statues have been interpreted as part of the library's ornamentation. However, the significance of this indirect evidence is lessened by the fact that these bases were discovered in secondary locations, mainly in late walls; it is therefore unclear whether the statues were originally displayed in the sanctuary of Athena or in other buildings of the acropolis, such as the palaces. Moreover, differences in the script and material used for the various bases is proof that they were not part of a coherent programme. It is most probable that these depictions were independent offerings of a type often attested in Greek sanctuaries.[36]

Finally, further indirect support for the identification was taken from short descriptions of the Alexandrian Museum, viz. the topographic link between such a royal institution as the museum or the library and the palaces (Figure 6.1). The Alexandrian Museum and library were located in the district of *Broucheion*, the royal district. While no literary evidence mentions the location of the Attalid library in Pergamum, it has been inferred that it most probably stood in close proximity to the royal palaces,

---

[34] Kohl 2002 especially 233–6.

[35] Two other statues and one marble head of Athena found in the debris of the *stoa* are also free copies of Attic works of the fifth and fourth centuries; see Winter 1908: 13–33 (no. 22–3) and 46–7 (no. 25).

[36] Bases for such statues are often found in sanctuaries throughout the Greek world. They are also frequently mentioned in ancient narratives, such as Pausanias' *Description of Greece* and Strabo's *Geography*.

on the city's acropolis. This tenuous argumentation has been used to place the library in the important sanctuary of Athena, an association seemingly reinforced by the association of the goddess with wisdom and cultural institutions in the Greco-Roman world.[37] However, even if the comparison with Alexandria were of value here, many other buildings in the acropolis could have better accommodated the library than the sanctuary of Athena, whose connection with the institution remains purely hypothetical: one or several rooms in one of the palaces,[38] an unidentified Hellenistic building under the massive Roman remains of the Trajaneum, *et cetera*.

Conclusions

The library of Pergamum is one of the best known Hellenistic cultural institutions. It was considered by ancient writers to be the greatest rival to the Alexandrian library. Its supposed identification in the sanctuary of *Athena Polias* in the late nineteenth century was therefore welcomed. As the only Greek library physically identified, it was used as a model to reconstruct or identify other libraries in the Hellenistic world. During the century that followed its discovery, several reconstructions were proposed for its organisation and its physical settings, but its identification has rarely been challenged. Some recent studies have, however, contributed to raise doubts on this identification. It appears today most probable that the great hall in the north-eastern corner of the sanctuary was used as a banquet room and/or a repository for offerings. With the rejection of this room as a repository of books, the argumentation leading to the identification of the area as the Attalid library is singularly weakened, consisting mainly in vague comparisons with contemporary or later libraries.[39] Other elements that have been taken as offering support for the identification appear much too common in the Greek public landscape and can equally well be explained by the location of the rooms inside Pergamum's main sanctuary, dedicated to *Athena Polias* and *Nikephoros*.

Recent reconstructions of the library – however attractive – should as a result be treated with great caution, and 'one should give serious

---

[37] Höpfner 2002a: 41.
[38] W. Höpfner, while against the location of the Attalid library in the palaces, proposed to reconstruct a small library in Palace V: Höpfner 2002d: 95–6.
[39] Comparison with the literary descriptions of the Alexandrian library or with Roman libraries' remains.

consideration to situating the library in other rooms'.[40] With this observation, the Hellenistic library of Pergamum is again a building-less institution that lives only in the literary descriptions and legends surrounding its foundation and its rivalry with the similarly unidentified Alexandrian library. Consequently, it is important to reassess our knowledge of all Hellenistic libraries and to base their location and their physical settings on definite evidence rather than on a flawed comparison with the rooms of Pergamum's sanctuary of Athena.

[40] Radt 1998: 18.

7 | Priests, patrons, and playwrights

Libraries in Rome before 168 BC

MICHAEL AFFLECK

Aemilius Paullus and the library of Macedon

According to convention the history of libraries in Rome begins in the year 168 BC.[1] Plutarch, writing some 300 years after the event, records that in that year Aemilius Paullus defeated the Macedonians at the battle of Pydna and, as part of the spoils of victory, gave the library of the Macedonian court to his sons to take back to Rome.[2] Yet it is incredible that Rome had nothing resembling a library prior to 168 BC. By the middle of the second century BC, Rome had been a literate society for at least four centuries, in repeated and close contact with societies that had produced books in Greek, Punic, Etruscan, and Oscan languages. From the beginning of the third century, Roman expansion in Italy had involved the plunder of cities in which dramatic productions, gymnasial education, philosophical schools, and patronage of scholarship were as well established as they were in Macedon.[3] The earliest extant Latin texts are simple inscriptions. But the very earliest Latin literature is marked by an intense intertextual engagement with Hellenistic genres and ideas. That would seem to be a convenient starting point for any study of early Roman libraries. This chapter does not aim to gather testimony of pre-second century libraries: such testimony does not exist. But it is possible to present some likely scenarios for the prehistory of library culture in Rome on the eve of the wholesale looting of Hellenistic libraries that began with Aemilius Paullus, and to ponder the consequences of such early developments for the ways in which Roman libraries developed their own unique characteristics.

Firstly, I would like to examine whatever literary testimony exists that might suggest the presence of libraries in Rome before 168 BC. The first such testimony comes from Polybius, taken hostage after the battle of Pydna and brought to Rome at the same time as the library of Macedon. Those books had been given by Aemilius Paullus to his sons, described by Plutarch

---

[1] For example, see Thompson 1940: 27; Dunlap 1972: 29.
[2] Plut. *Aem.* 28.7: μόνα τὰ βιβλία τοῦ βασιλέως φιλογραμματοῦσι τοῖς υἱέσιν ἐπέτρεψεν ἐξελέσθαι.
[3] For some suggestive comments, see Purcell 2003.

as already passionate about literature. One was the future Scipio Aemilianus who would be Polybius' pupil and patron at Rome. As part of his polemic against the historical methods used by Timaeus of Tauromenium, Polybius noted that "you can make inquiries from books without risk or labour, provided only that one takes care to have access to a town possessing many documents or with a library nearby."[4] The clear implication of this statement is that libraries appear to be fairly common in the middle of the second century BC. It has been suggested that Polybius was in fact referring only to the Greek world. Timaeus composed his history of the west in Hellenistic Athens. But that implication is by no means obvious from the context of the passage. Perhaps Polybius (who seems to have had no difficulty accessing texts during his long exile in Rome) is making no distinction here between the Greek and Roman worlds, and instead implies that anywhere in the world where a literate culture exists, libraries should exist as a natural feature of that society. Certainly the expansion of Roman power that Polybius documented brought Romans into contact with libraries in Italy and Carthage as well as in the capitals of Hellenistic kingdoms and the major Greek cities of the east.

A second piece of testimony comes from Isidore of Seville, who is not generally regarded as the most credible of sources for this period, if for no other reason than that he was writing in the sixth century AD. However, on the subject of libraries, there is every reason to regard Isidore as well informed since his material most likely comes from Marcus Terentius Varro, one of the foremost ancient authorities on libraries. Varro was the writer of the only known work on libraries from the classical world, *De Bibliothecis*, now sadly lost. Varro was also tasked by Julius Caesar with establishing what would have been Rome's first public library. Isidore indicates that "Aemilius Paullus was the first to bring a copious supply of books back to Rome," therefore not necessarily the first to bring a library to Rome, but the first to bring in a sizeable collection of books, the clear implication being that collections of a smaller size already existed there.[5] This ties in with what is known of the situation in the city at this time with regard to the supply of books. There were no booksellers as such, and clearly the importation of books in large numbers from sources in the Greek world would have been very expensive. However, just as clearly, by this time books

---

[4] Polyb. 12.27.4: δὶ ἥν δ' αἰτίαν ταύτην ἔσχε τὴν αἵρεσιν εὐχερὲς καταμαθεῖν: ὅτι τὰ μὲν ἐκ τῶν βυβλίων δύναται πολυπραγμονεῖσθαι χωρὶς κινδύνου καὶ κακοπαθείας, ἐάν τις αὐτὸ τοῦτο προνοηθῇ μόνον ὥστε λαβεῖν ἢ πόλιν ἔχουσαν ὑπομνημάτων πλῆθος ἢ βυβλιοθήκην που γειτνιῶσαν.
[5] Isid. *Etym.* 6.5.1.

were trickling into Rome in quantities sufficient to endow at least modest libraries.

The main significance of the Aemilian seizure of the Macedonian royal library is the size of the library involved. It must have presented a real culture shock for Rome. The Roman aristocracy certainly had possessed private collections of books before this, but it seems likely that they were modest in size and perhaps limited in their range. The exact scale of the Macedonian royal library is unknown. But given that Macedonian patronage of writers predated Alexander's conquests, it is likely to have been quite large, if perhaps not comparable with the royal libraries of Alexandria and Pergamum.[6] However, compared to existing libraries in Rome at the time, it would haveseemed huge. It is possible too – although it is a matter of speculation – that a collection of this kind may have embodied some of the principles of organization that were already in use in Alexandria and that would be employed in the libraries of imperial Rome. Here, then, is the real significance of the Aemilian capture of this library, not that it was the first library in Rome, but that for the first time, the Romans could see, in their own midst, the sort of collection being built up in the Hellenistic East. It showed the Romans what a library could be.

Priests and books in Republican Rome

Before considering the implantation of literary cultures in Rome, I want to examine one earlier feature of Roman culture that would have a strong role in the development of Roman libraries, namely, the role of texts in religion. I am not suggesting that libraries as we know them existed in Rome's temples, but temples fulfilled an important archival function nevertheless in Republican Rome, and it is worthwhile examining how this developed.

Johnson was one of the few scholars to examine this possibility. He argues that from the earliest times, Roman temples must have possessed collections of texts for the education and training of the priests if nothing else.[7] This is possible, although becoming a priest may have been as much a matter of tutelage within the college. But the need for the priests to keep collections of books goes much deeper than this, being fundamentally linked to the essential nature of the Roman religion itself. It is well known that Roman religion was characterized by strict contractual obligations between gods and men, and also that the gods were believed to have demanded

---

[6] Strootman 2010.　　[7] Johnson 1970: 69.

strict adherence to designated forms of ritual, including the use of specific ritual formulae.[8] Any deviation from accepted forms of ritual was seen as potentially disastrous, in fact the slightest deviation from the proper form might lead to the entire performance having to be repeated.[9] This would seem to argue for the keeping of meticulous records of the form of each ritual and the wording of particular prayers. Given the number of different ceremonies for each cult, and the number of festivals and rites conducted each year, the potential number of ritual texts detailing these ceremonies could have been staggering. This would seem to suggest the need for a comprehensive and well managed system of archives within the temples.

This reconstruction, however, has been challenged in recent years. Scheid, for instance, strongly denies that there was ever a written tradition in Roman religion and argues that the forms of ritual were mainly passed down orally.[10] Current work emphasizes rituals as performances rather than as endlessly repeated formulae.[11] Yet there is a literary tradition for such records going back to the earliest history of Rome. Livy writes that as early as the Regal Period King Numa's organization of the public priesthoods gave a special role to written instructions for the regulation of rituals:

Then as Pontifex he appointed Numa Marcius the son of one of the senators, and entrusted to him all the regulations bearing on religion, written out and sealed. Here was laid down with what victims, on what days, and at what temples the various sacrifices were to be offered, and the sources of revenue from which the expense of each of them were to be funded. He placed all other sacred functions, both public and private, under the supervision of the Pontifex, in order that there might be an authority for the people to consult, and so all trouble and confusion arising through foreign rites being adopted and their ancestral ones neglected might be avoided. Nor were his functions confined to directing the worship of the celestial gods; he was to instruct the people how to conduct funerals and appease the spirits of the departed, and what prodigies sent by lightning or in any other way were to be attended to and expiated.[12]

Given that Livy himself admits that most of the records from before the Gallic sack no longer existed in his day, we should perhaps be skeptical about the veracity of this statement. But his testimony about events in later, more historically verifiable periods, indicates the continued prominence of texts in Roman religion. From the late third century, Livy records a city praetor named Marcus Aemilius issuing an edict that anyone holding written texts of prophecy, prayer or ritual should hand them in. "(Marcus

[8] Westrup 1929: 6.   [9] Klinghardt 1999.   [10] Scheid 2006: 14.   [11] Rüpke 2004: 25.
[12] Livy 1.20.5–6.

Aemilius) issued a decree that whoever had any books of prophecy or prayers or a ritual of sacrifice that was in written form should bring all such books and writings to him before the first of April."[13] Albeit that these texts did not derive from public cults, the incident indicates a well established notion of religiously authoritative texts. Varro also refers to the *pontificii libri*, which seem to record the exact details of sacrificial ritual.[14] Similarly, Tacitus makes a reference to the *libri caerimoniarum*.[15] There is evidence also that the priests, who had control over Roman law for a long time, also possessed texts relating to these laws, as indicated by Dionysius.[16] There is also considerable evidence for the priests having held collections of other kinds of texts as well. A particularly interesting reference regarding the aedileship of Gnaeus Flavius around 300 BC comes from Livy.

He published the formulae of the civil law, which had been kept stored in the secret places of the priests... [17]

As Oakley notes, there is considerable speculation among scholars as to what these legal formulae actually entail.[18] Cicero describes them as *actiones*.[19] It seems likely that they were forms of words used for bringing a claim before a court.[20] The significance of Flavius' action has generally been seen as wresting the practice of jurisprudence away from the secretive clutches of the pontiffs. The story might be compared with the traditions surrounding the *ordo scribarum* and the influence they gained from their proximity to magistrates and their privileged access to texts.[21] However, it also seems to suggest that the priests, from an early period, held some collections of texts associated with legal matters. While this does not mean that the priests held fully fledged legal libraries, they would have needed access to a considerable amount of written material relating to the law to perform even informal advisory functions.

The augurs too had their collections of texts, as is mentioned on several occasions by Cicero.[22] The augural archives may also have played an indirect part in Aemilius Paullus' decision to remove the library of Macedon to Rome. As Plutarch records, Aemilius was an augur, and apparently was particularly devoted to his augural duties, especially praised for his knowledge of religious ceremonial.[23] It is possible that this exposure to the augural

---

[13] Livy 25.1.12. [14] Varro, *Ling*. 5.98. [15] Tac. *Ann*. 3.58.
[16] Dion. Hal. *Ant. Rom*. 10.1.4. [17] Livy 9.46.5. [18] Oakley 1997: 609.
[19] Cic. *De Or*. 1.186; *Att*. 6.1.8.
[20] Jolowicz and Nicholas 1972: 90; Schulz 1946: 9; Stein 1966: 11.
[21] Purcell 2001. [22] For example, *Rep*. 2.31.54. See also the discussion in Linderski 1985.
[23] Plut. *Aem*. 3.2.

archives induced in him a particular respect for the collection of books and was one incentive to him to seize the library of Perseus.

Can these archives and collections of books be recognized as libraries, or even proto-libraries? There is little doubt that the Romans, for whom libraries seem always to have had a literary connotation, did not recognize them as such. The word *bibliotheca* does not appear in Latin until the mid-first century BC, and it is noticeable that Livy uses that word nowhere in the whole length of his work. In the modern sense they would possibly qualify as special libraries, in other words libraries devoted to a particular subject or related subjects, serving a particular clientele.[24] The documents held by the temples of Rome were predominantly archival. Certain temples are identified with particular documents, for example, the Temple of Jupiter Capitolinus held international treaties, while that of Saturn was the home of the treasury and held financial records. The vast majority of references to documents being held in temples clearly refer to what we would recognize as archives; however, in a few cases, such as the books of ritual and prophecy I have mentioned, they are often referred to by the word *liber*. This would suggest that they were thought of as true texts and not archival records. This is by no means a clear cut distinction, but perhaps parts of these collections might reasonably be distinguished from archives and thought of as true libraries.

Temple libraries in Republican Rome?

Is it possible to identify any particular temples or related structures where such collections might have been held? The most secret texts were evidently held in temples rather than in the pontiffs' civic offices. Livy records that when Gnaeus Flavius published the formulae of the law, he brought it forth from the *penetralia* of the pontiffs.[25] *Penetralia* is used numerous times in Latin literature and has a clear connotation of the inmost sacred recesses of a shrine or temple. It is possible that all major temples had their own archives or collections of books. But a few temples can be identified as potential candidates because they are known to have been repositories of documents of various kinds. The temples of Jupiter, Ceres, and the *Atrium Libertatis* are all recorded as being repositories of particular documents.[26] The *Atrium Libertatis* is of special interest because it was in this building

---

[24] See Martínez and Finn Senseney (this volume). [25] Livy 9.46.5.
[26] Cic. *Mil.* 73; Livy 3.55.13; Dion. Hal. *Ant. Rom.* 6.89.3; Polyb. *Hist.* 3.26; App. *Syr.* 39; cf. Stambaugh 1978: 582.

that Asinius Pollio established Rome's first public library in the last years of the last century BC. Another candidate is the Regia, the meeting-place of the pontiffs. The Regia was the place where the *tabula dealbata*, the whitewashed boards which recorded the pontifical annals and which were on display outside, were stored, and later condensed into the *Annales Maximi*, often considered an important source for later historians of the Republic. Archaeological excavations have discovered a deep cistern in the lowest level of the Regia which contained numerous broken writing tablets and writing implements, indicating that a certain amount of writing and record-keeping was carried on here.[27] However, militating against its use as a library for the college of pontiffs was its small size and the fact that it burned down at least four times during the history of the Republic.[28]

The location of the augural archives presents a problem, as no particular centre is known for their activities. One passage from Orosius seems to indicate that the augurs had a base on the Capitol.[29] This is backed up by the discovery of an inscription at the base of the Capitol which records the names of a number of augurs. It is not known, however, which of the temples on the Capitol was their base. One possibility is the Temple of Juno Moneta, as there is evidence linking the augurs with here. The temple is immediately adjacent to the Auguraculum, the open space on the Arx where the augurs performed their observations of the sky. There is also tentative evidence suggesting the existence of a library or archive in this temple.[30] The *libri lintei* (linen books) are known to have been stored here.[31] Moneta, coming from the verb *moneo*, has usually been translated as "Warner." However, on the basis of a fragment of Livius Andronicus' *Odyssey*, in which the Greek goddess of Memory, Mnemosyne, is translated in Latin as Moneta, the term has more recently been interpreted to mean Remembrancer or Recorder, which would certainly be appropriate for a temple containing a library or archive.[32] Another possible clue to the archival function of this temple is that the Capitol was the location of the structure known as the Tabularium, a building which has usually been thought of as a repository for Rome's state documents, although this is now debated.[33] If this was the function of the building, it might make sense to locate it near a structure which already contained a store of texts.[34]

[27] Brown 1935: 67–88.   [28] Cf. Roberts 1918: 55–65.
[29] Oros. *Historiarum adversum paganos* 5.18.27.   [30] Tucci 2005: 7–33.
[31] Livy 4.20.8; cf. Meadows and Williams 2001: 29; Ogilvie 1958: 40.
[32] Liv. Andron., *Od.* fr. 30 (Warmington 1935), cf. Palmer 1974: 30.   [33] Purcell 1993: 125–55.
[34] Culham 1989 makes a strong case that the Romans did not practice centralized archiving, and documents were either posted publicly or held in private domestic archives. However, Culham does concede that the priests did hold the annals which were displayed publicly as the *tabula*

The real significance of these priestly archives for the history of Roman libraries is that they established an early precedent for the keeping of documents and texts. I have already suggested that someone like Aemilius Paullus may have been influenced in his attitude to collections of texts by his knowledge of the augural archives. In the long term, there is some reason to think these early priestly collections influenced the development of Roman libraries in general. It cannot be coincidental that when the emperors did establish public libraries in Rome, so many of them were associated with temples. This at least was not borrowed from the Hellenistic world from which Rome took so much inspiration in cultural and literary matters. Libraries in the Greek world were usually associated with gymnasia and schools, not temples.

Book collections and the origins of Latin literature

The beginnings of Roman literature are usually dated to 240 BC. In this year, the playwright Livius Andronicus produced what is generally regarded as the first known work of Latin literature. At the *Ludi Romani* in that year, he produced on the stage the first Latin comedy and the first Latin tragedy. Both were adapted from existing Greek plays. It is from this key fact that we can derive the next evidence for the existence of early libraries in Rome. Casson declares that Livius must have had access to a substantial collection of Greek originals, which at this time would only have been available from Greek booksellers in the south of Italy, the procurement of which would have been beyond the resources of a freedman like Livius.[35] Casson therefore argues that the only possible source of Greek originals for Livius was the wealthy patron of whom Livius was formerly a slave and then a client, who must have possessed a private library of Greek literature.[36] This is a logical and entirely possible scenario.

From the time of their first contacts with the Greek world in the south of Italy and beyond, the Roman upper classes had become deeply interested in Greek culture, and it seems entirely logical that they would procure, through purchase or conquest, collections of literature. This, after all, is

---

dealbata, and that treaties, agreements etc. were held in temples so as to make them sacred objects so that the breach of them amounted to sacrilege and an offense to the gods.

[35] What is believed to be the first evidence of a library in Italy comes from Tauromenion in Sicily, where the remains of what appears to be a library catalogue on the wall of the second-century BC gymnasium were found. Cf Battistoni 2006.

[36] Casson 2001: 62.

what Aemilius Paullus had done after his conquest of Macedonia, and there is no reason it could not have happened at least a generation or two earlier, or indeed a century or more.[37] There were two periods of violent contact with Greek cities between the start of the third century BC and the middle of the second century. The second period involves the Macedonian wars and the Syrian wars against Antiochus, and from this period ensued the Aemilian capture of the Macedonian royal library. But it has recently been remarked by a number of scholars that Roman efforts to create a literature for themselves preceded the military engagement with the Hellenistic kingdoms of the east.[38] The earlier period of conflicts included the Pyrrhic and Punic wars. There seems no reason why similar capture and removal of libraries, albeit on a smaller scale, may not have happened in this period, without necessarily being recorded. After all, if it were not for Plutarch and Isidorus, both writing hundreds of years later, the Aemilian removal of the Macedonian library would also be unknown. During the war in Sicily, for example, the Roman nobility were exposed at length to the Greek culture of Syracuse and other cities, including libraries. It is quite likely that books were brought back to Rome, just as statuary and other art works were. Perhaps such plunder included the collections of Greek classics which Casson argues that Livius Andronicus and other early writers required.

Livius and the playwrights that dominated Roman literature for the next century, such as Plautus and Terence, derived their fame from producing Latin versions of Greek plays. Plautus in particular was extremely prolific, having been credited with writing 50 comedies, about 20 of which have survived. Six of the surviving works are known definitely to have been based on plays of the Greek New Comedy. With their bread-and-butter work based on adaptations of Greek plays, the question must be asked, where did these writers gain access to the large numbers of Greek originals they would have needed in order to produce their plays? In the case of Livius, there is not a real problem, as Casson argues, as he was the client of a wealthy family, the Livii. He may well have had access to any private collections they possessed or at least to the funds needed to acquire the necessary books from the south of Italy.[39] Casson argues that Plautus, in particular, a notably poor individual, had no access to a library of Greek originals through a wealthy patron as Livius Andronicus did. For some of the playwrights of the time, it may not have been too great a problem. Ennius

---

[37] Purcell 2003.
[38] For a selection of recent formulations see Gruen 1992; Habinek 1998, 2005; Hinds 1998; Feeney 2005; Hunter 2006; Wallace-Hadrill 2008.
[39] Casson 2001: 61.

is known to have had a number of wealthy patrons and associates, including M. Fulvius Nobilior, P. Scipio Africanus, Ser. Sulpicius Galba, and P. Scipio Nasica.[40] His connections with the Greek world in southern Italy, where he had been born, may also have aided him in acquiring texts.[41] Terence is also known to have had patronage and to have traveled to Greece to seek copies of plays, although it is also believed that he was not wealthy, with no house and his known worldly assets amounting to one small block of land on the Appian Way.[42] However, Plautus was a working playwright, with no wealthy patron, who likely derived his living entirely from selling his plays.[43] He is known to have struggled financially at times.[44] Certainly it could be assumed that the expense of importing books from southern Italy or elsewhere in the Greek world would have been beyond him. The only possible solution is that he had access to a collection of scripts of some description.

A number of possible candidates for the collections that playwrights like Plautus must have been able to access have been proposed. For example, it has been suggested that the state archives may have held copies of plays. It is believed, backed up by evidence from Plautus' contemporary Terence, that the aediles responsible for public entertainments such as festivals and plays bought the play from the writer and then arranged for the play to be performed.[45] Over time the state archive wherein these works would have been held may have accumulated sizeable collections of plays. Another possibility is that theatre managers acquired plays from writers and other sources and in this manner they acquired collections of works that may have been available.[46]

I would like to suggest another possibility, one that might have led to the establishment of a significant library or libraries as early as 207 BC. Livy records that, as a reward for Livius Andronicus composing a hymn which was credited with changing Rome's fortunes for the better, the writers and actors of Rome were given the Temple of Minerva on the Aventine, as a place to meet and make sacrifices.

So when Livius Andronicus in the Second Punic War wrote a hymn which was sung by the virgins... the Temple of Minerva on the Aventine was officially granted, where the *scribae* and *histriones* might assemble and make offerings; in honour of Livius because he used both to write plays and set them.[47]

---

[40] Cic. *Tusc.* 1.3, *Brut.* 29, *Arch.* 22, *Acad. Pr.* 2.51, *De or.* 2.276; Livy 38.56.4.
[41] Strabo 6.3.5.   [42] Suet. *Vita Ter.* 5.   [43] Hor. *Ep.* 2.175–6.   [44] Gell. *NA.* 3.3.14.
[45] Ter. *Eun.* prol. 2.19–21; Suet. *Vita Ter.* 2; cf. Clift 1945: 6.
[46] Ter. *Hec.* prol. 2.50–5, also *Hec.* 57; *Eun.* 20; Plaut. *Cas.* 7–12; cf. Beare 1950: 154; Duckworth 1952: 73.
[47] Festus 446L.

Livy supplies the date of 207 BC.[48] The choice of the Temple of Minerva is significant. Minerva's association with writers and musicians is well established, with evidence recording her as patroness of artistic guilds.[49] This reference is believed to be the first evidence of collegiality for Rome's writers.[50] The possibility therefore arises that the formation of a guild gave the writers sufficient resources to establish their own library of the necessary Greek originals and other required texts, or more likely gave them enough clout to attract a wealthy patron. The association of Livius Andronicus with this collegium gives further weight to this idea. Perhaps he used his connections to provide resources for the guild, either through direct donations from his patron or through copying of works held in the family library. There is evidence of this type of practice, albeit from a much later date. An inscription from the second century AD records the gift of a library to an association of writers and musicians by a wealthy benefactor.[51] Can such a possible benefactor be identified for the late third century or early second century BC?

The Livii were certainly not alone in this period as being a literate family who in all probability possessed a library. There are a number of other Romans of the time, who through demonstrated interest in literature, philosophy or science, would seem to be prime candidates for the ownership of a private library. Two of Rome's earliest prose writers who almost certainly possessed libraries of some description were Fabius Pictor and Cato the Elder. Fabius wrote one of the earliest known histories of Rome in Greek around or just after the time of the Second Punic War. Fabius is known to have followed the accounts of some Greek writers, including one Diocles of Peparethos. It is noted that he came from a family famed for their culture and education, so possibly he had access to a family library of such texts, or else acquired them during travels to the south of Italy or elsewhere.[52] It seems very likely that Cato the Elder had a library as he is acknowledged to have been a prolific writer, the first known to have written in Latin prose, with works on agriculture, medicine, law, and military matters to his credit. Most notably, his *Origines*, the first recorded history of Rome in Latin, must have required access to a substantial collection of Greek texts. As Astin notes bluntly, Cato did not write in a vacuum, and is known to have utilized the works of Timaeus, Fabius Pictor and a substantial number of Greek sources

---

[48] Livy 27.37.7; note that this date has been disputed and an alternative date of 249 BC suggested. Cf. Barwick 1933: 203; Mattingly 1957: 159.
[49] Ov. *Fast.* 3.834; Varro, *Ling.* 6.17.   [50] Jory 1970: 226; Garton 1972: 57–8.
[51] Milkau 1955: 125.
[52] His brother was a renowned painter, hence the name Pictor. Cic. *Tusc* 1.4; Plin. *HN* 35.19; cf. Rose 1954: 112.

in writing the *Origines*.⁵³ In his later years he is said to have devoted himself to gaining as wide as possible a knowledge of Greek literature, therefore it seems very likely that by the end of his life he had acquired a substantial collection of books.⁵⁴ Another individual who almost certainly possessed a library of some sort is Gaius Sulpicius Gallus. Gallus served under Aemilius Paullus in the Macedonian War, but it is likely that even before the war he was noted for his learning. It is recorded in several sources that he provided the soldiers of Paullus' army, who had been frightened by a lunar eclipse, with the explanation that it was a natural and predictable event. Cicero provides other examples of his astronomical knowledge and praises him for his learning.⁵⁵ It seems likely, since Gallus predicted to the soldiers of Paullus' army that the eclipse was a good omen, that he was in fact, like Paullus, an augur. It is possible that Gallus, as I have suggested for Paullus, was another who gained an appreciation of the value of books through contact with augural or pontifical libraries. Other possible candidates for the possession of private libraries during this period include Servius Fabius Pictor, who is described by Cicero as a man learned in law and letters, and who wrote one of the earliest histories of Rome.⁵⁶ Aulus Postumius Albinus is described by Polybius, in less than flattering terms, as nevertheless an individual steeped in Greek learning.⁵⁷ Titus Quintius Flaminius is another whose intellectual achievements are mentioned. He is known to have been fluent in Greek, and apparently composed his own inscriptions in Greek verse.⁵⁸

However, in searching for a possible benefactor for the donation of a library to a writers' collective, one candidate stands out among the others. Around 187 BC, Marcus Fulvius Nobilior erected the Temple of Hercules Musarum in the Circus Flaminius in commemoration of his victory over Ambracia in 189 BC.⁵⁹ In the temple Nobilior placed the statues of the nine Muses which he had looted from Ambracia as well as a statue of Hercules Musagetes (Hercules the Lyre-player), which was subsequently depicted on coins issued during the first century BC.⁶⁰ Because of its association with the Muses and the creative arts in general, the temple became strongly associated with writers, musicians, and artists. Nobilior himself, the patron of Ennius, deposited a copy of his *Fasti* there.⁶¹ The temple is associated with the much-debated *Collegium Poetarum*, an association of writers mentioned, among others, by Horace and Martial, which may or may not have been a direct descendant of the association of *scribae* and *histriones* from Minerva

---

[53] Astin 1978: 182, 230. [54] Plut. *Cat. Mai.* 2; Plin. *HN* 29.14; cf. Rose 1954: 92.
[55] *Brut.* 78; cf. Val. Max. 8.11.1. [56] *Brut.* 81. [57] Polyb. 39.1.
[58] Plut. *Flam.* 5.5, 12.6–7; cf. Gruen 1984: 256. [59] *Pan. Lat.* 9.7.3.
[60] Cic. *Pro. Arch.* 11.27; Plin. *HN* 35.66. [61] Macr. *Sat.* 1.16.

on the Aventine.[62] Thus Nobilior becomes a strong candidate for the type of benefactor who could have established such a library for the writers of Rome. There is no direct evidence of Nobilior having established such a library, but the fact of his having deposited his *Fasti* in the Temple is suggestive.

Conclusions

I hope I have been able to demonstrate some of the possibilities for the existence of libraries, or at least substantial collections of books, in Rome before the arrival of the royal library of Macedon captured by Aemilius Paullus. Perhaps what is most important is the foundations that these early collections seem to have laid for library establishments in later years. First, there is definitely a link between Rome's temples and libraries, one that was not obviously borrowed from the Greeks, and it would seem, may relate to the very early establishment of archives in priestly buildings. Second, a number of Roman aristocrats and writers seem, for their own reasons, to have realized the potential value of collections of (mostly Greek) texts. This trend would later give rise to the large private libraries of noble Romans in the last century BC[63] and also the use of the new public libraries of the principate by Rome's writers as a means of expanding their readership in the early first century AD. It is in these areas that the real significance of pre-second-century book-collecting lies.

[62] Val. Max., 3.7.11; Mart. 3.20.8–9, 4.61.3–4; Hor. *Sat.* 1.10.37–8, *Ep.* 2.2.92–4; cf. Sihler 1905: 1–21; Kunihara 1963: 85–99; Crowther 1973: 575–80; Horsfall 1976: 79–95.
[63] See Houston and Dix (this volume).

8 | Libraries in a Greek working life

Dionysius of Halicarnassus, a case study in Rome*

DANIEL HOGG

Introduction

The Second Sophistic, it has been said, is a 'world not just of the book, but of the very big book'.[1] A recent collection on ordering knowledge in the Roman Empire has drawn further attention to the scale of organisation required by the establishment of the Empire in the early centuries AD. Indeed, the co-editors of the volume refer to the accumulation of information in 'often enormous bulk'; they also draw attention to the very broad range of their own study, which by its very incompleteness further demonstrates the extraordinary scale upon which knowledge was organised in the Roman Empire.[2] My question relates to what happened before the Second Sophistic. The germ of the phenomenon of the massive book seems to be found earlier in Rome, though the picture revealed is a rather different one. I suggest that this is related to the practical nature of book production in the ancient world. I will concentrate on a case study, the *Antiquitates Romanae* of Dionysius of Halicarnassus, to explore the implications of this hypothesis in more detail.

Another way of forming the question is to ask, how would a Greek historian such as Dionysius of Halicarnassus have worked in first-century BC Rome? My question presupposes that a historian of the ancient world would hope not just to read and discuss books in libraries, but would also like to put his own books in them – in other words, I consider the question of an historian's audience, but from the point of view of books rather than people.[3] For reasons of space, I will leave aside *recitatio*, the public reading

---

* I would like to express my gratitude to Chris Pelling and Rhiannon Ash, as well as the editors, for reading and commenting on previous drafts.
[1] Goldhill 2008: 96; cf. Ath. 1.39.
[2] J. König and Whitmarsh 2007 at 3. Murphy 2004: 4–6 and 129–164 considers the accumulation and organisation of knowledge by Pliny the Elder in terms of Pliny's support of the Roman Empire, and the Empire's authority over the world.
[3] I will not concentrate on the question of which libraries Dionysius could or would have used. This has already been answered in part by Luraghi 2003: 269–70; Delcourt 2005: 65–9. Hidber 1996: 2–8 has contextualised Dionysius as part of the wave of Greek intellectuals moving to Rome after the Mithridatic War. See further Schultze 2000.

of works, which was very possibly an important means of dissemination, at least on a local level, for Dionysius.[4] Nor will I consider the role of *bibliopolae*, booksellers, in distributing books.[5] I rather consider the impact of the book on the final form a history may take. I argue that we should understand the first book of Dionysius' *Antiquities* as being separable from the rest of the *Antiquities*, since it has a different format and function, and was likely also published separately. I conclude by arguing that this separateness is explained by, and itself sheds light upon, the nature of ancient book collections in Rome and the Greek diaspora.

This essay will start from the suggestion that the spread of the Roman Empire changed the way Greek writers measured the scale of their works of literature. That is not to say that authors writing in Greek were not able to conceive of prodigious, grand works before the conquest of Greece in the second century BC. Big books may have become fashionable during the Second Sophistic, but Greek works requiring huge levels of scholarship had been possible for a long time before this, as Herodotus, Aristotle and the Alexandrian poets testify. Works of huge scope, such as Polybius' or Timaeus' history, existed from the Hellenistic period onwards.[6] But they became more common after the end of the Mithridatic War in the first century BC.[7] The aftermath of this war saw more works that are massive both in size and in terms of the scholarship that has gone into them, such as Diodorus' *Bibliotheca*, and Nicolaus of Damascus' history, both produced in the middle of the first century BC, the latter comprising over 140 books.[8] We also see in this period more works spanning Greek and Roman spheres, which we may call *Kolossourgiai*, 'colossal works'. So Strabo's *Geography* is a 'colossal work' because, as Sarah Pothecary has argued, it spans the Greek and Roman worlds, bringing them together, just as the Colossus itself spanned the harbour entrance at Rhodes.[9] Dionysius gives his twenty-book

---

[4] Sen. *Controv.* 4. praef.; see esp. Johnson 2000. It is unlikely that Dionysius could have insisted, like Claudius, on an annual public reading of his history at Alexandria (Suet. *Claud.* 42.2).

[5] See e.g. Plin. *Ep.* 1.2, 9.11 on the role played by booksellers in distributing works.

[6] Polybius sneers at Timaeus for spending sixty years researching in books (Polyb. 12.25d.1), though rather because in Timaeus' case, the sixty years dulled his sensibility to real history, turning him into a bookworm.

[7] We might also consider here universal history. Universal history is tightly defined by Alonso-Núñez as a history of the whole world from its beginnings to nearly the present day. See further Martin 1993: 193–214; Alonso-Núñez 1983: 411–26 laid down the terms for the subsequent debate. Cf. Fromentin 1998: 221; Ferrary 1976: 283–9; Clarke 1999b: 250.

[8] Posidonius' continuation of Polybius was fifty-two books long. Suetonius says that Ateius, an Athenian scholar who lived at Rome and advised Sallust, compiled 800 books' worth of encyclopaedic material; see further Kaster 1995.

[9] Strabo 1.1.23; Pothecary 2005, though Pothecary's interpretation of Strabo's use of *Kolossourgia* is arguable. Cf. Clarke 1999a and b. Under this definition, Polybius' history, argued by some to

Dionysius and the libraries of Rome   139

history of Rome a similar intellectual impetus, arguing that the Romans and the Greeks share a common blood origin.

Publishing in antiquity

The structures that support such mass organisation of knowledge were moved into place in Rome in the first century BC.[10] Crucial were the libraries, and the Greeks and Romans willing to dedicate large quantities of time and money to organising them. Creative intent was also key. The late Republic has been characterised as a period of concern, despair and revolution, which created a drive for order and systematisation.[11] Previously a stream, the Roman elite started to produce a flood of highly literate, soldiering men who imposed their own sort of literary order on the world. Chief among these was M. Terentius Varro, who by his death in 27 BC had written seventy-four works in around 620 books.[12] Yet it is remarkable that, in Roman historical writing, the organisational gaze is turned inwards; the *urbs* is in some degree co-extensive with the *orbis*. Even as the Romans conquer the known world, and produce a history as long as Livy's 142-book *Ab Urbe Condita*, they produce no *world* history to parallel the many Greek ones.[13] By the time the principate is established, the focus has narrowed further, and it is difficult to dissociate intellectual enquiry from the emperor himself.[14]

---

be an attempt to unite the Greek and Roman worlds under a common cultural banner, is also a *Kolossourgia* (see e.g. Champion 2005). The language of 'unification' in universal history appears at e.g. Alonso-Núñez 2002: 95: 'The Augustan empire means the political unification of the Mediterranean world under the command of a monarch who rules apparently under republican forms'; though cf. Verdin 1974: 291 and Hill 1961, who argue that Dionysius' identification of Greek origins is a reaction *against* Augustan propaganda. Alonso-Núñez 2002: 111: Dionysius 'symbolises the fusion of the Greek culture with the Roman one.' Cf. Martin 1993: 209; 2002.

[10] J. König and Whitmarsh 2007: 8–10, who also identify Strabo's geographical history as part of this trend of organising knowledge in Rome, in Strabo's case connected to how the spread of Roman imperial rule reconfigured the way people thought about space.

[11] Moatti 1991 and Wallace-Hadrill 1997; I thank Christopher Smith for showing me his unpublished paper on Varro, where he stresses the 'moral energy' of Varro's work, characterising it as a 'literature of confidence', and situates antiquarian history more generally at the centre of intellectual progress in the late Republic.

[12] Varro was the only living writer to have a statue placed in the first public library at Rome (Plin. *HN* 7.30.115).

[13] Walter 2004: 339.

[14] So Vitruvius, for example, has been interpreted as making writing architecture analogous to writing the Empire, at the heart of which is the emperor himself (McEwan 2003, summarised in Smith unpubl.; cf. A. König 2007 on Frontinus addressing his emperors, Nerva and Trajan,

It was no simple matter to publish a large work in the late Republic, since literature was still produced in cumbersome book-rolls. Such a monumental effort as Livy's consisted of 142 book-rolls, about the same size as a small library, and was published in smaller sets over a long period.[15] The codex, leaves of papyrus glued together like a modern book, would substantially improve the compactness of a given work, but this would not appear until the middle of the following century.[16] In what follows, I argue that Dionysius of Halicarnassus' *Antiquitates Romanae* was composed at a time when the ambition of literature was outgrowing its physical framework, the book-roll. Dionysius' solution, I suggest, was to create a work which takes account of the physical and logistical difficulties in producing literature on an international scale. The format of his work was adventurous, in that it combined the flexibility of the single-volume history with the substantial, monumentalising form of the multi-volume history.

Authors who composed in smaller units than a history, such as the Augustan poets, were thinking increasingly in global terms.[17] Others who managed quick, large-scale dissemination of their works, such as Pliny's acquaintance Regulus, had to pull considerable strings to do so.[18] Regulus distributed 1,000 copies of a memoir of his deceased son's life, and had them read aloud in the cities of Italy and beyond. But owing to differences in scale, this global approach is more manageable with poetry and memoirs than with massive prose works such as Livy's *Ab Urbe Condita* or Nicolaus' universal history. Complete collections of these works, numbering over 140 books each, would have a much more limited distribution, to a particular city, say, such as Rome, or among an intellectual elite with access to large collections,[19] because it is that much more difficult to disseminate large

---

in a comparable way). On the usefulness of the terms Augustan and anti-Augustan, see especially Kennedy 1992; for a different view, Davis 2006: 9–22. As for Dionysius and Augustus, for the *status quaestionis*, see Goudriaan 1989: 300–7; Delcourt 2005: 364 with n. 3. Crouzet suggests (2000: 159), not quite fairly, that affirmations of Dionysius' pro- or anti-Augustanism tend to rest on an analysis of the first books on the mythical history of Rome, such as Martin 1971, 1972, which are focused discussions of particular episodes and passages in the *Antiquitates Romanae*.

[15] Mart. 14.190; Blanck 1992: 86; Livy 6.1.

[16] The earliest literary reference is Mart. 1.2, who appears to refer to an innovation (Roberts and Skeat 1983: 24–30 at 27–8).

[17] E.g. Hor. *Carm.* 2.20.17–20, in which Horace says his fame will reach Scythia in the east and Spain in the west; Parker argues (2008: 186) that this passage should be taken literally.

[18] Plin. *Ep.* 4.7.2.

[19] See Johnson 2000: 615–24 on reading in elite Roman society. I leave aside the question of literacy in Rome, on which see e.g. Habinek 2008. One cannot of course create a uniform shape and size of a Roman history. Velleius Paterculus' history was two books long; Varro's *De Gente* and *De Vita* were each four books long (though his *Antiquities* were much longer;

collections of books nationally or internationally. Regulus may have produced 1,000 copies of his son's memoir, but 1,000 books of Livy or Nicolaus would only produce six or seven complete versions of each.

Even if it were realistic to produce dozens of complete versions of authors like Livy, there were not many places to store them. The huge collections of Rome and Alexandria were the exception; public libraries, though common in the Greek world, were normally much smaller than these. Hadrian's library in Athens can have housed a mere few thousand book-rolls; Casson estimates that the library at Ephesus could hold about 3,000 rolls.[20] Private book collections were dominated by the canon, Homer, Euripides, Pindar and so forth.[21] Access to many books in the Roman world was limited to visitors to large private libraries such as Lucullus', or Philodemus' in the Villa of the Papyri at Pompeii.[22] Only the largest or specialist collections had the space and resources to house large numbers of works, and books were expensive. Neither Lucullus' nor Philodemus' cases solve the problem of the general accessibility of non-canonical works by those outside Rome and the villas belonging to Rome's elite: most of Lucullus' library was plundered, and plundering and inheritance seem to be a common source of book collections.[23] Philodemus' library, on the other hand, may contain over 1,800 papyrus rolls, but most of these rolls are Philodemus' own works. At state level, it was only in the late first century that libraries, as the infrastructure for Roman knowledge, began to be organised, abortively by Varro and then successfully by Asinius Pollio.[24] We may reasonably ask the question, then, in practical terms: what size audience could a historian's books expect to reach?

A Greek historian resident in Rome could expect his work to enter somewhere onto Roman shelves.[25] If Dionysius could place it in a library as open as Lucullus', the historian could expect his work to be accessible to both Greek and Roman scholars.[26] International dissemination is a different

---

Gellius refers to a twenty-fifth book at *NA* 17.3); the Lives of Cornelius Nepos were also relatively short. Sallust wrote very short works, the *Bella Jugurthinum* and *Catilinae*, and a longer *Historia*. Cf. Walter 2004: 350.

[20] Casson 2001: 113, 115–16.
[21] Houston 2009: *passim*. On Dionysius' attempt to find his way onto this list, see Payen 2005.
[22] See the contribution of Houston in this collection.
[23] Bequeathing libraries: Diog. Laert. 5.52, 5.62 (Platthy 1968: nos. 81 and 83). Booty: Posidon *apud* Ath. 5.214d–e (Platthy: no. 84); Plut. *Sull.* 26.1–2 (Platthy: no. 70); Isid. *Etym.* 6.5.1 (Platthy: no. 98), Plut. *Luc.* 41.1–2 on Lucullus (on whom Dix 2000).
[24] Suet. *Div. Iul.* 44; Plin. *HN* 7.30.
[25] Cf. Horsfall 1993, who considers the efforts of Roman poets in this period to get their works into the Library of Apollo on the Palatine.
[26] Plut. *Luc.* 42.1–2; Cic. *Fin.* 3.2.7; Dix 2000: 455–6; Luraghi 2003: 269–70. In the case of the libraries Dionysius could have used himself, beside the public ones, we are on slightly trickier

matter. Its possibility is implicit in the view of Emilio Gabba: 'His [Dionysius'] audience consists of the upper classes of imperial society, above all those in the Greek cities.'[27] Books could certainly reach over a wide area in a lifetime. Pliny is delighted, for example, that his works are available for sale in Lyon, and Livy's work may have reached as far as Cadiz.[28] However, the evidence provided by ancient booklists and testimonia would suggest that Dionysius could at best expect to gain entry only to the largest, public collections.[29] An investigation of the booklists preserved on papyri reveals that while there was a range of sizes of ancient collections, they were generally much smaller than collections today.[30]

Our knowledge of the contents of actual ancient book collections has been driven forward in the last decade.[31] The information we have is unfortunately much too partial to draw conclusions based on absence, and individual papyri or inscriptions containing booklists give teasing but insufficient suggestions. So the inscription of a library catalogue found in Rhodes lists

---

ground. We may accept a professional, hierarchical relationship of some sort between Dionysius and Q. Aelius Tubero. We may then consider the words that Cicero puts into the mouth of Quintus' father, Lucius Tubero, in the *Republic*: tum ille: 'mihi vero omne tempus est ad meos libros vacuum; numquam enim sunt illi occupati; te autem permagnum est nancisci otiosum, hoc praesertim motu rei publicae.' *Then he said, 'For my part at least, there is always time available for my books; for they are never occupied; but it is a very valuable thing to find you at leisure, especially during this restless period for the state.'* Cic. *Rep.* 1.9.14.

Does this refer to a library in Lucius' possession before the Civil War (cf. Dix 1986: 5, 267)? And then, if it was in Lucius' possession, did it still exist after the Civil War, to be passed onto Quintus, perhaps, and to be used by Dionysius himself? He certainly refers to access to one archive collection in private possession (Dion. Hal. *Ant. Rom.* I.74.5). But since libraries were there to be plundered – Lucullus' fell victim to Antony in the proscriptions – and lacking concrete evidence, we can only posit the possibility that Dionysius had access to Lucius' 'library'.

[27] Gabba 1991: 80; at 213–16 Gabba considers later Greek authors who knew Dionysius' work to varying degrees, including Plutarch, Appian, Eusebius and Josephus.
[28] Pliny and Lyon: Plin. *Ep.* 9.11.2. Livy and Cadiz, if the anecdote is credible: Plin. *Ep.* 3.2. Cf. Blanck 1992: 120–32.
[29] Here I draw substantially on the presentation of such material by Houston 2009, Otranto 2000 and Platthy 1968.
[30] Houston 2009: 247.
[31] Ancient book lists on papyri have been collected by Rosa Otranto and recently analysed further by George Houston, who has isolated eight lists which appear to be inventories of actual collections. Otranto 2000; Houston 2009: 238–9, table 10.1. Inventories created from papyrus finds, for example by Grenfell and Hunt and Breccia at Oxyrhynchus, are inadmissible here, because I am looking for *absence* as much as presence (see Houston 2007 and 2009: 247–8 on the caution one needs to bring to an analysis of these finds). Another well known papyrus, *POxy.* 2192 (Otranto no. 11, pp. 55–61), contains a request for particular books (col. 2, lines 28–9). It cannot be known whether the requester only wanted these two books, or already had copies of the others.

Dionysius and the libraries of Rome 143

over thirty works,[32] and where numbers are given next to the works the number is predominantly one. Does this mean volumes or copies? Both are arguable; it was not unknown for private collectors, for example, to own multiple copies of books.[33] A papyrus which may preserve an inventory list of the dialogues of Plato is more expressive.[34] But even in this case, it is not possible to determine the bounds or the scheme of the inventory list very clearly.

Nevertheless, the evidence suggests that it would be difficult for Dionysius to place his twenty-book *Antiquities* in a private collection. These seem to have exceeded a few hundred rolls in only exceptional cases.[35] The canonical authors, especially poets, are dominant. For example, a papyrus from the Arsinoite nome in Egypt from the mid-first century AD appears to represent almost a full list of a library's holdings.[36] Almost a third of the seventy-five rolls on the list are books of Homer, and Callimachus and Hesiod form the bulk of the rest. To speak more hypothetically, if someone had a collection of one hundred rolls, a complete Homer and Plato would occupy ninety-five of them. There is not much room left for a modern historian like Dionysius.

One solution may be that Dionysius' work was not intended to be held in private collections, but in larger, public libraries. Plutarch, for one, considers the prerequisite for historical research to be residence in a large city, and does not mention private ownership of many books.[37] Indeed, the problems of limited individual ownership were sometimes offset by the loaning of books; but this solution was more effective in some places than in others.[38] Ovid, exaggerating, laments being cut off from books in exile,

---

[32] Platthy no. 117 = Maiuri no. 11. The inscription is on marble (perhaps suggesting permanency?), and appears to be an inventory of the books held in the public library in Rhodes (see also Maiuri no. 4). The date suggested by Maiuri is second to first century BC.

[33] This is the evidence from the library of Philodemus, and Houston determines (2009: 234–7) that Otranto no. 16 represents a collection (rather than, say, a list of desiderata) partly on the ground that it contains multiple copies. However, compare Platthy no. 162 (*IG* IV.1445), where the numbers next to Hermogenes' works clearly indicate the number of volumes in each work.

[34] Commenting on this list, Houston 2009: 235 suggests that 'we can probably infer that each line represents the contents of one papyrus roll'. The list also contains the entry '*Xenophon: Cyropaedia* 8', which is likely to indicate either that the owner possessed (a) all eight books of the *Cyropaedia*, or (b) only book eight. There is no room to discuss this here in the detail it requires. The other inventories have an emphasis on poetry, which does not elucidate my argument about not just *whether* historical works are present in book collections, but *how* they are present.

[35] E.g. Isid. *Etym.* 20.6.6 (Platthy no. 179). [36] Otranto no. 3 = *P Vindob Gr.* inv. 39966.

[37] Plut. *Dem.* 2. Cf. Ovid, *Trist.* e.g. 1.1–4, 75–80.

[38] Cic. *Q Fr.* 3.5.6, *Att.* 1.7, 13.32.2 (Marshall 1976: 253–4). Cf. Houston 2009: 241 n. 26.

and Horace and Catullus sometimes have to drag their own collections around with them.[39] But Dionysius does not target exclusively an audience of professional historians, who might carry their books around with them, or be willing to travel in order to consult collections. Furthermore, one cannot disregard Dionysius' own evidence regarding the publication of book 1 of his *Antiquities*, to which I turn now.

Antiquitates Romanae, Book I

Dionysius' life was an international one. He arrived in Rome from Halicarnassus in the early twenties BC,[40] and spent the following years engaged in intellectual activity, much of it professional, as a teacher of rhetoric.[41] Some of his works preserved for us are commissions from Romans; his most important patron, to the best of our knowledge, was Q. Aelius Tubero, whose father knew Cicero.[42] Dionysius mentions several other individuals in his correspondence, but these are mostly unknown to us outside Dionysius' writings.[43] The exceptions are Metilius Rufus, a Roman, and Caecilius of Caleacte, a 'dear friend' of Dionysius, to whose own *On the Sublime* [Longinus'] *On the Sublime* is a response.[44] According to the evidence we have, Dionysius was part of a network of Greek and Roman intellectuals;[45] while the nucleus of this network was probably in Rome, there is no reason

---

[39] Ov. *Trist.* 1.105–6; Hor. *Sat.* 2.3.11–12; Catull. 68.33.   [40] Dion. Hal. *Ant. Rom.* 1.7.2.

[41] But how high-ranking a teacher? Schultze 1986: 123–4 suggests he taught 'at a fairly high level'. Weaire 2005: 248–52 at 249 suggests that Dionysius' didactic method, of careful scrutiny of texts, marks him out as low-ranking; but Suetonius, speaking of the late Republic, says that teaching method depended on personal preference, and makes no mention of rank (Suet. *Gram.* 25.4).

[42] Hidber 1996: 6, cf. Bowersock 1979: 71, Gabba 1991: 43. Weaire 2005: 246 is more cautious, and Schultze 1986: 122–3 is a little more bold. Dionysius' commissioned works have most recently been analysed as attempts to define and represent parameters of Greek culture (rather than simply as rhetorical analyses of orators) by Payen 2005 and Weaire 2005.

[43] The others are Cn. Pompeius Geminus, Ammaeus, Demetrius and Zeno. See Hidber 1996: 2–4 (followed by de Jonge 2008: 25ff.). The only contemporary of Dionysius to mention him is Strabo, who describes Dionysius as a 'historian' (Strabo 14.2.16). Delcourt 2005: 32 argues that via Strabo Dionysius may have come to know the Seii, and hence perhaps even Sejanus himself; Bowersock 1979: 70 is more cautious (cf. Schultze 1986: 122 n.9). On the similarity of the projects of Strabo and Dionysius, see Goudriaan 1989: 272–4.

[44] Dion. Hal. *Pomp.* 3.20; [Long.] *De Subl.* 1.2.

[45] The consensus has consolidated to the extent that the only arguments left are semantic, i.e. whether this grouping is a circle or a network, and hierarchical, i.e. what was Dionysius' position in it. I follow de Jonge 2008: 25ff. in preferring 'network' to 'circle', since it is looser and allows for a more varied range of connections and associations, and also because it obstructs speculation about a hierarchy in a specific group. *Contra*, Delcourt 2005: 36–7.

to suppose Dionysius' Greek correspondents were based there as opposed to in the wider Greek world.[46]

History, says Dionysius, is a monument to the historian; and so the *Roman Antiquities* are a monument to Dionysius.[47] Published in 7 BC, they are a history of Rome in twenty books from the very beginnings of Rome to the first Punic War. In the later tradition, the books were normally divided into pentads and decades.[48] This would seem a reasonable structure for Dionysius to have originally imposed, especially in the light of Livy's very similar practice in the same period. Indeed, the midpoint of the *Antiquities* breaks off in a way that suggests a cliffhanger of artistic design, and recommences with a methodological preface, in a way comparable with the end of Livy's first pentad.[49] Crucially, however, Dionysius himself offers a different way of arranging the *Antiquities*, saying of the first book:[50]

For I promised at the end of the first Book (γραφή),[51] which I composed and published concerning their origin, that I would demonstrate this thesis by countless proofs, by citing time-honoured customs, laws and institutions which they preserve down to my time just as they received them from their ancestors.[52]

The implication is that the book was not just conceived and arranged independently (συνταξάμενος), but also published (ἐξέδωκα) separately. That the first book is different in tone and structure from the rest of the work

---

[46] *Pace* Delcourt 2005: 32–3.
[47] Dion. Hal. *Ant. Rom.* 1.2: 'For I am convinced that all who propose to leave such monuments of their minds to posterity as time shall not involve in one common ruin with their bodies, and particularly those who write histories, in which we have the right to assume that Truth, the source of both prudence and wisdom, is enshrined, ought, first of all, to make choice of noble and lofty subjects.'
[48] Fromentin 1998: liv–lxxvii at liv (n. 229 for further bibliography); see also Fromentin 1989: 37; 1993: 102–3; Schnäbele 1989: 9.
[49] Dion. Hal. *Ant. Rom.* 10.60.6 and 11.1. On Livy, see especially Stadter 1972.
[50] Dion. Hal. *Ant. Rom.* 7.70.2: ὑπεσχόμην γὰρ ἐπὶ τῷ τέλει τῆς πρώτης γραφῆς, ἣν περὶ τοῦ γένους αὐτῶν συνταξάμενος ἐξέδωκα...

Gabba 1991: 98 had already made a similar point in less detail: 'Book I of his *History* is in many respects different from the rest of that work... From the evidence of VII.70.1 [sic] one might also conclude that the first book was published separately.' Decades and pentads are not a universal structure for long prose works in the period before the codex, and Varro composed in sets of three and six as well as four. Cf. Birt 1882: 35.
[51] Dionysius uses γραφή for either an individual volume of the *Antiquities* (e.g. 1.5.1; 3.6.1, 32.3, 67.4) or for the work as a whole (1.7.1, 7.3). He uses ἱστορία to refer to the work as a whole at 1.8.1, and βίβλος of an individual book only at 1.90.2. Birt 1882: 11–21, 29–32 argues that βίβλος/βιβλίον can mean either 'book' or 'volume', but that the proper term for a multi-volume set is not βίβλος/βιβλίον but rather the plural form of these. Dionysius uses the plural method to describe the Sybilline books at *Ant. Rom.* 4.62.5.
[52] Dion. Hal. *Ant. Rom.* 7.70.2. English translations of the *Antiquities* are from Cary's Loeb except where stated.

has been expounded by Clemence Schultze.[53] In the first book, Dionysius sets out to prove the Greek origin of the Romans, clearly separating the task of the first book from that of books two to twenty:

> In order, therefore, to remove these erroneous impressions, as I have called them, from the minds of many and to substitute true ones in their room, I shall in this Book (γραφή) show who the founders of the city were, at what periods the various groups came together and through what turns of fortune they left their native countries. By this means I engage to prove that they were Greeks and came together from nations not the smallest nor least considerable. And beginning with the next Book (ἀναγραφή) I shall tell of the deeds they performed immediately after their founding of the city and of the customs and institutions by virtue of which their descendants advanced to so great dominion . . . [54]

There is further evidence within the text to suggest the separateness of book 1. At the end of the book, Dionysius writes:

> I shall now resume the thread of my narrative, after prefacing to the following Book (βίβλος) a recapitulation of what is contained in this.[55]

Dionysius recapitulates the narrative of book 1 in 74 lines of Teubner text (*Ant. Rom.* 2.1–2). Dionysius does not usually recapitulate much at all. Books 3 and 6–11 continue the narrative from where the previous book left off. Book 4 summarises Tarquinius Priscus' reign in five lines. The exception is book 5, which narrates the first years of the Roman Republic, and where Dionysius adds some details to the narrative of the end of book 4, the expulsion of the Tarquins and the election of the first consuls, in 21 lines of Teubner text. The case of books 1–2 is then unique.[56]

The content of book 1 speaks to a very different project from the rest of the work. Dionysius cites by name fifty-eight authors in the course of the *Antiquities*. Forty-eight of the names occur in the first book.[57] These are

---

[53] Schultze 2000, followed by Luraghi 2003: 269–70; see also Schultze 1986: 128–9, 139: 'Romans such as those whom Dionysius encountered will hardly have read his history for the novelty of its actual subject-matter (except for Book 1).'

[54] Dion. Hal. *Ant. Rom.* 1.5.1–2.   [55] Dion. Hal. *Ant. Rom.* 1.90.2.

[56] Again, Livy is a useful comparandum: he begins book 2 of his history with an unusually long recapitulation of the first.

[57] See especially Jacoby 1998: 1–4; Schultze 2000: §3.2–§5. Regarding Dionysius' access to libraries, Luraghi 2003: 269–70. Casson 2001: 102 has suggested that 'for serious study of Greek writings, scholars had to go to Alexandria'. This view is predicated on the huge Greek collection in Alexandria, and a supposed natural tendency towards collecting Roman material in Rome. Casson's view has not gained wide acceptance; the example of Dionysius is a useful further counterpoint to it. Whether he found the books in libraries or had them sent to him by his acquaintances outside Rome, the evidence of Dionysius' own testimony is that it *was*

mostly Greek authors, ranging from Homer and Sophocles to obscure historians. Dionysius arrays these names, often with direct quotations, to support his argument that the Romans are Greek in origin.[58] This ultra-scholarly style only occurs in the first book of the *Antiquities*, and matches quite closely what we call Roman antiquarianism. Yet the approach emphasises its own Greekness. Dionysius once criticises Roman sources, on which he relies elsewhere, because they have failed to cite Greeks (*Ant. Rom.* 1.11.1). If Dionysius is indeed directing this book towards a Roman audience, even a scholarly one, his citation of obscure historians such as Pherecydes (cited at 1.13.1), may even trivialise his case, since these minor authors lack the authority of a Homer or an Aristotle.[59] Rather, citing obscure authors is exactly the sort of Greek-facing, elitist obscurantism which would go down well in Alexandria. Indeed, the heavy-loading of direct quotation has a great deal in common with the compilatory works of the Second Sophistic, such as Aulus Gellius' *Attic Nights* and Athenaeus' *Deipnosophistae*.[60]

The great strength of Dionysius' one-book compilation is that it is, as we have seen, much more mobile than a larger history: one volume can fit into many more ancient collections than a larger work. But it is still small by ancient standards. Local works such as the *Atthides*, local histories of Attica, or Roman-facing works such as Sallust's *Jugurtha* or *Catiline* may be one or two volumes, but to achieve international glory a historian would need to produce a work fitting a larger scale, either one large work, such as Diodorus', or with a large total output, such as Xenophon's. Dionysius thus resolves a possible contradiction. To permit book 1 a life independent of the rest of the *Antiquities* allows Dionysius' work to spread beyond the large collections concentrated in the major public libraries. The *Antiquities* may then be truly international in more than an academic or abstract sense. The

---

possible for a Greek to engage in detailed scholarly research in Greek literature in late first-century Rome. On resources, see also Marshall 1976 and Rawson 1985: 39–53.

[58] Direct quotation at e.g. Dion. Hal. *Ant. Rom.* 1.12.3, 13.1, 19.3, 22.4, 28.2, 41.3, 48.2, 49.1. It has been suggested that, by quoting so many obscure sources, Dionysius both persuades by overwhelming the reader with the range of evidence and bolsters the impression of his own erudition. Dionysius also demonstrates the wealth of Greek material available in late Republican Rome. Schultze 2000: §4; Luraghi 2003: 270. Diodorus records the 'abundant supply' (χορηγία) of materials for research in Rome (Diod. Sic. *Bibl.* 1.4.2).

[59] Hose argues (2007) that ancient arguments normally gain weight by citing, and challenging, canonical authors. There is perhaps an article to be written which highlights the irony that Dionysius demonstrates Roman magnificence and wonder by hanging it on obscure Atthidographic hooks.

[60] As a contemporary parallel, one might consider here Strabo's efforts at the beginning of his *Geography* to be taken seriously, by engaging in detailed, scientific discussion of Homer and Eratosthenes, among others.

scholar who read and benefited from the first book could then turn to the full set, which would be held in fewer places. Within this larger work then resides Dionysius' claim to monumentality: within the single volume, his international reach.

Internationalism

Dionysius wrote his *Antiquities*, he says, for a dual purpose: for Greeks, to combat their ignorance of the early Roman period; and as a gesture of thanks towards Rome itself for his time spent in the city.[61] This clear duality between Greeks and Romans is reflected throughout the preface, and then further into the modern literature on Dionysius' intended audience for his history.[62] He pitches for as large an audience as possible: Greeks, Romans, political theorists, philosophers and those seeking pure entertainment.[63] Yet modern scholarship has been left unsatisfied by this, and rightly so: Dionysius' *Antiquities* comprise a learned engagement with theorising, highly literate Greek scholarship on the one hand,[64] and a very Roman sense of collective memory and history on the other.[65] Debate on Dionysius' audience has therefore crystallised in recent years into two competing churches. The larger church argues, deliberately vaguely, for a broadly Greek-literate audience for Dionysius' work. So Dionysius aims in his preface for as broad an audience as possible, a 'mixed' or perhaps even a 'democratic' one.[66] In favour of this argument is Dionysius' criticism of Thucydides, whose language Dionysius

---

[61] Dion. Hal. *Ant. Rom.* 1.6.5.
[62] For example in the list of seven Greek and seven Latin authors at 1.6.1–2, 7.3 (observed by Marincola 1997: 244–5; cf. Schultze 2000: §3).
[63] Dion. Hal. *Ant. Rom.* 1.8.3.
[64] For example, Matthew Fox's 1993 article, updated in his book of 1996 (and followed by Luce 1995), argues that Dionysius' works betray a highly abstracted sense of 'truth'. To delve further, Noè 1979 argues that Dionysius has a very Isocratean attitude, prevalent particularly in his account of the trial of Coriolanus (Dion. Hal. *Ant. Rom.* 7.21–66; cf. Verdin 1974); Goudriaan 1989: 442–54, 470–80, 691 suggests, persuasively, that Dionysius' overlap with Isocrates is rather superficial and contained in key words which would find common sympathy in many places, such as a concern for justice and the law.
[65] Dionysius' engagement with Roman ideas is true and deep, and not simply a Hellenisation of Roman sources (so Luraghi 2003: xx, against Gabba 1985: 805). His list of world hegemonies, for example, with which he starts the *Antiquities* (Dion. Hal. *Ant. Rom.* 1.2.3–3.3), stands in the Herodotean tradition in its inclusion of the Assyrians, and matches exactly those of the Romans Aemilius Sura and, slightly later, Velleius Paterculus (Hdt. I.95, 130; Vell Pat. 1.6.6; Martin 1993: 194 and 195 n. 8; Alonso-Núñez 2002: 49).
[66] 'Mixed': Schultze 1986; 'democratic': Delcourt 2005: 65–9. Weaire suggests (2005: 246) that the fluctuations and nuances within the *Antiquities* render inadequate a more precise answer.

sees as excessively difficult and accessible only to a narrow circle of scholars.[67] The second school of thought attempts to pick through the fluctuations and nuances to find a clearer, more defined answer. These can be fairly dogmatic statements, such as those of Gabba and Bowersock that the audience is, respectively, Greek or Roman.[68] More recently, however, Nino Luraghi has attempted to marry all these contrasting arguments under a single proposal. Luraghi evaluates Dionysius' status as a cultural outsider in Rome. He argues that while the moralising tone of Roman historiography has a strong influence on Dionysius, Dionysius' moral authority is destabilised by his social status as a client of the Roman nobility.[69] Owing to his dependence on the support of Roman patrons, Dionysius must mask or qualify his criticism of Rome. Dionysius, argues Luraghi, uses the *Antiquities* to criticise and instruct contemporary Romans, but does so within the context of educating Greeks about the ancient Romans.[70]

This is suggestive, but there is a risk here of diluting the international scope of the *Antiquities*.[71] Certain elements of Dionysius' argument, such as the description of Roman offices in Greek terms, broaden the *Antiquities* out, make them more international. But these elements are explained by Luraghi as masking the underlying, local purpose of the *Antiquities*,[72] namely guiding Romans towards nobler action. To be sure, the last nineteen books of the *Antiquities* are filled with great men and stories which both bolster the Roman image of its own past and challenge the present Romans to live up to this image. Nevertheless, it is not just the Romans who are lectured on proper behaviour. The Greeks do not come out of the *Antiquities* well at all. In book 19, Dionysius narrates with unconcealed disgust an embassy of the Romans to the self-consciously Greek city of Tarentum, where the inhabitants shame themselves by abusing the Romans for errors in

---

[67] Dion. Hal. *Thuc.* 51. [68] Gabba and Bowersock, cited at Luraghi 2003: 281–5 at 281.
[69] Luraghi 2003: 281–5 at 282; see qualification by Weaire 2005: 246.
[70] Lightfoot had already made a similar suggestion at Lightfoot 2000: 250, though to my knowledge no similar attempt to Luraghi's, to combine a Greek and Roman audience in this way, had been argued thoroughly before him.
[71] See e.g. Pelling 2007, who argues that the implied Greek audience acts as a 'reader over one's shoulder' to the reading Romans, and the implied Roman audience does the same for the Greeks.
[72] The use of Greek terms both broadens the audience that can understand the work, hence 'internationalising', and fixes the dialect of composition as classicising or atticising Greek. So for example Procopius, who, writing in the sixth century AD, uses classicising periphrases to describe Christians because there is no single *classical* word he can use, even though his mostly Christian audience would not have actually needed the explanation, and there were obviously contemporary words available.

their Greek, and shower them in excrement or urine.[73] Indeed, throughout the *Antiquities* the Greeks, especially the Spartans and the Athenians, come badly out of comparison with the Romans. When, in the successful Roman campaign following the Gallic Sack, the Romans treat their Tusculan prisoners magnanimously, Dionysius compares this admirable behaviour with instances of Spartan and Athenian brutality towards a defeated enemy. He recalls the Spartans' savage treatment of the Messenians in the seventh century BC, and Athenian cruelty towards the Samians in the Peloponnesian War.[74] Equally, when the senate agrees to expel the patrician Coriolanus from Rome, Dionysius presents this as a noble action, the senate sacrificing one of its own in order to placate the people and to avert civil war. This willingness to look beyond party lines is compared favourably with short-sightedness and partisanship in Greece, which during the Peloponnesian War led to the Corcyraean slaughter, and would later lead to other Greek atrocities.[75] To talk in terms of exemplarity, Dionysius' ancient Romans are not just exemplars for contemporary Romans, but they ought to be exemplars for Greeks, both within Dionysius' narrative and in the real world, as a potential audience for the *Antiquities*. Dionysius makes plain that there is a broader audience for the *Antiquities* than merely Rome itself. Moreover, the *Antiquities* gains its power from the narrator's willingness to criticise, both implicitly and explicitly, on an international scale.

The internationalism of Dionysius' work is about more than abstract affirmations of or challenges to identity, whether Greek or Roman. Dionysius' work has a global perspective, in that Dionysius attempts to speak to both Greeks and Romans. At the same time, he marries the academic interests of first-century Rome with the encyclopaedism and scale we associate with the Greek literature of the Second Sophistic. But to be international in practice as well as in theory, Dionysius' *Antiquities* must be mobile too, of a size that can be distributed around the world. So the *Antiquities* gain their force by combining a mobile, international history with a history large enough to be a monument. Dionysius' history represents an adoption by a Greek of local Roman trends of moralising and exemplarity in historiography, adapting them to a framework which stresses its internationalism. The combination of the local and international is reflected further in the structure which Dionysius gives to his work, which bears both the features of massive organisation of knowledge and small-scale, mobile information. Dionysius' attempt to encompass simultaneously these extremes of large

---

[73] On Tarentum: e.g. Barnes 2005; on Hellenism and Rome, Wallace-Hadrill 2008: 3–37.
[74] Dion. Hal. *Ant. Rom.* 14.5–6; cf. Livy 6.24–5.   [75] Dion. Hal. *Ant. Rom.* 7.66.

and small, even in the underlying format of the work, may explain why such divergent views on Dionysius' audience still persist.

The scale of Dionysius' *Antiquities*, then, is ambitious. It also reflects the nature of book production in the first century BC. Books were getting bigger, as was the potential global audience, but the structures were not yet in place to distribute and store many copies of large books over a wide area. One solution to this puzzle would be the codex, which could contain much more text on less material than a papyrus roll. This was invented in the first century AD, though it would not become popular until some time later. We know, of course, that booksellers played a role in determining the distribution of a work. But we ought to be more careful than we currently are when assigning a potential audience to an author. An author may have aimed ideally for an audience across the known world, or for one of future generations. But this ideal was not likely to have been matched by the actual, practical possibilities of a book reaching such a large audience in written form. I have argued that Dionysius took these difficulties into account when structuring his *Antiquities*; it may well be that other historians did the same.

9 | Libraries and intellectual debate in the late Republic

The case of the Aristotelian corpus

FABIO TUTRONE

Reading Aristotle at Rome

It is no exaggeration to say that it is impossible to study the history of culture without studying the history of book circulation. This becomes even more evident if we consider how often the work of scholars engaged on other more general topics becomes redirected to this field of research. Certainly this has been my experience. Over the last few years my attention has been focused on the role of animals and man-animal relationships in Lucretius' *De rerum natura*, as I have attempted to consider properly the importance of biology in the poem. Working on this theme, I was repeatedly struck by the frequent use of Aristotelian-like biological concepts in Lucretian passages dealing with animal behaviour and psychology.[1] The studies of J.-M. Pigeaud and more recently those of P. H. Schrijvers[2] have succeeded in showing how skilfully Lucretius managed to combine the tradition of Epicurean atomistic physics with some aspects of Hippocratic-Aristotelian thought, which conceived of living beings as continuous biological organisms and not as discontinuous atomic aggregates. Yet it remains unclear *how* a curious and educated Roman intellectual like Lucretius might have come into contact with an Aristotelian *corpus* of texts the fate of which has been much discussed by the past generations of scholars.[3] The main reason for this silence – or at least for

---

[1] I discuss this and other related problems in Tutrone 2012. The relevance of the Aristotelian biological tradition to Lucretius' scientific culture has become much more clear in the last years thanks to the work of Schrijvers 1999.

[2] See Pigeaud 1980 and Schrijvers 1999 especially 40–54 (on the man-animal relationship).

[3] The problem of the kind of contact – direct or indirect – that we might imagine between Lucretius and the Aristotelian tradition (and especially the *Historia animalium*, which seems to be very present in the poet's imagery) has been left unsolved by Schrijvers 1999: 54, who prudently states: 'cette question reste ouverte, étant donné le caractère fragmentaire de la tradition à l'époque hellénistique. En tout cas il nous semble improbable que sur ce point Lucrèce se serait inspiré directement d'Epicure lui-même.' On the long and varied scholarly discussion of the fate of Aristotle's esoteric works – and of Aristotle's personal library in particular – see Moraux 1973: I 3–31 and Jacob (this volume).

this lack of interest – can probably be found in the very complex question of the circulation of Aristotelian esoteric writings in Roman Italy in the first century BC. For some of the Aristotelian works by which Lucretius seems to have been most influenced – the biological works – belonged to the so-called esoteric or acroamatic *corpus*. Aristotle's philosophical production is usually divided into two branches: the so-called exoteric *corpus*, which is almost entirely lost and was characterised by a refined literary form, and the esoteric (or acroamatic) one, which is composed of unembellished treatises aimed at the internal activities of his school.[4] It is this latter body of work that is the subject of the discussion that follows.

My argument in this chapter is that we may be able to discover something unexpected and useful for our understanding of this problem if we move the focus of our inquiry to the cultural role played by libraries during the late Republic.[5] In the past the analytical attention of scholars has been captured and monopolised by just *one* library, that of Aristotle himself, the adventurous travels of which between the Greek east and Roman Italy are at the centre of the well known accounts of Strabo and Plutarch.[6] It was widely believed that this collection was the only one that actually contained copies of Aristotle's acroamatic works. Clearly this idea has distracted scholars' attention from the wider dynamics of transmission. Following Moraux's studies, however, it has become evident that we should avoid concentrating all our exegetic efforts on the story of Aristotle's personal collection,[7] or indeed on the chronologically uncertain edition of his works made by Andronicus, which, as Moraux states, 'cannot be considered as an *editio princeps* of the *Corpus*, even less of all the didactic writings'.[8] Instead, we should enlarge our perspective, beginning from the assumption that in the Hellenistic and Roman world there were a range of media through which the key components of the Aristotelian esoteric tradition were transmitted.

---

[4] This distinction, as well as the general chronology of Aristotle's works, has been variously discussed in the scholarly literature. For a short summary see e.g. Flashar 2004: 178–82.

[5] For a general survey of the role of libraries in Roman intellectual life, see Rawson 1985: 38–42, as well as Marshall 1976 and Fedeli 1988.

[6] Strabo 13.1.54.608–9; Plut. *Sull.* 26. A fascinating reconstruction of the sources' account on the destiny of Aristotle's library has been proposed by Canfora 1986a, who has exploited the flavour of 'detective story' offered in plenty by these two reports.

[7] Moraux 1973 especially I 3–94.

[8] See Moraux 1973 I 93: 'sicher ist auf jeden Fall, daß zumindest Teile des Corpus schon vor ihm (scil. Andronikos) zugänglich waren und daß seine Ausgabe nicht als editio princeps des Corpus und nicht einmal aller Lehrschriften angesehen werden kann'. On the wide bibliography concerning the place and the date of Andronicus' edition, see Moraux 1973 I 45–58. An interesting proposal on this matter has been presented by Gottschalk 1987: 1,095, who sees 60 BC as the *terminus ante quem* for Andronicus' edition.

Another factor which has distracted scholarly attention away from the role played by libraries in this historical-cultural process is the commonly held view that the ideas contained in Aristotle's esoteric works circulated in this period mainly through *indirect* means, in secondary works such as epitomes, *résumés, excerpta*. That view is not unreasonable. We cannot detect any certain *direct* use of the acroamatic writings even in famous authors of the imperial age like Seneca, Quintilian, Plutarch and Lucian who must surely have known of the Andronicus edition of the first century BC. As Düring remarks, 'the Andronicean edition does not seem to have been well known outside a narrow circle of specialists'.[9] It is probable that most of the non-Peripatetic educated public found it hard to follow didactic treatises themselves: in Lucretius' day, as well as in the Imperial age, many would have preferred to consult secondary works. Yet the production and the use of summaries and the like should not be separated from the fact that copies of those didactic treatises were contained in the libraries of Rome and Italy. Indeed, as I will try to show in this chapter, those collections were the basis for further intellectual undertakings. Consideration of some pieces of ancient testimony sheds light on precisely what was involved. Let us start by observing how relevant and widely diffused Aristotelian ideas and models were in the cultural debates of the first century BC both in Latin and in Greek. It will be sufficient to mention – besides Lucretius – the cases of two other important intellectuals who were active in Roman Italy at that time and seem to use clearly Peripatetic concepts and *exempla*: Cicero and Philodemus.

Cicero's knowledge and use of Peripatetic philosophy has been the subject of several surveys.[10] Here I would like to draw attention to his skilled use of Aristotelian zoological arguments – most of them drawn from the ninth book of our *Historia animalium* – in the second book of *De natura deorum*. His debt to Aristotle has been studied by S. Rocca[11] in a study that reveals how important the knowledge of Peripatetic scientific material could be from the point of view of a Roman intellectual like Cicero who aimed to integrate Aristotle's observational richness into the Stoic providentialist system. The

---

[9] Düring 1950: 40–1.
[10] E.g. Gigon 1959; Pahnke 1962; and the different studies collected in Fortenbaugh and Steinmetz 1989. An interesting discussion of Cicero's use of Aristotle's *Topics* can be read in Reinhardt 2003: 177–81, where it is assumed without too many difficulties that 'Cicero might have possessed a copy of Aristotle's *Top.*' (179). I am very grateful to Prof. Harry M. Hine for drawing my attention to the position of Reinhardt, and in general for reading the whole of my paper and making many valuable suggestions.
[11] Cf. Rocca 2003.

final result was an original compound of ethics and biology, a cosmological picture where anthropocentrism and humanism were mutually supportive.

This observation raises one of the most interesting aspects of our short survey, that is the *ethical* relevance of Aristotelian material for Greek and Latin authors of the first century BC. The adaptation and *re-writing* of Peripatetic philosophy, with all its *bioethical* implications, became a distinctive mark of the moral debates of this age. This is true of the work of Lucretius[12] and also of that of Philodemus, whose intense dialogue with Peripatetic thought – and with several of its exponents in particular – has been the subject of a very detailed essay by M. Gigante.[13] As Gigante has pointed out, Philodemus' interest in the Peripatetic tradition has one of its focal points in the discussion and development of ethical-moral problems such as the nature of human 'characters', a topic that Aristotle's school had dealt with in depth. One of the most relevant Peripatetic authors for Philodemus' philosophy is Aristo of Ceos, whose work concentrated on the theme of man's *ethē*.[14] It is also intriguing to notice how much Theophrastus' *Characters* influenced Philodemus' moral polemics.[15] The special relevance of this work for Philodemus brings us back to the dynamics of book circulation, for the most ancient text of the fifth character, Ἀρέσκεια or *Obsequiousness*, is one of the Herculaneum papyri (*PHerc.* 1457), actually transcribed by Philodemus himself.[16] According to Strabo and Plutarch, the works of both Theophrastus and Aristotle went mostly out of circulation until Andronicus' edition, and were conserved during this period in the famous library bought by Apellicon of Teos.[17] The evidence of Philodemus and the Herculaneum papyri challenges this simplistic view.

In spite of this, as I have already said, we should avoid thinking about frequent *direct* use of the Peripatetic texts in this period. Even during

---

[12] For the ethical implications of Lucretius' use of the Aristotelian biology see Tutrone 2006 especially 65–74. On the problem, in more general terms, of Lucretius' moral models, that are firmly founded on both scientific and epistemological concepts, see Marchese 1998: 97–136.
[13] Cf. Gigante 1999.   [14] See Gigante 1999: 123–33.
[15] See Gigante 1999: 93–5, and – from a more philological perspective – Kondo 1971.
[16] On this topic see Gigante 1999: 93–5, who also refers to the importance this discovery has had for the textual critic since D. Bassi published his edition of the *PHerc.* 1457 in 1914.
[17] Strabo 13.1.54.608–9; Plut. *Sull.* 26, 1–2. According to the sources (and in particular to Strabo), Theophrastus' library contained within it Aristotle's personal collection, which had been left by the founder of the Lyceum to his successor and pupil. On this particular see Moraux 1973 I 22, and Canfora 1986a: 190, who vividly compares this mechanism to the way 'Chinese boxes' contain each other. It is worth mentioning that in this period the names of Aristotle and Theophrastus were sometimes confused and works written by one ascribed to the other. This is, for example, what Philodemus does in his *On Economy*, where in a discussion of some passages of Aristotle's *Economics*, the text is ascribed to Theophrastus (see Moraux 1973: I 41).

the Imperial age, direct consultation of those texts remained unusual for those intellectuals who did not belong to the Peripatetic school. The fact that Cicero himself found it more comfortable to read handbooks and compilations, instead of directly consulting the works of Aristotle, has been remarked on by J. Barnes in his essay on the circulation of Aristotle in Rome.[18] What I would like to point out here is that this does not have to be ascribed, as it has been for a long time, to the objective impossibility of gaining access to Aristotle's esoteric works, the disappearance of which is borne out by the anecdotal accounts of the ancient sources. The trend towards using secondary texts should be explained as a consequence of the internal difficulty of the Aristotelian treatises themselves.[19] Consideration of the role played by libraries in this period turns out to offer some fruitful insights for our understanding of intricate problems of this sort.

My aim in this chapter is to show that libraries offered extremely lively frameworks for the intellectual life of the late Republic. Nonetheless, they are often undervalued in scholarly discussions dealing with cultural problems such as the spread of new philosophies at Rome. The case of Aristotle is perhaps an exception in this respect, since ancient accounts place special emphasis on the function of books and their transmission when they discuss the Peripatetic school. But in many cases, the main aim of modern scholars seems to have been to reconstruct the chronology of the revival of Aristotle's reputation through a history of his writings. In similar exegetic contexts libraries are usually regarded as means of transmission. Here I would like to go beyond this approach by focusing on the original social and cultural roles that libraries played in Roman circles in the period when Aristotelianism and other orientations gained new strength.

If we re-examine our sources with appropriate critical attention, it emerges that in Cicero's and Philodemus' time there were in Italy at least two important libraries which possessed copies of the Aristotelian acroamatic writings. Cicero's testimony in particular is a good guide to this rich intellectual milieu.

---

[18] Barnes 1997: 44–50. In Cicero, according to Barnes, 'genuine allusions, whether covert or overt, may derive from handbooks or from other sources. And the word "may" here does not mark a gratuitous scepticism'.

[19] The internal difficulty of the didactic writings – which was evident also for the Greek and Latin readers – has been regarded as a probable reason for the elaboration of an ancient tradition on Aristotle's temporary disappearance. Moraux 1973 I 25–6, reconnects the building of the sources' tale to the typical ancient habit of seeking explanations for complex critical matters in biographic and anecdotal particulars.

De finibus and the library of Lucullus

In *De finibus* we find a clear and precise picture of the situation of Aristotle's esoteric *corpus* in the Roman world, and at the same time, a fascinating description of one important private library that did contain Aristotle's works, that of Lucullus. This is the first library I shall focus on, as it also offers a vivid image of the cultural function of these private libraries in the lives of educated society in the first century BC. Cicero's report, however, is much more eloquent than any general assertions of the fact, despite its flavour of literary fiction. At the beginning of the third book of *De finibus* he relates a pleasant conversation he had in 52 BC[20] with Marcus Cato in the great library that the young Lucullus possessed in Tusculum, where Cicero also had an estate. Cicero had gone to Lucullus' house in order to make use of some books he knew he could find there; he also states he wanted to borrow them, as it was usual for him to do so.[21] When he arrived at the *villa*, he casually met Marcus Cato who was evidently there for similar reasons, as he was 'sitting in the library, surrounded by many books of the Stoics'.[22] A Stoic-oriented intellectual like Cato could clearly find in that precious collection writings which were closest to his own philosophical interests. What Cicero was looking for was maybe more peculiar, at least from our modern point of view. When Cato asks Cicero which books he was searching for (which books, Cato meant, that Cicero could not find in his own wide collection), the famous orator answered: 'I came to take away some commentaries by Aristotle (*commentarios Aristotelios*), which I knew were here and which I want to read as long as I have free time; which, I must say, does not happen to me often'.[23]

From this answer and from the passage as a whole we can learn at least two important things. Aristotle's acroamatic writings, which Cicero defines

---

[20] Cicero wrote the dialogue in 45 BC, but the scene he represents should have happened, according to the literary fiction, in 52. This is not a secondary particular, because it gives us a quite precise chronology for the diffusion of the Aristotelian *corpus*, which, as we will see now, was part of Lucullus' collection. For these chronological considerations, see Moraux 1973 I 39–40.

[21] *Fin.* 3.7: *nam in Tusculano cum essem vellemque e bibliotheca pueri Luculli quibusdam libris uti, veni in eius villam, ut eos ipse, ut solebam, depromerem.* The *puer Lucullus* Cicero mentions here is the young son of the famous Lucullus *Ponticus* who had established the library but had died in 56 BC. As Cicero himself tells us later in the dialogue (3.8–9), Lucullus had entrusted to him the task of educating the young boy (although, as Cicero says, this was actually Cato's *proprium munus*). On these relationships, see the Latin commentary of Madvig 1965: 349.

[22] *Ibid.* 3.7 *in bibliotheca sedentem multis circumfusum Stoicorum libris.*

[23] *Ibid.* 3.10 *commentarios quosdam, inquam, Aristotelios, quos hic sciebam esse, veni ut auferrem, quos legerem, dum essem otiosus; quod quidem nobis non saepe contingit.*

here as *commentarii* according to a basic distinction he makes clear in the fifth book of the same dialogue,[24] were potentially available in Italy at that time and could be borrowed by a writer who like Cicero was well connected within that network of social relationships that criss-crossed intellectual society in the late Republic. This does not mean of course that Cicero *usually* consulted the Aristotelian treatises directly: as we have seen this usage was not very common even in the imperial age outside Peripatetic circles, given the internal difficulty of these works. Nevertheless, copies of the esoteric writings could be found in the middle of the first century BC[25] in an important private collection such as the one of Lucullus. The second thing we can learn from Cicero's statements concerns the important role which libraries had for the cultural world of Cicero's time. If educated men belonging to different philosophical orientations like Cicero and Marcus Cato could go to Lucullus' house in order to use his book collection in a free and easy way, then there is a sense in which *private* libraries of this kind had a *semipublic* character.[26] This impression is vividly confirmed, in the case of Lucullus' library, by Plutarch in his life of Lucullus. According to Plutarch, this wealthy Roman politician opened his large book collection to everybody as well as the porticoes and reading rooms of the building where the library was housed.[27]

Perhaps it would be helpful in this context to be a bit more explicit about the meaning of the terms *public* and *private* for Greek and Roman societies in this period, since confusion between modern and ancient usage can be misleading. No concept of *public* opening in the modern sense could be employed for spaces such as the libraries of the ancient world, even when

---

[24] Ibid. 5.12: *duo genera librorum sunt, unum populariter scriptum, quod ἐξωτερικόν* (scil. Peripatetici) *appellabant, alterum limatius, quod in commentariis reliquerunt.* (There are two kinds of books, the former written in a popular way, which they (*scil.* the Peripatetics) called exoteric, the latter more sober, which they left in commentaries.) Cicero shows himself to be aware of the same division also in *Att.* 4.16.2.

[25] For the chronological collocation of the dialogue depicted in Cicero's *De finibus*, see *supra* note 20.

[26] Dix 2000: 457 remarks on the basic reliability of Cicero's testimony, but he casts some doubt on the fact that Lucullus' library was used so unconcernedly while the great general was still alive: 'while Cicero's dialogues may well be entirely fictional, surely the details of the setting are meant to be taken as genuine. Presumably Lucullus opened his library to his friends as well as to the Greek men of letters, and presumably Cicero and others began to use Lucullus' library while he was still alive; we may doubt, however, whether Cicero would have taken books from the library so nonchalantly while Lucullus was alive as he seems to have done when the library came into the possession of Lucullus' son'.

[27] Plut. *Luc.* 42.1–3. For Lucullus' library as a venue for cultural activities in the late Republic, see Rawson 1985: 40. The general features of such a famous library, which is also the setting of Cicero's lost *Hortensius*, are discussed by Dix 2000, who makes careful use of both literary and archaeological evidence.

we find the word *publicus* in a source. When we speak about public and private libraries (as well as public and private lectures, readings and so on) in a Roman context, we should always remember that in antiquity only a restricted range of people took part in active cultural life. Women, slaves, the poor and even people who were not sufficiently well connected, were frequently excluded from the use of book collections. This becomes even clearer if we consider the fact that books, above all those written on papyrus or parchment, were also considered to be precious material goods.[28]

Equally the concept of *private* covered a different semantic range. Private citizens who were engaged in a political career – we would probably say: on the *public* scene – had very good reasons to 'publicise', at least in part, their personal libraries. From the late Republic, individuals might win approval by advertising their sensitivity to literature and culture in general, and their commitment to making both more accessible. Naturally this depended to some extent on individual political orientations. One traditional viewpoint discouraged excessive love of the arts and of Greek culture in particular. Yet, men like Lucullus implicitly rejected such positions: in a moment I shall consider the analogous case of Sulla.

Thus, if we are aware of these basic *cultural* differences, we can probably accept the definition of *private* and *semipublic* libraries I used before: for it is possible to see as *private* collections the ones belonging to a man and open to his entourage, while these same libraries might become more and more *public* depending on who was granted access. The main reason for such an approach is the observation that in the late Republic intellectual circles and social relationships seem to have largely determined the use of book collections. Therefore, we should try to focus our attention on the importance *social networks* had for libraries and writers.[29] Seen in this light, the significance of book collections becomes more and more evident:

---

[28] For this period, see Fedeli 1988: 34: 'nel periodo della declinante repubblica l'acquisto di una biblioteca doveva essere un lusso costoso, destinato a restare un miraggio per i dotti squattrinati'. The general situation shows some variation over the course of classical antiquity (see next note). In particular, from the Augustan age onwards the foundation of *public* libraries – i.e. libraries established by public personages or local notables for the sake of the whole community – introduced a new element, even if the act of foundation by a named benefactor shows some continuity with the dynamics of the late Republic. See also Nicholls this volume.

[29] Citroni 1995: 3–56 rightly remarks on the role of circles, coteries and interpersonal exchanges for late Republican literature (although he redraws and in a certain sense widens the range of the public in this period). This situation gradually changed in the following centuries, and the role of libraries evolved consequently. In the imperial age, for instance, the extent to which libraries were made open was quite different (see Fedeli 1988: 48–59). But in no ancient case is it possible to find a perfect correspondence between our modern, post-Romantic view of cultural life and the ancient one.

through interpersonal connections of this kind texts and ideas might come to influence many members of the intellectual elite.

Lucullus' books may well have derived in large part from his military campaigns in Pontus, as Isidore says.[30] What is of greater interest for us is that he founded a cultural oasis which enriched and stimulated the intellectual milieu where it was situated. We should also add that this oasis offered something which was not very common at that time. Cicero's last remark (*quod quidem nobis non saepe contingit*) can be read as a simple reference to the fact that our author did not have much time for this kind of intellectual *otium* because of his many civil and political engagements. But it is not wrong, I think, to read behind these words an additional allusion to the restricted diffusion of Aristotle's esoteric works. For Cicero, we could say, it was rare to be *otiosus*, free from the tasks of his public life, but it was also rare to read in a direct way Aristotle's arduous *commentarii*. I do not need to add that such a statement corresponds perfectly to what we have already noticed about the diffusion of the Peripatetic tradition in this period. Nor should we undervalue the role that large and famous libraries like that of Lucullus' may have had for the book market. *Semipublic* libraries of this kind may have had a catalysing function not only for intellectual circles – the meeting of Cicero and Cato in Lucullus' house is a case in point – but also for the contemporary book trade.

The library of Sulla

In order to shed more light on this last matter, it is necessary to turn to a second library, the one that Sulla acquired when he captured Athens and which was regarded as the original library of Aristotle and Theophrastus. My intention is not to reopen the long and contradictory debate over the story of this itinerant library, which from Aristotle's and Theophrastus' personal possession allegedly travelled to Scepsis, and was then acquired by the unscrupulous bibliophile Apellicon and finally by Sulla, who brought it to Rome.[31] I have already said that I consider the thesis that there was a

---

[30] Isid. *Etym.* 6.5: 'At Rome the first man who brought a huge quantity of books was Aemilius Paulus, after he defeated the Macedonian king Perseus; then Lucullus did the same, taking his plunder from Pontus' [*Romae primus librorum copiam advexit Aemilius Paulus, Perse Macedonum rege devicto; deinde Lucullus e Pontica praeda*]. Plut. *Luc.* 42.1 simply says that Lucullus gathered together many and well written books, but he also says that their use was more honourable than their acquisition. See Dix 2000: 441–4.

[31] See the already quoted reports by Strabo and Plutarch, with the bibliographical review of Moraux 1973 I 3–31. Cf. Dix 2004. More briefly, see Jacob this volume.

Libraries and intellectual debate in the late Republic 161

total disappearance of Peripatetic texts to be completely groundless. For this reason it is fruitless to concentrate all our attention on the ups and downs of this particular library, as if it were the *only* source of the Aristotelian textual tradition. Instead we should perhaps consider the vicissitudes of this precious book collection critically, seeing it as just *one* of several sources which played a role in the diffusion of Peripatetic writings through the ancient world. Of course, its role is very particular and almost unique, for the copies it contained were said to date back to the origins of the Lyceum. But this need not distract us from analysing its story – and the many details provided by the sources in this context – as an example of testimony on the use and the function of libraries in the Greek-Latin culture. Some particulars reported by Strabo and Plutarch, in fact, seem to be more concrete and realistic than others which are evidently linked to the requirements of the narrative construction (for both reports show many elements of a typical *adventure story*, whose plot is dominated by the deeds of the library-hero).[32] Actually, after the arrival of the library at Rome in 84 BC the remarks of our two authors (and especially of Strabo, who is the more precise of the two) focus in an interesting way on the dynamics of the book circulation.

Sulla, Strabo says,[33] took Apellicon's Aristotelian library from Athens when he captured the city. Once the library had arrived in Rome it attracted the attention of some contemporary bibliophiles. I shall not deal here with the vexed question of Andronicus' edition, nor with Tyrannion's role in its production. But I do want to note what an important cultural event was constituted by the arrival of a major collection of Greek books, both for educated scholars like Tyrannion[34] and also for the book trade. One of the most

---

[32] This is not the place to develop a fuller account of the particular narratological features of Strabo's and Plutarch's stories, although it would be very interesting to do so. I just want to remark that Moraux's impressions about the typical 'ancient' nature of these two reports, which try to find a biographical and anecdotic explanation for a complex critical matter, might be supported by a structural analysis of them.

[33] Strabo 13.1.54.609. Schubert 2002 points out that Strabo's emphasis on the role of Rome and Tyrannion in the history of Aristotle's writings can be connected to his peculiar aims. He proposes a useful contextualisation of the account of Aristotle's library in the framework of Strabo's historical polemics. Similar remarks, however, strengthen the necessity of a critical and structural analysis of the sources.

[34] Tyrannion of Amisos was a very educated grammarian, brought to Rome as a slave after the Mithridatic War, who as a freedman came into contact with many members of the cultural elite including Cicero and Atticus. It seems Tyrannion had a particular competence in libraries, since we know he suitably rearranged Cicero's books in Antium (*Att.* 4.4a.1; 8.2) and was appointed to improve Quintus Cicero's library (*Q Fr.* 3.4.5; 5.6); he himself is said by the lexicon *Suda* (s.v. Tyrannion) to have possessed a library that contained 30,000 rolls. On the

interesting aspects of Strabo's tale, in fact, is the reference to some booksellers (βιβλιοπῶλαί τινες), who seem to have published Aristotle's works in a very inaccurate way by exploiting the contents of the Sullan library. In particular, they made use of bad copyists (γραφεῦσι φαύλοις χρώμενοι) and did not carry out any collation of the edited texts (οὐκ ἀντιβάλλοντες). Strabo's text is very problematic at this point, as the last part of the sentence evidently lacks the main verb (which should be referred to the βιβλιοπῶλαι). On this aspect, I agree with Barnes, who thinks that our text is corrupted and that maybe we have lost 'a sentence or two',[35] since Strabo does not mention here Andronicus whose edition is the very ending point of Plutarch's report. It is very likely that Plutarch's information is based on Strabo's reconstruction. If so, we are now reading this second account in a truncated form. So the bad booksellers we are talking about may have been entrusted *by Andronicus* with the publication of the Aristotelian works, as Barnes interrogatively supposes.

For our purposes, however, the most interesting element of the story is the evidence for a connection between libraries and the book trade. Strabo says that the lack of attention to textual quality was a frequent fault of books copied for commercial reasons. He specifies that this happened in his day (συμβαίνει) – i.e. in the Augustan age – both in Rome (ἐνθάδε) and in Alexandria, two of the main centres of the ancient book trade. That negative picture of commercial copies corresponds to the information we can draw from other reliable sources like Cicero and Catullus.[36] It seems that between the end of the Republic and the beginning of the Imperial age there was a sizeable market trading in poor quality copies in Italy and in the Mediterranean world more generally. Strabo's comment sounds quite plausible in this respect. It is therefore very likely that when he discusses the commercial use of Sulla's library he is reflecting on a common practice. Atticus, Cicero's erudite friend, possessed a very rich collection of books and was at the same time a successful book trader.[37] According to Cornelius Nepos he had copyists in his own house on the Quirinal hill.[38] It

---

life of this Greek scholar, as well as on his role in Aristotle's edition, however, see Moraux 1973 I 33–44.

[35] See Barnes 1997: 19–20.

[36] Cf. e.g. Cicero, *Q Fr.* 3.4.5; 5.6; Catull. 14. These and other testimonies about the situation of the late Republican book trade are discussed by Citroni 1995: 3–29 as well as by Rawson 1985: 42–5. In particular, Citroni 1995 points out the growth and influence of this market and recalls Strabo's significant discussion of it (26–7 n. 24).

[37] Cicero's letters indicate that Atticus' library was a precious source for his own work (see e.g. *Att.* 4.14.1; 13.31.2; 32.2). Moreover, Atticus was Cicero's editor and he could promote the sales of his friend's books in Athens and other Greek cities (*Att.* 2.1.2).

[38] Cf. Nep. *Att.* 13.3 (*plurimi librarii*).

would certainly be misleading to dissociate these two aspects of Atticus' activity.[39]

There is good reason to think that in the first century BC, libraries and the book trade were connected in a number of ways. On the one hand, library owners might have recourse to the book market in order to improve their collections, even if the quality available was not always equal to their taste.[40] On the other, the books kept in libraries were sometimes used as models by copyists creating books for resale. Perhaps Atticus had copies made of some of his books for resale on the market, at the point when Sulla's library became a focus of attraction for Roman booksellers. Either way, late Republican libraries seem to have been important engines of cultural transformation, through commercial enterprise as well as social networks. In an age of changes and debates, books had a certain impact on society, since a passion for literature and culture – above all, for Greek culture – was regarded as in some sense a *political* choice.

The case of Sulla is particularly illuminating in this regard. Sallust clearly depicts his passion for literature as a political matter. In the *Bellum Iugurthinum* Sulla is portrayed as an ambiguous figure, industrious and audacious, but at the same time a voluptuary. Sulla's interest in literature is one component of this rather shady characterisation.[41] It is no accident that in the same work Marius constructs a skillful 'anti-cultural' polemic for his own political purposes.[42] He presents himself as a *homo novus* and subjects the love of Greek literature among the Roman ruling class to a withering critique.[43] Indeed almost all the actors involved in the 'library stories' that have been related here – Lucullus and Sulla, Cicero

---

[39] See Fedeli 1988: 34: 'possessore di una notevole raccolta di volumi dovette essere Tito Pomponio Attico: ma si tratta di un caso particolare, perché il suo possesso di un ingente patrimonio librario è in stretto rapporto con la sua intensa e fortunata attività di editore, che si sviluppò con una tale ampiezza da portarlo a rifornire la stessa Atene di testi greci'.

[40] At *Q Fr.* 3.5.6, for instance, Cicero complains about the low quality of the Latin texts sold on the market.

[41] Cf. *Iug.* 95.

[42] See *ibid.* 85. On Marius' speech and its 'anti-cultural' polemic, see Picone 1976. The ethical contrast between culture and action, theory and praxis, was an important point of the Roman debate of this age, and Sallust's works reflect this situation. See, in particular, the discussion of Romano 2005.

[43] See e.g. *ibid.* 85.12; 32. In 85.12 Marius attacks those Roman generals who attached excessive importance to the study of Greek works on military strategy (*Graecorum militaria praecepta*). According to Cic. *Luc.* 2.1–10, Lucullus' competence as a general came mostly from his reading of historiography (*res gestae*) as well as from his conversations with specialists (*periti*). Cicero's account has a strong literary flavour, but it displays all the same a basic truth: like Sulla, Lucullus was an aristocratic lover of books and culture, and this evidently had a political significance.

and Cato – had roles to play in the cultural and political traumas of the late Republic. The libraries they captured, inherited or consulted were at the centre of complex intellectual phenomena, and their activity took place against the background of a Roman world refashioning its cultural identity. The patterns of use and access we can reconstruct for these libraries were founded on the influence of social networks, on the shared preoccupations of intellectual circles. I have tried to describe this situation by talking about a *semipublic* opening. It is no accident that the same description can be applied to the case of Sulla's Aristotelian library, to the final chapter of which I shall now turn.

When Sulla died in 78 BC the books that had once belonged to Aristotle and Theophrastus were inherited by his young son Faustus, who was left under Lucullus' *tutela*.[44] This is of course another indication of the operation of those social networks which had such an undoubted influence over Roman cultural life at the time. But there is much more. It seems that Apellicon's library did not remain in Rome – I mean *in the city of Rome* – for very long.[45] A letter of Cicero, written in spring 55 from Faustus Sulla's house in Cumae, makes clear that the library was now in Campania.[46] Cicero writes to Atticus that during his stay in what was, as it is well known, a resort favoured by many members of the Roman upper class,[47] he was enjoying Faustus' library (*ego hic pascor bibliotheca Fausti*). He asserts that he prefers to devote himself to the pleasures of literature, even though Campania also offered more common delights. Cicero then starts to make some sophisticated *allusions* to the kind of interests he was cultivating. He would have preferred, he writes, to sit on Atticus' little chair under Aristotle's portrait (*sub imagine Aristotelis*) than on Pompey's and Crassus' curule chairs. He also makes a very meaningful use of the verb *ambulare* and the term *ambulatio* (which can be easily reconnected to the περιπατεῖν typical of Aristotle's school), saying that he would have liked to 'stroll' with

---

[44] See Plut. *Luc.* 4.5. Barnes 1997: 49, n. 202, also supposed on this basis that Lucullus, who as we have seen possessed copies of the Aristotelian writings, 'might have bought the Sullan library'. But there is no evidence for this supposition.

[45] Both Strabo and Plutarch are rather clear in stating that Rome was the first place in Italy where the library was brought (although, as I said, their accounts are quite problematic). See Strabo 13.1.54.609 (δεῦρο) and Plut. *Sull.* 26.2 (εἰς Ῥώμην). In spite of this, Rawson 1985: 41, states that 'probably' Sulla's books 'had never been in Rome, but arrived from Athens by sea, conveniently, to Puteoli': so they would have always been in Campania.

[46] *Att.* 4.10.

[47] Many members of the senatorial elite owned comfortable *villae* in Campania, and in spring, when the political activities in Rome temporarily stopped because of the *senatus discessus*, the senate's recess, the territory of Cumae was so full of Roman people that it could seem a *pusilla Roma*, a little Rome, as Cicero says in *Att.* 5.2.2. On this topic, see D'Arms 1970: 48–55.

Atticus rather than with Crassus.[48] Crassus, however, is the person that Cicero must cultivate (*quocum video esse ambulandum*).[49] The whole letter helps us to understand how social relationships and the duties they entailed, might be intimately linked to cultural experiences such as reading the works of Aristotle.

Cicero's comments can clearly be connected to the story of the Sullan library and its contents. The fact that in 55 the library was in Cumae can be easily explained if we consider that at the end of his life Sulla, the father of Faustus, retired to his Cuman estate[50] where he died in 78. It is very likely that the Aristotelian collection remained in that *villa* after Sulla's death when Faustus inherited it. Nonetheless, it has been supposed that when Cicero writes his letter to Atticus and talks about the *bibliotheca Fausti* he is sitting in *his own* Cuman house, where he would have brought the library.[51] But this idea is based only on Plutarch's statement that when Faustus had to put up for auction his properties because of financial problems Cicero bought them.[52] Actually, Plutarch does not mention the library at all, and moreover we know that in 55 BC Faustus Sulla was not yet a ruined man, at least from a political and social point of view, since he was *quaestor* in 54 and as late as 52 was entrusted with restoring the *curia Hostilia* according to Dio Cassius (40.50.2–3).[53] We might add that in Cicero the word *bibliotheca* in the abstract meaning of 'book collection' is much rarer than its employment as a concrete term for library (i. e. 'the place where books are conserved').[54] So we can reasonably conclude that when Cicero says '*ego hic pascor bibliotheca Fausti*' he is referring to the actual library Faustus Sulla possessed in his Cuman villa.[55] In an analogous way, we can easily reject Usener's remark that Apellicon's Aristotelian collection was unsuited to a country house and so was probably conserved in Rome, and that the library Cicero mentions in his epistle must therefore be a smaller one which Sulla kept in Cumae.[56] This assumption is a gratuitous speculation which finds no support in our

---

[48] Cicero alludes to Pompey and Crassus when he says *in istorum sella curuli* (on their curule chair), and then only to Crassus when he says *cum eo* (with him). For these identifications and the related problems, see the commentary of Shackleton Bailey 1965–70: II 194–6.
[49] 'who I see I have to stroll with'.   [50] See App. *B Civ.* 1.104.
[51] Thus Münzer 1900c: 1516.   [52] See Plut. *Cic.* 27.6; *Reg. et Imp. Apophth., Cic.* 13.205C.
[53] For Faustus' biography, see Münzer 1900c, or the more concise note in *BNP* III 185.
[54] See e.g. *Top.* 1; *Div.* 2.8; *Fin.* 3.7; *Att.* 1.7; 4.5.3; *Q Fr.* 3.4.5. Cf. Dix 2000: 454 n. 43: 'Cicero uses *bibliotheca* of his entire collection of books, wherever housed; in the case of the smaller units of that collection housed within individual residences, he uses *bibliotheca* primarily of the room which housed the books'.
[55] This is also the opinion of D'Arms 1970: 30–2; Rawson 1985: 41, and Canfora 1986a: 65.
[56] See Usener 1913–14 III 153 (quoted and refuted in Moraux 1973: 45 ff.).

sources, and is only really useful for Usener's theory about the diffusion of Aristotle's works at Rome since 46 BC.

Concluding remarks

The life of libraries in the world of the late Republic was rich and dynamic. Collections like Lucullus' one in Tusculum and Sulla's in Cumae became important points of reference for some of the most active intellectuals of the city. The case of Cicero is maybe the most eloquent, as it shows us how influential the *social* connections underlying *intellectual* networks were in the *cultural* exploitation of libraries. More 'peripheral' writers like Philodemus[57] took part in philosophical and moral debates whose textual references were the same as those discussed by urban circles. The different parts of central and southern Italy were in any case connected by dense networks of contact, and especially by the mobility of individuals. Lucretius himself, who was an active and orthodox Epicurean, could be supposed to aim at integrating his physical teaching into this context, although the obscurity of his biography makes the question very difficult to answer.[58] However, the influence of libraries on such sophisticated writers should not be underestimated. They were both a resource for bibliographical research and a meeting point for curious intellectuals.

From this analysis we might draw the conclusion that a careful focus on *material culture* is always necessary when one considers the spread of philosophical and literary ideas. This is particularly true of classical antiquity, where the circulation of ideas was heavily determined – and often obstructed – by material media. After all, the lesson of historical materialism remains central to the work of classical scholars, at least as far as the practical organisation of cultures is concerned. In this respect, libraries need to be taken particularly seriously, as their very presence on a territory had the potential to change the course of textual tradition and ultimately the contents and nature of cultural life.

---

[57] In fact Philodemus' peripheral condition was more geographic than cultural: since, as Gigante 1990: 43–5 states, he aimed at Rome in spite of his living in Herculaneum. His influence on the Roman intellectual generations who lived between the late Republic and the Augustan age was significant.

[58] I discuss Lucretius' case in more detail in Tutrone 2006.

10 | Ashes to ashes? The library of Alexandria after 48 BC

MYRTO HATZIMICHALI

Introduction

The starting point and chronological framework for this chapter is provided by an especially celebrated episode in the history of ancient libraries, namely the fire that is said to have consumed the library of Alexandria in 48 BC, as a result of Caesar's actions during the Alexandrian War. Public interest and scholarly debate have concentrated on the various reports alleging the dramatic demise of the Alexandrian library, often at the expense of other factors that, as I will argue, played an equally if not more important role in the library's fate after 48 BC. It is not hard to see why the story of the fire receives so much attention. Its sentimental appeal is strongly connected with the sense of deprivation that inevitably accompanies the realisation that the surviving part of ancient literature is but a tiny fraction of what was actually produced. Within the history of classical scholarship, this realisation was reflected in the gradual transition during the Renaissance from hopeful searches for complete texts in European libraries towards collections of fragments, remnants of a 'literary shipwreck', in Politian's words.[1] The fire at the Alexandrian library thus began to be treated as a significant factor for this shipwreck, resulting in much nostalgic speculation on what might have been if the library had survived. In recent years this type of speculation has been called into question, notably by Bagnall, who drew attention to the gaps and contradictions that abound in the ancient and mediaeval reports on the Alexandrian library, its fate and its size. He also pointed out that the decline of the library was due to lack of sustained management and maintenance, rather than to a single dramatic event.[2] Similarly, the loss of so many classical texts is more the result of neglect and failure to make fresh copies from decaying books across the Greco-Roman world and over many centuries, rather than the outcome of the demise of one single library, however great.

These critical warnings call for a more nuanced approach to the fate of the Alexandrian library from the mid-first century BC onwards. It is not

---

[1] For these developments, see Dionisotti 1997: 21–30. [2] Bagnall 2002.

simply a case of destruction and crippling aftermath, but a more complex tale of continuity and change, one that raises questions of intellectual history and cultural development, and demands consideration of additional factors besides the fire. In this chapter, therefore, I will first examine briefly the ancient evidence on which we have to rely regarding the events of 48 BC, in order to evaluate the implications of the ancient narrative that provokes so much debate and speculation about the library's fate. In the main part of the chapter I will bring under consideration further factors that impacted upon the status of the Alexandrian library after the postulated watershed of 48 BC. These factors emerge mainly from an examination of the activity and achievements of intellectuals who worked in the library, a more promising path of inquiry into the library's history given the scarcity and the often controversial nature of direct references to the library and its material holdings, brought into sharp relief by Bagnall.[3]

I will be concentrating here on intellectuals who specialised in the study of Greek language and literature, both for reasons of brevity and because they are the ones who are particularly and explicitly associated with the library in our sources.[4] The focus will be on the way interests and methods evolved and took shape in the late first century BC, in comparison to those of the great scholars who were active during the heyday of the Alexandrian library in the third and second centuries BC. This almost mechanical reference to 'great scholars' of the more remote past already implies a value judgment working against the people to be discussed in what follows, and reflects a modern consensus that denies them much originality and intellectual acumen. But I will try not to linger on such value judgments, and to concentrate instead on what we can learn about the role of the Alexandrian library for intellectual life in the latter half of the first century BC from the work that was done during that period, even (and perhaps especially) from its derivative nature.

Fire and aftermath

Turning first to the evidence concerning the destructive fire, we should recall that in the period in question Caesar had gone to Egypt following the assassination of Pompey and became involved in the fight for the throne between Cleopatra and her younger brother Ptolemy XIII, taking sides

---

[3] The promising nature of this more positive line of inquiry is sketched out by Bagnall, too; see Bagnall 2002: 360–1.
[4] For other aspects of Alexandrian intellectual life in the first century BC, and philosophy in particular, see Hatzimichali 2011: 25–66.

against the latter. At some point in the course of the hostilities Caesar and his men were surrounded in the area of the royal palace, while Ptolemy's navy in the royal harbour was threatening to cut off any hope they had for assistance from the sea. Caesar thus took the decisive action that was required by the gravity of the situation, as he says himself (*Civ.* 3.111), and burnt all of Ptolemy's ships. From other sources we learn that the fire accidentally spread from the ships that were stationed in the harbour onto buildings near the sea, eventually destroying the library. The strongest report to this effect is found in Plutarch's *Life of Caesar*, where it is unequivocally stated that the great library was destroyed.[5]

Then he was first in danger of having his water supply cut off; for the channels were blocked up by the enemies. Secondly, as there was an attempt to cut him off from his navy, he was forced to fend off the danger by means of fire (διὰ πυρός), which spread from the dockyards and destroyed the great library (τὴν μεγάλην βιβλιοθήκην ἐκ τῶν νεωρίων ἐπινεμόμενον διέφθειρε). (Plut. *Caes.* 49.6–7)

The significance of Plutarch's testimony depends to a large extent on what one thinks about the setup and location of the library, which is not altogether certain. On the most plausible interpretation, the library would have consisted of a space with niches for shelves, as well as colonnades where the books could be consulted. Most importantly, these spaces formed part of the Museum complex, the famous institution of Ptolemaic Alexandria, where scholars would gather for common meals and lectures. This close spatial association between Museum and library is supported by both Greek and Egyptian parallels of book-collections within the complex of a temple or shrine. The main Greek parallels are Aristotle's Lyceum, which also included a shrine to the Muses on its premises, and the Pergamene library, located by some archaeologists in the sanctuary of Athena. From Egypt one may point to the Ramesseum at Thebes, among other examples.[6] The same spatial association is suggested by a frustrating reference in Athenaeus' *Deipnosophists*: 'on the number of books, the setting up of book stacks and their collection in the Museum what is there to say when all of this is well-known?' (Ath. 5.203e). We know further from Strabo that the Museum itself

---

[5] Plutarch goes on to describe how Caesar strove to rescue some private papers (his βιβλίδια) from the waters, while swimming to safety from his sunken dinghy (*Caes.* 49.5–8). For this interesting contrast effected by Plutarch between neglect for the great library and care for the private papers, see Zadorojnyi 2005: 133.

[6] See further Thompson 2008: 69–71; Canfora 1989: 77–82; Delia 1992: 1,450–6. On Egyptian temples, see in particular Ryholt (this volume). Regarding the Pergamene library, some serious doubts are cast on the traditional interpretation of the archaeological evidence by Coqueugniot (this volume).

was in the royal quarter, which was alongside the Great Harbour and thus not immune to a large and fast-spreading fire from the sea.[7]

In order to maintain that the library did not suffer any substantial damage, one would have to claim, as Canfora does,[8] that the palace walls surrounding the royal quarter offered sufficient protection and thus the fire did not proceed very far.[9] Support for the view that there was little or no damage to the library is sometimes sought in Dio, who speaks of 'storage-places' and puts books on a par with grain:

From this point onwards there were many battles between them, both during the day and by night. Many things were set fire to, with the result that the dockyard and the storage-places were burnt, both those of grain and of books (τάς τε ἀποθήκας καὶ τοῦ σίτου καὶ τῶν βίβλων καυθῆναι); the latter were very numerous and most excellent (πλείστων δὴ καὶ ἀρίστων), as they say. (Cass. Dio 42.38)

This may be taken to suggest that what was destroyed was in fact depots containing goods intended for export, or at any rate separate auxiliary storehouses near the dockyards. However, the word I have awkwardly translated as 'storage-places' (ἀποθῆκαι) can refer both to storehouses and to storerooms within a larger building or complex. The same expression is used by Lucian (*Ind.* 5) for the uneducated collector's book-cases. Moreover, Dio's superlatives on the number and quality of these books, read in conjunction with the information from our other sources that mention very high numbers, do suggest that Alexandria's book resources suffered a significant blow during the Alexandrian War.[10] There are good reasons for thinking

---

[7] Strabo 17.1.8: 'The Museum is also a part of the royal palaces; it has a public walk and an *exhedra* [an open recess or alcove with seating], and a large house in which the common meals of the learned men who are members of the Museum take place. This group have a common budget and there is a priest in charge of the Museum, appointed back then by the kings, but now by Caesar'.

[8] Canfora 1989: 69–70.

[9] See, however, Cherf 2008 for a survey of the circumstances at the Alexandrian harbour at the time of Caesar's desperate act of arson (dry weather, strong winds, highly combustible materials stored near the shore). Cherf concludes that they would have resulted in an extremely fast-spreading and destructive 'firestorm', comparable to the Great Chicago Fire of 1871.

[10] The following references to the fire are also recorded, yet they should be considered with Bagnall's cautionary remarks in mind concerning the exact figures: Caes. *B Civ.* 3.111 (Caesar was forced to set fire to the ships); Luc. 10.497–503 (the fire spread to buildings near the sea); Sen. *De tranq. anim.* 9.4–5 (40,000 books were destroyed); Amm. Marc. 22.12–13 (700,000 books were burnt – he locates two libraries at the Serapeum); Gell. 7.17.3 (70,000 or 700,000 books – the MSS offer the variant readings *septuaginta* and *septingenta* – were accidentally burnt by auxiliary soldiers); Oros. *Historiarum adversum paganos* 6.15.31 (400,000 books stored in buildings close to the sea were burnt). See also El-Abbadi 1992.

that the specific numbers reported in the sources are not to be trusted.[11] But we may hold on to the notion of a substantial destruction of what was considered an impressively large number of books according to the various sources that report the catastrophe (from Seneca, first century AD to Orosius, fourth–fifth century AD). I am therefore inclined to follow Fraser's tentative conclusion that 'the Mouseion building may have been damaged and the books therein at least seriously diminished'.[12]

It is, then, legitimate to treat Caesar's actions and their unintended consequences as a historical factor with an impact on the status of the Alexandrian library in the second half of the first century BC from the point of view of its material resources. At the same time, there are arguments against following the more extreme version of the ancient narrative and speaking of the 'end' of the library.[13] In fact, the clearest indication for continuing library provision in Alexandria even after 48 BC is the activity of scholars and authors who worked in the Egyptian capital from that period onwards. The scope of their work and the range of earlier authors that they were able to call upon indicate that they still had access to a considerable wealth of books.

The idea of partial destruction requires a cautious approach to the material aspects of library provision after 48 BC, because we have very little explicit information on which books were lost. At best we may speculate that the books most at risk of being entirely lost to posterity were those that could not be easily replaced from copies held elsewhere. These may have included lengthy learned treatises produced in the context of the library and unsuitable for broader circulation, or old and rare books that Alexandrian scholars had used as sources, often collected from different parts of the Greek world, and thus difficult to replace. El-Abbadi looked to Strabo for some evidence of books once held by the library that were not available by the time of Strabo's visit to Egypt in late 20s BC:[14]

Eratosthenes takes up all these facts as established through the testimonies of people who have been to these places, because he has consulted many treatises, which were readily available to him since he had access to a library as great (ὧν εὐπόρει βιβλιοθήκην ἔχων τηλικαύτην) as Hipparchus himself says. (Strabo 2.1.5)

---

[11] See Bagnall 2002: 351–6 who, however, may be underestimating the substantial growth of holdings after the third century BC from the point of view of works produced by scholars working in the library (which were often very voluminous), rather than acquired externally through special royal initiatives.
[12] Fraser 1972: 335; thus also Cherf 2008: 72–3.
[13] Of the ancient sources only Plutarch speaks of the library itself being destroyed, all others referring to numbers of books burnt.
[14] El-Abbadi 1992:177.

The implication would be that Strabo is reduced to speculation about possible authors consulted by Eratosthenes, unable to verify the sources for himself. We might be inclined to take this as an ironic comment (insinuating that these treatises were a figment of Eratosthenes' imagination), given the highly critical attitude displayed by Strabo towards the great third-century librarian. However, in this particular context Strabo is defending Eratosthenes against Hipparchus' charge that he relied on only one source.

A more crucial factor in the case of such old treatises and rare books is that they were probably decaying or lost even before the fire of 48 BC, given the humid climate of Alexandria and the lack of conservation techniques. The damage done by the fire, though not critical, may have served to heighten the consciousness of this loss, in ways not dissimilar to the repeated modern tendency to associate the fire with the loss of so many ancient texts (see above). Yun Lee Too recently drew attention to the importance of narratives in constructing the 'idea' of the ancient library out of separate collections of texts, whereby origins, lineage and fate play a key role.[15] In the Alexandrian library's narrative, destruction, loss and efforts towards reparation quickly became key motifs;[16] this must have had an impact on how intellectuals after 48 BC viewed themselves and their work vis-à-vis their predecessors.

Beyond the fire: post-Hellenistic intellectual trends

As suggested above, there are important considerations other than material damage that played a part in determining the status and prestige of the library in the second half of the first century BC. From a historical perspective, these include the demise of Ptolemaic monarchy after 30 BC, when Alexandria and all its institutions were placed under Roman control. Roman emperors did display an interest in the Museum and library of Alexandria, at least from an administrative point of view, but the nature of royal patronage for the library and its high-flying intellectuals must have undergone significant adjustments. For prominent scholars this meant a change from a close association with a ruler resident a few blocks away (an association often involving tutorship of the royal princes, see below), to a system of remote intervention in the form of appointments to the priesthood of the Museum.[17]

---

[15] Too 2010: 19–49, esp. 31–40.
[16] See, for example, the report that Antony presented Cleopatra with 200,000 volumes from the Pergamene library (Plut. *Ant.* 58–9).
[17] Strabo 17.1.8, *IG* XIV 1085.

A further consideration regarding the role of the library after 48 BC comes from an argument from silence, namely that we do not know of any prominent scholar who was head librarian during this period.[18] The absence of references to a librarian cannot be simply because there were no scholars important enough, and it is also hard to ascribe it to Hellenistic bias on the part of sources such as the *Suda* which contains many Roman-period intellectuals without calling them librarians; some key examples are discussed below. Didymus is a case in point: he was active up to the Augustan period and is referred to as 'the great' in the biographical tradition reflected in the *Suda* (s.v. Apion, α 3215), yet there is no information that he was librarian. In fact the latest datable librarian seems to be Onesander of Paphos in the 80s BC, a priest favoured by Ptolemy IX (we know of him from an inscription, *OGIS* 172),[19] who does not seem to have been of any scholarly distinction. By contrast, all the most important scholars of the third and second centuries BC, with the exception of Callimachus, are known to have presided over the library. The post of librarian in the case of these scholars often went hand-in-hand with that of tutor to the royal princes (see below on Zenodotus). The evidence for a Hellenistic 'succession' of librarians comes from a list preserved on a second-century AD papyrus from Oxyrhynchus, among other lists of 'famous men' and other historical and mythological information in summary form (*POxy* X 1241). The text emphasises the succession line from one famous scholar to the next (διεδέξατο, 'succeeded' col. ii l.6), and makes reference to the tutorship of royal princes (col. ii l. 4–5 and 13–15).[20] Similar information may be obtained from the biographical information on Alexandrian scholars preserved by the *Suda*, from which I quote the entry on Zenodotus as an example:[21]

Zenodotus of Ephesus (third century BC), author of epic verse and grammarian, pupil of Philetas, active at the time of the first Ptolemy. He became the first to produce a critical edition of Homer, and headed the libraries at Alexandria (τῶν

---

[18] For a possible exception in Dionysius the son of Glaucus (*Suda* δ 1173), see Bowie (this volume).

[19] The inscription reads τεταγμένον δὲ ἐπὶ τῆς ἐν Ἀλεξανδρείαι μεγάλης βυβλιοθήκης εὐνοίας [ἕνεκεν], 'appointed to the great library at Alexandria on account of favour'.

[20] The papyrus lists the names of Apollonius of Rhodes, Eratosthenes, Aristophanes of Byzantium, Apollonius ὁ εἰδογράφος ('the classifier of genres'), Aristarchus and Cydas ἐκ τῶν λογχοφόρων ('one of the spearmen'), all belonging to the third and second centuries BC. On this text, see also Pfeiffer 1968: 154; van Rossum-Steenbeek 1997: 137–9 and 322–3.

[21] Zenodotus' name is thought to have been mentioned in *POxy* X 1241 towards the end of col. i, which is mutilated. For other similar *Suda* entries, see α 3892 on Aristarchus and α 3419 on Apollonius and Eratosthenes.

ἐν Ἀλεξανδρείᾳ βιβλιοθηκῶν προῦστη), and educated the sons of Ptolemy (τοὺς παῖδας Πτολεμαίου ἐπαίδευσεν). (*Suda* ζ 74)

The lack of any distinguished librarian with royal connections after 48 BC suggests that the library had lost some of its prominence, particularly in terms of patronage and political clout.

It is now time to turn towards some of the scholars active in Alexandria in the late first century BC, following in the footsteps of the librarians of the third and second centuries, and to ask what alternative ways they had for a rise to fame and fortune, if the librarianship was not the obvious mark of distinction any more. One answer immediately suggests itself if we look at the biographical information on Philoxenus, who was an Alexandrian active in the Augustan period, but who practised his craft in Rome:

Philoxenus of Alexandria. Grammarian, who taught (ἐσοφίστευσεν) in Rome. [He wrote] *On Monosyllabic Verbs* (Περὶ μονοσυλλάβων ῥημάτων); *On the Critical Signs in the Iliad*; *On -mi Verbs*; *On Reduplication*; *On Metres*; *On the Syracusan Dialect*; *On Greek Usage* (Περὶ ἑλληνισμοῦ), 6 books; *On Conjugations*; *On Rare Words* (Περὶ γλωσσῶν), 5 books; *On Rare Words in Homer*; *On the Laconian Dialect*; *On the Ionic Dialect*; and so on. (*Suda* φ 394)

Emigrating to Rome and teaching there was a lucrative and attractive option as we will see in the case of other scholars too. Perhaps Rome's cultural and financial resources represented a competitive challenge that seriously undermined the Alexandrian library's claims to be *the* intellectual centre of gravity in the Mediterranean world. During the Hellenistic period Alexandria exercised a certain amount of centripetal power as far as scholarly mobility was concerned, with intellectuals travelling to and from other centres such as Athens, Rhodes, Pergamum (the main competitor) as well as Sicily (in the cases of Archimedes and Theocritus). Rome's transformation into an international cultural centre gained momentum especially after the Mithridatic War and the subsequent sack of Athens in 87–86 BC, when resources poured into the Italian capital through war booty, in the form of books, artefacts and skilled personnel.[22]

Returning to Philoxenus, we can see that the increasing importance of Rome was felt in his scholarship too, as he was concerned to show that Latin was originally an Aeolic dialect, and offered some admittedly questionable etymologies in order to prove it. This may be seen from the following

---

[22] On books as war booty, see the chapters by Affleck and Tutrone (this volume); for the effects of the Mithridatic War more generally, see Rawson 1985: 7–18, 69–70; Strabo 12.3.11.

fragments, which are thought to come from a separate treatise *On the dialect of the Romans* (Περὶ τῆς τῶν Ῥωμαίων διαλέκτου):[23]

(i) As Philoxenus says, the reason is that dual forms are later in origin; for duals were conceived of later. This is why not every dialect has the dual – the Aeolians have no dual forms at all, just like the Romans do not, who are Aeolian colonists (ἄποικοι ὄντες τῶν Αἰολέων). (Choerob. *in Theod.* 34.6–9 = fr. 323 Theodorides)

(ii) *nepos*: the 'new son' (νέος παῖς); this is how the grandson is called and it has a Greek etymology (ἐξ Ἑλληνικῆς ἐτυμολογίας) as Philoxenus has rightly pointed out. (Lyd. *Mag.* 1.42 = fr. 328 Theodorides)

The list of titles attributed to Philoxenus is indicative of another intellectual trend that was characteristic of this period of Greek scholarship and points to a shift of the library towards a more peripheral role. I am referring to the increasing dominance of what may be called formal grammar over text-based studies such as critical editions and commentaries. Earlier scholars may have dealt with difficult grammatical forms etc., but this was in order to solve *ad hoc* problems encountered, for instance, in establishing the correct Homeric text.[24] By Philoxenus' time we find systematic attempts at the construction of rules applicable to entire paradigms of declension and conjugation,[25] aimed at 'a fully fledged description of the morphology of Greek'.[26] Philoxenus' trademark contributions to this field of research consisted of observations on word-formation and etymology, and were characterised by a tendency to derive most Greek words from monosyllabic verbal stems (note his work *On Monosyllabic Verbs* in the *Suda* entry cited above).

This interest in global studies of various aspects of the Greek language is also evident in what we know about the work of Philoxenus' contemporary Tryphon:

---

[23] The title is cited explicitly at frs. 311–22 Theodorides. This connection between Greeks and Romans is not original to Philoxenus, but he added his own scholarly grammatical legitimatisation to it. The idea that the Romans' ancestors were in fact Greek and that the Aeolic dialect was disseminated in Italy and spoken even by Romulus is ascribed to Cato the Elder himself (D.H. 1.11.1; Varro fr. 295 Funaioli). See also Hogg this volume, and Ascheri 2011, esp. 65–71.

[24] See, for example, Aristarchus' interventions at Sch. *Il.* 1.114a, 5.269c[1], 11.454b[1]; A.D. *Pron.* 109.20. These matters are discussed fully by Matthaios 1999. See also Callanan 1987 for Aristophanes of Byzantium.

[25] Schenkeveld 1994: 281–3.

[26] Kemp 1991: 303; see also Morgan 1998: 160–2 for this development.

Tryphon, son of Ammonius, from Alexandria. Grammarian and poet. He lived in the time of Augustus, and earlier. [He wrote] *On Pleonasm in the Aeolic Dialect*, 7 books; *On the dialects in Homer, Simonides, Pindar, Alcman and the other lyric poets; On the dialect of the Greeks* (Περὶ τῆς Ἑλλήνων διαλέκτου) *and of the Argives, the people of Himera and Rhegium, the Dorians and Syracusans; On Analogy in the Oblique Cases* (Περὶ τῆς ἐν κλίσεσιν ἀναλογίας), 1 book; *On Analogy in the Nominative; On Comparative Words*, 1 book; *On Analogy in Monosyllables; On the Characters of Nouns*, 1 book; *On Analogy in Barytone Verbs*, 1 book; *On enclitic verbs, and infinitives, imperatives, optatives* and in brief all the moods; *On Orthography and problems therein; On breaths and tropes;* and more. (*Suda* τ 1115)

Tryphon is not known to have written any commentaries or monographs on literary criticism, and the titles cited by the *Suda* reveal a range of interests often overlapping with those of Philoxenus. These include detecting analogical patterns, classifying dialectal divergences and establishing normative rules (Apollonius Dyscolus speaks of rules formulated or clarified by Tryphon).[27] The pioneering value of Tryphon's work in dialectology is demonstrated by the titles listed above, which indicate that he made the distinction between 'literary' and 'spoken' dialects, as well as between general Greek usage and local dialects,[28] in both cases revealing a strong interest in Doric.

What is, then, the relationship between these types of study in formal grammar and dialectology and the Alexandrian library? On the one hand, the library must have provided the resources, in the form of scholarly treatises by predecessors whom we know to have been interested in rare dialectal words[29] as well as in establishing the correct grammatical form for problematic words found in literary texts. Source-material for scholars like Philoxenus and Tryphon would of course include the literary texts themselves, also to be found in the library. On the other hand, this new type of work had a strong orientation moving away from the library. As Morgan has shown, treatises specifying and advocating correct general Greek usage through the application of systematic grammatical rules were primarily targeted at advanced elite learners across the Greco-Roman world, aiming to deepen and solidify the understanding of authoritative forms of Greek language.[30] By contrast, earlier Alexandrian achievements in textual

---

[27] ἀποφαινόμενον τὸν προκείμενον κανόνα, 'setting forth the rule in question', A.D. *Adv.* 167.24–5.

[28] The *On the dialect of the Greeks* was probably a separate treatise identifiable with the *On Greek usage* (Περὶ ἑλληνισμοῦ) that we hear about in other sources, see Velsen 1853: 71–5.

[29] These may have included Callimachus' collection of dialectal words in his *Words of different peoples* (Ἐθνικαὶ Ὀνομασίαι, fr. 406 Pfeiffer 1949) and the *Words from Laconia* by Aristophanes of Byzantium (Λακωνικαὶ Γλῶσσαι, frr. 348–53 Slater 1986).

[30] See Morgan 1998: 162–89.

criticism, literary commentary, canon formation, colometry etc. were motivated by the drive to organise and establish the library's contents, even in those cases where this work achieved broader dissemination beyond the library.[31] In the period under consideration here, we observe a change in the focus of our grammarians' work; it is not so much on the library and its contents any more, but on the needs of the community 'outside', whether in Egypt, Rome or elsewhere. Thus we may add contemporary educational needs to the factors that contributed towards the Alexandrian library's loss of its undisputed status as intellectual focal point.

Another innovative feature of the period after 48 BC may be detected in the work of Theon, who was also from Alexandria and must have at least started his career there. His work crucially included commentaries on the Hellenistic poets, whereas up to his time all scholarly attention was drawn towards authors of the archaic and classical periods: we have explicit references to his commentaries on Nicander, Theocritus, Lycophron, Callimachus and perhaps also Apollonius of Rhodes.[32] Theon was thus instrumental in altering the canon of texts that represented the most significant holdings of the Alexandrian library. His influence is best appreciated if we recall Too's account of the library as a body of books that are canonically selected and preserved for posterity,[33] and now have been significantly expanded. The fact that Theon too was probably active in Rome in the Augustan period (based on the *Suda*'s information on his successor Apion)[34] invites the suggestion that his work may have had an influence on the literary tastes of Roman authors at the time, and on the nature of their access to Greek literature.

The weight of tradition: Didymus and meta-scholarship

Thus far I have discussed innovations and new areas of interest among scholars who spent at least some of their career after 48 BC studying and working in the library of Alexandria. I have tried to show how their lives

---

[31] The extent to which scholarly work from the library reached broader audiences is a contested issue; Cameron 1995: 24–70 reviews and challenges the image of the 'ivory tower', particularly as far as the poetry of authors such as Callimachus is concerned.

[32] I list *exempli gratia* the following references to Theon's commentaries: 'Theon in his commentary on Theocritus', *Et. Gud.* γ 323; 'Theon in his commentary on Lycophron', St. Byz. 176b; 'Theon in his commentary on *Aetia* I by Callimachus', *Et. Gen.* α 1316; 'Nicander in the *Theriaca* [...] and Theon and Plutarch who wrote a commentary on him', St. Byz. 166.

[33] Too 2010: 49.

[34] 'Apion, the son of Pleistonicus [...] taught in Rome under the emperors Tiberius and Claudius; he was the successor of Theon the grammarian and a contemporary of Dionysius of Halicarnassus', *Suda* α 3215.

and works reflect changes in the status and outlook of that great institution, coinciding with the aftermath of what must have been a sobering reminder that their heritage was not immune to calamity and destruction. I will now move on to another feature that can help us understand the nature of scholarly activity after 48 BC, looking more closely at the way in which its exponents engaged with the tradition and legacy established by their illustrious predecessors.

The field in which this engagement can be most fruitfully explored is that of Homeric scholarship, particularly textual criticism, where Aristarchus of Samothrace (second century BC) remained the most influential figure throughout antiquity. The marginal notes (scholia) that accompany the text of Homer in several mediaeval manuscripts offer much information on his work, but we also learn that this information was mediated through other authors, including two, Aristonicus and Didymus, who were active in the Augustan period. Our information comes from the following passage, which appears in more or less the same form at the end of most books of the *Iliad* in the 'Venetus A' manuscript (Venice, Biblioteca Marciana, gr. 822, tenth century):

παράκειται τὰ Ἀριστονίκου σημεῖα καὶ τὰ Διδύμου περὶ τῆς Ἀρισταρχείου διορθώσεως. τινὰ δὲ καὶ ἐκ τῆς Ἰλιακῆς προσῳδίας Ἡρωδιανοῦ καὶ ἐκ τοῦ Νικάνορος περὶ τῆς Ὁμηρικῆς στιγμῆς.

The text is accompanied by Aristonicus' *Critical Signs* and Didymus' *On the Aristarchean recension*. There is also some material from Herodian's *Iliadic Prosody* and from Nicanor's *On Homeric Punctuation*.

Aristonicus, who also enjoyed a career in Rome,[35] wrote *On critical signs*, explaining the use and meaning of signs such as the *obelos* (–) or the *diple* (>), which had been placed in the margin of copies of the Homeric text by scholars such as Aristarchus. We can thus detect an effort to systematise and make earlier achievements more accessible to the learned public of the late first century BC. Aristonicus' concern with the history of his discipline and the tradition of Alexandrian scholarship is also evident in the fact that he wrote a work entitled *On the Alexandrian Museum* (Περὶ τοῦ ἐν Ἀλεξανδρείᾳ Μουσείου, Phot. *Bibl.* 161. 104b 40), probably discussing its most famous representatives.

---

[35] The *Suda* (π 3036) says of him and his father Ptolemy that ἄμφω ἐπεδείκνυντο ἐν Ῥώμῃ ('they both taught at Rome'). See also West 2001: 46–7.

I have now come to the most important, certainly the most prolific, scholar of this period, Didymus 'with the brazen guts', on whom we have the following anecdotal information:

(i) Didymus, son of Didymus the fishmonger, an Aristarchean grammarian (γραμματικὸς Ἀριστάρχειος). He was from Alexandria and lived at the time of Antony and Cicero, and until Augustus. He was nicknamed 'brazen-gutted' (Χαλκέντερος) because of his perseverance with regard to books (διὰ τὴν περὶ τὰ βιβλία ἐπιμονήν); for they say that he wrote more than 3,500 books. (*Suda*, δ 872)
(ii) Didymus the grammarian – Demetrius of Troezen calls him 'book-forgetter' (βιβλιολάθαν) because of the number of books he published; for there are 3,500 of them. (Ath. 4.139c)[36]

The most spectacular report about Didymus, which gave rise to his nicknames, has to do with the sheer volume of his output, which alone can serve as evidence for the presence of rich library resources in Alexandria until the Augustan period.[37] Didymus wrote commentaries on a large number of classical authors (from Homer and Pindar to Demosthenes), several lexicographical works, as well as a sympotic miscellany (the latter is cited by Stephanus of Byzantium, 314.6). He cites a very wide range of earlier authors, including earlier grammarians and literary texts, as well as biographers and authors of local Attic history (in the case of his commentary on Demosthenes), since he had stronger historical, biographical and prosopographical interests than his predecessors.[38] Thus in a way Didymus' production was a repository of all previous Hellenistic scholarship, often functioning as the link in the transmission onto our late antique and mediaeval sources.

Didymus must have been conscious of his role as an heir and transmitter of earlier scholarship, as far as we can judge from his emphasis on his connection with and continuation of the Alexandrian tradition. He is called 'Aristarchean' in the *Suda* entry cited above, a characterisation which is highly uncommon in our sources and therefore may have been Didymus' self-representation. He was keen to point out an official Aristarchean 'lineage' in Alexandria, by saying that there was a 'school' of Aristarchus where

---

[36] Quintilian (*Inst.* 1.8.20) relates how Didymus condemned a story as being absurd (*vana*), only for one of his own books to be produced, containing the story in question.
[37] Despite the fact that our two sources agree on the figure of 3,500 books (Seneca, *Ep.* 88.37 mentions 4,000), it is still most likely an exaggeration; as Harding 2006: 1–2 points out, Didymus would have had to produce two books per week throughout a putative working career of forty years! We should retain the idea that Didymus was reputed for his extraordinarily large output.
[38] See Harding 2006: 20–39.

the latter was succeeded by Ammonius and eventually (one may infer) by Didymus himself:

'ἀθετητέον τοὺς τρεῖς στίχους, εἴ τι χρὴ πιστεύειν Ἀμμωνίῳ τῷ διαδεξαμένῳ τὴν σχολήν, ἐν τῷ Περὶ τοῦ μὴ γεγονέναι πλείονας ἐκδόσεις τῆς Ἀρισταρχείου διορθώσεως τοῦτο φάσκοντι [. . .]'. ταῦτα ὁ Δίδυμος περὶ τῶν στίχων τούτων.

'These three lines must be athetised, if we are to trust Ammonius who inherited the school, when he says so in his work *On there not having been many editions of the Aristarchean recension* [. . .]'. This is what Didymus has to say about these lines. (Sch. *Il* 10.397–9a.)[39]

Under these circumstances, it is particularly telling that Didymus chose to write a work specifically *about* Aristarchus' text of Homer (*On the Aristarchean recension*, see above in the extract from the Venetian manuscript), apart from his own commentaries on the *Iliad* and *Odyssey*. The purpose of this work was to report on and explain the readings put forward in Aristarchus' edition (which were not always readily available, as Didymus' reliance on Ammonius indicates), and not to conduct new independent research on the text. This account of the nature of Didymus' activity does not support West's thesis that it was Didymus who collated several manuscripts or sought information on different readings from multiple sources.[40] As a result, there is no compelling reason for thinking that books which had come to Alexandria before the second century BC from all over the Mediterranean, such as the copies of Homer from Massilia, Sinope and Cyprus, were still available in Didymus' time.[41] The following comments on *Il*. 1.423–4 ('for Zeus went yesterday to Oceanus, to the blameless Ethiopians for a feast') are central to the debate on these texts:

λέξις Ἀριστάρχου ἐκ τοῦ Α τῆς Ἰλιάδος ὑπομνήματος, 'τὸ μὲν μετ' ἀμύμονας ἐπ' ἀμύμονας, ὅ ἐστι πρὸς ἀμώμους, ἀγαθούς, τὸ δὲ κατὰ δαῖτα ἀντὶ τοῦ ἐπὶ δαῖτα· οὕτως γὰρ νῦν Ὅμηρος τέθεικεν. [. . .] χρῶνται δὲ καὶ πλείονες ἄλλοι τῶν ποιητῶν τῇ κατά ἀντὶ τῆς ἐπί. [. . .] οὕτως δὲ εὕρομεν καὶ ἐν τῇ Μασσαλιωτικῇ καὶ Σινωπικῇ καὶ Κυπρίᾳ καὶ Ἀντιμαχείῳ καὶ Ἀριστοφανείῳ. Καλλίστρατος δὲ ἐν τῷ Πρὸς τὰς ἀθετήσεις ὁμοίως, καὶ ὁ Σιδώνιος καὶ ὁ Ἰξίων ἐν τῷ ἕκτῳ Πρὸς τὰς ἐξηγήσεις.

A verbatim quotation from Aristarchus' commentary on book 1 of the *Iliad*: 'the expression "among the blameless" means "to the blameless", which in turn means "towards the flawless, the good". The expression "towards a feast" is used instead

---

[39] Cf. also *Suda* α 1641: 'Ammonius from Alexandria, son of Ammonius, an acquaintance of Alexander's; he took over the school of Aristarchus before Augustus became monarch'.
[40] West 2001: 46–85; his views were strongly opposed by Rengakos 2002 and Nagy 2003, esp. 489–501.
[41] For the dating of these texts, see West 2001: 68 with n. 69.

of "for a feast"; for this is how Homer put it on this occasion. [...] Many other poets use the preposition "towards" instead of "for" [...]. *We found* this reading in the versions from Massilia, Sinope and Cyprus and in those of Antimachus and Aristophanes'. Callistratus says the same thing in his *On the atheteses*, and so does (Dionysius) of Sidon and (Demetrius) Ixion in the sixth book of *On the commentaries*. (Sch. Il. 1.423–4)

Much of the controversy turns on the extent of the verbatim quotation and the subject of 'we found' (εὕρομεν): according to West it is Didymus, while Nagy's view that the verbatim quotation from Aristarchus continues past this point seems to me more plausible. Support for the view that Didymus did not here turn to pre-Aristarchean sources may be found in the fact that elsewhere he is ignorant of the background that informs Aristarchus' decisions, e.g.: 'and perhaps there was some reading according to which Homer maintained the standard usage. Otherwise Aristarchus would not have left the matter without comment' (Sch. Il. 16.467c).

What is particularly significant, as far as the role of the Alexandrian library for someone like Didymus is concerned, is that a major shift has occurred and we are now in a period of meta-scholarship: in the early period, the methods of textual criticism, metrical analysis and colometry, bibliography and canon-formation through eradication of spurious works were all developed almost from scratch as a response to the library's needs for good organisation and authoritative, comprehensive representation of Greek culture. By contrast, we notice that now, as Didymus seeks to reconstruct and transmit Aristarchus' Homeric recension, the focus is not any more on these initial concerns that bear directly on the setup of the library, but on the scholarly methods themselves.

Conclusions

In the course of this chapter I have examined a series of factors that marked the transition of the Alexandrian library from dynamic driving force to revered treasury of knowledge: the lure of Rome and developing educational needs encouraged scholars to engage more readily with the world outside the library; the work of Hellenistic poet-scholars was studied alongside the texts *they* worked on and they were assimilated into the catalogue of Greek culture. The books of the library were no longer simply to be endorsed as genuine or rejected as spurious and then arranged and corrected; now they also represented an intellectual heritage that included a tradition of eminent scholarly predecessors whose work had to be taken into account, as well as preserved through the meta-scholarly practices of quotation, commentary, excerption and compilation. These practices were developed and perfected by learned authors from Didymus onwards who, as Jacob has shown particularly for the case of Athenaeus,[42] strove to resemble, emulate and eventually incorporate and replace the library with their own texts.

The fire of 48 BC, even though it did not bring an end to Alexandria's wealth in books, caused material damage and challenged the prevailing narratives of totalising accumulation of knowledge by bringing the threat of large-scale loss of texts into sharp relief. As a result, the need for the preservation and safeguarding of scholarly resources was felt to be all the more pressing. The fire thus emerges as one factor that has to be considered alongside other developments impacting on Alexandrian intellectual life towards the end of the first century BC. These developments tell a story of marginalisation and loss of prestige in some cases, but also of preservation, transformation and progress. As a result, 48 BC cannot be singled out as the date of the Alexandrian library's demise, but it can still function as a helpful conventional benchmark for changes that took place over a longer period of time.

[42] Jacob 2000. See now also Too 2010: 116–42.

11 | The non-Philodemus book collection in the Villa of the Papyri

GEORGE W. HOUSTON

Over the course of the past several decades, papyrologists have made rapid and important advances in our knowledge of the carbonized papyri from the Villa of the Papyri in Herculaneum. Their careful and often spectacular work has produced improved readings, new identifications of texts, and editions of particular works.[1] As has long been known, more than half of the manuscripts found so far contain treatises by Philodemus, a poet, philosopher, and literary critic of the first century BC. Scholarly interest has naturally focused largely, but by no means exclusively, on Philodemus, his texts, and his era, and the collection of book-rolls from the Villa has most often been studied as a collection of the first century BC. In this chapter, I approach the material differently. First, I concentrate on the authors other than Philodemus; and second, I consider the collection primarily as it existed not in the first century BC, but in AD 79, when it was covered by the eruption of Vesuvius.[2]

The chapter is divided into two parts. Part 1 provides an analysis of the non-Philodemus collection and discussions of particular problems and topics that emerge from the manuscripts. The goal is simple: to see what we can learn about this ancient book collection. Part 2 consists of a descriptive catalogue of the manuscripts that contain works by authors other than

---

[1] The rediscovery of and early work on the papyri are described by Sider 2005: 16–23 and 46–57. Recent work is summarized by Janko 2002: 26–30 and set out in detail by Delattre 2007: lvi–cvii, especially xcvii–cvii. My great debt to the many papyrologists who have worked on the Villa materials will be manifest on every page. I would like to thank Keith Dix and William Johnson for reading and commenting on an earlier draft and Peter Parsons and Dirk Obbink for discussing particular aspects of the topic with me.

[2] I omit the Philodemus manuscripts from my primary analysis for several reasons. The works of Philodemus far outnumber those of any other author represented, so that including them distorts our picture of the collection and makes it difficult to define its characteristics. Second, it is reasonable to suppose that the non-Philodemus materials resemble, in some ways, other Roman-era collections of manuscripts that were produced over many years, while the manuscripts of Philodemus are a body apart, written by a single person and for the most part copied within a period of three or four decades. Finally, the manuscripts of Philodemus have been studied extensively already, and catalogues of them are available in, e.g., Delattre 2007: xlviii–lii and Delattre 2006: 76–7 and 137–41. We need not be rigid in drawing these distinctions, however, and we will not lose sight of the manuscripts of Philodemus, which can provide useful comparanda.

Philodemus. So far as I know, this is the first such descriptive catalogue of manuscripts from an ancient library.[3] It consists of a long table, and few will want to read it straight through, but it includes much information that I do not have space to discuss in Part 1, and its contents will convey, I hope, the nature of the manuscripts in this collection far more effectively than any summary can.[4] Taken together, the two parts will provide us with a more detailed look at the contents of an ancient book collection than has previously been possible.

Analysis and discussion of the non-Philodemus collection

Size of the Collection. Marcello Gigante's catalogue of all of the papyri from the Villa, published in 1979, listed 1,826 items; the total was later increased to 1,850 in two supplements.[5] Many of these are not whole papyrus rolls, but parts of rolls or fragments, and it is clear that there were many fewer rolls in the collection than there are *PHerc.* entries in Gigante's catalogue. For example, several of the entries in our catalogue consist of two separate *PHerc.* numbers (thus nos. 17, 28, 34, etc.), and one of the manuscripts of Metrodorus (no. 53) includes no fewer than five *PHerc.* entries. Current estimates of the villa's collection accordingly range from about 700 to "somewhere between 800 and 1,100 books."[6] Some 75 of Gigante's 1,826 items can be positively identified from their *subscriptiones*, and

---

[3] Gigante 1979 is a catalogue of all the papyri found in the Villa, vastly more extensive and detailed than the one presented here. Gigante's catalogue, however, was intended primarily for the use of papyrologists. It is arranged by *PHerc.* (*papyrus Herculanensis*) number, and for each *PHerc.* entry it provides a description of what survives: the number, size, and condition of the fragments, the title if known or conjectured, and full bibliography. The catalogue in this chapter is aimed primarily at scholars interested in library history. It is arranged alphabetically by author and title (like a modern catalogue), and it includes information on each manuscript such as date, scribal hands, possible origin, marginal notes, and possible owners.

[4] The catalogue is necessarily provisional, since new discoveries are being made all the time, and I have no doubt overlooked some items. In addition, we know that the Villa included at least two levels that have not yet been explored, so that more book-rolls may yet be discovered: De Simone and Ruffo 2003: 307–9.

[5] Gigante 1979. Capasso 1989 extended Gigante's catalogue numbers from 1,826 to 1,838, and Del Mastro 2000 added 12 further items, though he did not assign them *PHerc.* numbers, thus bringing the total to 1,850.

[6] The lower figure is from Delattre 2006: 22, the higher from Janko 2000: 4. I believe Delattre's estimates are more likely to be correct. Additional manuscripts may have been stored elsewhere in the Villa, but it is likely that we have most of the philosophical collection that was housed in the Villa in AD 79.

Philodemus is the author of 44, or 58 percent, of them.[7] If we applied this percentage to the whole collection, we would have some 375 to 640 volumes by Philodemus, and 275 to 460 by authors other than Philodemus. The non-Philodemus collection was, then, a significant one, hundreds rather than just a few volumes, but it was not huge and it did not run into the thousands of volumes.[8]

This is useful information, for despite its limitations it is one of the most reliable figures we have for the size of a book collection in the ancient world. Scholars have tended to accept, more or less at face value, such figures as the library of 62,000 volumes that Serenus Sammonicus is said to have owned, and the credibility granted to such numbers has made it easy to believe that the great public libraries of Rome and Alexandria contained hundreds of thousands of volumes.[9] Here, though, we have a library where there was a good motive – an obvious special interest – for making the collection large, and clearly the funds to do so, yet the collection of works by authors other than Philodemus, including Epicurus, seems to have numbered at most some 500 book-rolls (the equivalent of about 100 modern books), and it may have contained significantly fewer.[10] This, taken together with other evidence as it is coming in, suggests that personal collections in the Roman world may ordinarily have numbered a few dozen rolls or even fewer, and

---

[7] The *subscriptio* is the equivalent of a title page. In prose works, it usually gives the name of the author in the genitive and the title of the work in the nominative (or with περὶ plus the genitive), and sometimes additional information: Schironi 2010: 65–9. In extant papyri, such information is usually found at the end of the roll, after the text, hence the term *subscriptio*. Gigante 1979: 45–8 lists the manuscripts from Herculaneum in which the *subscriptio* survives entirely or in part. To his list we may add *PHerc.* 1380, *PHerc.* 1533, and perhaps *PHerc.* 78 (nos. 2, 56, and 65, respectively, in our catalogue).

[8] The number of book rolls that survived the eruption of Vesuvius is somewhat larger than the number that can be counted today because the early excavators at first mistook the carbonized rolls for wooden logs and destroyed them. It is likely that they destroyed several dozen rolls, so our totals could be increased by that many; but that will clearly not affect the counts given here in any significant way.

[9] Limitations in the Villa evidence: some papyri have been lost, and this is a specialized professional collection, not a general collection of Greek and Latin literature. We can, however, make allowances for those problems. Serenus Sammonicus: see e.g. Blanck 1992: 158 and Fedeli 1988: 39, each with some reservations. Serenus and his collection are almost certainly fictional: the figure comes from an unreliable source (the *HA*) and Serenus is otherwise completely unknown. Both Alexandria and the imperial libraries of Rome were probably smaller than most modern estimates would suggest. On Alexandria, see now Bagnall 2002; on the imperial libraries of Rome, see Dix and Houston 2006: 708–9 and Bowie (this volume).

[10] If we add the rolls by Philodemus, we have some 700 to 1,100 book rolls, as we have seen. The possibility remains that the Villa had also, perhaps separately, a collection of Greek and Latin literature. Even if we assumed that that collection was ten times the size of what survives, though, the entire collection in this sumptuous villa would not have numbered more than about 12,000 book rolls.

that personal libraries of more than some hundreds of book rolls were very rare.[11]

Authors and Titles. On the Greek side, the catalogue includes works, all prose, by seven Epicurean writers – Carneiscus, Colotes, Demetrius Laco, Epicurus, Metrodorus of Lampsacus, Polystratus, and Zeno of Sidon – as well as works by the Stoic Chrysippus and perhaps other authors. Epicurus and Demetrius account for roughly two-thirds of the manuscripts (41 of 64 Greek rolls), but the works included cover a wide range of topics and disciplines, reflecting the interests of the Epicureans: there are treatises on literary and textual criticism, music, logic, mathematics, geometry, astronomy, ethics, philosophical problems, and the history of philosophical thought.

Of Epicurus himself, the Villa collection certainly included one or more copies of Books 2, 11, 14, 15, 25, 28, and 34 of his great work *On Nature* (which ran to 37 books), and it is reasonable to suppose that the collection, at least at some point in its history, had one or more copies of each of the 37 books. As scholars have often pointed out, there were duplicate copies of Books 2 and 11, and at least three copies of Book 25.[12] It is possible that the collection included at least one matched set of all 37 books, since four of the surviving manuscripts (nos. 28, 33, 39, and 40) were all copied by Cavallo's scribe no. 1.[13]

What has not been emphasized previously is that *On Nature* is the only one of Epicurus' many works that has been identified in the Villa's collection so far. Diogenes Laertius tells us that Epicurus composed some 40 works, filling 300 book-rolls.[14] Some of those many other works may turn up, of course, but statistically it is very unlikely that the Villa collection included a significant number of Epicurus' other treatises.[15] This is of some interest.

---

[11] There is new evidence from Egypt, where several collections ranging from fewer than ten to a few dozen volumes are known: Houston 2009: 247–50. In the medieval and Renaissance periods, libraries, even famous and well-endowed ones, often numbered just a few hundred codices, and almost never more than 10,000: van Minnen 1998: 100; Dix and Houston 2006: 708 n. 263; and cf. Bagnall 2002: 356.

[12] Sedley 1998: 99–102 suggested that these books were particular favorites.

[13] The fundamental study of the scripts and hands in the Villa's Greek manuscripts is that of Guglielmo Cavallo. He was able to distinguish 34 different hands, which he called "Anonimo I," "Anonimo II," and so on: Cavallo 1983: 45–6. I refer to them as "Scribe no. 1" etc. The hands range in date from the third century BC to roughly the time of Augustus.

[14] Diog. Laert. 10.27–8. Diogenes tends to give round numbers – 300, 400, and the like – so we should not regard his figures as exact, but we can assume that they give a reliable approximate count.

[15] The math, briefly. We have the *subscriptiones* on 13 of the manuscripts of Epicurus. Every one of them identifies the manuscript as coming from the *On Nature*. If we assume (for example) that the collection included fifty rolls from the *On Nature* and fifty rolls containing other

The non-Philodemus book collection 187

We know that copies of at least some of Epicurus' other works were still circulating and sought after in the middle of the first century AD, because several of them are mentioned in a letter from Egypt.[16] Moreover, the later Epicureans clearly valued the letters of the early Epicureans, yet with the exception of one uncertain text there seem to be no papyri in the Villa that preserve letters.[17] The owner of the collection was, it appears, not especially interested in the work of Epicurus except for the *On Nature*.

A similar picture emerges if we look at the other authors represented in the collection. In Book 10 of his *Lives of the Philosophers*, Diogenes Laertius provides a list of what he takes to be the seventeen chief Epicurean writers. Of these, one or more works of only six – Colotes, Demetrius, Epicurus, Metrodorus, Polystratus, and Zeno – have been identified in the Villa papyri so far. Even allowing for future discoveries, the Villa collection can hardly have contained all of the works, or even all of the major works, of the majority of Epicurean writers. Diogenes tells us that Apollodorus alone wrote some 400 rolls and Epicurus 300, lists 22 titles of works by Metrodorus, and characterizes Zeno as a prolific author. We saw above that the Villa collection included some 275 to 460 book rolls by authors other than Philodemus. Given that fact, the collection clearly could not have contained all of Epicurus, Apollodorus, and Zeno, much less all of them plus the works of the other fourteen Epicureans. Gaps, and significant gaps, there must have been. Of all of these writers, Zeno of Sidon is perhaps the greatest mystery. Not only was he prolific, he was also one of Philodemus' own teachers, and we might expect him to be well represented in the Villa library.[18] In short, the Villa collection of Greek texts is a useful reminder

---

works of Epicurus, and that these other manuscripts too had *subscriptiones*, then the odds against our finding thirteen *subscriptiones* from the *On Nature* and no *subscriptiones* from other works are 2 to the 13th power, or 1 chance in 8,192. Of course, there may have been just a few rolls of Epicurus' other works, and that would explain why none of them has been identified yet. But that is the point: there were probably very few rolls from works other than the *On Nature* in this collection.

[16] *P.GettyMus. acc.* 76.AI.57 = Otranto 2000: 17–21; first century AD. The titles probably included *On Justice*, *On Pleasure*, and others now lost in a lacuna. Gigante 1985: 6 noted that we might reasonably have expected the Villa collection to include several of Epicurus' other works, including the three great letters quoted by Diogenes Laertius and the *Canon* mentioned by Diogenes (10.27).

[17] For the Epicurean interest in letters, see Militello 1997: 76. An awareness of the importance of letters goes back to the earliest days of Epicureanism. See, e.g., *POxy.* 76.5077 (forthcoming), probably by Epicurus himself. As for Philodemus, he cites letters of Epicurus to at least 17 correspondents; even if he knew the letters only second hand, the interest in the form is clear. The possible exception I mention in the text is catalogue no. 57.

[18] Dorandi 1997: 48 made the attractive suggestion that the texts of Zeno are not to be found because the compositions of Philodemus himself reproduced, to a considerable degree, the lectures and thought of Zeno.

of a basic fact of book collections: they are selective. Owners make choices. Even in the context of such wealth as is manifest in the Villa of the Papyri, works that we might have expected to find may be absent not because the owner could not afford them but because he did not care to acquire them.

On the Latin side, most of the manuscripts are highly fragmentary, making identifications difficult or impossible, but we clearly have both verse and prose. The verse includes the poem describing the battle of Actium (no. 67), a few scraps of what may be epic (no. 68), and possibly Ennius' *Annales* and a comedy by Caecilius.[19] On the prose side, parts of three orations survive (nos. 69, 70, and 73), there may be part of an historical work in eight or more books (no. 74), and Janko, working primarily from the Oxford *disegni*, has recently been able to suggest the nature of several small Latin fragments; they seem to be correspondence, legal documents, or speeches.[20] So far, then, the Latin texts are very different from those in Greek: several are in verse (in striking contrast to the all-prose Greek collection); there is no certain connection with Epicureanism (though Ennius could have provided such a connection; see n. s, p. 207); there is a clear interest in oratory and history; and the surviving fragments include personal and legal documents.

The Early Manuscripts. Among the non-Philodemus manuscripts, more were produced in the second century BC than in any other century. Cavallo noted this, and also that at least sixteen are in scribal hands for which he could not find parallels.[21] He suggested that many of them had been brought together by about 100 BC, that they formed a core collection (a "primo fondo di libri"), and that Philodemus took this core collection to Italy with him.[22] Philodemus then would have added a large number of his own compositions during the early and middle years of the first century,

---

[19] There has been much discussion of *PHerc.* 395 + 1829–31, which Kleve assigned to Lucretius (Kleve 1989 and 2007). See, most recently and at this point most conclusively, Beer 2009, arguing against the assignment to Lucretius. Kleve's other identifications have been doubted by some and accepted by others. Radiciotti 2009: 105 doubts all of them. Del Mastro 2005b: 188–9 estimates that some sixty of the Villa's rolls contained Latin texts.

[20] Janko 2008: 62–4 (*PHerc.* 413, perhaps a letter or a legal document), 69 (O "459," a letter or legal document), 76 (O "1082" *bis*, prose or verse), 90 (O "1419," oration or letter), and 93 (*PHerc.* 1816, prose). I do not include these fragments in the catalogue below. See also no. 73 in the catalogue, probably an oration.

[21] These are the manuscripts in his groups B and C, Cavallo 1983: 29–30.

[22] Cavallo 1983: 58–60. Cf. Gigante 1995: 18–19 (with the notes of Obbink) or Dorandi 1995b: 168–9 and 172. These early volumes consist very largely of volumes of Epicurus and Demetrius Laco, plus Carneiscus (no. 1), Metrodorus (no. 53), Polystratus (no. 55), and a few of our *incerti*.

plus a few other volumes, and after Philodemus' death the collection fell, Cavallo theorized, into relative disuse.[23] However plausible, such a history is impossible to prove, since any given manuscript could have been added to the Villa collection at any time after its creation.[24] Here, though, rather than deal with the entire history of the collection, I would like to call attention specifically to Cavallo's thesis that it was Philodemus himself who acquired the core collection and took it to Italy. It is not difficult to imagine, and find parallels for, scenarios that are different from Cavallo's. Perhaps a wealthy Roman purchased a Greek collection and brought it to Italy, just as Cicero bought, or hoped to buy, a Greek library with the help of Atticus.[25] Perhaps Philodemus did not bring the volumes, but rather was drawn to them after someone else had moved them to Italy, as the scholar Tyrannio and other Greeks were drawn to the libraries that Lucullus and Sulla brought back from the east; or the first Roman purchaser of the Villa collection might have invited Philodemus to organize it, as Cicero, returning from exile, asked Tyrannio to organize his library, and as, in a later generation, Augustus put the scholar Pompeius Macer in charge of organizing the Palatine library.[26]

Original Quality of the Manuscripts. The collection contained at least some high-quality manuscripts from every period: the third century BC (no. 33, Epicurus), the second (no. 1, Carneiscus), the first (no. 21, Demetrius), and the first century AD (no. 26, probably Demetrius). Many manuscripts contained large numbers of errors that were corrected by the original scribe (so, e.g., no. 2, Chrysippus, and no. 54, Polystratus).[27] A few (nos. 2, Chrysippus, a late text; 21, Demetrius; and 31, Epicurus) contain corrections by two or more hands. One of the two copies of Epicurus' *On Nature* Book 25 (no. 34, second century BC) was copied by a careless scribe and, in addition, torn in two, repaired, and then retained in, or purchased for, this otherwise mostly elegant collection.

No manuscript in the collection is known to be an opisthograph – that is, to have one text on the *recto* and another text, either literary or documentary,

---

[23] A similar history consisting of three stages, with the second being the most important for the formation of the collection, seems to emerge from the papyri unearthed by Grenfell and Hunt in their second great find. On that, see Houston 2009: 260–1.

[24] Nor do we know for sure where the Villa collection was housed, if it did exist in the first century BC. It could have been in Rome, for example. For a clear statement of the many unknowns, and of doubts regarding Cavallo's reconstruction of the history of the collection, see Porter 2007: 99–101, and cf. Costabile 1984: 599–600.

[25] Cic. *Att.* 1.7, 1.10.4, 1.11.3. On Cicero's library, see further the chapter by Keith Dix in this volume.

[26] Sulla's books (= the so-called library of Aristotle): Strabo 13.1.54 C 609. Tyrannio organizing Cicero's books: Cic. *Att.* 4.4a. 1–2, 4.8. Macer: Suet. *Iul.* 56.7.

[27] This is typical of the manuscripts from the Villa generally. Details in, e.g., Delattre 2006: 65–6.

on the *verso*, or a text that continues from *recto* to *verso*. A few rolls have writing on both sides, but in the six or seven known cases the writing on the *verso* appears to consist of notes or additions to what is found on the *recto*.[28] Although opisthographs seldom constitute a significant percentage of the manuscripts in collections known to us, there are almost always some in any collection, and it is striking that none has yet been identified among the Villa manuscripts.[29] The significance of the absence of opisthographs here is straightforward: there seems to have been no need to economize by reusing rolls; and no rolls had come to seem so irrelevant or expendable that they were reused.

Stichometric (Line) Counts. At least fourteen of the non-Philodemus Greek manuscripts include line or column counts of some sort. These are most often summary counts in the *subscriptio*, but sometimes there are running counts in the margins, once we find both, once the count is in an initial title, and once the column number is entered above every tenth column.[30] They appear in manuscripts of all chronological periods except the third century BC, and in manuscripts of at least six of the eight Greek authors (all but Metrodorus and Polystratus). The function of stichometric counts is not entirely clear. They almost certainly originated as a way for the scribe to reckon up the number of lines he had copied and thus determine the amount owed him.[31] If we were certain that they were always intended for that purpose, we could conclude that all manuscripts containing stichometric counts were produced commercially, either by a scribe on commission or by a scribe or bookseller who hoped to sell the text. Such professionally produced texts would not, then, have been produced in house by a slave belonging to the owner of the collection. There is, however, uncertainty regarding the nature of these counts. It is possible, for example, that a slave

---

[28] Capasso 2000, esp. 17–18. There may be opisthographs that are unknown to us, since the papyrus fragments are glued to a backing for support.

[29] In Grenfell and Hunt's second find, for example, two manuscripts out of a total of thirty-five (or 5.7 percent), are opisthographs: a copy of Callimachus' *Iambi*, and a lexicon of rare words. For these, see Houston 2009: 252–4 nos. 9 and 33. In one extreme case, the percentage of opisthographs is much higher. That is Grenfell and Hunt's first find, in which the fifteen papyri include six opisthographs: Houston 2009: 249 no. 3. In another extreme case, the compiler of the list of philosophical works on *P. Vars.* 5 *verso* specifically noted numerous opisthographic rolls: Otranto 2000: 98–9. In short, an ancient collection of book-rolls of more than just a few rolls was likely to include one or more opisthographs. The Villa collection is in this respect unusual.

[30] Counts in the *subscriptio*: nos. 4, 29, 30, 31, 32, 42, 56, and 60. Running counts in margins: nos. 6, 8, and perhaps 13. Both: no. 1. In initial title: no. 23. Column count in upper margin: no. 64.

[31] On stichometry, see Damschen 2008 or the much more detailed account in Bassi 1909. The counts could have had other, or additional, functions such as helping to guarantee that a given text was complete.

Table 11.1 *Marginal annotations in the non-Philodemus manuscripts*

Catalogue number	Author	Date of copy	Type of annotation
21	Demetrius Laco	First century BC	possible marginal notes
31	Epicurus	Second century BC	scholion
32	Epicurus	Second century BC	possible marginal annotations
39	Epicurus	Third or second century BC	possible scholia
54	Polystratus	Late first century BC	variant reading

of the household, who would presumably not be paid for his work, simply copied the stichometric count that he found in his archetype, right along with the rest of the text. Despite this uncertainty in individual cases, it is likely that the majority of manuscripts in which stichometric counts appear were produced commercially rather than by slaves working in-house.

If we accept this thesis, at least provisionally, interesting points emerge. Two of the manuscripts that contain stichometric counts (nos. 1, Carneiscus, and 13, Demetrius) were taken by Cavallo as belonging to the core collection that Philodemus brought to Italy. Assuming there was such a core collection, these two manuscripts may then indicate that at least part of it had been prepared commercially. Similarly, one of the latest manuscripts (no. 4, Chrysippus) contains a summary line count, and that may indicate that the owner(s) of the collection in the first century AD commissioned, or bought from a dealer, this manuscript and perhaps others. Most importantly, these dozen manuscripts provide solid, if not infallible, evidence for the presence in the collection of commercially prepared texts dating from every period except the very earliest.

Marginalia. A small number of the manuscripts contain marginal notes that may move beyond the usual corrections of mistakes. I list them in Table 11.1.

What is striking about this list is how short it is. Granted, many texts have yet to be edited carefully, and more annotations may eventually show up; but the texts published so far run to dozens of columns and yet do not reveal any significant number of marginal comments. This is of interest for several reasons. First, we might expect a scholarly collection to include scholia, glosses, and notes of various sorts. Thus the collection of papyrus fragments found by Grenfell and Hunt in their second find at Oxyrhynchus contains a remarkably high number of such notes: some 45 percent of the fragments they found contain marginal notes that explain terms in the text, cite variant readings, or add other information.[32] Moreover, we know that the Epicureans were keen philologists and that in their work they took up precisely such questions; yet the copyists have incorporated very few explanatory notes in these book-rolls. Finally, it has been suggested that papyri from Egypt in which there are few marginalia can be assumed to have come from gymnasia or public libraries, since people would (we might assume) be less likely to write in copies that were not their own. That assertion was disputed by Peter van Minnen, who argued that handsome copies of texts with few annotations may well have belonged to wealthy individuals, who wanted them for show, rather than to municipal or institutional libraries,[33] and van Minnen's general point, that clean, elegant manuscripts may come from private collections, is supported by the manuscripts from Herculaneum, which have few marginal additions.

Marcus Octavius. In two manuscripts (nos. 26, an early copy of Epicurus' *On Nature* 2, and 54, Polystratus, late first century BC), a Roman name, Marcus Octavius, is written in the margin below the next to last column. It is in the genitive case, in Greek cursive, and written out in full: Μάρκου Ὀκταουίου. The same person wrote the name in both manuscripts, and his hand is different from that of the scribes who copied the texts.[34] There has been much discussion concerning the identity of Octavius and the significance of the appearance of his name in the two manuscripts.[35] The most likely (though still not certain) explanation for the presence of his name, in the current state of our knowledge, is that at some point he owned the two volumes.

There is an interesting point here, not previously noted. It concerns Cavallo's thesis that Philodemus brought a core collection of texts with him from Athens to Italy. The Polystratus manuscript is dated on palaeographical grounds to the second half of the first century BC, and, since Octavius' name cannot have been added to the manuscript before it was created, we may

---

[32] Houston 2009: 258–9. Marginal comments in ancient manuscripts do not, as a rule, consist of the reader's personal reactions. Rather, they tend to be explanatory material copied from some source, and they were probably carried forward from one copy of a given work to the next. See McNamee 2007: 23.

[33] van Minnen 1998: 106–8.

[34] Indelli 1978: 90 for the text, placement of the name, and hand. Cf. Dorandi 1987: 37.

[35] For detailed discussions, see Indelli 1978: 90–3 and Capasso 1995, and cf. Delattre 2006: 18 n. 16. Octavius has generally been taken as a (previous) owner of the two book-rolls or as owner of the Villa, or both. It has also been suggested that he was a reader of the volumes, but that leaves the genitive case difficult to explain. He cannot be securely identified with any known historical person.

infer that Octavius lived in the first century BC or later.[36] That in turn shows that Octavius' name cannot have been added to the Epicurus text before the first century. This Epicurus roll was among those that Cavallo took as part of the collection brought to Italy by Philodemus, but if an Octavius really did own the manuscript at some point in the first century BC that is not likely.[37] It would require us to assume one or the other of two difficult scenarios: either Octavius acquired the manuscript early in the first century BC (presumably in Greece), wrote or had his name written in it, and then gave or sold it to Philodemus, all before Philodemus' move to Italy in about 80 BC; or Philodemus brought the manuscript to Italy as Cavallo suggested, but it then somehow became the property of Octavius, who entered his name in it and then gave or sold it to the owner of the Villa collection. In short, if we take Octavius as the name of an owner of the Epicurus manuscript, that manuscript was probably not brought to Italy by Philodemus.

It is possible that these two manuscripts never belonged to Philodemus at all and instead were acquired by Octavius and subsequently passed from him to the owner of the Villa collection by sale, gift, or bequest.[38] The exact sequence of events cannot be recovered in the present state of our knowledge, but the likelihood of Octavius' ownership and the implications of that possibility are important, for the Epicurus manuscript was copied by Cavallo's scribe no. 1, who also did the Villa's copies of *On Nature* Books 25, 28, and 34. Any or all of these, therefore, may also have belonged to Octavius and entered the collection together, at a relatively late date.[39] Despite the *non liquet* here, the problem serves as a useful reminder: we may accept Cavallo's thesis in its main outlines without thereby concluding that every early manuscript belonged to the core collection. Any given roll could have entered the Villa collection at any time, and by any one of a number of means.

The Special Interest of the Most Recent Manuscripts. Since a book-roll could, at least in theory, be added to the collection at any time after it was first created, we can never know for sure when a given manuscript was acquired. For this reason, the volumes copied during the last century of

---

[36] The date of the Polystratus manuscript is from Cavallo 1983: 43–4 and 65.
[37] For the hypothesis, see Cavallo 1983: 58.
[38] It would be reasonable to assume that Octavius bought the Epicurus volume and commissioned the Polystratus.
[39] Capasso 1995: 185 also suggested that all of these manuscripts entered the Villa collection at the same time. He noted that the name of Octavius certainly does not appear in the copy of Book 28 (no. 39), but that the other two manuscripts are too badly damaged for us to know if his name was written in them or not.

Table 11.2 *Greek manuscripts copied in the period after c. 50 BC*[40]

Catalogue number	Author, title	Cavallo group and scribe
2	Chrysippus, *On the Elements of Propositions*	[Not identified]
3	Chrysippus, *On Foresight* 1	Varie, 34
4	Chrysippus, *On Foresight* 2	R
7	Chrysippus?	M
8	Colotes, *Against Plato's Euthydemus*	Varie, 34
9	Colotes, *Against Plato's Lysis*	R
26	Demetrius Laco, *On the Form of the Divine*	I
43	Epicurus, *On Nature*	Q
47	Epicurus, *On Nature?*	K
48	Epicurus, *On Nature?*	R, 29
52	Metrodorus, *On Wealth*	R, 30
54	Polystratus, *Against Irrational Doubters*	R
63	*Incertus* (perhaps Demetrius)	M or I

the life of the collection are of special interest, because in the case of these volumes the time of accession must be fairly close to that of the time of copying. There are at least thirteen Greek manuscripts that can be dated to this last period. I list them in Table 11.2.

The texts in this group reflect, in broad terms, the interests revealed in the collection as a whole, but with additions. Epicurus' *On Nature* is still, it seems, the single most important text, but other Epicureans appear: Demetrius (nos. 26 and perhaps 63), Colotes, who is not known from any earlier manuscript, Metrodorus, and Polystratus.[41] There is also a certain amount of (pro-Epicurean) polemic: nos. 8, 9, and 54. A different interest is signaled by the manuscripts of Chrysippus, as has often been noted. At least two of the texts (nos. 4 and 8) include line counts and so may have been commissioned especially for the collection.[42]

---

[40] The list I give here differs somewhat from that of Delattre 2006: 78. Delattre includes five rolls by Philodemus, which I omit. I include no. 63, by an unknown author, which Delattre omits because he is interested in rolls that can be assigned to specific authors. The others that I include, but Delattre does not, are numbers 2, 7, 26, and 47. For the evidence on their dates, see the catalogue. Others could be added: thus *PHerc.* 1138, assigned by Cavallo to the first century AD, or *PHerc.* 1504, by scribe 29.

[41] As William Johnson has pointed out to me, the late copies of Epicurus' *On Nature* may well represent replacement volumes for rolls that had been damaged or worn out by use. Whether they are replacements or duplicates, they indicate a continuing interest in the *On Nature*.

[42] A change of interest on the part of the owners after the death of Philodemus is often taken for granted. See, for example, Delattre 2006: 78. It is far from certain, of course, for it is possible

The late manuscripts were copied in a wide range of what we might call styles (Cavallo's "gruppi"). Cavallo assigned them to no fewer than six groups of hands: I, K, M, Q, R, and "varie." Two of these are of special interest: the group Q, because it was influenced by Roman formal capitals, and the "varie" because Cavallo found no parallels for those hands. In this late group, only two rolls were identified by Cavallo as having been copied by the same scribe (nos. 3 and 8), and it is thus likely that the owner(s) of the collection in this relatively limited period acquired texts that had been copied by at least twelve different scribes.[43] We have, in sum, an owner or series of owners in this late period who went to the trouble of commissioning or buying copies of philosophical works done by a dozen different copyists, and who seem to have adjusted to some degree the focus of the collection. It may thus be that there was more interest in, and use of, the Villa's collection in this late period than has generally been assumed.[44]

The Find Spots of the Papyri. It is well known that the papyri were found in at least five different locations, many on shelves, some in portable wooden cases, and others, it seems, piled on the floor.[45] Scholars have explained these facts variously. Perhaps the Villa was undergoing renovations, and the manuscripts were in process of being moved out to storage. Or perhaps the owner(s) of the collection tried, during the hours of the eruption, to pack up and remove some of the book rolls.[46] I would add a third possibility: perhaps some of the rolls were currently in use and therefore stored casually or simply left out. But the important point is this: every one of these scenarios implies some interest in and appreciation of the value of the manuscripts in AD 79.

---

that a single person, interested primarily but not exclusively in Epicureanism, assembled the collection as we know it through a combination of, say, retrospective purchases and commissions for new copies. Cf. on this Porter 2007: 99.

[43] At least two of these rolls contain stichometric counts (no. 4, in the *subscriptio*, and no. 8, in the margins). That, plus the fact that they are almost all written by different scribes, may well indicate that the late rolls were not copied in house but rather commissioned or purchased from various outside copyists. If they had been copied in house, we might have expected to find more rolls copied by the same scribe or scribes.

[44] A few other signs of activity late in the first century BC or early in the first century AD can be adduced. Cavallo's Group P – some thirty manuscripts, most of them assigned to Philodemus – has its closest parallels in manuscripts of the first and second centuries AD: Cavallo 1983: 54–5. Cavallo himself declined to date this group, noting that the parallels may represent an archaizing script, but perhaps the manuscripts of Group P were copied early in the first century AD after all. Note also *PHerc.* 1697 (possibly Demetrius), which was found partially unrolled and thus presumably in use at the time of, or not long before, the eruption of Vesuvius. See on this Capasso 2007: 75.

[45] Longo Auricchio and Capasso 1987.

[46] Possible scenarios are set out by Capasso 1991: 53–4 and 81–2.

The Non-Philodemus Collection. The non-Philodemus volumes from the Villa of the Papyri provide us with invaluable, if still evolving, evidence for a particular type of manuscript collection, one that was specialized rather than general, and personal rather than public. Consisting of several hundred volumes, the Villa collection was focused on philosophy; within that, on Epicureanism; and within that, on Epicurus' *On Nature* and the works of Demetrius Laco, together with a certain number of other authors. There was apparently no interest in assembling a complete collection of Epicurean texts. There were also Latin texts and documents, and they reveal a completely different set of interests, namely poetry, history, and oratory.

As we would expect in a context of wealth, the manuscripts are often handsome and, although they often have many mistakes, those mistakes are generally corrected. Cavallo noted a number of indications of homogeneity in editorial practice, especially in the texts by Philodemus, but in the non-Philodemus collection there are numerous signs of heterogeneity. Some manuscripts were more than 250 years old (nos. 33, 39, 53, 61), others less than 100 (7, 26, etc.). A few had marginal notes, but most did not. One (31) was corrected by at least four hands. Some were written in an elegant script (1), others in scripts that varied (21), most in simple clear scripts. Mathematical and geometrical treatises (14, 15, 16) were illustrated. Two rolls are probably dedicated to Romans (19, to a Nero, and 26, to a Quintus). Among the last thirteen Greek manuscripts produced, there are at least six different styles of script and twelve hands. Similarly, at least six different scribes – three writing in capitals, three in cursive – can be identified among the surviving Latin manuscripts.[47]

Stichometric counts suggest the purchase of some volumes on the commercial market and are attested from every century from which we have manuscripts except for the third century BC. Some volumes, such as those including the name of Marcus Octavius, were probably obtained secondhand, and the collection seems to have included a mix of items commissioned, copied in house, and purchased from dealers, either new or used. We cannot at present know how the collection came into being, for there are too many unknowns and too many possible scenarios, but reasonable hypotheses (not least Cavallo's) can be advanced, and further discoveries may help to clarify the history of the collection. This then is what an ancient manuscript collection might look like. When we think of Cicero's library, say, or of the

---

[47] Janko 2008: 14–15. Of the cursive hands, one certainly and a second possibly copied works of literature: Janko's "Manus A" copied *PHerc.* 1082, an oration, and his "Manus B" copied *PHerc.* 1419, an oration or a letter.

great imperial collections that evolved out of the late Republican collections, we should keep in mind both the many variables and idiosyncracies of the individual manuscripts and the variations on the theme of book collection that are so vividly suggested by the collection from the Villa of the Papyri.

Descriptive catalogue of manuscripts by authors other than Philodemus that have been found in the Villa of the Papyri

This catalogue includes all manuscripts from the Villa of the Papyri that do not seem to be by Philodemus and that provide us with useful information. I list them in alphabetical order by author. Works by unknown authors are placed at the end, under "incerti."[48] Latin manuscripts follow the Greek. I give each manuscript a catalogue number for ease of reference; it appears in column 1. Column 2 gives the *PHerc.* number or numbers of a given manuscript, followed by its equivalent *LDAB* (*Leuven Database of Ancient Books* – www.trismegistos.org/ldab/) number. Column 4 gives the group and scribe to which Cavallo 1983 assigned the manuscript. In column 5, the numbers ordinarily refer to centuries: thus no. 1 was copied late in the second century BC. The dates come from Cavallo 1983 unless specified otherwise; both the Cavallo pages and later redatings are cited in column 6. In column 6, "Cav." means Cavallo 1983. I make no attempt to provide a complete bibliography for each manuscript, for which the reader is referred to the relevant entries in Gigante 1979 and in the *LDAB*.[49]

In addition to the items listed in this catalogue, several small fragments of Latin manuscripts have been published in Janko 2008. See n. 20 above for a list.

---

[48] I include manuscripts by unknown authors if they satisfy two criteria. First, we know something useful about the manuscript, such as date, scribe, or contents. Second, there is some reason to believe that the manuscript is not by Philodemus. Most of these manuscripts, for example, were copied before Philodemus' lifetime. I omit many manuscripts that were assigned to specific authors by earlier scholars if we know nothing else useful about the manuscript, and I omit a number of doubtful cases, even from the list of *incerti*, if there is a reasonable chance that Philodemus is the author. Thus, for example, I omit *PHerc.* 346, which was assigned to Polystratus by Vogliano, and *PHerc.* 1044 (the *Life of Philonides*), because these texts may well have been written by Philodemus: Capasso 1982: 39–40 and De Sanctis 2009: 108 n. 8 respectively. I include *PHerc.* 395 but assign it to an unknown author rather than to Lucretius. On this manuscript, see now Beer 2009.

[49] To compile the catalogue, I searched Gigante 1979, Cavallo 1983, *Cronache Ercolanesi* through 2009, the volumes resulting from the various papyrological congresses, and bibliographical aids such as *L'année philologique*. I have no doubt overlooked some manuscripts, but their addition would not, I think, change the main outlines of the catalogue.

Cat. no.	PHerc. = LDAB	Author and work	Cavallo group and scribe	Date of manuscript	Reference and comment
1	1027 = 535	**Carneiscus**, Philistas 2. Subscriptio	O, 24	Late 2 BC	Cav. 40, 54, 59. Probably copied east of Italy: Cav. 59, cf. Capasso 1988: 155. Elegant script, generous spacing, careful copy, few or no corrections: Capasso 1988: 140–4, 149–50. Stichometric count (3,238) in *subscriptio* and margins: Capasso 1988: 147–9. *Subscriptio* in same hand as text: Capasso 1988: 148
2	1380 = 109375	**Chrysippus**, On the Elements of Propositions.[a] Subscriptio		Late 1 BC or early 1 AD?	Title, date, and meaning of the title: Del Mastro 2005a. Numerous corrections by the first hand, and one by a second hand: Del Mastro 2007: 250
3	1421 = 546	Chrysippus, On Foresight 1. Subscriptio	Varie, 34	Late 1 BC	Cav. 44, 46, 57. *Subscriptio*: Gigante 1979: 315
4	1038 = 545	Chrysippus, On Foresight 2. Subscriptio	R	Late 1 BC or early 1 AD	Cav. 44, 56. Stichometric count in *subscriptio*: Bassi 1909: 356–7
5	307 = 549	Chrysippus, Problems of Logic. Subscriptio		50–25 BC	Title: in *subscriptio*. Date: Delattre 2006: 74 n. 155
6	1384 = 3642	Chrysippus (?)	I		Author: Antoni and Dorival 2007.[b] Group: Antoni 2007: 44. Stichometric count in margin: Antoni 2007: 45
7	1020 = 551	Chrysippus (?)	H	Mid-1 BC to early 1 AD	Cav. 35, 52. Scribal hand perhaps first century AD: Obbink 1996: 76 n. 1
8	1032 = 568	**Colotes**, Against Plato's Euthydemus. Subscriptio	Varie, 34	Late 1 BC or early 1 AD	Cav. 44, 46, 57. Stichometric counts in margins: Bassi 1909: 499
9	208 = 567	Colotes, Against Plato's Lysis. Subscriptio	R	Late 1 BC or early 1 AD	Cav. 44, 56. Crönert 1906: 162–7

Cat. no.	PHerc. = LDAB	Author and work	Cavallo group and scribe	Date of manuscript	Reference and comment
10	1258 = 593	**Demetrius Laco**, *On the aporiae of Polyaenus*, 1.[c] Subscriptio	R, 30	1 BC	Cav. 44, 46, 56
11	1429 = 597	Demetrius Laco, *On the aporiae of Polyaenus*, 5. Subscriptio	C, 4	2 BC	Cav. 30, 45, 56–7. From Greece or Asia Minor?
12	1083 = 600	Demetrius Laco, *On the aporiae of Polyaenus*	C, 4	150 BC	Cav. 30, 45, 56–7. From Greece or Asia Minor?
13	1647 = 599	Demetrius Laco, *On the aporiae of Polyaenus*	C, 4	2 BC	Cav. 30, 45, 56–7. From Greece or Asia Minor? Possible stichometric counts in margins: Bassi 1909: 501
14	1642 = 598	Demetrius Laco, *On the aporiae of Polyaenus* (?)	C, 4	2 BC	Cav. 30, 45, 56–7. From Greece or Asia Minor? Geometrical figure[d]
15	1822 = 595	Demetrius Laco, *On the aporiae of Polyaenus* (?)		1 BC or 1 AD	Author and title: Capasso and Dorandi 1979: 41–2. Geometrical figure: see no. 14
16	1061 = 596	Demetrius Laco, *On Geometry*. Subscriptio.	B, 2?	2 BC	Cav. 29, 45, 57. From Greece or Asia Minor? Geometrical figure: see no. 14
17	233 + 860 = 4341	Demetrius Laco, *On Music*	C, 4	2 BC	Author, title, hand: Janko 2008: 32–5.[e] Date: Cav. 30, 45, 56
18	188 = 601	Demetrius Laco, *On Poems* 1	B, 2	2 BC	Date and hand: Cav. 29, 45, 57–8. From Greece or Asia Minor? Author: Romeo 1988: 26–32. Perhaps long enough to have required two rolls: Romeo 1988: 73–4

(cont.)

Cat. no.	PHerc. = LDAB	Author and work	Cavallo group and scribe	Date of manuscript	Reference and comment
19	1014 = 602	Demetrius Laco, *On Poems*, 2. *Subscriptio*	B, 2	Late 2 BC or very early 1 BC	Date and hand (from Greece or Asia Minor?): Cav. 29, 45, 57. Corrections by original scribe: Romeo 1988: 76. Both Books 1 and 2 of the *On Poems*, or just Book 2, were dedicated to a Nero: Philippson 1943: 161–2, cf. Romeo 1988: 57[f]
20	230 = 117905	Demetrius Laco, *On Poems*, uncertain book	B, 2		Janko 2008: 29–32
21	1006 = 592	Demetrius Laco, *On Some Topics for Discussion Concerning the Manner of Life*.[g] *Subscriptio*	M	1 BC	Cav. 38, 53–4. Script varies from careful and deliberate to rapid, almost cursive. Ligatures, corrections, possible marginal notes: Assante 2008: 156. Generous margins and large script indicate a high-value manuscript: Assante 2008: 112–13[h]
22	1012 = 606	Demetrius Laco (?), *Textual and Critical Problems in Epicurus* (?)	I	2nd half 2 BC	Cav. 35, 52, cf. Cavallo 2005: 113. Author (not certain): Puglia 1988a: 126–7. At least some corrections by a second hand, with other corrections probably by the original scribe: Puglia 1988a: 116–18
23	1786 = 594	Demetrius Laco, uncertain work probably on ethics. *Initial title, in the same hand as the main text*		Late 2 or early 1 BC	Date: Capasso 2001: 185. Initial title: Del Mastro 2002: 255 n. 54, Caroli 2007: 56. Stichometric count in title: Bassi 1909: 355–6, Capasso 2001: 183
24	128 = 3694	Demetrius Laco. (*Rhetoric?*)	C	2 BC	Cav. 30, 56–7, 59. From Greece or Asia Minor? Author and work: Dorandi 1992b: 30 with n. 16, citing C. Romeo; Janko 1995: 86

Cat. no.	PHerc. = LDAB	Author and work	Cavallo group and scribe	Date of manuscript	Reference and comment
25	1013 = 604	Demetrius Laco (?) *On the Size of the Sun* (?)	B, 2	2 BC	Cav. 29, 45, 56–7. From Greece or Asia Minor? Author: Crönert 1906: 100. Title: Romeo 1979
26	1055 = 605	Demetrius Laco (?) *On the Form of the Divine* (?)	I	First half 1 AD	Cav. 35, cf. 52–3, pl. 27. Author: Santoro 2000: 23–6. Title inferred from content: Santoro 2000: 23–9. Date: Menci, cited by Santoro 2000: 73–4. Letters clear, ample interlinear spaces. Columns follow Maas's Law: Santoro 2000: 75–6. Corrections probably by the original scribe: Santoro 2000: 78. In the text, a Quintus is addressed, probably as dedicatee of the work: Santoro 2000: 25
27	1010 = 855	**Epicurus**, *On Nature* 2. *Subscriptio*	C	2 BC	Cav. 30, 56–7. From Greece or Asia Minor? On date, cf. Janko 2008: 71. This copy of Book 2 is less elegant than no. 28: Leone 2005: 25, cf. Leone 2010
28	1149 + 993 = 862	Epicurus, *On Nature* 2. *Subscriptio*	A, 1	3 or 2 BC	Cav. 28, 45, 50. A name, Marcus Octavius, is written in Greek cursive letters in the ms. and may be that of an owner: Indelli 1978: 90–3, Delattre 2006: 18, n. 16.[i] A high-quality copy: Leone 2005: 25
29	154 = 852	Epicurus, *On Nature* 11. *Subscriptio*	E	Late 2 BC	Cav. 32, 51, 58; cf. Cavallo 2005: 119. Probable stichometric count in *subscriptio*: Bassi 1909: 357–8
30	1042 = 860	Epicurus, *On Nature* 11. *Subscriptio*	E	Late 2 BC	Cav. 32, 51, 58. Stichometric count in *subscriptio*: Gigante 1979: 239
31	1148 = 856	Epicurus, *On Nature* 14. *Subscriptio*	D, 5	2 BC	Cav. 31, 45, 50; cf. Cavallo 2005: 119. Stichometric count in *subscriptio*: Gigante 1979: 276. A date (=301/300 BC) appears in the *subscriptio* and probably gives the date of composition: Longo Auricchio 2008: 194. Corrections and marginal annotations in at least four hands: Leone 1984: 25–8[j]

(*cont.*)

Cat. no.	PHerc. = LDAB	Author and work	Cavallo group and scribe	Date of manuscript	Reference and comment
32	1151 = 857	Epicurus, On Nature 15. Subscriptio	D, 5	2 BC	Cav. 31, 45, 50. Stichometric count in *subscriptio*: Gigante 1979: 278. A date (=300/299 BC) appears in the *subscriptio* and probably gives the date of composition: Longo Auricchio 2008: 194. Possible marginal annotations: Millot 1977: 12–13
33	1191 = 863	Epicurus, On Nature 25. Subscriptio	A, 1	3 or 2 BC	Cav. 28, 45, 50. Book number: Laursen 1987. Third century the more likely date: Laursen 1995: 16
34	1420 + 1056 = 858	Epicurus, On Nature 25. Subscriptio	D and A, 6	2 BC, repairs late 2 BC	Cav. 29, 31, 45, 50. *Subscriptio* at end of 1056: Laursen 1987: 77 and 1997: 50. Date and repairs: Laursen 1995: 27–31 and Puglia 1997: 40–2^k
35	419 = 853	Epicurus, On Nature 25	K, 15	2 or 1 BC	Cav. 36, 45, 53, 56. On date, cf. Laursen 1995: 36–8. Numbers 35 to 38 may all be from the same roll: cf. Dorandi 2000 and Laursen 1995: 31 and 36–8
36	459 = 4340	Epicurus, On Nature 25	K, 15	2 or 1 BC	Janko 2008: 67–9. See also on no. 35
37	697 = 854	Epicurus, On Nature 25. Subscriptio	K, 15	2 or 1 BC	Cav. 36, 45, 53. Date: Laursen 1995: 36–8. *Subscriptio*: Laursen 1987: 77–8 and 1997: 50. See also on no. 35
38	1634 = 859	Epicurus, On Nature 25	K, 15	2 or 1 BC	Cav. 36, 45, 53. Date: cf. Laursen 1995: 36–8. See also on no. 35
39	1479 + 1417 = 864	Epicurus, On Nature 28. Subscriptio	A, 1	3 or 2 BC	Cav. 28, 45, 50. Date: Janko 2002: 40. The *subscriptio* probably includes the date of composition: Longo Auricchio 2008: 194, cf. Puglia 1998. Corrections, and possible scholia, in a second hand: Sedley 1973: 12
40	1431 = 865	Epicurus, On Nature 34. Subscriptio	A, 1	3 or 2 BC	Cav. 28, 45, 50. Book number: Leone 2002: 23–4. Date (probably third century BC): Leone 2002: 24–6. Perhaps part of an edition of all or most of the *On Nature*: Leone 2002: 28–9, following Cavallo

Cat. no.	PHerc. = LDAB	Author and work	Cavallo group and scribe	Date of manuscript	Reference and comment
41	1413 = 848	Epicurus, unidentified book in *On Nature*, dealing with the subject of time	A	1st half 3 BC	Date: Janko 2008: 89.[1] Content: Cavallo 1983: 70. A high-quality copy, perhaps from Egypt: Crisci 1999: 54–6
42	1385 = 844	Epicurus, *On Nature. Subscriptio*		Before AD 79	Count of columns and *stichoi* in *subscriptio*: Bassi 1909: 488–9
43	362 = 850	Epicurus, *On Nature. Subscriptio*	Q	Late 1 BC	Cav. 43, 55–6, 65
44	989 = 842	Epicurus, *On Nature Subscriptio*	A	3 or 2 BC	Cav. 28, 50
45	335 = 117906	Epicurus, *On Nature*	5 (?)	3–2 BC	Janko 2008: 59
46	908 + 1390 = 841	Epicurus, *On Nature* (?)	C	2 BC	Cav. 30, 56–7. From Greece or Asia Minor?
47	1398 = 845	Epicurus, *On Nature* (?)	K	Late 1 BC or early 1 AD	Cav. 37, 53
48	1199 = 851	Epicurus, *On Nature* (?)	R, 29	Late 1 BC or early 1 AD	Cav. 44, 46, 56
49	1039 = 117907	Epicurus (?), *On Nature* (?)	D, 6	2 BC	Cav. 31, 45, 50. Possibly by Epicurus: Puglia 1988b
50	1113a = 590	Epicurus (?), *On Nature* (?)			Author and work (both uncertain): Porter, cited by Janko 2008: 80[m]
51	996 = 843	Epicurus (?), unidentified work	B	2 BC	Cav. 29, 56–7. From Greece or Asia Minor?
52	200 = 109360	**Metrodorus of Lampsacus,** *On Wealth. Subscriptio*	R, 30	1 BC, prob. late.	Cav. 44, 46, 56. Author and *subscriptio*: Tepedino Guerra 1979
53	255 + 418 + 1084 + 1091 + 1112 = 4337	Metrodorus, *Against the Dialecticians* (Spinelli) or *Against the Sophists* (Tepedino Guerra)	Varie, 31	Prob. mid-3 BC	Cav. 44, 46, 57–8. Author: Spinelli 1986. Title: Spinelli 1986; Tepedino Guerra 1992[n]

(cont.)

Cat. no.	PHerc. = LDAB	Author and work	Cavallo group and scribe	Date of manuscript	Reference and comment
54	336 + 1150 = 3847	**Polystratus**, *Against Irrational Doubters*. Subscriptio	R	Late 1 BC	Cav. 43, 56. The seven-line *subscriptio* is carefully centered: Delattre 2006: 57 n. 114. Clear hand, but there are numerous errors, often corrected, probably by the first hand: Indelli 1978: 87–9. A variant reading was recorded by the scribe at col. 32 line 8.[o] A name, M. Octavius, is written in Greek cursive letters in the margin below the penultimate column and may be that of an owner: Indelli 1978: 90–3[p]
55	1520 = 3697	Polystratus, *On Philosophy* 1. Subscriptio	E, 7	Late 2 BC	Cav. 32, 45, 51, cf. Cavallo 2005: 119 and Capasso 1991: 157
56	1533 = 10669	**Zeno of Sidon**, *Response to the "On Geometric Proofs" of Craterus*. Subscriptio		1 BC	Kleve and Del Mastro 2000. Stichometric count in *subscriptio*: Ibid
57	118a = 10357	**Incertus**. On Epicurus? Or a history of the School?		Before Philodemus	Contents and date: Obbink, email to PAPY list of 22 April 2005; cf. Militello 1997: 82–3[q]
58	1111 = 4353	Incertus. Citations of passages from a series of Epicurean works		Before AD 79	Obbink 1996: 300–1[r]
59	176 = 207	Incertus. Sketches of Epicureans, with quotations from their letters	Varie	2 BC	Cav. 44, 57, 60. Content: Militello 1997: 49–56, cf. Janko 2008: 43

Cat. no.	PHerc. = LDAB	Author and work	Cavallo group and scribe	Date of manuscript	Reference and comment
60	1041 = 4347	*Incertus.* Final illness of an Epicurean (?) *Subscriptio*	G	Mid- or late 1 BC	Cav. 34, 51–2. Subject: Crönert 1906: 73–4. Stichometric count in *subscriptio*: Bassi 1909: 343–5
61	439 = 117908	*Incertus.* Perhaps on the theory of atoms	*Varie*, 31	Mid-3 BC	Janko 2008: 64–5: same scribe as that of no. 53 (Metrodorus)
62	1696 = 4368	*Incertus.* Perhaps on ethics		Before AD 79	Capasso and Dorandi 1979: 37–41
63	831 = 591	*Incertus.* Possibly Demetrius Laco	M or I	Mid-1 BC or 3rd quarter 1 BC	Cav. 38, 54, cf. Cavallo 2005: 115; Dorandi 1995a: 36. Author: Philippson 1943: 148–9 and 156–62; Van Heel 1989: 190 n. 35; Sanders 1999; Delattre 2006: 78. Scribal hand perhaps from Group I: Dorandi 1995a: 36
64	1158 = 6912	*Incertus.* Possibly Stoic	D, 5	2 BC	Cav. 31, 45, 50. Possible Stoic content: Puglia 1993: 39–43. Column numbers above every 10th column: Puglia 1993: 32–3

Latin manuscripts in the collection of the Villa of the Papyri

65	78 = 459	**Caecilius Statius** (?), "The Usurer" (*Obolostates sive faenerator*) (?). *Subscriptio*		1 BC	Author, title: Kleve 1996. Doubts: Radiciotti 2009: 105. Informal script: Radiciotti 1998: 358
66	21 = 825	**Ennius** (?), *Annales* 6 (?)		50 BC	Author, title: Kleve 1990.[s] Doubts: Radiciotti 2009: 105. Informal script: Radiciotti 1998: 358
67	817 + 399 = 3870	*Incertus. Carmen de bello actiaco*[t]		1 BC to 1 AD	Zecchini 1987, Scappaticcio 2008 (on PHerc. 817), Janko 2008: 59–62 (on PHerc. 399) [u]
68	395 = 2583	*Incertus.* Epic (?) verse		1 BC	Verse: Beer 2009: 75–7.[v] Script a "cursive bookhand": Radiciotti 1998: 358, cf. Beer 2009: 74.

(*cont.*)

Cat. no.	PHerc. = LDAB	Author and work	Cavallo group and scribe	Date of manuscript	Reference and comment
69	1067 = 7735	Incertus. Oration addressed to the emperor? Subscriptio: L(uci) · M[anlii Torquati?]		1 AD	Subject of oration: Costabile 1984: 593–5, cf. Del Mastro 2005b: 191. Formal script: Radiciotti 1998: 357. Subscriptio: Del Mastro 2005b: 191–2. Manlius Torquatus (perhaps the praetor of 49 BC) as author of the speech: Costabile 1984: 597–9[w]
70	1475 = 7736	Incertus. Oration, probably judicial		1 BC or 1 AD	Content: Costabile 1984: 595–7, Radiciotti 1998: 361 with n. 25. Formal script: Radiciotti 1998: 357
71	1491 = 10518	Unidentified Latin prose[x]		1 BC	Date: Kleve 1994: 318; Radiciotti 1998: 365–70. Informal script: Radiciotti 1998: 358
72	1558 = 10516	Unidentified Latin		1 BC	Date and formal script: Radiciotti 1998: 365–70 and 357
73	238a = 117909	Incertus. Oration, probably political		1 BC ?	Janko 2008: 15, 19, and 35–40: early Roman cursive in large letters. Fragments include references to consul, quaestor, and names of places
74	863	Incertus. Prose (?), perhaps historical[y]		1 BC	Radiciotti 2009: 114: early Roman cursive; possibly a *subscriptio* mentioning the eighth book of some work

[a] The Greek title is Χ[ρυ]σίππου [πε]ρὶ τῶν [σ]τοιχείων [τ]ῶν λεγομένων. Exactly how to translate it is not clear. Del Mastro 2005a: 65 provides what he calls a "generic" translation, "parti degli enunciati." See also Del Mastro 2007: 256.

[b] PHerc. 1384 had earlier been taken as by Philodemus. Antoni 2004: 36–8 summarizes the scholarship.

[c] In this manuscript, a much fuller version of the title of this work is given. I use a standard short version known from some of the other manuscripts.

[d] This manuscript and the next two contain geometrical figures. For nos. 14 and 15, see Tepedino Guerra 1991: 95–6; for no.16, see Fowler 1999: 210 with plate 1. Fowler notes that another figure appears in column 11 of this papyrus. Tepedino Guerra 1991: 180 considers possible connections between nos. 10 to 15. Note that 11 to 14 were all copied by Cavallo's scribe no. 4.

[e] Janko would assign PHerc. 1671 to the same treatise (*On Music*) and perhaps the same book-roll.

[f] Philippson noted that Nero (clearly a Roman) was presumably a student or patron of Demetrius, or both. He could be identical with Drusus Claudius Nero, the grandfather of the emperor Tiberius (as Philippson noted), with Tiberius Claudius Nero, the friend of Varro (thus Gigante 1997: 152 n. 12), or with Tiberius Claudius (Nero), a *monetalis* whose term as moneyer was dated in 79 BC by Crawford 1974: 398 no. 383.

^{g} The Greek title is Περὶ τινων συζητηθέντων κατὰ δίαιταν. How to translate the title is not entirely clear: see Assante 2008: 110–13. My thanks to Peter M. Smith for advice on the range of meanings of the philosophical terms.

^{h} Earlier scholars thought that the *subscriptio* included a stichometric count, but Assante 2008: 111 found no evidence of any count in this manuscript.

^{i} Marcus Octavius and the implications of the presence of his name are discussed in Part 1 above, p. 192.

^{j} The scribe himself made many corrections. A second hand made grammatical corrections and rewrote some letters, in both cases occasionally erring. A third hand entered a marginal scholion to the right of column 38. This third hand is not much later than the others and so cannot be Philodemus'. A fourth hand added a note above column 35. That note offers an alternate reading and may be due either to a collation or to a reader's own suggestion.

^{k} Puglia provides a full history of this roll, which included both *PHerc.* 1420 and 1056. In brief: the original roll, containing all of Book 25, was written by a careless scribe ("Hand A" = Cavallo's Scribe 6) some time in the second century BC. Either that roll was damaged, or part of it was deemed too full of errors, so a second, more careful, scribe ("Hand B") made, late in the second century BC, a new copy of the damaged or faulty part of the roll. That section was then attached to what remained of the older manuscript.

^{l} Cavallo 1983: 29, 50, and 58, placed no. 41 in his group A, which includes some very early manuscripts, but dated it to the late second or early first century BC. Janko dates the hand as "probably contemporary with Epicurus' lifetime."

^{m} *PHerc.* 1113 has in the past been assigned to Demetrius Laco, but see now Janko 2008: 84–5, suggesting Epicurus, Zeno, or Philodemus for *PHerc.* 1113a.

^{n} Janko 2008: 56 suggests that *PHerc.* 390, 456, 1108, and possibly 1103 could all be by the same third-century hand. Thus they may be additional fragments of this treatise of Metrodorus or fragments from one or more other early works. I omit them from this catalogue since we have no other information about them.

^{o} Wilke, cited by Indelli 1978: 89, noted that the variant reading means that the scribe either was copying an exemplar that had been corrected or was copying from two distinct copies.

^{p} See also no. 28.

^{q} *PHerc.* 118a is still unedited. Militello follows Crönert and others in seeing it as containing quotations from letters of Epicurus or other Epicureans. It is not known if the manuscript quoted the letters in full, or simply cited passages from letters in the course of an argument.

^{r} This is a very short fragment, but it is not simply a catalogue or inventory. Obbink gives the full surviving text.

^{s} Suerbaum 1995: 32–4 noted that Book 6 of Ennius' *Annales* may have held particular interest for Epicureans because it could have included the story of Gaius Fabricius learning about the doctrines of Epicurus while in the camp of Pyrrhus. The story is known to us from Plut. *Pyrrh.* 20.3–4.

^{t} The title is modern. Zecchini 1987: 31 suggests *Bellum Actiacum et Alexandrinum*.

^{u} Janko noted that *PHerc.* 399 appears to contain the tops of six successive columns of the manuscript and includes speeches and military narrative. The relation of these fragments to those in *PHerc.* 817 cannot be established at present. The authenticity of *PHerc.* 817 has been questioned. In defense of its authenticity: Radiciotti 2000, Capasso 2003. The lines newly discovered by Janko in the Oxford *disegni* provide additional support for the authenticity of *PHerc.* 817.

(*cont.*)

[v] *PHerc.* 395 was identified as coming from Lucretius' *De rerum natura* by Kleve 1989 and Kleve 2007. Kleve also assigned *PHerc.* 1829–31 to the same work. On present evidence, his identifications appear to be unlikely and the author of the fragment in *PHerc.* 395 must be considered unknown.

[w] Costabile 1984: 597 assigned the *subscriptio* to *PHerc.* 1475 (my no. 70), but it seems to belong rather to *PHerc.* 1067: Del Mastro 2005b: 192.

[x] The fragment catalogued as *PHerc.* 1491 includes both Latin and fragments from at least two separate manuscripts in Greek: Macfarlane and Del Mastro 2007: 112–13.

[y] As of January 2011, this fragment appears not to have been entered in the Leuven Database.

12 | "Beware of promising your library to anyone"

Assembling a private library at Rome

T. KEITH DIX

Cicero's letters chart the growth of his library through a period of about twenty years, from the height of his public career until almost the end of his life. Combining the evidence in the letters with other sources, we gain a more complete picture of how aristocrats and men of letters at Rome assembled, housed, and used substantial libraries in the first century BC, as well as how those collections might be dispersed. I organize the evidence for acquisitions under the headings of purchases, gifts and inheritances, and miscellaneous acquisitions, then consider two instances of losses suffered by Cicero; I examine Cicero's patterns of library usage and conclude with speculation on the fate of his collection.

Purchases

The earliest references come in four letters of 67–66 BC from Cicero to Atticus, then in Greece. In the first letter, dated before the Ides of February, 67, Cicero says: "Please consider how you can obtain a library for me, just as you promised. All hope of the pleasure which I want to have when I come into some leisure, I have placed in your kindness."[1] By May, it seems, Atticus had the library in hand, for Cicero says, "Beware of promising your library to anyone, however passionate a lover you find. For I am reserving all my little grape harvests for it, in order to prepare that prop for old age."[2] Then in August, Cicero writes, "Beware of handing over your books to anyone; save them for me, as you write. The greatest enthusiasm for them holds me,

---

[1] *Att.* 1.7, before February 13, 67: *et velim cogites id quod mihi pollicitus es, quem ad modum bibliothecam nobis conficere possis. omnem spem delectationis nostrae, quam cum in otium venerimus habere volumus, in tua humanitate positam habemus.* I give Shackleton Bailey's dates for Cicero's letters throughout this chapter.

[2] *Att.* 1.10.4, c. May 67: *bibliothecam tuam cave cuiquam despondeas, quamvis acrem amatorem inveneris; nam ego omnis meas vindemiolas eo reservo, ut illud subsidium senectuti parem.* As Shackleton Bailey 1965–70 points out: "The double senses of *despondeas* ('promise' or 'betroth') and *amatorem* ('amateur' and 'lover') suit the gender." His translation is: "Mind you don't engage your library to anyone, no matter how ardent a wooer you may find. I am putting all my little gleanings aside to pay for this stand-by for my old age."

just as disgust for all other things."[3] Finally, in 66, Cicero says "Save your books and don't despair that I am able to make them mine. If I accomplish that, I will surpass Crassus in riches and I despise the hamlets and meadows of all."[4]

Subsequent letters do not reveal the end of this transaction, but we may assume that Atticus brought the books with him when he returned to Italy from Greece some time in 65. Whether or not Cicero ever took possession, these few sentences do raise interesting issues. First, Cicero must have owned a collection of books already: he was almost forty years old and already the author of speeches and a rhetorical handbook, so the collection acquired by Atticus in Greece can hardly have been the beginning of Cicero's library. We can assume that Cicero began to collect books while studying oratory and philosophy, particularly during his student days in Athens and Rhodes,[5] and he may have inherited a library from his father (see below). Cicero twice refers to the collection he hoped to obtain from Atticus as a *bibliotheca* ("Please consider how you can obtain a library for me, just as you promised" [*Att.* 1.7], "Beware of promising your library to anyone" [*Att.* 1.10.4]). He may well have made clear to Atticus in earlier communications that he meant a *Greek* library; or perhaps he judged whatever collection he already owned insufficient in size or breadth to deserve the title *bibliotheca*.

A second issue is how much Cicero was willing to pay for a library. Cicero three times asks Atticus to hold on to the library and not promise it to anyone else, which suggests that Cicero was unwilling, unprepared or unable to make immediate payment; on the other hand, when he says that he is "reserving all my little grape harvests for it," the diminutive *vindemiolae* suggests that Cicero is making a joke of his apparent reluctance to pay.[6]

The four letters about the Greek library provide some additional clues to the cost of the library (as well as Cicero's motives for acquiring the library). All four letters also mention the purchase of statuary for Cicero's villa at Tusculum.[7] In letters 1.7 (the first letter to mention the library) and 1.8,

---

[3] *Att.* 1.11.3, August 67: *libros vero tuos cave cuiquam tradas; nobis eas, quem ad modum scribis, conserva. summum me eorum studium tenet, sicut odium iam ceterarum rerum.*

[4] *Att.* 1.4.3, first half of 66: *libros tuos conserva et noli desperare eos <me> meos facere posse. quod si adsequor, supero Crassum divitiis atque omnium vicos et prata contemno.*

[5] Perhaps Cicero's sojourn in the Greek world resembled Thomas Jefferson's time as minister to France: "While residing in Paris, I devoted every afternoon I was disengaged, for a summer or two, in examining all the principal book stores, turning over every book with my own hand" (Hayes 2008: 283, quoting Jefferson's letter to Samuel H. Smith, September 21, 1814).

[6] See notes 2–4. Both Lewis and Short and the *Oxford Latin Dictionary* cite *Att.* 1.10.4 as the only instance of *vindemiola*.

[7] *Att.* 1.7, 1.10.3, 1.11.3, 1.4.3: mention of the statuary immediately precedes the library in all four letters. The following letters also mention purchases for the *Tusculanum*: *Att.* 1.5.7, 1.6.2

Cicero tells Atticus that he has made a payment of over 20,000 *sestertii* for a shipment of statuary for the *Tusculanum*, and in another letter (*Att.* 1.9.2) he tells Atticus to "trust my strongbox" for whatever purchases of artwork Atticus might make on Cicero's behalf.[8] Cicero's willingness to purchase art works, while he apparently hesitated to pay for the library, may indicate that the library represented a much greater expenditure. On the other hand, the purchase of statuary simply may have been more urgent a priority for Cicero at the time than immediate acquisition of a library; and there were probably many more buyers for Greek art than for Greek scrolls. The purchase of statuary may have involved payments to third parties, while Cicero's words suggest that Atticus was in fact the owner of the library.[9]

Perhaps Cicero mentions these two subjects, the Greek library and the art works, in tandem because both were commissions which he had entrusted to Atticus in Greece; more likely, however, is that Cicero intended the library, like the statuary, to furnish the *Tusculanum*. Several circumstances support this hypothesis. Possession of the *Tusculanum* was both a mark of Cicero's increased status and a support for his efforts to climb higher.[10] The *Tusculanum* seems to have been the first property acquired by Cicero,[11] and

---

(the first two letters in the collection, by Shackleton Bailey's reckoning: see Shackleton Bailey 1965–70 on the dates and sequence of the earliest letters), 1.8.2, 1.9.2, 1.3.2, 1.1.5. On Cicero's purchase of sculpture, see Marvin 1989.

[8] *Att.* 1.7: "I have arranged that I will pay 20,400 *sestertii* to L. Cincius on the Ides of February" (*L. Cincio HS $\overline{XX}$CD constitui me curaturum Id. Febr.*); 1.8.2: "I paid 20,400 *sestertii* to L. Cincius for the Megarian statues, as you had written to me" (*L. Cincio HS CCI⊃⊃ CCI⊃⊃ CCCC pro signis Megaricis, ut tu ad me scripseras, curavi*); 1.9.2: "Whatever you have of the same kind which seems suitable to you for the Academy, don't hesitate to send it and trust my strongbox" (*quicquid eiusdem generis habebis dignum Academia tibi quod videbitur, ne dubitaris mittere et arcae nostrae confidito*). In addition to payment for Megarian statues to L. Cincius, the agent of Atticus (*Att.* 1.7, 1.8.2), Cicero also records payment for transportation of statues (1.3.2, "I've sent someone who will pay for the shipping" [*misimus qui pro vectura solveret*]). Cicero mentions Atticus "buying" statuary in one instance (*emisse*, 1.7); elsewhere Cicero speaks of "commissioning" Atticus (*mando*, 1.5.7, 1.10.3), or of Atticus "sending" (*mitto*, 1.8.2, 1.9.2, 1.4.3) or "procuring" (*paro*, 1.11.3; *curo*, 1.3.2) statuary. Prof. Dennis Kehoe suggests that the arrangement between Cicero and Atticus was a good-faith contract of mandate, under which Atticus would buy statuary on Cicero's order and had the right to be compensated for his expenses.

[9] *bibliothecam tuam* (*Att.* 1.10.4), *libros… tuos* (*Att.* 1.11.3), *libros tuos* (*Att.* 1.4.3). Shackleton Bailey 1965–70 *ad Att.* 1.10.4 describes the library in this way: "Apparently acquired in Greece, perhaps in response to C.'s request: cf. 1.7. But the books were bought on Atticus' own account, not as a direct commission: cf. 1.4.3."

[10] Rawson 1983: 47–51.

[11] Cicero had already acquired the *Tusculanum* by November 68 when the letters to Atticus begin: he mentions the *Tusculanum* at *Att.* 1.5.7 and *Att.* 1.6.2. Cicero acquired the *Tusculanum* before his father's death in November 68 (*Att.* 1.6.2, "Our father died on the eighth day before the Kalends of December" [*pater nobis decessit a. d. VIII Kal. Dec.*]), when Cicero presumably took possession of the family estate at Arpinum and his father's house in Rome in the Carinae

he took great pride in its possession and delight in the task of equipping and decorating the villa.[12] As Cicero's only suburban villa, the *Tusculanum* was the natural spot for a library which he would have time to use probably only during periods of vacation from business in the capital.[13] Cicero makes explicit the connection between *otium* (leisure) and his enjoyment of the library, when he says in letter 1.7: "All hope of the pleasure which I want to have when I come into some leisure, I have placed in your kindness." A villa which included both an "upper gymnasium," called the *Lyceum*, and a "lower gymnasium," the *Academy*, as Cicero's *Tusculanum* did, surely would have been incomplete without a library.[14]

Third, what kind of collection did Cicero hope to obtain from Atticus? Cicero's words do not suggest that he knew in any detail the contents of the library acquired by Atticus, nor even that he was particularly concerned with the contents; but as the library almost certainly contained only works in Greek, Cicero's words do suggest that he believed that the best way to obtain a Greek library was through the purchase of an entire collection of books, already assembled, rather than through the purchase of individual volumes.

How often entire libraries came on the market in Greece in the first century BC, we do not know; but given the difficult economic conditions in Greece in the aftermath of the Mithradatic War,[15] the continued lively traffic in Greek art works for the Italian market, and an increased interest in at least the display of literary culture among members of the Roman

---

(although Cicero may well have occupied the house in Rome before his father's death). See Shackleton Bailey 1965–70 *ad Att.* 1.6.2, on Asconius 82.10 and the date of the death of Cicero's father. For the *Tusculanum*, see Schmidt 1899: 466–72; Ashby 1910: 231–8; Ashby 1927: 167; McCracken 1935: 261–77; Shatzman 1975: 404–5; Shackleton Bailey 1976: 209–10; Coarelli 1981: 118–19.

[12] See note 7.

[13] Cicero places these words in the mouth of the orator Marcus Antonius (*De or.* 2.14.60): "when I had studiously read those books at Misenum (for it's scarcely allowed at Rome)" (*cum istos libros ad Misenum [nam Romae vix licet] studiosus legerim*). D'Arms 1970: 21–2 shows that the reference is specifically to a *villa* at Misenum. Meyer 1955: 12 points out that both Sulla and Lucullus placed their libraries in a villa rather than at Rome, presumably for that same reason. For the connection between villas and leisure, see D'Arms 1970: 12–17, 55–61.

[14] Cicero sets a conversation between himself and his brother Quintus in the library, which was in the *Lyceum*. *Div.* 1.5.8: "For when, for the sake of a walk, we had come into the Lyceum (for that is the name of the upper gymnasium)" (*nam cum ambulandi causa in Lyceum venissemus [id enim superiori gymnasio nomen est]*); 2.3.8: "For when my brother Quintus had discussed those things about divination... and it seemed that we had walked enough, then we sat down in the library, which is in the Lyceum" (*nam cum de divinatione Quintus frater ea disseruisset... satisque ambulatum videretur, tum in bibliotheca, quae in Lycio est, assedimus*). For the association between "gymnasia" and libraries in Roman villas, see Dix 2000: 448–51.

[15] Habicht 1997: 328–37.

aristocracy, it should not be surprising that Atticus was able to find a library for sale. Indeed, Atticus was perhaps uniquely qualified to act as an agent for procuring art works and books. In his years of residence in Greece, he probably came to know those with something to sell; and his acquaintance with the philosophers of Athens may have given him greater access to the book trade there. In particular, art works and books may have come to Atticus through his loans to cities like Athens and Sicyon. Atticus apparently insisted on scrupulous repayment,[16] and in the case of Sicyon, he hoped to enlist the aid of the Roman governor to secure payment.[17] In 58, Sicyon was compelled to hand over the city's paintings in order to pay its debts (Plin. HN 35.40.127), and Atticus was presumably among the creditors who received them. Through such transactions as these, with debtors both public and private, Atticus could have come into possession of large quantities of luxury items, including art works and books, which he could supply to the voracious market in Italy.[18] If we take Cicero's correspondence with Atticus as evidence for a trade in books from Greece to Italy, then we have a wider context for the reports in hostile sources of Greek libraries taken as "spoils of war," by Sulla and Lucullus, for example: the seizure of famous collections by conquering Roman generals may have been simply the most visible instances of an inexorable drain of intellectual resources from east to west.[19]

From the book trade from Greece to Italy, we turn now to the book trade in Rome. Cicero was planning a project in 54 to improve the library of his brother Quintus: "About filling up your Greek library, exchanging books, buying Latin books, I would really like those things to be done, especially since they also tend to my advantage. But I don't have someone even for myself through whom I can do them. For they aren't for sale, at least, not the sort that are satisfactory, and they can't be obtained except by a man both experienced and diligent. But I will give orders to

---

[16] Nepos (*Att.* 2.4, 5) says that Atticus' insistence was for the city's own good.
[17] *Att.* 1.13.1, 1.19.9, 2.13.2, written in January 61, March 60, and April 59, respectively; and Shackleton Bailey 1965–70.
[18] When Pompey asked Atticus to collect the statues for his theater (*Att.* 4.9.1), he probably hoped to take advantage of more than the good taste of Atticus. It may not be coincidence that a painting by Pausias of Sicyon stood in the Porticus of Pompey (Plin. *HN* 35.40.126, 127).
[19] Sulla and the "library of Aristotle": Strabo 13.1.54, Plut. *Sull.* 6.1–3, Dix 2004. The library of Lucullus: Plut. *Luc.* 42.1–2, Isid. *Etym.* 6.5.1, Dix 2000. Posidonius' remark (Ath. 5.214d) on the Athenian bibliophile Apellicon is interesting in this connection: "He acquired the library of Aristotle and other collections, for he was very rich" (τὴν Ἀριστοτέλους βιβλιοθήκην καὶ ἄλλας συνηγόραζε συχνάς· ἦν γὰρ πολυχρήματος). For the art trade, see Coarelli 1983.

Chrysippus and I will speak with Tyrannio."[20] Cicero's remark that he also will benefit indicates that he intended to buy books for himself as well as for Quintus; so the project was probably designed to repair losses which Cicero's collection, and probably his brother's as well, suffered in the attacks on their residences during Cicero's exile, a subject to which I return below.[21]

Cicero divides the project into three parts: "filling up" Quintus' Greek library, exchanging books, and buying Latin books. The exchange of books may have been between the brothers, in order to eliminate any duplicates in a block purchase, but Cicero does not make that explicit; or the exchange may have been between the brothers and booksellers. Cicero emphasizes the difficulty of the project, particularly in the purchase of books – the quality of books one wanted were not for sale; and even Latin books were carelessly written and sold – and the importance of putting a very diligent man in charge.[22] Cicero promises to speak with the Greek grammarian and scholar Tyrannio, and to give orders to Chrysippus, a member of Cicero's household staff.[23] In a subsequent letter, Cicero complains that Tyrannio

[20] Q Fr. 3.4.5, October 24, 54: *de bibliotheca tua Graeca supplenda, libris commutandis, Latinis comparandis, valde velim ista confici, praesertim cum ad meum quoque usum spectent. sed ego mihi ipsi ista per quem agam non habeo. neque enim venalia sunt, quae quidem placeant, et confici nisi per hominem et peritum et diligentem non possunt. Chrysippo tamen imperabo et cum Tyrannione loquar.* Q Fr. 3.5.6, end of October or beginning of November 54: "Tyrannio is an idler about the books; I will speak to Chrysippus. But the business is difficult even for a very diligent man. I realize this myself, who accomplish nothing with the greatest enthusiasm. For Latin books, indeed I don't know where to turn; they are both written and sold so carelessly. But nevertheless, what can be done, I will not neglect" (*de libris Tyrannio est cessator; Chrysippo dicam. sed res operosa est et hominis perdiligentis. sentio ipse, qui in summo studio nihil adsequor. de Latinis vero quo me vertam nescio; ita mendose et scribuntur et veneunt. sed tamen, quod fieri poterit, non neglegam*).

[21] Quintus' Palatine house was damaged in an attack during the reconstruction of Cicero's Palatine house, if not before (*Att.* 4.3.2; Q Fr. 2.3.7, 2.4.2, 2.6.3).

[22] Strabo strikes the same note in his account of the "library of Aristotle": "And Rome contributed much to this [decline of the Peripatetic school]; for straightway after the death of Apellicon, Sulla, who captured Athens, carried off the library of Apellicon, and the library having been brought here, Tyrannio the grammarian a lover of Aristotle had it in hand, paying court to the man in charge of the library, and some booksellers using poor copyists and not collating, which also happens with the other books written for sale both here and in Alexandria" (πολὺ δὲ εἰς τοῦτο καὶ ἡ Ῥώμη προσελάβετο, εὐθὺς γὰρ μετὰ τὴν Ἀπελλικῶντος τελευτὴν Σύλλας ἦρε τὴν Ἀπελλικῶντος βιβλιοθήκην ὁ τὰς Ἀθήνας ἑλών, δεῦρο δὲ κομισθεῖσαν Τυραννίων τε ὁ γραμματικὸς διεχειρίσατο φιλαριστοτέλης ὤν, θεραπεύσας τὸν ἐπὶ τῆς βιβλιοθήκης, καὶ βιβλιοπῶλαι τινες γραφεῦσι φαύλοις χρώμενοι καὶ οὐκ ἀντιβάλλοντες, ὅπερ καὶ ἐπὶ τῶν ἄλλων συμβαίνει τῶν εἰς πρᾶσιν γραφομένων βιβλίων καὶ ἐνθάδε καὶ ἐν Ἀλεξανδρείᾳ).

[23] Three years later, while governor of Cilicia, Cicero assigned Chrysippus as a companion to young Marcus and Quintus Cicero, a post which Chrysippus abandoned (*Att.*7.2.8 and Shackleton Bailey 1965–70). Cicero then repudiated his manumission of Chrysippus. Among

has done nothing yet; after that letter, he makes no further mention of this project.[24]

Tyrannio had been taken prisoner by Roman forces in 71 BC in the capture of Amisus in Pontus, during the campaign of Lucius Licinius Lucullus against King Mithradates, and had been handed over to Lucius Licinius Murena, a kinsman and legate of Lucullus (Plut. *Luc.* 19.7); Tyrannio presumably came to Rome with Murena. Tyrannio is perhaps best known for his connection to the so-called "library of Aristotle" which Sulla had acquired in Athens in 84 and brought to Italy; Tyrannio is supposed to have gained access to that collection and furnished copies of the texts to Andronicus of Rhodes, who produced a new edition of Aristotle.[25] Atticus and Cicero knew Tyrannio by 59, when Cicero was hesitating to undertake a work on geography because, among other reasons, he thought Tyrannio might write one.[26] Tyrannio was at Cicero's house in Rome in March of 56, where he taught the cousins Quintus and Marcus; while he was with Cicero in Rome, he may have begun the project which he was to complete at Antium in June, the restoration of Cicero's damaged library (see below).[27] According to the *Suda*,[28] Tyrannio got rich at Rome and acquired more than 30,000 books: Tyrannio may have played a very important role in the book trade, acting as an intermediary between his aristocratic patrons and those with books to sell.

Cicero may have acquired one substantial collection of books at auction.[29] Writing to Atticus from Cumae in April 55, Cicero says, "Here I feast on the library of Faustus."[30] Scholars have assumed that Faustus Sulla inherited the possessions of his father, Lucius Sulla, and that the *bibliotheca Fausti* corresponds to the "library of Aristotle."[31] Cicero's reported comment on Faustus' auction (Plut. *Cic.* 27.3), that he preferred the "public notice" of Faustus (the list of goods for sale at auction) to the "public notice" of Faustus' father (Lucius Sulla's proscription list), has led some scholars to suggest that Cicero acquired the library of Faustus at auction and then

---

his other misdeeds, Cicero specifies *furta*. Given the case of Dionysius (see below), we may wonder if his thefts included books.

[24] On bookshops in Rome, see White 2009. As White points out (273–4), Cicero assumes that he must purchase the books he wants, and despite his complaints, he must resort to the book trade; if he wants books made to order, he must use professional copyists; and his strategy is to deal with booksellers through knowledgeable agents.

[25] Strabo 13.1.54, Plut. *Sulla* 26.1–3; Dix 2004. [26] *Att.* 2.6.1.

[27] *Q Fr.* 2.4.2; Hillscher 1892, 374 (n.8). [28] *Suda*, s.v. Τυραννίων.

[29] Books do seem to have been among the items for sale at auction in Rome: see Kleberg 1973, 1–5.

[30] *Att.* 4.10.1, April 22, 55: *ego hic pascor bibliotheca Fausti*.

[31] On the "library of Faustus," see Dix 2004: 67–9.

installed that collection in his own *Cumanum*.[32] On the other hand, I incline to the view that Cicero was feasting on the library of Faustus while paying a visit to his neighbor's villa at Cumae,[33] as Cicero did in the case of other neighbors;[34] that Cicero could make so little comment on an acquisition such as the "library of Aristotle" strikes me as unlikely.

Cicero mentions one other acquisition of a group of books. In two letters of 47, he writes to his freedman Tiro that he is sending books to the villa at Tusculum; he asks Tiro to put the books away and draw up a list of them. Cicero does not indicate how he acquired these books, but his instructions to Tiro, to draw up an *index*, show that the books were a new acquisition.[35]

Gifts and inheritances

Significant collections of books probably came to Cicero as gifts, particularly through inheritances, given the great number of legacies Cicero received and his enthusiasm for books.[36] One such collection may have been part of the family estate at Arpinum which Cicero inherited from his father.[37]

---

[32] Münzer 1900b: 1516; Wendel 1952: 112; Shackleton Bailey 1965–70, *ad Att.* 4.10.1. Faustus went heavily into debt because of his political career, and Cicero, in 49, names him as one of the Pompeians who hoped for proscriptions in order to deal with their creditors: *Att.* 9.11.4, March 20, 49; Shatzman 1975: 335–6.

[33] On the properties of Lucius and Faustus Sulla in Campania, see D'Arms 1970: 14–15, 30–6, 177; Shatzman 1975: 272. See also Tutrone this volume.

[34] Young Marcus Lucullus at Tusculum, for example: *Fin.* 3.2.7; Dix 2000.

[35] *Fam.* 16.18.3: "I will send the clock and books, if it's dry. But do you have no books with you? Or are you composing something Sophoclean?" (*horologium mittam et libros, si erit sudum. sed tu nullosne tecum libellos? an pangis aliquid Sophocleum?*). On *nullosne tecum libellos*, Shackleton Bailey 1977 comments: "This seems to be a joke. The books were being sent to be added to Cicero's library at Tusculum... Tiro may be supposed to have kept reminding Cicero to send them, so Cicero pretends to think that he wants them for his own amusement." On *an pangis*, Shackleton Bailey comments "I.e. 'or are you writing, not reading?' Or the books may have consisted of tragedies." *Fam.* 16.20: "Put away the books; draw up an index, when it pleases Metrodorus, since you must live under his direction" (*libros compone; indicem cum Metrodoro libebit, quoniam eius arbitratu vivendum est*).

[36] Cicero claimed to have received more than 20 million *sestertii* from inheritances (*Phil.* 2.40); see Shatzman 1975: 411. At some point libraries became common enough in inheritances that the jurists had to define *bibliotheca*: see *Dig.* 32.52.7, where *bibliotheca* is equated with *locus* ("room"), *armarium* ("cupboard"), and *libri* ("books").

[37] Cicero says of the estate at Arpinum (*Leg.* 2.1.3) "You see this villa, as it is now, constructed more lavishly through my father's enthusiasm: when he was in infirm health, he spent almost all this time here at his studies" (*hanc vides villam, ut nunc quidem est, lautius aedificatam patris nostri studio, qui cum esset infirma valetudine, hic fere aetatem egit in litteris*). Cicero was to do a great deal of writing at Arpinum (*Q Fr.* 3.1.11, September 54: *De re publica, Pro Scauro*,

Cicero anticipated a major addition to his collection in 60 BC, when Lucius Papirius Paetus gave Cicero the books left to Paetus by Paetus' relative, Servius Claudius.[38] The books seem to have been in Greece, for Cicero asked Atticus, then in Greece, to mobilize all his connections to ensure that nothing was lost from the collection and that it was sent to him.[39] Servius Claudius probably took up residence in Greece after his departure in disgrace from Rome; he was alleged to have plagiarized an unpublished work of his father-in-law, the antiquarian and grammarian Lucius Aelius Stilo Praeconinus (Suet. *Gram.* 3.1).

Cicero had no detailed knowledge of the contents of Servius Claudius' collection; he says in the first letter, "I really need both those Greek books

---

Pro Plancio, poem to Caesar; *Att.* 13.13.1, June 45: *Academica*; *Att.* 15.27.2, July 44: *De gloria*, something in the manner of Heraclides; *Att.* 16.13a.2, November 44: a history; *Att.* 16.14.3, November 44: *De officiis*); and he describes in some detail a specific place where he was accustomed to think, to write, and to read, a small island in the Fibrenus river furnished with a "modest palaestra." Cicero compares the island to the shrine of Amalthea beside the river Thyamis, on Atticus' estate in Epirus (*Leg.* 2.1.1, 2.3.6, 7). The palaestra seems a logical spot for a library.

[38] Cicero refers to Servius Claudius as the *frater* of Paetus (*Att.* 2.1.12: *Paetus... omnis libros quos frater suus reliquisset mihi donavit*). Shackleton Bailey 1977, on *Fam.* 9.16.4, says of the relationship between Paetus and Servius Claudius: "As often, we are left in doubt whether *frater* means brother, half-brother, or *frater patruelis* [cousin] (the different *nomen* might be due to an adoption)."

[39] *Att.* 1.20.7, after May 12, 60: "Lucius Papirius Paetus, an honest man and our friend, has bestowed on me those books which Servius Claudius left. Since your friend Cincius said that it is permitted to me to take them by the Cincian law, I said that I would gladly accept them if he brought them. Now if you love me, if you know that you are loved by me, work through your friends, clients, guests, your freedmen of course and your slaves, that not even a sheet be lost. For both those Greek books which I suspect, and the Latin books which I know he left, I really need. But more and more every day, whatever time is given to me from legal work, I relax in those studies. You will do me a great favor, a great favor, I say, if you are as diligent about this as you are accustomed to be about those matters which you think I really want" (*L. Papirius Paetus, vir bonus amatorque noster, mihi libros eos quos Ser. Claudius reliquit, donavit. cum mihi per legem Cinciam licere capere Cincius amicus tuus diceret, libenter dixi me accepturum si attulisset. nunc si me amas, si te a me amari scis, enitere per amicos, clientis, hospites, libertos denique ac servos tuos, ut scida ne qua depereat. nam et Graecis iis libris quos suspicor et Latinis quos scio illum reliquisse, mihi vehementer opus est. ego autem cottidie magis quod mihi de forensi labore temporis datur in iis studiis conquiesco. per mihi, per, inquam gratum feceris si in hoc tam diligens fueris quam soles in iis rebus quas me valde velle arbitraris*). *Att.* 2.1.12, c. June 3 (?), 60: "Paetus, as I wrote to you before, has bestowed on me all the books which his kinsman left. This gift of his is placed on your diligence. If you love me, take care that they are preserved and are brought to me. Nothing can be more welcome to me than this. And please diligently preserve both the Greek and especially the Latin ones. I will believe that this little present is from you" (*Paetus, ut antea ad te scripsi, omnis libros quos frater suus reliquisset mihi donavit. hoc illius munus in tua diligentia positum est. si me amas, cura ut conserventur et ad me perferantur. hoc mihi nihil potest esse gratius. et cum Graecos tum vero Latinos diligenter ut conserves velim. tuum esse hoc munusculum putabo*).

which I suspect he left and the Latin ones which I know he left," and in the next letter, "Please diligently conserve both the Greek books and especially the Latin ones."[40] Cicero thought the collection contained both Latin and Greek works; he had some idea what the Latin books were but was not sure what Greek works it contained. Nevertheless Cicero had good reason to suppose that the acquisition of the library was worth his trouble. In a letter to Paetus (*Fam.* 9.16.4), Cicero describes Servius Claudius as *litteratissimus* and mentions his ability to distinguish genuine lines of the comic playwright Plautus from spurious ones; and Servius Claudius seems to have produced a canon of authentic Plautine plays.[41] Cicero may have known Servius Claudius and his scholarly activities from Cicero's own studies with Lucius Aelius Stilo (Cic. *Brut.* 56.207). Claudius is likely, then, to have had an extensive collection of Latin authors; at the least, Cicero may have come into possession of the complete works of Plautus.

Cicero describes the collection as "those books which Servius Claudius left" (*libros eos quos Ser. Claudius reliquit*) and "all the books which his kinsman left" (*omnis libros quos frater suus reliquisset*): the last phrase suggests that Paetus' gift to Cicero may well have been the entire library of Servius Claudius. As in the case of the Greek library of 67, Cicero says nothing of eventual receipt of Paetus' gift; Atticus may have brought the books with him on his return to Italy, this time by December of 60,[42] unless his agent Lucius Cincius had already brought the books to Cicero.[43]

Nor does Cicero say anything about his plans for the collection of Servius Claudius, whether he intended to maintain the books from Servius Claudius as a separate collection, for example, and where he planned to house them. We have seen, in the case of the Greek collection acquired by Atticus, that Cicero anticipated the use and enjoyment of the books during future periods of leisure, but also needed them to furnish his suburban villa at Tusculum in a fashion appropriate not only to his intellectual but also to his social and

---

[40] See note 39.
[41] Gell. 3.3.1. Claudius also wrote *Commentarii*, which seem to have been glossographical in nature. The *commentarii* are cited by Gellius (13.23.19) and by Servius (*ad Aen.* 1.52, 1.176, 2.229). On Claudius' works, see Münzer 1900a: 65; Funaioli 1907: 95–8.
[42] *Att.* 2.2.3, 2.3.4; Shackleton Bailey 1965–70.
[43] *Att.* 1.20.7: "Since your friend Cincius said that it is permitted to me to take them by the Cincian law, I said that I would gladly accept them if he brought them" (*cum mihi per legem Cinciam licere capere Cincius amicus tuus diceret, libenter dixi me accepturum si attulisset*).

political standing. In the same way, Cicero may have needed the collection of Servius Claudius as furnishings, this time for his town house in Rome. Cicero had purchased a house on the Palatine in 62, and this house seems to have had a library by the end of 60.[44]

Miscellaneous acquisitions

Cicero must also have acquired individual volumes to fill gaps in his collection; and as an important figure in both political and intellectual life, he must have received many gifts of individual volumes. We can point to two sources of new books for Cicero's library.

One type of gift received by Cicero was the "complimentary copy." There was a lively exchange of new works among literary men at Rome. Prominent authors dedicated works to Cicero and must have sent him a copy of the dedicated work, Varro's *De lingua Latina* and Julius Caesar's *De analogia*, for example.[45] Others sent drafts of their latest literary efforts to Cicero for his comments and suggestions for improvements.[46] Cicero's closest associates, like Atticus and his brother Quintus, probably sent copies of all their works to Cicero, just as Cicero was accustomed to send his books to Atticus.[47]

---

[44] Acquisition of the Palatine house: *Fam.* 5.6.2, December 62. Writing to Atticus, perhaps from Antium, in December 60 (*Att.* 2.2.2), Cicero says: "I was holding the *Pellene* in my hands and by Hercules I had piled up a great heap of Dicaearchus before my feet... I think I have the *Corinth* and the *Athens* at Rome" (Πελληναίων *in manibus tenebam et hercule magnum acervum Dicaearchi mihi ante pedes exstruxeram...* Κορινθίων et'Ἀθηναίων *puto me Romae habere*). This implies that Cicero had a book collection at Rome. The presence in Cicero's house of the Stoic philosopher Diodotus, who lived there until his death in 59, also suggests that the house was equipped with a library, especially as Cicero tells us that Diodotus, who became blind, had books read to him night and day (*Att.* 2.20.6; *Acad.* 2.36.115; *Brut.* 90.309; *Nat. D.* 1.3.6; *Tusc.* 5.39.113). The one explicit mention of a library in the Palatine house comes in a letter of 46 (*Fam.* 7.28.2), where Cicero says that after the morning *salutatio*, he hides in the library (*abdo in bibliothecam*).

[45] Varro's dedication of *De lingua Latina*: Varro, *Ling.* 5.1; *Att.* 13.12.3; *Fam.* 9.8.1. Caesar's dedication of *De analogia*: *Brut.* 72.253. Brutus' dedication of *De virtute*: *Fin.* 1.3.8, *Tusc.* 5.1.1. Appius Claudius Pulcher's dedication of a book on augury: *Fam.* 3.4.1, 3.11.4. C. Trebonius' book on Cicero's witticisms: *Fam.* 15.21.1, 2.

[46] Aulus Caecina sends a work to Cicero, perhaps on oratory: *Fam.* 6.7 and Shackleton Bailey 1977. Aulus Hirtius sends his "Anti-Cato" to Cicero: *Att.* 12.40.1. Cicero asks M. Fabius Gallus to send his *Cato*: *Fam.* 7.24.2. Cicero reads Caesar's *Contra Catonem*: *Att.* 13.50.1. Brutus sends an oration to Cicero for correction: *Att.* 15.1a.2.

[47] Atticus sends to Cicero his *commentarium* on Cicero's consulship in Greek: *Att.* 2.1.1. Quintus sends his tragedies to Cicero: *Q Fr.* 3.1.13, 3.5.7, 3.7.6–7; and perhaps *Q Fr.* 2.16.3, see Shackleton Bailey 1980.

Cicero supplemented the resources of his own library by borrowing books from others' libraries: chiefly from Atticus,[48] but also from his brother[49] and from other friends.[50] In one instance, Cicero says he has copied a work lent him by Atticus and is returning Atticus' copy;[51] in another case, Cicero says he will pay for a book sent to him by Atticus, which suggests that Atticus had already made a copy for Cicero.[52] Thus, through borrowing and copying, Cicero sometimes added books to his own library; but since in many (perhaps most) cases, Cicero was borrowing books in order to gather

---

[48] Cicero borrowing from Atticus: a book by Serapion (*Att.* 2.4.1); books by Alexander of Ephesus (*Att.* 2.20.6, 2.22.7); an oration of Q. Celer against M. Servilius (*Att.* 6.3.10); a book *De concordia* by Demetrius of Magnesia (*Att.* 8.11.2, 13.32.2); a book by Tyrannio (*Att.* 12.6.2); a work of Brutus (*Att.* 13.8); works of Cotta (*Att.* 13.4.3); *On the Gods* by Phaedrus (*Att.* 13.39.2); eulogies of M. Varro and Ollius (*Att.* 13.48.2).

[49] Cicero borrowing from his brother Quintus: *Att.* 2.3.4: "Bring me Theophrastus *on ambition*, from the books of my brother Quintus" (Θεοφράστου περὶ φιλοτιμίας *adfer mihi de libris Quinti fratris*); *Att.* 13.8: "Please send me Brutus' epitome of Caelius and from Philoxenus, Panaetius *on providence*" (*epitomen Bruti Caelianorum velim mihi mittas et a Philoxeno* Παναιτίου περὶ προνοίας). Shackleton Bailey 1965–70 *ad Att.* 13.8 suggests that Philoxenus was in charge of Quintus' house in Rome.

[50] Cicero borrowed Nico's *On Heavy Eating* from Sextus Fadius (who is otherwise unknown), *Fam.* 7.20.3; and perhaps borrowed from Faustus Sulla, *Att.* 4.10.1, but see discussion above. A pair of references suggests that Cicero borrowed from the library of Cato the Younger: *Att.* 16.11.4, November 5, 44: "But I have sent for [Posidonius'] book and I have written to Athenodorus Calvus to send me a *précis*, which I'm awaiting. Please urge him on and ask for it as soon as possible" (*ego autem et eius librum arcessivi et ad Athenodorum Calvum scripsi ut ad me* τὰ κεφάλαια *mitteret; quae exspecto. quem velim cohortere et roges ut quam primum*); *Att.* 16.14.4, November 12 (?), 44: "There is no need for you to urge Athenodorus, for he has sent a pretty enough memorandum" (*Athenodorum nihil est quod hortere; misit enim satis bellum* ὑπόμνημα). Cicero's statement "I have sent for [Posidonius'] book" suggests that Cicero was borrowing from someone other than Atticus. Athenodorus Calvus has been identified with Athenodorus Κορδυλίων of Tarsus, the Stoic philosopher and Pergamene librarian (Diog. Laert. 7.34), whom Cato brought from Pergamum to live in his house at Rome (Strabo 14.5.14; Plin. *HN* 7.30.113; Plut. *Cat. min.* 10.16; Plut. *Cum princ. philos.* 1.777A). Cato died in 46; Caesar allowed Cato's property to go to Cato's children (Val. Max. 5.1.10; Plut. *Cat. min.* 73.1; Shatzman 1975: 394); and Athenodorus apparently remained a member of the household, for he is said to have died in Cato's house (Strabo). Athenodorus was probably both house philosopher and librarian for Cato, and we might expect Cicero to turn to Cato's library and Athenodorus to find copies of Stoic works, like those of Posidonius; particularly as Cicero seems to have been the guardian (along with Atticus) of young M. Cato, the son of Uticensis (see *Att.* 13.6.2 and Shackleton Bailey 1965–70).

[51] *Att.* 2.20.6: "I am copying and sending back" (*describo et remitto*); *Att.* 2.22.7: "I have sent back to you" (*tibi remisi*).

[52] *Att.* 2.4.1: "You have done me a great favor in sending the book of Serapion to me; from which indeed (which we can say between ourselves) I understand scarcely the thousandth part. I have ordered that cash on hand be paid to you for it, so that you don't enter the expense under 'gifts'" (*fecisti mihi pergratum quod Serapionis librum ad me misisti; e quo quidem eo, quod inter nos liceat dicere, millesimam partem vix intellego. pro eo tibi praesentem pecuniam solvi imperavi, ne tu expensum muneribus ferres*).

material for projected literary works,[53] he probably read the book, excerpted the material he needed, then returned it. The books requested by Cicero are usually rather rare ones; presumably his library included the basic literary works needed for his work and literary activities.

Some libraries were more accessible than others: Cicero says that he was accustomed to enter the library in the Tusculan villa of young Marcus Lucullus and himself carry out whatever books he wanted to his own villa,[54] and he had Atticus fetch books for him from the library of Quintus Cicero.[55] The library of Atticus, however, seems to have been another matter; for, despite the fact that Atticus regularly sent books at Cicero's request, even when Cicero was on campaign in his province of Cilicia,[56] Cicero still found it necessary to ask Atticus to instruct his household that Cicero be given the run of Atticus' library in his absence.[57]

Although Cicero frequently borrowed books from Atticus and others, we know of Cicero lending a book in only one case; and even here, Cicero may in fact be returning a book borrowed from Atticus.[58] The letters of Atticus to Cicero might have shown that Atticus frequently borrowed from Cicero; on the other hand, Cicero's literary endeavors would have required him to borrow more frequently. In any case, the much wealthier Atticus probably

---

[53] A work of geography: *Att.* 2.4.1, 2.20.6, 2.22.7; a work appealing for peace, in 49: *Att.* 8.11.7, 8.12.6, 9.9.2; a "Political Conference" at Olympia: *Att.* 13.31.2, 13.32; *De officiis*: *Att.* 16.11.4, 16.4.4. See Shackleton Bailey 1965–70 ad. locc.

[54] *Fin.* 3.2.7: *nam in Tusculano cum essem vellemque a bibliotheca pueri Luculli quibusdam libris uti, veni in eius villam, ut eos ipse, ut solebam, depromerem.*

[55] See note 49.   [56] *Att.* 6.3.10.

[57] *Att.* 4.14.1, May 54: "Please write to your house that your books be accessible to me just as if you yourself were present, both the others and those of Varro. For there are some things from these books which I must use for those which I have in hand; which, I hope, you will certainly approve" (*velim domum ad te scribas ut mihi tui libri pateant non secus ac si ipse adesses, cum ceteri tum Varronis. est enim mihi utendum quibusdam rebus ex his libris ad eos quos in manibus habeo; quos, ut spero, tibi valde probabo*). Although Cicero's request may simply have been for the sake of politeness, it may also be connected with his desire to use the *libri Varronis*. These books, which Cicero says he needed to consult for his *De re publica*, may have been Varro's *Antiquitates rerum humanarum*: Boissier 1861: 46–7; Della Corte 1954: 110. One consequence of Cicero's request to use Varro's books may have been that Atticus suggested to Cicero that Cicero include Varro in one of his works: Kumaniecki 1962: 228–9. Varro may have sent his friend Atticus a copy of this or some other work as a gift or for his comments; Varro may have asked Atticus not to show it to others, just as we know Cicero did with some works which he sent to Atticus (*Att.* 13.21a.1, 2; 13.22.3).

[58] *Att.* 4.11.2: "I am sending Demetrius of Magnesia's book to you immediately, so that there will be someone to bring back a letter from you to me" (*Demetri Magnetis tibi mitto statim, ut sit qui a te mihi epistulam referat*). Atticus may have asked Cicero to send him some book of Demetrius in Cicero's possession; or perhaps he had asked Cicero to return a book which Atticus had lent to Cicero. Cicero later asks Atticus to lend him a work *De concordia* which Demetrius had dedicated to Atticus (see note 48 above), which suggests that Atticus is more likely to have had works of Demetrius in his library than is Cicero.

had a better-stocked collection (at least in some fields) than did Cicero; and his frequent sojourns in Athens would have given Atticus readier access to Greek texts.

Losses

The first tale of loss involves the library in Cicero's residence at Antium. Cicero speaks explicitly of a *bibliotheca* at three of his properties: the suburban villa at Tusculum, the town house on the Palatine, and the house at Antium. Cicero had acquired the house at Antium around 60 BC.[59] Writing from Antium in 59, Cicero says that he has a "festive supply" of books at the house,[60] and during that visit he devoted himself to literature and considered writing a geographical work.[61] The words *festiva copia* suggest that Cicero did not have a substantial collection of books at Antium, but only those brought with him from Rome. In addition to the transferred meaning of *festiva*, "agreeable, pleasing," Cicero may also have in mind the literal meaning of "festal, belonging to a feast": that is, the supply of books he took with him when he left Rome during a holiday from public business – "reading for the holidays" or "enough books to last through the holiday."

Three years later, after his return from exile, Cicero clearly does have a library at Antium. Writing to Atticus in June of 56, Cicero says: "It will be very nice if you come to us. You will find Tyrannio's wonderful arrangement of my books, the remains of which are much better than I had thought."[62] Cicero's mention of "the remains of my books" led to the suggestion that the house at Antium, like his Palatine house and the villas at Tusculum and Formiae, was attacked by the gangs of Clodius in 58.[63] If that was the case,

---

[59] *Att.* 2.2.1, c. June 3 (?), 60: "Your boy met me on the Kalends of June as I was going to Antium" (*Kal. Iun. eunti mihi Antium . . . venit obviam tuus puer*). For the house at Antium, see Schmidt 1899: 473–5.

[60] *Att.* 2.6.1, April 59: "And so I delight myself with books, of which I have a festive supply at Antium, or I count the waves" (*itaque aut libris me delecto, quorum habeo Anti festivam copiam, aut fluctus numero*).

[61] *Att.* 2.4.1–3: Atticus sends books by Serapion, Cicero considering a geography; 2.5.2, 2.6.1, 2: the geography and a "Secret History"; 2.7.1: the geography and two speeches; 2.8.1: the "Secret History."

[62] *Att.* 4.4a.1: *perbelle feceris si ad nos veneris. offendes dissignationem Tyrannionis mirificam librorum meorum, quorum reliquiae multo meliores sunt quam putaram*.

[63] Meyer 1955: 54, who identifies the *villam apertam ac ne rudem quidem etiam nunc* ("a villa uncovered and not even rudely finished even now") to which Cicero hesitated to invite his friend M. Marius (*Q Fr.* 2.9.2), with Antium, rather than the *Tusculanum* or *Formianum*. On the date and place of *Q Fr.* 2.9, see Shackleton Bailey 1980, who prefers the *Tusculanum*. Cicero twice calls the residence at Antium a *domus* (*Att.* 9.9.4, 13.47a.1).

it is odd that Cicero makes no mention of it. He received no compensation for damages at Antium, as he did for the other three properties.[64] When he writes to his brother Quintus, in March 56, "I build in three places, I repair the rest," the three places must surely be the Palatine, the *Tusculanum* and the *Formianum*, and the house at Antium must belong among "the rest."[65] Indeed, Antium became Cicero's refuge during the reconstruction work at Rome and Tusculum.[66]

So a house which seems to have had no library in 59, does have a library in 56; and although the house seems to have gone undamaged during Cicero's exile, the library is in need of repair. The explanation is simple: when Cicero speaks of "the remains of my books," he is not referring to just the books at Antium, but to his entire collection of books, wherever housed before his exile. Cicero probably gathered up all his remaining books upon his return and deposited them in one place.[67] The repair and arrangement of the books would have been easier to accomplish when they all had been assembled in one spot. The house at Antium was the logical choice for the temporary storage of his damaged collection, for the house was not seriously damaged and was therefore able to provide storage space during the reconstruction at Rome and Tusculum; and Antium was near enough to Rome so that Cicero could use the books stored there (by having books sent from Antium to Rome), but far enough from the political turmoil at Rome to avoid new attacks on the property like that which befell the Palatine house in November 57.[68] Antium was also close to Troia, where Cicero was considering the purchase of a villa to replace his *Tusculanum*.[69] Thus, Cicero

---

[64] *Att.* 4.2.5.   [65] *Q Fr.* 2.5.1.   [66] Schmidt 1899: 474.
[67] Schmidt 1899: 474; Wendel 1943: 271–2. Upon his return to Rome, Cicero speaks of "gathering up and setting in order the remains" (*Att.* 4.1.3, September 57): "But in domestic matters – you are not unaware how they have been smashed, dissipated, plundered – I am really struggling, and I am in need not so much of your resources, which I consider my own, as of your advice, in gathering up and setting in order the remains" (*in re autem familiari, quae quem ad modum fracta, dissipata, direpta sit non ignoras, valde laboramus, tuarumque non tam facultatum, quas nostras esse iudico, quam consiliorum ad colligendas et constituendas reliquias nostras indigemus*).
[68] *Att.* 4.3.2.
[69] Of the *Tusculanum*, Cicero says (*Att.* 4.2.7, October 57) "I have put the *Tusculanum* up for sale, although not easily do I lack a suburban estate" (*Tusculanum proscripsi, <etsi> suburbano non facile careo*). For the reading <etsi>, see Shackleton Bailey 1965–70. It appears that the damage to the villa at Tusculum was so extensive, and the amount awarded by the consuls so inadequate, that Cicero decided to sell the villa and buy another property with the moneys from its sale and from the consuls. Writing to Atticus of a property at Troia which he had considered buying in 56, Cicero says (*Att.* 9.9.4) "I thought those gardens would be more agreeable to me because of the house at Antium which I had then and less expensive than if I had rebuilt the Tusculan villa" (*ego istos hortulos propter domum Anti quam tum habebam iucundiores mihi fore putabam et minore impensa quam si Tusculanum refecissem*). For this property, see also *Att.* 9.13.6 and Shackleton Bailey 1965–70 *ad loc.*

would have had continued access to a library while at a suburban villa. His announced intention to sell the *Tusculanum* might also have led him to remove any books remaining there.

The library at Antium, then, which Cicero does not mention until after his return from exile, was probably created only then, and created from the remnants of Cicero's collection of books previously housed at other properties.

Cicero enumerates several tasks in the repair: the "arrangement" of the books, which Tyrannio had taken in hand before the arrival of two skilled slaves sent by Atticus; and the repair of book-rolls, the provision of shelving, and painting.[70] What Cicero meant by "arrangement" is unclear: he uses the noun *dissignatio* in one letter and the verb *disposuit* in another;[71] but as his letters emphasize the physical appearance of the library, he may refer simply to the orderly and pleasing arrangement of the book rolls on the shelves.

Cicero anticipated that Tyrannio would employ Dionysius and Menophilus, the two *librarioli* sent to Antium by Atticus, as "book-binders" (*glutinatores*). Cicero mentions one task performed by the *glutinatores*, attaching small tags of parchment bearing the book title to the papyrus rolls. Dionysius and Menophilus may also have strengthened rolls in danger of breaking or cracking, by reinforcing the back with extra strips or patches of papyrus, and mended rolls already broken in two. If the roll had lost a column of writing, a copy of the missing section would be procured and pasted into the roll.[72]

---

[70] Att. 4.4a.1, 2: "And please send me two of your book men, whom Tyrannio can use as binders and as assistants for other things, and tell them to bring a piece of parchment, from which labels are made, which you Greeks, I think, call *sittybae*. But this, if it's convenient for you ... Do come, and about the book men, if you love me, be diligent" (*et velim mihi mittas de tuis librariolis duos aliquos quibus Tyrannio utatur glutinatoribus, ad cetera administris, iisque imperes ut sumant membranulum ex qua indices fiant, quos vos Graeci, ut opinor, σιττύβας appellatis. sed haec, si tibi erit commodum... tu fac venias, et de librariis, si me amas, diligenter*). Att. 4.8: "After Tyrannio has arranged the books for me, a soul seems to have been added to my house. And in that business the work of your Dionysius and Menophilus has been miraculous. Nothing is more attractive than those shelves of yours, after the *sittybae* have adorned the books" (*postea vero quam Tyrannio mihi libros disposuit, mens addita videtur meis aedibus. qua quidem in re mirifica opera Dionysi et Menophili tui fuit. nihil venustius quam illa tua pegmata, postquam sittybae libros illustrarunt*). Att. 4.5.4: "Your men have painted my library along with the shelving and the labels; please praise them" (*bibliothecam mihi tui pinxerunt cum structione et sittybis, eos velim laudes*).

[71] Att. 4.4a.1: *offendes dissignationem Tyrannionis mirificam librorum meorum*; Att. 4.8: *Tyrannio mihi libros disposuit*.

[72] Turner 1983 remarks that Cicero used *sittybae* for the book labels, but perhaps should have written *sillybi*. On what Cicero wrote (or should have written) and on the various tasks

Dionysius and Menophilus were also to assist with other tasks, which seem to have included the installation of beautiful bookcases, *pegmata*, provided by Atticus. *Pegmata* is, like *bibliotheca*, a Greek word; it is not found outside Cicero with the specific sense of "bookcase." Perhaps Cicero is using a bit of Graecizing slang here, like his use of *sittybae* in the same letters. The Greek noun πῆγμα is derived from the verb πήγνυμι, "fasten together, put together"; perhaps *pegmata* implies a kind of portable shelving which could be transported in pieces and assembled on the spot.[73]

Cicero sold the house at Antium between 55 and 49 BC.[74] It seems likely that Cicero had transferred the books housed there back to his Palatine house and the villa at Tusculum before the sale.[75]

Cicero's last mention of his collection comes in letters of 46 and 45. Writing to Publius Sulpicius Rufus, the governor of Illyricum, in August 46,

---

undertaken by *glutinatores*, see also Dorandi 1983, Puglia 1995, Puglia 1997: 99–119, Caroli 2005, Pintaudi 2006.

[73] In his last reference to the library, Cicero refers to the painting of the room. The manuscript reading for *Att.* 4.5.4 is *bibliothecam mihi tui pinxerunt constructione et sittybis*. Shackleton Bailey 1965–70 prints *bibliothecam mihi tui pinxerunt cum structione et sittybis*, and comments: "*structio* refers to the tiers of bookshelves (*pegmata*). Besides these and the book labels, the *librarioli* also painted the ceiling and walls, where visible: so Birt... *constructione* (or *constrictione* [Hertzberg]) is usually supposed to refer to binding (cf. 4.4a.1 *glutinatoribus*), but even if the word could have such a meaning it would consort oddly with *pinxerunt*..." Birt 1909, 469–70 proposed the emendation from *constructione* to *cum structione*, producing this translation: "Your slaves have painted my library along with the shelving and the book labels." Watt 1963, 21–3 pointed out that Cicero uses *pingere* in the sense of "beautify, embellish" only of literary or oratorical style, and that *pinxerunt* must here refer literally to "painting"; none of the meanings proposed for *constructione* accords with that meaning. Watt remarks that *structio* is a rare word and occurs only in late Latin; he suggests the reading *con<fecta pegmatum con>structione et sittybis*: "With the construction of the shelves and the book labels finished, your slaves have painted my library." Wendel 1943, 274 note 25, objects to the "learned Greeks" having to paint the room and the shelves; surely, however, this is no more menial a task than assembling the shelves, a task which he does assign to them. Menci 1988: 502 adopts the reading *constrictione*, referring the term *constrictio* to "the operations of gluing, binding and restoration executed by the *glutinatores*." Dorandi 1992a: 42–3 proposes the following emendation: *con<fecta librorum con>strictione*; he identifies *constrictio* as a book-roll cover and translates "Your *librarioli* have colorfully adorned my library with the book-roll sleeves and the labels."

[74] The latest letters from Antium come in 56 or 55. Doubts about date and place of origin attach to letters *Att.* 4.4a-12 (letters 78–86 in Shackleton Bailey 1965–70). Letters from Antium in this group, by Shackleton Bailey's reckoning, are: 4.4a, c. 20 June (?), 56; 4.8, shortly after the preceding; 4.5, soon after the preceding (these three letters, *Att.* 4.4a, 4.8, and 4.5, are the letters about the library at Antium); 4.12, end of June (?), 56; 4.8a, from Antium or Tusculum, c. 17 November (?), 56; 4.11, from Tusculum or Antium, June 26, 55. For the date and origin of all these letters, see Taylor 1949: 217–21; Shackleton Bailey 1965–70, vol. II, 233–5 (Appendix 2); and Shackleton Bailey 1977, vol. I, 319. Cicero speaks of ownership of the house at Antium in the past tense in 49 (*Att.* 9.9.4; see also *Att.* 9.13.6 and Shackleton Bailey 1965–70); in 45, Cicero says that Lepidus has the house which he sold (*Att.* 13.47a.1).

[75] Wendel 1943: 271–2.

Cicero asks Sulpicius to take into custody Cicero's runaway slave Dionysius, who while in charge of Cicero's library had stolen books from it.[76] The next governor of Illyricum, Publius Vatinius, learns of Dionysius from someone other than Cicero; Vatinius knows that Dionysius is an educated slave, as he calls Dionysius a reader (*anagnostes*), and he promises to find him.[77] Cicero replies that he will honor whatever promises Vatinius makes to Dionysius (presumably promises of lenient treatment by Cicero),[78] but the year 45 ends with Dionysius still on the loose.[79]

Cicero's reactions to this situation are very interesting. He characterizes his library as financially valuable (*meam bibliothecen multorum nummorum*), accuses Dionysius of pilfering many books (*multos libros surripuisset*), and calls Dionysius "truly shameless" (*vero improbus*). On the other hand, Cicero seems to deprecate his own request: "It's a small matter but a great grief to my spirit" (*res ipsa parva sed animi mei dolor magnus est*); but

---

[76] *Fam.* 13.77.3: "In addition I ask of you in greater measure by our friendship and by your uninterrupted devotion to me that you even make a great effort in this business: My slave Dionysius, who handled my very valuable library, when he had pilfered many books and thought he wouldn't go unpunished, ran away. He is in your province. Both my friend Marcus Bolanus and many others have seen him at Narona, but when he said that he had been manumitted, they believed him. If you take care of restoring him to me, I can't say how welcome it will be to me. It's a small matter but a great grief to my spirit. Where he is and what can be done, Bolanus will tell you. If I recover the man through you, I will feel that I have been done the greatest kindness by you" (*praeterea a te peto in maiorem modum pro nostra amicitia et pro tuo perpetuo in me studio ut in hac re etiam elabores: Dionysius, servus meus, qui meam bibliothecen multorum nummorum tractavit, cum multos libros surripuisset nec se impune laturum putaret, aufugit. is est in provincia tua. eum et M. Bolanus, familiaris <meus>, et multi alii Naronae viderunt, sed cum se a manu missum esse diceret, crediderunt. hunc tu si mihi restituendum curaris, non possum dicere quam mihi gratum futurum sit. res ipsa parva sed animi mei dolor magnus est. ubi sit et quid fieri possit Bolanus te docebit. ego, si hominem per te reciperaro, summo me a te beneficio adfectum arbitrabor*).

[77] *Fam.* 5.9.2, Publius Vatinius to Cicero, July 45: "I am told that your slave reader is a fugitive with the Vardaei. You have given me no orders about him, nevertheless I have ordered that he be sought on land and sea and I will certainly find him, unless he has fled into Dalmatia; and yet I'll root him out from there someday" (*dicitur mihi tuus servus anagnostes fugitivus cum Vardaeis esse. de quo tu mihi nihil mandasti, ego tamen terra marique ut conquireretur praemandavi et profecto tibi illum reperiam, nisi in Dalmatiam aufugerit; et inde tamen aliquando eruam*).

[78] *Fam.* 5.11.3, Cicero to Publius Vatinius, December 45: "About Dionysius, if you love me, accomplish it. Whatever promise you give him, I will fulfill; but if he is shameless, as he is, you will lead him as a captive in your triumph" (*de Dionysio, si me amas, confice. quamcumque ei fidem dederis, praestabo; si vero improbus fuerit, ut est, duces eum captivum in triumpho*).

[79] *Fam.* 5.10a.1, Publius Vatinius to Cicero, December 45/January 44: "About your Dionysius I extricate nothing so far, and so much the less because the Dalmatian cold, which ejected me from there, has also frozen me here. But nevertheless I won't desist from rooting him out someday. But nevertheless you demand all sorts of difficult things from me" (*de Dionysio tuo adhuc nihil extrico, et eo minus quod me frigus Dalmaticum, quod illinc eiecit, etiam hic refrigeravit. sed tamen non desistam quin aliquando eruam. sed tamen omnia mi dura imperas*).

even so, he will consider the capture of Dionysius the "greatest kindness" (*summo beneficio*) that he can receive from the governor. The simultaneous depreciation of request and multiplication of thanks seems dictated by the rhetoric of mutual favors among the Roman elite. Cicero does want the governors to undertake this service and so tries to convince them, first, that the service will prove easy for them to accomplish, and second, that it will earn them gratitude in excess of the effort expended as well as the prospect of favors in return; but should they fail, Cicero would not want that failure to color their relationship in the future.

Whether Cicero felt that Dionysius had betrayed Cicero's trust or was guilty of ingratitude for the education he had received, or whether he was influenced by some other emotion, lies beyond the available evidence and the scope of this chapter. Confining our speculation to what Cicero reveals in private correspondence to his familiars, we can say that Cicero's principal goal was the return of Dionysius. Cicero suggests that fear of imminent detection of his thefts led Dionysius to flee; and Cicero may have believed that he could still recover the stolen books, if only he could recover Dionysius. This hope would explain Cicero's pledge to honor the promises of Vatinius. Dionysius might have hidden away the stolen books, or taken them with him; or if he had sold them, he could reveal the identity of the buyers. Equally likely, it seems to me, is that Dionysius stole the books specifically to finance his escape, and may have left a trail of sold books behind him as he made his way to Illyricum and Dalmatia.

Patterns of use

As we saw above, Cicero speaks explicitly of a *bibliotheca* at three of his properties, the suburban villa at Tusculum, the town house on the Palatine, and the house at Antium. In the case of the Tusculan villa and the Palatine house, Cicero uses the term *bibliotheca* primarily of the room which housed his books. One characteristic of a collection of books which makes it a "library," of course, is the provision of a room for it. As I have argued above, the *bibliotheca* at Antium is of a different order: it was probably created only after Cicero's exile, from the remnants of his collection of books previously housed at other properties, and its contents returned to Cicero's other properties before he sold the Antium house.

That Cicero does not mention a *bibliotheca* at other properties does not mean that he kept no books in them: every residence might have a few scrolls left in it, although perhaps too few to merit a room exclusively devoted to their storage and to merit the designation *bibliotheca,* and some residences simply may have had *bibliothecae* which go unmentioned by Cicero. There would be advantages to keeping some books in each residence: reading material would always be at hand for the owner, no matter how sudden a visit he might make, or for guests, especially for those who might use the residence in his absence. Like vacation cottages, guest rooms, or dig houses, each of Cicero's residences may have had a small collection of scrolls available.[80]

Even the book owner who kept some volumes in each of his properties might house the bulk of his collection in one central location; he would take books with him or have them sent when he went to another residence. For a book lover like Cicero, who actually read his books and used them in his writing, a central location offered several advantages: centralization would eliminate the need for duplication (or the possibility of accidental duplication) of the same work in different properties, eliminate confusion about the location of individual works, allow better care and security for the collection, and reduce the number of persons needed to take care of it. Disadvantages would be the necessity to pack up and transport books whenever one traveled or to wait for the books one needed while a messenger went to the central location and then returned with the book.

Despite the (seemingly obvious) benefits of centralization, by the late 60s BC Cicero had two *bibliothecae* in locations only about sixteen miles apart. The two collections may have differed originally in contents – especially if the *Tusculanum* library began with the collection acquired in Greece by Atticus and the library in the Palatine town house received the collection inherited from Servius Claudius – and purpose. The *Tusculanum* was intended for *otium* and so probably consisted of philosophical and literary works,[81] while the Palatine may have been intended to support Cicero's political and

---

[80] Pliny the Younger seems to have had such a collection in his Laurentine villa (*Ep.* 2.17.8): "A bedroom is attached at the corner, curved into an apse, which follows the movement of the sun in all its windows. A cupboard is inserted into its wall in the appearance of a library, which holds books not for reading but for re-reading" (*adnectitur angulo cubiculum in hapsida curvatum, quod ambitum solis fenestris omnibus sequitur. parieti eius in bibliothecae speciem armarium insertum est, quod non legendos libros sed lectitandos capit*).

[81] Cicero writing at Tusculum: *De oratore,* November 55 (*Att.* 4.13.2); *De re publica,* October or November 54 (*Q Fr.* 3.5 (5–7).1); *Cato,* May (?) 46 (*Att.* 12.4.2), July or August 46 (*Att.* 12.5.2), July (?) 46 (*Fam.* 16.22.1); *Orator,* October (?) 46 (*Att.* 12.6a.1); Letter to Caesar, May 45 (*Att.* 12.51.2, 12.52.2, 13.1.3, 13.2, 13.27.1, 13.28.2); "Political Conference at Olympia," May 45 (*Att.* 13.31.2, 13.30.2, 13.32.2), June 45 (*Att.* 13.33.2, 13.6.4, 13.4.1, 13.5.1, 13.8, 12.5b); *De natura deorum,* August 45 (*Att.* 13.38.1, 13.39.2, 13.40.2); *Laudatio Porciae,* August 45 (*Att.* 13.48.2, 13.37.3).

forensic activity and so might have consisted primarily of rhetorical, legal, and historical works.[82] The Palatine library may also have been used to further the education of Cicero's son and nephew, who received instruction in his house.[83] During periods of enforced leisure for Cicero, such as the domination of the first "triumvirate" and then of Caesar, he was constrained to stay in Rome but play only a cautious and subsidiary role in affairs of state; under those circumstances, he expressed his desire to be allowed to devote himself entirely to his studies, and he would have felt the need to have a library at hand.[84]

I suggested above, in the section on gifts and inheritances, that Cicero inherited his father's book collection when he inherited the family estate at Arpinum. Cicero did a great deal of writing there, and the small island furnished with a modest palaestra, where he read and wrote, would be a logical setting for a library.[85]

For Cicero's other residential properties, we have no mention of a library but much evidence for literary activity. Cicero spent a great deal of time at the *Formianum*[86] from December 50 to June 49, the first months of the

---

[82] Cicero has the *Corinth* and the *Athens* of Dicaearchus at Rome (*Att.* 2.2.2), see note 44; Cicero consulting the *De iure civili* of Q. Mucius Scaevola: *Fam.* 7.22, Shackleton Bailey 1977, Fränkel 1957: 67.

[83] Boys studying with Aristodemus, April 59: *Att.* 2.7.5, Shackleton Bailey 1965–70; studying with Tyrannio, March 56: *Q Fr.* 2.4.2; studying with the *rhetor* Paeonius, September–October 54: *Q Fr.* 3.1.14, 3.3.4. Diodotus the Stoic also taught in Cicero's house. Cicero remarks that Diodotus continued to teach geometry even after he had become blind (*Tusc.* 5.39.113), and in a letter to Caesar (*Fam.* 13.16), Cicero recommends Apollonius, a freedman of the late P. Crassus (son of the triumvir) and a pupil of Diodotus, "for from a boy he was often at my house with Diodotus the Stoic, a most learned man in my judgment" (*nam domi meae cum Diodoto Stoico, homine meo iudicio eruditissimo, multum a puero fuit*).

[84] See, for example, *Fam.* 1.8.3 (February [?] 55), "that which most pleases me, that I return to my studies of literature" (*id quod mihi maxime libet, ad nostra me studia referam litterarum*); *Fam.* 9.1.2 (late 47/early 46), "know that I, after I came into the city, returned into friendship with old friends, that is with my books" (*scito enim me, postea quam in urbem venerim, redisse cum veteribus amicis, id est cum libris nostris, in gratiam*); *Fam.* 7.33.2 (end of July [?] 46), "For I have resolved, if only Caesar either allows or wants this, to put aside that persona, in which I have often proved myself to that very man, and to hide myself away entirely in literature and to enjoy the most honorable leisure with you and with other students of literature" (*mihi enim iudicatum est, si modo hoc Caesar aut patietur aut volet, deponere illam iam personam, in qua me saepe illi ipsi probavi, ac me totum in litteras abdere tecumque et cum ceteris earum studiosis honestissimo otio perfrui*).

[85] See note 37.

[86] On the *Formianum*, see Schmidt 1899: 348–55; Coarelli 1982: 365–6. He must have owned the *Formianum* at least by the end of 67, when he had statues intended for Tusculum unloaded at Caieta (*Att.* 1.3.2, "The statues which you provided for me, they have been unloaded at Caieta" [*signa quae nobis curasti, ea sunt ad Caietam exposita*]). In his next letter (*Att.* 1.4.3, dated to the first half of 66), Cicero says that the statues are in the *Formianum* ("The statues which you sent to me before, I have not seen yet; they are in the *Formianum*" [*quae mihi antea signa*

civil war between Pompey and Caesar.[87] As he wrestled with the issue of his own position in the war, Cicero often sought solace in reading and writing; he occupied himself with θέσεις, rhetorical exercises on invented themes. While the themes were clearly statements of his own political dilemma,[88] Cicero may have collected historical material for these exercises. His reading included the Seventh Letter attributed to Plato, in which the author speaks of Plato's detention at Syracuse by Dionysius II.[89] Cicero undertook to write some kind of political tract appealing for peace, and had Atticus send a book he needed for this tract to Formiae, although he eventually abandoned the

---

misisti, ea nondum vidi; in Formiano sunt]). Schmidt 1899: 348 suggests that Cicero acquired the *Formianum* before the *Tusculanum*, pointing to the traditional orientation of Arpinum towards Naples and the fact that the river Liris, which flows past Arpinum, ends in the Gulf of Formiae (an important consideration, since agricultural estates often moved their products by water); and he suggests that Cicero's mention of the *Formianum* at *Att.* 1.4.3 ("I will decorate Caieta, if ever I begin to have an abundance" [*Caietam, si quando abundare coeperis, ornabo*]) shows that he had become almost indifferent to the *Formianum* in contrast to the more recently purchased *Tusculanum*. On the other hand, perhaps Cicero had inherited the *Formianum*, as well, from his father.

[87] See *Att.* 7.3–10.18 (letters 126–210 in Shackleton Bailey 1965–70). For Cicero's activities and letters during this period, see Shackleton Bailey 1965–70, vol. IV, 428–37 (Appendix 1: "Ephemeris: 18 January–19 May 49").

[88] *Att.* 9.4.1–3, "But nevertheless, lest I give myself up entirely to grief, I have taken up some general questions as it were, which are both political and belonging to these times, in order to remove my mind from its complaints and to be occupied with that very thing which is at issue. They are of this sort: If one must remain in his fatherland under a tyranny, if one must work for the dissolution of tyranny in every way, even if the city is going to be entirely in danger through this… Occupying myself in these deliberations and arguing on both sides now in Greek now in Latin I both take my mind away from annoyances for a little while and I consider something useful" (*sed tamen, ne me totum aegritudini dedam, sumpsi mihi quasdam tamquam θέσεις, quae et πολιτικαὶ sunt et temporum horum, ut et abducam animum a querelis et in eo ipso de quo agitur exercear. eae sunt huius modi:* εἰ μενετέον ἐν τῇ πατρίδι τυραννουμένης αὐτῆς, εἰ παντὶ τρόπῳ τυραννίδος κατάλυσιν πραγματευτέον, κἂν μέλλῃ διὰ τοῦτο περὶ τῶν ὅλων ἡ πόλις κινδυνεύσειν… *in his ego me consultationibus exercens et disserens in utramque partem tum Graece tum Latine et abduco parumper animum a molestiis et* τῶν προὔργου τι *delibero*).

[89] Cicero recalls Plato *Ep.* 7.348a at *Att.* 9.10.2: "So day and night like that bird I look over the sea, I desire to fly away" (*ita dies et noctes tamquam avis illa mare prospecto, evolare cupio*), and quotes *Ep.* 7.329d at *Att.* 9.13.4: "But I do not fear the finesse of this one so much as the duress. 'For the requests of tyrants,' Plato says, 'you know that they are mixed with compulsion'" (*ego autem non tam* γοητείαν *huius timeo quam* πειθανάγκην. ʻαἱ γὰρ τῶν τυράννων δεήσεις' *inquit* Πλάτων ʻοἶσθ' ὅτι μεμιγμέναι ἀνάγκαις'). See Shackleton Bailey 1965–70. The *exempla* at *Att.* 9.10.3, although conventional and well known, also may point to Cicero gathering historical material: "But those things clung to me: Tarquinius acted wrongly who encouraged Porsenna, who encouraged Octavius Mamilius against his fatherland, Coriolanus impiously who sought aid from the Volsci, Themistocles rightly who preferred to die, Hippias son of Pisistratus, who fell in the battle of Marathon bearing arms against his fatherland, was impious" (*mihi autem haeserunt illa: male Tarquinius qui Porsennam, qui Octavium Mamilium contra patriam, impie Coriolanus qui auxilium petiit a Volscis, recte Themistocles qui mori maluit, nefarius Hippias, Pisistrati filius, qui in Marathonia pugna cecidit arma contra patriam ferens*).

project.[90] Cicero also tried to provide a tutor for young Marcus and Quintus during the family's sojourn at the *Formianum*.[91] All these things indicate that Cicero had books at Formiae during his lengthy stay; at the same time, it is clear that he was in daily contact with Atticus in Rome, and so could obtain books as he needed them from his own library in Rome and from Atticus.

Cicero's last property in Latium was the villa at Astura, which he had acquired perhaps by 46.[92] Astura was Cicero's refuge after the death of his daughter Tullia in February 45.[93] He spent his entire day reading and writing, Cicero says, and he found literary efforts no more difficult there than if he were at home.[94] He had books with him: philosophical works, the *liber annalis* of Atticus, political tracts of Aristotle and others;[95] and he wrote not only a *Consolatio* for himself, but the *Academica* and a political tract addressed to Caesar.[96] Cicero came to Astura in March from Atticus' house in Rome, and spent April in Atticus' *Nomentanum* before returning to Astura in May; many of the books which Cicero had with him at Astura, then, may have been borrowed from Atticus.[97]

---

[90] Demetrius of Magnesia *on concord*: *Att.* 8.11.7, 8.12.6, 9.9.2.

[91] Atticus' freedman M. Pomponius Dionysius: *Att.* 7.26.3, 8.4.1, 2, 8.5.1, 8.10.

[92] On the villa at Astura, see Schmidt 1899: 475–8; Coarelli 1982: 298, 300. On *Att.* 12.9, written from Astura in November 46, see Shackleton Bailey 1965–70.

[93] See *Att.* 12.13–12.44, 12.46, 13.26 (letters 250–87 in Shackleton Bailey 1965–70).

[94] *Att.* 12.13.1: "I miss only you; but I employ literature with no more difficulty than if I were at home" (*te unum desidero; sed litteris non difficilius utor quam si domi essem*); *Att.* 12.14.3: "I write all the day, not that I profit at all but meanwhile I am engaged – indeed not enough (for the force presses hard), but nevertheless I am assuaged" (*totos dies scribo, non quo proficiam quid sed tantisper impedior – non equidem satis [vis enim urget], sed relaxor tamen*); *Att.* 12.15: "In this solitude I lack conversation with all, and with the morning I conceal myself in a dense and rough forest, I do not come out from there before evening. After you nothing is friendlier to me than solitude. In that solitude all my conversation is with literature" (*in hac solitudine careo omnium colloquio, cumque mane me in silvam abstrusi densam et asperam, non exeo inde ante vesperum. secundum te nihil est mihi amicius solitudine. in ea mihi omnis sermo est cum litteris*). For more in the same vein, see *Att.* 12.16, 12.18.1, 12.20.1, 12.21.5, 12.28.2, 12.38.1, 12.38a.1, 12.40.2, 13.26.2; *Fam.* 5.15.3, 4.

[95] Philosophical works on grief: *Att.* 12.18.1, 12.21.5; *liber annalis* of Atticus: 12.23.2; the *Cyrus* of Antisthenes: 12.38a.2; the *Letter to Alexander* of Aristotle and of Theopompus: 12.40.2.

[96] *Consolatio*: *Att.* 12.14.3, 12.18.1, 12.20.2, 12.22.2, 12.23.3, 12.24.2; *Academica*: 12.23.2, 12.44.4; "Letter of Advice" to Caesar: 12.40.2, 13.26.2.

[97] *Att.* 12.14.3: "For there is nothing written by anyone about diminishing grief which I did not read at your house" (*nihil enim de maerore minuendo scriptum ab ullo est quod ego non domi tuae legerim*). Compare *Att.* 12.18.1: "those authors whom I read often now who say that it is right that that thing be done" (*quos nunc lectico auctores qui dicant fieri id oportere*); and *Att.* 12.21.5: "the most learned men... all of whose writings whatever on that opinion I not only read" (*doctissimi homines... quorum scripta omnia quaecumque in eam sententiam non legi solum*). Thus it seems that Cicero brought the philosophical works on grief with him from Atticus' house.

Cicero owned three properties on the Bay of Naples: at Pompeii, acquired by 60 BC;[98] at Cumae, acquired by 56;[99] and at Puteoli, acquired in 45.[100] Cicero undertook a great deal of composition while in residence at these villas, as his letters show;[101] and we might expect that he had a library in at least one of them, especially given their distance from Rome. As we saw above, some scholars have suggested that Cicero acquired the library of Faustus Sulla at auction and then installed it in his own *Cumanum*.[102] Other scholars have drawn a different conclusion from Cicero's remark, "Here I feast on the library of Faustus,"[103] namely, that Cicero did not have a library at his *Cumanum* and had to resort to that of Faustus.[104] At Tusculum, however, where Cicero did have his own library, he continued to consult the library of his neighbor Lucullus.[105]

Writing from Pompeii or Cumae in 54, Cicero makes what seems to be a special request for full access to the library of Atticus in Rome;[106] while this request was occasioned by the demands of the project he was then undertaking (the *De re publica*), it does indicate that even while in Campania Cicero could have books sent to him from Rome.

Conclusions

Cicero seems to have obtained much of his library in block acquisitions. Entire collections could be found for sale: Atticus bought a library in Greece for Cicero in 67, and Cicero may have purchased the library of Faustus Sulla at auction in 55. Cicero and his brother contemplated a joint purchase of books in 54. Gifts and inheritance were another source of books: Cicero received the library of Servius Claudius as a gift and probably inherited the books of his own father. Cicero must also have purchased individual volumes to fill gaps which appeared in his collection; he received gifts of new

---

[98] *Att.* 1.20.1, after May 12, 60: "When I had returned to Rome from my *Pompeianum* on the fourth day before the Ides of May" (*cum <e> Pompeiano me Romam recepissem a. d. IIII Id. Mai*). On the *Pompeianum*, see Schmidt 1899: 489–97; D'Arms 1970: 198.

[99] *Q Fr.* 2.6 (5).4, April 9, 56: "Returning, to look at my *Cumanum*" (*rediens aspicere Cumanum*). On the *Cumanum*, see Schmidt 1899: 478–86; D'Arms 1970: 198–200; Shatzman 1975: 405.

[100] On the *Puteolanum*, see Schmidt 1899: 486–9; D'Arms 1970: 200; Shatzman 1975: 406.

[101] A piece dedicated to Hortensius: *Att.* 4.6.3, from Cumae; *De re publica*: *Q Fr.* 2.13 (12).1, from Cumae or Pompeii; a "Secret History": *Att.* 14.14.5, from Puteoli, and 14.17.6, from Pompeii; *De gloria*: *Att.* 16.3.1, from Pompeii; the second *Philippic*: *Att.*15.13.1, 3, from Puteoli; *De officiis*: *Att.* 15.13a.2, from Puteoli or Cumae, and 16.11.3, 4, from Puteoli.

[102] Münzer 1900b: 1516; Wendel 1952: 112; Shackleton Bailey 1965–70 *ad Att.* 4.10.1.

[103] *Att.* 4.10.1, April 22, 55: *ego hic pascor bibliotheca Fausti*.

[104] Schmidt 1899: 481. [105] *Fin.* 3.2.7; Dix 2000. [106] See note 57.

Table 12.1

Year	Event	Property	Sources
79–77	Cicero a student in Athens and Rhodes		
By 68 (Nov.)	Cicero purchases the *Tusculanum*		
68 (Nov.)	Death of Cicero's father; Cicero inherits the family estate at Arpinum (and his father's library?)	Arpinum	*Att.* 1.6, *Leg.* 2.1.3
67–66	Atticus buys a library for Cicero in Greece	*Tusculanum*	*Att.* 1.7, 1.10, 1.11, 1.4
62	Cicero purchases a house in Rome on the Palatine		*Fam.* 5.6
60	L. Papirius Paetus gives Cicero the library (in Greece) bequeathed by Ser. Claudius		*Att.* 1.20, 2.1
58–57	Cicero's exile in Macedonia; Palatine house, *Tusculanum* and *Formianum* damaged by gangs of P. Clodius Pulcher; Cicero returns to Rome in September 57		
56	Repairs to the library at Antium, supervised by Tyrannio and aided by slaves of Atticus	Antium	*Att.* 4.4a, 4.8, 4.5
c. 55	Cicero acquires the "library of Faustus" at auction?	*Cumanum*	*Att.* 4.10
54	Project to improve libraries of Marcus and Quintus Cicero through purchases from booksellers; Cicero hoped to enlist Tyrannio		*Q Fr.* 3.4, 3.5
47	Cicero sends books to the Tusculanum	*Tusculanum*	*Fam.* 16.18, 16.20
46–45	Dionysius, in charge of Cicero's library, steals books then flees to Illyricum and Dalmatia		*Fam.* 13.77, 5.9, 5.11
Dec. 43	Proscription and execution of Cicero; confiscation of his properties		Vell. Pat. 2.14.3 (Palatine); Plin. *HN* 31.3.6 (*Cumanum*)
39	Treaty of Misenum, allowing the younger Marcus Cicero to return to Italy and perhaps to recover some of his father's property		
30	Younger Marcus Cicero suffect consul with Octavian		

works from other contemporary authors and borrowed and copied works from friends' libraries. Cicero was still acquiring books as late as 47. There were losses to his collection as well as acquisitions: his collection suffered both through the destruction of his house and villas during his exile, an episode which prefigures the confiscation of libraries during the civil wars, and through theft by a slave, which suggests one source of volumes for the book trade.

Cicero's properties and belongings, including his book collection, presumably fell into the hands of others as a result of his proscription: his house on the Palatine, for example, passed to a supporter of Marcus Antonius, Lucius Marcius Censorinus, and his *Cumanum* passed to Gaius Antistius Vetus, who joined Octavian after Philippi.[107] Libraries, like other objects of value, seem to have attracted the interest of the avaricious during the proscriptions; Varro, who escaped with his life, reported that his library had been plundered,[108] and Octavian, Antony, and Pollio may have acquired major book collections as spoils during the civil wars.[109]

Cicero's son may have been able to recover some of his father's property. He was in Greece in 43, and so escaped the fate of his father, uncle and cousin; he served Brutus and Sextus Pompey.[110] Modern scholars have assumed that he returned to Italy upon the conclusion of the Treaty of Misenum, under which the proscribed were to recover one quarter of their property.[111] By 30, the younger Cicero's personal and political fortunes were sufficiently recovered, and his loyalty to Octavian sufficiently assured, to win him a priesthood (probably the augurate) and suffect consulship with Octavian, who was in Egypt; Cicero subsequently became the governor of the province of Asia. The family line seems to have ended with him.[112]

Table 12.1 summarizes the evidence presented in this chapter.[113]

---

[107] The Palatine house: Vell. Pat. 2.14.3; Münzer 1930: 1,554–5. The *Cumanum*: Plin. *HN* 31.3.6; Klebs 1894: 2,558; D'Arms 1970: 69–70, 198–200.

[108] App. *B Civ*. 4.6.47; Gell. 3.10.7.

[109] Dix and Houston 2006, 679 and note 62, 687 and notes 111–12.

[110] App. *B Civ*. 4.4.19, 20; 4.6.51; 5.1.2.

[111] App. *B Civ*. 5.8.71, 72; Dio 48.36.4; Hanslik 1948: 1,285–6.

[112] App. *B Civ*. 4.6.51; Sen. *Suas*. 7.13, 14; Hanslik 1948: 1,285–6; Broughton 1951–2, vol. II, 426.

[113] My thanks to the organizers of the Ancient Libraries Conference and to the participants, to Professor George Houston for reading and commenting on a draft of this chapter, to University of Georgia graduate student Kevin Roth for his assistance with research, and to University of Georgia undergraduate Courtney Baron for her help with Greek fonts.

PART III

Libraries of the Roman Empire

13 | Libraries for the Caesars

EWEN BOWIE

Introduction

Imagine you are the great sophist Hadrianus of Tyre, and you have been persuaded to give up your post as imperial professor of rhetoric in Athens, to which you were appointed by the emperor Marcus around AD 176, and to take up the chair of Greek rhetoric in Rome,[1] which has now for a century, since its establishment by the Flavians, been the highest academic appointment for sophists. The time is the early 180s AD. Of course you have been to Rome before, but you want to know what it will be like to work there. What is the *library* provision? How many libraries have good collections of Greek literature – good enough to write a commentary on a classical Greek orator, or a political history, or a learned hexameter poem in which every myth and every word are obscure but are attested in at least one reputable author? You would like to know which libraries are best for which subject areas. How much overlap is there between the collections? Do they all have catalogues? Are these catalogues constructed on a uniform system? Does anyone actually have a central 'union' catalogue for some or all of these libraries? What are their opening hours? Which, if any, allow borrowing, whether by any reputable reader, or only by such people as yourself, the holder of a high imperial appointment?[2] Is there a recall system? Have some more comfortable or quiet reading spaces than others? Will you be given a personal room or space in any of the libraries? In which library is the staff of library slaves, *servi a bibliothecis*, most helpful? Or best informed about the collection for which they are responsible?

These are certainly the things one would want to know about libraries. But we in the twenty-first century can answer almost none of these questions for imperial Rome – though we do happen to know from Fronto that around AD 144–5 the future emperor Marcus had borrowed what were presumably the only copies of two speeches of Cato from the 'Libraries of Apollo', *Apollinis bibliothecae*, with the consequence that if his personal tutor in rhetoric and assiduous correspondent, M. Cornelius Fronto, were to want

---

[1] For this move, see Philostr. *VS* 2.10.589. [2] On the matter of access, see esp. Dix 1994.

to read them himself he would have to go elsewhere, chat up the librarian of Tiberius' library (*Tiberianus bibliothecarius*) and tip him for allowing him to borrow.[3] Would this apparent abuse of the system have to be concealed from the procurator in charge of libraries (*procurator a bibliothecis*), possibly at that date Volusius Maecianus?

What we *could* do, if Hadrianus of Tyre were interested, is give him a rough account of how the imperial library system had grown up. So before moving to an aspect of that system where *some* questions, at least, can be answered, let me give the briefest of such accounts.[4] I limit myself to the libraries established by emperors in the city of Rome: of course every imperial villa, like almost any wealthy Roman's villa, had its own library or libraries, but we know almost nothing about such libraries' organisation, and have only occasional windfall information about their content – such as the claim that a collection of sayings of Pythagoras that Apollonius of Tyana had emerged carrying from the Trophonium at Lebadeia (as well – it seems – as some letters of Apollonius himself) had been lodged by Hadrian in the library of the imperial villa at Antium.[5]

The libraries

In 47 BC Caesar had planned to establish a major public library in Rome, and had marked out Varro for undertaking the task, but that plan had not been implemented by the time of his death in 44 BC. Accordingly the first

---

[3] 'I read the speech of Cato "On the property of Pulchra" and another in which he prosecuted a tribune. "Wow!" You say to your slave, "Go as fast as you can and bring me these speeches from the libraries of Apollo." You are wasting your time sending him, for they have come with me. So the Tiberian librarian will have to be chatted up by you: some disbursement will be needed for this task, which he will split 50/50 with me when I come to town' (*legi Catonis orationem de bonis Pulchrae, et aliam qua tribuno diem dixit. 'Io' inquis puero tuo, 'vade quantum potes, de Apollinis bibliothecabus has mihi orationes apporta'. frustra mittis, nam isti me secuti sunt. igitur Tiberianus bibliothecarius tibi subigitandus est. aliquid in eam rem insumendum, quod mihi ille, ut ad urbem venero, aequa divisione impertiat*), Fronto, *Ep., ad M.Caesarem* 4.5 = 1.178 Haines = 68 Naber = 61.6–24 van den Hout.

[4] A fuller account, with thorough coverage of the archaeological evidence for library buildings, is to be found in Dix and Houston 2006, to which I am indebted in much of what I say.

[5] Philostr. *VA* 8.20: some of what Philostratus recounts he asserts that he heard from people in Lebadeia, but not apparently the presence of Pythagoras' sayings in the library at Antium. The prologue of the Latin version of Dictys' *Diary of the Trojan War* (p.3.11–13 Eisenhut) also claims (surely fraudulently) that *that* work was admitted 'to the Greek library' (*in Graecam bibliothecam*) by the emperor Nero, but without specifying *which* library: one in Rome seems to be implied, suggesting the author imagined the existence of both a Latin and a Greek library in the capital.

public library to be established in Rome[6] was that of C. Asinius Pollio, in the 'Hall of Freedom' (*Atrium Libertatis*), which has been argued by Nicholas Purcell to be the building we call the 'Record Office' (*tabularium*) rather than a site in the *forum*.[7] Pollio's reconstruction of the *Atrium Libertatis*[8] was financed by the victor's spoils (*manubiae*) of his Illyrian triumph, in 39 BC, so was under way in the 30s. Portraits in the library, which apparently had both a Greek and a Latin section,[9] included one of M. Terentius Varro, the only living person, we are told,[10] so to be honoured. The complex must have been completed, then, before Varro's death in 27 BC. Perhaps Pollio had asked Varro to organise it, just as Varro had been earmarked by Julius Caesar to set up his library; or perhaps the honour was simply a recognition of his huge literary production, over 600 books. The choice of Varro is perhaps less interesting than the implications of his being the only living person honoured: there can have been no statue or bust of Augustus or of any living member of his family. The library's proximity to the 'Record Office' (*tabularium*) suggests that one of its functions was to serve as a public archive: Coarelli notes two *tabularii a porta Fontinali* ('registry clerks attached to the Fontinal gate').[11] Its decoration included much Greek statuary of high quality.

It was very soon after, then, on 9 October 28 BC, that Augustus dedicated his temple of Apollo on the Palatine, to which was attached a pair of Greek and Latin libraries.[12] The rapidity with which the creation of this prestigious library followed that of Pollio can hardly be accidental. Built from his *manubiae*, Pollio's library would be a perpetual reminder of the status conferred on a *triumphator*, and will have put Pollio in the small group of senators whose military achievement, *gloria*, was in any way comparable with that of Augustus. Perhaps worse still, the library shifted the credit for Rome's first public library from the *gens Iulia*, where Caesar's implementation of his project would have banked it, to a representative of the traditional senatorial *ordo*. Augustus' decision to attach a library to his temple of Apollo may be seen as a move to regain *auctoritas* in the matter of the relation between the

---

[6] Ov. *Tr.* 3.1.71–2, Plin. *HN* 7.115, 35.10, Isid. *Etym.* 6.5.2.
[7] Purcell 1993.   [8] Suet. *Aug.* 29.
[9] Isid. *Etym.* 6.5.2. This division was already planned for Caesar's library if we trust Suet. *Iul.* 44.2. For the problems likely to have arisen from trying to give equal space to Greek and Latin literary works, cf. Horsfall 1993. For the relation between portraits and texts, see Petrain in this volume.
[10] Plin. *NH* 7.115.
[11] Coarelli 1993a, citing *CIL* 6.9921, 9514. As the editors have pointed out to me, the nature of public archives in the Roman Republic has been debated, see Culham 1989.
[12] Greek and Latin: Suet. *Aug.* 29, Dio Cass. 53.1.3.

populus Romanus and the propertied elite, educated in Greek and Roman culture, in the senatorial and equestrian *ordines*. Since Julius Caesar's project was not carried through, it is difficult to know what its objectives were, but they must have included maintaining his beneficent image in the eyes of the people and offering the population of Rome something that the major players in late Republican politics, with private libraries in both their town houses and villas, had never offered – not an optimate like Lucullus, not Crassus, not Pompey. Likewise Augustus' library on the Palatine might be seen as similar to his provision of both buildings and entertainments calculated to retain the *populus Romanus* in his *clientela*. Some may have reflected that the proximity of the library to the house of the *princeps* had some worrying precedent in Hellenistic monarchies – the great library at Pergamum was close to the Attalid palace. At the same time, however, its association with a temple complex seems to be an innovation, one that both drew a line between the Hellenistic and Augustan pattern and encouraged the perception that temple and library both belonged in the long list of new and reconstructed religious buildings that marked Augustus' reverence for the gods.

I shall return shortly to the problem of how these Greek and Latin libraries were organised, but for the moment I note that the only person attested as specifically in charge of the Palatine libraries during Augustus' principate is his freedman, the polymath scholar and language teacher (*grammaticus*) C. Iulius Hyginus.[13] At some stage that cannot be precisely determined, the ordering of 'libraries' (in the plural) was entrusted to Pompeius Macer, son of Theophanes, the Mytilenean wheeler-dealer who had advised and written about Pompey during and after his Mithridatic War.[14] When a second Augustan library was built in the Portico of Octavia (*Porticus Octaviae*) another freedman who was also, like Hyginus, a writer and language teacher (*grammaticus*), C. Maecenas Melissus, was put in charge of *its* running: Melissus' own literary activity consisted in developing a new form of drama with Roman settings and assembling a collection of jokes or amusing stories in 150 books.[15] One possible explanation of the few data we have is that Hyginus was put in charge of the Palatine libraries *ab initio*, that C. Melissus

---

[13] *praefuit Palatinae bibliothecae, nec eo secius plurimos docuit*, 'he was in charge of the Palatine library, but despite that he still had numerous pupils', Suet. *Gram.* 20.

[14] *Pompeium Macrum, cui ordinandas bibliothecas delegauerat*, Suet. *Iul.* 56.7. For Macer's career, see briefly Wachtel in *PIR*² P 625 (1998), noting the doubts of White 1992 about earlier reconstructions.

[15] Suet. *Gram.* 21: that his name was C. Maecenas Melissus follows from his having been Maecenas' slave before enfranchisement, and the name Maecenas is explicitly attested by Plin. *HN* 28.62, see Petersen in *PIR*² M 38 (1983).

was likewise in charge of the library in the Portico of Octavia *ab initio*, and that Macer was only brought into the picture when it was decided that some co-ordination was needed – which of course could have been when the library in the Portico of Octavia was built, or when Pollio died and such part as he had been playing in the administration of the library in the *Atrium Libertatis* had to be taken on by somebody else. This may not be the right explanation, but if it is then some sort of statement is being made by Augustus' decision to have each library in the charge of a freedman, in the case of the Palatine library one of his own freedmen. The library is presented as a private resource that is generously being made available to the *populus Romanus* – in particular, of course, to those members of the *populus Romanus* with an interest in consulting books and admiring the works of art that decorated the structure, the educated elite which included the senators and *equites* whose support for the regime still had to be fought for.

As to the structure itself, a lost fragment of the third-century Marble Plan of Rome (*Forma Urbis Romae*, fr. 28b) shows two parallel long rooms with an interior row of columns and an exedra at the end of each. These have been thought by some to be the Palatine libraries, but if they are they represent not the Augustan building but the reconstruction by Domitian when he remodelled the imperial complex on the Palatine. The most recent archaeological evidence points to the existence of only a single hall in Augustus' library.[16] A statue of Augustus as Apollo dominated this space,[17] and walls were decorated with portrait heads set in shields (*imagines clipeatae*) of poets and orators, including Hortensius and (later) Germanicus.[18]

The library attached to the temple of Apollo (*bibliotheca ad Apollinis*) may have been too close to the palace of Augustus (*domus Augusta*) for nervous readers' comfort: indeed there was a special access from Augustus' house to the temple area that will have reinforced the sense that this was Augustus' private space in which others were guests. Nor was that area always quiet: the temple itself could be used for meetings of the senate,[19] and imperial business could even be transacted in the library, as it was in

---

[16] See Dix and Houston 2006: 681, and the account of recent excavation by Iacopi and Tedone 2005/2006. I am extremely grateful to George Houston for directing me to this publication and for many valuable suggestions for improvement.

[17] Schol. Hor. *Ep.* 1.3.17, Servius on V.*Georg.* 4.10.

[18] Hor. *Ep.* 2.1.214–18 plus Porphyrio, schol. Hor. *Sat.* 1.4.21, Tac. *Ann.* 2.37 and 83. For the addition of images of Drusus and his son Germanicus on the latter's death, see Petrain in this volume.

[19] E.g. in AD 31, Dio Cass. 58.9.4–6, cf. Jos. *BJ* 2.6.1 80f.

AD 13 when Augustus received an embassy from Alexandria 'in the Roman library'.[20] Recitations and declamations took place either in the temple itself or the libraries – presumably the latter. Recitations must also have taken place in Pollio's *Atrium Libertatis*, since Pollio is recorded as having nurtured the practice of recitation, and it would be interesting to know who chose (or was chosen?) to recite in which building, and on what grounds. Where did Virgil test out passages of his *Aeneid*?[21]

The other library that Augustus and his family established in Rome was, as just mentioned, that in the portico of Octavia (*Porticus Octaviae*). The complex was a reconstruction of the portico of Metellus (*Porticus Metelli*),[22] undertaken by Augustus with the victor's spoils (*manubiae*) from his Dalmatian campaign, which was concluded in 33 BC.[23] Within the portico was a pair of libraries, Greek and Latin, dedicated to the dead young Marcellus by Octavia. Marcellus' death gives a *terminus post quem* of 23 BC, Octavia's own death gives a *terminus ante quem* of 11 BC.[24] As noted above, the first man in charge was a freedman of Maecenas, C. Melissus, but some intervention by Pompeius Macer, to whom I shall shortly turn, may have been associated with his appointment.

Other libraries were added in succeeding principates. The temple of Augustus (*templum divi Augusti*), built chiefly by Tiberius but only dedicated in AD 37 by Gaius,[25] also had a library, reconstructed by Domitian after a fire. Domitian also reconstructed the libraries of the portico of Octavia (*Porticus Octaviae*) which is among the buildings mentioned by name in Cassius Dio's account as destroyed in the fire of AD 80,[26] and his efforts to restock its collections went so far as sending for books from the world-class library in Alexandria.[27]

A further library had already been added in AD 75 by Domitian's father Vespasian, in the temple of Peace (*Templum Pacis*). Gellius, hunting for a copy of L. Aelius Stilo's 'Study of axioms' (*commentarius de*

---

[20] ἐν τῆ Ῥωμαϊκῆ βιβλιοθήκη, *POxy*. 2435 *verso* line 32. Dix and Houston 2006: 683, following a suggestion by Corbier 1992, may be right to take this to mean 'the Latin library' (thus offering evidence for a division into Latin and Greek libraries at this date) citing Plut. *Luc*. 1.7, *IDelos* 442b.132. Note also Jos. *AJ* 17.11.1 for Augustus dealing with the problems of Judaea in 4 BC 'in the temple of Apollo', ἐν ἱερῶι Ἀπόλλωνος.

[21] Schol. Hor. *Sat.* 1.10.38, Calp. *Ecl.* 4.157–9. For Pollio's part in developing the practice of recitation, see Dalzell 1955; Dix and Houston 2006: 676.

[22] Vell. Pat. 1.11.3.   [23] Dio Cass. 49.43.8.

[24] Livy, *Per*. 140, Plut. *Marc*. 30.11. That Octavia financed the construction is indicated by the expression 'her own generosity' (*sua munera*), Ov. *Ars am*. 1.69–70, but the funding is seen as that of Augustus, acting in his sister's name, by Suet. *Aug*. 29.4, Dio Cass. 49.43.8. For the problem of the date, see Dix and Houston 2006: 685 n. 102.

[25] Dio Cass. 57.10.2, 59.7.1.   [26] Dio Cass. 66.24.2.   [27] Suet. *Dom*. 20.1.

proloquiis), finds it 'in the library of Peace' (*in Pacis bibliotheca*).[28] It has been suggested that at least a part of the collection housed there came from that presumably kept by Nero in the now decimated Golden House (*domus aurea*).[29]

Domitian may also have reconstructed another library on or adjacent to the Palatine, that of the palace of Tiberius (*domus Tiberiana*), used in the 140s by Aulus Gellius.[30] Gellius, his teacher Sulpicius Apollinaris and others conversed there, and it may be that we are to understand that Sulpicius was actually teaching there: they seem randomly to be consulting old books, Fronto, as we saw (above n. 3), knows a 'Tiberian librarian' (*Tiberianus bibliothecarius*) and the *Augustan History*'s claim to have used it for its *Life of Probus*, even if fraudulent, shows fourth-century knowledge of the library.[31] Coarelli's identification of it with the church of Santa Maria Antiqua seems not to be widely accepted, and Houston has argued persuasively that the 'library' of the *domus Tiberiana* was not formally a public library, simply the part of Tiberius' palace that still housed his collection of books.[32] The recent publication of Galen's περὶ ἀλυπίας, 'On the avoidance of distress', has added to our knowledge of the collection in the *domus Tiberiana*.[33]

The construction of the forum of Trajan, dedicated in January AD 112, involved the addition of another pair of libraries, flanking the column at the forum's Capitoline end. Each of these had a reading room of 460 square metres:[34] perhaps (so suggests Coarelli) the collection was built around that of the 'Hall of Freedom' (*Atrium Libertatis*), now destroyed. The Ulpian library (*Bibliotheca Ulpia*) certainly seems to have housed some official documents: Gellius consulted old praetor's edicts there,[35] and the *Augustan History* asserts its usefulness for the lives of Aurelian and Probus.[36]

Two decades later a complex that very probably included libraries was established by Hadrian, called in Greek and Latin texts 'the Athenaeum'. Aurelius Victor puts its foundation after Hadrian's return from the Jewish war, i.e. around AD 135, and terms it a 'school of liberal arts' (*ludus*

---

[28] Gell. 16.8.2, cf. 5.21.9 for the library having a single book of letters of Sinnius Capito.
[29] Dix and Houston 2006: 692.   [30] *NA* 13.20.1.
[31] SHA *Prob.* 2.1. For the claim, compare that of the writer of SHA *Aurel.* 9.1 to have found the rolls (*scrinia*) of the City Prefect (*praefectus urbi*) and the linen books (*libri lintei*) of SHA *Aurel.* 1.7–10.
[32] Houston 2008.   [33] See Jones 2009; Tucci 2009a.
[34] Full architectural description by Packer 1995.
[35] *NA* 11.17.   [36] Linen books (*libri lintei*), *Aurel.* 1.7–10 cf. *Prob.* 2.

ingenuarum atrium).[37] Cassius Dio claims that it got its name from 'the training of those who were being taught there'.[38] If the complex which survived to the age of Sidonius was the same structure, it had a theatre-shaped lecture space divided into wedges (*cunei*). Like libraries it was vulnerable to being taken over for senatorial meetings, as it was in AD 193 when Dio himself was present,[39] or for judicial business. Here, if anywhere, Hadrianus of Tyre will surely have had his personal office. In 1945 Piganiol[40] proposed to identify the Athenaeum with a large Domitianic structure next to Santa Maria Antiqua. This was accepted by Coarelli,[41] and if they are correct it shows either that Aurelius Victor was wrong to credit the Athenaeum to Hadrian or, more probably, that Hadrian revamped an existing Domitianic complex. A pre-Hadrianic existence is perhaps also indicated by Martial's reference to 'the inner sanctums of our goddess Athena' (*penetralia nostrae | Palladis*).[42]

Let us leave Hadrianus of Tyre in the Athenaeum, making arrangements for his inaugural performance as the imperial professor of Greek rhetoric in Rome. Indeed we know from his *Life* by Philostratus that it was in the Athenaeum Hadrianus used to perform, attracting even students who were studying Latin and not Greek.[43] He had many libraries to turn to, and was not to know that in AD 191 a fire was to devastate the Palatine, perhaps destroying much of its libraries.[44] We are told by Philostratus that Commodus appointed him 'secretary for Greek correspondence' (*ab epistulis graecis*) on his death-bed, with apologies for not having done so sooner:[45] we know little of holders of the post 'secretary for libraries' (*a bibliothecis*) for the period after Pius, but we must wonder whether perhaps Hadrianus held that post too before his appointment *ab epistulis graecis*.

The librarians

This takes me into the topic of the second part of my paper. What sort of person did emperors choose for the post of 'secretary for libraries'

---

[37] Aur. Vict. *Caes.* 14.1.3. [38] τῆς ἐν αὐτῶι παιδευομένων ἀσκήσεως, Dio Cass. 73.17.4.
[39] Dio Cass. 73.17.4. [40] Piganiol 1945: 25–6.
[41] Coarelli 1993c. Two large halls, one with two terraces of steps facing each other, possibly for seating, have been excavated since 2009 in Piazza Venezia and claimed as the Athenaeum.
[42] Mart. 4.53.12. [43] *VS* 2.10.589.
[44] Gal. *de compos. medicin. per genera* 1.1 = xiii 362 Kühn, with further evidence now in Galen's περὶ ἀλυπίας discussed by Iacopi and Tedone 2005/2006.
[45] Philostr. *VS* 2.10.590.

(*a bibliothecis*)? What sort of career did these men have? What were their duties? Fortunately we can attempt at least some answers to these questions.

As we saw above, the first man known to us to have been put in charge of libraries as a whole was Cn.(?) Pompeius Macer, the son of the Mytilenean aristocrat Cn. Pompeius Theophanes who in the 60s BC established a connection with Pompey the Great, may have advised him in the Mithridatic War and secured liberty for his own city Mytilene around 62 BC: about that time too Theophanes was awarded Roman citizenship, and in the civil wars briefly held the post of 'military engineer' (*praefectus fabrum*), perhaps (as apparently in the case of some Greeks who are so described later) an honorific title which bore little relation to his job description. Strabo says he has shown himself to be 'the most distinguished of all Greeks', πάντων Ἑλλήνων ἐπιφανέστατον.[46] Theophanes had some literary aspirations, writing a history of Pompey's campaigns of which seven fragments survive. His son, Pompeius Macer, seems likely to have been born some time after 60 BC – though not necessarily as late as the 40s, as White insists – and to have built upon the position that his father had established in Roman society (and that survived the civil wars) to the point that in the early years of Tiberius Strabo could say of him 'and now he is numbered amongst the first of Tiberius' friends' καὶ νῦν ἐν τοῖς πρώτοις ἐξετάζεται τῶν Τιβερίου φίλων.[47] We can add from Tacitus that Macer's son or grandson was *praetor* in the year AD 15.[48]

How did this career evolve? In the same sentence Strabo says of the man his text calls Marcus Pompeius (Μάρκον Πομπήιον) that he was someone 'whom Caesar Augustus at one point made procurator of Asia' (ὃν τῆς Ἀσίας ἐπίτροπον κατέστησέ ποτε Καῖσαρ ὁ Σεβαστός). During this procuratorship Ovid seems to have been among his official companions (*cohors amicorum*):

Under your leadership we toured the magnificent cities of Asia
Sicily was seen by my eyes under your leadership.

Ovid, *Letters from Pontus* 2.10.21–2[49]

---

[46] Strabo 13.2.3 617–18. For a fuller discussion of Theophanes, see Bowie 2011.
[47] Strabo 13.2.3 618. It has been suggested that this son, possibly described as Marcus Pompeius (Μάρκον Πομπήιον) by Strabo (unless one emends to Macrus [i.e. Macer] Pompeius, Μάκρον Πομπήιον), was not natural but adoptive, and was indeed the son of an Italian immigrant to *provincia Asia*: White 1992 cf. Wachtel in *PIR*² P 625 (1998).
[48] Tac. *Ann.* 1.72.3. He was prominent enough to have to commit suicide in AD 33 (Tac. *Ann.* 6.18.2); eventually there is a consul suffect in 115 AD (*PIR*² P 628) whose nomenclature M. Pompeius Macrinus Neos Theophanes revived memories of Strabo's Theophanes.
[49] *Te duce magnificas Asiae perspeximus urbes* | *Trinacris est oculis te duce visa meis*, Ov. *Pont.* 2.10.21.

Since here Ovid also mentions seeing Sicilian cities in Macer's company, Pflaum conjectured that he also had a post in Sicily.[50] This is an attractive guess, and I accept Pflaum's proposed chronology: a procuratorial post in Sicily followed by the much more important one in Asia, where his father's Mytilenean power base and connections will have been helpful. Arguments put forward by Schwartz point to the winter of 21–20 BC as that which saw the arrival of Ovid and Pompeius Macer.[51] Only after these administrative posts, presumably discharged successfully, would his library appointment fall, an appointment we know from Suetonius:

Of these volumes [minor literary works of Caesar] Augustus vetoed the publication in a quite short and straightforward letter he sent to Pompeius Macer, to whom he had delegated the job of setting libraries in order.[52]

Macer was a cultivated and well connected administrator with a touch of culture – he apparently wrote poetry himself[53] – rather than a professional or even full time man of letters. His son was perhaps the earliest man of Greek descent to reach the praetorship (in AD 15),[54] and Macer himself must have been equally at home in Italian and in Greek company. How much he involved himself in the minutiae of library administration is impossible to tell.

As we have seen, however, we know another person to have been put in charge of the Palatine library by Augustus, his freedman C. Iulius Hyginus, also probably an addressee of the exiled Ovid.[55] Again our source is Suetonius.[56] Hyginus, from either Spain or Alexandria, and a pupil of Alexander Polyhistor, was certainly a *grammaticus* in the sense that he wrote commentaries on Virgil and other scholarly and historical works (on bees, agriculture, cities, families, religion) and also in the sense that he taught language and literature (Suetonius credits him with many pupils). He will have brought to his job a quite different range of skills from those of Macer, and there is no ground for seeing him as holding the same post as Macer, whether as his predecessor or (as Hirschfeld thought) his successor. His fief was the Palatine library, and perhaps his writ ran there for

---

[50] Pflaum 1960–1: 12.   [51] Schwartz 1951.
[52] *Quos libellos vetuit Augustus publicari in epistula, quem brevem admodum ac simplicem ad Pompeium Macrum, cui ordinandas bibliothecas delegaverat, misit*, Suet. *Iul.* 56.7.
[53] Ov. *Pont.* 2.10.13–18, *Am.* 2.18 (an epic), Quint. *Inst.* 6.3.96 (epigrams), Stob. *Ecl.* 4.24.52 (a tragedy, *Medea*).
[54] Tac. *Ann.* 1.72. That the praetor was son and not (as in the MSS of Tac. *Ann.* 6.18.2) grandson of Pompeius Macer was argued forcefully by Syme 1958: 748–9 and again 1978: 73–4, and also accepted by Wachtel in *PIR*² P 625 (1998).
[55] *Tr.* 3.14.   [56] *Gram.* 20.2.

some time before Macer was appointed. Thereafter he and Macer may have held their respective posts concurrently, although we do not know for how long. Under Hyginus, of course, was a staff at least some of whom were slaves.[57]

There remains the problem of C. Melissus. We have seen that Suetonius attests his appointment in connection with the libraries in the portico of Octavia.[58] White (1992) argued that his role of 'setting in order the libraries' (*ordinandarum bibliothecarum*) was parallel to that of Macer, and that each of these men was simply given the task of setting up the collections in the libraries. But the plural 'libraries' (*bibliothecas*) used by Suetonius in his reference to Macer's position,[59] and explained by White as referring to the Greek and Latin Palatine libraries, might rather point to a wider supervision, especially now that it seems clear on archaeological evidence that the Greek and Latin libraries in the Palatine were not clearly distinct spaces. As suggested above, Macer may have been brought in when the library in the portico of Octavia was built so that there should be some co-ordination between that and the Palatine library.

Our next librarian was discovered too late to be taken into account by Pflaum: an inscription from the city of Rome, published in 1959,[60] revealed a Ti. Iulius Pappus, son of Zoilus:

To the shades of Tiberius Iulius Pappus, son of Zoilus, of the tribe Fabia, companion of Tiberius Caesar Augustus, and also in charge of all the libraries of the Augusti from Tiberius Caesar until Tiberius Claudius Caesar.

This man's voting district (*tribus*), Fabia, and family name (*gentilicium*) make it almost certain that he, his father or grandfather was given Roman citizenship by a Caesar. I take him to be a Greek, probably from one of the cities of *provincia Asia*, perhaps somebody whom Tiberius came to know in his period on Rhodes, but there are many other possibilities: he might, for example, have been a crony of Macer. I think it is very unlikely that a

---

[57] Epigraphic attestation comes from rather later: 'Antiochus (the slave of) Tiberius Claudius Caesar, attached to the Latin library of Apollo' (*Antiochus Ti. Claudi Caesaris (servus) a bibliotheca Latina Apollinis*: *CIL* 6.5884) and 'Alexander the slave of Gaius Caesar Augustus Germanicus once owned by Pylaemenes, attached to the Greek library of the temple of Apollo' (*Alexander C. Caesaris Augusti Germanici servus Pylaemenianus ab byblothece Graeca templi Apollinis*: *CIL* 6.5188). For the Galatian Pylaemenes, see Cichorius 1922: 329.

[58] 'he undertook the task of setting in order the libraries in the Portico of Octavia' (*curam ordinandarum bibliothecarum in Octaviae portico suscepit*), Suet. *Gram.* 21.3.

[59] *Iul.* 56.7, quoted above n. 51.

[60] *D.M. Tiberio Iulio Zoili f. Fabiam Pappo, comiti Tiberi Caesaris Augusti, idemque supra byblothecas omnes Augustorum ab Tiberio Caesare usque ad Tiberium Claudium Caesarem*, van Buren 1959: 384 = *AE* 1960 no. 26.

man who became a companion (*comes*) of Tiberius is somebody who had once been his freedman (*libertus*) as was believed by Petersen and White.[61] It is possible that he was the son or grandson of Julius Caesar's freedman (*libertus*) C. Iulius Zoilus from Aphrodisias, whom Octavian described as his friend in 39–38 BC and who secured from him privileges for Aphrodisias, where he was a major player in city politics and benefactions.[62] But some grander description might then be expected in his epitaph from Rome, and he may be from a quite different family and city. His forename (*praenomen*) is not incompatible with descent from Zoilus, though it could equally suggest that Pappus is from a different family and that his citizenship was owed to Tiberius himself. We know of nothing to tell us whether he was a committed man of letters, or simply a Greek who was well-educated (*pepaideumenos*). Although his tenure spanned three reigns, the fact that the second, that of Gaius, lasted only four years, means his case does not constitute evidence of a strikingly long appointment.[63] The epitaph does show that he held no other post of significance. He is the first man we know explicitly to be described as in charge of all imperial libraries. Since he is also our first librarian whose post is epigraphically attested, the formula cannot be pressed, but it is an attractive idea that the setting up of a new library in the temple of Augustus impelled Tiberius to come up with a broader or clearer job description for an official who now had four libraries to run.[64] At the same time, as I have suggested above, it is possible that a co-ordinating role was already played by Pompeius Macer.

The next procurator may indeed be a freedman, Tiberius Claudius Scirtus: certainly a sepulchral inscription put up by his wife Vettia Tyche describes him as 'procurator of libraries' (*proc. bybl.*) as well as 'freedman of Augustus'.[65] That Vettia should make so little of her dead husband's attainment is surprising if he was in charge of the libraries at Rome. I am inclined to suspect he held an appointment in an imperial villa (cf. below on Q. Veturius Callistratus), a guess that might receive support from the discovery of the inscription in the area of Naples, or a subordinate procuratorial appointment in Rome (see below the case of Largus). That his appointment was in an imperial villa is made more likely by the attestation

---

[61] Meyer 1960, Petersen in *PIR*² I 447 (1966); White 1992: 214 n. 15.
[62] For the epigraphic texts documenting Zoilus, see Reynolds 1982: 156–64; for his monument, Smith 1993; see also Weaver 2004: 199–200; Osgood 2006: 274–6. For the possible relationship of Pappus to Zoilus, see Smith 1993, Houston 2008: 253.
[63] Like Tiberius' legate in Moesia, Poppaeus Sabinus: 24 years, Tac. *Ann.* 6.39.3.
[64] So Dix and Houston 2006: 690, Houston 2008.
[65] *Ti. Claud. Aug. l.* | *Scirti proc. bybl.* | *Vettia Tyche Scirti*, *CIL* 10.1739 = *ILS* 1587, *PIR*² C 1014.

in the *Fasti Antiates Minores* of a man whose name *may* be Scirtus and who was a librarian at the imperial villa at Antium.[66]

Thereafter there is a gap in our knowledge until Dionysius of Alexandria, whose career as a whole, according to the Suda, spanned at least three decades, from Nero to Trajan.[67] Pflaum's reconstruction is attractive:[68] in his view Dionysius succeeded his former tutor, the philosopher Chaeremon, as head of the Alexandrian library, an appointment made by the emperor; then, perhaps around AD 69/70, when Vespasian and Titus were in Alexandria, he was promoted to be the procurator in charge of libraries (*a bibliothecis*) in Rome. If we take the Suda correctly to imply that Dionysius was Chaeremon's immediate successor, that will have been in the reign of Claudius. Chaeremon is registered by the Suda as the teacher of Nero, so in Rome by no later than AD 50.[69] Dionysius would then have a career beginning under Claudius, not (as asserted by the Suda) under Nero. It is also possible, however, that it was the promotion to be head of the Alexandrian library that coincided with or was occasioned by Vespasian's visit to Egypt, and that the position in charge of libraries in Rome falls rather later. Much later, in a quasi-document of AD 113, a Dionysius who seems to be the same man is found defending the interests of Alexandrian Greeks before Trajan:[70] that would suggest a later career. It seems likely that this man's son is the Dionysius of Alexandria who wrote the hexameter *Periegesis of the inhabited world*, dateable to AD 130–8.[71] Father Dionysius, the librarian, is presumably someone who had his own writing career, perhaps one similar to that of Hyginus, given the Suda's term *grammaticus* (γραμματικός). After his library post, it seems, our Dionysius was in charge of correspondence (*ab epistulis*), perhaps specifically correspondence in Greek (*ab epistulis graecis*), an office held by a number of prominent Greeks, most of them intellectuals,

---

[66] Houston 2002: 145 nn. f and g. I am very grateful to George Houston for drawing this item to my attention.
[67] Suda Δ 1,173: Dionysius of Alexandria, son of Glaucus, a *grammaticus*, who associated with Caesars from Nero until Trajan, and was head of the libraries and in charge of correspondence and embassies and responses. And he was the teacher of Parthenius the *grammaticus*, and pupil of Chaeremon the philosopher, whom indeed he succeeded in his post in Alexandria (Διονύσιος Ἀλεξανδρεύς, ὁ Γλαύκου υἱός, γραμματικός, ὅστις ἀπὸ Νέρωνος συνῆν Καί<σαρσι> μεχρὶ Τραιανοῦ καὶ τῶν βιβλιοθηκῶν προὔστη καὶ ἐπὶ τῶν ἐπιστολῶν καὶ πρεσβειῶν ἐγένετο καὶ ἀποκριμάτων. ἦν δὲ καὶ διδάσκαλος Παρθενίου τοῦ γραμματικοῦ, μαθητὴς δὲ Χαιρήμονος τοῦ φιλοσόφου, ὃν καὶ διεδέξατο ἐν Ἀλεξανδρείαι).
[68] Pflaum 1961–2: 111–12.
[69] Suda A 1128, in the entry on Alexander of Aegeae, also said by the Suda to be Nero's teacher.
[70] *POxy.* vol. X. 1,242 lines 3–4 = Musurillo 1961 viii *Acta Hermaisci* p32 lines 3–4: 'Dionysius who had held many procuratorships' (Διονύσιος ὁ ἐν πολλαῖς ἐπιτροπαῖς γενόμενος).
[71] Bowie 1990: 70–9, esp. 77–9 on date and identification.

some of them sophists,[72] and then after that of embassies and responses (*a libellis*).

A single procurator in charge of imperial libraries, even if his tenure was long, cannot safely be taken as a basis for generalisation. Dionysius may have combined philological and managerial skills, and this combination may have commended him, but the other men who ran the libraries in Rome between AD 69 and 96 may have had different profiles, even though this is an era in which we know the Flavians were establishing chairs of rhetoric in Rome and a system of immunities for teachers in cities of the empire.[73]

Another procurator may be found in the addressee of an epigram of Martial, Sextus, described as the eloquent cultivator of Palatine learning and asked to arrange for the admission of Martial's poems.[74] Whether Sextus is the procurator in charge of libraries (who would thus be documented as having some control over accessions) or a man lower in the bureaucratic hierarchy cannot be determined on the basis of the poem.

Rather more is known of Annius Postumus, whose post as procurator in charge of libraries is attested epigraphically at Saldae in Mauretania Caesariensis and at Ostia. The former inscription presents him simply as 'procurator of Augustus for libraries' ([*p*]*roc. Aug. a bybliothecis*), the latter as 'procurator for (the) libraries of divine Trajan' (*pr. bibliothecarum divi Trajani*).[75] If this simply identifies the emperor under whom Annius Postumus held his post, then it gives us a date (AD 98–117) and puts him before Suetonius and after Dionysius and (if he was indeed procurator in charge of libraries) Sextus. Pflaum takes the phrase to mean that he was responsible for the libraries in Trajan's forum: that resource is indeed called 'the library of the temple of Trajan' (*bibliotheca templi Traiani*) by Gellius[76] – but with *bibliotheca* in the singular, not, as in the two Annius Postumus inscriptions, the plural (*bybliothecis / bibliothecarum*) and the singular term 'Ulpian library' for the libraries in Trajan's forum is also found in the *Augustan History*.[77] This, and the fact that no other procurator is so far attested as having responsibility for a specific library, makes me incline against Pflaum's view: rather we should suppose that Annius Postumus' remit covered all the imperial libraries in Rome. If I am right, we have in him a Trajanic

---

[72] See Bowie 1982.
[73] See the edict of Vespasian in his capacity as censor dated to 27 December AD 75 and the follow-up pronouncement (*responsum*) of Domitian from AD 93–4, FIRA I 77, TAPA 86 (1955) 348–9, McCrum and Woodhead 1961 no. 458: *editio princeps* SPAW Berlin 1935, 967–72.
[74] Mart. 5.5.   [75] CIL 8. 20684, CIL 14.5352; see Pflaum 1960–1: 316–19 no. 132.
[76] NA 11.17.   [77] Aurel. 1.7–10, Prob. 2.

procurator who bears no signs of having the literary interests or Greek connections of the Flavian Dionysius or of the known Hadrianic appointees; indeed, as is shown by the Ostia text, he held his post early in what became a straightforward administrative career – inheritance tax, the grain supply of Ostia, then a provincial procuratorship, Pannonia Inferior.[78] Such a choice by the hard-headed Trajan is not surprising.

With our next librarian we are on better charted territory: C. Suetonius Tranquillus, who indeed is himself one of few witnesses to matters concerning the early imperial librarians.[79] From literary sources it has long been known that Suetonius had an interest in a public career that culminated in his equestrian post in charge of correspondence (*ab epistulis*): a successful request channelled through Pliny for a post as military tribune (*tribunus militum*), which Suetonius then decided to transfer to one of his wife's family, Caesennius Sabinus, was followed by another successful request to Trajan, again through Pliny, for the privileges attached to the status of father of three children (*ius trium liberorum*);[80] then the post in charge of correspondence (*ab epistulis*) from which, according to the generally well informed *Life of Hadrian* in the *Augustan History*, he was summarily ejected during Hadrian's visit to Britain in the autumn of AD 121 for displaying excessive familiarity in the presence of Sabina.[81] Famously in 1952 the publication of an inscription from Hippo added his membership of select judges (*iudices selecti*), a post as priest of the imperial cult (*flamen*) at Hippo and posts in charge of education (*a studiis*) and in charge of libraries (*a bybliothecis*).[82] It may be guessed, as it was by Wallace-Hadrill,[83] that the posts in charge of education (*a studiis*) and in charge of libraries (*a bybliothecis*) were ones to which Suetonius was appointed by Trajan, perhaps precisely to undertake the stocking and arranging of the new Greek and Roman libraries in his forum, and so perhaps around AD 112; and that it was Hadrian who

---

[78] *Proc. vicesimae hereditatium, proc. Aug. ad annonam Ostiens., proc. Aug. Pannoniae inferioris.* Pflaum 1960–1: 317 notes that the procurator for the 5% inheritance tax is first attested under Hadrian, and thinks Annius belongs before AD 150.

[79] On Suetonius, see Syme 1980; Wallace-Hadrill 1983; on his equestrian career Pflaum 1960–1: 219–24 no. 96.

[80] Plin. *Ep.* 3.8.1 and 10.94–5.

[81] 'He appointed successors to Septicius Clarus, the praetorian prefect, and Suetonius Tranquillus, the master of correspondence, and many others, because they had then conducted themselves in the presence of his wife Sabina with too great familiarity in their exchanges with her than due respect for the imperial house required' (*Septicio Claro praefecto praetorii et Suetonio Tranquillo epistularum magistro multisque aliis, quod apud Sabinam uxorem in usu eius familiarius se tunc egerant, quam reverentia domus aulicae postulabat, successores dedit*), SHA *Hadr.* 11.3.

[82] E. Marec and H. G. Pflaum in *CRAI* 1952.76 = *AE* 1953.73. [83] Wallace-Hadrill 1983: 7.

appointed him to be in charge of correspondence (*ab epistulis*). As qualifications for the posts in charge of education (*a studiis*) and in charge of libraries (*a bybliothecis*) Suetonius had only some limited experience in public office but a much more prominent engagement in a literary career, already evident in a letter of Pliny of AD 105.[84] Millar saw Suetonius' official posts as a recognition of his literary distinction, and Wallace-Hadrill conjectured that Hadrian's appointment of Suetonius to the post in charge of correspondence (*ab epistulis*) 'celebrated' the recent appearance of his work 'On famous men' (*De viris illustribus*).[85]

If the appointments of Dionysius and Suetonius seem to establish a pattern, that of Eudaemon seems to be an exception. Pflaum infers from others who had similar career patterns that Eudaemon was a Greek and 'un homme de lettres réputé'.[86] As far as I know not a shred of evidence supports this guess. To me Eudaemon seems more like a career bureaucrat, even a workaholic bureaucrat, closer in his profile to Annius Postumus than to the others who have been considered so far. The key elements are furnished by almost identical texts from the bases of honorific statues in Ephesus (in Latin), and from the area of Beirut (in Greek). I offer a translation of the two texts:

To... procurator of the emperor Caesar Trajanus Hadrianus Augustus attached to the Finance Office in Alexandria, procurator of the Greek and Latin libraries, secretary for Greek correspondence, procurator of Lycia, Pamphylia, Galatia, Paphlagonia, Pisidia and Pontus, procurator of inheritances and procurator of the province of Asia, procurator of Syria, Hermes, freedman of Augustus, his assistant, to honour him.[87]

[The Council an]d the People (erected this) to [....]emon, procurator of the emperor Caesar Trajanus Hadrianus Augustus attached to the Finance Office in Alexandria, procurator of the Roman and Greek libraries, secretary for Greek correspondence, procurator of Lycia, Pamphylia, Galatia, Pisidia, Pontus, Paphlagonia and Lycaonia, procurator of inheritances and procurator of the province of Asia, procurator of the province of Syria,... proc....[88]

---

[84] Plin. *Ep.* 5.10.   [85] Millar 1977: 90–1, Wallace-Hadrill 1983: 8.
[86] Pflaum 1960–1: 264–71 no. 110, at p. 271.
[87] ....*proc(uratori)[(Imperatoris)] Caesaris Tra(iani) Hadriani [Aug(usti)] ad dioecesim Alexandr(eae),[p]roc(uratori) bibliothecar(um) Graec(arum) et Latin(arum), ab epist(ulis) Graecis, proc(uratori) Lyc(iae)Pamp(hyliae) Galat(iae) Paphl(agoniae) Pisid(iae) Pont(i), proc(uratori) hered(itatium) et proc(uratori) pro[vin]ciae Asiae, proc(uratori) Syriae Hermes Aug(usti) lib(ertus) adiut(or) eius h(onoris) c(ausa), CIL* 3.431 = *ILS* 1449.
[88] [ἡ βουλὴ κα]ὶ ὁ δῆμος ‖ [. . . . . .]ιμονι ἐπιτρόπωι | [αὐτοκράτορος Κ]αίσαρος Τραιανοῦ | [Ἀδριανοῦ Σεβασ]τοῦ ἐπὶ διοικήσεως | [Ἀλεξανδρείας, ἐ]πιτρόπωι βιβλιοθηκῶν Ῥωμαϊκῶν καὶ Ἑλ]ληνικῶν, ἐπὶ ἐπιστολῶν|[Ἑλληνικῶν, ἐ]πιτρόπωι ἐπαρχειῶν|[Λυκίας Παμφ]υλίας

Eudaemon's first position in Alexandria was chiefly, it would seem, financial; his second, in charge of libraries (*a bibliothecis*), was in Rome, and shared with his third, that of secretary for Greek correspondence (*ab epistulis Graecis*), the feature that it was often held by Greek men of letters. Perhaps Pflaum was right to exploit the *Augustan History*'s characterisation of Eudaemon as a man at one time in Hadrian's inner circle,[89] and to infer that Hadrian therefore appointed him to a post that had to be held in Rome when he, Hadrian, was himself in Rome, and then to the post of secretary for Greek correspondence when he was off on one of his imperial tours, so that Eudaemon was kept in the imperial entourage. That too, in Pflaum's view, might explain the Asian appointment, to be associated with Hadrian's visit to the province Asia in 129–30. He might have added that the move to Syria could be at the time of the Jewish War, AD 133–4: this is not incompatible with the *Augustan History*'s story of Hadrian turning against Eudaemon, which could well be in the bad, last years of his reign, AD 134–8. The Asian and Syrian posts look as hard-core financial as Eudaemon's first; but a gift for number-crunching can less easily explain that of secretary for Greek correspondence and is unlikely to be the most important reason for the libraries appointment as *a bibliothecis*. That Eudaemon is not *also*, it seems, 'secretary for education' (*a studiis*) might support the view that he is an administrator's administrator, and that idea might gain support from his later appointment by Pius to one of the top equestrian posts, Prefect of Egypt.[90]

L. Iulius Vestinus seems to fall into the pattern we have seen earlier. His career is known only from a copy of a lost inscription in a manuscript in the library of Einsiedeln:

For the high priest of Alexandria and all Egypt Lucius Iulius Vestinus, head of the Museum and in charge of the Roman and Greek libraries in Rome and in charge of education under the emperor Hadrian and the secretary of the same emperor.[91]

Γαλατίας Πι[σι]δίας [Πόντου Παφλα]γονίας Λυκαονία[ς, [ἐπιτρόπωι κλη]ρονομιῶν καὶ [ἐπαρχείας] ||[αρχείας Ἀ]σίας, ἐπιτρ[όπωι ἐπαρ]χείας Συρίας... ἐπιτ..., *IGR* 3.1077.

[89] 'For he drove into poverty Eudaemon, who had earlier been a party to the government of the empire' (*nam Eudaemonem prius conscium imperii ad egestatem perduxit*), SHA. *Hadr.* 15.3: cf. Pflaum 1960–1: 264–71. Like stories of Hadrian's turning against and persecuting Dionysius of Miletus, Favorinus of Arelate and Apollodorus of Damascus, this allegation should be treated with caution, cf. Bowie 1997.

[90] He is in post by 18 July AD 142, *POxy.* 237 col. viii 7–8 and 18.

[91] ἀρχιερεῖ Ἀλεξανδρείας καὶ Αἰγύπτου πάσης Λευκίωι Ἰουλίωι Οὐηστίνωι καὶ ἐπιστάτηι τοῦ Μουσείου καὶ ἐπὶ τῶν ἐν Ῥώμηι βιβλιοθηκῶν Ῥωμαϊκῶν καὶ Ἑλληνικῶν καὶ ἐπὶ παιδείας Ἀδριανοῦ τοῦ αὐτοκράτορος καὶ ἐπιστολεῖ τοῦ αὐτοῦ αὐτοκράτορος, *CIG* 5900 = *IG* 14.1085 = *OGIS* 659 = *IGR* 1.136. For Vestinus, see Pflaum 1960–1: 245–7 n. 105.

The combination of 'high priest' and directorship of the Museum has a precedent in the career of Ti. Claudius Balbillus[92] and may have been frequent – the summary notice on Dionysius in the Suda certainly does not show that he was not also high priest of Alexandria. Pflaum's story about Vestinus is plausible enough: Hadrian encountered him in Alexandria when he visited Egypt in AD 130 and approved of him, and hence had him appointed to run the Roman and Greek libraries (*a bibliothecis*) and at the same time education (*a studiis*). Pflaum seems to want this joint appointment to fall after Hadrian's return to Italy in AD 134, which leaves little time (albeit just enough) for Vestinus also to be Hadrian's 'secretary for Greek correspondence' (*ab epistulis Graecis*). Stein and Petersen in their *PIR* entry also put the post at the end of Hadrian's reign, tendentiously claiming the support of the inscription.[93]

Some further data deserve notice. First, Vestinus' scholarly activities, noted briefly by Pflaum. For knowledge of these activities we are indebted to the Suda:

Vestinus, named Iulius, a sophist. (He wrote) an epitome of Pamphilus' *Rare words* (94 books); a selection of words from the works of Demosthenes; a selection from those of Thucydides, Isaeus, Isocrates and the rhetor Thrasymachus and the other rhetors.[94]

This looks like a man who can turn his hand to rhetoric but is chiefly immersed in linguistic and particularly lexicographic scholarship.

Second, another possible sighting – in Athens in AD 131/2, where he is responsible for the pattern poem called the *Altar of Besantinus* (Βησαντίνου βωμός) by the manuscript that transmits it: it can be written out so as to give the shape of an altar, an altar to Hadrian on which Hadrian himself is urged to sacrifice, with the acrostich 'Olympian, may you sacrifice for many years' (ΟΛΥΜΠΙΕ ΠΟΛΛΟΙΣ ΕΤΕΣΙ ΘΥΣΕΙΑΣ).[95] Like the sophist Marcus Antonius Polemo, who delivered the celebratory speech at the dedication

---

[92] Pflaum 1960–1: no.15. The office of 'high priest' (a Hadrianic innovation analogous to the post of *idios logos*, the chief finance officer) seems more likely to have had responsibility for managing temples and associated estates than for imperial cult (like ἀρχιερεῖς in the provinces of Asia Minor or the *sacerdos ad aram* at Lyon), cf. Bowman 1989: 67, 179ff.

[93] *PIR*² I 623.

[94] Οὐηστῖνος, Ἰούλιος χρηματίσας, σοφιστής. Ἐπιτομὴν τῶν Παμφίλου Γλωσσῶν βιβλία ϞδʹἘκλογὴν ὀνομάτων ἐκ τῶν Δημοσθένους βιβλίων, Ἐκλογὴν ἐκ τῶν Θουκυδίδου, Ἰσαίου, Ἰσοκράτους καὶ Θρασυμάχου τοῦ ῥήτορος καὶ τῶν ἄλλων ῥητόρων, Suda O 835 s.v. Οὐηστῖνος.

[95] The poem is found in Book 15 of the *Palatine Anthology* and in the fourteenth-century Vatican MS 434 (which also has the *Altar* or Dosiadas and the *Axe* of Simmias): on Vestinus' career and on his poem (offering a Greek text and English translation), see further Bowie 2002a: 185–9.

Libraries for the Caesars 255

of the temple of Olympian Zeus in 131/2, the sophist Vestinus is doing his bit to ratchet up the razzamatazz. It is hard to think that at this point he is in Rome, as Pflaum would have him.

Third, an unnoticed datum from Smyrna in AD 124, an inscription that lists benefactions contributing to the reconstruction of public spaces, parks and buildings in Smyrna;[96] they culminate in a list of generous gifts in cash and kind and privileges obtained from Hadrian for Smyrna 'by Antonius Polemo'. Many rich Smyrnaeans are on show, including rich women, among them Claudia, daughter of one of the previous generation's greatest sophists, Claudius Nicetes, and a group of 'former Judaeans' (οἵ ποτε Ἰουδαῖοι), perhaps migrants from Judaea rather than apostate Jews. High in the list (in fifth place) is a Lucius Vestinus, who in lines 11–12 promised 'that he would pave the basilica near the council chamber and would supply it with bronze doors'.[97] The previous contributor in the list, one L. Pompeius, had promised 50,000 drachmas, and the order in which names are listed seems to be that of the extent of their bearers' financial commitment. What Vestinus promised must therefore have committed him to something approaching 50,000 drachmas – equivalent to 200,000 sesterces, precisely the annual salary on which Pflaum puts him a few years later. We may of course be encountering a different Vestinus: but his first name (*praenomen*) and perhaps the association with Polemo support the notion that this is the same Vestinus. Perhaps, then, it was he, and not Eudaemon, who was the immediate successor of Suetonius in charge of correspondence (*ab epistulis*) in AD 121 or 122, and also, rather earlier, to Suetonius' posts in charge of education (*a studiis*) and in charge of libraries (*a bybliothecis*), holding them, say, 117–21. When we find him in Smyrna around the time of Hadrian's first tour of the province Asia he would thus be in the imperial entourage in his capacity of *ab epistulis*, perhaps indeed involved in the negotiations between Polemo and Smyrna concerning Hadrian's own substantial contribution to the scheme, and might feel obliged (nudged by the emperor?) to play the game and to promise virtually a year's salary.

Our last known librarian before the arrival in Rome of Hadrianus of Tyre is not much later: L. Volusius Maecianus, another career administrator, who outpaced the others, even Eudaemon, in making it to two top posts, both prefect in charge of Rome's grain supply (*praefectus annonae*) and prefect of Egypt (in AD 161), followed by adlection to the senate and ultimately election to the consulate. I print here only the two most informative of four

[96] *CIG* 3148 = *IGR* 3.1431 = *IKSmyrna* II.1.697 (= *IK* 24.1.697) re-edited by Puech 2002.
[97] ♦ Λούκιος Βηστεῖνος | τὴν βασιλικὴν στρώσειν ♦ τὴν | πρὸς τῶι βουλευτηρίωι καὶ χαλ|κᾶς τὰς θύρας ποιήσειν *hed.*, lines 11–12.

epigraphic texts from Ostia, one of which documents the last two steps in his impressive career (some earlier posts are here supplemented from the other inscriptions):

To Lucius Volusius, son of Lucius, Maecianus, consul designate, prefect of the Treasury of Saturn, prefect of Egypt, prefect of the grain supply, minor pontiff, secretary for petitions and reviews of status of the emperor Antoninus, secretary for education and procurator of libraries, prefect of transport, secretary for petitions of Antoninus Caesar, prefect of the first Aelian naval cohort, prefect of works, patron of the city, Lucius Volusius Mar . . .[98]

To Lucius Volusius, son of Lucius, Maecianus, jurisconsult, prefect of Egypt, prefect of the grain supply, minor pontiff, secretary for petitions and reviews of status of the emperor Antoninus, secretary for education and procurator of libraries, prefect of transport, secretary for petitions of Antoninus Caesar under the divine Hadrian, prefect of the first Aelian naval cohort, prefect of works, patron of the city[99]

Pflaum has unpacked the stages of Maecianus' career, much better documented than any of his predecessors, but it is still not quite clear what sort of man he was. He is not a military man (*vir militaris*) – his early post of 'military engineer' (*praefectus fabrum*) was already losing its military character in the time of Theophanes in the middle of the first century BC – and he serves only one of the three usual equestrian military appointments (*militiae equestres*): perhaps he had thought of serving more, but the posting of his cohort to Britain, perhaps even a visit to the Tay, changed his mind. His next post was in Rome, as an assistant (*adiutor*) to one of the commissions (*curae*) held by senior senators, in this case the commission for public works (*cura operum publicorum*). This was followed by another post which on Pflaum's view was used to keep in Rome somebody the administration wanted there and not elsewhere. Pflaum believes Maecianus' legal skills were relevant to his appointment.

His next move is appointment by Pius on his adoption by Hadrian to the important post of 'secretary for petitions and reviews of status' (*a libellis*

---

[98] L(ucio) V[olus]io L(ucii) f(ilio) | Ma[e]ciano | cos(uli) desig(nato), praef(ecto) aer(ari) Satur[n(i), pr(aefecto)Aeg(ypti),]) pr(aefecto) ann(onae), pontif(ici) m(inori), a libell(is) et [cens(ibus) Imp(eratoris)] | Antonini, a studiis et pro(curatori) [biblioth(ecarum)], | pr(aefecto) vehic(ulorum), a libell(is) Antoni[ni Caes(aris), pr(aefecto)] coho(rtis) I Aeliae class(icae), pr(aefecto) fabr[um, p(atrono) c(oloniae) L(ucius) V[olusi]us Mar. . . H. Bloch NSA 1953, 270 no. 33 = AE 1955.179, from Ostia. For Vestinus, see Pflaum 1960–1: 333–6 n. 141.

[99] [L(ucio) Volusio L(ucii) f(ilio) Maecian]o [iuris cons]ulto,[praefecto Aeg](ypti), [prae(fecto) annonae, pontif(ici) m(inori), a libe]llis [et censibus Imp(eratoris)] Antonini Aug(usti) Pii, [a studiis et pro(curatori) [biblioth(ecarum), p]raef(ecto) vehic(ulorum), [a libellis Antonini Aug(usti) Pii sub divJo Hadriano, [adiutori o(perum) p(ublicarum), praef(ecto) c]oho(rtis) I Ae[liae classicae, praef(ecto) fabr[um, patrono coloniae, CIL 14.5348 from Ostia.

et a censibus), a post that he cannot have taken up before that adoption on 25 February 138, and that he demitted on Pius' accession on 10 July. His next post is again, in Pflaum's view, simply a device to keep him in Rome, prefect of transport (*praefectus vehiculorum*). Only after this does Maecianus get the job that is at issue here, secretary for education and procurator for libraries (*a studiis et procurator bibliothecarum*). Between that and his prefecture of Egypt, dated no later than November AD 161, Maecianus held both the same post, 'secretary for petitions and reviews of status' (*a libellis et a censibus*), under Pius as emperor that he had briefly held on Pius' staff in the months before his accession, and the important post of prefect of grain supply (*praefectus annonae*), this no later than AD 152. We cannot tell how the three posts of prefect of transport (*praefectus vehiculorum*), secretary for education and procurator for libraries (*a studiis et procurator bibliothecarum*) and 'secretary for petitions and reviews of status' (*a libellis et a censibus*), were distributed over the years AD 138 to 152 – a pity, because if we knew how long he was in charge of libraries we might judge better how careful and appropriate a choice he was for the job.

Pflaum makes much of his legal knowledge: 'un des grands savants, dont les princes ne veulent plus se séparer':[100] and certainly by the end of his career his designation as a jurisconsult (*iuris consultus*) shows he had been given the 'right to issue responses' (*ius respondendi*). But how early did he hone these skills? Were they in any way relevant to his running of the libraries? Or is he another of the men whose financial skills are important, useful perhaps to control or even to cut library expenditure?[101] What is clearly lacking is evidence of involvement in literary culture (*paideia*) other than study of the law. In the generation of Salvius Iulianus, knowledge of the law is not a science to be underestimated, but my guess is that Maecianus is a rather different animal from Suetonius and Vestinus, and rather more like Eudaemon. He is indeed a writer, but not of 'literary' or 'scholarly' works. As well as his work on trusts (*fidei commissa*), on the public courts (*judicia publica*) and a collection of Rhodian laws relating to maritime affairs, he compiled a treatise on numerical divisions, weights and measures (*distributio*) most of which is extant, if little read. Of course he may have other cultural accomplishments too that have predictably escaped the honorific inscriptions: epigraphy alone would not have revealed the literary activities of Suetonius and Vestinus. We do not even know where Maecianus

---

[100] Pflaum 1960–1: 335.
[101] For Pius' interest in cutting expenditure, cf. the case of the citharode Mesomedes, SHA *Ant. Pius* 7.8.

came from: Pflaum insisted metropolitan Italy, Syme conjectured Africa.[102] But one might also bring the Greek world into the picture: a rhetor Maecius Faustinus is attested for Corinth, and Avidius Cassius seems to have married a Maecia or a Volusia Maeciana who may be our Volusius' daughter.[103] Work on Rhodian maritime law might stem from attachment to Greek origins, and Volusius Maecianus could conceivably come from the east, which would enhance his ability to assess the importance of Greek texts in the libraries of Rome.

This is an appropriate context to mention another library official with legal knowledge, T. Aelius Largus. The text honouring Largus at Praeneste describes him as 'procurator of libraries of Augustus' and as 'most skilled in public and private law'.[104] It mentions no other post. His name suggests that he or an ancestor received Roman citizenship from Antoninus Pius: perhaps indeed his post was under Pius, after Volusius Maecianus, and that man's legal skills had shown themselves in some way relevant to library administration. But this dating can only be a guess, and it may be doubted if he was the procurator in charge of libraries: Pflaum assumes his rank to be lower, with a salary of 60,000 sesterces.[105]

Two names pertinent to Roman libraries after the arrival of Hadrianus must be mentioned. First L. Baebius Aurelius Iuncinus, for whom an inscription from Sardinia attests a series of procuratorial posts, with the libraries post his first, at the salary (the text specifies) of 60,000 sesterces (the lowest grade in the procuratorial career).[106] In this inscription his career climaxes in his appointment as prefect of Egypt, where he duly appears on three papyri, one of which dates his activity as prefect to AD 213.[107] His first post, as procurator for libraries, presumably belongs around AD 180–90. If he is a descendant (more likely grandson than son) of L. Baebius Iuncinus, probably from Sicilian Messana, who held four equestrian military posts before becoming an administrator and ending up (probably under Hadrian) in the second highest post in Egypt, minister of justice (*iuridicus*),[108] his career may owe something to family influence with an emperor. The evidence betrays no sign of special qualifications for work with libraries, and at 60,000 sesterces he cannot have been the official in overall charge.

Our last evidence from the High Empire concerning imperial libraries concerns the Christian philosopher and scholar Sex. Iulius Africanus from

---

[102] Pflaum 1960–1: 335, Syme 1988: 698.
[103] *Corinth* 8.3 264; for Maecia, Syme 1988: 698.
[104] *iuris publici et privati peritissimus*, *CIL* 14.2916.   [105] Pflaum 1960–1: 1023.
[106] *CIL* 10.7580 = *ILS* 1358. See Pflaum 1960–1: no. 251, *PIR*² B 13.   [107] *P.Giss.* 40. II.
[108] *CIL* 10.6976 = *ILS* 1434, *PIR*² B 18.

Aelia Capitolina (the city that had been Jerusalem until Hadrian's Jewish war). A successful embassy to seek the status of a city for Emmaus brought him to Rome in the reign of Severus Alexander (AD 222–35) and he writes that in Rome, in the same reign, he built a library in the Pantheon next to the baths of Alexander. We owe this item to a papyrus fragment of his 24-book miscellany, *Charmed Girdles* (Κέστοι), a work completed by c. AD 231 and also dedicated to Alexander Severus.[109] There was presumably still a procurator in charge of libraries (though none has so far been attested in the now diminishing epigraphic record),[110] and how Africanus' initiative (if we believe it happened) related to his responsibilities we cannot tell. Perhaps one reason for setting up a new collection was the destruction of much of the Palatine libraries in AD 191 or 192.[111]

Conclusions

The emperors' building of libraries in the imperial city of Rome, all containing works in both Latin and in Greek and most explicitly divided into a 'Roman' and a 'Greek' library, asserted their own role as participants in and supporters of the Greco-Roman literary culture which had become the habitus of the western elite. It may also have allowed them on rare occasions to exercise discreetly some control over what some sections of that elite read. In most cases the imperial inclusion of a library in a larger monumental programme was a response to cultural expectations nurtured by the progressive Hellenisation of Rome and Italy[112] – so, certainly, the libraries associated with the temple of Apollo on the Palatine and with the portico of Octavia, and later those of Trajan's forum. This is less obviously the case for the library in the temple of Peace, and not at all for that in the house of Tiberius. Hadrian's Athenaeum (if Hadrian's it was) falls in a rather different category: a complex whose functions seem entirely or predominantly to relate to literary culture, and hence necessarily equipped with a library.

---

[109] *POxy.* 312, from book 18, where his term (line 67) is 'I was architect of', ἠρχιτεκτόνισα. The context, Africanus' insistence that lines of *Odyssey* 11 missing from other manuscripts had been found by him in books in Aelia Capitolina, Nysa and the library he had built in Rome, does not inspire confidence in any of its claims. Other testimonies are assembled in *PIR*² I 124.

[110] Matthew Nicholls has kindly drawn my attention to the *vir egregius* Q. Veturius Callistratus, attested c. AD 240 by *CIL* vi 2132 as 'procurator of the final accounts of the private libraries of Augustus' (*proc. rationum summarum privatarum bibliothecarum Augusti*): if my translation is correct (taking *privatarum* with *bibliothecarum*), we have a unique piece of evidence for the organisation of private imperial libraries, presumably including those in imperial villas.

[111] Gal. *de compos. medicin. per genera* 1.1 = xiii 362 Kühn.

[112] For Italy especially, see Wallace-Hadrill 2008.

If any pattern at all can be detected in emperors' choices of librarians then it reflects the issues both of culture and control, at least in the broader sense of ensuring that imperial institutions were run effectively and economically. The appointments known before the development of the equestrian procuratorial system point the way: Pompeius Macer, an equestrian, indeed held at least one, and perhaps two, posts as procurator, before he got his library job, and that may have been intended either (at least initially) to get the new libraries up and running or to put in place some co-ordination between imperial libraries, each of which had its own, freedman administrator. Both his double identity (a man with a Greek father, but himself forging a career in Latin-speaking Rome) and his apparently amateur activity as a poet complemented presumed organisational skills. One of the other Augustan appointments, the freedman Melissus, may or may not be a more professional writer than Macer, but Hyginus is undoubtedly a scholar and writer who recalls some of Alexandria's librarians. The relevance of scholarly involvement seems again to be important for some later procurators – Dionysius, Suetonius and Vestinus: but for all three the post is part of a longer administrative career. Too little is known about Scirtus or Zoilus to assess their 'qualifications', but both Hadrian's other attested appointee, Eudaemon, and Pius' man Volusius Maecianus, seem on our evidence to be career administrators with no involvement in literature, despite the latter's responsibility for education (*a studiis*) as well as libraries. But we know far too little of the circumstances of any single appointment to be able to reconstruct with confidence on what criteria a man *was* selected.[113] We cannot say who alternative candidates were, whom an emperor might have thought it better *not* to appoint, what sort of pressures were brought by friends and family, whether by the later second century the career structure of the equestrian 'service', settling into a pattern, added its own pressures. As so often, we must be content with a set of data which, though in some ways remarkably rich and informative, is insufficient to establish a pattern in which we can have confidence.

[113] Just as what books went into a library must have depended on many factors unknown to us, cf. Dix and Houston 2006: 673.

14 | Roman libraries as public buildings in the cities of the Empire

MATTHEW NICHOLLS

Bibliothecas quas maximas posset publicare

References to the new libraries of Augustan Rome often use the verb *publicare* or its cognates:

bibliothecas Graecas Latinasque quas maximas posset publicare

[Julius Caesar aimed] to make public the biggest possible Greek and Latin libraries. (Suetonius, *Iul.* 44)

bibliothecas publicavit Pollio Graecas simul atque Latinas

Pollio made public both Greek and Latin libraries. (Isidorus, *Etym.* 6.5.2)

bibliotheca, quae prima in orbe ab Asinio Pollione ex manubiis publicata Romae est

The library which was made public at Rome, the first in the world, by Asinius Pollio from his booty. (Pliny, *HN* 7.115)

Asini Pollionis hoc Romae inventum, qui primus bibliothecam dicando ingenia hominum rem publicam fecit

This [the placing of author portraits in libraries] was the invention of Asinius Pollio at Rome, who was the first to make the genius of men public property by dedicating a library. (Pliny, *HN* 35.10)

What might this mean? We learn from other references to these public libraries that they could be thought of as nominally open, putting their literary contents on public display: Ovid wrote that 'whatever men of old or the present day have conceived in their learned hearts lies open to be inspected by those who would read (*lecturis inspicienda patent*)'.[1] We can also compare the language used of similar acts of cultural benefaction in other fields by the emperor and his circle, and consider (for example) the opening up of Rome's gardens, and the provision under Agrippa of the city's first public bathhouse. The verb *publicare* seems to have become commonly attached to this sort of activity in this period; Agrippa, for example, used the word *publicandis* in the title of his pamphlet *On the necessity of making public*

---

[1] Ov. *Tr.* 3.1. 63–4.

all pictures and statues.[2] The new regime seems to have surveyed the wealth of cultural property piling up at its disposal and decided that the proper ideological tactic was the conspicuous public disposition of this material, much of which had previously been part of private aristocratic collections. In its scope and scale this was something new.

But there remains the vexed question of how public these and other 'public' libraries in the Roman world really were: buildings and institutions that are nominally public can present a wide variety of faces, from an open-door policy accessible to all comers to tightly regulated access favouring only a few known and trusted visitors. It is often presumed that Rome's public libraries tended towards the latter end of the spectrum, open only to the 'learned and respectable',[3] a stratum of society that is naturally presumed to be narrow. Consequently, a relatively small number of library users is envisaged.

However, the architecture of surviving libraries tells a rather different story. My intention here is simply to look at several firmly identified surviving libraries at Rome and in the provinces, and to observe that their location and architecture seem intended to place their façades and contents on display to large numbers of people, not just to visiting readers.[4] This intention necessarily involved choices, of sites, budgets, priorities and design: the public aspect of these libraries was a deliberate part of their intended function.

If Roman public libraries were meant only to store large numbers of books for the use of a narrow literary elite, then they were designed with a cavalier inefficiency and a marked profligacy of both space and materials. They incorporated large areas of open floor space and lofty halls from their earliest development, judging by surviving remains and literary references to the senate meetings in Augustus' Palatine library, for example, or the fifty-foot-tall bronze Apollo kept in Tiberius' library of the Temple of the Deified Augustus.[5] Books seem to have been relegated to wall-mounted

---

[2] *de tabulis omnibus signisque publicandis*: Plin. *HN* 35.9.26.
[3] In this instance: Harris 1989: 228.
[4] There is an obvious risk of circularity in the interpretation of the available archaeological evidence: the best-attested public libraries seem to be large buildings with niches, so large buildings with niches tend to be claimed as libraries and other candidates overlooked. It may well be that other sorts of library eschewed monumental public display and have disappeared from the record for just this reason. Nonetheless, there is a marked consistency in firmly identified examples of Roman public libraries that fits with the description of form and use given here and seems to have been typical.
[5] For an overview of Roman library buildings, see Makowiecka 1978, but note difficulties with the typology of library buildings as discussed above. For descriptions of buildings in Rome: *LTUR*, s.v. *bibliotheca*; Dix and Houston 2006. It has been suggested that the Roman

cases (common to all known public library buildings) and protected from the central floor area by a high podium. At the same time, library buildings such as those of Trajan's forum and the Palatine in Rome and of Celsus at Ephesus and Rogatianus at Timgad had wide doorways which would have placed the contents on display to passers-by (and admitted light for readers). This combination of features suggests a tension in the intended function of these buildings between housing and protecting valuable books and accommodating and impressing large numbers of people, both inside and outside the library.

Moreover, as David Petrain's paper in this volume shows, Rome's public libraries were also furnished from the outset with works of art alongside their books which 'communicated to viewers about the significance of their holdings' – not just author portraits, but separate highly prized antiquities and pictures and sculptures of various sorts[6] – and often stood in monumental public complexes which were themselves noted for their artworks.[7] The libraries, with their ranks of book cupboards and smart fittings visible from the outside, were surely intended to function as part of this display as well as being working resources, attracting visitors to the imperial spaces in which they were located and contributing in no small measure to the impression of cultural prestige they engendered: their visitors, even those who were illiterate, could in some sense be counted among the intended audience for such libraries, even if not as 'library users' in the conventional sense.

Authors like Galen who record their use of the libraries for reading and writing are, therefore, representative of only one among a number of categories of people who experienced the buildings in one way or another.[8] The sources, in fact, give a picture of libraries that were fairly lively and busy places, used by people belonging to different groups by background or age – prestigious intellectuals, but (as Gellius records) also pupils and students,

---

development of window glass, probably for large public baths, made it possible for the first time to locate substantial book collections in large and well lit spaces without the danger of rainwater penetration: Höpfner 1996: 9 (though the argument here is not entirely convincing), Baatz 1991.

[6] Author portraits: e.g. Isid. *Etym.* 6.5.2, Plin. *HN* 35.2.9–11, Suet. *Tib.* 70, Sid. Apoll. *Epist.* 9.16. Other portraits: Tac. *Ann.* 2.37 with Tabula Hebana X; cf. Tabula Siarensis fr. II Col. C, lines 15–18. Other important works of art in the *Asinii Pollionis monumenta*: Plin. *HN* 36.23–5, 33–4. An ancient bronze inscription from Delphi in the Palatine libraries: Plin. *HN* 7.210, and see David Petrain's chapter elsewhere in this volume. Art works in the library of the Temple of the Deified Augustus: the famous giant statue of Apollo Temenitus taken from Syracuse: Suet. *Tib.* 74 (cf. Cic. *Verr.* 2.4.119, Plin. *HN* 34.43); a painting of Hyacinthus by Nicias which Augustus had liked: Plin. *HN* 35.131.

[7] E.g. the Porticus Octaviae: Plin. *HN* 35.66; 35.114; the Templum Pacis: Plin. *HN* 34.84, Amm. Marc. 22.16.2. For the Palatine, see below.

[8] For Galen's use of libraries at Rome, see Nicholls 2011.

or young people seeking to learn from the real or figurative presence of established authors, as 'Dio' proudly claims for his statue in the library at Corinth.[9] The public library thus acted as a place of encounter between living generations, as well as between authors of the past and the present. To these types of library user we can add the sort of non-specialist reader whom a Quintilian or Apuleius can tell to go and look something up,[10] people who came to look at the artworks on display, and those who attended meetings and lectures there, such as the public recitals that Asinius Pollio, founder of Rome's first public library, offered in Rome for the first time, or the senate meetings discussed elsewhere in this volume by David Petrain and Ewen Bowie.[11] The design of many public libraries suggests that we can add those who simply walked past their impressive façades, perhaps noting the dedicatory inscriptions or observing through the entrance screen the statues, paintings and rows of book cupboards within.

None of this was inherently a part of what we might have imagined to be a library's 'core function', housing and allowing access to books for readers – though aspects of their design certainly provided intelligently for this purpose. The library needs of literary-minded aristocrats and their circles of litterateurs, if they were the only intended audience, could have been perfectly well served by private structures on a far smaller scale, judging by the relatively modest book room in the Villa of the Papyri at Herculaneum.

Roman public libraries therefore seem to have been designed from the outset with an ostentatious public function in mind, as monuments displaying works of art and providing a magnificent backdrop for cultural activities of various sorts. They provided in a library room or rooms the public equivalent of various aspects of the private luxury of a villa like that at Herculaneum – architectural, decorative, artistic, as well as bibliophilic – and were often part of complexes that manifested different elements of this broad intent. The imperial regime's efforts to be seen to be adorning Rome with public benefactions, noted above, suggest that making these gestures visibly magnificent was a political aim in itself, separate from (though not incompatible with) the actual working life of the libraries in question. The fact that they existed, and were talked of as public, mattered whether or not the actual reading usership was large, or of mixed status.[12] The regime's

---

[9] Gell. 13.20, Dio Chrys. *Or.* 37.8. The 37th oration attributed to Dio is now generally considered to be by another hand, probably that of Favorinus. Cf. König 2001.

[10] Quint., *Inst.* 10.1.57; Apul *Apol.* 90–1.

[11] Dalzell 1955. For recitations in public libraries, see below notes 16 and 40.

[12] A brief modern comparison might be useful. There was a total of 486,867 reading room visits to the British Library in 2007–8, representing a small proportion of the UK's population, but

generosity must have been well publicised, after all, for news of the library foundations to have reached Ovid in Tomis.

Augustus and the Palatine library

Augustus' Palatine complex provides an excellent early example, incorporating a public library in the heart of metropolitan Rome as part of a scheme with a wider political, cultural and functional remit. The library room (apparently at first a single hall, later joined by the twin visible on the marble plan)[13] was part of the famous suite of buildings that included the Temple of Apollo dedicated in 28 BC, a portico and the *princeps'* own house. Many art treasures were housed and displayed here: the temple's collection of artworks, the elaborate pair of golden cases for the Augustan recension of the Sibylline books, the collection of jewels and signet rings dedicated by Marcellus and much else, including an ancient inscription from Delphi and portraits of authors and statesmen in the library room itself.[14]

This whole area was of course unmistakably under the tutelary gaze of its august inhabitant, but it carefully transcended the traditional functions of a mere private house by sustaining public, civic and religious functions. The library there was part of this programme, combining its various literary functions with a civic role. Both Ovid and Horace suggest that reading was possible in the library,[15] while Horace also suggests more performative literary events such as recitations.[16] But it is well known that the library room was also used by Augustus for the reception of embassies, revision of the jury lists and meetings of the senate.[17]

---

the library as an institution and a building is deliberately designed to present itself to the general public in an accessible way, broadening its audience beyond its usership. It has a prominent public location with a large public square facing the Euston Road, a free ground floor exhibition space, a cafe, a shop, a monumental display of the books of the King's Library in the central atrium, and temporary exhibitions and events, and is regarded as a prominent London landmark and national cultural asset even by those who never go there to read. Figures: The British Library 2008.

[13] Fr. 20b. For a recent archaeological account, see Iacopi and Tedone 2005/2006, with discussion in Nicholls 2010a: 16–19.

[14] Sibylline books: Suet. *Aug.* 31; Marcellus' jewels: Plin. *HN* 37.11; Delphic inscription and author portraits: see above note 6.

[15] Hor. *Epist.* 2.1.214–15: *qui se lectori credere malunt | quam spectatoris fastidia ferre superbi* ('those [authors] who prefer to entrust themselves to a reader than to bear the haughtiness of an arrogant spectator'); Ov. *Tr.* 3.1.63–4. *lecturis inspicienda patent* (see above).

[16] Hor. *Epist.* 2.2.92–105 and *Sat.* 1.10.38 with Acron's commentary; perhaps Calp. *Ecl.* 4.157–9 and Juv. *Sat.* 7.36–7.

[17] Alexandrian embassy: *POxy.* 2435 verso. Cf. Joseph. *BJ* 2.82. Jury lists: Suet. *Aug.* 29.3; senate *ibid.* and Tac. *Ann.* 2.37. Thompson 1981, Corbier 1992; D. Palombi, 'Curia in Palatino', *LTUR* I, 334.

Such uses do not, of course, prove that the Palatine library had a genuinely 'public' aspect in anything like the modern meaning of the word; access could still have been restricted and surely was when important political events were held there. Nonetheless, the library does seem from its inception to have been part of a wider programme of cultural display and intended for use as a venue for events involving a lot of people, of a public quality at least insofar as they pertained to the *res publica* rather than the world of purely literary *otium* or leisure.

As it happens, an insight into the perceived function and status of this Augustan public library can be found in the contemporary writer Vitruvius. In *De Architectura* Book 6.5.2 he writes that the private houses of aristocrats holding public office should contain impressively appointed hallways, atria, courtyards, groves, walkways and 'libraries, picture galleries and basilicas like those in public buildings' because 'in their houses both public counsels and private decisions and judgments' are made. This is a surprising statement: the public library was a new institution in Rome at this date, though Vitruvius makes it sound commonplace, and there is little record if any of the great Republican figures having basilicas in their houses or transacting public business in their private libraries. The tiny library room of the Villa of the Papyri could scarcely have housed such activities, and even Lucullus' larger library acted, says Plutarch, as a 'lodging of the muses'[18] and home to Greek scholars rather than a venue for public business. At any rate Lucullus' library, like those of Cicero, Atticus and Pliny, was not in Rome but at one of his country villas at Tusculum, a place for learned *otium*, not public business.[19] Rather, Vitruvius must have had in mind the new public libraries of Augustan Rome, which we know to have been used in just this way: perhaps the Porticus Octaviae, where the senate also met,[20] and the Atrium Libertatis, which housed the headquarters and archives of the censors, but above all Augustus' new residential complex on the Palatine, where the *princeps* was trying to develop a new, decorous idiom of palace architecture that could sidestep charges of excess grandeur by claiming a public function.

An approving reference to Augustus' Palatine project is wholly consonant with the spirit of Vitruvius' work, which is dedicated to Augustus. It suggests that from the outset the library here was intended to be seen, like the rest of the palace-temple complex, in a wider civic-religious-public context. Reports of its uses suggest that Augustan authors picked up on

---

[18] Plut. *Luc.* 42.   [19] Cic. *Fin.* 3.2.7.
[20] Cass. Dio, 55.8.1 – the senate met at least once in the Porticus Octaviae.

this intention and discussed the new buildings in those terms. In Augustus' new Rome, quite apart from their use by readers and scholars, which was and continued to be considerable, Rome's public libraries formed part of a grand backdrop suitable for the conduct of public business, setting a pattern for their successors.

Location, location, location: some provincial public libraries

So far we have been dealing with privileged spaces, and mainly considering library interiors. The public business transacted in and around these libraries, and the collections of art and other treasures housed in or near them, suggest a monumental public identity, but cannot demonstrate a mass audience. The location as well as the design of Rome's public libraries was significant, making them part of the grandiose landscape of imperial architectural euergetism or civic philanthropy that reshaped and defined the city. While we might suspect a large potential audience, however, we simply cannot be sure what proportion of the population had access to libraries in the Augustan Palatine complex or spaces like the *Atrium Libertatis* and the libraries of the Imperial Fora.[21]

If we consider the physical location and context of well known provincial Roman public libraries, however, we can see that some trouble and expense has been taken to present a bold public façade to as many people as possible, using the outside as well as the inside of the building to advertise their patrons' generosity and virtues. The builders of these public libraries clearly saw prominent public display as part of the role of the public library. They were aware of the Roman aristocratic and imperial tradition of library collection and wanted to engage with it, as their buildings demonstrate; they were also part of a local municipal tradition of philosophical schools and gymnasia. As they were often men with good connections to the upper echelons of Roman government, and their own library buildings abound in architectural echoes of those at Rome, we might see their efforts as a useful analogue to the way libraries were understood to function in the capital.

The Austrian anastylosis or reconstruction of Celsus' early second-century library at Ephesus provides the most striking surviving example of a rich library exterior. It is important to note that much of the

---

[21] I leave aside the separate question of whether Rome's imperial bathhouses had libraries, which would have markedly increased the public aspect discussed here. It is certainly possible, though all commentators point out the paucity of the evidence: see e.g. Dix and Houston 2006: 701–6.

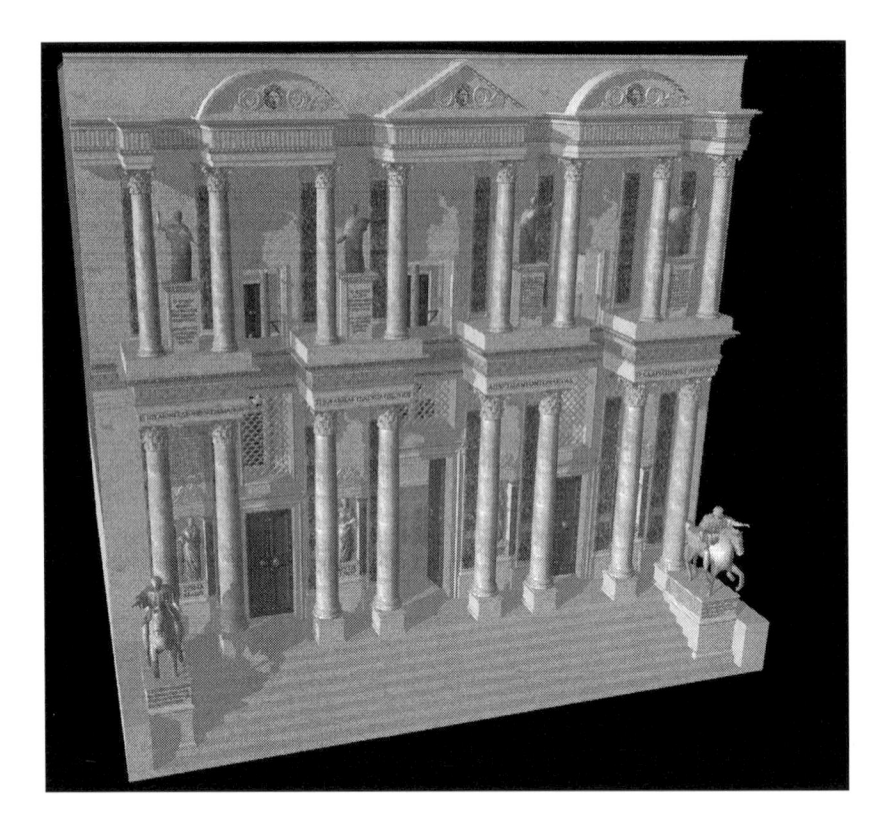

Figure 14.1 The façade of the library of Celsus at Ephesus

architectural effort expended on this building was directed towards the public face it presented to the street. The library's enormous and elaborate façade, covered with inscriptions and statues, addresses the casual passer-by as well as the reader or visitor who ventured within. Moreover, it must be considered not in isolation but in its specific location within the city.

The library is situated at the culmination of the city's principal thoroughfare ('Curetes Street') which leads from the Upper Agora into the heart of the city, funnelling traffic into the city between two high hills. By the time Celsus and his heirs built the library in the early second century AD, Curetes Street had undergone several decades of adornment with a distinctive blend of local architectural ebullience and imperial loyalist symbolism. The effect is that the library caps a series of elaborate architectural expressions of Ephesian prosperity and loyalty, joining imperial monuments such as the gate and shrine of Hadrian and the nymphaeum of Trajan. The library shares some of their decorative architectural vocabulary and also contains echoes of metropolitan Trajanic Rome.[22] Celsus had served library-building emperors as consul and curator of public works in Flavian Rome, and would have known the city's libraries, especially if we believe that he was the intellectual figure his own library claims him to have been. It is interesting, then, that he regarded prominent public visibility as a suitable priority for his own scheme.

The library sits at an important right-angle bend, dominating the little piazza on which it sits like a theatrical *scaenae frons* and forming the focal point of the view down the entire length of the street.[23] As such it must have been one of the town's most prominent buildings in antiquity, as it is today. Its single large book room opens straight onto the street through three large doors in its grand façade and a broad staircase running the entire width of the building, increasing its visual impact but compromising its security. We have already seen this tension in library design; to protect valuable books from pilfering and damp, libraries like this one might more easily have been located in compact and modest accommodation on an upper floor (like many medieval libraries). The need for a large and visually impressive space, visible and directly accessible from street level, must therefore have outweighed practical concerns for the builders of the surviving public libraries; this indicates a wider constituency than a small clique of regular readers.

This deliberately public aspect is also attested by the Celsus library's epigraphic and decorative programme. The famous sequence of four statues of Celsus' personified intellectual virtues (the 'Wisdom', 'Virtue', 'Understanding', and 'Knowledge of Celsus') and the bilingual career inscriptions on the lower level[24] blazon an unsubtle celebration of the patron's merits to those passing by as well as those who enter the building, forming part of a very dense concentration of commemorative texts in this word- and image-rich part of town. Statues of Celsus himself and his son dedicated by other family members adorn the upper level, their own statuses and careers inscribed on the bases. In short, the library, which also houses Celsus' tomb, was intended to function as a sort of billboard proclaiming the family's virtues (and promoting their standing) in one of the busiest parts of the city. With its mix of architecture, statuary and bilingual text, it was comprehensible to townspeople and visitors with varying degrees and types of literacy. Like much Roman euergetistic and funerary architecture, the building goes all-out to catch the attention of people whose interest in it might well have been

---

[22] Strocka 1978.   [23] For the development of this part of Ephesus over time, see Burrell 2009.
[24] *IvE* 5,102–3.

marginal and transitory; indeed, the interior, though far less well preserved, seems to have been rather plainer than the extraordinary façade, to which it bore little architectural correspondence.

The long foundation inscription of the library is particularly interesting.[25] It describes a fund for the operation of the library and also for the thrice-annual garlanding of Celsus' statues and especial adornment of all his images (here and elsewhere in the city?) on his 'festival day', whose date is given – presumably his birthday, the date when the library staff's salary was also to be paid from the library's endowment. This is an attempt to make the library part of a euergetistic gesture that encompassed the civic landscape of Ephesus and was refreshed regularly. The family's foundation was intended to be not just a library building, of interest only to a relatively small number of Ephesian intellectuals, but a commemorative, living benefaction, staking out a place for itself in a civic landscape crowded with competing philanthropic structures and events. Like the building's prime location and busy façade, this was an appeal for attention and memory: the range of commemorative events, linking the library to public statues and an annual festival, were intended to keep the memory of Celsus alive, refreshing the impact of his library and his statuary display every year, and to extend the potential constituency of his library benefaction to the city's wider population. We might compare the famous procession of Vibius Salutaris, another roughly contemporary euergetistic foundation at Ephesus that integrated physical gifts of statues with civic distributions and a regular commemorative procession;[26] Celsus and his heirs tried to make their library the epicentre of a similar addition to the civic life of the city.

Another attempt to broaden or at least reinforce the impact of a library benefaction comes from a near-contemporary dedication at Dyrrachium. The younger Pliny, in the letter describing his library foundation at Comum, says that it was not likely to win as much instant favour among the townsfolk as the gift of a gladiatorial combat.[27] At Dyrrachium the patron Gaetulicus (an officer, like Celsus, of one of the greatest library-building emperors, Trajan) hedged his bets by providing both:

To Lucius Flavius Aemilius Tellur(ius) Gaetulicus, son of Titus, honoured as Public Knight by the emperor Caesar Trajan Augustus, Prefect of the II Cavalry Cohort of Spaniards in Upper Germany, Duovir Quinquennalis, Priest, Patron of the Colony, who by spending 170,000 HS for the purchase of the ground for the construction

---

[25] *IvE* 5,113. [26] See Rogers 1991. [27] Plin. *Ep.* 1.8.

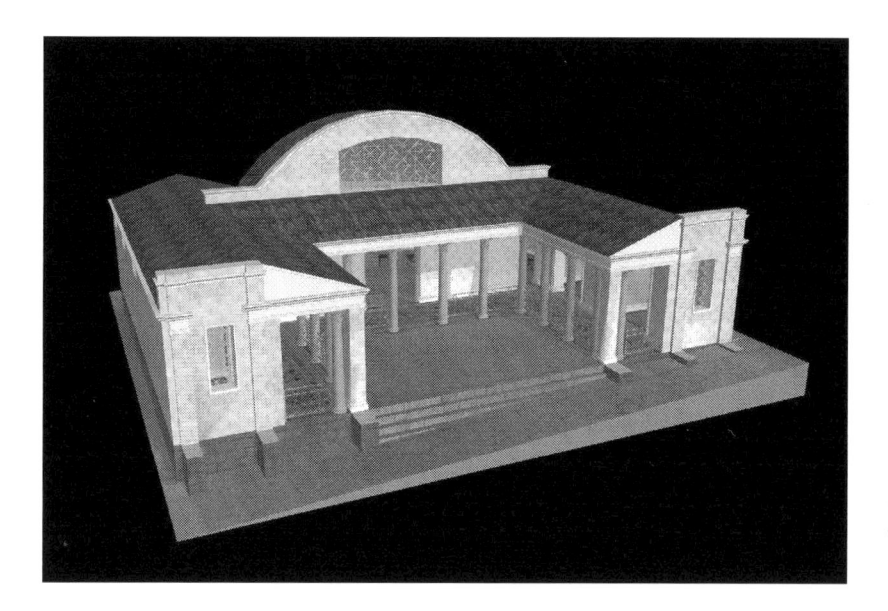

Figure 14.2 The library of Rogatianus at Timgad viewed from the street

of the library freed the public exchequer from the expense and at its dedication provided twelve pairs of gladiators at his own expense. (*CIL* III 607)[28]

The library building at Dyrrachium does not survive, but where we do find library remains we tend to see that their builders, as at Ephesus, went to some trouble to put them on public display. The library of Rogatianus at Timgad in modern Algeria, for instance, occupies an entire block in the centre of the colony's grid of streets, one block north of the junction of the Cardo and Decumanus. The library is therefore right in the central district of the town and close to other large public monuments including the forum, theatre and macellum. Since Timgad outgrew its original orthogonal grid of streets and spilled out to the west into organically growing suburbs, where various public complexes which needed a lot of land were located, building land in the central part of the city seems to have been expensive and prestigious (as the land for the library at Dyrrachium must have been, to cost as much as 170,000 sesterces); the decision to take up a whole block here with the library, which is usually dated to the third century AD (well into the period of the town's expansion) cannot have been taken lightly.[29]

The Timgad library building faces deliberately onto the Cardo Maximus, taking care to present an ornamented façade and open courtyard to the city's

---

[28] I am grateful to my colleague Peter Kruschwitz for his assistance with this inscription.
[29] For dating and details, see the not unproblematical Pfeiffer 1931.

busiest street leading to the forum, thereby risking the attendant hazards of noise and theft. A porticoed courtyard approached from the Cardo by a short, wide flight of steps provides an open public library forecourt (graffiti on the columns suggest that people could loiter there). Like the Ephesus library, this building is at pains to show itself and its ground-floor book holdings off to the general public of the town. In order to achieve this, the library faces west – not east to catch the morning sun and avoid damp damage to the books, as Vitruvius suggests.[30] In fact several known public libraries ignore Vitruvius' suggested orientation, preferring to align themselves with their monumental context.[31] The Timgad library entirely ignores the less prominent street behind it to the east; indeed, its apse extends out into this rear street, partly obstructing it. The architectural features of the Timgad library are consistent with this prominent location and public aspect. The neat, even elegant building, with its semicircular book room and helical columns, shows a degree of architectural flair and innovation consonant with its eye-catching location: it is designed to impress townspeople and visitors, passers-by and readers alike.

Another earlier and larger library which fills an important urban position is that built at Athens by Hadrian in AD 131/2, famous for its luxury and enthusiastically received by Aristides and Pausanias.[32] The map of Hadrianic Athens shows that Hadrian accelerated rapidly a process of expansion that Roman builders had been imposing on the ancient city since the days of Augustus and Agrippa. Hadrian's library is clearly related to other major Roman structures by scale and alignment, and in particular to the adjacent and coaxial Roman agora, a project begun by Caesar and completed by Augustus.[33] The alignment, scale and overall scheme of these neighbouring buildings is very similar; each consists of an enclosed porticoed square with high boundary walls and a monumental entrance to the west, and they seem to form a pair. Indeed, at the same time as Hadrian built his own complex he repaved and repaired the neighbouring agora, inscribing one of the laws of his revision of the Athenian constitution on its main entrance.[34]

The overall effect of this cluster of civic and religious buildings was to reshape this section of the city, between the old agora area and the new Hadrianic residential quarter, and to stamp a Roman imperial presence firmly in the city, just as the famous inscription on Hadrian's arch boasts.[35]

[30] Vitr. 6.4.1; cf. 6.7.3.
[31] E.g. Palatine libraries – prob. faced NW; Trajan's libraries NE/SW; Ephesus SE; Hadrian at Athens W; *Templum Pacis* prob. NW.
[32] Aristid. *Panathenaicus* 13.188; Paus. 1.18.9.   [33] See Boatwright 1983; cf. Shear 1981.
[34] *IG* II^2, 1,100.   [35] *IG* II^2 5,185.

The location of these buildings ensured that they would be prominent landmarks within the reshaped Athens, with major roads routing large volumes of traffic around them. Independently of its literary function, then, the Hadrianic public library achieved on a grand scale the same conspicuity that Celsus aimed for in Ephesus and, later, Rogatianus in Timgad. Provincial library donors (whose numbers peak dramatically in the early second century AD) seem to have been influenced by the notable examples set by Hadrian and his predecessor Trajan.[36]

Before Hadrian's benefactions reshaped Athens, another privately donated Trajanic public library had in fact already been located in a prominent location spanning the old Greek and modern Roman faces of the city in a similar way. This library of Pantainos is best known for the famous inscription of its rules.[37] Another inscription from the building tells us that the library, its stoa and peristyle, and all its books and furnishing were dedicated from the personal resources of one T. Flavius Pantainos, Priest of the Wisdom-Loving Muses and son of an Athenian teacher (διάδοχος), to Athena Polias, the emperor Trajan, and the City of the Athenians.[38] Pantainos' dedication suggests a moderately large building with spaces for meeting and discussion as well as a library, perhaps allowing for the continuation of Pantainos' father's school-teacher role. Excavation confirms this impression, and graffiti on the courtyard columns and the stern epigraphic prohibition on book-borrowing suggest heavy use.

The building also incorporated a measure of public sculpture display, like Celsus': outside stood statues of the *Iliad* and *Odyssey* personified, and somewhere in the complex a statue of Trajan trampling on a Dacian was dutifully erected. The prominent location of Pantainos' library echoes this carefully expressed dual Graeco-Roman identity: adjacent to the Stoa of Attalos, the library opened on one side onto the ancient Panathenaic Way and the Greek agora, and on the other side to the new road (the 'Plataia') linking this area to the Roman agora and the future site of the library of Hadrian. Pantainos' building was thus located at an important corner of two busy streets linking some of the city's principal public areas: again, a library was used to attract the attention of passers-by as a prominent act of high-minded civic euergetism, enhanced by public displays of sculpture and epigraphy together with a politically astute blending of local culture and Roman loyalty that caught the mood of the age. Pantainos' conspicuous loyalty to Rome and his fellow citizens paid off, since he seems to have

---

[36] Nicholls 2005: 287–8.
[37] Thompson and Wycherley 1957: 150 Agora I 2,729 = Platthy 1968: 113 no. 37.
[38] Thompson and Wycherley 1957: 150 = Platthy 1968: 112 no. 36.

become archon in AD 102: a herm dedicated to him in this capacity was found inside Hadrian's library.[39]

Libraries as cultural centres: spaces for audiences and visitors

The potential constituency for several public libraries, including those at Athens, was expanded by the inclusion of facilities for public meetings, lectures, or recitations. Such events could attract large and mixed audiences, especially in the lively intellectual civic milieu of the Second Sophistic. Apuleius, speaking from the stage of the theatre in Carthage, says that if his audience hears anything especially learned they should imagine that they are listening to him in the town's library, as if it were a familiar venue for intellectual or literary performance.[40] We might also note that some libraries seem to have had a role in the education of the young, like the Pantainos library, the library in Corinth where 'Dio' says the students might be inspired by his portrait bust, the library that Pliny endowed at Comum as part of his educational patronage of the town, or the Domus Tiberiana where Gellius sets an anecdote that implies the presence of a mixed group of scholars and at least one student.[41] Although students who required a library for their studies would have been a privileged minority in a Roman city, their numbers would still have contributed to a rather more lively and busy library scene than is sometimes envisaged.

We have already seen that library buildings, where they survive, typically incorporated a large open central floor area flanked by a podium, which could in itself have accommodated a fairly sizeable number of people for formal or informal gatherings. As we saw in the case of Augustus' Palatine libraries, this was part of the intended function of the Roman public library from its origins. Furthermore, some libraries seem to have been associated with larger and more formally appointed spaces for public events. An inscription shows that at some point an auditorium was constructed near the Celsus library, for example.[42] It has been suggested that this would have been used for the hearing of legal cases. But the proximity to the library could imply a cultural or entertainment function as well (and at any rate, the rhetorical fireworks of Second Sophistic forensic oratory, with the library's theatrical façade as a backdrop, could well be categorised as such).[43]

---

[39] *IG* II 2,017.   [40] *Flor.* 18. Cf. Mart. *Ep.* 12 preface.
[41] Dio Chrys. *Or.* 37.8; Plin. *Ep.* 1.4; Gell. 13.20.   [42] *IvE* 3,009.   [43] Burrell 2009: 85–8.

Other libraries were located alongside auditoria: the second-century medical writer and noted library user Galen names the library of the Templum Pacis in Rome as a pre-eminent centre of Roman intellectual life in the late second century AD, and implies that a set-piece medical disputation, in which he confronted his critics by producing huge armfuls of books, took place in 'one of the auditoria' of this Flavian complex.[44] The exact disposition of the southern end of the Templum Pacis is imperfectly understood, but it is tempting to reconstruct the suite of rooms there as library chamber(s) and lecture rooms of the sort Galen describes. This would imply a similar plan to the Hadrianic library at Athens, where it seems likely that the spaces flanking the central library room contained twin auditoria or lecture rooms as well as spaces suitable for meeting, reading, or discussion.[45]

We might note that this Roman-style library built by Hadrian at Athens looks rather like descriptions of the academy known as the Athenaeum which Hadrian built at Rome as a school for the liberal arts, augmenting the literary connections between the two cities.[46] The location and architectural form of this Athenaeum remain unknown,[47] but the functions attributed to it by various ancient authors suggest it would have included spaces like those which we have now encountered in various imperial public libraries. As well as a library room it contained an assembly hall used for literary declamations and readings,[48] as well as meetings of the senate[49] and judicial gatherings.[50] A series of impressive Hadrianic halls with marble-paved shallow steps for a seated audience have recently been discovered in the Metro C excavations in Rome, close to the libraries of Trajan's forum and with decorative details closely corresponding to those buildings. It has been suggested that these were part of Hadrian's Athenaeum, but in any case the close conjunction of libraries and lecture halls is instructive.[51]

Public library buildings in the provinces of the Empire, as well as imperial buildings at Rome and elsewhere, therefore seem to have incorporated or been associated with spaces in which large numbers of people could gather

---

[44] *Libr. Propr.* 2.21–2.
[45] Personal communication with site director Dimitris Sourias. Cf. Boatwright 2000: 153–7; Travlos 1971 s.v. 'Hadrian, Library of': 244–52; Spetsieri-Choremi 1995: 137–47.
[46] Aur. Vict. *Caes.* 14.2–3.
[47] The *LTUR* (Coarelli, s.v. Athenaeum) fairly convincingly locates it in the forum at the head of the Vicus Tuscus, behind the temple of Castor and Pollux, communicating with the Domus Tiberiana.
[48] SHA *Pert.* 11.3; *Alex. Sev.* 35.2; *Gordian* 3.4.   [49] Cass. Dio, 74.17.
[50] Symmachus, *Ep.* 9.89.2.
[51] Libraries in the Athenaeum: Sid. Apoll. *Ep.* 2.9.4. See also Claridge 2007: 76–80 which proposes, before the rest of this building with its seating steps came to light, that this hall was itself a library building. See now Coates–Stephens 2012: 326–8 with n. 6.

for events such as debates and recitations, popular forms of entertainment in the imperial period, increasing their potential 'usership' to non-specialist and even illiterate visitors. A sense emerges from these examples that library patrons seem to have tried, naturally enough, to display their foundations to as wide a range of their townsfolk as possible. They were expensive buildings, and the logic of civic philanthropy (and in Celsus' case, as in Trajan's, Roman funerary architecture) required them to catch the eye. While Roman public libraries were designed to hold large book collections and to make them available in intelligent ways to readers, that was not their only role: they also acted as landmarks, venues for public meetings, recitations and debates, or informal discussions and teaching groups, and as reminders of their patrons' generosity and family pride.

Given the value of the book collections and the measures that library architects took to protect and preserve them, the decision to expose the buildings and their contents to the public gaze came at a cost, as the Pantainos library's pointed prohibition of borrowing implies; in all the examples above, prominent display seems to have won out over discreet protection of the books. This means that it is not right to restrict the 'audience' or constituency for these acts of library euergetism solely to the literary communities of the recipient towns: the consistent choice of prominent, expensive locations and ebullient architecture suggests a wider appeal. These richly appointed library buildings, occupying prominent spots in the town, were in some sense addressed to the entire populations who enjoyed their architecture and decoration, walked past them, or waited in their shade.

15 | Flavian libraries in the city of Rome

PIER LUIGI TUCCI

My aim in this chapter is to examine a group of Flavian libraries and to construct an accurate picture of what they were like and how they functioned.[1] I have chosen the Flavian age because Rome's first public libraries, built from the end of the first century BC, have not been identified so far, the only exception being the library of Apollo on the Palatine hill. Domitian, the last emperor of the Flavian dynasty, was particularly concerned with these buildings: he restored the library in the Porticus of Octavia after the fire of AD 80, as well as the already mentioned library of Apollo (not necessarily as a consequence of the same fire). Nothing is preserved of the former, but we know for certain that the reconstruction of the library on the Palatine was a faithful copy of the original single hall, which Domitian even duplicated by adding *ex novo* a twin hall on its right side. The suggestion that Domitian demolished Rome's first public library, built by G. Asinius Pollio between 39 and 27 BC, must remain an hypothesis. But it is possible to demonstrate that the library of the *Templum Pacis*, the complex dedicated by Vespasian in AD 75, was built *ex novo* by Domitian himself: the destruction and construction of the two libraries may be closely related. In this case, too, the model of the new library of Peace was the original single hall of the library of Apollo. I shall first focus on the library of the *Templum Pacis* and explain why it should be identified with the hall towards the Via Sacra, corresponding to the basilica of SS. Cosma e Damiano, which is currently (and wrongly) regarded as a Severan addition.[2] Secondly, I shall highlight the architectural similarities between the libraries of Peace and Apollo. Then I shall reconsider the information on books and libraries provided by Galen (AD 129–216) in his treatise *On the avoidance of grief*. This work, which

---

[1] I presented an early version of this chapter at the 111th Annual Meeting of the Archaeological Institute of America, held at Anaheim in January 2010. I thank Greg Woolf, who attended my lecture, for his invitation to contribute to this volume and his comments. On Rome's libraries see Dix and Houston 2006, with previous bibliography; I thank G. W. Houston and M. Nicholls for having shared their thoughts on Roman libraries with me. I also thank M. L. Haack, my graduate students at Johns Hopkins University and the friars of SS. Cosma e Damiano. I owe a debt of gratitude to the late L. Cozza.

[2] The original hall of the library is very poorly preserved due to late antique, medieval, and Baroque restorations.

reveals previously unknown details on the fire of Rome of AD 192, is relevant because all the places mentioned by Galen, such as the *Templum Pacis*, the imperial palace, and the Domus Tiberiana, as well as the storerooms along the Via Sacra and the Clivus Palatinus, destroyed and/or damaged by the fire, were Flavian buildings. Though the content of the library of Peace is not mentioned, Galen's silence is telling. Just as this library was a copy of an Augustan building, it is likely that most of the works available there were copies as well – not comparable to the most precious collections of the imperial palace. These, I argue, might have been stored not only in the monumental library halls on the Palatine but also in otherwise ordinary warehouses together with archival records.

The Domitianic library in the *Templum Pacis*

The *Templum Pacis* consisted of a rectangular enclosure with three porticoes and a group of halls on its rear side. The actual Temple of Peace was located in the axial hall, but its name was also applied to the whole building.[3] Its plan was reconstructed only in the 1930s, although the ancient hall corresponding to the basilica of SS. Cosma e Damiano was not taken into consideration.[4] Despite the contribution of the excavations carried out in the last decade in the square and in the axial hall, a comparison between the plans by I. Gismondi (1941–6), G. Gatti (1959) and the archaeologists of the Soprintendenza Comunale (2007) shows that the hall of SS. Cosma e Damiano has "disappeared" from the Flavian complex (Fig. 15.1).[5] In fact Gismondi's and Gatti's drawings refer to the fourth century AD and show all the building phases in the same plan.[6] In the recent plans produced by the Soprintendenza Comunale the omission of the hall implies that it did

[3] Throughout my text I shall refer to the whole complex as *Templum Pacis* and to the axial hall as "Temple of Peace."
[4] See Colini 1937.
[5] Gismondi's plan: Lugli 1946 tav. 5 (adapted from Gismondi's original of 1941); Gatti's plan: Gatti 1960: 219; for the 2007 plan: Meneghini, Santangeli Valenzani 2007: 5 (which is not reliable especially for what concerns the halls of SS. Cosma e Damiano and of the Forma Urbis). The same plan and reconstruction are published in Meneghini 2009: 39–40 (plates I and II): surprisingly the actual walls, rated as a few fragments of masonry ("pochi lacerti murari") and the evidence provided by recent scholarship are not taken into consideration. For the recent excavations, see Coarelli 2009a.
[6] Their drawings of the original phase do not include the hall towards the Via Sacra. See Colini 1937 plate IV and the version by S. E. Gibson in Ward-Perkins 1981: 66 fig. 30. The survey published in Castagnoli, Cozza 1956–8: 119–42 did not make any distinctions for what concerns the dating of the squared-stone masonry of the hall towards the Via Sacra, considered one and the same with the hall of the monastery.

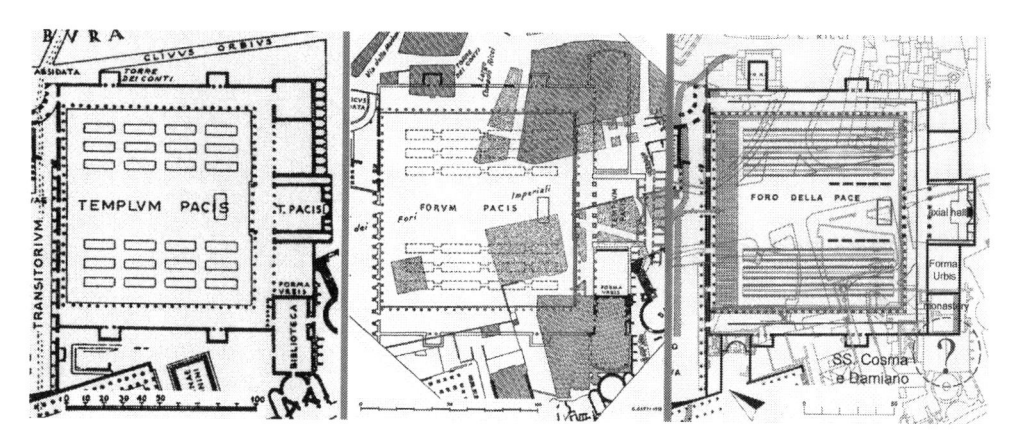

Figure 15.1 The plan of the *Templum Pacis* according to the investigations of
I. Gismondi (in 1941–6), G. Gatti (in 1959) and Bianchi-Meneghini (in 2007)

not exist before the Trajanic age – thus leading astray those who are not familiar with topographical and architectural matters.

Over the last decade I have carefully studied the remains incorporated into the monastery and basilica of SS. Cosma e Damiano and I can demonstrate that the hall towards the Via Sacra was built in the Flavian age, though not necessarily under Vespasian.[7] The Flavian and the Severan brickworks are easy to distinguish. The Flavian module (a conventional unit of five courses of bricks and five joints of mortar) is higher than the Severan, and the Flavian joints are systematically raked (Fig.15.2). As for the squared-stone masonry, in the rear wall of the *Templum Pacis* one can see both the original structure, built with blocks of Tufo Lionato, and the Severan restoration made with blocks of *Lapis Albanus* (the so-called peperino) (Fig. 15.2).

Also the lifting devices were different: the Flavian blocks were lifted by means of forceps, whereas the Severan ones were lifted through lewis irons. The joints of the latter were also painted with a red coat, which makes it possible to date the squared-stone masonry, and even to distinguish the blocks of travertine used in both the Flavian and the Severan phases.[8] The distinctive building techniques of each period reveal the extent of the Severan restoration even when the blocks do not exist anymore, as in the case of the rear wall of the hall of the Marble Plan, whose imprint on the buttress

---

[7] These technical details will be discussed at length in my forthcoming book on *The* Templum Pacis *and the Influence of Classical Art and Architecture in Imperial and Late-Antique Rome*. A preliminary mention of this issue is in Tucci 2009b: 164.
[8] See Tucci 2011.

Figure 15.2 Flavian and Severan brickwork (inside the monastery) and squared-stone masonry of the rear wall of the *Templum Pacis* (towards the Basilica of Maxentius). On the right, imprint of the Flavian (two lowermost courses) and Severan blocks (I-XXI and cornice) of the rear wall of the *Templum Pacis* on the buttress of the Basilica of Maxentius

of the Basilica of Maxentius shows that the original Flavian structure, after the fire of AD 192, was preserved for a height of circa 2 m (Fig. 15.2, right). Each of the four surviving halls at the rear of the *Templum Pacis*, from the axis of the Vespasianic complex up to the Via Sacra, has been tentatively identified with the library of Peace. Now it is finally possible to date them, discuss their possible function, and identify the library. My conclusion is that the hall towards the Via Sacra is as Flavian as the Colosseum – though added as an afterthought – and was the actual library.

The partial excavation of the axial hall has brought to light its Severan marble floor, a podium, and a tall base on which certainly stood the goddess Peace. The presence of a statue would not be unusual in a library (see below), but the four basins on each side of the podium are unheard of in a library hall and suggest a religious ritual.[9] The side wall (with no niches

---

[9] Before the excavation it had been claimed that in the libraries built after the Augustan age there would be an association of religious and cultural functions – hence the axial apse – and an example would have been precisely the axial hall of the *Templum Pacis*: see Gros 2001a: 407.

even in the original Flavian phase) was characterized by small *lesenae* whose capitals, decorated with *bucrania*, laurel garlands, ox-skulls, and sacrificial tools, confirm the religious function of the hall. The identification with the library of Peace was suggested by the similar plans of the *Templum Pacis* and of the (much smaller) "Library of Hadrian" in Athens, the axial hall of which, however, had sixty-six niches on three levels.[10] Another difference of substance of the Athenian from the parent building in Rome is that "the principal room, being a library, not a temple, did not call for the gabled pronaos that breaks the line of the inner portico of the Templum Pacis."[11] After all it is unlikely that the library of Peace had such a prominent location inside the *Templum Pacis*, moreover in a hall that was almost completely open towards the SE portico, like the nearby hall of the Forma Urbis. The function of the latter hall depends very much on the function of the Marble Plan: decorative, administrative, or propagandistic? It has been often suggested that an archive was housed there, but the link between the Praefectura Urbi and the cadastral office (not explicitly located here) is attested only from the fourth century AD.[12] Recently a detailed reconstruction has been presented, showing the interior of the hall with benches and tables for consultation, wooden cupboards near the walls, and the boundaries between the fourteen Augustan regions, as well as the relevant numbers, marked on the Marble Plan. This drawing is nice but mistaken – many architectural details are missing or misunderstood. Considering also the absence of niches, it is unlikely that the library of Peace was inside this hall.[13]

---

[10] Cf. Makowiecka 1978: 49; Coarelli 1991: 79–81. Libraries and archives are attested in and/or next Roman temples, but the details of their arrangement are unknown. The hall of the Temple of Peace, however, seems unfit for this purpose.

[11] Ward-Perkins 1981: 269. Indeed in the *Templum Pacis* the columns before the axial hall were much higher than those of the porticoes. The two corner halls in the rear side of the Athenian building had sloping seats (supported by barrel vaults) which could be approached by means of two staircases located along the side walls. These features are generally overlooked, since the "canonical" plan of the library of Hadrian does not show the substructures but just the sloping seats. In the corner hall of the *Templum Pacis* the windows recorded by Peruzzi, the lack of walls supporting sloping vaults and seats, as well as the shallow apse, make any comparisons with the Athenian building unfruitful: the hall towards the Via Sacra was not an auditorium, but the actual library of Peace.

[12] See Coarelli 1991: 79–81; Gros 2001b: 113; cf. Tucci 2007: 469–80.

[13] For the drawing of the hall, see Meneghini, Corsaro and Pinna Caboni 2009. Just to give an example of its inaccuracy, the existence of the windows in the rear wall is dismissed by the imprints of the blocks on the buttress of the Basilica of Maxentius (see my Fig. 15.2). The folders in which the plates are kept look quite anachronistically similar to the folders of the Catasto Pio-Gregoriano in the State Archive of Rome. Only Dudley 1967: 131–2 suggested that at the time of Vespasian the hall of the Forma Urbis housed a library.

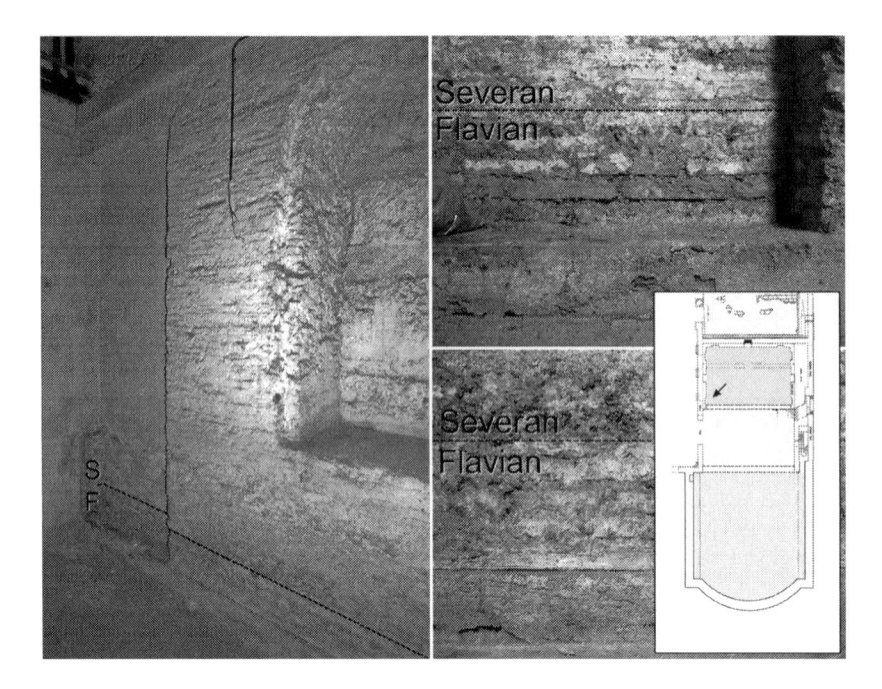

Figure 15.3 The wall with niches – the one on the left is original – incorporated into the monastery of SS. Cosma e Damiano

The next hall, incorporated into the monastery of SS. Cosma e Damiano (just behind the wall of the Forma Urbis), has been sometimes identified with the library of Peace because of the presence of nine niches in a reinforcement of the original walls, and due to a misinterpretation of a passage by Galen.[14]

However six niches are *circa* 20 cm deep, not enough for bookrolls, and only three (those in the middle of each side, showing traces of a marble veneer) are 60 cm deep, the customary dimension of library niches. The brickwork looks completely Severan and has suggested a radically new intervention after the fire of AD 192.[15] Only recently, however, I observed that the lowermost courses consist of a Flavian brickwork (Fig. 15.3), which means that the niches were merely rebuilt under Septimius Severus. Nevertheless the Flavian wall with niches was an afterthought, in that it modified the layout of the hall (which had no niches at all). The main

---

[14] Castagnoli, Cozza 1956–8. Cf. Tucci 2008 as updated in this present chapter. The fragment of a monumental inscription and a few remains of architectural sculpture, found in this hall during my survey and still unpublished, will be presented in my forthcoming book on the *Templum Pacis*.

[15] See Gatti 1960: 214–15 n.19.

entrance, originally on the axis of the hall, was walled up and shifted towards the corner of the porticoes, whereas the opposite entrance towards the Clivus ad Carinas was modified. The reinforcement was built against the original surfaces only in the NE half of the hall, towards the wall of the Marble Plan, and – more importantly – directly on the original marble floor, as attested by a very precious yet unpublished photograph taken in the 1940s. Apparently the modification of the rectangular hall in the S corner of the Vespasianic complex – basically divided into two different halves – was made in connection with the addition of a new apsed hall towards the Via Sacra, which turned the axis of the original hall 90 degrees (cf. Fig. 15.3). A new entrance was opened on the same axis as the SW portico of the *Templum Pacis* and, through the insertion of two transversal walls (disappeared after the late-antique restorations, but the foundation of one of them is still visible), an intermediate space was created which extended the SW portico and gave access to the new apsed hall. As for the building techniques, two sixteenth-century drawings by Baldassarre Peruzzi (Uffizi, Arch. 382–3) show very clearly that the materials used in the construction of the original surviving portion of the rear wall of the *Templum Pacis* were Tufo Lionato and travertine as in the Colosseum (the *Templum Pacis* and the Flavian amphitheater were built at the same time) and that the next stretch towards the Via Sacra, corresponding to the SE side of the new hall and destroyed in the seventeenth century under pope Urban VIII, was also Flavian, with a Severan restoration above made with blocks of Lapis Albanus and probably due to the fire of the wooden beams of the roof (Fig.15.4). Peruzzi could not see the inferior part of this wall, already buried, but he recorded a row of three windows.

The opposite corner of the hall, connected to the rear wall of the SW portico, is still preserved, with traces of a niche, originally measuring 90 by 315 cm, surmounted by a window which was at the same level as those seen by Peruzzi on the opposite side of the hall. The thickness of the side walls was *circa* 1.5 m and the niches might have been 60 cm deep. Further elements, such as the floor level, the staircase, and a curvilinear foundation help to reconstruct the interior of the hall, characterized by two architectural orders on both sides, framing two rows of possibly forty niches.[16] The hall (apse excluded) measured 19.15 by 18.35 m, or 15.75 by 18.35 m considering that its width was reduced by the side columns (not visible in my

---

[16] The large Flavian halls were all provided with shallow apses (see the *triclinium* of the *Domus Flavia* on the Palatine or, even better, the nearby axial hall). Also the libraries next to the Temple of Apollo on the Palatine had large shallow apses, either in the original Augustan phase or in the Domitianic reconstruction.

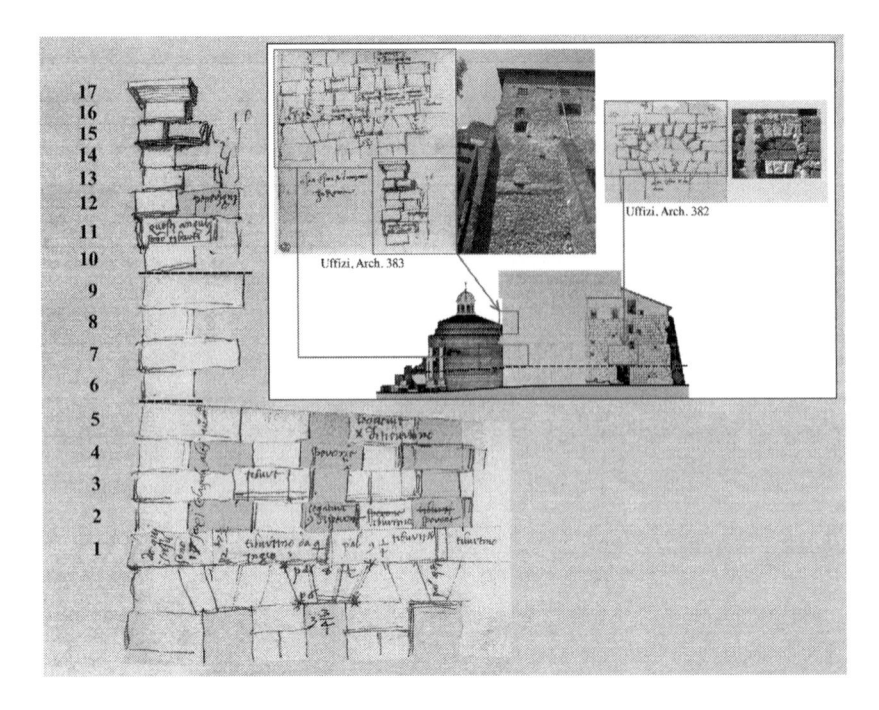

Figure 15.4 The corner of the hall towards the Via Sacra in a drawing by B. Peruzzi (Uffizi, Arch. 383, adapted from Bartoli, A. [1914–22] vol. II. fig. 216). In the box, the rear wall of the *Templum Pacis* along the Clivus ad Carinas (elevation adapted from B. M. Apollonj Ghetti, "Nuove considerazioni sulla basilica romana dei SS. Cosma e Damiano," *Rivista di Archeologia Cristiana* 50 (1974) fig. 28; B. Peruzzi's drawings (Uffizi, Arch. 382–3) from Bartoli, A. [1914–22] vol. II, figs 215–16; photos author)

Figs. 15.3 and 15.5). In Roman libraries the height of the niches ranged from 2.60 to 3.80 m, with an average of 3.20 m.[17] At the *Templum Pacis* the lower niches were 3.15 m high, slightly less than in Trajan's libraries (3.23 m). Unfortunately it is not possible to ascertain the presence of a stepped podium along the side walls as well as the existence of a base for a statue in the apse.

I have already stressed that this hall was very likely an afterthought. It is not clear what the function of the original hall may have been, since it had no niches and, in contrast to the axial hall and the hall of the Marble Plan, it was the only one to open off the SE portico by means of a great entrance. The new "extension" is undoubtedly Flavian, and might even be credited to

[17] See Callmer 1944: 188. The capacity of the W library of Trajan has been estimated by Packer as 10,412 rolls (one row of rolls on a single shelf) – see Packer 1997: 453–4 – although it has been argued that there were fewer niches, so the total would be inferior: see Meneghini 2002a. At the *Templum Pacis*, with niches 0.90 m wide and 3.15 m high, the capacity would have been between 7,200 rolls (one row of rolls per shelf) and 21,600 rolls (three rows).

Vespasian, but I believe that a library was not part of his original project and that a Domitianic dating seems more likely.[18] In the former case, the change would have taken place during the construction of the complex in AD 71–5, or in the last years of Vespasian's principate (between AD 75–9). Otherwise the library would have been completed or begun by Domitian at the same time as the construction of the imperial palace and of the new library of Apollo on the Palatine, or during his preliminary work in the site eventually occupied by the Forum of Trajan (see below). The possibility should also be considered that Domitian made other modifications at the *Templum Pacis*, such as the new front wall towards the Argiletum.[19] I also found evidence that the lower part of the wall supporting the Marble Plan already existed in the Flavian age but was another afterthought. Statius (*Silvae* 4.3.16–17) claims that Domitian added a statue of Peace in the *Templum Pacis* – "he who... puts Peace back in her own home" ("*qui... Pacem propria domo reponit*"). His *ecloga tertia* celebrates the completion of the Via Domitiana in AD 95 and the passage quoted above refers to Domitian's building activity, so the mention of Peace should not be just symbolic. Considering that the *Templum Pacis* was dedicated by Vespasian in AD 75, the lack of a cult statue would be at least suspect. Statius' *reponit* might imply a second dedication after more consistent alterations.[20] Finally, the existence of a library (and of a marble plan) in the *Templum Pacis* is not attested by Vespasianic sources referring to the dedication of the complex, but only later by Aulus Gellius (see below); of course the absence of sources on a possible Domitianic intervention would be easily explained by the *damnatio memoriae* of the last Flavian emperor.

---

[18] Not Trajanic or later because of the raked joints of mortar of the brickwork and other technical details.

[19] Blocks of *Lapis Albanus*, without red layer, are used in the Domitianic Forum of Nerva (inaugurated in AD 97), whereas in the hall towards the Via Sacra they were confined to the top of the walls and belonged to the Severan restoration. Several sectors of the *Templum Pacis* were restored with blocks of *Lapis Albanus*, which excludes their belonging to a Domitianic intervention (indeed they are the actual Severan restorations). Apparently the addition of the library hall was built with the same materials as in the original phase of the *Templum Pacis*, either for the sake of homogeneity (the exterior wall would have been visible) or because the builders had these materials at hand. The use of Tufo Lionato in the second (Domitianic) phase of the *Templum Pacis* might even suggest a dating to the early 80s, considering that the construction of the Forum of Nerva had already began around AD 85–6 (Mart. 1.2.7–8).

[20] It has already been noticed that Statius "seems to ascribe" the completion of the *Templum Pacis* to Domitian, but his intervention was just linked to the NW wall towards the Forum Transitorium (from AD 86): Coleman 1988: 12–3 and 108. I would add that Suetonius (*Otho* 7.1) and Tacitus (*Hist.* 1.78) use the verb *reponere* for re-erect, "to set up again," suggesting that the statue of Peace had been removed and eventually put back on public display – the goddess had to vacate her temple while it was being renovated.

The library of Apollo as a model for the library of Peace

The hall added to the *Templum Pacis* was very similar to the Augustan library of Apollo on the Palatine hill, built by Octavian (Augustus) in 36–28 BC (Suet. *Aug.* 29.3) and eventually reconstructed by Domitian (Fig. 15.5). The Augustan building was referred to both in the singular and the plural by ancient authors, but the literary evidence is not sufficient to argue that its original phase had separate Latin and Greek halls and still less that such bicameralism was standard practice. A recent survey has in any case made it clear that this Augustan library was a single apsed hall, located along the short SE side of the rectangular portico of the Danaids and at the same level as the temple of Apollo. Traces of contemporary tufa walls exclude the presence of a second adjacent library room in the Augustan phase (which could not exist on the opposite side of the rectangular portico, limited by the *Scalae Caci*). Under Domitian the Augustan library was rebuilt and a second identical hall was added, intruding into the symmetrical scheme of the original portico: these twin rooms appear on the lost fragment 20b of the Marble Plan (cf. Fig.15.5), and are still visible today.[21]

The original Augustan library hall was probably the model for the library of Peace. The two Domitianic halls on the Palatine were each 19.5 m deep (apse excluded) and 17.5 m wide, whereas the new hall at the *Templum Pacis* was 18.35 m deep but 19.15 m wide – longer than it was wide – though, as I said, its width was reduced to 15.75 m if we take into account the colonnades on either side.[22] They were not exactly identical, but shared the same plan and possibly the same architecture, with niches and side colonnades. In the Domitianic library of Apollo the side walls were characterized by seven niches, each 3.80 m high (3.15 at the *Templum Pacis*), 1.80 m wide (only

---

[21] Iacopi, Tedone 2005/2006: 351–78. It was previously believed that the rectangular portico of the Danaids was a Flavian intervention and that the Augustan library was *circa* 9 m beneath the Domitianic portico and library, on the level of the lower terrace of the House of Augustus. I would stress that the three columns visible on fragment 20b of the Marble Plan before the second library hall, and the corner of the portico, suggest a widening of the Augustan enclosure, in order to have the twin libraries on the new transversal axis. Domitian may have widened the portico of the Danaids and turned it into the squarish *Area Apollinis*, mentioned after the Flavian age (Forma Urbis, Ludi Saeculares of AD 203 – *CIL* VI 32327, 23 – and Solinus 1.37). According to Carandini, Bruno 2008, the apsed hall next to the Temple of Apollo was the Curia, whereas two libraries would have been on both sides of it (see their fig. 25). In the second part of the book, however, Bruno on pp. 213–19 implies that the Augustan library was one and the same with the apsed hall (indeed the twin halls on its side are not attested by archaeological evidence).

[22] It is also worth recalling that the plan of the library of Peace had to be adapted to the pre-existing walls of the *Templum Pacis*.

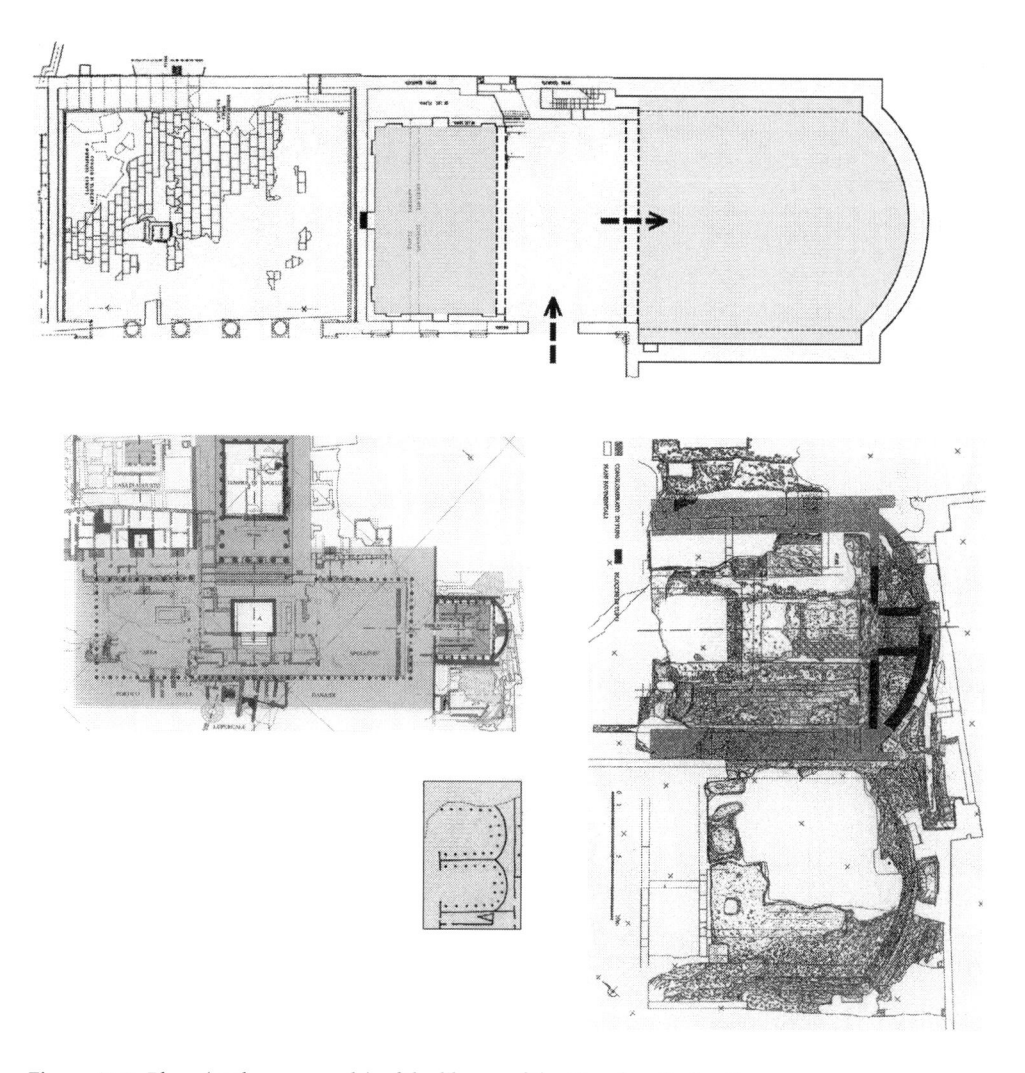

Figure 15.5 Plans (at the same scale) of the library of the *Templum Pacis* – the arrows indicate the entrances (above, right) and the Flavian library of Apollo (below). Drawing, author; Apollo's library from Iacopi (2007) 13 and Iacopi, Tedone (2005/2006) tav. 2; the lost fragment 20b of the Marble Plan from Carettoni, Colini, Cozza, Gatti (1960) *La pianta marmorea di Roma antica*. Rome, plate XXII

0.90 at the *Templum Pacis*) and 60 cm deep.[23] The niches were twenty-eight in total (instead of the forty smaller niches at the *Templum Pacis*) and at the centre of the apse was a larger niche framed by an aedicula. Nothing else is preserved, and so the remains of the library of Peace might be the only indirect testimony of the elevation of the Augustan/Domitianic library on

[23] Callmer 1944: 157 (for the library of Apollo).

the Palatine. Not by chance they both had two free sides – whereas the halls in the imperial forums were not opened towards the exterior – and, as a rule, were not independent buildings. Interestingly, both the halls of Apollo and of Peace were on the right side of a temple.

In the *Templum Pacis* there was no twin hall next to the library and it is uncertain whether there was a symmetrical hall on the opposite corner. The library was not built after a fire, and the reason for its addition might be that Domitian had to demolish the library of Pollio, Rome's first public library, which stood behind the Forum of Caesar on the ridge between the Capitoline and the Quirinal. (This library might have been damaged by the fire of AD 80, since the Forum of Caesar was heavily restored in the Domitianic and Trajanic periods.) The "Terrazza Domizianea" and the massive retaining walls on the NE slope of the Arx attest that it was Domitian who began to clear the site that was eventually occupied by the Forum of Trajan.[24] I suggest that Pollio's library – and also his collection of Greek statuary if displayed in the *Atrium Libertatis* (Pliny, *HN* 36.4.23–4, 25, 33–4) and the ancient cadastral documents kept in the same building – was "moved" to the *Templum Pacis*, on the opposite side of the great porticoed squares of the imperial forums, slightly after AD 80.[25] Perhaps it is just a coincidence, but we only have two explicit mentions of the contents of the library of Peace, and one refers to the personal notebooks of Aelius Stilo on axioms (Gell. 16.8.1–4).[26] Lucius Aelius Stilo Praeconinus (154–74 BC), the earliest

---

[24] Tortorici 1993; Amici 1991: 65–74.

[25] The location of the *Atrium Libertatis* on the so-called Tabularium, suggested by N. Purcell in 1993, has not won wide acceptance: see Coarelli 1993a: 124–5 and 140–1. It is worth noting that at least part of the archive of the censors associated with the *Atrium* might have been moved to the NE exedra of the Basilica Ulpia, as attested by the Forma Urbis – which makes the survival of Pollio's books likely as well. As for the plans, Granius Licinianus (28.35) tells that in 172 BC the task of recovering land parcels from public land in Campania led to the engraving of a *forma* on bronze which was placed in the *Atrium Libertatis* (*formamque agrorum in aes incisam ad Libertatis fixam reliquit*). The censors' *tabulae publicae* included lists of public lands and, very likely, also maps and plans (cf. *CIL* VI 919), eventually engraved on marble slabs: these documents may have been moved to and stored in the *Templum Pacis*, which would explain the recovery of fragments of marble plans different from the Forma Urbis in its area (they all survived simply because marble is not as perishable as papyrus, and so their presence should not be overestimated). This does not imply the existence of an active "cadastral office" but simply of a sort of deposit/archive, not differently from the archives of the imperial procurators mentioned by Galen in *On the avoidance of grief*, § 8: the discovery (in 1997) of the fragment of a marble plan beneath the floor of the Forum of Nerva suggests that at least some of these documents were "useless."

[26] Wishing to know the meaning of what the logicians called "an axiom," which Varro called either "propositions" or "preliminary statements," Aulus Gellius went personally to the library of the Temple of Peace and read a commentary on that subject written by Aelius Stilo: "and

Roman philologist, was the teacher of Varro (as stressed by Gellius himself in the passage mentioned above), and Varro had received a portrait in Pollio's library during his own lifetime (Pliny, *HN* 7.115). Though Varro's personal library was almost completely plundered after 43 BC (Gell., 3.10.17), it is not unlikely that the notes of his teacher Aelius Stilo might have reached the library of Peace via Varro himself, then Pollio and finally Domitian (who may have also considered that Varro was born in Reate, near the birthplace of his father Vespasian). At the end of the passage cited (Gell. 16.8.1–4), Gellius, being dissatisfied with Aelius Stilo's notes, returns to his Greek books. It is not clear whether he is still referring to the library of Peace, but if this is the case, it is worth noting that immediately thereafter (Gell. 16.8.6) he quotes Varro's *De Lingua Latina*.[27] These hints might explain why Domitian gave Rome another public library. It is also possible that the library of Peace was more similar to Pollio's than to the library of the temple of Apollo. Be this as it may, the architecture of the Augustan age influenced the Flavian library in the *Templum Pacis*; this is not surprising, because in the design of the *Templum Pacis* there are many references to the Forum of Augustus, such as the architectural orders of both porticoes and temple.[28]

At this point it is possible to draw together some general conclusions. As far as we know the first public libraries were installed in single halls, as clearly shown by the Augustan library of Apollo. Between the creation of that library and the foundation of the library of Peace only the library of the Templum Divi Augusti was built. This was constructed by Tiberius some time between AD 14–37, but it has not so far been identified. It lay between the Palatine and the Capitoline hills, and perhaps opened off a portico which

---

finding it *in the library of Peace*, I read it. But I found in it nothing that was written to instruct or to make the matter clear, but Aelius seems to have made that book rather as suggestions for his own use than the purpose of teaching others. I therefore of necessity returned to my Greek books" (Gell. 16.8.1–4). On another occasion, Gellius reports that a friend, in order to demonstrate to "a very audacious critic of language" that one who says *pluria* and *compluria* speaks good Latin, invited this critic to check a volume deposited in the *Templum Pacis* and containing numerous letters of Sinnius Capito, a grammarian of the Augustan age (Gell. 5.21.9–13).

[27] Papini 2005: 134 implies that as Gellius returned to his Greek books he began to quote a number of passages going back to Chrysippus, on the basis (Papini's n. 52) of Holford-Strevens 2003: 274 (see also 230) who, however, found these references in other books of the *Attic Nights*. It is likely that Chrysippus' works were available in the library of Peace, but after the mention of Aelius Stilo there is just a second-hand quotation of Chrysippus (cf. Diog. Laert. 8.65) which, in fact, might even imply the absence of Chrysippus' works. On Papini's suggestion, see Meneghini 2009: 89 and 91; 2010: 36.

[28] Tucci 2009b. Cf. Isager 1976.

surrounded the temple of the Divus Augustus. It must have been another large, tall, and single hall, due to the presence of a single colossal statue of Apollo which was fifty Roman feet (*circa* 15 m) in height, the same height as the columns of the temple of Castor and Pollux. The statue is mentioned by Pliny and Suetonius.[29] Next Domitian added the single hall in the *Templum Pacis*, and only at this point do we meet with double halls, starting precisely with the Domitianic restoration of the library of Apollo and, later, with Trajan's libraries. So it is in the Flavian age that the transition from single to double halls (to bicameral libraries) first takes place. Even so the later library of Celsus at Ephesos and the library of Hadrian in Athens were once again constructed with single halls. The library of the *Templum Pacis* towards the Via Sacra was a single hall and the possibility that a matching hall existed on the opposite side of the SE portico, although it cannot be excluded, is not necessary for the sake of symmetry (see the Curia Senatus in the Forum of Caesar and the library of Apollo itself); in addition, the presumed twin libraries in the *Templum Pacis* would have been *circa* 100 metres apart. The library of Apollo was also a *templum* and a *curia*, and so an inaugurated space. The *Templum Pacis*, as the name itself implies, must have occupied another inaugurated site (Galen uses the word *temenos*) and probably the same was true of the new Domitianic extension. It is worth remembering that Pliny (*HN* 36.28–9) mentions a *Curia Octaviae* in the Porticus of Octavia and it is likely that when the senate met there, at least on one occasion (Dio Cass. 55.8.1), it convened in the library. I do not mean that this was a general rule, but at least two Domitianic libraries also shared this peculiar status. All these library halls were also associated with large open areas suited for the display of art collections: this was the case of Pollio's library (next to the Atrium Libertatis), of the library of Apollo, which opened off the portico of the Danaids, of the library of Octavia, another Augustan building restored by Domitian which was surrounded by an impressive collection of Greek masterpieces, and of the library of Peace (see for instance Plin. *HN* 34.19.84).

As for the interiors, in the age of Tiberius the library of Apollo contained the bronze portraits of Roman orators; Germanicus and his father Drusus also received clipeate portraits, to be placed on the architrave above the columns of a fastigium which housed an image of Apollo/Augustus (*Tabula Hebana*, line X; Tac. *Ann.* 2.37 and 2.83). The first use of authors' portraits as decoration for libraries in Rome was attributed by Pliny (*HN* 35.2.9–10)

---

[29] See Torelli 1993. Nothing is known about the founding of the library in the Domus Tiberiana.

to Asinius Pollio, the founder of the public library mentioned above.[30] Just to give a few other examples, the writings (*scripta*) and the busts (*imagines*) of three Hellenistic poets were placed by Tiberius "in the public libraries among those of the eminent writers of old" (Suet. *Tib.* 70), while Caligula decided to remove the writings and the busts (*scripta et imagines*) of Virgil and Livy from all the libraries (Suet. *Cal.* 34).[31] Did the libraries of Apollo and of the *Templum Pacis* share the same ornaments? Moreover, both the Temple of Apollo and the "Apollinis bibliotheca" (Fronto, *Ad M. Caes.* 4.5.2) had statues of Apollo, and so both the actual Temple of Peace and the "Pacis bibliotheca" (Gell. 16.8.1–4) might have been decorated with statues of Peace (as perhaps is implied by Statius). But since in the two "Augustan" libraries there were statues of Apollo, Augustus' favourite god, we might also imagine that the new hall next to the original library on the Palatine might have housed a statue of Minerva, Domitian's favourite goddess, and we might imagine the same situation in the new library of the *Templum Pacis*.

Storerooms, library halls, and books around the Palatine hill

In AD 192, during the reign of Commodus, a great fire destroyed the *Templum Pacis* and reached the Palatine hill: the halls of the Flavian building were all severely damaged, as is proved by the Severan restorations. The blaze is described by Dio Cassius (73.24.1–3) and Herodian (1.14.2), but Galen mentions it in many of his works and most of all in the recently re-discovered treatise *On the avoidance of grief*.[32] In the present paper I can add a long passage, so far overlooked, which appears at the end of the eleventh book of Galen's *Anatomical procedures* (11.12) preserved only in an Arabic transcription but published and translated into English in 1962:

---

[30] It is worth noting that Pliny died before the addition of the library in the *Templum Pacis*. A clipeus made of stucco (d = 85 cm) with the portrait of Apollonius of Tyana, whose name was painted red on the circular cornice, was found in a room near S. Martino ai Monti: *BullCom* 12 1884: 48–9 tav. V: it might have belonged to a private library, showing that the use of clipeate portraits was widespread also during the second century AD.

[31] See also the Horatian scholia *ad Serm.* 1.4.21.

[32] Tucci 2008: 133–4 on Galen's accounts on the fire; Jones 2009; Tucci 2009a, with previous bibliography. See also Nicholls 2010a; Nicholls 2010b; Kotzia and Sotiroudis 2010: 63–150; Roselli 2010; Nicholls 2011. I have not quoted a number of just published and forthcoming papers because they are not yet available. Boudon-Millot and Jouanna: 2010 xxii–xxiv and 41–2 report that V. Nutton, in his forthcoming edition, adds two short references to the fire of AD 192 – one of which already published in Nutton 1979: 49–50 – from the German translation of the Arabic transcription of Galen's *In Hippocratis VI Librum Epidemiarum Commentaria*; apparently they are unaware of the passage from *Anatomical procedures*, quoted here.

in addition to my previous burden another great burden has been laid upon me. For after I had written out the books of the works "On Anatomical Dissections", as I was very nearly at the end of them, it so happened that there broke out that great fire in which the Temple of Peace was burnt down together with many warehouses and storehouses in the Via Maxima [Sacra], in which were stored those books of mine on Anatomical Dissections, together with all my other books. None of my works survived, except what I had already handed over to be transcribed. At that time I had already published eleven books of the present work also; but as for the books which will follow these [i.e. Books XII–XV], and which were then burnt, I am returning to compose them for the second time. There were also burnt many other books on anatomy which I had not revised sufficiently to allow me to publish them. For I used to write them and note them down bit by bit in disconnected passages every time I was dissecting an animal.[33]

This information adds significantly to what Galen says in his other passages known so far, where he mentions the copies of his own works and lost books he had to rewrite. It also questions the recent suggestion that Galen would have found it useful to keep rolls and writing equipment in the storerooms at the Via Sacra, close to the libraries where he found his source material, "to avoid the need to carry them daily to and from his house and to enable him to have complete and ready access both to his own books and to the libraries during the course of his researches."[34] In fact we now know that the burnt storehouse contained also the notes on Galen's dissections, which had nothing to do with libraries and no doubt were not taken in that area. Indeed he used to practise long hours in private, and certainly not in the nearby libraries or auditoria (his presumed dissection at the *Templum Pacis* was a rather special event: see below) and not even in his storeroom, I presume. In other words, it is unlikely that Galen deposited his books in the storerooms of the Via Sacra just because of the proximity of the libraries. Galen seems to mention his lost works in relation to whatever topic he is discussing at the time – hence the new mention of the last four books burnt in the fire of AD 192 in *Anatomical procedures*, similar to that of the treatise *On prognosis* (in his *In Hippocratis VI Librum Epidemiarum Commentaria*) or of the first two books of *On composition of drugs according to kind* lost on the same occasion. The focus on books and libraries in *On the avoidance of grief* just covers part of Galen's interests and no general conclusions should be drawn from it.

---

[33] Lyons and Towers 1962: 107–8. Galen's observation is important also because it attests his use of professional copyists.
[34] Nicholls 2011.

Anyway, in this latter treatise Galen tells explicitly that not only the warehouses along the Via Sacra, but also the collections of the imperial palace were destroyed:

the fire spread not only over the *apothēkai* located along the Via Sacra, and (but also?), before them, over those located next to (in?) the *Templum Pacis*, and after them, over those located in the vicinity of (inside?) the *Palatium* and the *domus* called *Tiberiana* where, here also [in the Domus Tiberiana], there was a library, filled with several books of different kinds (ch. 18).

Galen goes on to mention a group of rolls (copies?) which

at present are completely useless and cannot be unrolled since the sheets have pasted together because of moisture: the area indeed is marshy and very deeply enclosed and is stifling in summer (ch. 19).

The description in chapter 18 may be interpreted in different ways, depending on the meaning of *apothēkai* and *bibliothēkai*. The general sense also changes if the former were *next to* or *inside* the buildings to which they are associated, and even the translation of *Palatium* is not decisive, since it might indicate either the imperial palace or the whole Palatine hill (although in chapter 18 the Palatium is mentioned together with the Domus Tiberiana). Each interpretation, of course, has consequences for what concerns the identification of the libraries and the location of their collections. In either case, however, it is possible to discover further information not only about the Flavian library of the *Templum Pacis* but also on the general organization of the libraries in the area.

In chapter 8 Galen specifies that the *apothēkai* of the Via Sacra, watched over by a military guard because the archives of four imperial procurators were kept there, consisted of many individual storerooms (*oikēmata*) with wooden doors. These storerooms were rented and Galen used to keep there books and other objects. Of course there is little in common between such warehouses and the library halls, and the *apothēkai* or *oikēmata* of the Via Sacra cannot be assimilated to a library just on the basis of the presence of archival records and private books. There was no "library of the Via Sacra," but simply a group of storerooms which also contained books. In the words of G. W. Houston, "an *apothēkē* is not a *bibliothēkē*."[35] Thus Galen's *apothēkai* (without further specifications as for their content) would be not only the warehouses/*horrea* located along the Via Sacra, but also those *near* the *Templum Pacis* (not *inside* it) and along the Clivus Palatinus, between the

---

[35] Houston 2003: 45–51.

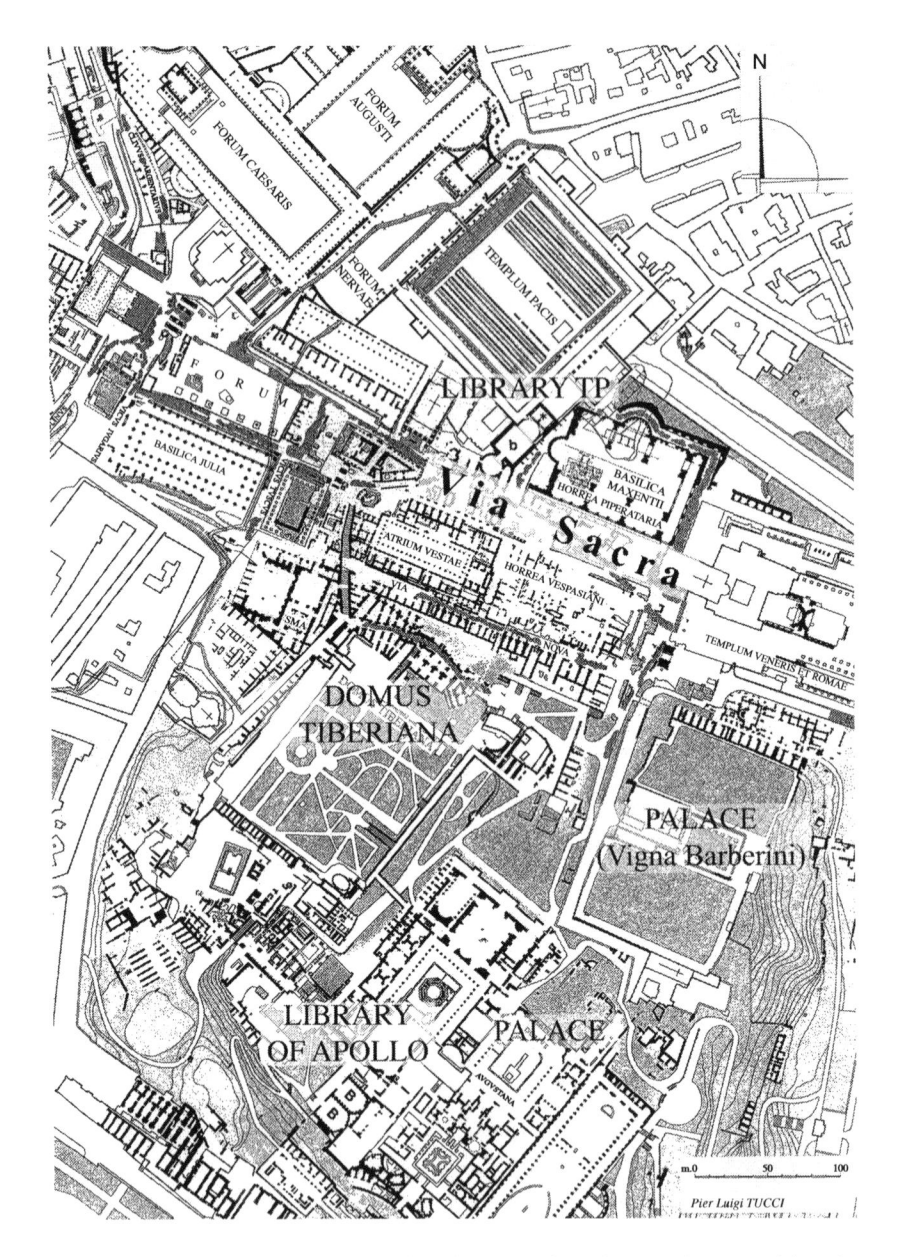

Figure 15.6 The area involved in the fire of AD 192, from the *Templum Pacis* (above) to the Palatine hill (below)

Palatium and the Domus Tiberiana. Indeed there were hundreds of storerooms in the Palatine substructions that actually belonged to the imperial palace, although the existence of a NE wing of the palace in the area of the Vigna Barberini is generally overlooked (Fig. 15.6).

Flavian libraries in the city of Rome 295

In his digression on the destruction of his books and of those of the Palatium, Galen (like Dio Cassius) describes the path of the fire with a focus on the storerooms in the area. After his mention of the destruction of the deposits at or by the Domus Tiberiana, Galen states that there was also a *bibliothēkē* (singular) in the Domus Tiberiana itself. He does not say that there was a *bibliothēkē* in the *apothēkai* (which were destroyed by the fire), but that there was one actually inside the Domus. Thus the *apothēkai* may have been storerooms which had nothing to do with the library hall of the Domus Tiberiana, otherwise Galen would have said that the *bibliothēkē* of the Domus was inside those *apothēkai* (plural). I shall argue below that it is likely that the books were kept in the Domus Tiberiana library hall as well as in other storerooms. Apparently by *bibliothēkē* Galen did not mean a physical space – the actual library – but more likely a collection of books.[36] This would confirm my first guess and indicate that 1) the library hall of the Domus Tiberiana was not necessarily involved in the fire; 2) the *apothēkai* were just storerooms; and 3) the *apothēkai* next to the palace would also be storerooms, but – I add – storerooms which may have contained the destroyed collections of books. If so, it is not necessary to assume that the twin library halls of Apollo were burnt. Galen writes of rare collections of books *circa* 200 years old which might have been stored together with the archival records located by Dio Cassius in the palace, possibly along the Clivus Palatinus. Finally, considering that after the age of Domitian Rome's libraries were invaded by copies, and that the library of the Domus Tiberiana was probably filled with further copies of books plundered in the 160s, Galen's digression in chapter 19 might refer precisely to these books or copies, possibly deposited in other storerooms that might be located not only along the Clivus Palatinus, but also towards the Via Nova and in the area of Santa Maria Antiqua. In the case of the famous library of Alexandria, too, we have a fire, burnt deposits of books, and an endless debate: it is likely, however, that the library was not damaged at all.[37] Of course the Roman context is different, but in chapter 18 Galen seems to refer to the destruction

---

[36] Strabo 13.1.54 tells that the *bibliothēkē* of Theophrastus, which included that of Aristotle, was inherited by the philosopher Neleus, and also that the *bibliothēkē* of Apellicon was carried off from Athens to Rome (see also Plut. *Sull.* 26): of course these were collections of books.

[37] In *Hippocratis Epidemiarum III et Galeni in illum Commentarius* 2.4 (Kühn 17a.606–7) Galen reports that the books taken by Ptolemy III Euergetes (246–221 BC) and destined for the Great Library in Alexandria were stored in *apothēkai*, since the king's emissaries "did not take books straight to the *bibliothēkē*, but heaped them first in some houses (*oikoi*)." Also the deposits of books burnt by Julius Caesar in Alexandria in 47 BC were called *apothēkai* by Dio Cassius (42.38.2), and it had been argued that their destruction meant the destruction of the Great Library, too: instead these store buildings – explicitly associated with books – were next to granaries and far from the library. See Canfora 1988: 20–3, and Hatzimichali this volume.

of such storage places.[38] This is the interpretation I have preferred so far, also because our other sources on the fire of AD 192 do not mention the Domus Tiberiana at all.

Many translations of *apothēkai* reiterate that the fire of AD 192 destroyed the "dépôts" (Boudon-Millot/Jouanna), "storehouses" (Jones), "repositories" (Nutton), "warehouses" (Nicholls), "depositi" (Garofalo), which were associated with the *Templum Pacis*, the imperial palace, and the Domus Tiberiana, and assume that the fire must have destroyed the three buildings, libraries included.[39] As we have seen, the word Galen uses for the horrea of the Via Sacra, *apothēkai*, means "warehouses" at the beginning of chapter 18; so in the same sentence it would also imply "libraries". In fact Lucian of Samosata, in his *Remarks addressed to an illiterate book-fancier* (5), uses *apothēkai* for library stacks ("unless you think that your very *bookcases* acquire a tincture of learning, from the bare fact of their housing so many ancient manuscripts"). Dio Cassius does the same for the libraries of Apollo on the Palatine (53.1.3), of the Porticus of Octavia (49.43.8), and probably of Trajan's Forum (68.16.3). Both Lucian and Dio specify that what was stored inside were books (*apothēkai tōn bibliōn*). Otherwise in Dio Cassius the *apothēkai* are either the storehouses of Egyptian and Arabian wares destroyed in the fire of AD 192 (73.24.1–3) or the granaries and the deposits of books burnt in Alexandria in 47 BC (42.38.2).[40] Yet nowhere does Galen use *apothēkai* to indicate an actual library hall and his usual word is *bibliothēkē* (implying collections). For instance, in *De compositione medicamentorum per genera* 1.1 (Kühn 13.362) Galen tells us that in the fire of AD 192, beside his *apothēkē* along the Via Sacra and the whole *Templum Pacis*, "the great *bibliothēkai* of the Palatine" were also burnt down. Until recently this was the only source attesting the (presumed) destruction of the library of Apollo.[41] Galen, however, does not mention the *apothēkai* or *bibliothēkē* of the *Templum Pacis*, and not even the *apothēkai* of the imperial palace. This might confirm that he refers to the "great" collections of the palace and that chapter 18 of the new treatise deals with actual warehouses.

---

[38] Claridge 2007: 78, dealing with the libraries in and around Trajan's Forum, notes that for any sizeable collection extra storage must have been provided elsewhere. No independent storerooms are attested in the *Templum Pacis* (unless they correspond to the row of rooms built along the Clivus ad Carinas) and next to the library of Apollo on the Palatine: see Mar 2009: 262.

[39] Boudon-Millot and Jouanna 2010: 71 (at page 48, however, they reiterate that there were seven libraries on the Palatine hill); Jones 2009; the other translations derive from my correspondence by e-mail.

[40] Fowler and Fowler 1905: 267. Richmond 1914: 201, translates Dio's mention of the libraries of Apollo on the Palatine hill as "the magazines of the books."

[41] See Lugli 1960: 112, and the comment by Thompson 1981: 338 n. 21.

I am aware that in chapter 18 "books" might be implied and consequently the *apothēkai* of (not *near*) the *Templum Pacis*, the palace, and the Domus Tiberiana, might indicate the relevant libraries (although with the possible anomalies of the deposits of the Via Sacra, and of the "library of the Palace," which is unheard of and might be different from the library of Apollo). If so, chapter 18 would contain Galen's first and only explicit mention of the library in the *Templum Pacis* and of the destruction of the library in the Domus Tiberiana.

Unfortunately Galen's account is ambiguous: and nobody can claim to have the only possible interpretation at hand.[42] However, I believe that since the *bibliothēkē* (collection of books) of the Domus Tiberiana was not (or not entirely) inside the destroyed *apothēkai*, then Galen made a distinction between storerooms and actual library halls and so the usual identification or translation of *apothēkai* with library halls is dubious. Apparently in chapter 18 Galen also makes a clear distinction between the Palatium and the Domus Tiberiana – they are mentioned at the same time – and he always uses the plural for the *bibliothēkai* of the Palatium (as in chapter 12b, his first mention of the burnt books, where he even talks of "*all* the libraries of the Palatium," suggesting quite problematically more than one or two halls, if interpreted as physical spaces). In fact these should be identified with *all* the collections of the imperial palace (although this would take us back to the starting point, because we should assume that also the main library halls were burnt).[43] But it is worth noting that Galen never mentions the library of Apollo by name, nor the Greek and Latin subdivision of its collections attested by literary and epigraphical sources. In the "new" passage quoted above from *Anatomical procedures* he does not even mention the Palatine, and the library of Apollo was not in the imperial palace proper.[44] I would also stress that after the fire of AD 192 the nearby sector of the palace was not

---

[42] To sum up, the *apothēkai* might be: 1) warehouses; 2) warehouses containing also the books of the libraries; 3) deposits of books far from the libraries; 4) deposits of books next to the libraries; 5) the library halls.

[43] I cannot figure out why he says "all" the libraries, or "the great" libraries (were there "small" libraries?). So far as we know, there were perhaps two: the Apollo library and the Domus Tiberiana library. There might have been a library in the NE wing of the imperial palace (Vigna Barberini), and that would make three. Or maybe, if there was "off-site" storage, Galen thought of the warehouses. This certainly seems like a clear logical sequence: storerooms burn, Palatine collections now lost – and the losses do not seem to be connected to the burning of the library halls that probably housed less valuable books.

[44] The toponym *in Palatio* (see the Tabula Hebana) refers to the complex of Apollo before the construction of Domitian's imperial palace. If it is impossible to say whether the library of Apollo was touched by the fires of AD 80 (the older collections survived, perhaps providentially saved) and 192, what can we say about the library of the Domus Tiberiana, which has not even been identified so far?

damaged, since on March 28 of AD 193 we find the troops of the Praetorian Guard making their way through the portico up to the first court, which went by the name of Sicily, and to the great banquet hall just north of the libraries of Apollo.[45] This would mean that the fire did not reach the Augustan/Domitianic library and would support the thesis of the possible storage of the most precious collections in the warehouses, which are central in Galen's account of the fire.

What follows in chapter 19 (rolls *at present* deteriorated, marshy place, etc.) does not help. This seems to be a digression on the Domus Tiberiana collection, and seems to indicate that the books there were not burnt but simply unusable because they had been subject to theft and damaged by dampness. There would not seem to be much point for Galen to complain about theft and dampness if they had been all burnt up. Does Galen introduce this section because the Domus Tiberiana might have been a source of archetypes, to help replace what was lost in the fire? Copies are implied in Fronto *ad. M. Caes.* 4.5.2. Galen's account might imply that the rolls were not completely destroyed – after all he claims that only the books of the palace were completely lost – and even suggests a possible location for that library and its deposits in the complex of Santa Maria Antiqua. Otherwise it is not unlikely that a fourth site located in a marshy area, possibly next to the Palatine hill, is hidden in chapter 19 (or is simply not mentioned: Galen would just indicate it as, say, "the site of the books/copies"). If some of them by chance survived the fire of AD 192, they might have been deposited temporarily (during the reconstruction of the buildings on the top of the hill) in the Forum extension of the Domus Tiberiana, where there were rows of Hadrianic rooms with suspensurae under the floors, which suggests a marshy place and makes me think of the granaries and deposits of books of Alexandria. Other interpretations of chapter 19, based on different reconstructions of the original text of Galen's treatise, include C. P. Jones's identification of the damaged rolls with the books of the imperial villa at Antium – but when one tries to read the previous chapters as a logical sequence, it does not seem possible to bring in Antium since the focus is on Rome throughout.[46] V. Nutton favours the Athenaeum, which has not been

---

[45] *Hist Aug.*, Capitolin. *Pertin.* 11 (4–6); cf. Dio Cass. 73.9. Boudon-Millot and Jouanna 2010: 40, reiterate that there were nine (!) libraries on the Palatine and overlook the difference between Palatium and Domus Tiberiana. Roselli 2010: 135 suggests that Galen refers to the library of Apollo.

[46] Jones 2009; Tucci 2009a. Jones's suggestion has been dismissed by Nutton and Jouanna, too, but as far as I know other works about Antium are in press.

identified so far (it might even be in the Domitianic complex at Santa Maria Antiqua).[47]

I would also exclude a recent suggestion by J. Jouanna. According to him, the place (χωρίον) mentioned in the controversial chapter 19, in which the papyri "cannot even be unrolled because decay has caused the pages to stick together, for the place is marshy and extremely low-lying, and stifling in summer," would be one and the same with the χωρίον of chapter 8: so it would correspond to the warehouses of the Via Sacra.[48] He claims that Galen's copies of the libraries' rolls would have been kept there and survived the fire but, when Galen is writing, "les rouleaux de papyrus de son dépôt qui n'ont pas été complètement carbonisés ont pourri par suite de l'humidité et de la chaleur lors de l'été qui a suivi l'incendie." In fact in the new treatise (see, e.g., chapter 50b) and in all his other references to the fire of AD 192 Galen attests explicitly that *all the things* he kept in his deposit at the Via Sacra were burnt to ashes and destroyed (not damaged) because of the fire. Jouanna's interpretation would imply that Galen used to keep his works and remedies (a long established habit) in a marshy place and so did the procurators with their archives and the dead grammarian with all his books. A single summer, however, would have sufficed to provoke the damage. Was the prudent Galen really so foolish as to store dry goods such as spices and papyrus rolls in a damp marshy place? The condition of the "place" as described by Galen is a permanent one – marshy and enclosed always, stifling only in summer – so the damage might have occurred at any time, even before the fire and the summer of AD 192. The reason why Galen wanted to send his books to Campania at the beginning of summer was not humidity, but the arrival of the Etesian winds – and other copies

---

[47] See Coarelli 2009a. The recent identification of the Athenaeum with an Hadrianic hall found at Piazza Venezia is uncertain: see Coates-Stephens 2010: 52–4. The real Athenaeum was provided with a cavea, possibly made of wood, with curvilinear and not straight steps (cf. Sid. Apoll. *Epist.* 2.9.4; 9.14.2). In addition, the hall at Piazza Venezia was "the central component of a trio of similar structures" and was not large enough to contain a meeting of the senate (cf. Dio Cass. 74.17.4).

[48] Boudon-Millot and Jouanna 2010: 74; see also 34 and lix (and xix). *Contra* Roselli 2010: 146 and esp. note 89. Also in the case of the warehouses along the Via Sacra, χωρίον has a broad sense, but cannot be identified with the χωρίον of chapter 19. The only element in common is that they refer to a wide area, like the imperial estates where the young Commodus resided (Galen, *On prognosis* 9.7–8) or the area of the Vatican circus created by Caligula south of the later basilica of St Peter's, located by Tacitus in the Vatican valley (*Ann.* 14.14) and described by Dio Cassius (59.14.6) with the word χωρίον. The same word is used again by Galen (*De temperamentis*, 2; Kühn I.630) to indicate wet places such as Rome (presumably the low areas, otherwise all the papyrus rolls in the city would have suffered from the same problem): "phlegm descending from the head, on the other hand, is extremely common, especially in Rome and other such wet places."

would have remained in Rome: chapter 23a. Even pretending that the fire was so selective as to spare the rolls of Galen's copies (indeed his own works were completely burnt and he had to rewrite them), it is unlikely that damp would have damaged those copies in a few months, along the Via Sacra. Even assuming that this problem revealed itself only after the fire of AD 192, the rolls would have remained on the site during the summer – implying that such an important area was not cleared for months? – and the "imperturbable" Galen would have searched in the debris to recover (very much like Adso, the monk of *The Name of the Rose*, after the fire of the abbey[49]) entire rolls that however were semi-carbonized and could not be unrolled.[50] If so, how could he identify them? If useless, why did he save them as "souvenirs" from the summer of AD 192 until he writes (cf. chapter 19)? Jouanna's parallel with the charred rolls of the library of the Villa dei Papiri at Herculaneum is not pertinent: Galen's rolls would have appeared like carbon blocks, very difficult to open but not for the reasons mentioned in chapter 19 (Galen never says that the rolls were charred or, for instance, damaged because of the water used to put out the fire). Last but not least, the stretch of the Via Sacra from the Roman Forum to the Temple of Venus and Rome climbs on the slopes of the Velia and was some 30 m wide (Fig. 15.6). This neighborhood can hardly be defined "au plus haut point marécageux" and "encaissé."[51]

Copies and originals

That said, the topographical puzzle outlined above is of no great importance. After all Galen was not concerned with topographical issues and his primary goal was to create a dramatic setting for the subsequent discussion on his avoidance of grief.[52] Galen's Greek is not easy (and the text we have is not

[49] Eco 1994: 500. Cf. Cuvigny 2009: 47 for the description of the real discovery of a room filled with papyri burnt in a fire precisely in the late second century AD; those which had escaped the fire were reduced to a kind of brownish paste. Otherwise, also due to the pressure of the collapsed ruins, the charred rolls "cannot typically be unrolled... in most case, the very thin charred layers of papyrus are stuck and more or less pasted together": cf. Frösén 2009: 92. Galen's description – which however does not refer to rolls directly involved in the fire – may purposely have been depressing, especially if compared to the actual damage provoked by damp which is described by ancient sources.

[50] I assume that Jouanna does not argue that the rolls were eventually kept in a new building reconstructed along the Via Sacra. If so, although very lucky in the recovery of these precious copies, Galen would have continued to keep his rolls in that unfavourable place.

[51] There is archaeological evidence for damp only in the S wing of the House of the Vestals, just below the Via Nova and close to Santa Maria Antiqua (cf. Lanciani 1900: 206–7).

[52] As I stressed in Tucci 2008: 133 n.1.

even certain), but it would be interesting to know whether his addressee in Pergamum, or his audience, may have understood what he was telling. Be that as it may, it is clear enough that in any case Galen does not list any books available in the *Templum Pacis*, because his own burnt copies were linked to the lost Palatine books. As a matter of fact, Galen was indifferent to the destruction of the library of Peace, as is confirmed by his other works: in *On the avoidance of grief* Galen refers to the whole Vespasianic building in passing. There might well have been books which were important and of high quality, but these were just not of interest to him, and this is one of the few conclusions that are not questionable. I cannot find any place where Galen is clearly lamenting the loss of particular books there. Of course the next step is to understand why those books were not of interest to him. We can safely state that the rare collections he mentions were not kept there. Perhaps, together with ancient documents (older than the library itself and possibly coming from Pollio's library[53]), there were just copies (or less accurate editions) and "new books" also available in other libraries.

It is worth recalling that Domitian "provided for having the libraries, which were destroyed by fire, renewed at very great expense, seeking everywhere for copies of the lost works, and sending scribes to Alexandria to transcribe and correct them" (Suet. *Dom.* 20). Perhaps it is not coincidental that Dionysius of Alexandria had been appointed director of the libraries under Vespasian or Titus.[54] Some copies might have filled also the new library of Peace. In Rome "the libraries were the emperor's, a central fact: the collections were his, part of the Palatine property even when housed off that hill," and he made his personal collections available to friends and scholars "by placing the books in halls that were located in public spaces."[55] Not by chance, researching (in Rome) a variant in the *Epidemiae* of Hippocrates that Dioscorides recorded as occurring in only two copies, Galen looked deliberately at "all the *copies* in the 'public libraries' [*dēmosiai bibliothēkai*]" and all those in the libraries of his friends (*Hippocratis Epidemiarum VI Commentarius* IV.21: Kühn 17b.194–5).[56]

---

[53] Cf. Dix and Houston 2006: 672–3 (and 692 specifically on the hypothetical provenance of the books in the library of Peace).
[54] See Houston 2002: 161, and Bowie this volume.
[55] Houston 2002: 172; Dix and Houston 2006: 672.
[56] No doubt the public who used them was restricted, like the circle of scholars mentioned by Aulus Gellius and Galen himself. It has been suggested that the *Tabularium Principis*, too, was located in the imperial palace, while its copies might have been available in the *Templum Pacis*: see Coarelli 1991: 77–8. Also to be considered is the case of the archives of the four imperial procurators that Galen locates in the warehouses of the Via Sacra.

The choice of the *Templum Pacis* for the copies would not be surprising: not only was the Vespasianic building very close to the palace, but already under Vespasian the spoils from the Temple of Jerusalem had been divided between the two sites. The spoils visible at the Arch of Titus and also "the vessels of gold from the temple of the Jews, on which he (Vespasian) prided himself" (Joseph. *BJ* 7.5.7, 158–61) were displayed in the *Templum Pacis*, but "the law of the Jews" and "the purple hangings of the Temple" (of Jerusalem) were kept in the imperial palace.[57] In the rabbinic literature there are two other passages referring to furnishings of the Temple of Jerusalem in Rome after AD 70, located both in the *Templum Pacis* and the palace.[58] The *Templum Pacis* was also a perfect place in which to gather scholars to discuss literature, philosophy or medicine, as it was provided with a wide porticoed square like the Greek *gymnasia*. It would also have required less security than the palace. Galen tells us that the *Templum Pacis* "even before the fire was the general meeting-place for all those engaged in learned pursuits" (*De libris propriis*, 2: Kühn 19.21–2; cf. SHA *Tyr. Trig.* 31.7–12, both reconsidered below), referring to both the Flavian and Severan periods. No doubt it was one of those sites where Roman citizens could engage with Greek culture. The philosophers depicted in the School of Athens by Raphael (1510–11) may give an idea of the scholars strolling under the porticoes and in the open square, or sitting on the steps of the *Templum Pacis*. There might also be a similarity with the Serapeum in Alexandria, built in the third century BC and a temple as well, which housed an offshoot collection of the Great Library. Epiphanius, writing in the fourth century AD, tells that after the first library was built in the palace area, eventually (after Ptolemy II Philadelphus) "another library was built in the Serapeum, smaller than the first, which was called the daughter of the first one." It was here that Vespasian consulted the oracle in AD 69–70, and Titus in AD 71.[59] As reported by Aphthonius in the late fourth century AD, at the Serapeum the "precincts (*sēkoi*) of the stoas have been built inside, some as storehouses (*tameia*) for the books, open to those eager to study, and they lift the entire city up to the possibility of acquiring wisdom" (*Progymnasmata* 12).[60] The "daughter" library received duplicate copies from the Great Library and "did not collect scrolls from far and wide . . . there were nothing but copies,

---

[57] See Yarden 1991. [58] Cf. Noy 2005: 373–85.
[59] McKenzie 2003: 50–6; McKenzie, Gibson and Reyes 2004: 99–100 and 103 nn. 160–1 for the Flavian emperors. Not by chance a sacred cubit for measuring the water level was kept in the Temple of Serapis at Alexandria and a statue of the Nile surrounded by sixteen children, a symbol of his fertility and of the ideal rising of the river which equals 16 cubits, was displayed in the *Templum Pacis* (Plin. *HN* 36.58). See also Henrichs 1968: 73–4 and 79–80.
[60] McKenzie, Gibson and Reyes 2004: 105.

excellent copies, of the good editions prepared in the Museum."[61] No doubt Galen would not have trusted such editions.

We also know from Strabo (13.1.54) that certain booksellers "used bad copyists and would not collate the texts – a thing that also takes place in the case of the other books that are copied for selling, both here (in Rome) and at Alexandria" (cf. Mart. 2.8). Near the *Templum Pacis* there was a concentration of booksellers: *circa* AD 86 Martial (1.2.8) locates Secundus' bookshop "*behind the entrance to the temple of Peace* and the Forum of Pallas" and recalls the *Vicus Sandaliarius*, "the area of Rome with the largest concentration of booksellers," where a century later Galen would discover a work falsely ascribed to him.[62] There is no clear evidence for the identification of this *Vicus* with the street running NE of the *Templum Pacis* (nowadays Via del Colosseo) which, indeed, reached the entrances to the Forum of Nerva and the *Templum Pacis*. The *Vicus Sandaliarius* was in any case located in the IV Augustan region, just as was the *Templum Pacis*. I would remark the possible link with the *Horrea Chartaria*, a warehouse of unwritten papyrus rolls located in the same Augustan region and not far from the *Apollo Sandaliarius*.[63]

I have already mentioned the personal notebooks of Aelius Stilo on axioms, which could have been put in a bookcase containing original manuscripts coming from the just demolished library of Pollio together with the letters of Sinnius Capito.[64] Galen's silence about the *Templum Pacis* collections is important and telling, because after all he reveals what was *not* available there. He says very clearly that, because of the destruction of the books of the palace, "it is no longer possible to find what is rare and cannot be found anywhere else, among those things which are absolutely ordinary but are demanded because of the exactness of their writing"; among these, there were "the original books of several ancient grammarians, orators, doctors and philosophers" (chapter 13). He also mentions his own copies of most of the books of Chrysippus and of all the ancient doctors that he had found in the palace (chapter 15). Thus we might conclude that the books in the library of Peace were not rare and original, and did not include the

---

[61] Cf. Canfora 1989: 63–4.
[62] *On my own books*/Kühn 19.8–9 and *On prognosis* 4/Kühn 14.620.
[63] Coarelli 1999a: 189. See also Nutton 1979: 89, 95, and 175; White 2009: 271. It is not clear why the Horrea Chartaria are considered Severan in date by Rickman 1971: 164.
[64] Cf. Dix and Houston 2006: 691–3. See also Coarelli 2009a. The works of Aelius Stilo and Varro, cited by Sinnius Capito, by Verrius Flaccus, and finally by Aulus Gellius – see Rowell 1952 – might suggest another link between Pollio's library and the library of Peace.

books of the doctors.[65] However, the bronze head of Chrysippus, found in the recent excavations next to SS. Cosma e Damiano and dated to the original phase of the *Templum Pacis*, suggests the existence of his works in that library (though Galen did not care for them). So there might have been: 1) some "nominative collections" (as in the palace) such as the notebooks of Aelius Stilo and the letters of Sinnius Capito; 2) copies of Greek and Latin works together (but not the rare authenticated copies available in the Palatine collections); and 3) new books.

Galen tells that doctors and even the ill used to discuss in the *Templum Pacis* how to define various pulse rates (*De pulsuum differentiis*; Kühn 8.495). This suggests that doctors were attracted there, and would confirm that the library had a collection of texts on medicine.[66] For instance, the seventeen books of Galen's *The usefulness of the parts of the body*, in which he attempted to show the design and foresight of Nature in terms of the usefulness or purpose for which each component of the body was formed, seem to have been available in the *Templum Pacis* or, at least, to have been familiar to the scholars who gathered there.[67] Galen (*De libris propriis*, 2: Kühn 19.21–2) tells that:

The usefulness of the parts, too, had reached a wide readership, on account of the enthusiasm of virtually every doctor with a training in traditional medicine, as well as that of philosophers of the Aristotelian persuasion: for Aristotle himself had written a treatise of a similar kind. And so of course certain malicious individuals put about the city the slander that I was in the habit of describing things which were simply not visible in dissections, so as to gain a reputation as having made discoveries far beyond those of my predecessors; for, they said, such matters could not have failed to be noticed before. To those men my only response was that of contemptuous amusement; but they excited the anger of my friends, who begged me to give a public demonstration before a large audience [*kata ti tôn megalōn akoustēriôn*] of the truth of my anatomical writings. When I refused (for my disposition even then was to care nothing for what men thought), those slanderers attributed my high-mindedness to fear of refutation rather then to contempt for their stupidity; and every day they would go to the *Templum Pacis* – which even

---

[65] According to Casson 2001: 101, the library of Peace ("Vespasian's library") might have been specialized in works of the grammarians.

[66] Dix and Houston 2006: 692 n. 146 suggest "translations into Latin of books taken from Mithridates by Pompey more than a century earlier."

[67] In *On the avoidance of grief* Galen gives great importance to public libraries outside of Rome in the process of distribution or publication. Of the two copies of each of his new works, one was intended to satisfy the requests of Galen's friends in Pergamum who asked him for copies of his new works so that they could deposit them "in a public library" – and several of his books were available in other towns (chapter 21). Very likely they were available in the *Templum Pacis*, too.

before the fire was the general meeting-place for all those engaged in learned pursuits – and mock me continually. I was, then, compelled by my friends to give a public demonstration, wherein, over a period of several days, I proved that I had not been lying, and that there were many matters of which previous authorities had been ignorant. At my friends' behest, too, I wrote up these demonstrations and arguments; and the work is entitled *Lycus' ignorance in anatomy*, for the following reason.[68]

According to some scholars the public building explicitly mentioned for these public demonstrations was the *Templum Pacis*. In particular, the hall of SS. Cosma and Damian would have been the place where, during the second century AD, the meetings and the debates of the physicians were held (a *schola medicorum* would have been there), and where Galen himself would have confuted his detractors in public – thus implying that the library would have been the dark hall corresponding to the monastery. This interpretation, however, is based on a limited knowledge of the structures and architectural phases of the *Templum Pacis* and on a mistaken identification of the library hall (see above). Moreover, had Galen's anatomical demonstration taken place in the *Templum Pacis*, and if a *schola medicorum*, an auditorium or an important collection of books had been there, we would expect Galen to mention them. No doubt the provocations against Galen happened in the *Templum Pacis*, but at no point does Galen say that he held his public demonstration there. We need not even assume that Galen himself was at the *Templum Pacis* when "those slanderers" mocked him! He just heard the rumors. Galen's friends suggested "a great *akoustērion*," not a library or a presumed lecture hall inside the *Templum Pacis*.[69] In fact *akoustērion* is

---

[68] Singer 1997:9 translates *kata ti tôn megalōn akoustēriôn* as "in one of the great auditoria."
[69] There are no explicit sources on Galen's demonstrations in the *Templum Pacis* according to Gleason 2009: 97 (and personal communication). Instead this view is supported by Debru 1995: 70 and 75, Palombi 1997–8 and 2007, and other scholars who simply quote Palombi's papers; it can be found already in Temperini 1994: 5. Meneghini 2009: 85, 94 (esp. note 21) supports Palombi's view – see also Meneghini 2010: 35–8, esp. 37 – and apparently has not been able to understand the reasons of my disagreement in Tucci 2008. In fact I had simply discussed the architectural remains in the S corner of the *Templum Pacis* – the same walls and hall that Meneghini omits from his plans (although their inclusion would help him to follow my argument) – and disclosed that Galen's anatomical demonstrations and the *schola medicorum* have nothing to do with the *Templum Pacis*. Beside the *schola* in the *Templum Pacis*, Palombi 1997–8 had also identified the library of Peace with the hall of the monastery (but see above) and Galen's storeroom with the official residence of the doctor of the imperial court (the later discovery of *On the avoidance of grief*, however, has shown that this was not the case). The total absence of any references in Galen's works to a professional body of physicians in Rome to which he or his opponents belonged is clearly highlighted in Nutton 1971: 62; see also Pazzini 1935. Despite this, and overlooking also the late antique phases of the halls in the S corner of the *Templum Pacis*, Meneghini keeps on producing "creative" arguments to reinforce

another ambiguous term which usually means an audience, as elsewhere in Galen (see *De venae sectione adversus Erasistratum* 1; Kühn 11.194) or in Porphyry of Tyre (AD 234–305) (*Plot.* 15.12), and a large audience does not necessarily imply a great assembly hall.[70] In any case there is no certain link with the *Templum Pacis*.

After AD 163 Galen had renounced the practice of giving public demonstrations and public lectures in Rome, due to the hostility displayed by a few detractors.[71] The comments against him, as we have seen, were a consequence of the publication of his *The usefulness of the parts of the body*, written between AD 165 and 175 (or AD 161–80, in any case before the fire of AD 192). Eventually he changed his mind and accepted the challenge:

> I placed the works of all the anatomists before me and invited everyone present to choose whatever part he wished to be dissected. My claim was that I would show the extent of the divergence of the facts – which had been accurately described in my own works – from the accounts of my predecessors. Someone chose the chest. Now, as I was taking up the books of the most ancient of medical authorities, whom I intended to be my starting-point, some very reputable doctors who were sitting in the front row told me not to waste my time: Lycus of Macedon who had been a disciple of Quintus, the greatest expert in anatomy, had written down all the discoveries made up to his own time, and so I should forget about the rest and subject his work alone to examination against mine. It was, then, in accordance with their request that I proceeded, with respect to every proof that was demanded of me from one day to the next.[72]

It is also unlikely that dozens of animals were dissected in the library hall of a *templum*. No doubt Galen would have mentioned the destruction of all these books, had they been available in the *Templum Pacis*: he does so for the books of the palace, using the same expression in *On the avoidance of*

---

the plausibility of Palombi's suggestions, without any proof. He claims that the Gallic roses which decorated the square of the *Templum Pacis* would relate to the activity of the *schola medicorum* – Meneghini 2009: 97 n. 58, *contra* himself (!) at page 81; a dedication to Asclepius found in the Cloaca Maxima would be another proof – see Meneghini 2009 n. 21 – together with the medical records attested in the sanctuaries of Asclepius in Greece, whose relevance to the *Templum Pacis* (where documents of this kind have never been found) is not clear. Fogagnolo, Rossi 2010a: 93 and 2010b: 36 claim that "Galeno (Gal. *libr. propr.* 19, ed. Kühn, p. 19) ricorda inoltre come... andó bruciata... un'aula del *Templum Pacis* dove si svolgevano dispute mediche, annessa con ogni probabilità ad una biblioteca" (!) and mention "la sede di una scuola medica che nei testi di Galeno... viene ricordata nel *Templum Pacis*."

[70] On the *auditoria*, cf. Tamm 1963 and Gros 2001a: 416–17; they both do not consider this passage of Galen, probably because it does not refer to an actual building.
[71] Cf. Nutton 2004a.
[72] *On my own books* 2 (Kühn 19.21): from Singer 1997: 9–10. Lycus of Macedon, only a few years before Galen arrived in Rome in AD 162, had published a substantial manual of dissection that dealt with vivisection and dissection: see Nutton 2004b: 212–14.

grief (chapter 13 and mostly 15: "the books of all the ancient doctors"). And it would have been useless to take all the books on anatomy: once agreed on the author, it would have been sufficient to take a single volume – the proximity of a library was not indispensable and the libraries of Galen's friends were also provided with medical texts.[73]

I have already recalled that Galen says that the scholars used to gather every day in the *Templum Pacis* even before the fire of AD 192 (which means also *after* the fire). Similar information is provided by the SHA *Tyr. Trig.* 31.7–12. The author, writing under the name of one Trebellius Pollio, in the *Life of Victoria*, a leader of the so-called Gallic Empire in the late third century AD, expresses himself concerned about the reception of his work by the scholars of the *Templum Pacis*. Despite the possibility of some fictional content in this passage, it is very likely that the author intended to provide a realistic setting for his dialogues, one that would correspond to the experience of his readers. Indeed this anecdote corresponds to Galen's account of his own new books and of the slanderers in the *Templum Pacis*, thus confirming that new works were "presented" or published there.

As for the other libraries in the area, it has been suggested that from the Flavian period onwards they "may have assigned each a field on which to concentrate."[74] Perhaps, instead, it was a matter of organization and the quality of the works available. Apparently the first libraries ran out of space and it became necessary to find room somewhere to put up more shelves, hence new library halls and also the creation of separate storage areas for books. The total capacity of Rome's library would be less than in Pergamum and Alexandria, but with the storerooms – which did not exist before the Flavian age – the number increased. There might have been a new organization precisely from the Flavian age onwards. A work such as Galen's *The usefulness of the parts of the body*, in seventeen books, would have occupied *circa* one row in any shelf of the library of Peace, and Galen's corpus alone (listed in *On his own books*) would have required more than one niche ("one must imagine at least six or seven hundred rolls containing his own writing alone," according to Nutton)[75] – just to give an idea of the problems of storage, either for an individual scholar such as Galen or a public library (not to mention the catalogues). The Roman poet Persius (AD 34–62) bequeathed his friend and mentor, the philosopher Lucius Annaeus Cornutus, his collection of "libros circa septingentos Chrysippi sive

---

[73] There is much more to say about the discussions on medical matters in the *Templum Pacis* and in the Baths of Trajan, and on the places in which public demonstrations were actually held and the bloodshed of Galen's dissections (see my forthcoming book on the *Templum Pacis*).
[74] Casson 2001: 100.   [75] Nutton 2009: 20–1.

bibliothecam suam omnem" (Suet. frg. p. 74). Pliny the Elder (*HN*, praef. 17) claimed that "by perusing about 2,000 volumes... we have collected in 36 volumes 20,000 noteworthy facts obtained from one hundred authors." The emperor Gordian II (AD 238) would have inherited up to 62,000 volumes – "and this raised him to the seventh heaven, for being now possessed of a library of such magnitude and excellence, thanks to the power of letters he became famous among men" (SHA *Gord.* 18.2–3). This would be more than any library hall could contain: where did he store them? After all, like Galen who had his own house but used a storeroom, the emperor, too, who had his own residence and magnificent library halls, is likely to have used the storerooms around the Palatine (he might have said the same things as Galen – the storerooms looked safer than his "house," but the fire destroyed the storerooms). It is now clear that the archives too expanded outside of the palace.[76] All of the imperial libraries in Rome could be considered a single *bibliotheca*, i.e. the emperor's collection, which he kept stored in many different buildings. However, the sole function of the monumental library halls might have become to serve those who came to consult the books: they were simply handsome spaces in which to work. Of course I do not mean that there were empty shelves and no public at all.[77]

The Augustan libraries might have been partially "empty."[78] But 220 years after their construction (28 BC–AD 192), when the fire destroyed the area around the Via Sacra, it is not unreasonable to assume that the majority of the works had been deposited in the Flavian storerooms. The ancient documents might have been in the warehouses, available upon request – we know from some two dozen inscriptions that public libraries in Rome were staffed by slaves from the imperial household[79] – and the library halls might have housed just the most recent works. Otherwise, why does Galen concentrate his attention largely on the *apothēkai*? Is it just because they are the buildings that, topographically, best define the path of the fire, or is it because they contained books and so are relevant to his point? In addition,

---

[76] According to Nutton 2009: 20, Galen gives the impression that much of his library was normally kept in the storeroom at the Via Sacra.

[77] Claridge 2007: 78, thinks that niches would be more appropriate for a gallery of statues and would constitute an essential part of the decor in the reading hall of a public library. This, however, does not mean that the library of Peace might have been used for Galen's demonstration. In the West library of Trajan there are no traces of shelves, and the famous relief (now lost) from Neumagen, showing rolls stacked in three levels on a shelf, refers to a wooden structure and not to actual niches. For Trajan's library, see Meneghini 2002a: 684; cf. Dix and Houston 2006: 696.

[78] See Horsfall 1993: 62.   [79] Houston 2004: 5–13.

the library of Apollo was more than half a km distant from the *Templum Pacis* (and I have stressed that the structures next to the twin halls were in good condition the year after the fire): is it possible that there was not the time to save the collections in the Palatine library?[80] And, during the Domitianic reconstruction of the library of Apollo, considering the survival of the older collections – either saved from fire or just removed to allow the works – where were they stored? There remains the possibility that some of the Apollo library's collection was stored off-site, in warehouses, and that might be all that Galen is saying. My own feeling is that the Atticiana etc. were part of the Apollo library's collection – a peculiarity of the palace – although the precious books were not at hand. Galen might have had access to these repositories and this is how he found unknown works.

If the warehouses were used for overflow, or perhaps as safe places for specific valuable collections, that would be useful to know. After all, after the fire of AD 192 there were other libraries in Rome, but apparently they did not compensate for the loss of the Palatine collections, as for the quality at least. The library of Peace could even be re-created soon after its reconstruction, as suggested by Galen, the *Historia Augusta*, and the remains of the hall itself, only to disappear forever after the transformations of the same hall in the first half of the fourth century AD.

---

[80] According to Herodian (1.14.2) the Vestals saved the Palladium and brought it on to the Palatine hill.

Addendum
Galen *On the avoidance of grief* 19: Rome or Antium?

This chapter builds on an interpretation of this passage first advanced in two articles published in the *Journal of Roman Archaeology* in which I argued that the place where Galen states that some papyrus rolls had suffered from their marshy environment was to be located at Rome.[1] C. P. Jones' alternative suggestion[2] that it should be located in the imperial villa at Antium has been answered already. But the Antium hypothesis still has defenders,[3] and it seemed useful to the editors and to myself that I should respond very briefly to their arguments here.

Stramaglia criticizes my suggestion on the grounds that it is implausible to locate a marshy and deeply enclosed area in the Domus Tiberiana "sul colle Palatino": in fact I argued that the library was located in the forum extension of the House of Tiberius. A good deal of evidence has been gathered to show the existence of marshy areas around Antium. Stramaglia states that miasma from the Pontine Marshes reached the library at Antium (although his source, Gregorovius, refers to local climate in 1854 – specifically to summer fevers provoked by the "caldo tiepido e voluttuoso che sale dal mare" – and if this was the problem, no doubt Galen would have mentioned the sea). Stramaglia also refers to the frogs and mosquitoes reported by Horace in 38 BC along the Decennovium canal parallel to the Via Appia, at least 30 km east of Antium, and Rothschild and Thompson mention three marshy areas described in 7 BC by Strabo and conclude that "the entire coast of Latium is spotted with marshes." As it happens Strabo adds that Antium "is situated on masses of rock." Much of this testimony is of limited relevance. There is no doubt there were marshy areas in both Rome and in coastal Latium, but no conclusions about the location of the library in question can be drawn from general characterizations of either landscape. The matter therefore turns on the interpretation of the text itself. Rothschild and Thompson note that I acknowledge that "τὸ χωρίον could mean 'hall,'" but that "standard usage and contextual cues suggest that the best interpretation of τὸ χωρίον in Ind. 19 is 'region'." This was precisely my interpretation, and the region I suggested was the valley between the

---

[1] Tucci 2008; 2009a. [2] Jones 2009. [3] Stramaglia 2011; Rothschild and Thompson 2012.

Capitoline and Palatine hills, and the Roman Forum.[4] When Galen mentions a humid χωρίον, he talks of Rome explicitly (cf. n. 48 in the present chapter). Defenders of the Antium thesis are, to be sure, handicapped by the corrupted state of Galen's text in the Vlatadon manuscript. Antium might occur three times, but the fifteenth-century copyist may equally well have misinterpreted the original, or carefully copied a faulty text. For all these reasons there seems no compelling reason to take chapter 19 to refer to the imperial villa at Antium rather than the imperial collections in Rome.

---

[4] Tucci 2009a: 398–9; cf. Lanciani 1900: 6–7.

16 | Archives, books and sacred space in Rome

RICHARD NEUDECKER

Life in the library

Aulus Gellius is one of the best-known readers in the libraries of ancient Rome.[1] On one occasion, during the reign of Marcus Aurelius, he chanced to be sitting in the library of the temple of Trajan (*'in bibliotheca templi Traiani'*) and looking for something else, when the edicts of the ancient praetors (*'edicta veterum praetorum'*) fell into his hands, and he thought it worthwhile to read them and become acquainted with them. Then he came across a strange expression and a friend who sat beside him – *'quispiam nobiscum sedens amicus'* – immediately remembered a passage in *De Origine Vocabulorum* by Gavius.[2] This frequently quoted passage demonstrates that juridical rarities could be found in the library. But it also gives us an idea of life in the library: people seeking out and finding things, communicating with each other, and demonstrating their knowledge and scholarship to each other, not just the fictional *'quispiam amicus'* to be sure, but Gellius himself as well. And not just inside the library but also out of doors *'in area fori'* where an eye-catching building inscription immediately elicits an etymological discussion of the term *'ex manubiis'*, all for the sake of showing off with quotations from Cicero, Aristophanes, Cato, Homer and constitutional texts.[3]

It was all a matter of cultivating one's image. An arrogant critic of words *'reprehensor audaculus verborum'* who 'had read very little and that of the most ordinary sort' makes a big fuss about the proper use of the word *plura* instead of *pluria* and is well and truly put in his place with a stream of quotations from Cato, Quintus Claudius, Valerius Antias, Lucius Aelius, Publius Nigidius and Marcus Varro.[4] These were excerpts that Gellius had committed to memory from the 'very learned' Sinnius Capito whose letters (as one of Gellius' friends then remembered) were to be found collected in a book of which there was a copy in the temple of Peace *'in templo Pacis'*.

---

[1] For Gellius, see Holford-Strevens 1988; Michel 1998 and Keulen 2009. For Roman libraries, still most valuable Dziatzko 1897 and Wendel 1954; short introductions Cavallo 1989 and Fedeli 1988; recent literature Neudecker 2004; Dix and Houston 2006 and Blanck 2008.
[2] Gell. 11.17.1.   [3] Gell. 13.25.2.   [4] Gell. 5.21.9–17.

Archives, books and sacred space in Rome 313

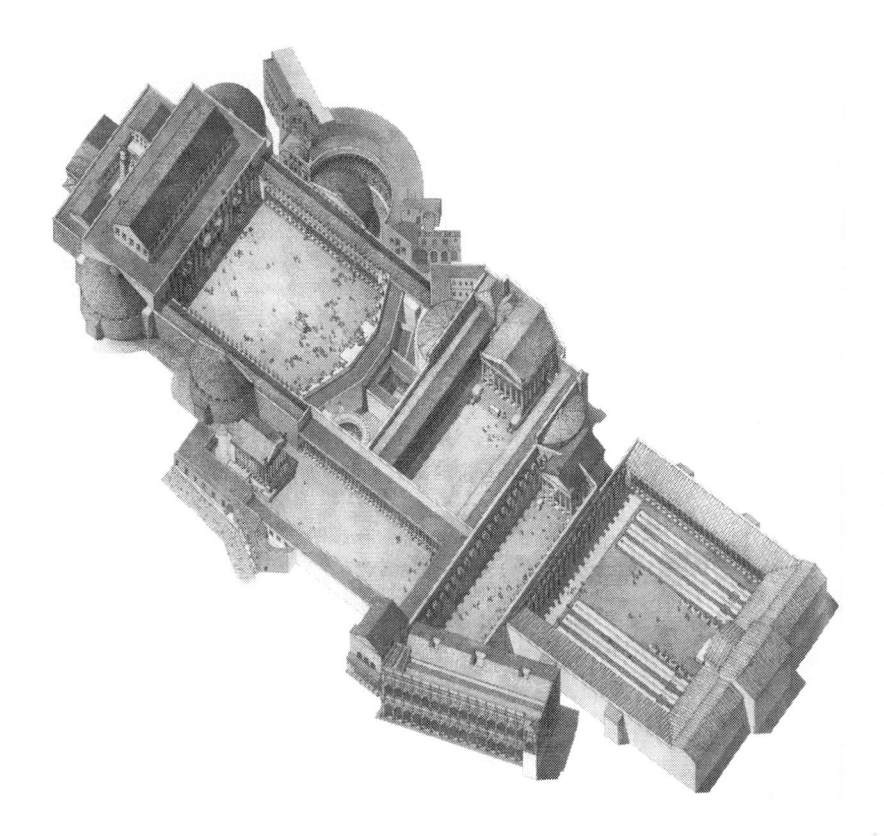

Figure 16.1 Rome's Imperial Fora

And, just to show off a bit, Gellius 'the eternal student'[5] throws into his report some quotations from Plautus and Cato.

Everybody raided the libraries for excerpts, digging around for interesting bits from all genres of texts, in effect, recycling information. This was not intended to produce deep erudition but rather the kind of knowledge that was expected in smart circles. It was an exercise in keeping up with the refined conversation of society at large.[6] Gellius' *Noctes Atticae*, a conversation guide of which I myself shall make liberal use in these pages, were themselves a part of this game. This recycling of texts went through a sort of inflation during the Imperial period. It needed facilities – the archives – where one might discover these bits and pieces in documents, in literature, in scientific texts, in recorded speeches. One such location was the Forum of Trajan (Fig. 16.1).

---

[5] So Fantham 1996: 246–52.
[6] For the intellectual climate, see Zanker 1995: 190–206, 234–42; Krasser 1995, Krasser 1999 and Bowie 2000; for techniques of memorising, see Small 1997 with review by Horsfall 1998.

Of all the public buildings in Rome, this is the most complex, and one component was the library.[7] Over 23 metres in height, and with three tiers of niches, the figure of 21,000 *rotuli*, which Packer thought would fit into it, is definitely on the low side. The upper niches were accessible via outside staircases.

Not every question concerning the proper functioning of the library's various rooms has been answered. Consulting books was not an activity restricted to the halls, so my main interest is with the functional complexity of the entire building. One component, the apses of the bordering Basilica, was used as law courts. When Gellius and Favorinus discussed the *manubiae* inscription mentioned above they were waiting for a friend who was still busy in court. Gellius, a judge himself, knew very well that in legal practice it was essential to be able to find the right precedent for a formula or an edict in the archives and to have it quickly to hand. The library was an important part of the administration of justice, precisely because of the importance of such documents.[8] Gellius' anecdote points to a further, non-textual source of information in the Forum. Beneath the standards of military units, which Gellius mentions in passing, there was a series of fifty-four portraits of members of the Imperial family and historical personages. In Meneghini's reconstructions it becomes apparent that the decoration of the monument might actually have been perceived as a compressed illustration of history (Fig. 16.2).[9] Like the building inscription, it offered further material for gaining and displaying knowledge.

In the pages that follow, I should like to establish what it is that unites the collections of books, of administrative documents and of non-textual material. Most of the varying designations of these archival spaces employ terms that recur in the sacral sphere: '*bibliothecae templi Traiani*' or '*divi Traiani*',[10] the '*bibliotheca Pacis*'[11] and the '*bibliotheca ad Apollinis*'.[12] Sanctuaries were public spaces. Public admittance applied to the libraries, too. We take this for granted, or treat the claim as an empty one. Yet during the founding years of Rome's first public library in the *Atrium Libertatis* the question of public admittance was part of a political discourse over *publicatio* in a wider sense.[13]

---

[7] Packer 1995, 1997; Meneghini 2001, 2007 and most complete Meneghini 2009: 146–51; for a short overview, see Meneghini 2002a; Meneghini 2002b with doubts about the definition of the library; about contents of the library Sbordone 1984.
[8] Meneghini 2002b: 668; in general, see Tuori 2010.
[9] Illustrated in Packer 1997: 89, Meneghini 2007 figs. 93 and 104 and Meneghini 2009 figs. 142–5. On the wider issue of images and books in libraries, see Petrain this volume.
[10] Gell. 11.17.1; *CIL* 14.5352. [11] Gell. 5.21.9. [12] Suet., *Aug.* 29.3.
[13] On *publicatio*, see Nicholls this volume.

Figure 16.2 Rome, Forum of Trajan

The *Atrium Libertatis*

The *Atrium Libertatis*[14] as architecture is lost to us. We have to rely on a few mentions in textual sources which inform us about the 'prehistory' of the library. During a fire, presumably in 210 BC, many bronze plates with laws '*fixa in atrio Libertatis*' were destroyed. Cato the Censor knew one of them, the law on the punishment of fallen Vestal Virgins, noted and quoted in a speech *De Auguribus*, which was found by Festus, and used by him to explain the notion '*probrum*'.[15] Under 169 BC Livy records an attempt to impeach the censors who reacted by going on strike. They went to the *Atrium Libertatis*

et obsignatis tabellis publicis, clausoque tabulario, et dimissis servis publicis, negarunt se prius quicquam publici negotii gesturos.[16]

they sealed the books of the public accounts, shut up the office, and dismissed the clerks; affirming, that they would do no kind of public business until the sentence of the people was passed on them.

Tabellae publicae were census lists, the same from which in 168 BC the tribus for the Liberti was publicly chosen by lot in the *Atrium Libertatis*.[17] The

---

[14] Coarelli 1993b; Canfora 1993: 32–7; Castagnoli 1946 on the literary sources.
[15] Festus 277 L; *ORF*³ fr. 220; Astin 1978: 102.
[16] Livy 43.16.13, see Astin 1986: 131–4, and Moatti 1993: 67; for censors, still Mommsen 1887: 360–2; see also Suolahti 1963: 33–40.
[17] Livy 45.15.1–5.

occasion for the conflict of 169 was measures taken by the censors against illegal buildings on the Via Sacra. Obviously, the censors also disposed of cadastral maps. Indeed, when the praetor P. Cornelius Lentulus divided the *ager Campanus*, he had the '*formam agrorum in aes incisam ad Libertatis*', that is an inscribed bronze tablet with the plan of the land registry, set up in the *Atrium Libertatis*. We owe this piece of information to one of the collectors and researchers of Gellius' day, Granius Licinianus.[18] Clearly, the *Atrium Libertatis* was a building housing public administration, in which a survey of the population and the territorium was kept.[19]

Caesar had a project in mind for it, probably developed no later than 47 BC when he commissioned Varro to organise a library.[20] But a library building was never actually completed on that occasion. It was not until ten years later that the library in the *Atrium Libertatis* was founded, this time by Asinius Pollio.[21] It is commonly presumed that it was a realisation of the Varronian project because 'Varro is said to have been the only living person who was given a portrait there', as if to honour him as the *spiritus rector* (driving force).[22] If this inference is correct, it means that Caesar had already planned a fundamental reorganisation of the entire institution of the *Atrium Libertatis*. In fact, according to Suetonius, he

proposed to reduce the civil law to a reasonable compass, and out of that immense and undigested mass of statutes to extract the best and most necessary parts into a few books; to make as large a collection as possible of works in the Greek and Latin languages, for the public use; the province of providing and putting them in proper order being assigned to Marcus Varro.[23]

Without doubt his idea was based on establishing some relationship between state archives and books, and the need for accessible order. By adding

---

[18] Granius Licinianus, 28.35–6; Moatti 1993: 84–5.
[19] For archives in general, see Memelsdorff 1890 especially 6–8; Dziatzko 1895; Cencetti 1940 especially 26–9; Dibelius 1950; for cadastres see Nicolet 1988 and Culham 1989;. Cic. *Arch.* 8 is a good example for using anagraphical registers during a hearing.
[20] Isid. *Etym.* 6.5.1; Suet. *Iul.* 44; Fernández Uriel and Rodríguez Valcárcel 2006.
[21] For the building, see Castagnoli 1946, Coarelli 1993a, 1993b and 1999d: 6–9; for the library, see Fehrle 1986: 50–61.
[22] Plin. *HN* 7.115 '... *Varronis, in bibliotheca quae prima in orbe ab Asinio Pollione publicata Romae est, unius viventis posita imago est.*' For Varro, see Griffin 1994: 701–7.
[23] Suet. *Iul.* 44. *ius ciuile ad certum modum redigere atque ex immensa diffusaque legum copia optima quaeque et necessaria in paucissimos conferre libros; bibliothecas Graecas Latinasque quas maximas posset publicare, data Marco Varroni cura comparandarum ac digerendarum.*

'bibliothecae Graecae simul atque Latinae'[24] a further type of text was to be added for the first time to the administrative files.[25]

Pollio did not stop here. He extended the original project by adding portraits of the authors – *'additis auctorum imaginibus in atrio'* – according to Pliny an innovation of Pollio.[26] This recalls Varro's *Hebdomades vel de imaginibus libri quindecim*, a picture book of 700 portraits accompanied by epigrams, published to coincide with the opening in 39 BC.[27] We do not know what Varro's illustrations looked like; if they were clipeus portraits of the kind known from late antique book illustrations,[28] they would have been similar to Pollio's portrait gallery which probably also took the form of clipei. All in all, it was a combined database of text and illustration.

Caius Asinius Pollio was 37 years old. He had just triumphed over the Dalmatians when he completed his project. As a result he could offer even more. He put on show art treasures funded from the booty – *'de manubiis magnificentissimum instruxerat'*.[29] Pliny listed them in his catalogues, extracting the titles from the inscriptions.[30] The collection of books was complemented with a collection of works of art, that was not only noted by Pliny, but also visited and examined by a larger public (*laudatur*). These *monumenta sua* – which means Pollio's – comprised war booty and became tangible documents of history, especially of Pollio's history who, as Pliny put it, 'just as he was a man of fierce passion, so he wanted his monuments to be seen' (*ut fuit acris vehementiae sic quoque spectari monumenta sua voluit*).[31] Appropriately enough he also wrote his own historical account, which will have had a place of honour in his library.

For the first time, then, we have here assembled all the main components of an enlarged centre of information. Like the Forum of Trajan, this was no profane administrative edifice. The label *monumenta* alludes to the traditional exhibitions of art put on in sanctuaries, like the famous *Monumenta Catuli* at the Temple of *Fortuna huiusce diei*.[32] The *Atrium Libertatis* was a *templum*, even if the day of its consecration in Ovid's *Fasti* 4, 623–4 is given incorrectly. Not without sarcasm Ovid laments that admission was refused

---

[24] Isid. *Etym.* 6.5.2.
[25] For the combination of books and documents, see Rodríguez Valcárcel 2006–7; for Egyptian archives as a case in point, see Burkhalter 1990.
[26] Isid. *Etym.* 6. 5. 2 and Plin. *HN* 35.10.   [27] Gell. 3.10.17.
[28] Like e.g. in Weitzmann 1959: 122–4 pl. 60.   [29] Isid. *Etym.* 6.5.2; André 1949.
[30] Plin. *HN* 36.23–5 and 36.33–4; Becatti 1957; Sellers 1896 index s.v. Asinius Pollio with commentary.
[31] Plin. *HN* 36.33–4; see Zecchini 1982 about Pollio's historiographical work.   [32] Gros 1995.

to his *docta libella* by Libertas.[33] For most of the juridical acts executed there, the sacral nature of the space was essential.[34]

This brand-new functional complex was closely linked to the political slogan of *publicatio*, literally 'making public'. The sources do not talk about *bibliotheca publica*, but report that *bibliotheca publicata est*, that what was hitherto closed to the public was now made accessible. For the first time a library claimed to have made '*ingenia hominum – rem publicam*', a public business. *Publicatio* had been a hot political topic in the late Republic, and Caesar had taken a definite stance in his testamentary *publicatio* of his *horti*, making his gardens open to the public.[35] Yet in essence, the discourse did not aim at a democratisation of enjoyment of art. Rather, in my opinion, it was about using the state archives.[36] They were vitally important in political life, for the preparation for lawsuits. But access was regulated by personal connections. This applied even to those in positions of authority. Cato the Younger spent five talents when he was quaestor, in order to get copies of fiscal documents in the archives, and to put an end to the abuse of bribing employees.[37] In all archives it was the same game. Cicero complained that as a consequence the laws were what the attendants wished them to be: *eae leges sunt, quas apparitores nostri volunt, a librariis petimus*. The *apparitores* were doubtless acting on behalf of the most influential people.[38] Cicero, when preparing a political speech he had to deliver in Olympia, gives us an idea of the annoyance. In a series of letters to Atticus, he laments the impossibility of gaining access to state documents concerning a diplomatic mission of Mummius, but he finds it just as difficult to trace rare historical works with the help of his friends.[39] Access to information was in the hands of groups who maintained their importance by controlling access to texts. This powerplay by a few was broken by Caesar through *publicatio*. What made it so remarkable is that this power was not limited to archival material but extended to various types of texts, to what we call literature. Nevertheless, I suppose that much of the contents of the first public libraries was not

---

[33] See Ov. *Tr.* 3.1.71–2 *nec me, quae doctis patuerunt prima libellis, atria Libertatis tangere passa sua est.*

[34] Gros 2001b: 112–13, underlining the latent sacrality of such spaces 108–9; see also Kroll 1926 for the Atrium's sacred aspect which is denied by Wendel 1949: 414–16.

[35] Cic. *Phil.* 2.109.

[36] For archival practice in general, see Posner 1972 and Mantovani 2000; for more, see Cencetti 1940, Nicolet 1988: 135–6, Williamson 1995 and Moatti 2003.

[37] Plut. *Cat. Min.* 16 and 18; Culham 1989: 113–14, also about Cicero's problems.

[38] Cic. *Leg.* 3.20.36.

[39] Cic. *Att.* 13.30, 32, 33.5.4; *Att.* 13.33.3 on searching for books. Cicero needs a written permission for using Atticus' library when he is absent: Cic. *Att.* 4.14.1; see Steinby 1956: 545–55 and more generally Marshall 1976: 254 and Fehrle 1986: 54–7.

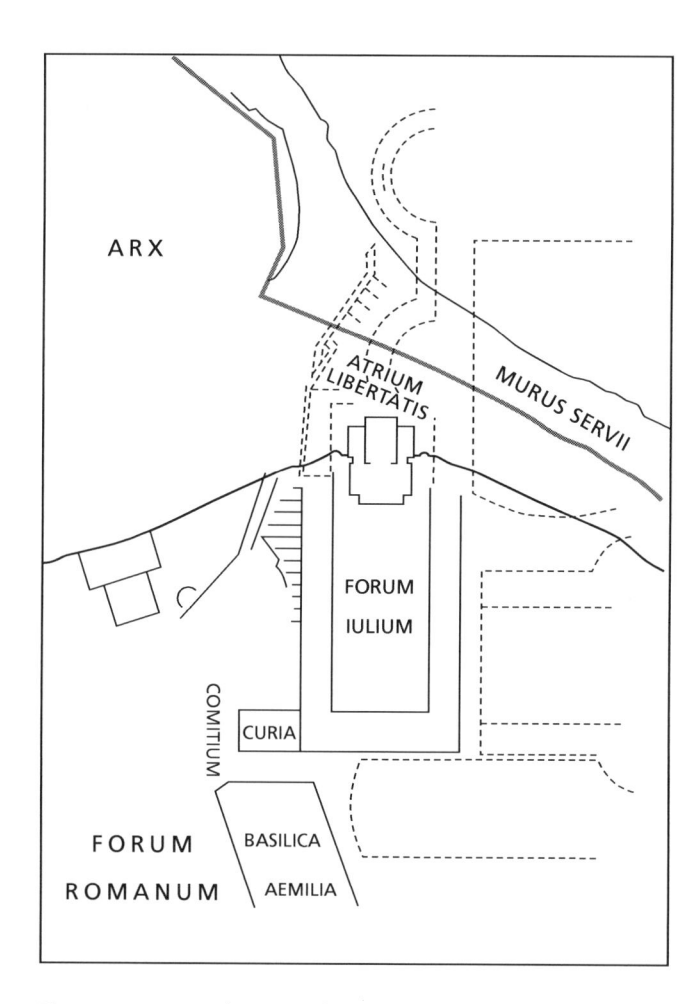

Figure 16.3 Rome, location of the *Atrium Libertatis*

Alexandrine poetry anyway, but historiographic and rhetorical works, that were in constant demand. The borderline between documents and literature is fluid.

The architecture of this information centre is as obscure as its location, which we do not know more than approximately (and even this has been the subject of debate).[40] If we accept the traditional location to the north of the *Forum Iulium*, it must have been destroyed in AD 95 in order to create space for the Forum of Trajan (Fig. 16.3). At least, the vicinity

---

[40] Cic. *Att.* 4.16.8 (July 54 BC) *usque ad Atrium Libertatis explicaremus* about the project, see Castagnoli 1949, *contra* Purcell 1993 who is disproved by Coarelli 1994: 65 and 1999d: 6–9.

of the *Forum Iulium* makes sense. The Forum was after all a place of jurisdiction, and documents from the archives would frequently have had to be at hand – especially for divorce proceedings, if we are to trust Ovid.[41]

The Temple of Apollo and the *Bibliotheca Tiberiana*

Augustus completed the *Forum Iulium*[42] and at once started work on the construction of law courts which were visibly connected to his person, the *Forum Augustum*.[43] Just a few years later, in 28 BC, the same desire to stamp Rome's cityscape with his own public institutions, led him to add a porticus '*cum bibliotheca Latina Graecaque*', a second public library for the city, to the Temple of Apollo on the Palatine.[44] The plan of the libraries on the *Forma Urbis Romae* shows the successor building from the time of Domitian, but what remains from the Augustan building does not seem to have looked much different (Fig. 16.4).[45]

It has been suspected that compared to the Greek department the shelves reserved for Latin texts had rather a lot of spare capacity, even if they were not entirely empty.[46] Instead, the library seems to have been filled with important '*auctores eloquentiae*', like the political attorney Hortensius, accompanied from the time of Tiberius by Germanicus and Drusus.[47] Although Tiberius insisted that they were only to receive the usual author's portraits for their *eloquentia*,[48] their writings were surely more of a documentation of their political activities and only to a lesser extent literary treasures. Placing their portraits '*supra capita columnarum*' flanking the '*simulacrum Apollinis*' was in fact a political statement. The information comes from the *Tabula Hebana*.[49]

---

[41] Ov. *Ars am.* 1.81–8; for further juridical uses, see Maiuro 2010.
[42] *Res Gestae Divi Augusti* 4.20.3.   [43] Neudecker 2010 with a selection from the vast literature.
[44] Suet., *Aug.* 29; Dio Cass., 53.1.3.
[45] Gros 1993 and Palombi 1993; for a quick overview, see Balensiefen 2002; for the actual state of knowledge, confronted with the design on the *Forma Urbis*, see Iacopi and Tedone 2005/2006.
[46] Hor. *Epist.* 1.3.15–20 about Greek texts copied by the plagiator Celsus; Ov. *Tr.* 3.1.59 for Latin texts; Horsfall 1993 for inadequacies of the Latin department.
[47] Castagnoli 1949, Sengelin 1983: 189, and Neudecker 2004: 297.   [48] Tac. *Ann.* 2. 83.
[49] For the *Tabula Hebana*, dated to 19–20 AD and containing part of the SC de Pisone, see full text in Minto and Coli 1947, especially '*in porticu quae est ad Apollinis in eo templo in quo senatus haberi solet... viri illustris ingeni Germanici Caesaris et Drusi Germanici patris eius naturalis, Ti. Caesaris Aug. fratris, qui ipse quoque fecundi ingeni fuit, imagines ponantur supra capita columnarum quibus simulacrum Apollinis tegitur,*' and see below n. 50.

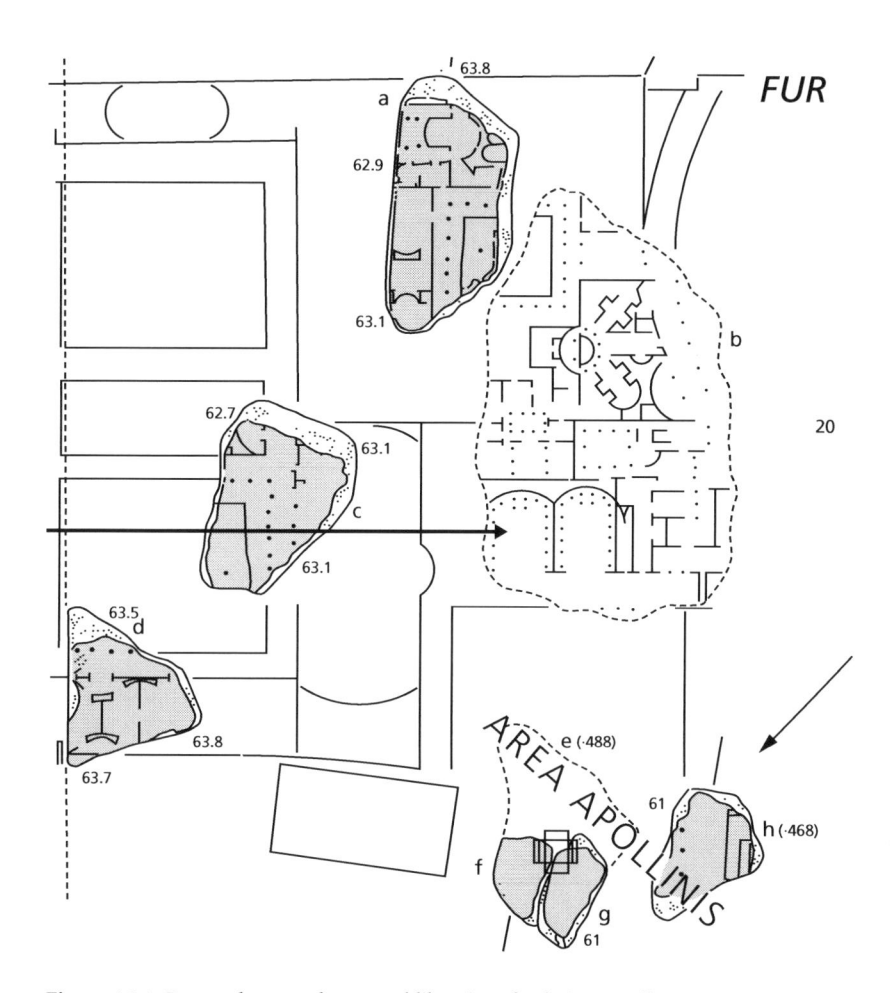

Figure 16.4 Rome, the sacred area and libraries of Palatine Apollo

Meetings of the senate and elections of the *decuriae iudicum* were organised here by Augustus on a regular basis.[50] For this reason the library is called a '*templum*' in some of the documents. The *Tabula Siarensis*, which reports the '*Senatus consultum de Pisone*' from the year 20 AD, was documented and signed here '*in porticu quae est ad Apollinis*'.[51] Copies were to be preserved amongst the '*tabulae publicae*'. Presumably the library

---

[50] See e.g. Tac. *Ann.* 2.37 and in general Suet., *Aug.* 29 '*iam senior saepe etiam senatum habuit decuriasque iudicum recognovit*' for juridical sessions; for the Senate, see Thompson 1981: 355, and Moatti 1993: 131; for the political significance of the space, see Bonnefond-Coudry 1989 and 1995.

[51] For the *Tabula Siarensis*, see Eck, Caballos and Fernández 1996.

behind the porticus was the place to keep them, alongside a copy of the *Tabula Hebana* which contains the *rogatio* of the senate about those portraits. At all events, the institution of this library had a strong political flavour. Augustus had established a library primarily dedicated to legal writing.[52] Significantly, the Sibylline Books, perhaps the most important documents belonging to the Roman state, were kept by Augustus in the base of the cult statue of Apollo in the temple.[53]

In this '*delubrum Apollinis*' was exhibited a collection of Greek masterworks '*ex manubiis*'[54] (from booty) which we may dub '*Monumenta Augusti*', by analogy with Republican usage. The whole sanctuary became a place of *memoria*, a historically pregnant archive of books, documents, portraits and works of art. And yet, the library right in the centre of the palace was accessible to private citizens, open for any reader to inspect – '*lecturis inspicienda patent*', as Ovid writes.[55] It was in easy reach of anyone who lived on the Palatine or had any business being there. During the forties of the second century, the young Marcus Aurelius, vacationing in the countryside, reported to Fronto in Rome that he had read two speeches by the elder Cato, obviously rare finds, which he is very proud of having located.[56] Fronto, he surmises, will immediately order his slave to go and find them in the Palatine library – '*vade quantum potes, de Apollinis bibliotheca has mihi orationes adporta*' – but in vain, because Marcus himself has taken the books away with him to the villa. Fronto would therefore be forced to turn to the librarian of the *Tiberiana*, and to bribe him.[57] With the money, the librarian and Marcus on his return would go out to 'paint the town red' that evening.

Marcus could easily have met Gellius in the *Bibliotheca Tiberiana*, as both were of more or less the same age. When Gellius once happened to be sitting with his teacher Apollinaris, and a few others known to one or other of them '*et quidam alii mihi aut illi familiaris*' exactly in that library, again by pure chance a book was brought with the title '*Marci Catonis Nepotis*'. And again an erudite discussion ensued, the result of which was confirmed later through the consultation of the '*Laudationes Funebres*' and the '*Liber Commentarius de familia Porcia*'.[58]

---

[52] Schol. Iuv. 1.128 '*bibliothecam iuris civilis et liberalium studiorum in templo Apollinis Palatini*', see Tuori 2010: 52.
[53] Suet. *Aug.* 31.1.　　[54] Zanker 1983.　　[55] Ov. *Tr.* 3.1.9.　　[56] Fronto, *Ep.* pp. 68–9 N.
[57] For the bribing of librarians, see Fedeli 1984: 165–8; Piacente 1988.　　[58] Gell. 13.20.1.

The *Templum Pacis*

Within the *Bibliotheca Tiberiana* such lexicographical works were obviously not to be found.[59] For complex research there were better places. Again Gellius tells us, some other time when he was eagerly searching – (*studiose quaesivimus*) – for the *Commentarium de Proloquiis* by the learned Lucius Aelius, he found it in '*Pacis bibliotheca*': the book did not answer his questions, but he was keen to tell us the story all the same.[60] Special researches and controls were common, and fussy readers were much at home particularly in the *Templum Pacis*. At the very least, even 'Trebellius Pollio', self-appointed composer of the *Historia Augusta*, seems to have read about it: 'No one in the *Templum Pacis* should be able to claim that I dubbed the queens "*tyrannos, tyrannas videlicet vel tyrannides*", and make me a laughing stock.'[61]

The *Bibliotheca Pacis* was part of the sanctuary or *templum* of the goddess Pax. A lot about its architecture has become clear in recent years (Fig. 16.5).[62]

The sanctuary was built in 71 to 75 AD by Vespasian and reconstructed by Severus after a fire under Commodus without any major changes to the layout. An area of 110 by 105 metres was enclosed on three sides by porticoes. An altar in front of the temple figured as a central monument. Two large halls were connected to the temple on the southwest side. A hall on the west end, which later has been converted into the church of Santi Cosma e Damiano, tallies well with a library-building (Fig. 16.6).[63]

From the *diverticulum* behind, an entrance leads to a stairwell; a second entrance was from the porticus. The identification of this hall as a library has recently been supported by the find of a bronze portrait of Chrysippus in the west portico (Fig. 16.7). It measures no more than 14 cm, just like the authors' portraits from the Villa dei Papiri.[64]

---

[59] For the location of the building, Krause 1993; see Galen's newly found text and discussion in Jones 2009, *contra* Tucci 2009b.
[60] Gell. 16.8.2 making us believe that all his adventures in Rome's libraries really happened.
[61] SHA *Tyr. Trig.* 31.10.
[62] Coarelli 1999d, La Rocca 2001: 195–207, Rizzo 2001: 234–44, Meneghini 2009: 79–97, and Meneghini 2010.
[63] For the library rooms, see the first fundamental research by Biasiotti and Whitehead 1924–5; Colini 1937; Castagnoli and Cozza 1956–8; recently Tucci 2009a with a doubtful reconstruction.
[64] See Papini 2004 and 2005; Meneghini 2009 fig. 106 for the philosophers' busts from Villa dei Papiri.

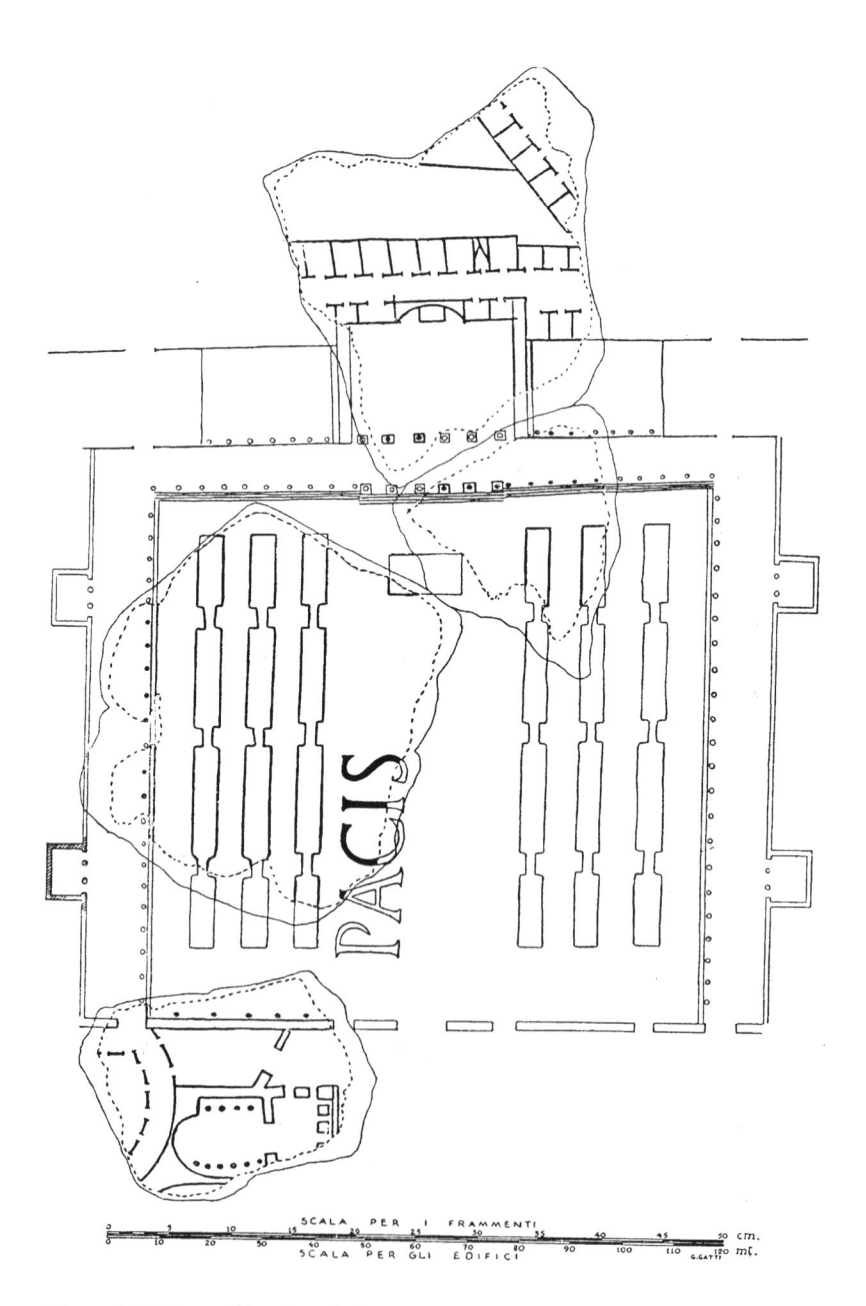

Figure 16.5 Rome, *Templum Pacis*

Much better known and perfectly visible is the eastern outer wall of SS. Cosma e Damiano, in fact the library's eastern wall, which corresponds to the inner wall of the hall next to the temple. This hall was open towards the porticus with a line of columns, and light could stream in through

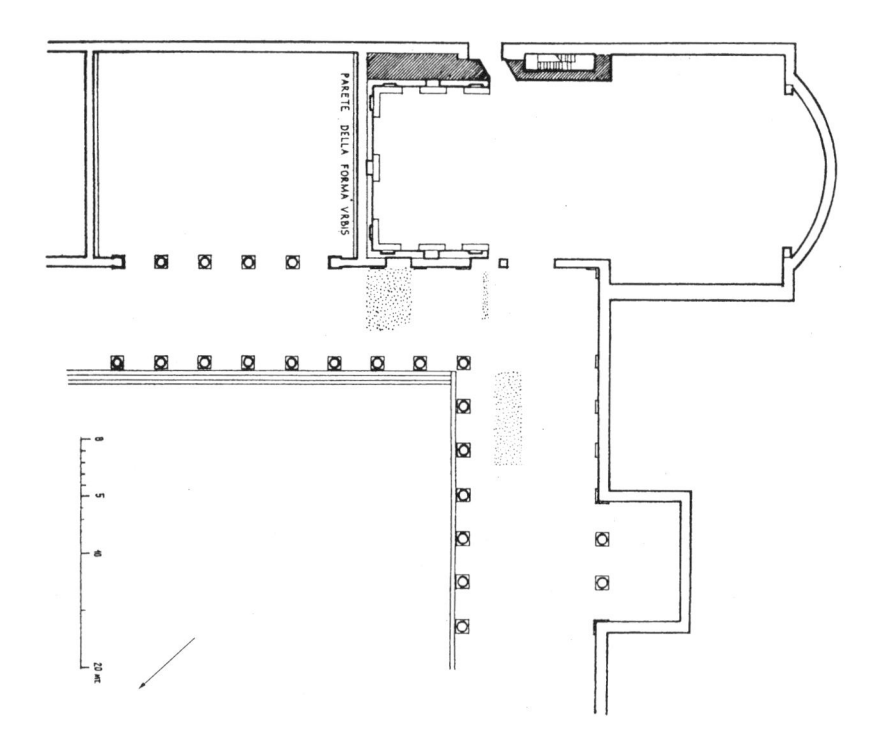

Figure 16.6 Rome, library and map room of *Templum Pacis*

Figure 16.7 Portrait of Chrysippus from the area of the *Bibliotheca Pacis*

openings above the roof of the porticus. The wall is where the 150 slabs of the Severan *Forma Urbis Romae* were fixed, forming a map of the city with the scale of 1:240.[65] Some of the fragments which have been newly found were part of maps which are dated earlier and show remarkable details. The boundary of the *Regio* near the *Circus Maximus* is marked in red, indicating administrative information. Other slabs are more detailed than the Severan plan and readable from close up, particularly the references to properties, which are totally missing on the Severan plan. All versions derive from a cadastral plan which covered the complete administrative territory of the city of Rome.

Like all monumental inscriptions, the marble map is not the original document, but a monument celebrating the efficiency of the public authority which was responsible for the overview of the territory, the *Praefectura Urbi*. There we would find the real register of residents, organised by *vici*, there the *domini insularum* notified their *professiones*.[66] But the central seat of the *Praefectura Urbi* was located '*in Tellure*', around the temple of Tellus about 200 metres to the south east.[67] Therefore, it is rather improbable that a cadastral office – in Greek called βιβλιοθήκη τῶν ἐγκτήσεων[68] – was located within the *Templum Pacis*.[69] This does not in any way diminish the significance of the Marble Plan as an indicator to those archives. In some way, the plan could even have been used as a source of information. The fourth-century *Notitia Urbis Romae* and the *Curiosum Urbis Romae* evidently compiled information from such plans, as is shown by identical entries.[70]

In 1952, slabs of the opposite wall were found.[71] Filippo Coarelli deduces from a few traces of red colour that there was a second map, the '*Italia picta*'. The idea remains a hypothesis even if we would like to adopt it – after all, at the time of Varro there existed such a map on the temple of Tellus.[72] If Coarelli is right, then the incised 'cadastre of the Urbs' would have been combined with a 'painted overlook of Italia' as a significant monument.

---

[65] Published by Carettoni, Colini, Cozza and Gatti 1955; Rodríguez Almeida 1981; see also Castagnoli and Cozza 1956–8 for the wall; for recent excavations and research, see Meneghini 2009; for the marble plan, see Meneghini and Santangeli Valenzani 2006; Meneghini 2007 with literature about the cadastre, Trimble 2007, Wilson 2007: 292, and Wallace-Hadrill 2008: 290–312.

[66] Nicolet 1988: 173–9, Coarelli 1997, and Chastagnol 1997.

[67] Coarelli 1999d; for the *Praefectura* see Gros 2001b: 113, and Palombi 1997: 149–68.

[68] Posner 1972: 147.

[69] Coarelli 2009b: 73–4 identifies the hall with the prefect Fabius Cilo's bureau.

[70] Compare the lists in Nordh 1949.

[71] See photos in Carettoni, Colini, Cozza and Gatti 1955: 194 figs. 26–7.

[72] Coarelli 1999b: 69, see Varro *Rust.* 1.2.1–3; for the plan in the temple, see Nicolet 1988: 257.

Archives, books and sacred space in Rome 327

Figure 16.8 Rome, *Templum Pacis*

The *Templum Pacis* did not only offer information about the city and specialist scholarship. Pliny exploited it for his lists of sculptors and painters, as he did the material from the *Atrium Libertatis*.[73] He reports from notes taken during his visits and claims that most people will be kept from such scientific observations through duties and business[74] (and according to Juvenal also by amorous adventures).[75] Even Procopius still has some memory of the sanctuary as an art historical reference collection. He does recall 'some works of Phidias, or of Lysippos; also a second one by Phidias, according to the inscription'.[76] We can speculate on how the collection of classical masterpieces was exhibited and imagine them in the porticoes, which are five steps high above the area, and form galleries of 12.50 metres in depth, subdivided in their length by marble barriers. Behind these barriers it was possible to display statues and paintings safely (Fig. 16.8).

Flavius Josephus went to visit the new sanctuary, and he gives us an explanation about the collection, which fits well with Pliny's account:[77] 'After

---

[73] For *Templum Pacis*, see La Rocca 2001: 195–207 and Bravi 2009 for all testimonies; Sellers 1896 Index s.v. Rome Peace for Pliny alone; for Pliny and his 'collections in paper', see Carey 2003: 75–101 and Citroni Marchetti 2005.
[74] Plin. *HN* 37.27.   [75] Juv. 9.22–6 and Schol.   [76] Procop. *Goth.* 4.21.
[77] Joseph. *BJ* 7.5.7, not without irony, see Mason 2005; compare Plin. *HN* 36.101 ' all the wonders of the world piled up in Rome'.

the triumph Vespasian built the sanctuary of Eirene... and decorated it with paintings and statues. Everything was gathered together and kept in this sanctuary, for which people hitherto had to travel all over the world.' It is not by chance that the exhibition resembles the collections of sculptures in villas. There, peristyle gardens created a pseudo-Greek world through copies. Here, the original inventory of the world's masterpieces was constituted in the context of public libraries. Taken together with maps, cadastres and book collections, the sanctuary actually represented a gigantic archive.[78]

In AD 192 the sanctuary was burnt down.[79] The fire cost Galen the loss of unpublished work of his – beside some rather expensive pharmaceutical material – inducing him to compose a treatise about how it feels to lose unpublished texts. The manuscripts were burnt ἐν τῇ κατὰ τὴν ἱερὰν ὁδὸν ἀποθήκῃ 'in the apotheke by the Via Sacra'; Galen had to start again and did it even better than before.[80] Unfortunately the complete text, which has only recently been found, does not definitely end the disputes about the exact location of Galen's books.[81] In Greek, libraries are often called ἀποθῆκαι,[82] and this one had an entrance in fact quite near the Via Sacra; but tabernae, too, are called ἀποθῆκαι. I suppose that the ἀποθήκη on the Via Sacra does in fact refer to the public library, where ἑτέρων τε πολλῶν βιβλία were burnt among which had been medical texts.[83]

If all this is true, the existence of a section of medical literature in the library gives us a further lead. Domenico Palombi[84] has shown that the area of *Carinae ad Telluris* bordering to the south had been a medical centre since the late Republic. Lenaeus, who was the first to write a Latin treatise on pharmacology, lectured there.[85] He also translated the medical library of Mithridates, which had been brought there by Pompey.[86] These books seem to have been incorporated into the *Bibliotheca Pacis* where Gellius was able to quote from them. Galen had placed such books ready at hand, when he – like

---

[78] Plin. *HN* 36.84 reports on the statues' origin from the Domus Aurea and their *publicatio* in old Republican tradition; about the imperialistic aspect, Murphy 2004; see Plin. *HN* 3.66–7 for a statistical representation of Rome's greatness.

[79] Dio Cass.72. 24.1–2.

[80] Gal. *Comp. Med.* 1 (Kühn 13, 362) and Gal. *Libr. Propr.* 2 (Kühn 19, 19); for Galen, see De Filippis Cappai 1993: 118–51.

[81] The newly discovered text has been published by Boudon-Millot 2007.

[82] See Posner 1972: 147; Houston 2003 thinks of *horrea* as the storeroom of Galen's books because 'apotheke is not a bibliotheke'.

[83] Gal. *Comp. Med.* 1 (Kühn 13, 362); Tucci 2008 excludes the *Templum*'s library as storeroom, but see Herodian 1.14. 2 for private storerooms within the *Templum Pacis*.

[84] Palombi 1997–8.   [85] Suet. *Gram.* 15.

[86] Plin. *HN* 25.3.5–7; also Gellius works with this library, see Gell. 17. 16. 1–4; see De Filippis Cappai 1993 for medical culture in Rome in general.

other medics – gave spectacular lectures on anatomy in the dissecting room of the *Templum Pacis*.[87] His hands-on experiments, by the way, soon led to an acrimonious challenge to the authority of these books, as Galen demonstrated their shortcomings.

Medical texts may have been placed in an important specialised section of the *Bibliotheca Pacis*. If so, one could pursue this medical aspect in the light of a recent article by Lorenzo Perilli[88] which enquires into the role medical texts played in the formation of libraries. Some of the earliest collections of texts were medical records kept in the sanctuaries of Asclepius, like those written by Rufus of Ephesus in the imperial period.[89]

Libraries and sacred space

At the same time, another type of archive developed in sanctuaries: lists of votive offerings. It is perhaps in this long tradition that the public libraries of Rome are in the end to be viewed, always combined with art collections, which were actually collections of votives. The sacred space seems to have been the obvious place for government archives, museum archives and archives of knowledge.

Rome's imperial sanctuaries seem first of all to be spaces for the representation of power. The *Templum Pacis*, Pollio's *Atrium Libertatis*, the sanctuary of Apollo and the sacred Forum of Trajan, and also the *Porticus Octaviae* with its library, were explicitly constructed *ex manubiis*. Nominally, they were the property of a deity, and what holds all the objects in any archive together is unity of ownership. Consequently, granting access becomes a sign of power. Access to state documents is never taken for granted. The author of the Life of Aurelian in the *Historia Augusta* is not writing nonsense when he invents the following story: the *Praefectus Urbi* is said to have pointed out to him the *Ephemeridas* and promised that he would see to it that the Ulpian library would provide him with the linen books on which Aurelian's activities were recorded each day: '*curabo autem ut tibi ex Ulpia Bibliotheca et libri lintei proferantur*'.[90] The *princeps* also decided whose literary works were admitted into public libraries.[91] Ovid did not only think of his future literary fame, but also about the rehabilitation of his status, when

---

[87] Gal. *Libr. Propr.* 2 (Kühn 19, 21–2); see Schlange-Schöningen 2003: 204–5 and Nutton 2000.
[88] Perilli 2006.   [89] See translations in Ullmann 1978.
[90] SHA *Aurel.* 1.7–10 and SHA *Tac.* 8.1; about permissions for the consultation of archives in Alexandria, see Posner 1972: 152–4, and Cencetti 1940: 46–7.
[91] Purcell 1988 for power over archives; censorship over libraries, see Canfora 1993 and Suet. *Iul.* 56; on the emperor's personnel, see Houston 2002 and Neudecker 2004: 297 and 300.

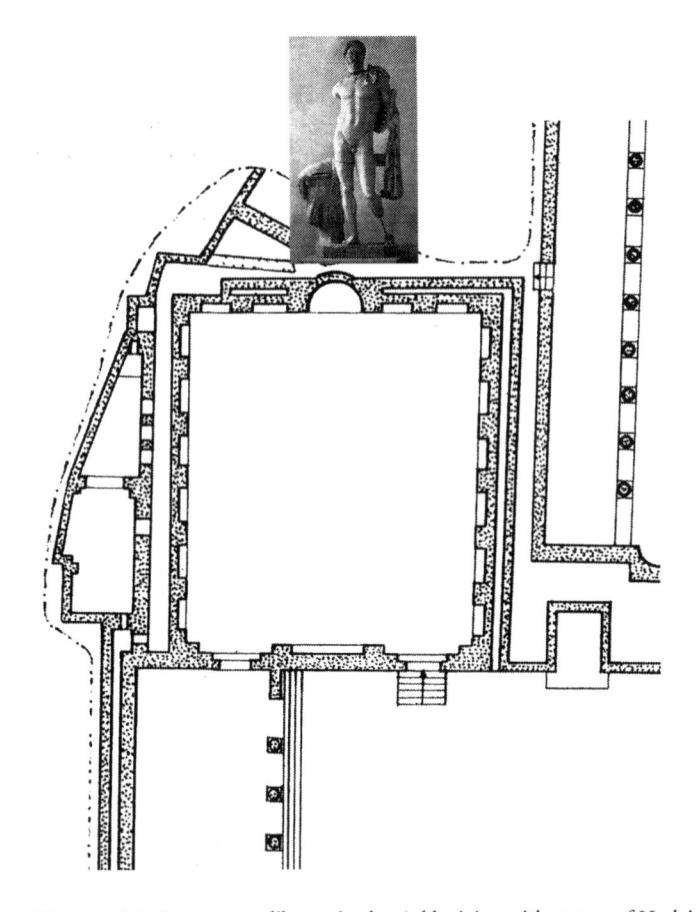

Figure 16.9 Pergamum, library in the *Asklepieion* with statue of Hadrian

he begged Tiberius to let his works have entry into the *Palatina*.[92] He insists on the fundamental difference between '*statio publica*' and '*privatus locus*' of all books. Whoever has the power to decide about access to documents, also has the right to destroy them with all the consequences that follow. So Hadrian had the *syngraphai* of tax liabilities burnt right in the middle of the Forum of Trajan, as Trajan had done before.[93] This leads one to believe that administrative documents, which might be useful at the time, were also kept there in case they were needed again.

The library on the Palatine was under the protection of Apollo whose statue is named in the *Senatus consultum Pisonianum*.[94] Tacitus, instead,

---

[92] Ov. *Tr.* 3.1.
[93] For Trajan, see *CIL* 6.967; for Hadrian, see SHA *Hadr.* 7. 6; see also SHA *Aurel.* 39. 3.
[94] See above n. 49 and n. 51.

mentions a statue of Augustus, which a scholiast explains as a portrait of Augustus in the shape of Apollo.[95] Since the first Republican archives were deposited in the *Atrium Libertatis*, it was important to make the gods responsible for their safety. They offered religious protection for the words. During the Empire, the *princeps* appropriated the gods' role as the keeper and publisher of books and archives. The emperor alone ruled on the basis of universal knowledge. His statue, like that of Hadrian in the *Asklepieion* of Pergamum (Fig. 16.9), was soon to be found at the centre of library halls, as a sort of heavenly guardian of books. Political and cultural lives met each other in the protected archives of intelligence.

[95] Schol. Hor. *Epist.* 1.3.17; Serv. *Georg.* 4.10; Porph. Hor. *Epist.* 1.3.17; Tac. *Ann.* 2.38, 83; Suet. *Aug.* 29; see Sengelin 1983: 178 for Apollo, and Juv. 1.128 '*iurisque peritus Apollo*'.

17 | Visual supplementation and metonymy in the Roman public library

DAVID PETRAIN

The Hellenistic age saw the creation of a range of spaces designed both to store and to showcase collections of books, from the elaborate royal libraries in Alexandria and Pergamum to the more modest ones associated with local gymnasia. Romans responded to this fashion, and from at least the second century BC onward installed in their own homes collections that, as often as not, had been taken as war booty from the Greek east. By the end of the first century BC Rome had acquired public libraries to rival those of the Hellenistic dynasts.[1]

The appearance of public libraries in Augustan Rome seems to have coincided with the development of a new type of building, one that provided facilities for displaying collections of Greek and Latin literature in a form both visually striking and ideologically pointed. Simply by creating a building type specifically designed to house their libraries, the Romans broke with Greek practice. To the best of our knowledge, the earlier libraries of the Hellenistic age had in essence been complexes of several common, pre-existing types of structure that fulfilled the functions of a library only in combination: small, undistinguished storage rooms housed the texts themselves; these opened out onto a portico, perhaps with an associated exedra, that provided light and space for reading; a larger hall nearby would offer a venue for the library's users to meet, converse, or dine. None of these structures is individually distinctive, and it can be difficult to infer from an excavated floorplan alone that a given grouping of storeroom, portico, and hall had once functioned together as a library. No excavated Hellenistic gymnasium, for instance, has yet yielded definitive architectural evidence for the presence of a library, though we know that gymnasium libraries existed.[2] Even the great library at Pergamum has proved elusive.[3]

---

[1] The history of the ancient library has been told many times, though in recent years much of the evidence used to reconstruct this history has been undergoing critical re-evaluation (cf. the present volume, *passim*). Despite its title ("Römische Bibliotheken"), Strocka 1981 is an excellent analysis of the development of the library's architecture in the Greek as well as the Roman world; Fedeli 1988 and Blanck 1992: 133–214 survey the literary and archeological evidence, while Höpfner 2002f offers chapters each devoted to a single library. Casson 2001 is an accessible popular account.

[2] Strocka 2000: 161; cf. Scholz 2004: 125–6.   [3] See Coqueugniot (this volume).

At the instigation of Julius Caesar and later Augustus, however, the public library in Rome emerged from architectural anonymity and innovatively combined the functions of storage room, reading area, and meeting hall in a single, recognizable blueprint.[4] In effect these buildings monumentalized the storage of papyrus rolls by incorporating them into an impressive architectural setting. The following chapter will explore what impact this innovative layout may have had on its viewers, how it converted the prestige of famous authors and literary works into an immediately accessible experience. Roman public libraries, I suggest, spurred the creation of a new, visual language for communicating ideas about the organization and significance of literature. They established systematic links between authors and specific visual cues such as portraits, links so close that the portraits themselves became objects of interest, even longing, and could be manipulated for ideological ends.

The state of the evidence usually precludes us from inquiring closely into the layout and ornamentation of any one library, but in the case of Augustus' library on the Palatine just enough information survives to give us a glimpse of the varied pictorial and inscribed material that once adorned this space. I begin with a case study and explore an inscription dedicated in the Palatine library and how its meaning may have been affected by the works, both Greek and Latin, that surrounded it. I continue with the feature of the imperial libraries that perhaps had the most wide-ranging consequences in the visual realm, namely their use of imposing cabinets or *armaria* as conspicuous, even constitutive elements in their decorative programme. A final section uses the debate attending the decision to place a portrait of Germanicus in the Palatine library as a window on to the complex meanings a library's decoration could express.

Greek and Latin letters in the Palatine library

Completed by Augustus around 28 BC, the Palatine library is one of the earliest surviving examples of the new monumental building type, despite the fact that the remains currently visible belong not to the original structure

---

[4] For the innovations of the Roman library vis-à-vis Hellenistic models, see the standard accounts at Strocka 1981; Blanck 1992: 191–214. Höpfner 1996 suggests that Hellenistic libraries, particularly the library in Pergamum, already showed key features of the putative "Roman" type, but it seems rash to draw any conclusions on the basis of reconstructions of this problematic space; cf. the response of Strocka (2000) and Coqueugniot (this volume).

but to a Domitianic rebuilding.[5] In this later incarnation we see a double floorplan with two identical but separate halls – one for Greek and one for Latin, presumably – that were placed side by side and opened out onto the same portico, but did not communicate one with the other.[6] The contours of the previous, Augustan building are hard to trace. One recent reconstruction outfits the library of Augustus with just one hall, as opposed to Domitian's two,[7] but the question is not yet definitively decided.

Regardless of the number of halls, literary and epigraphic testimonia make it certain that the Palatine library did house from its inception distinct Latin and Greek collections.[8] The way in which the structure expressed this linguistic and cultural divide may have changed over time: if Domitian truly did double its floorplan and thus spatially segregate the languages for the first time, he would simply have rendered more salient a contrast already present in the original conception of the project. The emphasis on comparison and competition between the two literatures is an unmistakable feature, certainly the fruit of deliberate reflection on how a public library should function in the city of Rome. When Julius Caesar conceived the project of creating what was to have been Rome's first public library, he stipulated that it should house both Latin and Greek works,[9] thus setting the stage for the places of literary *synkrisis* that the libraries of Rome were destined to become.

The backdrop formed by this architectural staging of cultural contestation could guide viewers' interpretations of individual objects on display within it. According to Pliny the Elder, an old Greek inscription installed in the library on the Palatine served to demonstrate the near-identity of the Greek and Latin alphabets at an early period (*HN* 7.210):

veteres Graecas fuisse easdem paene quae nunc sint Latinae, indicio erit Delphica antiqui aeris, quae est hodie in Palatio, dono principum Minervae dicata in bibliotheca cum inscriptione tali: ΝΑΥΣΙΚΡΑΤΗΣ ΑΝΕΘΕΤΟ ΤΑΙ ΔΙΟΣ ΚΟΡΑΙ ΤΑΝ ΔΕΚΑΤΑΝ

---

[5] For an excellent, bracingly skeptical survey of the evidence pertaining to all of Rome's public libraries, see Dix and Houston 2006 (680–5 for the Palatine library).

[6] For the relevant sources see, besides Dix and Houston, Blanck 1992: 191–4 (with footnote 13 on p. 236); Iacopi and Tedone 2005/2006. Nicholls 2010a has recently reminded us that there is no direct evidence for the separation of Greek and Latin holdings into two distinct halls.

[7] Iacopi and Tedone 2005/2006 (esp. 355).

[8] The sources are helpfully collected at Lugli 1960: 109–13, to which may be added a papyrus that records an embassy received by Augustus in the temple of Apollo "in the Roman library" (ἐν τῇ Ῥωμαϊκῇ βιβλιοθήκῃ, *POxy.* 2435 *verso*, adduced in this connection by Corbier [2006: 173; first published 1992]).

[9] Suet. *Iul.* 44.2 (for Caesar's plans see Dix and Houston 2006: 673–5).

The old Greek letters were almost the same as the present Latin ones: this may be shown by an old Delphic bronze that today is on the Palatine, by a gift of the emperors dedicated to Minerva in the library, carrying the following inscription: Nausikrates dedicated to the daughter of Zeus the tithe...

Pliny's text here has had a chequered history. Leaving aside problems in the transmission of the Greek,[10] the phrase *in bibliotheca* was bracketed as spurious by Mayhoff in both editions of his Teubner text, so that Pliny would simply be locating the bronze "on the Palatine." Mayhoff does not seem to have explained his intervention, and most subsequent editors have restored the phrase.[11] I see no reason to suspect it.

Which library on the Palatine did Pliny mean? Besides Augustus' library there is just one plausible candidate, the library of the *Domus Tiberiana* on the northwest part of the hill.[12] Yet this library is first securely attested only in the middle of the next century;[13] in a recently discovered work that discusses both libraries, furthermore, Galen appears to refer to the *Domus* as a structure distinct from the Palatine.[14] It is reasonably sure that Pliny refers to the library founded by Augustus.

Let us turn to the inscription itself. At this point in the *Natural History* Pliny is detailing examples of consensus among the peoples of the inhabited world, and he cites the Delphic bronze as evidence of a general agreement to adopt a uniform writing system.[15] In the immediate context of the Palatine library and its holdings in two languages, however, I believe the inscription will have suggested an additional meaning. Its script hovering between Greek and Latin seems also to endorse, in almost overdetermined fashion, the Palatine library's project of drawing comparisons and equivalencies between the two literatures: the inscription's age lends an aura of antiquity to the project, while its provenance from Delphi seems specifically to claim

---

[10] For these, see Schilling 1977.
[11] *in bibliotheca* is retained by Winkler (responsible for the Latin text in König 1975), Schilling 1977, G. Ranucci (editor of book 7 in Barchiesi *et al.* 1982–8). Cf. the brief accounts of Mayhoff's editorial practice, and his tendency to intervene too drastically in the text, at Schilling 1977: xxi–xxii and Barchiesi *et al.* 1982–8: 1.lxviii.
[12] Dix and Houston place the Temple of Divine Augustus and its library "on or very near the Palatine," potentially giving us one more library to choose from (Dix and Houston 2006: 689, with earlier bibliography); their evidence (*ibid.*) suggests, however, that this building was at best at the foot of the Palatine, and perhaps between it and the Capitoline.
[13] Dix and Houston 2006: 690–1.
[14] ταῖς [sc. ἀποθήκαις] κατὰ τὸ Παλάτιόν τε καὶ τὴν Τιβεριανὴν καλουμένην οἰκίαν, ἐν ᾗ καὶ αὐτῇ βιβλιοθήκη τις ἦν (*περὶ ἀλυπίας* 18). The *editio princeps* is Boudon-Millot 2007. On the sense of Παλάτιον here (probably "Palatine hill" rather than "imperial palace"), see *ibid.* 104 n. 240 (the same remarks are repeated at Boudon-Millot and Jouanna 2010: 48).
[15] *gentium consensus tacitus primus omnium conspiravit ut Ionum litteris uteretur* (7.210).

the sanction of Apollo, god of poetry as well as the divinity to whom Augustus' entire complex was dedicated.[16]

Pliny's notice of the Delphic bronze offers a precious glimpse into the variety of objects that might once have adorned the halls of Rome's libraries. We know that Hellenistic gymnasia, with their associated libraries, often boasted a kaleidoscopic variety of texts and images in their decor, from statues to altars to shields carrying depictions of mythological narratives;[17] an inscription from Rhodes whose text is, unfortunately, not fully published, mentions inscribed stelai erected in the library of the island's gymnasium.[18] In Rome, lack of evidence cuts us off from the multimedia experience that the imperial libraries might have been, but Pliny's text both reminds us of what we are missing and, more importantly, suggests the dynamic relationship that could obtain between the space of the library and the objects within it. In the case of the Delphic bronze, the Palatine library focuses viewers' attention on the connection between Greek and Latin supposedly substantiated by the object.

Armaria, visual supplements, and metonymy

Though the inclusion of two literatures was a key characteristic of Rome's new imperial libraries, the feature that arguably had the greatest impact in the visual realm is the new technology for the display of books that they utilized. Ungainly and prone to damage, a roll of papyrus does not naturally lend itself to monumental display. Indeed the libraries of the Greek world had kept their holdings out of sight, the rolls collectively hidden from view in storage rooms until individually consulted by a patron. Libraries in the Greek style were thus somewhat schizophrenic places, in which the texts that constituted their avowed *raison d'être* played no part in their decoration, however sumptuous.

The Romans finessed this difficulty by housing their papyri in wooden cabinets or *armaria* that they installed in niches lining the walls of the library's main rooms. Though the *armaria* themselves do not survive, their

---

[16] At 34.14 Pliny mentions bronze cauldrons for tripods that were known as *Delphicae* "because they were mostly dedicated to the Delphic Apollo as gifts" (*quoniam donis maxime Apollini Delphico dicabantur*).
[17] See von den Hoff 2004 and Martini 2004.
[18] *SEG* 37.699. Papachristodoulou 1986, the initial publication, offers only a partial text (see page 270 for the mention of the stelai, lines 38–9 on the stone). See also Papachristodoulou 1990 (no text).

presence is implied by physical evidence from surviving niches[19] and seems confirmed by the tendency of our literary sources to associate *bibliothecae* and *armaria*, sometimes specifying that the latter are embedded in the wall.[20] The dimensions of extant niches – the Palatine library's are 1.8 m wide, 3.8 m high, 60 cm deep – give an idea of the imposing size of the cabinets, which would have been constructed of precious woods, their doors perhaps inlaid with ivory.[21] Profligate of space and utilizing a common architectural feature, the wall niche, in a novel way,[22] this ostentatious mode of book storage required a large hall and walls thick enough to receive the niches, a design that showcased the wealth and means of whoever commissioned the building.[23] The bookshelves themselves likely became one of the most striking elements in the library's decoration.

The Palatine library may serve as an example. In its Domitianic phase, the walls of each of its reading rooms are lined with a series of rectangular niches for the *armaria*, interrupted in the middle of the apsidal back wall with a larger recess meant to accommodate a cult statue.[24] A continuous podium runs under all of the niches, and provides access to them by means of a set of steps in front of each niche.[25] To judge from the better preserved remains of the libraries in Trajan's forum,[26] the interior of the Palatine library might have been unified by a marble revetment that further set off the

---

[19] See Sève 1990 (esp. 178–9): surviving niches are at least twice as deep as the length of an average papyrus roll, which implies that extra space has been left to allow the insertion of the wooden cabinets whose backing, doors, and other elements required the additional room.

[20] Association of libraries and *armaria*: Vitr. 7 *praef*. 7 (*armaria* in the library of Alexandria – evidence at least for Vitruvius' conception of a library's furnishings if not for the Alexandrian structure itself); Sen. *Tranq*. 9.6; Augustine, *Contra Cresconium* 3.29 (*posteaquam apertum est in bibliothecam, inuenta sunt ibi armaria inania*). *Armaria* embedded in walls: Plin. *Ep*. 2.17.8 (*parieti . . . in bibliothecae speciem armarium insertum est*); *Dig*. 30.41.9 (*in bibliothecis parietibus inhaerentibus*). A key passage is *Dig*. 32.52.3, 7: there the jurists distinguish different senses of *bibliotheca*, noting that the word is often synonymous with *armarium* (as at *Dig*. 30.41.9 above) but that the bequest of a library may not include *armaria* that are fixed in place because these are part of a building's structure (*si mihi proponas adhaerentia esse membro armaria vel adfixa, sine dubio non debebuntur, cum aedificii portio sint*). (On *Dig*. 32.52, see now Spallone 2008.)

[21] For the measurements see Dix and Houston 2006: 683. For the materials, cf. Sen. *Tranq*. 9.6 (*armaria e citro atque ebore*); *Dig*. 32.52.7 (*eboream bibliothecam*). Stern and Thimme reconstruct an elaborately decorated *armarium* from elements of wood, plain veneer, ivory, and bone excavated at the port of Kenchreai (2007: 281–94).

[22] On niches in Roman architecture, see Hornbostel-Hüttner 1979.

[23] For this point, see Wendel 1974: 158.

[24] The earlier, Augustan hall likewise terminates in an apse with a rectangular structure (perhaps a base) at its center, but the elevation of its walls does not survive (Iacopi and Tedone 2005/6: 353–5).

[25] Blanck 1992: 193; Dix and Houston 2006: 683.

[26] See Packer 1997: 1.120–6; Meneghini 2010: 38–40.

armaria with frames of colored stone. While the Palatine library's eventual division into two halls is an innovation virtually confined to the libraries of Rome,[27] the design of its individual halls enjoyed a much wider influence: the features of their layout that we have just touched on – rows of niches for *armaria* reached by a stepped podium, a central recess for a cult statue – recur in libraries throughout the empire,[28] a testament to the success of the Romans' solution to the problem of how to monumentalize collections of books.

Though collectively impressive, the rows of identical *armaria* that graced the library's hall would have been somewhat anonymous, insufficient on their own to communicate precisely which prestigious texts they concealed behind their doors.[29] This possibility of concealment may, indeed, have been part of the point: in his classic article "Empty shelves on the Palatine," Horsfall drew attention to the fact that the organizers of the Palatine collection might initially have found many more Greek texts to include than Latin. Wouldn't this asymmetry – a preponderance of green Loebs over red! – have stuck out like a sore thumb? Perhaps not: any numerical discrepancies, or conspicuous "empty shelves" set aside for a Latin literature not yet written, could remain hidden from view so long as the *armaria* were shut. Once promoted to the library's main hall and the viewer's immediate awareness, then, these bookshelves effaced the books and favored the introduction of supplements for them, that is, additional decorative elements that could communicate to visitors about the identity and importance of the authors whose works the *armaria* held – a visual discourse about literature that was alienated from the materiality of the book or the number of holdings in each language. We may contrast here the open shelves of Cicero's library at Antium, where no such alienation was possible because the colorful labels that provided identifying information and visual interest were attached to the papyri themselves.[30]

The type of ornament that most commonly performed the function of supplementation was the authorial portrait. Though statues and busts of authors did appear in Greek-style libraries,[31] it was only in Rome's imperial

---

[27] For possible exceptions see Blanck 1992: 205–6; Ferrari 1999.
[28] See Strocka 1981: 315–29; Blanck 1992: 168–76, 205–14.
[29] I presume that a library's *armaria* would usually be shut to protect the fragile papyri (for doors and locks on *armaria*, cf. *Der neue Pauly* s.v. armarium; *Dig.* 32.53.9, *sunt tamen quaedam, quae omnimodo legatum sequuntur: . . . armariis et loculis claustra et claves cedunt*).
[30] See *Att.* 4.4a.1; 4.5.4; 4.8.2 (with Shackleton Bailey 1965–70), with Fedeli 1988: 43 and Blanck 1992: 156. Dorandi 1984: 189–91 collects the literary and material evidence for such labels.
[31] Cf. Cic. *Att.* 4.10 (a bust of Aristotle in the library of Atticus); Strocka 1981: 299 (the Villa of the Papyri in Herculaneum).

libraries that these were deployed more systematically. An author's works and his likeness formed an indissoluble unit,[32] and when emperors added or removed authors from the imperial libraries, their actions encompassed both the authors' writings and their likenesses, as when Caligula threatened to remove the *scripta et imagines* of Virgil and Livy from all libraries.[33]

We may gauge the impression that these portraits could make on a viewer from Pliny the Elder's enthusiastic praise of Asinius Pollio for first introducing them into his library at the *Atrium Libertatis* (*HN* 35.9–10):[34]

Non est praetereundum et novicium inventum, siquidem non ex auro argentove, at certe ex aere in bibliothecis dicantur illis, quorum immortales animae in locis iisdem locuntur, quin immo etiam quae non sunt finguntur, pariuntque desideria non traditos vultus, sicut in Homero evenit. quo maius, ut equidem arbitror, nullum est felicitatis specimen quam semper omnes scire cupere, qualis fuerit aliquis. Asini Pollionis hoc Romae inventum, qui primus bibliothecam dicando ingenia hominum rem publicam fecit. an priores coeperint Alexandreae et Pergami reges, qui bibliothecas magno certamine instituere, non facile dixerim.

I should not omit a newly established practice either: in libraries they dedicate portraits – if not of gold or silver, at least of bronze – to those whose immortal spirits speak in the same places. Indeed, they even make up portraits that have no factual basis, and their desires give birth to faces that have not been handed down by tradition, as has happened in the case of Homer. Hence, as far as I'm concerned, there is no greater proof of good fortune than that everyone should always wish to know what a person looked like. In Rome this practice was established by Asinius Pollio, who was first to dedicate a library here, and in so doing to make men's genius public property. Whether the kings of Alexandria and Pergamum, who competed fiercely in setting up their libraries, had begun to do this earlier, I couldn't easily say.

Significantly, Pliny's account of the library in Pollio's Atrium occurs in a section of the *Natural History* devoted to portraiture, hard on the heels of his treatment of the wax ancestor masks displayed in the atria of noble families (*HN* 35.6–8); his one other mention of the library concerns a portrait as well, the likeness of Varro that was the only image of a man still alive on display in the Atrium (*HN* 7.115). For Pliny, the visual experience provided by the library is as important as the literary monuments to be found there, the novel *imagines* of authors as stirring as those of the ancestors once were (Pliny suggests that the latter have fallen into neglect, *HN* 35.6). The author

---

[32] For a conspectus of sources, see *TLL* 2.1957.54–72 s.v. "bibliotheca."
[33] Suet. *Cal.* 34: *sed et Vergili ac Titi Livi scripta et imagines paulum afuit quin ex omnibus bibliothecis amoveret.* Cf. id., *Tib.* 70.
[34] For the *Atrium Libertatis* library, see Dix and Houston 2006: 675–80.

portraits are a focus of emotion, inspiring longing (*desideria*) for any likeness that is missing, and it is precisely this *desire* to know (*scire cupere*) that Pliny views as a mark of felicity, even if a portrait is an imaginative invention rather than a correct likeness (*quae non sunt, finguntur*). The portraits generate such an effect of palpable presence that in the library the authors themselves seem to breathe and speak (*immortales animae in locis iisdem locuntur*). The younger Pliny also attests to the strong feelings author portraits could arouse, to the point of excess in the case of Silius Italicus who did not just own but even venerated his *imagines* of authors, that of Virgil above all.[35] I suggest that the halls of Roman public libraries engendered in their visitors what we might refer to as a "metonymic habit," a readiness, even a keenly felt need to perceive close connections between literary works and the visual supplements associated with them. The supplements stand in for – one might say, speak for – the texts, even eclipse them in importance.[36]

Once established, the metonymy between an author's work and his portrait could be utilized to make nuanced assertions about literature without direct reference to literary texts themselves. It is easiest to observe the cultural work that these portraits could accomplish in the Palatine library, where the evidence is, once again, most abundant. Here the author portraits followed a standard format, with each author's likeness engraved on a metal shield or *clipeus*; these portraits are mobile, not set in stone like, for example, the shields with the face of Jupiter Ammon carved into the attic of the forum of Augustus.[37] The shields thus render the literary canon literally manipulatable: by moving them around in space, by placing certain images in places of special prominence, statements can be made about the relative value of authors and, as we shall see, their connection to Augustus and his successors.

---

[35] *imaginum quas non habebat modo verum etiam venerabatur, Vergili ante omnes* (*Ep.* 3.7.8; for more temperate examples of devotion, cf. *Ep.* 1.16.8, 4.28.1).

[36] I see here an intriguing contrast with Too's notion of the walking library, a figure who, like Athenaeus' banqueters, transmits and orders cultural knowledge through performative feats of memory (Too 2000). If such a figure is a "breathing library" (βιβλιοθήκη τις ... ἔμψυχος, Eunap. *VS* 4.1.3), then we might say that Rome's visually impressive public libraries are designed to take his breath away, in more ways than one. The author portraits not only inspire awe, but also seem to speak for themselves and so deprive others of the chance: as we shall see, their arrangement fixes in place an authorized view of the literary tradition that will be defended against individual, revisionist performances. I thank Greg Woolf for alerting me to this reference.

[37] Cf. Blanck 1992: 194, Corbier 2006: 174–7. It is likely that the other imperial libraries also displayed such *imagines clipeatae*, though our sources are not quite explicit on this question.

Because meetings of the senate were often held in the Palatine library (Suet. *Aug.* 29),[38] members of the senatorial class would have been intimately familiar with this gallery of portraits on shields. Tacitus (*Ann.* 2.37) preserves a speech in which Marcus Hortalus, asking financial support of Tiberius during a meeting in the library, gestures toward the likeness of his own ancestor, the orator Quintus Hortensius, on display there, as well as toward one of Augustus (more on the likeness of Augustus below).[39] Tacitus notes that Hortensius' image was "placed among the orators" (*Hortensii inter oratores sitam imaginem*), so that we may assume the shields were grouped in such a way as to convey relationships of genre.

Tacitus' mention of this detail is unlikely to be casual or merely intended to inform readers about the Palatine library's layout. In his dyspeptic response to Hortalus (2.38), Tiberius refuses the request and scolds him: if all paupers were given a handout, he grumbles, the *res publica* would fail (*res publica deficiet*); nor should a senatorial meeting be interrupted to further one's private business and personal finances (*ut privata negotia et res familiaris nostras hic augeamus*). Hortalus has violated a boundary between public and private – in more ways than one. He was attempting to treat the *imago* of Hortensius like an ancestor portrait, displayed in his house and acting as guarantor of his family's prestige and worthiness. The strategy is ineffective, for in *this* space Hortensius is placed among the orators, not kinsmen, and family ties are subordinate to the hierarchies established by the library and its proprietor, the emperor. The author portraits may resemble other types of commemoration, such as the wax masks set up in the cupboards of an atrium, but as Hortalus discovered, they obey a different set of rules and impose a different set of values.

A portrait for Germanicus

Besides being an imposing presence at senatorial proceedings, the shield portraits were themselves sometimes the subject of debate. In the wake of Germanicus' death in AD 19 a number of honors were proposed for him, among them a portrait shield in the Palatine library to honor his literary pursuits. Once again Tacitus records the discussion of the proposal (*Ann.* 2.83):

---

[38] For senate meetings in the Palatine library, see Thompson 1981, Corbier 2006: 171–4.
[39] [M. Hortalus] *modo Hortensii inter oratores sitam imaginem, modo Augusti intuens*...

cum censeretur clipeus auro et magnitudine insignis inter auctores eloquentiae, adseveravit Tiberius solitum paremque ceteris dicaturum: neque enim eloquentiam fortuna discerni et satis inlustre si veteres inter scriptores haberetur.

When they proposed a shield that would stand out among the authors of eloquence by virtue of its size and the fact that it was made of gold, Tiberius retorted that he would decree one of the usual sort, and equal to the others: distinctions in eloquence, he said, are not made on the basis of one's fortunes, and it would be honor enough if [Germanicus] were counted among the writers of old.

This passage and the debate it records are remarkable for the ease with which they move between evaluating physical attributes of the portraits and articulating ideas about literary value. The rows of uniform shields evidently conveyed a potent image of the authors as belonging to an ordered canon, and deriving equal prestige from the simple fact of being included; the metonymy of literary work and (standardized) portrait effaced distinctions between individual authors and rendered their merits commensurable, so that Germanicus could be placed on a par with the older authors or, on a broader scale, Latin literature balanced against Greek.

The Palatine library's decorative programme was thus a sophisticated tool allowing the emperor to harness and manipulate the prestige of the literary tradition, and as such its details were publicized throughout the empire. A bronze tablet discovered in the Tiber valley near ancient Heba contains part of the senatorial decree that detailed Germanicus' honors; the preserved portion of the text commences with a careful description of the placement of the new shield portrait (*Tabula Hebana* 1–4):[40]

utique in Palatio in porticu quae est ad Apollinis in eo templo in quo senatus haberi solet [inter ima]/gines virorum inlustris ingeni Germanici Caesaris et Drusi Germanici patris eius naturalis [fratrisque]/ Ti(beri) Caesaris Aug(usti) qui ipse quoque fecundi ingeni fuit imagines ponantur supra capita columna[rum eius fas]/tigi quo simulacrum Apollinis tegitur.

[And they decreed] that on the Palatine, in the portico that is by Apollo's [temple], in that temple in which the senate is customarily held, among the likenesses of men of renowned talent, likenesses of Germanicus Caesar and of Drusus Germanicus, his natural father and the brother of Tiberius Caesar Augustus, who himself also possessed a fertile talent, should be placed over the capitals of the columns of the pediment that covers the statue of Apollo.

---

[40] For a text, discussion, and bibliography for the *Tabula Hebana* and related fragments, see Crawford 1996: 1.507–47 (the commentary misunderstands the nature of Germanicus' and Drusus' portraits, however).

A fragment of the same text came to light in Spain (the *Tabula Siarensis*), a testament to how widely the decree circulated; this tablet includes the interesting detail that a bronze copy of the decree was to be set up in the library's hall together with the shield portraits (b.2.20–1). The text of the decree presupposes a broad familiarity with both the layout of the Palatine library and its commemorative strategies, registering the presence of author portraits as well as the recess topped by a pediment that contained the cult statue of Apollo.

As an orator and poet Germanicus might have had some claim to be included in the library, but the same cannot be said for his father Drusus, on whose literary activity our sources are silent.[41] The primary reason for so honoring both men is of course that they were members of the imperial family, as the *Tabula Siarensis* makes clear when it instructs that copies of the decree should be set up "so that *the piety of all orders toward the house of Augustus* and the consensus of the entirety of the citizens in honoring the memory of Germanicus Caesar might be more readily apparent."[42] Nonetheless the lines quoted above are eloquent in the way they scrupulously indicate the specific nature of commemoration in the library, where *ingenium* ("talent") is the official criterion of inclusion. The clause pertaining to Drusus has provoked consternation because "fertile talent" (*fecundi ingenii*) is an unusual phrase, while "eloquent talent" (*facundi ingenii*, requiring the change of just a letter) is better attested;[43] yet the clause is essentially a bit of special pleading, so that the oddity and vagueness of "fertile talent" may well be designed to gloss over the fact that Drusus lacks the proper credentials to appear in this space beside his son. Once again, then, the Palatine library's portrait gallery follows its own rules that differ from those of other portrait collections, such as the galleries of Roman heroes and Augustus' ancestors that occupied the porticoes of the *forum Augustum*.[44] The rules could be bent, as Drusus' inclusion shows, but they also gave Tiberius the power to refuse to Germanicus the distinction that might be due to him on the basis of kinship, and to assert that by the measure of eloquence he was no better than anyone else.

The precise positioning of the two new portraits may be read as a compromise between Tiberius and the senators: while the emperor may have

---

[41] See Dix and Houston 2006: 684.

[42] *quo facilius pietas omnium ordinum erga domum Augustam et consensu<s> universorum civium memoria honoranda Germanici Caesaris appareret* (b.2.22–3). On the role of the imperial family in the honors decreed for Germanicus, see Severy 2000: 320–7 (325–6 for the term *pietas* in the *Tabula Siarensis*).

[43] Weinstock 1957: 144 proposes the alteration to *facundi*.

[44] For the *forum Augustum*, see *LTUR* 2.289–95 s.v. (V. Kockel).

insisted that the shield portraits remain uniform, their location over the central cult statue nonetheless does distinguish Germanicus and his father from the other authors. This is a subtle message, but one expressed in a visual language that those familiar with the library would be adept at reading. It is significant that the mobility of the shields allows the collection to be recentered around newly added figures in a way that, say, the statues of Augustus' forum would not.

The prominence of the cult statue in the senate's decree is no accident, for it may have been the ideological lynchpin of the entire complex. Scholiasts to Horace tell us explicitly that the statue of Apollo in the Palatine library actually depicted the emperor Augustus with the attributes of the god.[45] If the statement is accurate, this statue would presumably be the same likeness (*imago*) of Augustus mentioned by Tacitus in his account of Hortalus' speech; if not, it at least implies that a connection between the statue and Augustus might be perceived by the library's visitors.[46] To be sure, Augustus refused temples and divine honors in Rome, even melting down statues dedicated to him and using the proceeds to dedicate golden tripods in the very temple of Apollo to which his library was attached.[47] Yet Suetonius preserves a rumor that Augustus did appear in the guise of Apollo at a private banquet (*cena secretior*, *Aug.* 70), and such artworks as the Gemma Augustea, a cameo that depicts Augustus with attributes of Jupiter, support the notion that the emperor might choose to be represented as a divinity in private contexts like those in which the cameo would circulate.[48] The presence of a statue of Apollo with Augustus' features would mark the Palatine library as a quasi-private venue, open to a "public" of political elites and complementing the official face of the regime and different strategies of memorialization to be found in spaces like Augustus' forum.[49]

According to the specialized logic of the library's decoration, each portrait points metonymically to specific texts stored behind the doors of the *armaria*. To which texts would the statue of Apollo-as-Augustus refer? Given its central position and greater size (full-sized statue versus shield bust), the obvious answer is that Augustus would be claiming a stake in *all* the works

---

[45] E.g., *Caesar in bibliotheca statuam sibi posuerat habitu ac statu Apollinis* (pseudo-Acron ad *Ep.* 1.3.17). For the other sources, see Lugli 1960: 109.
[46] Cf. Neudecker 2004: 297 for a similar point.   [47] Suet. *Aug.* 52.
[48] Naturally this latter point is valid only if the cameo was commissioned during Augustus' lifetime. For the Gemma, its dating, and the contrast with public depictions of Augustus, see Kleiner 1992: 69–72.
[49] See Neudecker 2004: 294–302 on the users of the Palatine library, and Johnson (this volume) for differences between "public" libraries and other types of public spaces in Rome.

stored in his library as the one responsible for bringing them together, giving visual form to the resultant canon, and regulating the admittance of newcomers.[50] The guise of the god of poetry, whose right to a position in the middle of the library is self-evident, would naturalize Augustus' special relationship to the library's texts by connecting it with a divine prototype.[51] Standing directly beneath the newly decreed portraits of Germanicus and Drusus, the image of Apollo watching over the bookshelves with Augustus' features would have served as a visual analogue for Tiberius' own efforts in controlling just how Germanicus should be honored within the library's halls.

Conclusions

I have tried to offer a sketch of the processes through which the decoration of Rome's imperial libraries communicated to viewers about the significance of their holdings. The evidence is patchy and widely scattered, and it is symptomatic of the difficulties involved that my exploration of the libraries' visual impact had to focus more on texts than images. The inscription in bronze from Delphi is nonetheless a tantalizing indicator of the varied adornments the libraries may once have possessed, and Pliny's remarks suggest too how individual objects might acquire complex layers of meaning when displayed in the libraries' halls.

I have argued that the emperors' decision to monumentalize the storage of papyrus rolls in their libraries encouraged the introduction of visual supplements to distinguish the authors whose works were held behind the *armaria* doors. The shield portraits in particular functioned as metonymies for the authors they depicted that could generate meaning independently from whatever the authors actually wrote: this is a visual rhetoric whose subject was the literary canon and its place in the empire. Viewers familiar with the library's layout and adornment, whether from personal visit or secondhand description, learned to negotiate easily between texts and multifarious representations evoking those texts; to read in the physical attributes of these representations – their arrangement in space, their size, their material – visual arguments about the significance of the works themselves; and to attribute the entire complex of text and image to the activity of

---

[50] For Augustus as gatekeeper of the Palatine library, cf. Hor. *Ep.* 2.1.214–18 and Horsfall 1993.
[51] In the provinces it was possible to honor the emperor more directly: at Pergamum one Flavia Melitine dedicated a library in the city's *Asklepieion* and installed there a statue of "the god Hadrian" (θεὸν Ἀδρίανον, *IvP* 3.6 = Habicht 1969: 29–30; cf. Blanck 1992: 209).

an organizing figure who reciprocally both bestows prestige upon authors and works, and enhances his own prestige from the same.[52] Architecturally dazzling and pervasively politicized, Rome's public libraries were spaces designed to effect the transmutation of the literary tradition's prestige into visual experience and the assertion of power.

[52] On the popularity of libraries as conspicuous displays of euergetism, see Neudecker 2004: 302–7.

18 | Libraries and reading culture in the High Empire

WILLIAM A. JOHNSON

Introduction

In the last thirty years, a revisionist view of Roman public libraries has gradually come to challenge in various ways comfortable assumptions about the goals, logistics, and usage of the public libraries.[1] In this chapter, I try to situate some apparent anomalies in the institution and usership of the public libraries in the much broader terms of the reading system as a whole (what I call the *reading culture*).[2] By keeping at the centre ancient *habits and attitudes* – the use of texts, the situation of texts, the control and validation of texts, and the broad socio-cultural system behind these – I will try to make more sensible some of the ways in which Roman public libraries appear to have differed from our own.

I will focus my remarks on the early and High Empire, and I begin with the observation that the trail of evidence for the *use* of the "public" imperial libraries is remarkably thin. We are accustomed to seeing images like that from Packer's study of the library in Trajan's Forum (Figure 18.1), an image that is familiar and comfortable, to my mind disquietingly so: not very different from the reading room at Yale's Sterling Memorial Library where I grew up (Figure 18.2a), and so similar to the Biblioteca Angelica in Rome that one wonders if it served as inspiration to the artist (Figure 18.2b). I say "disquieting" because Packer's much repeated image[3] powerfully asserts various implicit roles for the library that match modern notions but that are at best debatable. For instance: that there was a lot of light; that there were desks; that there were throngs of readers. Or, more essentially: that the library's *purpose* had to do with *broad use by a public of readers*.

Let's keep our attention on that last. In fact, there is an almost eerie silence in the ancient record about users of public libraries. We commonly

---

[1] Most influential has been the pathbreaking work of Keith Dix and George Houston, for which see the bibliography (esp. Dix 1994, Dix and Houston 2006, Houston 2002, 2004, 2007, 2009) and the contributions by Dix and Houston in this volume.
[2] For detailed treatment of "reading culture" in the High Empire, see Johnson 2010.
[3] Such as, for example, on the cover of Casson's handbook treatment (Casson 2001).

Figure 18.1 Forum of Trajan. James Packer's reconstruction of the SW library

assume that the book trade made use of these libraries and, though I don't doubt that they sometimes did, there is no direct evidence for it.[4] There are no images of people reading in libraries,[5] nor of the interior of libraries

---

[4] For what we do know, White 2009.
[5] Cavallo has read this fact as "an indication that [libraries], whether private or public, were primarily intended for the storage of books" (*Der Neue Pauly* s.v. "Book"). The interesting question however also arises: how would an ancient artist identify a scene as one *in a library*? Do we know enough to say? I'm not sure that we do.

Figure 18.2 (a) Sterling Memorial Library. (b) Biblioteca Angelica, Rome

at all, aside from the doubtful possibility of a much-reproduced drawing of a lost relief from Trier of uncertain date, but certainly late.[6] Vitruvius

---

[6] The relief is known only from an ectype in Christoph Brouwer, *Antiquitatum et annalium Trevirensium libri XXV*, 1670, reproduced in Birt 1907: 247 and often since; the relief was already lost in Birt's time. Depictions of writing at desks are almost unexampled: see Turner

(*De arch.* 6.5),[7] writing of the private libraries of persons of high rank, tells us that they need high, princely vestibules and spacious atria and peristyles (*vestibula regalia alta, atria et peristylia amplissima*) not to accommodate readers, but since "public councils and private trials and arbitrations" are held there. We will come to the literary evidence in a moment, but we can say at once that that evidence is sparse, and from an interestingly limited number of sources. None of this is meant to imply, arguing *e silentio*, that the imperial libraries did not have users. But it does seem to suggest that whatever the historical realities, there is something in the Roman *view* of the public libraries that is somehow not quite analogous to, say, the forum or the senate or the temples, public locales (with their implicit activities) that do routinely find depictions of their use.

Fronto, Gellius, and Galen on the libraries of Rome

Let us start with a direct examination of the central evidence.[8] There are only a handful of direct witnesses to the use of ancient imperial libraries: to reading in them, trying to locate books in them, or doing things in them other than reading or locating books. The passages are well known and we can work through these rapidly. The earliest is in a letter from Marcus Aurelius to his teacher Fronto, *Ep. ad M. Caes. et invicem* 4.5 (c. 145 AD).

After the hunt, I was reading two volumes of Cato's speeches. "Ho" you cry to your boy "go as fast as you can and fetch me those speeches from the libraries of Apollo" (*de Apollinis bibliothecabus has mihi orationes apporta*). It is no use your sending, for those volumes among others have followed me here. So you'll have to stroke one of the Tiberian library's Bookmeisters (*Tiberianus bibliothecarius tibi subigitandus est*).[9] A little douceur will be necessary, in which he and I can go shares when I come back into town....

This is a real letter, so we can interpret it straightforwardly. What it seems to tell us is that an emperor-designate could freely remove a volume from the "public" library; that his intimate friend and teacher Fronto would know

---

1980: 2 and 190; Nicholls 2011: 139 n. 81 cites a late fourth-century relief from Ostia (inv. 130), of a different era and depicting use of codices or tablets.

[7] Further on this passage in the contribution by Petrain in this volume.

[8] The passages from Fronto, Gellius, and Galen are treated more extensively (though also to different purpose) in Johnson 2010, chapters 5, 6, and 7.

[9] For the translations "stroke" and "Bookmeister," see Houston 2004: 11–12. *Subigitare* is however not simply playful, but jocular and crudely explicit: the meaning is "to excite sexually by fondling" (translation from *OLD*; my thanks to colleague Francis Newton for pointing this out).

to look for it in the Temple of Apollo and could assume the right to have his "boy" fetch the volume; also that, as a devotee, Aurelius knew where the only other copy of this rare book was located (in the Tiberian library); and that there Fronto might have to do some persuading to get one of the librarians to cooperate in releasing the book.

By far the most substantial set of evidence comes, however, in the pages of Fronto's contemporary Aulus Gellius. Why that is so is itself a question worth posing, and I will in due course try to answer it. Gellius's *Attic Nights*, a curious miscellany of about 400 short essays that tell "fun stories" and "fun facts to know and tell," mostly about matters of language and literature, was written in probably the 170s or 180s AD, with the dramatic date for most of the passages of interest here set in the 150s.[10]

At *NA* 5.21, Gellius tells the story of an unnamed friend who is attacked for using *pluria* instead of *plura*, and who after some back and forth then silences his interlocutor by saying:

Quite a few letters of Sinnius Capito have been deposited in a single book-roll in, I think, the Temple of Peace (*Sinni Capitonis... epistulae sunt uno in libro multae positae, opinor, in templo Pacis*). The first letter was written to Pacuvius Labeo, and carries the heading (*titulus*), "*pluria*, not *plura*, ought to be spoken." In that letter he puts forth the grammatical rules for why *pluria* and not *plura* is correct Latin. (trans. after J. C. Rolfe)

There is more to notice here than the simple fact of a book deposited in the library of the Temple of Peace. First is the intellectual game (which is also a social game): to establish his authority, the *amicus* cites an obscure, antiquarian text (Sinnius Capito was a marginally important collector of linguistic and historical minutiae in the late Republic). But notice the details of how he does this. The friend gives not only the author and name of the book, the number of the epistle, the exact heading of the epistle, and the addressee, but also the place, and likely the only place, where one can find it (Temple of Peace). The implication seems to be, "this obscure antiquarian book-roll can, if I recall correctly, be found only in the Temple of Peace, where it was deposited, and to which I am one of the few to have access" (though it's unclear whether because he is one of the few to know about it, or because he has special connections to gain access, or both).

Since Gellius is an author more often cited than read, it seems worth making clear that this emphasis on special knowledge of and access to obscure texts is pandemic in the *Attic Nights*. Gellius packs his text with

---

[10] Houston 2004 discusses Gell. 11.17 and 13.20.

obscure references. I think in particular of the ranks of (mostly older) philological commentators that he brings into play,[11] but literary texts are also commonly cited in such a way as to carry the implication that they are rare, and not easily come by.[12] Along similar lines are the many claims for authority from ancient – i.e. rare or unique – manuscripts. At 18.9.5, for example, Gellius reports that he discovered a manuscript "of true antiquity" at the library at Patrae that to his mind settles a question of spelling in the text of Livius Andronicus; at 9.14.1, he resolves a textual problem in Claudius Quadrigarius by "inspecting several antique manuscripts"; at 2.3.5, Gellius reports that the grammarian Fidus Optatus showed him once a copy of *Aeneid* 2 "believed to have belonged to Virgil himself."[13] The extravagant pedigrees claimed for these manuscripts have sometimes been doubted,[14] but it is the very extravagance of the claims that illustrates the almost desperate measures that Gellius will deploy in order to assert the privileged status of the intellectual community he espouses, a special knowledge of what texts to seek, and where to locate them. The fact that so much of our ancient testimony to exotic MSS of this type comes in the pages of Gellius is not happenstance, but a reflex of the program of the text, which seeks to claim special status for a certain type of elite intellectualism.

The net result is a work suffused with claims to special access: to archives, to rare books, to famous contemporary teachers, to knowledge of famous teachers in the recent past. Gellius's references to libraries are best read in this context. Baldly stated: the *Attic Nights* accounts for so large a percentage

---

[11] Some examples of philological commentators cited by name in the *Attic Nights*: Aelius Gallus, Annaeus Cornutus, Antistius Labeo, Asconius Pedianus, Caesilius Vindex, Servius Claudius, Gavius Bassus, Publius Lavinius, Nigidius Figulus, Iulius Hyginus, Sempronius Tuditanus, Valerius Probus, Verrius Flaccus, Volcacius Sedigitus.

[12] Some examples where the context suggests rarity or difficulty of access: the *Problems* of Aristotle (2.30.11), *Letters* of Capito (5.21), *Annales* of Q. Claudius Quadrigarius (9.14), edicts of a praetor (11.17), Aristotle's *De animalia* (13.7.6), a speech of M. Porcius Cato "Nepos" (*RE* #11, an obscure grandson of Cato the Elder; 13.20), letters of Augustus (15.7.3), an old speech of Favorinus (15.8), *Commentaries* of Probus (15.30), *Commentary on Proloquia* of Aelius Stilo (16.8), the (now lost) *Physica* of Aristotle (19.5), Laevius' *Alcestis* (19.7).

[13] Other examples of Gellius's citation of rare or unique manuscripts: his teacher resolves a textual question in Ennius by procuring a book-roll "almost certainly emended by the hand of Lampadio" (18.5); he cites Hyginus who bases his reading on a copy of the *Aeneid* that "had come from the home and family of the poet" (1.21.2); a reading is said to have been verified by a copy of Virgil written in the poet's own hand (9.14.7); and cf. the old copy of the *Annals* of Fabius mentioned at 5.4, of Cato's *Contra Tiberium Exulem* at 2.14, of Cicero's *In Verrem* at 1.7.1.

[14] Zetzel 1973, esp. 230ff.; Zetzel 1984, 60–2. Other positions on this question are gathered by McDonnell 1996: 478 n. 41. For the lampoon of such enterprise in Lucian's *Adv. Indoctum*, see Johnson 2010: 158–70.

of references to visits to the imperial libraries at Rome[15] precisely because Gellius is so eager to highlight exclusive or difficult-to-access sources. The remaining references to public libraries in the *Attic Nights* exemplify this theme. In the Temple of Peace, Gellius finds an obscure commentary by Aelius Stilo that he had long sought after (*NA* 16.8.1–3). In the library "at Trajan's temple" he is looking for "something else" when the rarity of a book of edicts of the early praetors "fell into my hands" (*NA* 11.17.1). In the library of the *domus Tiberiana*, another rare book by happenstance presents itself. Let us pause for a moment to look at this, again, well known tale:

When Sulpicius Apollinaris and I were sitting in the library of the *domus Tiberiana*, along with some others, friends of his or mine, by chance a book was brought to us that had inscribed as its author, M. Cato Nepos. (*NA* 13.20.1)

As with Fronto, the text is Cato (though neither of the famous Catos, as it will turn out) and the setting is the Tiberian library. Gellius is not alone, but with his teacher Sulpicius Apollinaris and unnamed others. Sulpicius was not just anyone, but one of the illustrious grammarians of the day – the fact that he had the future emperor Pertinax as one of his pupils gives an idea of his standing and circle of acquaintance. This is, then, an exclusive group, and an exceedingly rare text. Similarly, Gellius tells us that he found an obscure source – an ancient MS of Q. Claudius Quadrigarius – in the library at Tibur (*NA* 19.14.3); and in a different chapter (*NA* 19.5.4), we find him at the villa of a "rich friend" where, when a dispute arises over the healthiness of drinking water from melted ice, one of the company, a *vir bonus* of the peripatetic school, fetches a volume of Aristotle from the library at Tibur (in the Temple of Hercules) to prove his point. Again, this is not just anyone, but a distinguished philosopher and guest of a rich man who offers his villa as venue to an intellectual gathering. Moreover, he seeks at the library not a run-of-the-mill volume, but a relatively obscure work of Aristotle.

In similar fashion, we see Galen, of roughly the same generation, the polymathic medical man and, famously, the court physician of Marcus Aurelius, looking for a variant in the *Epidemiae* of Hippocrates, that Dioscorides records as occurring in only two copies, thus a rare variant: to research this point, Galen looks "deliberately at all the copies in the public libraries and all

---

[15] Temple of Peace: 5.21, 16.8 (*Letters* of Capito, commentary of Aelius Stilo); Forum of Trajan: 11.17 (edicts of praetors); suburban library at Tibur: 9.14, 19.5 (*Annals* of Q. Claudius, Aristotle on water); Domus Tiberiana: 13.20 (speeches of Cato "Nepos"). Primary references to libraries in Rome or its suburbs are collected in Boyd 1915.

those in the libraries of my friends" (*in Hipp. epid. VI Comment.* 17b.194–5 Kühn) and finds that the variant in fact is in all these copies. Note that he gains access to the public libraries not to check out a romance or book of poetry or even a volume of Hippocrates, but to look into a manuscript variant. His boast is that he can gain access to all the copies in Rome, whether in the public libraries or in the libraries of his (many) connections, and this is the authority he wields in refuting his rival, Dioscorides.[16] Galen's focus on libraries, public and private, is that they were endowed with rare, unique texts.[17]

We find supporting evidence in a new treatise of Galen, *On the avoidance of grief*, itself a vivid reminder that the age of miraculous discovery is not past us in any realm of Classics. In this case, a persistent researcher managed to uncover in January 2005 a new treatise hidden in plain view in a Galenic manuscript in the Vlatadon monastery in Thessaloniki.[18] In the treatise, Galen describes how he avoided grief even on the occasion of the loss of many of his most cherished personal treasures in the fire of March 192 that destroyed the Temple of Peace and the Palatine library, among much else. In the course of all this, he talks about the losses in the Palatine library itself. Given his theme, it is of course natural that Galen focuses upon the rare items, yet it is still interesting that in detailing the losses he speaks *only* of unique items, with a heavy emphasis on items important to a scholar looking for reliable manuscript attestations. Irreplaceable losses from the fire, he tells us, included

manuscripts of the collection of Callinus, of Atticus, of Peducaeus, and most certainly the two book-rolls of Homer owned by Aristarchus and those of Plato owned by Panaetius, and many others of this kind, because these famous writings were kept there [in the Palatine library] – writings that those men who gave their names to the books either had well copied each of them by their own hand or had had them well copied by others. And indeed there were the autographs of several ancient grammarians, orators, doctors, and philosophers.... (Galen, *On the avoidance of grief*, 13; trans. after P. L. Tucci).[19]

[16] *Der Neue Pauly* s.v. Dioscorides, #9.
[17] For discussion of what the papyri have to tell us about the active use by readers of unique textual witnesses, see Johnson 2010, chapter 9.
[18] See Boudon-Millot 2007 for the history of the discovery and for the *editio princeps* of the treatise; and see now Boudon-Millot *et al.* 2010 (*non vidi*) for a critical edition with commentary.
[19] Tucci 2008: 142; for Peducaeus, see Jones 2009: 393. See now Nicholls 2011, who discusses the passage and its implications in detail (and my thanks for a preview of the article prior to publication).

Galen's sole focus in describing the collection of this public library is on autographs and texts attached to scholars or other men famed for learning and bookish care – all unique copies, the sorts of materials we associate with a rare book archive today. Note also the display of learning here, that Galen *knows* which were the particularly valuable book-rolls located in the Palatine library, and by implication knows also the details of why, exactly, these are so valuable.

This quick survey of Antonine sources allows us, perhaps, to do something useful with the evidence in the *Historia Augusta*, a later and highly problematic source. The consensus has formed that the writer of the *Historia Augusta* has a tendency to fabricate sources, and this is particularly true of the later lives, in which all the evidence for libraries lies. "Vopiscus" writes, for instance, in defense of his digest of the life of the emperor Aurelian that – at the advice and by special arrangement of the consular Junius Tiberianus (*cos.* 281, 291) – he has consulted the detailed journals Aurelian wrote *ex libris linteis* and goes on to say that anyone who is skeptical can "demand the linen books themselves, which the Ulpian library will furnish you whenever you desire" (SHA *Aurel.* 1.5–10; and cf. 8.1, 24.7). Scholars today see these linen journals as fictitious, an invention based on the *Libri lintei* of the Republic, said to have contained lists of the early magistrates of Rome.[20] Yet we can observe that the account of the writer of the *Historia Augusta* – whatever its (dubious) historicity – does still fall within the *view* of public library here suggested, in which there is this notion of special access to exclusionary zones. The linen books and ivory laws (SHA *Tac.* 8.1) are kept in a sort of special treasury, available only to the few – that is, the place known as the "public" library.[21]

---

[20] The *Libri lintei* were named as sources by C. Licinius Macer and Q. Aelius Tubero (first century BC: cited at Livy 4.7.12; 23.2) but are considered apocryphal by many modern scholars. The Ulpian library is a favorite locus for rare source materials cited by Vopiscus: SHA *Tac.* 8.1 ("lest anyone think that I have rashly put faith in some Greek or Latin writer, there is in the Ulpian library, in the sixth case [*in armario sexto*], an ivory book [*elephantinum*] in which is written out this decree of the senate, signed by Tacitus himself with his own hand"); SHA *Prob.* 2.1 ("I have used ... chiefly the books from the Ulpian library, in my time in the Baths of Diocletian, and likewise from the *Domus Tiberiana*, as well as registries [in the Forum of Trajan] ... and the *acta senatus et populi*").

[21] Other stories of libraries include the information that the Palatine library was used by Augustus and some of the early emperors as a meeting place for the senate and for juridical proceedings (Suet. *Aug.* 29.3, Tac. *Ann.* 2.37), which, as Dix 1994: 287 points out, "suggests that access to [the public libraries] was, or could be, restricted."

Great men and book collections

The question arises, then, how Romans came to such a view of their public libraries.[22] I'm not so interested in the historical fact that Fronto, Galen, and Gellius gained access to the libraries – Fronto and Galen were imperial intimates, after all, and Gellius but one step removed – nor in the historical question of who exactly did or could gain access. Rather, I'm interested in the viewpoint, the *mentalité* – that, even as imperial favorites, these men speak of libraries as repositories of exotic information, and themselves as rare bearers of that information. If I'm seeing this at all clearly, it appears that the (admittedly thin) trail of direct evidence in Gellius and elsewhere implies an essential link between libraries and the construction of elite circles and exclusivity.

In this context, it may be helpful to go down some side tracks to see if we can get a better understanding of the Roman view of libraries more generally. Let us first consider one of the paradigmatic images of library usage in Rome, in this case a private library and in the time of the Republic. The scene, from book three of Cicero's *De finibus*, is the library of Lucullus, a man of legendary wealth[23] who deployed that wealth aggressively in his estates, which he rebuilt with costly edifices, ambulatories, and baths, and peppered with paintings and statues.[24] Particularly famous was the library at his estate at Tusculum, which seems to have included, among much else, a considerable collection of philosophical texts.[25] Cicero used it as a setting both here, and in the lost *Hortensius*, where he makes Lucullus one of the principal interlocutors. We know a little bit about this library from the life of Lucullus by Plutarch. We are told that "the book collection was made open to all" – meaning of course the elite with access to his villa – and that "the places for walking and being at leisure were made accessible without hindrance for the Greeks" who flocked there, as to "an abode of the Muses," to spend their days in (philosophic) discussion.[26] Lucullus himself "often spent his leisure hours among them, walking about in the arcades with the *philologoi*," a sort of coterie of Greek philosophers who frequented the spot.[27] In *De finibus*, Cicero makes a trip to Lucullus' library, he says, in

---

[22] Further discussion in Too 2010 which, however, should be used with caution.
[23] "The richest man in Rome" (Diod. Sic. 4.21.4). [24] Plut. *Luc.* 39.2.
[25] Inferred from Plut. *Luc.* 42, and Cicero, below, and in *Academica priora* book 2. Generally on the library of Lucullus, see the detailed study in Dix 2000. On the question of the specialization of the collection, Dix 2000: 445–6 (Dix supposes a more comprehensive collection).
[26] Plut. *Luc.* 42.1.
[27] Plut. *Luc.* 42.2. See Dix 2000 for discussion of some probabilities (Archias, etc.) for the leading philosophers attending Lucullus. To be sure, the idea of the villa that was a "home and

order to fetch a volume of Aristotle he knows to be there, so that he can copy it for himself; when he arrives, he finds to his surprise and delight none other than Cato, who is sitting and reading.[28] They strike up a conversation on Stoicism, which constitutes the dialogue of this and the subsequent book. Note that this is not a documentary account, but the author's deliberate choice of a setting. Why does Cicero choose this particular scene? First to notice is that Cicero imagines himself going in person to the library – he does not send a servant – even though the task is simply to pick up a book. He mentions explicitly that Lucullus' son[29] has given him liberty to take a book away. Second, we notice that Cato is there, perusing volumes. The scene suggests that even men as distinguished as Cicero and Cato happily come in person to the library, in order to gain access to the collection and to assert their privilege as insiders. Cicero's presence there and his ability to borrow a rare volume seem chosen – just as in the *Hortensius* – as a sort of boast of connection and access to the household of Lucullus and to the famous book resources available to the *amici*. The scene, in short, encapsulates the way in which the library, itself a sort of memorial to Lucullus as Great Man, is the centerpiece and embodiment of a particular, intellectualist mode of high elite self-fashioning.

Other paradigmatic library stories from the Republic can be situated similarly. One thinks of the royal Macedonian library brought to Italy by Scipio's father L. Aemilius Paullus (Plut. *Aem.* 28.6, Isid. *Etym.* 6.5.1), which probably informs the romanticizing of Scipio and his friends by Cicero, who makes them into a close coterie (Cic. *Rep.* and *Amic.*, 69).[30] Similarly prominent is the library of Atticus, which Cicero made important use of,[31] and which along with other book-related services seems to have been

---

prytaneion for the Greeks" may be influenced by correlation with the parallel life of Cimon who makes his house a "public *prytaneion*' (*Cim.* 10.7; see Duff 1999: 60 n. 30, Tröster 2008: 30), and there may well be other distortions. But the notion that Lucullus had deep-seated interest in Greek learning and philosophy does at least accord with Cicero's presentation in *Academica priora* book 2 and elsewhere. On Plutarch's sources for the life of Lucullus, see generally Tröster 2008: 22–5; for Lucullus and philhellenism, Tröster 2008: 27ff., and esp. 30 on the Plutarch passage here quoted.

[28] *De fin.* 3.2.7–10. *Commentarios quosdam Aristotelios* (3.2.10) is of uncertain meaning, but perhaps, as often asserted, some of the esoteric works (Powell 1995: 18).

[29] The dramatic date is 52 BC; Lucius Lucullus was dead by 56. The son inherited the Tuscan estate and library, as *De fin.* 3.2.8 makes clear.

[30] Cicero's presentation of the "Scipionic Circle" may in part accommodate to the use of the library resources of Cicero himself, who had the likes of Archias and Tyrannio among his intimates, and Diodotus the Stoic as a resident Greek scholar (*Tusc.* 5.39.113; cited by Dix 2000: 463).

[31] As, for example, when writing his *De re publica*. See Dix 2000: 458f. Less well known, but similar in its social construction, is Cicero's use of Faustus Cornelius Sulla's library (perhaps

central to the *Freundschaftdienst* that the super-rich Atticus used to cement his cultured and powerful circle of friends.[32] The telling parodies of this behavior in Petronius (*Satyricon*) and Lucian (*Adversus Indoctum*) spring to mind, where bibliomania is confused with cultural advancement and elite status. And, to return to the High Empire at a stroke, we find similar scenes in Gellius as well. In one episode (*NA* 1.2), Gellius is together with many others at Cephisia, the villa of Herodes Atticus, consular and famous orator, another man legendary both for wealth and for assembling around him an intellectual coterie. A youth brags at immoderate length that he alone understands thoroughly the Stoic tenets (an indirect affront to the learned Herodes, of course). Herodes shames the fellow by summoning from his library a book of Epictetus and having a passage read in which just such a youth is condemned. Similarly, in a scene Gellius sets in Rome (*NA* 19.10), a group of learned men hang about Fronto in his mansion on the Esquiline. Fronto was also a consular and an illustrious orator of great wealth. A chance use of *praeterpropter* ("more or less") gives rise to a spirited philological debate, towards the end of which a friend, Julius Celsinus, observes that the word is used in the *Iphigenia* of Ennius and asks that the book be produced; at which, Fronto summons the book and the passage is read. What is striking in these and other similar passages[33] are two things. First, there is a strong sense of coterie about the *vir magnus*. Second, there seems an implicit assumption that the Great Man has to hand the relevant texts. In an intellectual coterie in antiquity, the wealthy and powerful formed points of nexus, and a natural inference, one borne out by scenes such as the above, is that these Great Men, as leaders of an intellectual community, held their central position in part on the basis of their book collection, their library.[34] We see a direct example of this in Herculaneum, where what the Great Man – in this case the Great Family – offers is not a

---

part of the Aristotle library acquired by his famous father): writing to Atticus from Cumae, Cicero says, *ego hic pascor bibliotheca Fausti* (*Att.* 4.10). (Marshall 1976: 259 speculates that Cicero has bought Faustus' library and is reading at home, but evidence for that is lacking; the "financial trouble" he cites from *Att.* 9.11.4 comes six years later.)

[32] Iddeng 2006. These included Octavian: Horsfall 1993.
[33] See Marshall 1976 for further examples. Not mentioned by Marshall is Athenaeus, in which the wealthy host Larensis is similarly a man with a very large library, used to like purposes by his guests: *Ath.* 1.3.
[34] Forming an intellectual community was of course but one option; then as now many elites chose rather to take leadership and form community on other grounds, such as politics or material pursuits or shared entertainment. Cf. Plutarch, *De amicorum multitudine* 97AB, who lists some options for how friends form connections: "reading books with the scholarly, rolling in the dust with wrestlers, following the hunt with sportsmen, getting drunk with drunkards, canvassing with politicians." Further at Saller 1982: 137–8; Johnson 2010: 36.

general library of classics (at least so far as we can tell), but a rare library of Epicurean texts, not exclusively but especially the collected works of Philodemus.[35] It was the acquisition and maintenance of this collection of texts[36] that made the *Pisones* the focal point to an intellectual coterie.

That then brings us to a remarkable, and somewhat neglected, passage written by Galen during his stay in Rome.[37] In his treatise, *On the passions and errors of the soul*, Galen reports a conversation with one of his intimate friends on the question of moderation. The young friend (49–50), like Galen himself (48), is extremely wealthy, but has the problem that he cannot control his passion for yet more wealth. Galen urges a controlled appetite for luxury, such that he spends just enough to preserve his wealth, with no net increase or decrease. Galen goes on to delineate in detail the ways in which his friend does not, but, by implication, *should* be spending his extra money:

I see that you cannot bring yourself to spend your wealth on noble pursuits, neither on the purchase and preparation of books, nor on the training of scribes, whether in shorthand ability or in fine and accurate writing – nor even on lectors who read well. Too, I never see you sharing anything the way you see me constantly sharing my clothing with members of my household, or assisting people with food or medical care. You have even seen me discharging other people's debts. (*De an. aff. dign. et cur.* 5.48 Kühn)

A wealthy gentleman, in Galen's view, is expected not to hoard but to share with his circle, and at the top of the list are the expenses important to *intellectual* sharing: buying books and having them made, training scribes, training lectors.[38] The several servants involved make clear that Galen is thinking of a *large* book collection. Moreover, the collection needs to be discriminating, containing only worthwhile books, as we see from Seneca and other sources.[39] Why a wealthy man should do this is clear from the context: in order to share these resources. As a matter of course sharing

---

[35] On the library at Herculaneum, Sider 2005 with Johnson 2006; Houston, this volume. For a thorough review of the question of ownership by the family of Calpurnius Piso, see Capasso 2010.

[36] Something that to our eye looks more like a "philosophical library for professional use" – Cavallo and Chartier 1999: 68. Similarly, the satirist Persius owned a specialized library of 700 volumes of Chrysippus that he left to the influential intellectual and teacher Cornutus: Suetonius, *Persius*; Snyder 2000: 17–18 and 39–40.

[37] The second stay, from 168 to *c.* 205.

[38] The expense was considerable. Seneca sets 100,000 sesterces as the cost of a skilled copyist: *Ep.* 27.6–7. Other examples of wealthy men with in-house copyists: Atticus, of course, but also Crassus, Plut. *Crass.* 2.

[39] Sen. *Tranq.* 9.6: the goal is not foolishly to accumulate books that include unknown or discredited authors (*ignotum auctorum aut improbatorum*); cf. Lucian, *Adv. indoct.*

intellectual resources includes not only books, but also an in-house capability for making copies, and, importantly, good lectors so as to be able to share the books *viva voce* among the circle of friends. Galen's ideal community, for which he serves as model, contains then not only a setting where rich man and intellectual can commune (and ideally are one and the same), but also a *culture of sharing* wherein group activities surrounding the maintenance and dissemination of knowledge become peculiarly important. The sharing of books, knowledge, intellectual discourse, is what – in ideal terms – forms the core of an elite community of this stripe.[40]

There were, to be sure, strong practical motivations behind this culture of sharing. Books were expensive and many were rare: the Elder Pliny, for example, was offered 400,000 sesterces for the *excerpts alone* – not, notice, the full texts – of the many volumes he researched for his *Natural Histories*.[41] Galen remarks in the context of laying out some basic information on the properties of wine: "Since it is the case that, due to scarcity and unavailability, we often have to wait a long time to read many of the books in which the detail of remedies is given in full, probably now anyone would pardon us for our manner of teaching, if it does not display exact brevity" (*De san. tuenda* 5.7 = 6.347–8 Kühn). Essential to the reading community is the practical matter of access to the data. Rareness of resource required sharing of books and discussion of their contents, if knowledge was to be expanded and maintained.[42]

Yet there is more at stake than mere practicality for the reader: the Great Man with his book collection – "great" because wealthy and socially important, and usually also politically or intellectually prominent – forms an important focal point in the delicate negotiation among the intellectual elite with regard to their own *writings*. There was, of course, no one who acted as a publisher in antiquity, and thus the gatekeeping role – whose work would be validated, circulated, perpetuated, and whose would not – was negotiated within the circles of the intellectually involved.[43] One important mechanism within that negotiation was, I think, the book collection. When a poet dedicates a *libellus*, or an historian his *liber*, and presents the dedicated copy to an *amicus* of rank, he is asking that the book be accepted into the

---

[40] See Johnson 2010 chapter 5 and Mattern 2008 for detailed discussion of the Galenic community and its ideals.
[41] Mentioned by his nephew at *Ep.* 3.5.17. Pliny the Younger sets the cost of the library he donated to Comum at one million sesterces (*Ep.* 1.8.2). Cicero says only that his library was worth *multorum nummorum* (*Fam.* 13.77.3, 46 BC).
[42] For evidence of parallel habits among Greek reading communities in second-century Egypt, see Johnson 2010 chapter 9.
[43] On the social mechanics of negotiating literary value, see Johnson 2010: 52ff.

book collection and made available to the circle of people with access to that collection.

Sociologically, a central use of a library then is to focus the circle of readers, and also of writers, more particularly around the Great Man, much as the physical space of the villa does. For group interactions among the intellectually inclined, libraries are emblematic of a commitment to shared resources as well as of practical benefit. Moreover, by virtue of the selective nature of the collections, libraries are an important component in determining what forms the subject of *studia* – important, that is, in the negotiation of which literary texts are considered to have enduring value.

Emperors and book collections

If we accept that book collections in Rome tended to center around a Great Man, who offered his library as a symbiotically status-gaining resource to his *amici* and *contubernales* and their hangers-on, then what follows as we turn back to reconsider the imperial "public" libraries? We see at once that, in sociological terms, a sort of disconnect arises. When Augustus founded the monumental Palatine library next to his palace, the "public" libraries were at first, naturally, taken to be Augustus's book collection. As Nicholas Horsfall has eloquently discussed,[44] everyone with literary ambitions at first rushed to get their book-rolls on those "empty shelves on the Palatine,"[45] since in that way the book-rolls can gain immediate status as worthy literary texts.[46] Or at least that seems to be the initial Roman "take" on the public library: what it means, what it stands for.[47] But as time passes and the empire expands and develops, this notion of the public library – as the resource of a Great Man, the *princeps*, and implicitly bearing his stamp of

---

[44] Horsfall 1993.   [45] Horsfall 1993, paraphrasing Hor. *Ep.* 2.1.217–20.
[46] This seems the implication at Hor. *Ep.* 2.1.214–18 (cf. Brink 1982; also Farrell 2009 on Ode 1.1.35f.), and, for the contrary case, we recall Ovid's travails: *Tristia* 3.1 laments how Ovid sent his poem first to the Palatine library, and then to two others, finding however rejection from all (cf. also *Trist.* 3.15.5ff.). The tradition of such rhetoric continued into the High Empire: cf. Martial 5.5, 12.3. Dix 1994: 289; Horsfall 1993: 60–1.
[47] The "public" libraries were also places to store archival documents. This is a natural development since the personal book-roll collections of Great Men traditionally contained central state records. In pre-imperial times censorial records were stored not by the state but in the household of the censor's family – Dionysius of Halicarnassus claims to visit the "many illustrious men of censorial families who preserve these records" in order to uncover details of early Rome (*Ant. Rom.* 1.75.5) – and senatorial resolutions were similarly reliant on the private archives of the consuls (Cic. *Leg. agr.* 2.37).

approval – is not readily scalable. The institution of the "public" library[48] is too grand, and attracts too many book deposits,[49] for the intimate, traditional model to continue to operate – that model in which the Great Man with intellectual interests interacts closely with a coterie of *amici* in a way that makes use of the shared book resources. In a 1976 study, Anthony Marshall wrote that Augustus was in respect to his libraries a "Republican patron writ large." This is true in some respects and continues to hold some truth for later emperors as well. There is at least the illusion that the public libraries continued as the emperor's personal resource: he himself had ready access and gave it to his relatives and intimates, as we saw with Marcus Aurelius and Fronto. He could have a book removed, with the implicit disapproval of the book and its circulation.[50] But even this aspect of libraries seems quickly to get overwhelmed, and by Galen's and Gellius's day the public libraries seem to operate mostly as a public depository for an author's works.[51] When we *do* see a Great Man having an intellectual interchange, the situation is normally in his own house, using his own book collection; the public library doesn't seem to come into the equation, except as a resource for rare textual variants and *obscurata*.[52]

When, finally, we revisit the question with which we started – what was it about the Roman notion of "library" that might influence or even direct the light imprint that the imperial public libraries have left on the literary record – we see that this fact – that eerie silence on usership – makes sense

---

[48] On the ideology, Dix 1994.

[49] We know frustratingly little about how a book came to be in a public library; for what we do know, see Houston 2004. We also know little about how the books were accessed, but here too a disconnect arises between the smaller collection of a *vir magnus*, for which a personal slave or two (and often the Great Man himself) would have control over the contents, and the imperial libraries, which seem to have had surprisingly small staffs (see Houston 2002) and whose deposits, less personal, would have been also less well controlled and accessible. (The overall contents of imperial libraries were however documented in some sort of accession list kept off site, or such seems to be the implication of Domitian's decision to restore the book-rolls in the "libraries destroyed by fire" by sending copyists to Alexandria [Suet. *Dom.* 20]. For possible evidence on library catalogues in the new Galen treatise, see the discussion in Nicholls 2011.)

[50] For the emperor controlling what books were in the public libraries: Suet. *Caesar* 56 (Macer forbidden by Augustus from making available the youthful works of Caesar); several complaints in Ovid's works from exile (esp. 3.1.59ff.); Suet. *Calig.* 34 (Caligula thought of "destroying Homer" – *de Homeri carminibus abolendis* – and did remove the works and *imagines* of Livy and Virgil from all the libraries – *ex omnibus bibliothecis*). Further examples (including also books added and promoted by imperial favor) are collected in Marshall 1976: 261–3, and in Nicholls 2011.

[51] This can include works not intended for broad circulation: see Johnson 2010: 85ff. 131f.

[52] The depiction of Galen's library activities sketched in Nicholls 2011 depends on Galen's own assertions of his exceptionalism, thus the (perhaps rather exaggerated) exception that proves the rule.

in the larger terms of the reading culture of the times. Writers negotiated their position within the context of text-centered activities that were deeply embedded in the exclusionary domain of elite circles. These circles were self-supporting, in the sense that the activities of reading, writing, sharing, vetting, comparing, researching, all took place within the circle, using shared resources (meaning lectors and books, but also the *amici* themselves, a resident intellectual or two, and suitable venues such as a large house with porticoes to walk in and dinners over which to talk). Even more public events like recitations, in contradistinction to Greek habits, seem to have taken place almost always in domestic circumstances (despite assertions to the contrary, there is no solid evidence for recitations in public libraries).[53] Again, unlike the library at Alexandria, and also in opposition to our own inclinations, the great imperial libraries did not, interestingly, lay claim to the goal of bringing together all accumulated knowledge; nor was there any Roman analogue to a library-centered scholarly shop like the Mouseion.[54] With this as the cultural context, it is perhaps not, then, so surprising that elite writers did not regard the public libraries as a central part of the enterprise of writing and reading and the sociabilities devolving therefrom, and thus, in the literary texts that survive, public libraries draw only rare and limited mention of the sort we have examined.[55]

[53] See Johnson 2010: 47 n. 36, following White 1993: 293.
[54] Despite misguided and speculative efforts to identify such: Horsfall 1993. The closest was the initial attempt by Asinius Pollio (as part of Julius Caesar's campaign to remake Rome as a world capital): Plin. *NH* 35.29, *Asinius Pollio qui primus bibliothecam dicando ingenia hominum rem publicam fecit.*
[55] My thanks to George Houston for helpful, incisive comments on this chapter.

19 | Myth and history

Galen and the Alexandrian library[1]

MICHAEL W. HANDIS

The interest which the famous Ptolemy [i.e. Euergetes, 247–222 BC] took in collecting ancient books is mentioned as not a small sign of interest for the people of Athens, inasmuch as he gave as a deposit 15 silver talents and received the books of Aeschylus, Sophocles and Euripides, but only to copy and return them intact in no time. When he had prepared a magnificent copy on the best of paper, he kept the books which he received from the Athenians and he sent the copies back to them, asking them to keep the 15 talents and accept the new books instead of the old originals which they had given him. Even had he not sent the new books back to the people of Athens and kept the old ones, they could have done nothing since they had accepted the silver on condition that they might keep it if he would keep the books. Therefore they accepted the new books, and kept the money.[2]

The story is told by Galen in his commentary on the third book of Hippocrates' *Epidemics*. This chapter will explore what this anecdote, and others like it, tell us about the Roman-period mythologizing of the Alexandrian library. The anecdotes examined come from authors writing during the Roman Empire, centuries after the founding of the Alexandrian library. Nonetheless, these stories constitute what we know about the library; no contemporary accounts of its founding and early operations exist. Galen's belief in such a fantastical story is but one example of a process that recurs over centuries whenever historians have treated the Alexandrian library, which Roger Bagnall calls "the library of dreams." The mythologizing of the Alexandrian library did not start in the Middle Ages but in antiquity.

Background and context of Galen's story

An official compilation of the texts of Aeschylus', Sophocles', and Euripides' plays had apparently been carried out in the fourth century BC in accordance with a law proposed by the Athenian statesman, Lycurgus, aimed

---

[1] I would like to thank Dr. Alexei V. Zadorojnyi at the University of Liverpool for his help with Galen's anecdote, and Dr. W. Gerald Heverly at New York University for advice and lively discussions on Galen and libraries in the ancient world.

[2] Galen, *Comm. II in Hippocratis Epidem. libri III*, 239–40, cited in Platthy 1968: 118–19.

at ensuring the accuracy of the lines said by actors during performances.[3] These official copies were believed to be the closest texts to what the tragedians actually wrote.[4] The possibility that errors might have been introduced when manuscripts were copied explains the Ptolemies' desire for the oldest exemplars.[5] It is possible that the official edition created in the time of Lycurgus still existed one hundred years later during the time of Ptolemy III.[6] Ptolemy therefore sought to obtain the originals for the Alexandrian library. The Alexandrian library was founded some time during the third century BC.[7] It is certain that the library had copies of the plays but whether or not these copies were indeed the official Athenian copies from the time of Lycurgus remains debatable.[8]

The anecdote of the Ptolemaic acquisition of Athenian master copies of the three classic tragedians survives by chance, in a casual display of his polymathy by the physician Galen.[9] Galen is addressing a controversy over a medical book in the Alexandrian library, part of what we know as the Hippocratic Corpus: "The case histories in *Epidemics III* are followed by shorthand symbols, Greek letters that seem to summarize in code the salient factors in the disease. Their meanings and origin have been disputed by the earliest students of the text."[10] Who added these symbols, Hippocrates or someone else? This created a controversy that lasted, according to Galen, for over a century in early Alexandria. For Galen, clear, understandable writing – his own and Hippocrates' – is easily read; symbols or letters are not needed. Such markings, concludes Galen, indicate a forgery by those seeking to promote their own interests in the medical field.[11] Galen then recounts the story told by the physician Zeuxis, whose works in Galen's time were rare

---

[3] Plut. *X orat.* 841 F cited in Platthy 1968: 118.
[4] For some background on what the Athenians were looking for in regards to "authentic," see Blum 1991: 42.
[5] Casson 2001: 34.
[6] Bagnall 2002: 358–9. He states that papyrus could "last hundreds of years under good conditions." However, he concludes "The likelihood is that by the reign of Tiberius relatively little of what had been collected under the first Ptolemies was still useable."
[7] No one is sure which Ptolemy founded the library. Generally Ptolemy I Soter (c. 367–c. 283 BC, reigned 323–283) is credited with planning and perhaps beginning construction, but it was his son, Ptolemy II Philadelphus (309–246 BC, reigned 283–246), who is credited with the initial creation of the collection.
[8] Blum 1991: 42 discusses the Alexandrian scholars' attitudes towards the works attributed to Aeschylus, Sophocles, and Euripides.
[9] On Galen, see most recently Yount 2010, Gill *et al.* 2009, Mattern 2008, and Hankinson 2008a. On the motif of the transfer of books, see Jacob, this volume.
[10] Smith 1979: 63.
[11] Vallance 2000: 104 believes Mnemon did what college students have done for years: marked up the library copies they used before returning them to the library. Then of course Mnemon would know the meanings of the letters.

and none of whose writings have survived. Zeuxis' story takes place during the reign of Ptolemy III, about a century earlier.[12] The physician Mnemon from Side in Pamphylia was known to be able to translate these letters found in the margins of the *Epidemics III* copy in the Alexandrian library. At this point Galen introduces the story of the Athenian tragedies and Ptolemy III. Galen believes the story Zeuxis tells of Mnemon, that he wrote the letters in the margins of *Epidemics III*. How Mnemon got his copy of the book into the Alexandrian library would be easy, concludes Galen: because of the bibliomania of the Ptolemies. The story of the official Athenian tragedies illustrates the great lengths to which the Ptolemies would allegedly go in order to obtain books for their library.

Galen experienced this protectionist attitude towards medical knowledge firsthand. In Galen's time, knowledge relating to medicine was carefully guarded. The medical profession was highly competitive. Many works in circulation were inaccurate, having transcription errors or lines altered or missing; in some cases, copies of titled works were completely falsified, as Galen reports.[13] It was not unknown for a practitioner to pass off another's techniques or written works as his own. This was a way to generate business, especially if the treatment being used was effective. Even Hippocrates' works were falsified and tampered with by others for their own unscrupulous gains, as Mnemon's letters in the margins of *Epidemics III* demonstrates. People seeking medical help would go to people such as Mnemon, believing that he understood the "secret knowledge" of the letters in the margins of Hippocrates' book. Galen had no use for charlatans like Mnemon who sought to profit from people's misery. Galen originally visited Alexandria because of its reputation for the study of medicine.[14] He wanted to study the works of Numisianus, the famed anatomist, and he stayed in Alexandria from four to six years. Unfortunately, most of Numisianus' works were unavailable. The only existing copies of these works were in the custody of his son, Heraclianus, who was also a physician. Galen was not allowed to examine Numisianus' works, nor would anyone teach him Numisianus' ideas, not even his teacher Pelops, who had been a pupil of Numisianus. When Heraclianus died, he left instructions for all of his father's works to be burned. Thus, all knowledge learned by Numisianus was lost.

---

[12] Smith 1979: 199. [13] Zadorojnyi, this volume.
[14] On Galen's stay in Alexandria, see Von Staden 2004.

Of the works available, there were three ways of obtaining copies. "Public libraries and private book collections make up the terrain where Galen's research is taking place."[15] There were also the book markets. Galen made his way through the book markets of Alexandria, conducting his own extensive research and developing strategies to find what he needed. Galen spent his time analyzing works in libraries and correcting his own copies of medical books in an attempt to establish the authentic passages, and even having works he discovered duplicated.[16] He found libraries woefully inadequate, since they also contained corrupted copies of the works in question. This burgeoning fake book industry is blamed on the Ptolemies' book-collecting as well as that of their rivals, the Attalids of Pergamum; Galen asserts that it did not exist before their bibliomania.[17] If the Ptolemies and the Attalids had not been spending so much money acquiring old books regardless of the pedigree, Galen concludes, then there would have been no forgeries. Therefore, his research would have been much easier by having fewer texts to analyze. Mnemon's annotated copy of Hippocrates' work is but one example of this corruption. The compilation of the official copies of Aeschylus', Sophocles', and Euripides' works is another, since there would have had to have been a sifting through of many false titles and copies to create the canonical texts.[18]

Galen also disliked libraries because they were impermanent. It has been estimated that in Rome alone, more than twenty libraries were destroyed by fire, war or neglect in the course of antiquity.[19] Galen had personal experience with libraries and fire. In 197 AD, a fire destroyed the Temple of Peace in Rome. This temple, like many others, had storehouses where people kept their valuables. In Galen's case, he not only archived books by other writers but also many of his own manuscripts. Galen did not have duplicates made of his library collection; the books stored in the temple were the only copies. Years of editing works to identify authentic passages and lines were gone. In the case of his manuscripts, he would try and rewrite

---

[15] Zadorojnyi, this volume for a discussion of Galen's attitudes towards libraries and his own library.

[16] Nutton 2009: 22

[17] Galen, *Comment. In Hippocratis De natura hominis liber I*, 127, cited in Platthy 1968: 162. Fraser 1972 I 325 endnote 152 notes that there were forgeries in existence before the Ptolemies and the Attalids began their book-collecting.

[18] Blum 1991: 42 believes that textual criticism was probably not done on the plays in Athens, but some "test of authenticity" was performed, and that Lycurgus' classmate, Aristotle, was probably involved in the compilation.

[19] Ward 2000: 165.

some of them. Everything was lost.[20] Most of his library could not be replaced.[21]

For all their limitations, libraries are a part of culture; only advanced civilizations have libraries. The Alexandrian library functioned, in part, to show the world that the Ptolemies were refined and civilized. For example, the first public library in Athens, the old center of Greek learning and culture, was supposedly founded by Pisistratus when he ruled the city.[22] It was supposedly under him that the first compilation of Homer's works also took place.[23] One story claims that Ptolemy II rivaled the Athenian tyrant's library when he established the Alexandrian library.[24] However, there was more going on in Alexandria than cultural aggrandisement and the promotion of the ruler. It was important for Ptolemy and his successors to connect their kingdom to Alexander and, through him, to the cultural heritage of Greece. The Mouseion and, by extension, the library, helped to create another tradition by which the Ptolemies reinforced Greek culture in Alexandria. Aristotle's Lyceum in Athens was claimed as a model for the Mouseion and library in Alexandria, and Aristotle had been Alexander's tutor – more examples to reinforce the Ptolemaic connection.[25] The story of Pisistratus and Ptolemy II also reinforced Ptolemaic ties with Greece, specifically Athens, the old Greek cultural center.[26] Thus the creation of Alexandria as a Greek city assured the Ptolemies of cultural supremacy through their voracious book-collecting for the library and the editing of classical texts by members of the Mouseion. The Ptolemies never militarily dominated the Hellenistic world, but their new Greek cultural and learning center, the city of Alexandria, eclipsed Athens and would dominate the Greek East for centuries; Alexandria was second only to Rome in the early empire.

---

[20] See Nutton 2009: 19, who lists the citations for Galen where he discusses his loss.

[21] On Galen's account of this loss in the *Peri alypias* (*On the avoidance of sorrow*) recently discovered in a known manuscript, the *Vlatadon Codex* 14, see Nicholls 2011 and Tucci and Johnson this volume with reference to earlier bibliography.

[22] Gell. 7.17.1–2 cited in Platthy 1968: 100; *Ant. Pal.* 9, 442. Most scholars consider these stories fabrications since no public library earlier than Roman times has been found in Athens.

[23] Cic. *De or.* III, XXIV, 37; Strabo 9.1.10; Paus. 7.26.13.

[24] Tert. *Apol.* 18. See Platthy 1968: 97–110 for a list of entries dealing with Pisistratus.

[25] For analysis of Greek cultural imperialism in Egypt, see Erskine 1995 and Maehler 2004. For the association of book accumulation and monarchy, see Jacob, this volume.

[26] Both Ptolemies and Attalids gifted Athens with buildings. One of the Ptolemies gave the city a gymnasium, the Ptolemaion, which contained a library. Attalus II built a stoa in the Athenian agora. The Ptolemaion has not been found, but the rebuilt Stoa of Attalus serves as the agora museum.

The idea that the early Ptolemies were bibliomaniacs could have been reinforced during the reigns of the early Roman emperors. The early Caesars founded many libraries and they made sure that they were staffed with slaves, sometimes from their own households.[27] The early emperors were interested in Rome's libraries and steadily increased their number, as well as adding libraries to public baths.[28] One of the last Roman references to the Alexandrian library is made by Suetonius, when he reports that Domitian rebuilt one of the libraries in Rome and went to great lengths to restock it; the emperor sent his agents to the Alexandrian library to verify the authenticity of some of the books.[29] The Roman emperors were following a cultural pattern started by the early Ptolemies.

Galen may have failed to realize that the Ptolemies were looking for authentic texts just as he was, but going about it in a different way. The library and Mouseion may have been created, in part, as cultural icons, but over time book-collecting led to textual analysis. The Ptolemies used their vast resources to buy up texts of authors, transferring them to the library where scholars in the Mouseion could sift through and analyze the different texts to identify the authentic passages and then bring them together in an official canon of works. In effect, the members of the Mouseion did what Galen was trying to do with his own copies only on a much larger scale.[30] There is some evidence that medical texts were in the Alexandrian library and that textual criticism was performed on them.[31] This should have made the copies more accurate and closer to what the author intended. One has to wonder whether or not Galen ever visited the library. Perhaps Galen believed Seneca's statement about the Ptolemies, that they collected books for no other reason than to display their wealth and power.[32]

The legacy of the Alexandrian library

If the Alexandrian library was as grand as the ancient stories led us to believe, then why, as Bagnall rightly asks, do we know so little about its specifics? We do not know who founded the Alexandrian library or when. We can guess

---

[27] See Dix and Houston 2006. [28] Casson 2001: 92, and see Bowie, this volume.
[29] Suet. *Dom.* 20 discussed in Casson 2001: 103.
[30] Fraser 1972 I 326 states that the Alexandrian scholars worked to counteract forged texts and provide more accurate ones.
[31] For a more detailed analysis, see Vallance 2000.
[32] Sen. *De tranq. anim.* 9.5 as mentioned by Delia 1992: 1,457.

that the library was built somewhere in the middle of the third century BC. Galen lived around 400 years after the library was founded, in the second century AD. No contemporary writings exist on its establishment; no one is even sure where it was located.[33]

Yet the mythologizing of the library began very early. One of the earliest testimonies is *The Letter of Philocrates*, dated to the second century BC and ascribed to one "Aristeas."[34] The story tells how the Septuagint, the translation of the Hebrew scriptures into Greek, was created, under the auspices of the Mouseion in Alexandria. Much of the information is contradicted by more credible sources; there is no evidence that Ptolemy II commissioned Jewish scholars in Judaea to come to Alexandria and create the Septuagint.[35] The letter claims that Demetrius of Phalerum was appointed the first librarian and that his efforts resulted in the creation of the Septuagint. Demetrius was a graduate of Aristotle's Peripatetic School in Athens but was an advisor to Ptolemy I and not his son; he may well have helped to initially organize the library, but he was not the first librarian nor did he ever serve in that capacity.[36] This "letter" served to link the Hellenistic Jews, a substantial minority in Alexandria, with the great Ptolemaic library and its collection.

Many other stories of Ptolemaic bibliomania have been passed down: that ships were seized and any book aboard was taken to be copied, the originals going to the library, the copies returned to the ships; that once catalogued, these books' tags carried the moniker "from the ships";[37] that newly acquired books were kept in warehouses by the docks until they were transferred to the library.[38] Strabo states that Aristotle taught the kings of Egypt how to organize libraries.[39] Then there is the tradition that the libraries in Alexandria and Pergamum were in rivalry with one

---

[33] El-Abbadi 2000: 172 and 1992: 153–6 believes that Strabo's silence about the Alexandrian library meant that the fire started by Julius Caesar's troops in 48 BC destroyed the library. See Delia 1992: 1,459 footnote 44 for her response. For an assessment of whether or not the library was destroyed during Caesar's siege of Alexandria, see Hatzimichali, this volume.

[34] El-Abbadi 1992: 90–1 believes the letter was written in the second century BC and is of "somewhat doubtful historical value." Fraser 1972 I 84 dates the letter to the reign of Ptolemy VI Philometor (180–145 BC). Hadas 1951: 1–54 discusses the factors involved with the dating. He opts for a date "shortly after 132 BCE."

[35] Bagnall 2002: 349–50. He calls *The Letter* "Jewish propaganda." El-Abbadi 1992: 99 says that the Septuagint was translated piecemeal in the third and second centuries BC. See also 208 endnote 88.

[36] He was later exiled by Ptolemy II for advising Ptolemy I not to choose Philadelphus as his successor. Zenodotus was the first librarian.

[37] Galen, *Commentarii in Hippocratem Epidem.*, iii, 4–11.

[38] Galen, *Commentarii in Hippocratem Epidem.*, xvii, a 606–7.

[39] Strabo 13.1.54–5. El-Abbadi 1992: 97 interprets this as Aristotle being the spiritual father of the Alexandrian library since it was those from his Peripatetic school who influenced the

another;[40] that this rivalry grew to the point where the Egyptians stopped exporting papyrus, at which point parchment was invented by the Pergamenes.[41] Even the obviously false story of Mark Antony giving the Pergamene library to Cleopatra VII to add, presumably, to the holdings of the Alexandrian library,[42] was another fanciful tale.[43] There are even two stories about the fate of the library of Aristotle. The first is that Aristotle bequeathed his library to Theophrastus, who in turn left his library (which included Aristotle's works) to Neleus,[44] who took them to Scepsis. Ptolemy II purchased the collection from Neleus,[45] and then moved it to Alexandria. The other story is that when Sulla sacked Athens in 68 BC, he carried off to Rome the library of Apellicon the Teian, which contained the works of Aristotle and Theophrastus; it was in Rome that Tyrannio the grammarian worked on compiling and editing Aristotle's works.[46] The mythos of the great library with a huge collection was alive and well during the Roman Empire.

No one knows whether the Alexandrian library was a separate building or part of the Mouseion. Hellenistic and early Roman libraries were often connected to gymnasia and/or temples.[47] Ptolemy III built "the daughter library" of the library in the Serapeum,[48] a temple sacred to the god Serapis. Augustus Caesar built the Palatine library in the Temple of Apollo.[49] It was not until well into the imperial period that libraries were housed in separate buildings, such as the library of Pantainos (*c.* 100 AD) in Athens and the

---

library's early stages. However, the statement taken literally means that Aristotle did organize the library. This would only have added to the belief during the Middle Ages that Aristotle taught in Alexandria.

[40] Canfora 1989: 48 states that the story of Ptolemy's borrowing of the plays was made up in Pergamum to discredit the Egyptians. Because of the special relationship between the Alexandrians and Aristotle's Peripatetic School in Athens, Canfora says, the copies of these works would have made their way to Alexandria long before the time of Ptolemy III. Barnes 2000: 74 says, "Canfora's book reads like a detective novel, and parts of it are pure fiction." MacLeod 2000b: 1–2 refers to Canfora's book as "a non-fiction novel."

[41] Varro *apud* Plin. *NH* 13. 70. Cf. Isid. *Etym.* 6.2. 1, cited in Platthy 1968: 163. Erskine 1995: 45–7 thinks the story may be exaggerated. However, he believes that the rivalry between the two cities was real.

[42] Plut. *Ant.* 58.

[43] Plut. *Ant.* 59. Plutarch reports that this charge, like most leveled against Antony, was false.

[44] Diog. Laert. 5.52; Strabo 13.1.54.

[45] Ath. 1.3a–b. See Tanner 2000 for the argument that the works Aristotle prepared at Mieza when he was Alexander's tutor were those deposited in the Alexandrian library.

[46] Strabo 13.1.54; Plut. *Sull.*, 24.1–2.

[47] One of the Ptolemies built the Ptolemaion, a gymnasium for the Athenians with a library inside the building.

[48] El-Abbadi 2000: 172 believes that Ptolemy built the Serapeum library because the main library had run out of room.

[49] See Affleck, this volume and Neudecker, this volume.

library of Celsus (second century AD) in Ephesus. Library rooms have been identified from the archaeological evidence at Pergamum;[50] they are not elaborate and are part of a complex, which leads to the question: if rivalry did exist between Pergamum and Alexandria, would not the Attalids have tried to imitate the Alexandrian library in the design of their own library?[51] No remains of the Alexandrian library and the Mouseion have been found.

There is no agreement on what was in the collection. *The Letter to Philocrates* tells us Ptolemy II gave huge sums of money to the library with the aim of collecting copies of all the books in the world.[52] Ptolemy II supposedly had the Septuagint created for the library's collection. Besides the official tragedies compiled by Lycurgus in Athens, the library was also thought to contain the Egyptian "sacred records" used by Hecataeus of Abdera to write his *Aegyptiaca*; the Egyptian priest Manetho's comprehensive work on Egypt was also included in the collection.[53] Berossos, a Chaldaean priest, wrote the history of Babylonia in Greek.[54] The Alexandrian library certainly did not hold all the books in the world; it did not even have all the Greek authors.[55] There may have been some Latin literature in the library added in the time of the Ptolemies.[56] The library was primarily a Greek language institution, but also housed translations of works from other languages,[57] like the "sacred records" that Hecataeus used to write his history.

The number of volumes housed in the library is unknown, and what we have are spectacular numbers. The aforementioned *Letter to Philocrates* gives the number as 200,000 but expected it to rise to half a million,[58] which agrees with Josephus;[59] John Tzetzes, a Byzantine grammarian who lived in the twelfth century, believed that the Alexandrian library housed

---

[50] But for doubts about the identification, see Coqueugniot, this volume.
[51] Fraser 1972 I 324.   [52] *The Letter to Philocrates* 9, in Hadas 1951: 97.
[53] El-Abbadi 1992: 98.
[54] Syncellus p. 32 = Manethon, by Waddell (Loeb) fr. 3, cited in El-Abbadi 1992: 208 endnote 84.
[55] Fraser 1972 I 329–30 states that several Greek works were not in the library's collection. El-Abbadi 2004: 171 and 1992: 95 believes that the number and range of the Greek works suggests "the whole corpus of Greek literature was amassed." Maehler 2004: 9 asserts that only selected authors' complete works were created by the Mouseion.
[56] Fraser 1972 I 330; II 487 endnote 185.
[57] Ward 2000: 167 calls the library "principally a Greek language institution." Fraser 1972 I 330 believes that translations of books into Greek from other languages were probably added.
[58] *The Letter to Philocrates* 9–10, in Hadas 1951: 97. Maehler 2004: 5 believes that the reference was only for Greek books or books translated into Greek.
[59] Joseph, *AJ.* 12.2.1.

closer to 490,000 volumes;[60] Aulus Gellius and Ammianus Marcellinus, nearly 700,000 volumes.[61] Athenaeus does not even give a number: "And concerning the number of books, the establishing of libraries, and the collection in the Hall of the Muses, why need I even speak, since they are in all men's memories?"[62] In his analysis, Bagnall uses the *Thesaurus Linguae Graecae* to estimate how many works in ancient Greek survived as well as how many works were probably written; he concludes that all the numbers given for volumes in the library are grossly inflated.[63] Just how many volumes the library held is debatable.

When was the library destroyed? We know that Julius Caesar set fire to his enemy Pompey's ships in the harbor of Alexandria in 48 BC, which spread to the docks. Did Caesar destroy the library? There are scholars who believe he did,[64] just as there are scholars who dispute the claim.[65] Was the library destroyed in 215, when Caracalla's troops looted property and slaughtered Alexandrians for an insult done to him? In 273, when Aurelian retook Alexandria from the usurper Zenobia of Palmyra, much of the palace district – where the library and Mouseion were supposedly located – was destroyed.[66] In 297, Diocletian brutally crushed a revolt in Egypt and deported half the population of Alexandria.[67] There were earthquakes in 319/20 and 365, which damaged Alexandria. Was the library destroyed with the Serapeum library in 391, when Christians sought to enforce Theodosius II's decree to close all pagan temples?

Neither the Alexandrian library nor the Pergamene library were public even in the sense in which the term was used of the imperial libraries in Rome; they were royal libraries accessible only to those who were authorized. We have no stories of cooperation between Alexandria and Pergamum – or any other libraries for that matter – only rivalry and one-upmanship.

---

[60] John Tzetzes, *Ploutos* (Kaibel), 19–20, cited in Delia 1992: 1,458 footnote 38.
[61] Aul. Gell. 7.17.3, Amm. Marc. 22.16.13. Cited in El-Abbadi 1992: 150–1.
[62] Ath. 5.203e.   [63] Bagnall 2002: 352–3.
[64] Fraser 1972 I 335 notes that Roman references were all to the Serapeum library, which leads him to conclude that the library was either destroyed or "seriously diminished"; El-Abbadi 1992: 156 believes the library was destroyed. Delia 1992: 1,459 and footnote 44 disagrees with El-Abbadi over Strabo's silence about the library; Strabo's silence is a main reason why El-Abbadi believes the library was destroyed in 48 BC.
[65] Delia 1992: 1,462 states the fact that the Mouseion "which the main library serviced, flourished into the third century AD implies the library's continued survival." Delia cites Livy for support. See 1,450 footnote 6.
[66] Barnes 2000: 73.
[67] Delia 1992: 1,463 believes that some part of the Mouseion and library might have survived Aurelian's sack but whatever was left was definitely destroyed by Diocletian. She cites a Mouseion monument being inscribed and used by a private citizen at the time of Diocletian's sack as proof that the Mouseion and library were destroyed.

Few scholars worked in both cities.[68] The best-known story is that of Aristophanes of Byzantium, who served as the librarian of the Alexandrian library. The Attalids asked him to come to Pergamum and work for them, but when Ptolemy V heard of the offer, he promptly imprisoned Aristophanes where he stayed until he died.[69] Did the Ptolemaic avid book-collecting affect Greek literature, making works more accessible, canonizing the written words of authors and thereby assuring the survival of such works, or in the end did it only serve to promote the aims of the two dynasties with no bearing on the survival of Greek literature? In short, did the Alexandrian library truly make a contribution to Greek literature, or was it an intellectual exercise lost to history? There is evidence that the scholars of Alexandria exerted some influence over the organization of Homer's *Iliad* and classical Greek poetry in general, but there is no evidence for other subjects.[70] If the texts housed in the Alexandrian library were copied and distributed to individuals and to other libraries then the scholars would have had an influence that would be undetectable. There is just no way to know.

Bagnall asserts, "Indeed, no more books would have survived antiquity if the library had not been destroyed (deliberately or accidentally) than did so anyway. The destruction is simply not important."[71] All the libraries of antiquity were destroyed. Byzantine and Islamic medieval libraries were also dispersed and torched, many works never to be seen again. Wars destroy cultural artifacts, including libraries. "This is a sobering thought, which must ultimately call in question the wisdom of large concentrations of books, in ancient or modern times.... Human efforts to bring all literature together may ultimately be doomed to frustration, but there is no doubt that large libraries contribute enormously to the advancement of knowledge while they exist and are maintained."[72] The major difference between Alexandria and the huge, national and academic libraries of today is that there is cooperation and exchange of scholarly works. Before the Internet, many libraries would make copies of their manuscripts available, whether in facsimile reprints, microfilm or microfiche, thereby increasing the survival rate of the text.[73] With digitization initiatives, one can argue that manuscript collections now online are made available to anyone who has

---

[68] Fraser 1972 I 470 reports that "... there was, no doubt, some intercourse between the two centres... it is likely that such migrations... represent a change in individual scholarly loyalties rather than a general dilution of the hostility between the two schools."
[69] Erskine 1995: 46.
[70] See Fraser 1972 I 475–9 on texts and the legacy of Alexandrian scholarship.
[71] Bagnall 2002: 352–3.   [72] Barnes 2000: 75.
[73] An argument for the manuscript as a cultural object can be made here, but nothing lasts forever. Many of these manuscripts were copies of copies of copies, so errors and changes in

access to a computer; if the manuscripts are destroyed, their images exist in cyberspace.

By Roman times, the heyday of the Alexandrian library was over.[74] The first Ptolemies were the visionaries who built the collection of the library and lured scholars to Alexandria. These monarchs were within walking distance of the library and had regular contact with the librarian and the Mouseion scholars. The emperors ruled from Rome, not Alexandria. But over time, the Alexandrian library came to symbolize all libraries in the ancient world. "In the Western tradition, the romantic lament for the lost wisdom of the ancient world is reserved for the great library at Alexandria."[75] The legend of the library even inspired a modern novel about an imaginary, medieval library as great as the ancient one in Alexandria.[76] The more the library's fortunes declined, the more stories about the Alexandrian library were told.[77] Bagnall's sub-title, "library of dreams" comes from operating under the inflated *idea* of the Alexandrian library rather than its reality. The view that the library was a wondrous place filled with lost manuscripts and knowledge that can never be recovered is rejected by Bagnall. As should be clear by now, there is too much conflicting information on who founded it and who organized the collection. This is complicated by mismatched facts and figures that cannot be substantiated. Bagnall summarizes three reasons why the Alexandrian library is important: one, the Mouseion compiled and edited the texts of Greek authors – the first time such an activity was done – and the library became the repository of their work, from which the texts would have been disseminated throughout the Roman world; two, the library served as a repository to support other scholarly endeavors; and three, the image of the library as an all-encompassing center of knowledge.[78]

Regardless of whether or not the Alexandrian library's destruction is important in our collective memory or if civilization truly lost priceless works, today's libraries are greater. Modern libraries – the Library of Congress, Harvard and Yale university libraries, the British Library, the Bibliothèque Nationale de France, to name just a few – hold far more books in hundreds of languages than the Alexandrian library ever hoped to have, as well as manuscripts, rare books and materials in formats that Galen

---

text were, in most cases, made unintentionally, but the original manuscripts have long turned to dust.
[74] But see Hatzimichali, this volume, for new kinds of scholarship in Alexandria after Actium.
[75] Delia 1992: 1,464.
[76] See Ward 2000 on analyzing Umberto Eco's library in *The Name of the Rose*.
[77] Barnes 2000: 76 says that "The Alexandrian Library became a legend well within its own lifetime."
[78] Bagnall 2002: 360–1.

never dreamed of: serials, videos, DVDs, CDs, and access to the Internet and digitized materials. Yet we still look to the past, to that library, truly "the library of dreams." One could rightly ask whether, without the stories of the mythical Alexandrian library, today's great national and academic libraries would exist? In effect, modern endeavour has created today's great libraries to rival the *idea* of the Alexandrian library.

There is a new library in Egypt, a modern construct: "The new Library of Alexandria, the new Bibliotheca Alexandrina, is dedicated to recapture the spirit of openness and scholarship of the original Bibliotheca Alexandrina."[79] This library, though, is Egyptian and not Greek; it is not a royal library with restricted access like the ancient library; and its holdings will (hopefully) mirror those of the other great modern libraries. But this library is the most recent example of the mystique of the Alexandrian library exercising its magic. The Roman stories of the library – it was a universal library, collecting in languages from all over the world, that it was open for all to use, and that the collection was massively huge – is still exerting power over modern minds. The Bibliotheca Alexandrina is the latest library built to "rival" the ancient library but will, in reality, exceed its ancient predecessor.

Conclusions

Galen's story of Ptolemy III stealing the official copies of the plays of Aeschylus, Sophocles, and Euripides from the Athenians is just one of the many stories that contributed to the perception of the early Ptolemies as motivated by bibliomania and the Alexandrian library as a vast and multi-lingual treasurehouse of ancient knowledge. Such myths about the Alexandrian library started in antiquity. The library was part of the Mouseion; no contemporary writings record the details of its construction or holdings. It was only after the fortunes of the Ptolemies, and those of the library, waned that interest in the library peaked in the Roman period. This *idea* of the Alexandrian library still haunts us today, truly a "library of dreams."

[79] Bibliotheca Alexandrina, the New Library of Alexandria, About the Library page (www.bibalex.org/aboutus/overview_en.aspx; viewed 2010 February 20).

20 | Libraries and *paideia* in the Second Sophistic

Plutarch and Galen*

ALEXEI V. ZADOROJNYI

Now you see them, now you don't

It is widely accepted that the libraries of the High Roman Empire symbolised and reinforced the alliance between paideia and power.[1] Literary, epigraphic and archeological data on libraries, public as well as private,[2] jigsaw into discourse(s) of authority and knowledge-ordering. Architecturally, libraries were a feature of elite lifestyles.[3] For a literary text a place in a library marks recognition of its sociocultural (that is poetic, pedagogical, or scientific) merit.[4] At times the princeps himself might take an interest in library holdings and decor; Caligula's sweeping, albeit unrealised, ban of Virgil's and Livy's 'books and portraits... from all libraries' (*scripta et imagines... ex omnibus bibliothecis*, Suet. *Calig.* 34.2) cannot fail to impress.[5] Libraries are also tied up with the dynamics of public euergetism. The list of known library sponsors is a good cross-section of the ruling class – emperors, a prominent senator (Plin. *Ep.* 1.8.16; *CIL* 5.5262), a Roman army officer (*CIL* 3.607), a provincial fat cat,[6] Greek and Roman

---

* My thanks go to the co-editors as well as to the discussants at the 2008 St Andrews conference and at the Exeter Classics seminar (November 2010) for their friendly feedback and advice; I am grateful to William Johnson for letting me read his (then) unpublished work.
[1] Neudecker 2004; Dix and Houston 2006: 710; Winsbury 2009: 68, 74–5; Keulen 2009: 246–7; Nicholls, this volume.
[2] Scholarship – e.g. Marshall 1976: 256–7, 261–2; Bruce 1981: 566; Dix and Houston 2006: 671–2, 678, 682, 691, 709–10; Fedeli 1988: 45–6, 56–8; Winsbury 2009: 67–8; Too 2010: 41, 222, 228–9; several papers in this volume – notably that of Johnson – argue that in the case of Roman libraries the distinction between private and public may be irrelevant, since these libraries a) cater for the elite literati who are b) a high-visibility group ('public') yet c) defined by and reliant upon networks of personalised relationships ('private').
[3] Sen. *De tranq. anim.* 9.7; Vitr. 6.5.2; Petron. *Sat.* 48.4, with Starr 1987 and Too 2010: 109–10. Generally Fedeli 1988: 46–7; Knüvener 2002.
[4] E.g. Hor. *Ep.* 2.1.216–18; Mart. 5.5.5–8 and 9 *praef.*; Quint. *Inst.* 11.3.4; Apul. *Flor.* 18.9; *MAMA* VIII no. 418b.14–18 = Roueché 1993 no. 88.ii.14–18; Gal. Περὶ ἀλυπίας 21; 'Dictys' prologue *ad finem*; also Ov. *Tr.* 3.1.59–72 and the (unrealised) negotiations in Ael. Arist. 32.40.
[5] Too 2010: 204. Further examples and references in Marshall 1976: 262–3; Zadorojnyi 2006a: 373; Mülke 2008: 17 and 207–8.
[6] At Timgad: *L'année épigraphique* 1908, no. 12, with Wilson 2007: 315–16; cf. also *CIL* 5.7376 (from Tartona, Liguria).

intellectuals (Plin. *Ep.* 10.81; *POxy.* 412 col. ii.63–8), and an upper-class woman.[7]

Libraries were equally flashpoints in the contest for cultural and societal status. The Greco-Roman literati perceived themselves as a community solidarised around vintage texts and highbrow reading practices.[8] Aulus Gellius' *Noctes Atticae* demonstrates how episodes of study and debate in libraries both in Rome (11.17; 13.20.1; 16.8.2) and elsewhere (Tibur: 9.14.3, 19.5.4; Patrae: 18.9.5) might add to one's image as an insider in terms of elite erudition;[9] pertinently, in a polemical context the library address of an authoritative *and* recherché antiquarian bookroll ('in the Temple of Peace...') can be brought into play against a wilful smart aleck (5.21.4–13), thus highlighting the divide between the undereducated impostor (5.21.4 'he had read very little, and that of the popular range', *perpauca eademque a uolgo protrita legerat*) and the true expert (5.21.1 *uir adprime doctus*).[10] The library space itself is sometimes literally at stake too: one famous and much-discussed example is the controversy over Favorinus' statue in the library precinct at Corinth ([Dio Chr.] 37).[11] Dio was involved in broadly similar acrimony in his native Prusa where complaints were made that he was turning a public library into a family mausoleum (Plin. *Ep.* 10.81).

For the purposes of euergetic self-presentation, libraries may have been an exciting option yet they were apparently not the default choice; Herodes Atticus, arguably the greatest indigenous benefactor of Roman Greece,[12] did not sponsor libraries as far as we can tell.[13] Furthermore, the literary sources of the Second Sophistic[14] are not all enthusiastic about libraries. The orator Aper in Tacitus' *Dialogue* sarcastically remarks on the poetastering by Julius Caesar and Brutus:

---

[7] Flavia Meletine: *Altertümer von Pergamon* VIII.3 no. 38 (84–5).
[8] Johnson 2010: 11–13, 39–40, 94, 202–5, and *passim*; also Johnson this volume.
[9] Johnson 2010: 134–5 and in this volume; also Jacob 2000: 102; Keulen 2009: 246–7, 315–16; generally Beall 2004: 219–21.
[10] Johnson 2010: 131 and also Johnson this volume 351 on the defeated pseudo-insiders ('poseurs') of elite textual culture in the *Noctes Atticae*, see Johnson 2010: 210–11; further, Vardi 2001.
[11] Swain 1989; Gleason 1995: 8–20; Korenjak 2000: 155–6; Whitmarsh 2001: 119–21; König 2001.
[12] Tobin 1997: 162–210, 295–331; Galli 2002.
[13] Cf. Dix and Houston 2006: 710 on the silence about the foundation of the Palatine library in Augustus' *Res Gestae*.
[14] Using the term as a catch-all name for Greco-Roman intellectuals from the first to the third centuries AD, though many of them were distant from or hostile to sophistic as such.

for they wrote poems too and placed them in libraries (*in bibliothecas rettulerunt*). They did no better than Cicero – but they were luckier (*non melius... sed felicius*), since even fewer people know they wrote verse. (21.6)

A library does not safeguard texts from oblivion, it seems. Acquisition of culture through libraries is not a given either. Seneca as a Stoic moralist and Lucian as a protean satirist disparage people who set store by expensive literary paraphernalia.[15] Seneca stresses that the expansionist approach to books leads down an intellectual cul-de-sac:

Wherefore the countless books and libraries, of which the owner has managed to read, in his lifetime, just the tables of contents? <...> it is far more adequate to commit oneself to a few authors, rather than to go astray among many.

quo innumerabiles libros et bybliothecas, quarum dominus uix tota uita indices perlegit? <...> multoque satius est paucis te auctoribus tradere quam errare per multos. (*De tranq. animi* 9.4)

The Senecan example (9.5) of such futile book-collecting is the archetype itself – the Great Library of Alexandria. Quantities of texts may produce a delusion of paideia (Lucian *Ign. bibl.* 29) but miss out on the real thing.[16]

So how important were libraries in the self-perception and self-promotion of the discursively active class of the Second Sophistic? To gauge the problem it is useful to examine texts where an intellectual is facing – describing, praising, lamenting, castigating – a city. Some authors would salute and frequent libraries. For Martial, libraries (*bibliothecas*) are integral to the refined and pleasurable ambience of Rome (12 *praef.*).[17] Aelius

---

[15] Luxury editions: Lucian *Ign. bibl.* 2 and 7; decorated bookcases: Sen. *De tranq. animi.* 9.5–7. Marshall 1976: 256; Fedeli 1988: 47.

[16] On Lucian's essay see most recently Johnson 2010: 158–70. Cf. the argument in Dio Chr. 4.30 that to value acquaintance with many books is the way of the superficial, 'human' (*vs* true and 'divine') paideia (νομίζουσι... καὶ πλείστοις ἐντυγχάνοντα βιβλίοις τοῦτον σοφώτατον καὶ μάλιστα πεπαιδευμένον). Quintilian's repudiation of the very idea of library when identifying good stylistic models (10.1.104 'we sample genres, not search through libraries', *nos genera degustamus, non bibliothecas excutimus*; cf. 10.1.57) bespeaks a more pragmatic need to show off literary culture while avoiding the impression of scholasticism – but this is perhaps not totally unrelated to the 'philosophical' demurral of Seneca and Dio.

[17] Conversely, Ammianus Marcellinus in the fourth century sees 'the permanent tomb-like closure of libraries' (14.6.18 *bybliothecis sepulcrorum ritu in perpetuum clausis*) as a symptom of Rome's cultural and moral collapse.

Aristides in the *Panathenaicus* briefly dwells on the libraries of Athens as a unique cultural asset:[18]

warehouses of books such as are not seen anywhere else in the world and very much the beautiful speciality of Athens

βιβλίων ταμιεῖα οἷα οὐχ ἑτέρωθι γῆς φανερῶς, καὶ μάλα τῶν Ἀθηνῶν κόσμος οἰκεῖος (354)

Pausanias, who usually sidesteps the more recent architecture,[19] makes an exception for Hadrian's library in Athens, designating it somewhat obliquely[20] as 'the buildings... where books are kept' (1.18.9 οἰκήματα... κατάκειται δὲ ἐς αὐτὰ βιβλία).

Nevertheless when talking about a puny Phocian settlement Pausanias omits a library from the inventory of must-have elements in a polis (10.4.1 'if the name "polis" is applicable to people who have no town hall or gymnasium, no theatre, no agora, no water reservoir...'). Aelius Aristides in his prose lament for Smyrna in the wake of the earthquake of AD 178 does not single out the library[21] in his list of the destroyed structures across the city (18.6; cf. 19.3); this is hardly a tacit indication of the library's survival. In Aristides' description of the prosperous Pax Romana (26.97) 'everything is full of gymnasia, fountains, gateways, temples, craftsmen and teachers' – but where are the libraries?

Our best witness to how inconspicuous the libraries are in the Second Sophistic cityscape is the epideictic textbook by Menander Rhetor. When laying down guidelines for praising a city[22] Menander either does not include a library in the generic catalogue of admirable features[23] or telescopes libraries into *mouseia*.

from the beauty of [the city's] appearance, for instance: its colonnades, harbours, acropolis, splendid temples and statues. Then he will praise the festivals and holidays, *mouseia*,[24] theatres and competitions. (2.431.3–7)

---

[18] Too 2010: 47, 196–7. The teasingly vague θησαυροὶ γραμμάτων on the streets of Corinth in Aristides' *Isthmian* (46.28) can imply bookshops as well as paintings – but certainly not libraries.

[19] Arafat 1996: 37–44, 212–14.   [20] 'Almost as an afterthought': Too 2010: 197.

[21] Mentioned by Strabo 14.1.37.

[22] Within a gamut of possible contexts; see Webb 2009: 155–61; cf. Trapp. 1995: 168.

[23] E.g. 2.386.23–6 colonnades, temples, harbours, race-courses, baths, 'flowing waters' (aqueducts?), groves; also 2.382.15–16; 2.429.16–17; 2.433.15–16.

[24] Following the text printed in Russell and Wilson 1981; the manuscripts read μουσικά.

Menander's coverage of Athens is particularly rich in references to *mouseia* as part of the enlightened climate of the city:[25]

to mention Athens itself... the hierophants and torch-bearers, the speech-contests and the *mouseia* (καὶ λόγων ἀγώνων καὶ μουσείων),[26] the teachers, the youths... (2.392.15–18)

the passion (πόθος)... for the [Athenian] mysteries and initiations, *mouseia* and theatres of discourse (μουσεῖα καὶ θέατρα λόγων), the literary competitiveness of the teachers (παιδευτῶν φιλοτιμίαι περὶ τοὺς λόγους)... the Areopagus, the Lyceum, the beauty of the Acropolis... (2.396.26–30)

The Athenians pride themselves on ancient tales, *mouseia*, and literature (μουσείοις καὶ λόγοις)... but our *mouseion* is not inferior to theirs. (2.426.26–31)

Juxtaposed with *logoi* and teachers, *mouseion* certainly points towards intense textual activity. Elsewhere the word is known to imply specifically literary learning. Thus the philosopher Longinus is famously described by Eunapius as 'a living library and walking museum' (*VS* 456b βιβλιοθήκη τις ἦν ἔμψυχος καὶ περιπατοῦν μουσεῖον);[27] the Younger Pliny refers to his country retreat, where he is busy reading and writing (*Ep.* 1.9.4 *aut lego aliquid aut scribo*, 1.9.5 *cum libellis loquor*) as his 'true and hermitical *mouseion*' (1.9.6 *uerum secretumque* μουσεῖον); in Plutarch's *Table-Talks*, 705E the theatrical pleasures are distinguished from the pleasures of the *mouseion*, which may be an allusion to reading. But *mouseion* (or for that matter *gymnasion*)[28] is still not *bibliothēkē*. Menander's idiom seems to connect *mouseia* more with sophistic performance (2.398.7 ἅμιλλαι λόγων ἐπὶ τῶν μουσείων, cf. 2.396.28 μουσεῖα καὶ θέατρα λόγων) than with written texts – in effect, he fades out the books. This trend did not start with Menander. In Dio Chrysostom's *Alexandrian Oration* the Great Mouseion is hailed as a kind of shrine of high-calibre culture the citizens should be looking up to (32.100), but never explicitly associated with books and text-centred scholarship.[29] Whether we are talking about Athens, Alexandria or

---

[25] Cf. Ath. 5.187d: 'the city of Athens, the *mouseion* of Greece'.
[26] μουσείων here is, again, editorial emendation of the manuscript reading μουσικῶν.
[27] Further Too 1998: 209–10; 2000 and 2010: 84, 90–4.
[28] The archaeology of Greek libraries firmly brackets many of them with *gymnasia*: Blanck 1992 149–51; Höpfner 2002c. For the implied link between gymnasia and textual lore, cf. e.g. Arist. *Or.* 46.28 'the gymnasia, schools, knowledge, stories' (τὰ γυμνάσια, τὰ διδασκαλεῖα, καὶ μαθήματά τε καὶ ἱστορήματα).
[29] '... so that your Mouseion appears not just as a place in the city (τόπος ἐν τῇ πόλει), as indeed there are, I imagine, other places with meaningless names (μάτην προσαγορεύονται), since they do not possess the substance (τὸ πρᾶγμα μὴ ἔχοντες) to go with the name'; Trapp 1995: 171, 173. Contrast Men. Rhet. 1.360.23–4: the Alexandrians are proud 'even nowadays

an unspecified polis, a term that connotes holiness and harmony ('sacred place of the Muses') while steering clear of writtenness *per se*[30] amounts to evasion of literacy as a cultural factor. The books are invisible both in Dio's Alexandria, which may be in a moral crisis, and inside the paideutically flourishing cities of Menander Rhetor.

Why do libraries have such a low-key presence in the polis-oriented rhetoric of the Greek *pepaideumenoi* of the empire? The question promises no uncomplicated answers. Illiteracy (partial literacy, basic education...) among the wider audience of the sophistic performances[31] is a feasible yet not a decisive constraint, because the sociology of literacy and the reception of literacy are, bluntly, not the same thing. While libraries obviously matter more to the educated elite, it does not follow that non-readers and semi-literates would not have been able to relate and react to the notion of a library as the headquarters of book culture – even if quite unfamiliar with the texts therein. Nor should we exaggerate the generic orality of the sophistic discourse. The ancient sources themselves are not in the habit of creating a polar opposition between texts and performances – in fact written texts and declamation can form a handy partnership: the sophist Proclus of Naucratis (Philostr. *VS* 604) 'had at home a cache of books (θήκη βιβλίων) which were available to the audience as supplement to the lectures (ἐς τὸ πλήρωμα τῆς ἀκροάσεως)'.[32] The imperial Greek sophists are, it goes without saying, on intimate terms with books (e.g. [Arist.] *Rhet.* 2.78; Arist. 4.3–5; Ath. 13.567a; Philostr. *VS* 488, 490), but they somehow do not give full justice to libraries. Is this enough to overthrow the far-reaching thesis that '[t]he representation of antiquity's library dramatizes the institution as a vehicle for elite cultural definition' (Too 2010: 9)? Probably not, however, it should make us seek a more nuanced picture of the negotiation of literary materiality by the *Kulturträger* of the High Empire.

---

because of grammar, geometry and philosophy'. The Mouseion is not mentioned at all – the paideutic curriculum takes precedence over the site.

[30] Cf. Libanius' comment that many senators of fifth-century AD Constantinople have 'military rather than cultural' qualifications (*Or.* 1.76 ἐξ ὅπλων ἢ μουσείων τὸ πλέον); *mouseia*-based experience is, once again, education at large.

[31] Korenjak 2000: 49–57.

[32] Cf. Paus. 6.23.7; Plut. *De aud.* 43F; Maternus in Tac. *Dial.* 39.1 complains that the energy of contemporary oratory has been sapped by the 'lecture-halls and record-offices' (as opposed to the Republican forum) where the cases are heard (*quantum uirium detraxisse orationi auditoria et tabularia...*); the politically slanted passage is short of anti-archival philosophy *tout court*. In the undeniably hyper-elitist setting of Athenaeus' banquet, the sophistic guests 'bring knapsacks of literature' with them (1.4b κομίζοντας τὰ ἀπὸ τῶν στρωματοδέσμων γράμματα); yet see n. 64 below.

Libraries and paideia in the Second Sophistic   383

The task therefore calls for a body of text guaranteeing no less than thoroughbred elite literacy. In the remainder of this chapter I am going to consider Plutarch and Galen as authors whose works are not only unmistakably written literature aimed at genteel and educated Greco-Roman readership, but also macrotextual transcripts of intellectual identity. (Hereafter, 'macrotext' stands for voluminous output and, what is more, the bedrock ideological cohesion across assorted and ostensibly distinct narratives and/or arguments; in the Galenic corpus such an axis is medical professionalism, whereas the Plutarchan *Lives* and *Moralia* fill out philosophical benchmarks.) It will be shown that Plutarch and Galen envisage libraries quite differently. For Plutarch, libraries belong within the ethico-political problematics of culture and power that straddle the past and the present. Galen's attitude to libraries, on the other hand, is grounded above all in his broader concerns about knowledge and language. Having said that, the differences arising from the *sunkrisis* between Plutarch and Galen can be mapped onto a panoramic spectrum of ancient reflection about books as the ontological and social interface of paideia.

Plutarch: library as example

Plutarch is an author who reveals few details about his research and writing routines. Not that he is indifferent to displays of scholarly prowess, casually pointing up his expert knowledge of the Platonic corpus (*Quaest. conv.* 718C) or coyly describing the book he just referred to as 'uncommon' (675B τῶν οὐκ ἐν μέσῳ). Yet on the whole Plutarch's macrotext is reticent on the process of working with others' texts.[33] When there is a glimpse of technique, it serves to remind us of higher, philosophically charged priorities. The essay *On Tranquillity of Mind* claims to be a rapid, half-baked composition knocked up out of Plutarch's notes (*hupomnēmata*),[34] for ethical profit must come before style:

I gathered together from my note-books (ἀνελεξάμην ... ἐκ τῶν ὑπομνημάτων) those observations on tranquillity of mind which I happened to have made for myself (ἐμαυτῷ), believing that you, in turn, requested this discourse not for the sake of reading a piece that pursues elegant style (οὐκ ἀκροάσεως ἕνεκα θηρωμένης καλλιγραφίαν) but for the constructive use ... (464F)

---

[33] In the hands-on technical sense, that is. Literary and philosophical criticism abounds in Plutarch but is seldom staged as follow-up to the act of reading; yet cf. *Adv. Col.* 1107E (ἀναγινωσκομένου τοῦ συγγράμματος).
[34] Van der Stockt 1999; generally on *hupomnēmata* Dorandi 2000b: 84–101.

Another key passage is the proem to *Demosthenes-Cicero*. Here Plutarch admits that his kind of research is bibliographically demanding:

> for a man who has undertaken to compile a *historia*, the textual sources (ἀναγνωσ-μάτων) of which are not immediately at hand, since they are foreign and scattered elsewhere, the first concern must be to base himself in a famous, cultured and well populated city (τὰν πόλιν εὐδόκιμον καὶ φιλόκαλον καὶ πολυάνθρωπον), so that with access to plenty of various books (ὡς βιβλίων τε παντοδαπῶν ἀφθονίαν ἔχων) ... he produces a work that is not missing any relevant material. (*Dem.* 2.1)

The proem purports, however, to vindicate Plutarch's authority precisely in the absence of such conducive milieu.

> But I live in a small town, and I care to stay there (φιλοχωροῦντες) so that it does not get smaller... (*Dem.* 2.2)

Earlier on it is declared that our raison d'être should be ethical virtue which is realisable anywhere (*Dem.* 1.1–4); the big city with all its books pales by comparison.

The nondescript and malleable 'plenty of various books' in the anonymous great city of *Demosthenes*, 2.1 allows Plutarch to blur or indeed to eschew the concept of metropolitan library as institutionalised venue.[35] A similar strategy is used in the preface to the dialogue *On the Delphic E*, addressed to the Stoic and poet Sarapio.[36] By offering the dialogue, Plutarch invites Sarapio and his friends 'over there' (αὐτόθι) to reciprocate in kind,

> ... since you have a great city at your disposal and enjoy greater pastime among many books and various discussions (ἐν βιβλίοις πολλοῖς καὶ παντοδαπαῖς διατριβαῖς) (384E)

Sarapio's whereabouts are most definitely in Athens, but Plutarch chooses not to name the 'great city'. Once again, he looks forward to the unidentified 'many books', leaving the libraries – the Athenian κόσμος οἰκεῖος, as Aelius Aristides will later call them – out of the picture.

To appreciate the scale of the Plutarchan non-engagement with contemporary libraries across the extant corpus, one has to weigh up some

---

[35] Zadorojnyi 2006b: 113–19 argues that the passage develops intertextual dialogue with Polybius' disapproval of the armchair historian (12.27.4) who is either ensconced in a city 'with records aplenty' (πόλιν ἔχουσαν ὑπομνημάτων πλῆθος) or relies upon a neighbouring library (βιβλιοθήκην που γειτνιῶσαν). Plutarch's βιβλίων... ἀφθονίαν tallies with the Polybian ὑπομνημάτων πλῆθος, but 'the library next door' is not there; the link between scholarhip and libraries willy-nilly thins out.

[36] For this figure, see Flacelière 1951; Jones 1978: 228–31; Puech 1992: 4874–8; Babut 1993: 206–8; Geagan 1991; Bowie 2002b: 45–6; 2004: 121–2.

of the most patently missed opportunities. Plutarch may not have lived to see Hadrian's library in Athens[37] or to witness the dispute around Favorinus' statue[38] in the library precinct at Corinth. Yet the medium-size library sponsored by Titus Flavius Pantaenus and dedicated in Athens between AD 98 and 102,[39] falls safely within Plutarch's lifetime; he surely knew about it but mentions neither Pantaenus nor the building. Another intriguing silence much closer to home is the library at Delphi constructed between AD 99 and 102. The man in charge of its construction was Flavius Soclarus (*Syll.*³ 823B), who happened to be a close friend of Plutarch, or maybe that friend's son.[40] Plutarch had a lifelong connection with the Delphian sanctuary (*An seni* 792F) and quite likely was on the Amphyctionic board that funded the library. But despite his proximity to it, he never talks about the project.[41] Likewise, not a word on the grand twin libraries of the Forum of Trajan in Rome, inaugurated on 1 January AD 112. It is also known that Plutarch visited Alexandria at least once (*Quaest. conv.* 678C 'upon our return from Alexandria'), yet there is nothing on his experience of the Great Library.

A particularly interesting 'omission' is the so-called Celsus library in Ephesus, datable to the first quarter of the second century.[42] Erected in honour of Tiberius Iulius Celsus Polemaeanus, a Greek from Sardis who had an illustrious career in the Roman imperial hierarchy,[43] the edifice was sponsored (although not brought to completion) by his son Tiberius Iulius Aquila Polemaeanus, himself a Roman senator and consul suffect in AD 110.[44] The inscriptions and façade of the Celsus library epitomise the criteria of self-display by the imperial Greek elite seeking to integrate the cultural optics of Hellenism with the imagery of Roman power.[45] Neither the Polemaeani nor their library are mentioned by Plutarch. Nonetheless the odds are that he knew of this family, considering that Aquila's colleague as

---

[37] On which see Callmer 1944: 172–5; Strocka 1981: 318–20; Blanck 1992: 171, 210–11; Boatwright 2000: 153–7; Höpfner 2002b.
[38] At the very least he knew Favorinus personally: *Quaest. conv.* 734F–735C, *De prim. frig.* 945F.
[39] Strocka 1981: 304–6; Camp 1986: 187–91; Blanck 1992: 170–1; Höpfner 2002c: 78–80. On Pantaenus' inscription, see Oliver 1979.
[40] *Amat.* 749B; *De soll. an.* 959D and esp. 964D; *Quaest. conv.* 640B–641A, 654C–655C, 682A–B, 694E–F, 726B. For the debated allocation of these references between Soclarus Snr and his son, see Jones 1971: 22 n. 15 and Puech 1992: 4879–83 *vs* Ziegler 1951, cols. 684–5 and Babut 1999.
[41] It borders on ironic that Plutarch's own statue (herm?), of which the inscribed base survives (*Syll.*³ 843A), could have been standing within or near that very library.
[42] Wildberg et al. 1953; Callmer 1944: 170–1; Strocka 1981: 322–9; Blanck 1992: 172–4, 206–7; Outscher 1995; Höpfner 2002e, also Nicholls, this volume.
[43] *Procos. Ponti et Bithyniae c.* AD 84/85, *cos. suff.* AD 92, *procos. Asiae c.* AD 105/107. *PIR*² J 260; Halfmann 1979: 111–12.
[44] *PIR*² J 168; Halfmann 1979: 133.   [45] R. Smith 1998: 73–5; Burrell 2009: 78–82.

consul suffect in AD 110 was C. Avidius Nigrinus, one of the dedicatees of the Plutarchan essay *On Brotherly Love* as well as an attested benefactor of Delphi (*Syll.*³ 827).[46] It is always possible to read reticence as muffled confrontation; proving it is usually harder. Plutarch is of course wont to inscribe ideology upon contemporary Greek statesmanship.[47] In a memorable passage of *On Tranquillity of Mind* his opinion is provocatively pungent.

> Yet some man (a Chian, Galatian, or Bythinian) would not be happy with whatever fame and power among his fellow-citizens that has fallen to his lot, but weeps because he does not wear the patrician shoe (πατρικίους); if he does wear it, then because he is not yet Roman praetor (μηδέπω στρατηγεῖ Ῥωμαίων); if he is a praetor, because he is not a consul (μὴ ὑπατεύει); and if a consul, because he is proclaimed not first, but second. (470C)

As scholars have rightly commented, Plutarch objects not to Greek participation in the Roman hierarchy but to the overly ambitious attitude[48] embodied in certain unnamed individuals.[49] There is no way to be sure that the target here is specifically the Polemaeani, as there were other upper-class Greeks in Plutarch's day and age who rose to senatorial and consular rank; with at least two of them Plutarch kept company.[50] Nor is it clear whether the Plutarchan essay and the Celsus library – as work-in-progress at best? – could be contemporaneous. Rather, the text and the building clash at the level of mindsets. The contrast we are entitled (I believe) to draw is, ultimately, between the high-wrought euergetism of the Celsus library and the homely modesty of Plutarch's writing that is shrewdly flagged in the proem of *Tranquillity* (464F).

The libraries that Plutarch does mention are all found in the Roman *Lives* and located invariably in the past. Absorbed by the ethico-political narrative, these libraries are treated as sites where powerful Romans interact, sometimes drastically, with book culture. The victorious Sulla in Athens grabs Apellicon's collection of Aristotelian books (*Sulla* 26.1 ἐξεῖλεν ἑαυτῷ τὴν ... βιβλιοθήκην); Augustus' sister Octavia dedicates a library to the 'honour and memory' of her son Marcellus (*Marc.* 30.11);[51] Antony

---

[46] *PIR*² A 1408; Jones 1971: 32–3, 52–4; Puech 1992: 4840.
[47] See esp. Trapp 2004.   [48] Swain 1996: 169–70; Stadter 2002: 124–5.
[49] *Pace* Russell 1973: 9: 'The whole development may well be on a universal moral plane, with no special pointedness in the example.'
[50] C. Iulius Antiochus Philopappus: *PIR*² J.151; Jones 1971: 59; Puech 1992: 4,870–3; Halfmann 1979: 131. C. Iulius Eurycles Herculanus: *PIR*² J.302; Jones 1971: 41; Puech 1992: 4850–5; Halfmann 1979: 125–6. Prosopography of the Greek high-flyers in the period: Halfmann 1979; Birley 1997.
[51] For this library see Dix and Houston 2006: 685–8.

transfers the library holdings of Pergamum to Alexandria as a favour to Cleopatra (*Ant.* 58.9 τὰς ἐκ Περγάμου βυβλιοθήκας).

Plutarch seems characteristically reluctant to approve or condemn but this does not prevent him attempting to engineer an evaluative response on the part of the readers. Such 'descriptive' (as opposed to directly protreptic) moralism is at work throughout the *Parallel Lives*.[52] The story of Julius Caesar and the library of Alexandria (*Caes.* 49.5–8) is arranged so that the unspoken message is almost unmissable. First we are told how the fire started on Caesar's orders during the fighting in Alexandria accidentally destroyed the Great Library (*Caes.* 49.6 τὴν μεγάλην βιβλιοθήκην . . . διέφθειρε). Next, Plutarch cues in a close-up on Caesar's narrow escape in a naval skirmish. Caesar swims for his life and still manages to rescue his notebooks (49.7–8 βιβλίδια). The juxtaposition of μεγάλη βιβλιοθήκη and the diminutive βιβλίδια is striking. Resourceful and self-seeking as ever, Caesar has precipitated a bibliographical disaster yet succeeded in protecting his own documents.[53]

The longest and happiest Plutarchan passage on Roman 'librarianship' is the panegyric on the library of Lucullus.[54] Books are the recipe for configuring the retired general's villa(s) as a perfect paideutic habitat.

> His provision of books (τὰ περὶ τὴν τῶν βιβλίων κατασκευήν) deserves praiseworthy mention, for he collected many high-quality copies (πολλὰ καὶ γεγραμμένα καλῶς συνῆγεν). And the use they were put to was even nobler than the acquisition (ἥ τε χρῆσις ἦν φιλοτιμοτέρα τῆς κτήσεως). The libraries were open to everybody (ἀνειμένων πᾶσι τῶν βιβλιοθηκῶν); their promenades and reading rooms welcomed without restriction all Greeks who would come and spend time there as if in an abode of the Muses (ὥσπερ εἰς Μουσῶν τι καταγώγιον), escaping gladly from other occupations. Lucullus often spent time there himself, joining the scholars (τοῖς φιλολόγοις) in the promenades and giving his advice to politicians who required it. His house was a sort of home-hearth and Hellenic prytaneum for those who came to Rome (καὶ ὅλως ἑστία καὶ πρυτανεῖον Ἑλληνικὸν ὁ οἶκος ἦν αὐτοῦ τοῖς ἀφικνουμένοις εἰς τὴν Ῥώμην). He was fond of the whole of philosophy . . . Cicero wrote an excellent treatise (σύγγραμμα . . . πάγκαλον) in defence of this sect [the Academics], using Lucullus as his mouthpiece in the argument in favour of comprehension, and his own person for the opposite argument. The title of the book is *Lucullus* (Λεύκολλος δ' ἀναγέγραπται τὸ βιβλίον). (*Luc.* 42.1–4)

---

[52] Pelling 2002: 237–51; Duff 1999 esp. 68–71 and 2007/2008.
[53] Further Zadorojnyi 2005: 132–3.
[54] For a rich and searching discussion of the testimonia and comparanda, see Dix 2000; I am much indebted to his insights. See also Tröster 2008: 30, 32; Tutrone and Dix in this volume; Too 2010: 42 and 227–30, who does not refer to Dix.

Lucullus ticks all the right boxes: having collected first-rate books, he generously shares them with the Greek expats[55] and ends up by effectively becoming a book himself (42.4).[56] Such idealisation fits in with the tenor of the *Life* that is favourable towards Lucullus.[57] Critically, Plutarch is careful to whitewash the fact that most of Lucullus' books were looted from the Greek East;[58] the reference to 'usage more noble than acquisition' (42.1) is tactful and conciliatory. Plutarch likes it when eminent Romans strive after Hellenic paideia[59] and so is ready to exonerate their marauding bibliophilism.[60] Aemilius Paulus is praised for having picked books from the spoils of Macedon as a gift for his 'letter-loving' (φιλογραμματοῦσι) sons (*Aem.* 28.11). Sulla gets no stick for taking Aristotle's books either; indeed the upshot proves agreeable because in Italy the texts are edited and put into circulation by Andronicus (*Sull.* 26.2 εἰς μέσον θεῖναι).[61]

While historically Lucullus' library may have been modelled on the Mouseion of Alexandria,[62] the phrase 'home-hearth and Hellenic prytaneion' (ἑστία καὶ πρυτανεῖον Ἑλληνικὸν) alludes to a Delphic oracle about Athens, which is cited by Athenaeus (5.187d ἑστίαν καὶ πρυτανεῖον τῶν Ἑλλήνων).[63] Lucullus' ideal library is a therefore a mini-Athens 'recreated' (Too 2010: 229) in the bosom of Latium. The Romanness of the host space is important, since in the *Parallel Lives* it is the Romans that deal with large book collections. As if to offset his eschewal of contemporary libraries, Plutarch paints the library of Lucullus as a paradigmatic template of Greco-Roman elite relations. Amidst books, Hellenic paideia and Roman power consummate their mutually beneficial union. The scenario is no doubt meant to resonate with political and ethopoeic expectations about Plutarch's imperial present. Thus the Roman addressee of *Against Colotes* – a dialogue framed as impromptu colloquium during a group reading of an Epicurean treatise (1107E) – is credited with the view that 'to recall

---

[55] On the clientele of Lucullus' library, see Dix 2000: 454–5; Too 2010: 230.

[56] For the person-as-text metonymy, see *De Is.* 379A: 'we describe the man who is buying the books by Plato as "buying Plato"'; cf. Sen. *De ben.* 7.6.1.

[57] Swain 1990: 143–5 and 1992; yet see also Tröster 2005 and 2008: 28–31, 53–60, 70–1, 150 on the negative traits.

[58] Swain 1990: 144 n. 106; Dix 2000: 442–3. Cf. Isid. *Etym.* 6.5.1 'from the Pontic spoils' (*e Pontica praeda*).

[59] Swain 1990; Tröster 2008: 41–4.

[60] Zadorojnyi 2005: 135–6. Pompey's expropriation of books from a stock of civil war spoils (*Pomp.* 4.2) is more problematic (he is taken to trial over this), but then civil war is an especially fraught ethico-political context.

[61] The passage goes on to add that Andronicus wrote up the catalogues 'which are in circulation today' (τοὺς νῦν φερομένους πίνακας) – another rare peek into Plutarch's scholarly 'now'!

[62] So Jacob 2000: 88; Canfora 1988: 20; Fedeli 1988: 33.

[63] Cf. 6.254b; the allusion was sighted by Dix 2000: 456 n. 46.

and have in hand the arguments of the ancients is the most regal activity' (*ibid.*, βασιλικωτάτην διατριβήν). We should probably be thinking about the Platonic philosopher-kings here, but the word *basileus* is elastic enough to signify the emperor too (e.g. *De def. or.* 419E).

The description of Lucullus' library as 'open to everybody' shows that for Plutarch the division between public and private libraries is a porous one. By keeping an open house Lucullus provides for the community of statesmen and Greek *pepaideumenoi* as stakeholders in literary culture, leadership and philosophy. It may even appear that the oral voice of this community eclipses the books altogether. Peter White astutely observes that in Plutarch's passage the books actually 'remain in the background', the focus being on live discussion and 'the liberal give-and-take among intellectual peers' (White 2009: 283).[64] At the end of the day, the library matters not so much for its contents but as a setting for good discursive praxis. And yet the last word belongs to a 'sterling text' (42.4 σύγγραμμα... πάγκαλον) that has captured Lucullus-the-philosopher in action, namely Cicero's *Academica*. Plutarch does not bother to tell how he came across it – so not necessarily in a library...

Galen and the frail text

Notwithstanding his dislike of 'sophistry',[65] Galen is a dextrous (if grouchy) self-promoter well-versed in the challenges and discursive stratagems of the Second Sophistic.[66] A key component of Galen's intellectual persona[67] is the emphasis he lays on the thoroughness and encyclopaedic exhaustiveness of his research. He rarely forgets to press home his expert mastery (punctuation and all: Περὶ ἀλυπίας 14) of the relevant texts. In the

---

[64] Cf. Too 2010: 229–30. The situation is not fundamentally dissimilar in Athenaeus' *Deipnosophists*. The dining intellectuals in Athenaeus associate literary data with libraries (14.648c ἐκ ποίας βιβλιοθήκης), and their host Larensis is described as an eminent book-collector (1.3a–b). Yet his library is but 'la toile de fond' (Jacob 2004a: 149) of the banqueters' cultural display that oralises the texts by way of 'live' dialogical *recall* of citations: Jacob 2000: 89–91, 104–10; 2004a esp. 157–63 (163 'tout passe par la voix et l'écoute') and 2004b: 135–8, 154, 157–8; Too 2000: 120–2.

[65] E.g. *De loc. aff.* 3.3 = VIII 144 K; *De puls. diff.* 1.1 = VIII 493–4 K; *De dieb. decret.* 1.5 = IX 794 K; *De praecogn.* 1 = XIV 605 K. Pearcy 1993: 452; Brunt 1994: 51–2; Von Staden 1997: 34–6; Schlange-Schöningen 2003: 149, 300.

[66] *Pace* Brunt 1994: 43–5: see Bowersock 1969: 66–9, 74; Nutton 1972; Kollesch 1981; Pearcy 1993: 449–56; Swain 1996: 357–79; Von Staden 1997; Schlange-Schöningen 2003 esp. 153–60, 165–6 n. 116, 292 and 300; Mattern 2008: 7–10, 23, 70–1.

[67] Further Nutton 1972; Boudon 2000 and Boudon-Millot 2009.

setting of medicosophistic performance[68] Galen pits his own anatomical expertise against the collective voice of the extant tradition summoned to the show in the guise of books (*De libr. propr.* 3.16–17 = XIX 22 K).[69] As a Hippocratic commentator[70] Galen repeatedly underscores his effort to collate manuscripts in order to clinch the most accurate and authentic reading. He takes on and sifts through the messy, controversial textual plurality (normally, other editors or commentators are at fault) towards bona fide phrasing or titles.[71] This is where libraries enter the frame. Public libraries and private book-collections make up the terrain where Galen's research is taking place.[72]

in all the manuscripts which I read, having purposely checked every copy in the public libraries and every copy that my friends had (ἐξεπίτηδες ἅπαντα μὲν ἰδόντες τὰ κατὰ τὰς δημοσίας βιβλιοθήκας, ἅπαντα δὲ τὰ παρὰ τοῖς φίλοις), I found this reading... (*In Hipp. VI epid.* 4.21 = XVII.B 194–5 K)

Then I went straightaway to every library and bookseller (εὐθέως περιῆλθον ἁπάσας μὲν τὰς βιβλιοθήκας, ἅπαντας δὲ τοὺς βιβλιοπώλας), as well as to the doctors whom I knew to take this monograph... seriously. I made up my mind to get hold of the book (εὐπορῆσαι τοῦ βιβλίου προῃρημένος) which could help me somewhat to discover the cure, rather than the spot of the affect. (*De loc. aff.* 3.5 = VIII 148 K)

In both passages libraries are central to Galen's self-portrait as a relentless, no-stone-unturned researcher. The Galenic inquiry homogenises libraries and privately owned books – he must be seen to be looking everywhere.

We also hear Galen calling for libraries to become databanks of authoritative, pukka record. In a polemical essay he wishes scientific literature were vetted before release into the public domain, as supposedly used to be the custom in Egypt.

For it should have been (ἐχρῆν) as in Egypt of old. There each new scientific discovery, having been examined by a general council of educated men (ὑπὸ κοινοῦ συνεδρίου τῶν πεπαιδευμένων), was inscribed on stelae put up in sacred places (ἐν ἱεροῖς χωρίοις). Just so we need a council of fair-minded as well as educated men

---

[68] Debru 1995; Von Staden 1997: 37–43, 48–51; Gleason 2009.
[69] Snyder 2000: 192–3; Johnson 2010: 88–90; Nicholls 2011: 128–9.
[70] On Galen's hermeneutic strategies and range, see Bröcker 1885; Mewaldt 1909; W. Smith 1979: 124–76; Manuli 1983; López Férez 1992; Manetti and Roselli 1994; Mansfeld 1994: 135–9, 148–64; Hanson 1998; Von Staden 1998, 2002 and 2009; Manetti 2003; Strohmaier 2004; Wilkins 2007; Flemming 2007.
[71] E.g. *In Hipp. VI epid.* 1.1 = XVII.A 793 K; *ibid.* 3.30 = XVII.B 98 K; *In Hipp. de off. med.* 1.1 = XVIII.B 630–1 K; cf. *In Hipp. humor.* 1.1 = XVI 2–3 K. Further Von Staden 2009: 145–7; Mülke 2008: 221–3.
[72] Johnson 2010: 93; Nicholls 2011: 124.

(τι συνέδριον ἀνδρῶν δικαίων τε ἅμα καὶ πεπαιδευμένων) who would examine new writings (συγγράμματα) and install the good ones in public places (θήσουσι... ἐν δημοσίοις χωρίοις) but destroy all the bad ones. (*Adv. Iul.* 1.2 = XVIII.A 247 K)

Under this ideal censorship libraries – assuming they qualify as 'public places' for *suggrammata* – would have the same function as the sacred sites had in Egypt: although the precedent invoked by Galen is an Egyptomaniac (almost Herodotean!) fantasy,[73] the desire for clusters of epistemically worthy texts looks as good as genuine.

That utopia reflects on Galen's dissatisfaction with the books and libraries of his lifeworld. He is too aware that many scientific books out there are unsound (e.g. *De simpl. med. temp. et fac.* 6 proem = XI 796 K). The malaise of ill-advised writing inevitably looms over libraries.[74] A *bibliothēkē* might end up stockpiling gratuitous material, be that philosophico-medical anthologies or the endless case studies of the Empirical school.

If you wish, you could fill not a few books (οὐκ ὀλίγα πληρώσει βιβλία) with sayings by those three men [Plato, Theophrastus and Chrysippus]. And if you have leisure, like Julian had in Alexandria, you could fill a whole library (ὅλην βιβλιοθήκην πληρώσει) with phrases picked out from all the different Stoics or Peripatetics. (*Adv. Iul.* 4 = XVIII.A 260 K)

What library would have space for research of this length (τίς ἂν ἔτι βιβλιοθήκη τὴν τοσαύτην ἱστορίαν χωρήσειε), what soul can hold memory of so many cases? (*De exper. med.* 7.1 = Deichgräber pp. 102.18–104.20)

Worse, libraries are not safe from malicious corruption. Wicked people (*panourgoi*) are known to tamper with pharmacological books:

some even distort the copies they received from others (καὶ διαστρεφόντων... ἀντίγραφα). Library books that use letter-signs for numbers are easily fiddled with (τὰ δὲ δὴ βιβλία τὰ κατὰ τὰς βιβλιοθήκας ἀποκείμενα, τὰ τῶν ἀριθμῶν ἔχοντα σημεῖα, ῥαδίως διαστρέφεται). 'Five' they change into 'nine' [scil. ε into θ], and 70 likewise [ο into θ], also 10 and 3 [ι and γ], with one stroke of letter added or erased... (*De antidot.* 1.5 = XIV 31 K)[75]

Public libraries that ought to house true knowledge are, in practice, infected with fraudulent textuality![76]

---

[73] Nutton 1993: 24; Von Staden 1997: 46–7; yet see also Schlange-Schöningen 2003: 94 n. 150. On Galen's opinion (not unreservedly eulogistic) of Egypt, see Nutton 1993 and Von Staden 2004.
[74] Some consolation perchance in the fact that Galen's own works were sought after by the public library at Pergamum and beyond: Περὶ ἀλυπίας 21 with Nicholls 2011: 140–1.
[75] I thank Peter Parsons and William Johnson for clarifying the graphology in this passage. Cf. López Férez 1992: 199; generally Touwaide 1994: 1939–40.
[76] Von Staden 1998: 82–4.

Galen knew from first-hand experience that a written piece of work is not secure intellectual property. The treatise *On My Own Books* refers to unauthorised publication, contamination, plagiarism and outright forgery; in the opening scene Galen watches with wry amusement how a text offered for sale under his name is exposed as spurious.[77] Even against this tangled backdrop there is something special about textual corruption via libraries. The failure of libraries as an institution to guarantee authenticity cuts deep into the tensions embedded in the relationship between culture and its sociopolitical packaging. Galen briskly historicises the roots of the problem, stating that the upsurge of book forgeries was prompted by the bibliophile interests of Hellenistic royalty.[78]

For before the kings in Alexandria and Pergamum got zealous about buying old books (ἐπὶ κτήσεις παλαιῶν βιβλίων φιλοτιμηθέντας), no counterfeit text had been written (οὐδέπω ψευδῶς ἐπεγέγραπτο σύγγραμμα). But when those who delivered texts by an ancient author started to receive a fee (μισθὸν), people got to faking and submitting many titles (πολλὰ ψευδῶς ἐπιγράφοντες ἐκόμιζον). (*In Hipp. de nat. hom.* 42 = XV 105 K)

Ironically, the demand for creditable 'ancient' books results in cultural pollution.

The fullest Galenic treatment on the subject is the lengthy excursus in the *Commentary on the Epidemics Bk III*, 2.4 (XVII.A 603, 606, 608 K = CMG 5.10.2.1 pp. 77–80). Here Galen argues[79] that the enigmatic symbols (*charaktēres*) accompanying the Hippocratic case studies are a scam traced back to a Hellenistic physician called Mnemon who inserted the symbols into Hippocrates's text so as to sell his own 'unique' exegesis of their alleged mystery (μόνον γὰρ ἐπίστασθαι λέγων ἑαυτόν... μισθὸν τῆς ἐξηγήσεως... εἰσεπράττετο). Two alternatives are considered as to how he actually did it: a) Mnemon either tampered with the book in the Alexandrian library, using a matching ink and handwriting (μέλανι καὶ γράμμασι παραπλησίοις), or b) the pre-sabotaged copy was planted in the baggage of somebody (Mnemon himself?) travelling to Alexandria.

---

[77] Nutton 1972: 53; Mansfeld 1994: 126–7; Hanson 1998: 22–4, 29–30; Schlange-Schöningen 2003: 28–30; Mülke 2008: 220 n. 682; Winsbury 2009: 131–3; Johnson 2010: 85–6; also Strohmaier 1976: 118–19. As Boudon 2000: 121 rightly points out, such abuse of Galenic texts in circulation was the foreseeable 'rançon du succès' for Galen. For broader discussion of the ancient anxiety about one's texts being interfered with, see Mülke 2008: esp. 14–75.

[78] Cf. Speyer 1971: 112, 133–4; Canfora 2008: 18–19; Too 2000: 117 and 2010: 37, 89–90.

[79] For the sources and scope of Galen's debate, see Manetti and Roselli 1994: 1595–6; Hanson 1998: 38–42; Von Staden 2006: 34–5 and 21 n. 27.

Libraries and paideia *in the Second Sophistic* 393

It is said that Ptolemy the king of Egypt was so ambitious about books (φιλότιμον... περὶ βιβλία) that he ordered the books of all who had arrived by sea to be brought to him (πρὸς αὐτόν); these he transcribed onto new papyri (εἰς καινοὺς χάρτας γράψαντα) and gave the transcript to the owners (that is, the folks who had sailed in and had their books brought before the king). The handed-in books themselves were placed in the libraries (εἰς δὲ τὰς βιβλιοθήκας ἀποτίθεθαι); they were tagged FROM THE SHIPS. (*In Hipp. III epid.* 2.4 = XVII.A 606 K)

Thus the forger's volume would have been simply added to the hoard:

Among them was discovered the Book III of the *Epidemics*, with the tag FROM THE SHIPS: EDITED BY MNEMON OF SIDE – although some say there was no EDITED, just Mnemon's name, because the royal servants would mark every voyager's books with his name during the transfer to storage. For they did not take the books to the libraries right away but in the first instance deposited them in some buildings, in heaps (καὶ τῶν ἄλλων ἁπάντων τῶν καταπλευσάντων ἅμα βιβλίοις ἐπέγραφον οἱ τοῦ βασιλέως ὑπηρέται τὸ ὄνομα τοῖς ἀποτιθεμένοις εἰς τὰς ἀποθήκας. οὐ γὰρ εὐθέως <εἰώθεσαν> εἰς τὰς βιβλιοθήκας αὐτὰ φέρειν, ἀλλὰ πρότερον ἐν οἴκοις τισὶ κατατίθεσθαι σωρηδόν). (*ibid.*)

Galen, however, favours the former version that has Mnemon doctor the library manuscript.

... it is more plausible that he tweaked the text laid up in the library, for his explanation was going to look far more convincing if the symbols were found in a book from the royal library (πιθανώτερόν ἐστι τὸ κατὰ τὴν βιβλιοθήκην ἀποκείμενον ὑπ' αὐτοῦ διεσκευάσθαι. πολὺ γὰρ ἀξιοπιστότερον ἔμελλεν αὐτῷ τὸ τῆς ἐξηγήσεως ἔσεσθαι, τῆς βασιλικῆς βιβλιοθήκης <βίβλου τινὸς> ἐχούσης τοὺς χαρακτῆρας). To have the book brought from home would have made him suspicious. (*ibid.*, XVII.A 608 K)

The likelihood of a fraudster taking advantage of the Great Library's authority throws into relief the flaw in the Ptolemaic cultural solution. Galen cleverly splices the variant histories of Mnemon's bluff; the adulterated *Epidemics*, while not necessarily a book 'from the ships', cannot help being framed by the narrative about those indiscriminately seized books. The bibliographical regime at Alexandria (in which the king himself is emphatically involved[80] – note πρὸς αὐτόν and the singular form of γράψαντα –) is a wholesale and totalitarian pursuit of authenticity:[81] every original must be requisitioned and retained. But the voracious nature

---

[80] Ptolemy's predatory appetite for books is further detailed through the story of the Athenian tragedies (*ibid.*, XVII.A 607 K): see Handis in this volume.
[81] Cf. Jacob 1996: 51–5; Too 2000: 133 and 2010: 35–6, 122–3, 173–4.

of this mega-library means that the books are not processed in the best way. 'In heaps', σωρηδόν is suggestive of haphazard profusion.[82] So the interim storage of the confiscated book-rolls foreshadows inadequate monitoring of their contents.[83] Mnemon gets away with his interpolation because in such a throng of scripts, who can tell?

There is a paradigmatic ring to the anecdote, then.[84] Designed for embracing the maximum number of texts, the Alexandrian library squares with the intrinsically noble, in Galen's eyes, sociocultural imperative to 'purchase and prepare books' (εἰς τὰ καλὰ τῶν ἔργων... εἰς βιβλίων ὠνὴν καὶ κατασκευήν, *De an. aff. dign. et cur.* 9 = V 48 K).[85] Yet the aggressive Ptolemaic policy of acquiring originals[86] gives rise to an environment where originality itself may be hijacked[87] by a cheeky interloper. As the ultimate experiment in κατασκευὴ βιβλίων, the Great Library according to Galen is embarrassing and vulnerable at the same time.

Galen also has much to say about directly physical threats to libraries such as theft, rot and fire. When Galen first arrived in Rome the palatial library of Domus Tiberiana was, he claims retrospectively,[88]

on the brink of extinction... due to serial and frequent thefts which were overlooked.

---

[82] For the semantics, see e.g. Polyb. 1.34.5, 3.79.10, 15.14.2; Dion. Hal. *Ant. Rom.* 9.67.2; Philo, *De spec. leg.* 2.8; Hdn. 4.6.1; Heliod. 1.30.2; esp. Alex. Aphr. *In Met.* 11.3, *CAG* I p. 676,10 σωρηδὸν καὶ ὡς ἔτυχε. The lexicographer Hesychius defines σωρηδόν as κατὰ σύστημα σεσωρευμένον (Σ 3083) but also gives the word (at Χ 816) as a synonym for χύδην and εἰκῇ.

[83] It may be appropriate to think of Galen's remarks in Περὶ ἀλυπίας 16 on the errors and omissions in the Catalogue (ἐν... πίναξι) of the Palatine library; on this passage, see Nicholls 2011: 135–6.

[84] The popular suggestion (Canfora 1986b: 59; Blanck 1992: 139; Erskine 1995: 47) that Galen is biased against the library practice at Alexandria, as a native of its arch-rival Pergamum, is valid but a bit narrow. It is still curious that, having studied in Alexandria, Galen records no personal impressions of either the Mouseion or the Serapeion: Nutton 1993: 19; Hanson 1998: 39. For the awareness among the ancient intelligentsia about the Ptolemaic championing of libraries, cf. Ath. 5.203e: 'What need is there to even refer to the multitude of books and the establishment of libraries and the assemblage in the Museum, since this is remembered by all?' (περὶ δὲ βιβλίων πλήθους καὶ βιβλιοθηκῶν κατασκευῆς καὶ τὴν εἰς τὸ Μουσεῖον συναγωγῆς τί δεῖ καὶ λέγειν, πᾶσι τούτων ὄντων κατὰ μνήμην;)

[85] Further, Schlange-Schöningen 2003: 34–5 n. 14; Johnson 2010: 93–4 and this volume.

[86] Which Galen does not explicitly deplore – but consider the poignantly deadpan τοῖς δεσπόταις (XVII.A 606 K) describing the book owners who had to give up their books.

[87] Libraries as an avenue for bogus literary authentication: cf. Porphyrio on Hor. *Epist.* 1.3.15; Speyer 1971: 68–70; Dix and Houston 2006: 682, 696–7.

[88] The text used is that of Boudon-Millot 2007.

διὰ τὴν ἀμέλειαν τῶν ἑκάστοτε λῃστευομένων ἐκ διαδοχῆς αὐτὰ ... ἐγγὺς ἦν τοῦ διεφθάρθαι[89] (Περὶ ἀλυπίας 18)

And the books that were not stolen have since sunk into unrecoverable decay:

today they are completely useless and cannot be unrolled because putridity has caused the sheets to stick together.

νυνὶ δὲ τελέως ἐστὶ ἄχρηστα μηδὲ ἀνελιχθῆναι δυνάμενα διὰ τὸ κεκολλῆσθαι τὰς χάρτας ὑπὸ τῆς σηπεδόνος (ibid., 19)

But the worst nemesis was to be fire. In a good handful of passages Galen speaks of his texts that were kept in a storehouse (apothēkē)[90] near the Temple of Peace in central Rome and perished when the district burned in AD 192.[91] Saliently, to Galen this is representative of the endemic insecurity of libraries and books in general.[92] A book can be neglected or deliberately suppressed (*In Hipp. de nat. hom.* 1 = XV 23–4 K), but

leaving all the other causes aside, I'll remind you of just two events that recently (ἔναγχος) happened in Rome. Sacred precincts, which often burn and often are brought down by earthquakes or by some other reason, are evidently responsible for destruction of not a few books (πολλάκις μὲν ἐμπρησθέντες σηκοί, πολλάκις δὲ ἐν σεισμοῖς καταπεσόντες ἢ κατ' ἄλλην αἰτίαν οὐκ ὀλίγων βιβλίων ἀπωλείας αἴτιοι γεγονέναι φαίνονται). (*ibid.*, XV 24 K)

---

[89] Tucci 2008: 143 mistranslates as 'about to be destroyed' and proceeds to ponder over the otherwise unknown 'decision to destroy the library of the Domus Tiberiana in 162' (*ibid.*, n. 29). Jones 2009: 393–7 would amend the manuscript's awkward ἐναντία to ἐν Ἀντίῳ, which changes the location of the decayed library in Περὶ ἀλυπίας 18–19 from the Domus Tiberiana to the imperial villa at Antium – yet see objections by Tucci (2009a); further, Nicholls 2011: 138–9 n. 78. In any case, Galen is describing degradation of books kept on VIP premises.

[90] For the latest controversy on the function and location of Galen's *apothēkē*, see Dix and Houston 2006: 692 n. 150; Tucci 2008: 137–9 and Johnson 2010: 87; Nicholls 2011:124–9.

[91] Περὶ ἀλυπίας 2, 4–6, 10, 14, 29, 37; *De libr. propr.* 14.9 = XIX 41 K; cf. *ibid.*, 3.7 = XIX 19 K; *In Hipp. VI epid.* 8, *CMG* V 10.2.2, p. 495, 2–10; *De antidot.* 1.13 = XIV 66 K. *De anat. adm.* 1.1 = II 216 K must be referring to an earlier fire in which Galen's *hupomnēmata* also perished. Fire of AD 192: Cass. Dio *epit.* 73.24.1–2; Hdn. 1.142–3. See Hanson 1998: 50–1; Schlange-Schöningen 2003: 27–8 n. 37; Dix and Houston 2006: 700–1; Hankinson 2008a: 21–2; esp. Tucci 2008.

[92] Galen's teacher Pelops of Smyrna did not see his unpublished anatomical writings burn (*De anat. admin.* 14.1 = p. 184 Duckworth *et al.*) – he was lucky to be already dead.

Moreover, a sense of parallelism between the fate of Galen's books in the *apothēkē* and that of the imperial libraries is subtly[93] insinuated.

> I had written on this subject before; two of the earlier books have been made public. They were deposited, along with other stuff, in the storeroom by the Via Sacra (ἐν τῇ κατὰ τὴν ἱερὰν ὁδὸν ἀποθήκῃ) at the time when the Temple of Peace burned to the ground and the big libraries of the palace compound too (κατὰ τὸ παλάτιον αἱ μεγάλαι βιβλιοθῆκαι). This was when many others' books, including my own in that depot (κατὰ τὴν ἀποθήκην ἐκείνην), were lost, and none of my friends in Rome proved to own a copy (ἀντίγραφα) of the first two. (*De comp. med. per gen.* 1.1 = XIII 362–3 K)

> all the libraries on the Palatine burned on that day < ... > Those [books] on the Palatine were destroyed on the same day as mine ...
>
> τῶν ἐν τῷ Παλατίῳ βιβλιοθηκῶν πάσων κατακαυθεισῶν ἐν ἐκείνῃ τῇ ἡμέρᾳ < ... > διεφθάρη δὲ νῦν τὰ μὲν ἐν τῷ Παλατίῳ κατὰ τὴν αὐτὴν ἡμέραν τοῖς ἡμετέροις (Περὶ ἀλυπίας 12 and 18)

This accent on the shared demise, and the timing thereof, is significant rhetorically as well as ideologically. The libraries 'on the Palatine' were home to many unique[94] and valuable editions (Περὶ ἀλυπίας 13, 16–17) which Galen might have used to repair his decimated book collection – no chance of that now (*ibid.*, 12). Galen's loss of scientific literature, his own works included, along with medical tools and drugs in the *apothēkē* is irreversible (*ibid.*, 5–6, 12). The calculatedly restrained (Thucydides-style, as it were) appraisal underlines the pathos of the situation. Yet the tactic of contextualising the lost books against other staple library resources of Rome[95] conveys a deeper pessimistic acknowledgement that written texts, however culturally prized or grandly accommodated,[96] are habitually liable to nasty material mishaps.

---

[93] *Contra* Hanson 1998: 51–2. Her study pre-dates the discovery of Περὶ ἀλυπίας. On the 'deep' conformity between Galen's scientific writing and the Roman Empire, see Flemming 2007: esp. 245–7, 257–8, 263–8, 271–7.

[94] Johnson in this volume, 394–5; Nicholls 2011: 130–4, 136.

[95] Signally, bibliophile 'friends', as the next equivalent of 'public libraries' in the Galenic research protocol (*In Hipp. VI epid.* 4.21 = XVII.B 194–5 K) also feature in the aftermath of the AD 192 fire, though this time they are unable to lend a hand (*De comp. med. per gen.* 1.1 = XIX 363 K); Johnson 2010: 87–8.

[96] The Palatine library may not be the only prestigious library in Galen's sights in Περὶ ἀλυπίας. He says that his books, silverware and other medical gear in the *apothēkē* 'perished in a pile' (10 σωρευθέντα διαφθαρῆναι) – maybe an allusion to the storehouses of Ptolemy's Alexandria where the confiscated bookrolls were kept σωρηδόν (*In Hipp. III epid.* 2.4 = XVII.A 606 K)? Galen is certainly no stranger to either sarcasm or self-aggrandisement ...

Galen reports that a certain grammarian[97] whose books also burned in AD 192 got depressed, developed insomnia and fever, and died. Clearly, for a practitioner of paideia to have lost his books in this way was 'a great blow' (Nutton 2009: 19). Galen coped better and, as he doggedly insists in Περὶ ἀλυπίας (29, 31, 49–53, 58–61, 65, 76–8, and *passim*), did not despair – he has been, after all, fortified against eventualities by his philosophical training.[98] For sure, Greco-Roman philosophy excels at trivialising the external 'goods' and accidents. But because the books Galen was deprived of by the fire are objects that contain scientific value, this ethics might need to be backed up by another rationale of a properly epistemological nature.

Galen believes that knowledge is achievable, through a great deal of trial and error, by balancing a priori principles against sensory observation (e.g. *De meth. med.* 1.4 = X 30–2 K)[99] and crucially by correlating verbal information with understanding and practice. Language in Galen's epistemology is not a self-sufficient medium for true knowledge but a tool of didactic communication that must facilitate learning, not dominate it. In the end, the Galenic goal is to grasp the *pragmata* rather than to be preoccupied with the *onomata*.[100] This hard-nosed approach to language spills over into Galen's Hippocratic exegesis (*In Hipp. Progn.* 3.18 = XVIII.B 267 K) and leads to further downgrading of written texts as words handicapped by their detachment from autoptic practice and live pedagogical exchange. Time after time Galen decries the limitations of knowledge acquired solely from books;[101] in some of his grumpiest passages he asserts the high probability of a published text getting misunderstood by the world (*De ord. libr. propr.* 1.2 and 1.5 = XIX 50–1 K).[102] In this light it befits Galen to project himself as an author who is not keen on authorship,[103] announcing that he does not wish to put his name on his own books (*De meth. med.* 7.1 = X 457–8 K) and would

---

[97] By the name Phil<ipp>ides (Περὶ ἀλυπίας 7) or Callistus (*In Hippocr. VI epid.*, CMG V 10.2.2, p. 486, 19–24).
[98] Hankinson 2008a: 22.
[99] Frede 1981: 75–7; García Ballester 1981: 32–6 and 1994: 1643–6; Mattern 2008: 42; Hankinson 1992: 3517–18; 2008b esp. 175–80; 2009: 219–22; Boudon-Millot 2009: 182–3.
[100] *De puls. diff.* 1.1 = VIII 493–4, 496 K; *De marc.* 6 = VII 690 K; *De tum. pr. nat.* 3 = VII 716 K; *De opt. corp. const.* 1 = IV 738–9 K. Hankinson 1994: 166–87; Sluiter 1995: 528–9; Morison 2008, esp. 139.
[101] *De alim. fac.* 1.1 = VI 480 K; *De libr. propr.* 8.4 = XIX 33 K; *De comp. med.* 6.1 = XII 894 K; *De anat. adm.* 1.2 = II 223–4 K; *De simpl. med. temp.* 6 proem = XI 796–7 K; *De comp. med. per gen.* 3.2 = XIII 604–5 K. See Roselli 2002: 36–42; Del Corso 2005: 55–6; further Boudon-Millot (2004).
[102] König 2009: 55; further references in Mattern 2008: 210 n. 58.
[103] Von Staden 2002: 133; König 2009: 51–8.

choose to stop publishing if the polemics turned obnoxious (*De ord. libr. propr.* 1.11 = XIX 52 K).

Mastery of texts for Galen coexists with entrenched wariness about their alethic capacity. Indeed he recognises that the price of writtenness is attrition of the text's integrity due to misspellings, conjecture or physical damage to the book-roll (*In Hipp. De off. med.* 2.23 = XVIII.B 778–9 K). One could say, his stance on textuality is consistent with the medical perspective on the human body as a difficult, fragile and entropy-ridden system which the doctor is duty-bound to diagnose and aid. Just so Galen would not idealise the text but remains committed to accurate textual investigation and surgery. As Susan Mattern puts it, to Galen

> a text is not a fixed phenomenon but something constantly in flux, subject to deliberate or accidental alteration, falsification and deterioration (not to mention that the work might be ambiguous, unclear, or otherwise poorly written in the first place); it was something to be scrutinised, questioned and, if possible, corrected. (Mattern 2008: 12)

It is likely that the same epistemological strictures apply to libraries as congregations of texts. Galen is under no illusion about the libraries' built-in sickliness (case study: Domus Tiberiana) and mortality ('sanctuaries burn frequently...'). But equally he does not take for granted the written knowledge stored in the libraries. Fraudulent manuscripts may be extreme examples; shoddy and intellectually flawed publications are rife, alongside valuable material. The formula of the Galenic involvement with books and libraries is plucky, undeterred defeatism. He is compelled to ransack Roman libraries and bookshops in search for a medical tractate he is interested in (*De loc. aff.* 3.5 = VIII 148 K). Yet this happened, he adds, when he was young (ἔτι νεώτερος ὤν) and lacking a teacher locally – and the book itself was a disappointment.

Conclusions: beware of hardware

The Plutarchan and the Galenic macrotexts exemplify quite different visions of the library. While Galen engages with libraries as an unsentimental trouper in the battle for philological and epistemological integrity, Plutarch prefers the route of narrativised ethopoeic paradigms that oscillate between history and transferable 'timelessness'[104] (this approach is not entirely alien

---

[104] Pelling 2002: 241–2, 253–62.

to Galen too: think the Mnemon-story or the fantasy about scientific censorship in Egypt) and keeps his distance from contemporary libraries. Plutarch and Galen are both members of the empire's elite echelon of readers-cum-writers, hence their reflection on, and around, libraries bears out the claim that literary construal of libraries in antiquity pertains to 'elite self-definition' (Too 2010: 9). But of course the beautiful resilience of Too's thesis is that it can encompass the qualms, understatements and blanks which all have no less a role in self-definition than overt negativity.

The library culture of the Second Sophistic is a paradox. On the one hand, libraries ('public' and 'private') are crucibles of intellectual action and an arresting feature of many imperial cityscapes as hubs for the symbolic imbrication of power and paideia. Yet in the literary sources libraries often get airbrushed out of cities. We also ought to factor in the paucity of Greco-Roman narrative where library books and ambience enter the story in their own right[105] rather than as a backcloth for erudite display (Aulus Gellius, Athenaeus) or as a litmus test of political and moral conduct (Plutarch); Galen is exceptional in the way he zooms in on several libraries – ironically, he wishes to problematise, not to celebrate, the texts located there.

Libraries (like empires) operate on two levels, that of material organisation but also as platforms of sociocultural imagination.[106] The crux of my argument is that the intelligentsia of the Second Sophistic espoused a relatively weak phenomenology of libraries; the idea of library *qua* chamber of paideia is present on their discursive horizon, however, references to libraries and library usage in high-profile texts of the period are less prominent and not as upbeat as we might have expected. William Johnson in this volume suggests that in imperial Rome the public library had limited impact anyhow on the elite's textual regimen or 'the sociabilities devolving therefrom', because the overarching exclusivity of 'text-centered' culture would be more naturally and smugly achieved by sharing 'intellectual resources' (books as well as learned conversation about books) within personalised privileged surroundings (for example, at the villas). Johnson's interpretation thus focuses on the algorithms of networking and self-fashioning among the ancient readers. But perhaps there is a case for reopening the

---

[105] Hutchinson 2008: 37 n. 51; Johnson in this volume. The narratory potential of a Roman library may have been greater than that of a typical Greek *bibliothēkē*, which historically was just a room for storing (not reading!) book-rolls – that is to say, a plain and confined space, poles apart from the ambitious and evocative layout of Rome's major libraries; cf. e.g. Casson 2001: 88. But then many among the imperial Greek intellectuals were savvy about the latter too, and library architecture in the east followed suit (Hadrian's library in Athens, Celsus's library), cf. Nicholls 2011: 141.

[106] Too 2010: 4–6, 12, 169, 214–15, 242, and *passim*.

much more global question of how these readers responded to the written materiality of the text as the core common denominator of libraries and book collections.

What I have tried to show is that the elite narrative of the High Empire (Plutarch, Galen, Seneca; the list could go on a bit...) tends to feel uneasy over the whole issue. The muted or explicit misgivings range from the physical and hermeneutic vulnerability of books en masse to the existential inferiority of the written word vis-à-vis live learning and normative ethics. (Let us not forget that some Greco-Roman literati would have been wide awake to the Platonic critique of writing in the *Phaedrus*.) [107] Libraries are at risk from fire, decay (Gal. Περὶ ἀλυπίας 19),[108] forgery, confiscation by kings and warlords, and last but not least from the readers' incompetence[109] – when the contents of one's bookcases are but dead weight (Sen. *De tranq. animi* 9.4). Behind all this there lies a resistant awareness about making the paideutic capital contingent upon its medium and location: about entrusting software to hardware, so to speak.

Caught between insight and artifact, writing remains a faultline in the Greek and Greco-Roman consciousness.[110] My final contention is that the inhibited and wary library mentality of the imperial literate class stems from a teleological urge to ring-fence culture from outside pressures, including culture's own paraphernalia. There are multiple reasons as to why the book is never completely up to us (to poach a phrase from the Stoic school), therefore it is sensible to loosen the bond between the book and the text; while knowledge of the latter is requisite for elite status and must be paraded, the former could become a liability if relied on too eagerly. Like the guests of the Plutarchan Lucullus or Athenaeus' Larensis, one should be at home in the library yet touch not a single book-roll under the gaze of one's fellow sophists – or rather, of the sophisticated narratees.

---

[107] E.g. Trapp 2001; Ní Mheallaigh 2007; Marinčič 2007; Zadorojnyi 2010 and 2011.
[108] More infamous 'nightmare scenario' (Too 2010: 89) is the story of Aristotle's books in Strabo 13.1.54.
[109] The incompetent bibliophile is thus the opposite of the idealised polymath ('the walking library'): see Too 2000.
[110] *Contra* the optimistic assessments, such as Too 2010: 223 ('suspicion about the written word disappears') or Del Corso 2005: 33.

21 | The professional and his books

Special libraries in the ancient world*

VICTOR M. MARTÍNEZ AND MEGAN FINN SENSENEY

The idea of the ancient library has captivated scholars for generations, but one of the most fundamental questions in this academic field of inquiry continues to elude us: what constituted a library in the ancient world? In order to approach an answer, it is imperative to combine an analysis of the literary evidence and the archeological record for libraries in the ancient world with a thorough exploration of the history of libraries and the roles that libraries played as institutional entities in ancient society. Despite the interdisciplinary nature of the topic, few studies have combined knowledge gained by preparation in classical studies with training in librarianship and information theory.[1]

Traditional scholarship upholds a dichotomous framework for defining ancient libraries by identifying collections as either public or private. Unfortunately, this model precludes a more nuanced approach to the functional analysis of textual repositories, which might identify libraries that blur the line between public and private or otherwise fall outside the scope of the conventional model. In this chapter, we invite the reader to reconsider the model of the ancient library, beginning with the library of Alexandria and its depiction among nineteenth-century scholars as an idealized and universal library, a concept that gained considerable traction during the rise of the Public Libraries Movement in the 1850s. We then propose the model of the special library, which serves as a modern alternative to customary modes of service and collection development, as a point of departure for exploring textual repositories that may have developed in tandem with ancient professions and fields of inquiry that relied on the written word. Though a complete reappraisal of all the ancient evidence for libraries is well beyond the scope of this chapter, our intention is to suggest alternative methodologies and perspectives through which ancient evidence might be viewed in future research.

---

* The authors wish to express their thanks to the editors for their openness in including the perspective of contemporary library and information science. Our thanks also go to D. Gavio, J. Senseney, J. Sienkewicz, and J. Weinheimer for their comments on earlier drafts. Any errors or omissions remain our own.

[1] Notable exceptions are Holmes 1980, du Toit 2002.

The myth of the universal library

Through the nineteenth century, the scholarly study of ancient libraries in the United States evolved in tandem with concerns related to the democratization of education, the development of free, public libraries, and the growth of librarianship as a profession supported through allied organizations and associations.[2] Even current scholarship reflects an ontological understanding of the library that is steeped in the traditions and preoccupations of nineteenth-century librarianship. Bearing this historical tendency in mind, a brief examination of the cultural movements in library and information science during the nineteenth and twentieth centuries is crucial in evaluating the perspective – and prejudices – of the narratives that have shaped library history.

In *Memoirs of Libraries*, a joint study combining library history with an analysis of contemporary library administration published in two volumes in 1859, Edward Edwards idealizes the library at Alexandria as the perfect model of a so-called "true" library: a democratic institution that is "publicly administered, free, and accessible to all" with an eye toward the universal collection of literary and historical textual documents.[3] This definition conforms all too well to the nineteenth-century ideal of the public library, and it indicates Edwards' bias as one of the leading figures in the Public Libraries Movement.[4] A more likely interpretation suggests that the library at Alexandria was established by powerful public figures because books represented significant cultural capital and served as an expression of power.[5] Whatever intentions the Ptolemies may have had in establishing the library, Edwards' ideal of universal accessibility depends on total literacy within a culture, but less than 10 percent of the population is likely to have achieved so much as "craftsman's literacy" at any given time in the ancient world.[6] In fact, one of the only aspects of the library's administrative policies that appears to remain undisputed is its aggressive collection development mission in the interest of creating a complete, universal library that contains the entirety of society's textual output.[7]

Though utopian in its yearnings, the dream of the universal library is untenable. In evaluating the organization and use of ancient documentary deposits, Jacqueline du Toit dismisses Edwards' ideal in no uncertain terms:

The universal collection of information is per definition indiscriminate and therefore negates the existence of a function of selection of information, thus limiting

---

[2] du Toit 2002: 20. [3] Edwards 1964 [1859]: 27. [4] du Toit 2002: 27.
[5] Too 2010: 9. [6] Harris 1989: 7, 114, 157. [7] Too 2010: 88.

the import of the act of collection within the information theory continuum: if accumulation is indiscriminate, then collection becomes a blanket act of inclusion, rather than a conscious distinction between the essential and the ephemeral.[8]

In short, centralizing vast stores of information in a single repository is anathema to actual library practices and ultimately negates the mission of the library.

The acquisition of books is but a single component of the library. It is vital to understand that a library is a carefully cultivated repository of information that has been skillfully selected and organized in the interest of aiding those who seek knowledge and that all libraries are characterized by the systematic collection and organization of information for access or preservation. If a body of information fails to meet these criteria, it ought not to be considered a library. These defining characteristics do, however, allow for the possibility of a multitude of variations. Indeed, several fields of librarianship have evolved over the centuries due to differing perspectives on collection development, freedom of information, and the tenuous relationship between access and preservation. By placing the library within its functional and historical context, scholars may re-evaluate the potential roles libraries may have played in ancient societies. Of course, an analysis of the contemporary library should not – and cannot – lead to a prescriptive approach when applying library theory to classical history. Ultimately, this chapter seeks to broaden the general perspective on the variety of textual collections that might constitute a library, regardless of the terminology used across cultures and generations, and to provide methodological frameworks through which the evidence could be re-evaluated.

Special libraries

If the so-called "public" library of the ancient world was, in fact, founded by the cultural elite for the cultural elite, it might be useful to consider how literate craftsmen who were not quite initiated into the upper echelons of society would have collected and utilized texts. W. V. Harris describes skilled craftsmen as far more literate than the population as a whole, citing a professional motivation for gaining literacy and making use of the written word.[9] If craftsmen were collecting texts for use and reference within the context of their vocation, then the model for such a collection might have

---

[8] du Toit 2002: 148.   [9] Harris 1989: 22.

more in common with the modern day special library than their better-known public counterparts.

The formal origins of the special library are decidedly obscure, but such collections could be identified at least as early as the late Middle Ages.[10] At the turn of the twentieth century, librarians and documentalists organized the Special Libraries Movement to address professional needs associated with specialized collections developed to serve the requirements of specific institutions. One of the leaders of the Special Libraries Movement was John Cotton Dana, a public librarian and prominent figure in the American Library Association (ALA), who in 1909 spearheaded the establishment of the Special Library Association at an annual ALA conference.[11]

In a 1914 essay entitled "The Evolution of the Special Library," Dana explores the role of books in the promotion of culture from antiquity to the present and examines the flow of information from conception to obsolescence using the metaphor of the special librarian as a fisherman knee-deep in a rushing stream. He writes:

> The proper view of printed things is, that the stream thereof need not be anywhere completely stored behind the dykes and dams formed by the shelves of any library or of any group of libraries: but that from that stream as it rushes by expert observers should select what is pertinent each to his own constituency, to his own organization, to his own community, hold it as long as it continues to have value to those for whom he selects it, make it easily accessible by some simple process, and then let it go.[12]

Dana's view of information science is service oriented and dedicated to seeking out only the most up-to-date and appropriate information desired by a particular constituency. The primary difference between special libraries and their public counterparts is the fact that these collections were developed within a larger institutional context to serve the specialized information needs of a well defined user group.

Special libraries do not share the monumental characteristics of their public counterparts. They do not serve as a symbolic gesture to the power of knowledge and literary culture, nor do they provide the general community with gathering spaces or organized events. To the contrary, the contemporary special library is rarely more than a few crowded rooms housed within the context of a larger building. As such, the library is neither a prominent feature of the organization nor is it a primary element of the building's architecture. Despite its humble position, the library serves an

---

[10] Jackson 1994: 597; Chodorow 2007: 8. [11] Williams 1997: 775.
[12] Dana 1991: 59–60.

essential role in assuring that the information needs of an organization are met efficiently and accurately.

E. G. Bierbaum identifies five distinguishing characteristics of a special library: size, setting, funding, collections, and clientele.[13] The foremost characteristic of any special library is an exceptionally discriminating collection development policy, resulting in small collections dedicated to one particular field of study or research. Subject specialists are committed to monitoring developments in the field in order to keep the collections current and to discard items whose use has obsolesced. Because such specialists are interested in maintaining the most current and useful information in a field, there is little regard for long-term preservation of collections that are necessarily fluid in nature. This philosophy of librarianship suggests that allowing outdated materials to clutter the collections decreases accessibility: searching among vast stores of information takes a greater amount of time, and search results are less likely to be accurate if the information found is no longer applicable to the research at hand. Collections are, however, often remarkable for their diversity of formats, including books, periodicals, ephemera, and unpublished manuscripts more generally associated with archival repositories. In many cases, the library and corporate archives exist as a single department within a parent institution.

Special libraries in the ancient world

The case for special libraries in the ancient world is not self-evident; however, the process of identifying such collections may offer a more nuanced understanding of book culture in the ancient world, as well as an expanded view of the types of individuals who may have been using texts on a regular basis. Certainly the demands for, and clientele of, special libraries would have been significantly different in antiquity. Yet, one can generalize that only professions with an intellectual tradition or a need for specific, and sometimes technical, information would have relied on special libraries. Bierbaum's five characteristics of a special library cannot all be identified in the literary and archaeological evidence for ancient libraries, nor should one attempt to conform the evidence to her definition. The characteristics do, however, offer a set of criteria by which one can evaluate what we do know for similar or related types of collections.

[13] Bierbaum 1993: 7.

The first consideration for developing a special library is the perceived need for small, field- or subject-specific book collections among ancient professionals. In this regard, one may point to three factors that could have acted as catalysts for the emergence of special libraries: efficiency, accessibility, and content – the very hallmarks of the special library. Efficiency can be defined as the ability to retrieve information readily in order to address a specific problem or question. This criterion would have been critical for professionals such as physicians who may have needed to diagnose or treat a patient immediately or priests who may have needed to review sacred rites or procedures.[14] Prior to the establishment of public libraries in Rome, individuals would have relied on either personal ownership of texts or smaller, subject-specific collections as the primary means for text-based inquiry. It is likely these small holdings of texts were more akin to special libraries than traditional libraries. Likewise, the advent of public libraries did not signify the disappearance of organizations with discriminate holdings. If anything it may have promoted broader dissemination of subject-specific collections.

Accessibility goes beyond the potential to consult a specific work or group of works. Rather, the focus is on the availability of texts *and* the means for readily consulting those works. Repeated and prolonged need for specific works necessitated a different collection policy than that for private or public libraries. In this respect, one might see ancient special libraries as existing somewhere between purely public or private libraries. Galen, for example, had an extensive private collection of texts that included both medical writings and other literature. While he certainly may have lent his literary texts, the professional relationship between Galen and other physicians gave them the opportunity to borrow from a library with a specialized acquisition policy and collection that included medical notes and other related ephemera.[15]

According to Konstantinos Staikos a more corporate model might be found in the guild of writers and actors (*Collegium scribarum histrionumque*), which acquired copies of theatrical works that its members could have accessed for inspiration, emulation, or outright copying.[16] Through alternative mechanics of book acquisition, the "special libraries" of the ancient world may also have avoided the pitfalls and frustrations of dealing with booksellers.[17]

---

[14] Cf. Affleck in this volume.   [15] Nutton 2009: 21.
[16] Staikos 2005: 168. This institution is later to be identified with the *Collegium poetarum*, cf. Schmidt 2003: 535.
[17] White 2009 esp. 271–6.

The final criterion, content, ultimately is what made the special library effective. While the large public libraries of the early imperial period could certainly have sustained diverse literary tastes and interests through their extensive holdings, the special library similarly existed to meet the needs of a like-minded group, but also included in its holdings "texts" in formats other than papyrus rolls. Returning to the *Collegium scribarum histrionumque*, located in the Temple of Hercules Musorum in the Campus Martius, we might consider the example of the *fasti* of M. Fulvius Nobilior, which is described only by Macrobius in the early fifth century AD.[18] The *fasti* most likely existed in the form of a wall painting rather than a scroll, but its format is secondary to its content. Regardless of its format, the original document was available for copying or consultation in the meeting place of the *Collegium*.[19] Fulvius's *fasti* was a unique source that could not have been copied without the consent of the *Collegium* or at least the temple authorities.

An equally important consideration is the constituency of special libraries. Who would have used or relied on such a specialized collection? An idea of who may have used a special library can be inferred from the examples already cited, but in general, any profession that relied on books could have benefited from a specialized book collection. A more thorough argument, thus, might be made for special libraries within the medical, legal, and theatrical fields, but probably for several other professions as well.[20] For example, Roman doctors, who were sometimes viewed as mere craftsmen whose expertise was mechanical and hands-on, were also engaged in the intellectual tradition. Originally from Ostia, an early fourth-century AD sarcophagus in the Metropolitan Museum of Art illustrates the more learned type of medical practitioner.[21] Here, the physician is shown reading a scroll while seated beside a cabinet that contains a case with his surgical instruments as well as other tools of his trade and several additional scrolls. The relief illustrates the balance between the physical skill of his craft and the intellectual needs of his profession. While we may be skeptical that the image of the seated man is no more than an artistic trope for an intellectual, even this is significant. The relief's motif makes it clear that physicians could be counted among the intellectual classes. It is precisely this type of

---

[18] Schmidt 2003: 535; Rüpke 2006.
[19] Rüpke emphasizes the fact that even in the second century BC literary composition was still a relatively new phenomenon and that the very idea of writing down history rather than just narrating it orally would have been novel and perhaps a point of pride for the guild members, 2006: 510.
[20] Medical: Perilli 2007; legal: Chodorow 2007, esp. 8; theatrical: Schmidt 2003.
[21] Inv. no. 48.76.1. Illustrated in Casson 2001: 83 fig. 6.2.

physician who relied upon knowledge from special medical texts or who might wish to consult such books in order to review case histories.

While doctors, playwrights, and other professionals may have used the great libraries of Rome, the literary evidence is notoriously silent as to their presence. Dix and Houston put it rather succinctly: "No woman, no slave on his own, no tradesman or craftsman, no administrator seeking public records is ever mentioned in any public library in Rome."[22] The reality may not have been as bleak, but it is likely that the practical realities of the public library made alternative collections attractive. M. E. Soper's analysis of why individuals create and maintain private collections rather than use readily available institutional or research libraries makes some interesting observations from which we might draw conclusions regarding the constituency of ancient special libraries.[23] Soper makes three points that are particularly relevant. First, individuals prefer their own book collections to institutional ones because the former are easier to use and have been amassed to reflect the owner's specialized needs.[24] Second, personal collections are favored because their organization reflects individual needs and interests. They may be located in appealing and productive environments, for example, and they are flexible and responsive.[25] Lastly, personal collections are often created in reaction to institutional library practices: individuals do not like to use libraries where they cannot get what they want when they want it.[26] Soper's explanation reflects contemporary attitudes to large public libraries or academic research collections, but the impetus for choosing alternative collection models is relevant to the study of ancient libraries. Indeed, ancient professionals, whose immediate needs for efficiency, accessibility, and specialized content were not easily met in the public libraries of Rome, may have shared her criticisms. Moreover, given the expense and difficulties of creating and maintaining a personal, specialized library, institutional affiliation for special holdings would offer a happy compromise.

The type and nature of the holdings also set special libraries apart from public or private libraries. Evidence is particularly compelling for doctors and lawyers. Although knowledge of medical and surgical techniques certainly relied heavily on first-hand experience and apprenticeship, education and knowledge from books was a necessity. Literary sources allude to the existence of medical texts that formed a critical part of the physician's

---

[22] Dix and Houston 2006: 709.   [23] Soper 1976.
[24] Soper 1976: 414. Her conclusion builds upon previous research that indicates researchers preferred using collections with ease of access over using those with superior holdings, Soper 1976: 398.
[25] Soper 1976: 409.   [26] Soper 1976: 409.

training. Pliny the Elder, for example, recounts how, at the great Asklepieion at Kos, patients who had received successful treatments for their ailment would be obliged to recount their remedies or treatments to officials in the temple so that future patients and physicians might benefit from that knowledge (*HN* 29.2.4). Pliny goes on to remark that Hippocrates was said to have copied these prescriptions and then burned down the archive so that no subsequent person would have access to them. While we may doubt the veracity of Pliny's anecdote accusing Hippocrates of destroying such invaluable information, this narrative clearly attests to a collection of special medical texts as at least one source for his training. Other sanctuaries to Asklepios seem also to have held similar tablets: Strabo mentions that at Epidauros and Tricce similar tablets could be found in their respective sanctuaries to the god (*Geographia* 8.6.15).

Lorenzo Perilli argues that tablets similar to the ones discussed in Strabo and Pliny should be connected with the *pinakes* mentioned in inscriptions from the Asklepieion at Epidauros and perhaps to the votives from that site. Although he cites no specific examples, he argues, based on analogy with Egyptian and Mesopotamian examples, that such clinical notes must have existed at the Asklepieia.[27] A good parallel for these *pinakes* may be the sixth-century BC wooden tablets from Pitsa dedicted to the nymphs.[28] Lynn LiDonnici is correct to point out that the survivability of these tablets was not great given their material (wood and plaster), but allusions to their content and form can be found in the later stone votive inscriptions from Epidauros.[29]

On the basis of the inscriptions from Epidauros, Perilli further argues that the term *pinakes* can best be translated as "memorandum books."[30] These so-called "memorandum books" were probably files describing individual cases, which the sanctuary would have preserved for future consultation exactly like those mentioned by Pliny and Strabo.[31] The accumulated memorandum books would then have served as an archive of primary case files for later clinical consultation. Perilli adds that the tablets found along with other medical instruments at the sanctuary should be seen more than as mere votives for cures, but as tools that formed part of the technical equipment of the physician.[32] Further, he posits that such *pinakes* were used on the job-site by physicians who would record the illnesses and treatments of patients at the sanctuaries. In order for the records to be universally accessible to physicians, the descriptions would then be transcribed on more

---

[27] Perilli 2007: 57.   [28] Van Straten 1981 pl. 13.   [29] LiDonnici 1995: 45.
[30] Perilli 2007: 64. Cf. *IG* I² 91, 11.   [31] Perilli 2007: 64.   [32] Perilli 2007: 64.

durable materials, and put into more formal and technical language, thus creating a reference handbook for use by colleagues. Perilli sees the content and structure of these standardized files as similar to the cases described in books like the *Epidemiae* that formed part of the *Corpus Hippocraticum*.[33]

Several elements stand out from the perspective of library and information science both in the literary sources mentioned above and in Lorenzo Perilli's analysis of the primary documents from Epidauros. If one accepts that these so-called memorandum books existed and functioned in the manner that Perilli lays out, then the basis for the collection at Epidauros appears to include components of both libraries and archives. Perilli's transcribed archival texts were probably copied and organized by the library's administration, however it might be conceived. Perilli is surely correct to associate these transcribed texts with books that could easily have formed part of the *Corpus Hippocraticum*. Not only were these books highly structured and consistent in form, but they also gathered together different primary evidence into edited volumes.

It is, therefore, not a stretch of the imagination to assume that the great healing sanctuaries maintained a balance between their religious appeal and the more pragmatic therapies of their physicians who were dependent upon the documentary sources of the sanctuary. There is good evidence for the building of libraries at other numerous Asklepieia in the east: Kos (mid-first century AD, dedicated by Gaius Stertinius Xenophon), Epidauros (probable second-century AD dedication mentioned in a fragmentary inscription), and Pergamum (Hadrianic, dedicated by Flavia Melitine), whose holdings may have included a specialized medical collection.[34]

The case for special legal libraries is no less compelling and may even offer more potential information for the study of ancient libraries in general. We cannot present a complete argument here, but some basic points can be made. First, although most Roman litigation was rooted in oral argumentation, legal authority was inscribed into written texts from an early period as a tangible record of legal discourse. At one end of Roman history are the Twelve Tablets (fifth-century BC), which were highly restricted in their accessibility, and at the other is the Theodosian Code (fifth-century AD), which was more widely circulated. In fact, authorized copies of the latter were kept in the appropriate Palatine office and in the offices of provincial

---

[33] Perilli 2007.
[34] Petsalis-Diomidis 2010: 217. Callmer 1944: 175–6 similarly argues for a specialized library in the Asklepieion at Pergamum, while Petsalis-Diomidis 2010: 218 is skeptical ("[t]he idea of a specialized medical library is perhaps anachronistic" and Deubner 1938: 84–5 prefers a "general" public library).

prefects, presumably to be used by lawyers, jurists, or judges in order to adjudicate cases.[35] Between these two unique sources separated by about a millennium, other official *tabulae* and the commentaries of Roman jurists provide a broader view into the nature of Roman law and development of special law collections. According to Elizabeth Meyer, "[t]ablets, their uses, and their efficacy form the link: they are part of a continuous tradition linking earliest and latest Roman thought and practice, Roman history, and Roman law."[36]

Wooden *tabulae* were not the stenographic notepads of antiquity, as is often assumed, but were instead traditional, perhaps even venerable, records of acts that gave structure to both individual and state affairs.[37] The *tabulae* of the *pontifex maximus*, for example, were recorded at the end of the year, presumably distilled from the *acta diurnia*. These more permanent tablets then provided the reference sources for further commentaries.[38] Organizationally, the collection of generated texts shows a close relationship among ephemeral writings (*acta diurnia*), archival material (*tabulae* and perhaps some *acta*), and literature (*libri commentarii*).[39] Both *acta* and *tabulae* represent discrete sets of reference materials, while the *libri* need to be acquired, regardless of whether they were internally generated by its membership or created by outside readership.

It is precisely this last category of writings that is at the heart of the records documenting the commentaries of the Roman jurists. Initially, the growth of the Roman state resulted in the increased importance of jurists' oral opinions for legal proceedings.[40] The authority of the juristic opinions gave way to their role as written precedents, casebooks, and teaching aids.[41] The most respected and important of the juristic opinions were culled together to form the basis of Justinian's *Digest*.[42] The process of composing such a text was a major achievement in legal scholarship and implies the existence of collections of written sources that included the opinions of jurists. The format of the archives is unclear, but it must certainly have been a unified collection, even if not comprehensive. With the increased importance of case models for judgments by magistrates or arbitrators – most notably used in the fourth and fifth century AD Donatist trials in North Africa – case precedents (*praeiudicia*) were copied, collected, and organized into groups by subject.[43] These *praeiudicia*, actual juristic opinions, and compendiums, such as the *Digest*, form a comprehensive collection of texts necessary for any legal training or practice. As a collection, these sources were certainly

[35] Humfress 2007: 90. [36] Meyer 2004: 2. [37] Meyer 2004: 22. [38] Meyer 2004: 30–2.
[39] Meyer 2004: 30–3. [40] Frier 1985: 281–2. [41] Humfress 2007: 131.
[42] Stein 1999: 33–4. [43] Humfress 2007: 130.

not one that could be easily amassed by private lawyers. The breadth of the collection, the nature of the material (archival documents as well as books), and all of the costs associated with acquisition and cataloguing made such specialized legal libraries possible to few institutions.

Significantly, several of our textual examples straddle the line between library and archival materials, and it is necessary to tread carefully in terms of vocabulary and definitions when applying the modern concepts of "archive" or "special library" to ancient collections. Indeed, we do not envision an institution where archives and libraries were separate and mutually exclusive. Rather, because the medical library, for example, was a special library, it was both archive and library combined.[44] In order to understand the true nature of the repository, we must also take into consideration the community in which the collections were used. In this instance, the very existence and development of the medical profession depended not only on knowing the traditional literature, but also reviewing recent case files. While libraries such as those at Alexandria, Pergamum, and Rome would certainly have held medical texts, the combination of primary files and secondary texts, immediately next to the patients themselves, made the sanctuaries ideal locations for special medical libraries.

Hugh Taylor and Cynthia Durance, both prominent archivists, suggest that "[i]t is entirely possible, and not infrequent, that one person's archive is another person's library."[45] Arguably, the distinction between archives and libraries may prove a false division, and distinguishing between the two becomes particularly perplexing when studying the written record prior to the development of the publishing industry. We contend that an analysis of the types of records being created within an institution must determine whether these documents are of an archival nature, or if they might be incorporated into an argument for viewing the repository as a special library. Two record types in particular support the idea that special libraries and archives may have served similar functions within an ancient organization or association: records generated for practical purposes that are briefly retained while useful and discarded when no longer needed, and records generated during the course of business that serve as original research. The first type aligns with contemporary records management programs that often fall within the purview of a corporate archive but also reflect the same short-term view of information services found in many special libraries. The second type falls outside the guidelines set forth by Ernst Posner for

---

[44] Likewise, the archival records of early Christian communities could form the basis of other special libraries (cf. Van Elderen 1998).
[45] Durance and Taylor 1992: 44.

identifying archival records in his seminal study *Archives in the Ancient World* (1972).

Posner describes six "basic types of records that may be called constants in record creation, whatever the nature of governmental, religious, and economic institutions."[46] These include records continuously created and retained as evidence of past administrative action, laws, financial and accounting records, tax records and land documents, documentation asserting control over persons, and notarial records documenting business transactions. Broadly speaking, archives serve the function of preserving administrative documents and documenting policy, precedent and procedure through an institution's recordkeeping. Similarly, Margaret Cross Norton defines modern archives as "business records of a government, a business firm, an ecclesiastical body, or even an individual, preserved as a memorandum of business transactions, and particularly because they are potential evidence for any court or other legal proceedings which involve matters recorded in such memoranda."[47]

In contemporary repositories, unpublished materials that do not meet the above criteria belong primarily to libraries as manuscript collections, preserved on account of their research or historical value, and, in cases where the manuscript collections are administered by archivists on account of their format, they are treated as discrete entities, quite separate from records of business. Thus within the context of ancient textual repositories, any original records that do not serve as business transactions or legal records might reasonably be considered library materials. Moreover, the nature of records that are created within an archival context may be transformed over time through physical transcription and dissemination or through the context of its environment, as we discuss elsewhere in this chapter. Due to the kinship between libraries and archives in professional settings, an in depth review of the evidence for ancient archives may provide further insights regarding a variety of information resources for the ancient professional.[48] Individuals who created and maintained archival documents demonstrate a prerequisite degree of literacy and a potential professional motive for cultivating a small library of technical handbooks or similar reference materials.

Posner's study of ancient archives also provides compelling evidence for framing an argument in favor of a more nuanced approach to the characteristics of libraries in the ancient world. In discussing the departments of the

---

[46] Posner 1972: 3–4.   [47] Norton 2003: 81.
[48] In recent years, a series of publications, collected under the title *La Mémoire Perdue*, has revitalized scholarly interest in ancient archives in Rome. See: Demougin 1994; Moatti 1998; Moatti 2000.

imperial chancery, Posner names only one office *a memoria* that was likely to have been housed on the Palatine in or near the palace. All other departments were scattered throughout the city, and each maintained separate records at their respective place of business.[49] The argument for decentralized archival recordkeeping further supports the notion that each office or organization would have a small repository of records generated during the course of business along with a collection of textual documents used for the purposes of reference or research. This combination of library and archives is precisely the model that many modern special libraries uphold to support contemporary business practices. Though today's specialist librarian manages periodicals, electronic resources, print materials, and any number of information formats, the principle is the same: build a collection of resources that supports the needs of the institution and its members and gather evidence of the legal decisions, administrative practices, or business transactions relating to the organization to comprise a joint library and archives.

A final anecdote from Posner's study describes the practice of legal recordkeeping as part of court proceedings in ancient Rome. Posner focuses on the survival of a textual document that provides evidence for the practice of transcribing minutes from trials and court proceedings:

That a verbatim record of court proceedings was prepared and preserved is confirmed by the proceedings against early Christian martyrs. The so-called martyr records – about a dozen genuine ones have survived – are nothing but copies of the minutes of their trials before the competent Roman officials. These minutes were in the custody of the judge's *commentariensis*, the keeper of his daybooks. He could turn a profit by making them accessible to the Christians, who were eager to obtain copies of them for the purpose of fortifying their brethren in the faith or arousing the sympathies of the heathen. In one case they had to pay 200 *denarii* for permission to transcribe the proceedings.[50]

Beyond Posner's interest in evidence of archival recordkeeping, this anecdote also offers a compelling insight into how the nature of an archival document transforms as it is created, copied, and disseminated. At what point does archival material transform from an original administrative document into a text with persuasive literary merit? This example illustrates the fluidity of the distinction between archives and libraries: the original text, located among the judge's daybooks, is inherently archival in nature; however, once the text is transcribed and disseminated to Christians, it may presumably have joined a collection of similar texts assembled for missionary purposes,

[49] Posner 1972: 192.   [50] Posner 1972: 200–1.

at which point we can imagine its inclusion in a special library devoted to Christian theology and the missionary cause.

How materials were acquired represents a final component for forming the special library. Some of the same mechanisms used for amassing private and public collections in antiquity would certainly have been possible – booksellers, gifts, and copying, for example. We have already mentioned how the *Collegium scribarum histrionumque* may have acquired some of its texts through the participation of its members. The collection of books from the Villa of the Papyri at Herculaneum was particularly strong in its holdings of works by Philodemus and Epicurean philosophy.[51] While the collection may be that of a single individual, it may also have been a "specialized collection" used by a professional group.[52] Books were an expensive luxury available only to those with the financial means and intellectual interest.[53] Thus, some special libraries may have evolved from the personal holdings of individual professionals, subject specialists, or patrons.[54]

Closely tied to the acquisition of books is the size of the collection. Emphasis is usually on the extent of a library's holding, but size did not always matter. Mount and Massoud distinguish several levels of collecting for special libraries. In decreasing order of completeness, they are: an exhaustive level in which everything of a serious nature on a given topic is sought; a research level that cultivates a collection large enough to support independent research; a working level that includes only select works and aims to keep current; and, finally, a browsing level, which includes focused material that appeals to a small group.[55] Mount and Massoud's hierarchy is useful for assessing book collections and reminding us that the special library type is not monolithic in its definition. This last point is especially important for identifying small collections that could be overlooked, despite their importance. Although dealing with a much later period, Chodorow makes the important argument that even small specialized collections could define a field:

The law library supporting the professional study of law in the mid-fifteenth century consisted of nine volumes... [t]he small number of books in this library brings home two notable points: the core professional library was and is a teaching library, and it is a minimum, not a maximum, collection. At its base, it was and is the library of works that a professional lawyer had to master and that formed the core of his reference collection as a practitioner or judge. Put another way, you could define a lawyer as one who had mastered these books. The library defined the

---

[51] Houston 2009: 256, table 10.2 no. 1. [52] Houston 2009: 257. [53] Dix 1994: 282.
[54] Cf. Dix and Houston 2006: 672. [55] Mount and Massoud 1999: 10.

professional... So, "THE" library of the late middle ages, as opposed to "a" law library from that period, consisted of nine books.[56]

If a field as rigorous and important as law could define itself by its small library, then one cannot ignore the possibility that an apparently small collection of texts could just as well be a vibrant special library.

Conclusions

The evidence for special libraries is admittedly scant, perhaps even more tenuous than for ancient libraries in general, and this study offers a modest first step. Nevertheless, we contend that much is to be gained by considering the methodologies and theories of library and information studies. There are several advantages to be gained by introducing new terminology derived specifically from library and information science into the dialogue of early library history.

First, and foremost, one might refine the current definition of a library in antiquity. It is clear that the terms public and private are insufficient as exclusive library types in the Roman world and antiquity in general. Second, the term special library offers some relief to the burden carried by the terms private and public. Moreover, the flexible and accommodating nature of special libraries further allows us to identify and consider other textual deposits, both real and literary, as possible libraries. Third, even if the current evidence for such smaller library types is obscure, perhaps acknowledging their very existence will allow new evidence to surface in the future.

The literature produced by professionals in library and information science provides a number of ontological perspectives on the nature of libraries, archives, documents, and records. As Ranganathan explains in his *Five Laws of Library Science*, the library is a growing organism.[57] That is to say, with changing user needs and social dynamics, the library, too, must change. Special libraries also illustrate the dynamic potential of information and knowledge when actively incorporated into the professional lives of citizens in the Roman world, regardless of time or place. It is fitting that the motto of the Special Library Association is, "Putting Knowledge to Work."[58]

Library science does not seek to supplant the authority of classical scholarship in the study of ancient libraries nor are its methodologies better suited for understanding them. Rather, the same concerns and crises of

[56] Chodorow 2007: 7–8. [57] Ranganathan 1957: 382. [58] Christiansen 1993: 785.

identity that contemporary libraries face with changes in technologies and documentary media may help one understand the challenges and shifts of purpose that defined ancient libraries. It is not only classical scholarship that stands to gain from such reappraisals of the evidence; most special librarians are more concerned with the practicalities of the profession in which they work than with an inquiry into its past, but our study suggests that librarians may be well served by looking to past continuities and transformations while struggling to lay a foundation for a better future.

Bibliography

Allen, J. P. (2005) *The Ancient Egyptian Pyramid Texts*. Atlanta.
Alonso-Núñez, J. M. (1983) 'Die Abfolge der Weltreiche bei Polybios und Dionysios von Halicarnassos'. *Historia* 32: 411–6.
  (2002) *The Idea of Universal History in Greece: From Herodotus to the Age of Augustus*. Amsterdam.
Amici, C. M. (1991) *Il foro di Cesare*. Florence.
André, J. (1949) *La vie et l'oeuvre d'Asinius Pollion*. Études et Commentaires 7. Paris.
Antoni, A. (2004) 'Deux citations d'Euripide dans le *PHerc.* 1384: vers une nouvelle identification de ce livre de Philodème?' *CErc.* 34: 29–38.
  (2007) 'Nouvelles lectures dans le *PHerc.* 1384', in *Proceedings of the 24th International Congress of Papyrology, Helsinki, 1–7 August, 2004*, eds. J. Frösén and T. Purola, 2 vols. Helsinki: 43–52.
Antoni, A. and Dorival, G. (2007) 'Il *PHerc.* 1384: una nuova ipotesi di attribuzione'. *CErc.* 37: 103–9.
Arafat, K. (1996) *Pausanias' Greece. Ancient Artists and Roman Rulers*. Cambridge.
Arnott, W. G. (1996) *Alexis: The Fragments. A Commentary*. Cambridge.
Ascheri, P. (2011) 'The Greek origins of the Romans and the Roman origins of Homer in the Homeric Scholia and in POxy. 3710', in *From Scholars to Scholia. Chapters in the History of Ancient Greek Scholarship*, eds. F. Montanari and L. Pagani. Berlin and New York: 65–86.
Ashby, T. (1910) 'The classical topography of the Roman Campagna, part 3, section 2'. *PBSR* 5: 231–8.
  (1927) *The Roman Campagna in Classical Times*. London.
Assante, M. G. (2008) 'Per un riesame del *PHerc.* 1006 (Demetrio Lacone, *Alcune ricerche comuni sul modo di vita*)'. *CErc.* 38: 109–60.
Assmann, J. (2001) 'Libraries in the ancient world – with special reference to ancient Egypt', in *Building for Books. Traditions and Visions*, eds. S. Bieri and W. Fuchs. Boston: 50–67.
Astin, A. E. (1978) *Cato the Censor*. Oxford.
  (1986) 'Livy and the censors of 214–169 BC', in *Studies in Latin Literature and Roman History* 4 (Collection Latomus 196), ed. C. Deroux. Brussels: 131–4.
Baatz, D. (1991) 'Fensterglas, Glasfenster und Architektur', in *Bautechnik der Antike. Kolloquium Berlin 1990*, eds. A. Hoffman and E.-L. Schwander. Berlin: 4–13.
Babut, D. (1993) 'Stoïciens et stoïcisme dans les *Dialogues Pythiques* de Plutarque'. *ICS* 18: 203–27.

(1999) 'Sur Soclaros de Chéronée et sur le nombre des enfants de Plutarque: méthodologie d'une mise au point'. *RPh* 73: 175–89.

Bagnall, R. S. (2002) 'Alexandria: Library of dreams'. *PAPhS* 146 (4): 348–62.

Baker, H. D. (2002) 'Approaches to Akkadian name-giving in first millennium BC Mesopotamia', in *Mining the Archives: Festschrift for Christopher Walker on the Occasion of his 60th Birthday*, ed. C. Wunsch. Dresden: 1–24.

Baker, H. D. and Pearce, L. (2001) 'Nabû-zuqup-kēnu', in *The Prosopography of the Neo-Assyrian Empire, 2/II: L–N*, ed. H. D. Baker. Helsinki: 912–13.

Balensiefen, L. (2002) 'Die Macht der Literatur. Über die Büchersammlung des Augustus auf dem Palatin', in *Antike Bibliotheken*, ed. W. Höpfner. Mainz: 117–22.

Bandini, M. and Dorion, L.-A. (eds.) (2000) *Xénophon. Mémorables*, I. Paris.

Barchiesi, A., Calvino, I., Conte, G. B., Frugoni, C., Ranucci, G. (eds. and transl.) (1982–8) *Storia naturale: Gaio Plinio Secundo*. 5 vols. Turin.

Barnes, C. L. H. (2005) *Images and Insults: Ancient Historiography and the Outbreak of the Tarentine War*. Stuttgart.

Barnes, J. (1997) 'Roman Aristotle', in *Philosophia Togata II: Plato and Aristotle at Rome*, eds. M. Griffin and J. Barnes. Oxford: 1–69.

Barnes, R. (2000) 'Cloistered bookworms in the chicken-coop of the Muses: the ancient library of Alexandria', in *The Library of Alexandria: Centre of Learning in the Ancient World*, ed. R. MacLeod. New York: 61–77.

Bartoli, A. (1914–22) *I monumenti antichi di Roma nei disegni degli Uffizi di Firenze* (six volumes). Rome.

Barwick, K. (1933) 'Das Kultlied des Livius Andronicus'. *Philologus* 88: 203–21.

Bassi, D. (1909) 'La sticometria nei papiri ercolanesi'. *RFIC* 37: 321–63 and 481–515.

Battistoni, F. (2006) 'The ancient pinakes from Tauromenion: some new readings'. *ZPE* 157: 169–80.

Beagon, M. (1992) *Roman Nature: the Thought of Pliny the Elder*. Oxford.

Beall, S. M. (2004) 'Gellian humanism revisited', in *The Worlds of Aulus Gellius*, eds. L. Holford-Strevens and A. Vardi. Oxford: 206–22.

Beare, W. (1950) *The Roman Stage*. London.

Beaulieu, P.-A. and Rochberg, F. (1996) 'The horoscope of Anu-belšunu'. *JCS* 48: 89–94.

Becatti, G. (1957) 'Letture Pliniane. Le opere d'arte nei monumenta Asini Pollionis e negli Horti Serviliani', in *Studi in onore di Aristide Calderini e Roberto Paribeni* 3. Milan: 199–210.

Beck, F. A. G. (1975) *Album of Greek Education. The Greeks at School and at Play*. Sydney.

Beer, B. (2009) 'Lukrez in Herkulaneum? – Beitrag zu einer Edition von PHerc. 395'. *ZPE* 168: 71–82.

Biasiotti, G. and Whitehead, P. B. (1924–25) 'La chiesa dei SS. Cosma e Damiano al foro Romano e gli edifici preesistenti'. *RPAA* 3: 83–122.

Bidmead, J. (2002) *The Akītu Festival: Religious Continuity and Royal Legitimation in Mesopotamia.* Piscataway, NJ.
Bierbaum, E. G. (1993) *Special Libraries in Action: Cases and Crises.* Englewood, CO.
Birley, A. R. (1997) 'Hadrian and Greek senators'. *ZPE* 116: 209–45.
Birt, T. (1882) *Das antike Buchwesen in seinem Verhältnis zur Literatur.* Berlin.
   (1907) *Die Buchrolle in der Kunst: Archäologisch-antiquarische Untersuchungen zum antiken Buchwesen.* Leipzig.
   (1909) 'Zu Cicero ad Atticum IV5, 5'. *RhM* 64: 469–70.
Black, J. A. (2008) 'The libraries of Kalhu', in *New Light on Nimrud,* eds. J. Curtis, H. McCall, D. Collon and L. al-Gailani Werr. London: 261–6.
Blanck, H. (1992) *Das Buch in der Antike.* Munich.
   (2008) *Il libro nel mondo antico. Edizione rivista e aggiornata.* Transl. R. Otranto. Bari.
Blum, W. (1991) *Kallimachos: The Alexandrian Library and the Origins of Bibliography,* transl. H. H. Wellisch. Madison, WI.
Boatwright, M.T. (1983) 'Further thoughts on Hadrianic Athens'. *Hesperia* 52 (2): 173–6.
   (2000) *Hadrian and the Cities of the Roman Empire.* Princeton, NJ.
Bohn, R. (1885) *Altertümer von Pergamon 2: Das Heiligtum des Athena Polias Nikephoros.* Berlin.
Boissier, G. (1861) *Étude sur la vie et les ouvrages de M. T. Varron.* Paris.
Bonnefond-Coudry, M. (1989) *Le sénat de la république romaine* (Bibliothèques des écoles françaises d'Athènes et de Rome 273). Rome.
   (1995) 'Princeps et sénat sous les Julio-Claudiens. Des relations à inventer'. *MEFRA* 107: 225–54.
Boudon, V. (2000) 'Galien par lui-même. Les traités bio-bibliographiques (*De ordine librorum suorum* et *De libris propriis*)', in *Studi su Galeno. Scienza, filosofia, retorica e filologia,* ed. D. Manetti. Florence: 119–33.
Boudon-Millot, V. (2004) 'Oral et écrit chez Galien', in *Médicine grecque antique: actes du 14e colloque de la Villa Kérylos à Beaulieu-sur-Mer, les 10 et 11 octobre 2003,* eds. Z. Zouanna and J. Leclart. Paris: 199–218.
   (2007) 'Un traité perdu de Galien miraculeusement retrouvé, le *Sur l'inutilité de se chagriner*: texte grec et traduction française,' in *La science médicale antique. Nouveaux regards. Etudes réunies en l'honneur de Jacques Jouanna,* eds.V. Boudon-Millot, A. Guardasole, and C. Magdelaine. Paris: 72–123.
   (2009) 'Galen's *bios* and *methodos*: from ways of life to path of knowledge', in *Galen and the World of Knowledge,* eds. C. Gill, T. Whitmarsh and J. Wilkins. Cambridge: 175–89.
Boudon-Millot, V., Jounanna, J. and Petrobelli, A. (eds.) (2010) *Galien tome IV: Ne pas se chagriner.* Paris.
Bowen, A. C. (2002) 'The art of the commander and the emergence of predictive astronomy', in *Science and Mathematics in Ancient Greek Culture,* eds. C. J. Tuplin and T. E. Rihll. Oxford: 76–111.

Bowersock, G. W. (1969) *Greek Sophists in the Roman Empire.* Oxford.
  (1979) 'Historical problems in late Republican and Augustan classicism', in *Le classicisme à Rome aux Iers siècles avant et après J.C.* Fondation Hardt Entretiens, 25: 57–75.
Bowie, E. L. (1982) 'The importance of sophists'. *YCIS* 27: 29–89.
  (1990) 'Greek poetry in the Antonine age', in *Antonine Literature*, ed. D. A. Russell. Oxford: 53–90.
  (1997) 'Hadrian, Favorinus and Plutarch', in *Plutarch and his Intellectual World*, ed. J. M. Mossman. London: 1–15.
  (2000) 'Literature and sophistic' in *CAH* 11 (2nd edn.): 898–921.
  (2002a) 'Hadrian and Greek poetry', in *Greek Romans, Roman Greeks*, ed. E. Ostenfeld. Aarhus: 172–97.
  (2002b) 'Plutarch and literary activity in Achaea: A.D. 107–117', in *Sage and Emperor: Plutarch, Greek Intellectuals and Roman Power in the Time of Trajan (98–117 A.D.)*, eds. P. Stadter and L. Van der Stockt. Leuven: 41–56.
  (2004) 'Poetry and music in the life of Plutarch's statesman', in *The Statesman in Plutarch's Works. Vol.1: Plutarch's Statesman and His Aftermath: Political, Philosophical, and Literary Aspects. Mnemosyne* Suppl. 250 (1), eds. L. De Blois, J. A. E. Bons, T. Kessels and D. M. Schenkeveld. Leiden and Boston: 115–23.
  (2011) 'Men from Mytilene', in *Greek Identity in the First Century B.C.*, eds. T. Schmitz and N. Wiater. Stuttgart: 49–63.
Bowman, A. K. (1989) *Egypt after the Pharaohs (332 BC–AD 642).* Berkeley and Los Angeles.
Bowman, A. K. and Woolf, G. D. (eds.) (1994) *Literacy and Power in the Ancient World.* Cambridge.
Boyd, C. E. (1915) *Public Libraries and Literary Culture in Ancient Rome.* Chicago.
Bravi, A. (2009) 'Immagini adeguate. Opere d'arte greche nel templum Pacis', in *Divus Vespasianus. Il bimillenario dei Flavi*, ed. F. Coarelli. Milan: 158–67.
Brink, C. O. (1982) *Horace on Poetry. Epistles Book II: The Letters to Augustus and Florus.* Cambridge.
Brinkman, J. A. (2006) 'The use of occupation names as patronyms in the Kassite period: a forerunner of Neo-Babylonian ancestral names?' in *If a Man Builds a Joyful House: Assyriological Studies in Honor of Erle Verdun Leichty*, eds. A. K. Guinan, M. Ellis and T. Rutz. Leiden: 23–43.
British Library, The (2008) *Annual Report and Accounts 2007–8.* London.
Bröcker, L. O. (1885) 'Die Methode Galens in der literarischen Kritik'. *RhM* 40: 415–30.
Broughton, T. R. S. (1951–2) *The Magistrates of the Roman Republic*, 3 vols., American Philological Association Philological Monographs 15. New York.
Brown, F. E. (1935) 'The Regia'. *MAAR* 12: 67–88.
Bruce, L. D. (1981) 'A reappraisal of Roman libraries in the *Scriptores Historiae Augustae*'. *JLH* 16: 551–73.
Brunt, P. (1994) 'The bubble of the Second Sophistic'. *BICS* 39: 25–52.

Burkard, G. (1980) 'Bibliotheken im alten Ägypten'. *Bibliothek. Forschung und Praxis* 4: 79–115.

Burkhalter, F. (1990) 'Archives locales et archives centrales en Egypte romaine'. *Chiron* 20: 191–216.

Burrell, B. (2009) 'Reading, hearing, and looking at Ephesos' in *Ancient Literacies. The Culture of Reading in Greece and Rome*, eds. W. A. Johnson and H. N. Parker. Oxford: 69–95.

Cagnat, R. (1906) 'Les bibliothèques municipales dans l'empire romain'. *Mémoires de l'Académie des Inscriptions et Belles Lettres* 38 (1): 8–39.

Callanan, C. K. (1987) *Die Sprachbeschreibung bei Aristophanes von Byzantz (Hypomnemata 88)*. Göttingen.

Callmer, C. (1944) 'Antike Bibliotheken'. *OpArch* 3 (3): 145–93.

Cambiano, G. (1988) 'Sapere e testualità nel mondo antico', in *La memoria del sapere*, ed. P. Rossi. Rome and Bari: 69–98.

  (2007) 'Come confutare un libro? Dal *Fedro* al *Teeteto* di Platone'. *AntPhilos* 1: 99–122.

Cameron, A. (1995) *Callimachus and his Critics*. Princeton, NJ.

Camp, J. M. (1986) *The Athenian Agora: Excavations in the Heart of Classical Athens*. London.

Canfora, L. (1986a) *La biblioteca scomparsa*. Palermo.

  (1986b) *La véritable histoire de la bibliothèque d'Alexandrie*. Paris.

  (1988) 'Le biblioteche ellenistiche', in *Le biblioteche nel mondo antico e medievale*, ed. G. Cavallo. Rome and Bari: 3–28.

  (1989) *The Vanished Library: A Wonder of the Ancient World*. Transl. M. Ryle. London.

  (1993) 'Nascita delle biblioteche a Roma'. *Sileno* 19: 25–38.

  (1996) *Il Viaggio di Aristea*. Bari.

  (1999) 'Aristotele "fondatore" della biblioteca di Alessandria'. *QS* 50: 11–21. Repr. (2002) in *Scritti in Onore di Italo Gallo*, ed. L. Torraca. Naples: 167–75. Repr. in French (2003): 'Aristote "fondateur" de la bibliothèque d'Alexandrie', in *La nouvelle bibliothèque d'Alexandrie*, ed. F. Pataut. Paris: 39–55.

Cantino Wataghin, G. (2010) 'Le biblioteche nella tarda antichità: l'apporto dell'archeologia'. *Antiquité Tardive* 18: 21–62.

Capasso, M. (1982) *Trattato etico Epicureo (PHerc. 346). Edizione, traduzione e commento*. Naples.

  (1988) *Carneisco, il secondo libro del Filista (PHerc. 1027)*. Naples.

  (1989) 'Primo supplemento al catalogo dei papiri ercolanesi'. *CErc.* 19: 193–264.

  (1991) *Manuale di papirologia Ercolanese*. Galatina.

  (1993) 'Nascita delle biblioteche a Roma'. *Sileno* 19: 25–38.

  (1995) 'Marco Ottavio e la villa dei papiri di Ercolano'. *Eikasmos* 6: 183–9.

  (2000) 'I papiri ercolanesi opistografi', in *Atti del V convegno nazionale di Egittologia e papirologia Firenze, 10–12 Dicembre 1999*, ed. S. Russo. Florence: 5–25.

(2001) 'Tre titoli iniziali interni in papiri ercolanesi', in *Atti del XXII congresso internazionale di papirologia, Firenze, 23–29 Agosto 1998*, eds. I. Andorlini, G. Bastianini, M. Manfredi, and G. Menci. Florence: 177–86.

(2003) 'Scrinia curva. V.*XXVII*. Perseverare è umano. Ancora sulla pseudofalsificazione del carme *De Bello Actiaco (PHerc.* 817)', in *Dal restauro dei materiali allo studio dei testi. Aspetti della ricerca papirologica*, ed. M. Capasso. Papyrologica Lupiensia 11/2002. Galatina: 249–51.

(2007) 'I rotoli ercolanesi: da libri a carboni e da carboni a libri', in *Akten des 23. Internationalen Papyrologen-Kongresses. Wien, 22.–28. Juli 2001*, ed. B. Palme. Vienna: 73–7.

(2010) 'Who lived in the Villa of the Papyri at Herculaneum – a settled question?', in *The Villa of the Papyri at Herculaneum: Archaeology, Reception, and Digital Reconstruction*. Sozomena: Studies in the Recovery of Ancient Texts: Edited on Behalf of the Herculaneum Society, 1, ed. M. Zarmakoupi. Berlin and New York: 89–113.

Capasso, M. and Dorandi, T. (1979) 'PHerc. 1696 e 1822'. *CErc.* 9: 37–45.

Carandini, A. and Bruno, D. (2008) *La casa di Augusto. Dai "Lupercalia" al Natale*. Rome and Bari.

Carettoni, G., Colini, A. M., Cozza, L. and Gatti, G. (eds.) (1960) *La pianta marmorea di Roma antica. Forma urbis Romae*. Rome.

Carey, S. (2003) *Pliny's Catalogue of Culture. Art and Empire in the Natural History*. Oxford.

Caroli, M. (2005) 'ΣΙΛΛΥΒΟΙ o ΣΙΛΛΥΒΑ? (Cicerone, *Ad Attico* 4, 4a; 4, 8, 2; 4, 5, 4)'. *S&T* 3: 39–49.

(2007) *Il titolo iniziale nel rotolo librario greco-egizio*. Bari.

(2010) '"Un acquisto per l'eternità". La pubblicità dei libri nel mondo antico', in *Antichità e Pubblicità*, ed. F. De Martino. Bari: 107–76.

Carrié, J.-Ph. (2010) 'Les lieux des lettres dans les *villae* occidentales de l'antiquité tardive'. *Antiquité Tardive* 18: 63–74.

Casson, L. (2001) *Libraries in the Ancient World*. New Haven, CT and London.

Castagnoli, F. (1946) 'Atrium libertatis'. *RendLinc* 1: 276–91.

(1949) 'Sulla biblioteca del tempio di Apollo Palatino'. *RendLinc* 4: 380–2.

Castagnoli, F. and Cozza, L. (1956–8) 'L'angolo meridionale del Foro della Pace'. *BCAR* 76: 119–47.

Cavallo, G. (1975) *Libri, editori e pubblico nel mondo antico. Guida storica e critica*. Rome and Bari.

(1983) *Libri, scritture, scribi a Ercolano: introduzione allo studio dei materiali Greci*. Naples.

(1988) 'Cultura scritta e conservazione del sapere: dalla Grecia antica all'Occidente medievale', in *La memoria del sapere*, ed. P. Rossi. Rome and Bari: 29–67.

(1989) 'Libro e cultura scritta' in *Storia di Roma 4. Caratteri e Morfologie*, eds. A. Momigliano and A. Schiavone. Turin: 718–25.

(2005) 'La scrittura greca libraria tra i secoli I a.C. – I d.C. Materiali, tipologie, momenti', in *Il calamo e il papiro. La scrittura greca dall'età ellenistica ai primi secoli di Bisanzio*, ed. G. Cavallo. Papyrologica Florentina 36. Florence: 107–22.

(2010) 'Libri, lettura e biblioteche nella tarda antichità: Un panorama e qualche riflessione'. *Antiquité Tardive* 18: 9–19.

Cavallo, G. (ed.) (1988) *Le biblioteche nel mondo antico e medievale*. Rome and Bari.

Cavallo, G. and Chartier, R. (eds.) (1999) *A History of Reading in the West*. Transl. by L. G. Cochrane. Studies in Print Culture and the History of the Book. Boston.

Cencetti, G. (1940) 'Gli archivi dell'antica Roma nell'età repubblicana'. *Archivi* 7: 7–47.

Champion, C. B. (2004) *Cultural Politics in Polybius' Histories*. Berkeley, CA.

Chastagnol, A. (1997) 'Le fonctionnement de la préfecture urbaine', in *La Rome impériale. Démographie et logistique. Actes de la table ronde Rome 1994*. Collection de L'Ecole française de Rome. Rome: 111–19.

Cherf, W. J. (2008) 'Earth, wind and fire. The Alexandrian fire-storm of 48 B.C.', in *What Happened to the Ancient Library of Alexandria?*, eds. M. El-Abbadi and O. Fathallah. Leiden and Boston: 55–73.

Chodorow, S. (2007) *Law Libraries and the Formation of the Legal Profession in the Late Middle Ages*. Austin, TX.

Christianson, E. B. (1993) 'Special libraries', in *World Encyclopedia of Library and Information Services*, ed. R. Wedgeworth. 3rd edn. Chicago: 785–96.

Cichorius, K. (1922) *Römische Studien*. Leipzig.

Citroni, M. (1995) *Poesia e lettori in Roma Antica. Forme della comunicazione letteraria*. Rome and Bari.

Citroni Marchetti, S. (2005) 'Le scelte di un intellettuale. Sulle motivazioni culturali della *Naturalis Historia*'. *MD* 54: 91–121.

Clancier, P. (2009) *Les bibliothèques en Babylonie dans la deuxième moitié du Ier millénaire av. J.-C.* Münster.

Claridge, A. (2007) 'Hadrian's lost Temple of Trajan'. *JRA* 20: 55–94.

Clarke, K. (1999a) *Between Geography and History: Hellenistic Constructions of the Roman World*. Oxford.

(1999b) 'Universal perspectives in historiography', in *The Limits of Historiography: Genre and Narrative in Ancient Historical Texts*, Mnemosyne Suppl. 191, ed. C. Kraus. Leiden, Boston and Cologne: 249–79.

Clauss, J. J. and Cuypers, M. (eds.) (2010) *A Companion to Hellenistic Literature*. Malden MA and Oxford.

Clift, E. H. (1945) *Latin Pseudepigraphia: A Study in Literary Attributions*. Baltimore.

Coarelli, F. (1981) *Dintorni di Roma*. Rome and Bari.

(1982) *Lazio*. Rome and Bari.

(1983) 'Il commercio delle opere d'arte in età tardo-repubblicana'. *DialArch* Ser. 3, v. 1.1: 45–53.

(1991) 'Le plan de via Anicia. Un nouveau fragment de la Forma Marmorea de Rome', in *Rome. L'espace urbain et ses représentations*, ed. F. Hinard and M. Royo. Paris: 65–81.

(1993a) 'Atrium libertatis'. *LTUR* 1: 133–5.

(1993b) 'Bibliotheca Asinii Pollionis'. *LTUR* 1: 196.

(1993c) 'Athenaeum'. *LTUR* 1: 131.

(1994) 'Moneta. Le officine della zecca di Roma tra repubblica e impero'. *AIIN* 38–41: 23–66.

(1997) 'La consistenza della città nel periodo imperiale', in *La Rome impériale. Démographie et logistique. Actes de la table ronde Rome 1994*. Collection de L'Ecole française de Rome 230. Paris: 89–109.

(1999a) 'Vicus Sandaliarius'. *LTUR* 3: 189.

(1999b) 'Pax'. *LTUR* 4: 67–70.

(1999c) 'Praefectura Urbana'. *LTUR* 4: 159–60.

(1999d) *La colonna Traiana*. Rome.

(ed.) (2009a) *Divus Vespasianus. Il bimillenario dei Flavi*. Milan.

(2009b) 'I Flavi a Roma', in *Divus Vespasianus. Il bimillenario dei Flavi*, ed. F. Coarelli. Milan: 73–4.

(2009c) 'Le biblioteche dei Flavi', in *'Bibliotheca Flavia' ad Templum Pacis. I libri antichi delle biblioteche reatine ricostruiscono idealmente quella edificata dall'Imperatore Vespasiano nel Foro della Pace*, ed. C. Moroni. Rieti. Catalogue of the exhibition at Rieti, December 11, 2009–February 11, 2010: 9–15.

Coates-Stephens, R. (2010) 'Notes from Rome'. *CWA* 42: 51–6.

(2012) 'Notes from Rome 2011–2012'. *PBSR* 80: 325–34.

Cohen, M. E. (1988) *The Canonical Lamentations of Ancient Mesopotamia*. Bethesda, MD.

Coleman, K. M. (ed.) (1988) *Statius. Silvae IV*. Oxford.

Colini, A. M. (1937) 'Forum Pacis'. *BCAR* 65: 7–41.

Conze, A. (1884) 'Die Pergamenische Bibliothek'. *SBBerlin*: 1259–70.

Corbier, M. (1992) 'De la maison d'Hortensius à la curia sur le Palatin'. *MEFRA* 104: 871–916. Repr. as (2006) '*In Palatio*: la "Curie" du Palatin, lieu de mémoire', in M. Corbier, *Donner à voir, donner à lire: mémoire et communication dans la Rome ancienne*. Paris: 163–79.

Costabile, F. (1984) 'Opere di oratoria politica e giudiziaria nella biblioteca della Villa dei Papiri: i *PHerc*. Latini 1067 e 1475', in *Atti del XVII congresso internazionale di papirologia (Napoli, 19–26 Maggio 1983)*. Naples: 591–606.

Coulton, J. J. (1976) *The Architectural Development of the Greek Stoa*. Oxford.

Crawford, M. H. (1974) *Roman Republican Coinage I*. Cambridge.

(ed.) (1996) *Roman Statutes*. 2 vols. London.

Crisci, E. (1999) 'I più antichi libri greci: note bibliologiche e paleografiche su rotoli papiracei del IV–III secolo a.C.' *S &C* 23: 29–62.

Crönert, W. (1906) *Kolotes und Menedemos, Texte und Untersuchungen zur Philosophen- und Literaturgeschichte*. Munich. Photographic reprint Amsterdam, 1965.

Crouzet, S. (2000) 'Les *excerpta* de Denys d'Halicarnasse, un reflet de l'idéologie romaine du premier siècle av. J.C.' *Pallas* 53: 159–72.

Crowther, N. (1973) 'The collegium poetarum at Rome: Fact or fiction?' *Latomus* 32: 575–80.

Culham, P. (1989) 'Archives and alternatives in republican Rome'. *CPh* 84 (2): 100–15.

Curtis, J., McCall, H., Collon, D. and al-Gailani Werr, L. (eds.) (2008) *New Light on Nimrud*. London.

Cuvigny, H. (2009) 'The finds of papyri: the archaeology of papyrology', in *The Oxford Handbook of Papyrology*, ed. R. S. Bagnall. Oxford: 30–58.

Dalzell, A. (1955) 'Asinius Pollio and the introduction of recitation at Rome'. *Hermathena* 86: 20–8.

Damschen, G. (2008) 'Stichometry'. *BNP* 13: 834–5.

Dana, J. C. (1991) 'The evolution of the special library', in *Librarian at Large: Selected Writings of John Cotton Dana*, ed. C. A. Hanson. Washington, DC: 55–64.

Danzig, G. (2003) 'Did Plato read Xenophon's *Cyropaedia*?', in *Plato's Laws: From Theory into Practice*, eds. S. Scolnicov and L. Brisson. Sankt Augustin: 286–97.

  (2005) 'Intra-Socratic polemics: the Symposia of Plato and Xenophon'. *GRBS* 45: 331–57.

D'Arms, J. (1970) *Romans on the Bay of Naples. A Social and Cultural Study of the Villas and Their Owners from 150 B.C. to A.D. 400*. Cambridge, MA.

Davis, P. J. (2006) *Ovid and Augustus: A Political Reading of Ovid's Erotic Poems*. London.

Davison, J. A. (1962) 'Literature and literacy in ancient Greece'. *Phoenix* 16: 141–56, 219–33.

Debru, A. (1995) 'Les démonstrations médicales à Rome au temps de Galien', in *Ancient Medicine in its Socio-Cultural Context: Papers Read at the Congress Held at Leiden University, 13–15 April 1992*, vol. I, eds. P. J. Van Der Eijk, H. F. J. Horstmanshoff and P. H. Schrijvers. Amsterdam and Atlanta: 69–81.

De Filippis Cappai, C. (1993) *Medici e medicina in Roma Antica*. Turin.

Delage, E. (1930) *La géographie dans les Argonautiques d'Apollonios de Rhodes*. Bordeaux and Paris.

Delattre, D. (2006) *La Villa des Papyrus et les Rouleaux d'Herculanum. La Bibliothèque de Philodème*. Liège.

  (2007) *Philodème de Gadara sur la musique livre IV*. 2 vols. Paris.

Del Corso, L. (2003) 'Materiali per una protostoria del libro e delle pratiche di lettura nel mondo greco'. *S&T* 1: 5–78.

(2005) *La lettura nel mondo ellenistico*. Rome and Bari.

Delcourt, A. (2005) *Lecture des antiquités romaines de Denys d'Halicarnasse*. Brussels.

Delia, D. (1992) 'From Romance to rhetoric: the Alexandrian library in Classical and Islamic traditions'. *AHR*. 97 (5): 1449–67.

Della Corte, F. (1954) *Varrone: il terzo gran lume romano*. Genoa.

Del Mastro, G. (2000) 'Secondo supplemento al catalogo dei papiri ercolanesi'. *CErc*. 30: 157–242.

(2002) 'La *subscriptio* del *PHerc*. 1005 e altri titoli in caratteri distintivi nei papiri ercolanesi'. *CErc*. 32: 245–56.

(2005a) 'Il *PHerc*. 1380: Crisippo, *Opera Logica*'. *CErc*. 35: 61–70.

(2005b) 'Riflessioni sui papiri latini ercolanesi'. *CErc*. 35: 183–94.

(2007) 'Un opera logica di Crisippo nel *PHerc*. 1380', in *Proceedings of the 24th International Congress of Papyrology, Helsinki, 1–7 August, 2004*, eds. J. Frösén and T. Purola, 2 vols. Vol. I: 249–57. Helsinki.

Demougin, S. (ed.) (1994) *La mémoire perdue: à la recherche des archives oubliées, publiques et privées, de la Rome antique*. Histoire Ancienne et Médiévale 30. Paris.

De Sanctis, E. (2009) 'Il filosofo e il re: osservazioni sulla *Vita Philonidis* (*PHerc*. 1044)'. *CErc*. 39: 107–18.

De Simone, A., and Ruffo, F. (2003) 'Ercolano e la Villa dei Papiri alla luce dei nuovi scavi'. *CErc*. 33: 279–311.

Detienne, M. (ed.) (1988) *Les savoirs de l'écriture en Grèce ancienne (Cahiers de Philologie, 14)* Lille.

Deubner, O. (1938) *Das Asklepieion von Pergamon*. Berlin.

Dibelius, M. (1950) 'Archiv'. in *RAC* 1: 614–33.

Diès, A. (1950) *Platon. Oeuvres complètes*, vol. VII.2. 2nd edn. Paris.

Dillery, J. (2005) 'Chresmologues and manteis: independent diviners and the problem of authority', in *Mantikê*, eds. S. Iles Johnston and P. T. Struck. *Studies in Ancient Divination*. Leiden and Boston: 167–231.

(2007) 'Greek historians of the Near East. Clio's "other" sons', in *A Companion to Greek and Roman Historiography*, ed. J. Marincola. Malden and Oxford: 221–30.

Dionisotti, A. C. (1997) 'On fragments in classical scholarship', in *Collecting Fragments – Fragmente Sammeln (Aporemata: Kritische Studien zur Philologiegeschichte 1)*, ed. G. Most. Göttingen: 1–33.

Dix, T. K. (1986) *Private and Public Libraries at Rome in the First Century B.C.: A Preliminary Study* (PhD Diss. University of Michigan).

(1994) 'Public libraries in ancient Rome. Ideology and reality'. *L&C* 29 (3): 282–96.

(1996) 'Pliny's library at Comum'. *L&C* 31 (1): 85–102.

(2000) 'The library of Lucullus'. *Athenaeum* 88 (2): 441–64.

(2004) 'Aristotle's "Peripatetic" library', in *Lost Libraries: The Destruction of Great Book Collections since Antiquity*, ed. J. Raven. New York: 58–74.

Dix, T. K. and Houston, G. W. (2006) 'Public libraries in the city of Rome from the Augustan age to the time of Diocletian'. *MEFRA* 118 (2): 671–717.

Doody, A. (2010) *Pliny's Encyclopaedia. The Reception of the Natural History*. Cambridge.

Dorandi, T. (1983) 'Glutinatores'. *ZPE* 50: 25–8.

(1984) 'Sillyboi'. *S&C* 8: 185–99.

(1987) 'Stichometrica'. *ZPE* 70: 35–8.

(1992a) 'Fünf buchtechnische Miszellen'. *AfP* 38: 39–45.

(1992b) 'Per una ricomposizione dello scritto di Filodemo sulla poetica'. *ZPE* 91: 29–46.

(1995a) 'Un papiro ercolanese a Leiden'. *ZPE* 109: 35–8.

(1995b) 'La "Villa dei Papiri" a Ercolano e la sua biblioteca'. *CPh* 90: 168–82.

(1997) 'Lucrèce et les Epicuriens de Campanie', in *Lucretius and his Intellectual Background*, eds. K. A. Algra, M. H. Koenen and P. H. Schrijvers. Amsterdam: 35–48.

(2000a) 'Un libro del ΠΕΡΙ ΦΥΣΕΩΣ di Epicuro trasmesso in tre esemplari', in *EPIEIKEIA: Studia Graeca in Memoriam Jesús Lens Tuero*, ed. M. Alganza Roldán. Granada: 103–11.

(2000b) *Le stylet et la tablette. Dans le secret des auteurs antiques*. Paris.

Dover, K. J. (1968) *Lysias and the Corpus Lysiacum*. Berkeley and Los Angeles.

(1993) *Aristophanes. Frogs*. Oxford.

Downey, S. B. (1998) *Mesopotamian Religious Architecture: Alexander through the Parthians*. Princeton, NJ.

(2003) 'Review of Kose 1988'. *JAOS* 123: 188–9.

Drews, R. (1988) 'Pontiffs, prodigies and the disappearance of the "Annales Maximi"'. *CPh* 83 (4): 289–99.

Duckworth, G. E. (1952) *The Nature of Roman Comedy: A Study in Popular Entertainment*. Princeton, NJ.

Dudley, D. R. (1967) *Urbs Roma*. Aberdeen.

Duff, T. E. (1999) *Plutarch's Lives: Exploring Virtue and Vice*. Oxford.

(2007/2008) 'Plutarch's readers and the moralism of the *Lives*'. *Ploutarchos* 5: 3–18.

Dunlap, L. W. (1972) *Readings in Library History*. New York.

Durance, C. J. and Taylor, H. A. (1992) 'Wisdom, knowledge, information and data. Transformation and convergence in archives and libraries of the western world'. *Alexandria* 4 (1): 37–61.

Düring, I. (1950) 'Notes on the history of the transmission of Aristotle's writings'. *Symbolae Philologicae Gotoburgenses, Acta Universitatis Gotoburgensis* 56 (3): 37–70.

(1954) 'Aristotle the scholar'. *Arctos* N.S. 1: 61–77.

(1957) *Aristotle in the Ancient Biographical Tradition*. Göteborg.

du Toit, J. S. (1998) 'Ancient Near Eastern collection development: reappraising the problematic nature of the description of ancient archival and library practices', in *Intellectual Life of the Ancient Near East*, ed. J. Prosecký. Prague: 389–96.

(2002) *The Organization and Use of Documentary Deposits in the Near East from Ancient to Medieval Times: Libraries, Archives, Book Collections and Genizas* (Ph.D. Diss. McGill University).

Dziatzko, K. (1895) 'Archive'. *RE* 2.1. Stuttgart: 553–64.

(1896) 'Die Bibliotheksanlage von Pergamon'. *Sammlung Bibliothekswissenschaftlicher Arbeiten* 10: 38–47.

(1897) 'Bibliotheken'. *RE* 3.1: 405–24.

Eck, W., Caballos, A. and Fernández, F. (1996) *Das Senatus Consultum de Cn. Pisone Patre*. Munich.

Eco, U. (1994) *The Name of the Rose*. Transl. W. Weaver. Orlando.

Edwards, E. (1859) *Memoirs of Libraries: Including a Handbook of Library Economy*. Rep. 1964. New York.

El-Abbadi, M. (1992) *Life and Fate of the Ancient Library of Alexandria*. Paris.

(2004) 'The Alexandria library in history', in *Alexandria, Real and Imagined*, eds. A. Hirst and M. Silk. Aldershot and Burlington, VT: 167–83.

El-Abbadi M. and Fathallah, O. (eds.) (2008) *What Happened to the Ancient Library of Alexandria?* Leiden and Boston.

Empereur, J.-L. (2003) 'La destruction de la Bibliothèque d'Alexandrie: la voix de l'archéologie', in *La Nouvelle Bibliothèque d'Alexandrie*, ed. F. Pataut. Paris: 179–93.

Erskine, A. (1995) 'Culture and power in Ptolemaic Egypt: the Museum and library of Alexandria'. *G&R* 42 (1): 38–48.

Fabian, K. (1992) *Callimaco, Aitia II: testo critico, traduzione e commento*. Alessandria.

Fantham, E. (1996) *Roman Literary Culture from Cicero to Apuleius*. Baltimore.

Fantuzzi, M. and Hunter, R. (2004) *Tradition and Innovation in Hellenistic Poetry*. Cambridge.

Farrell, J. (2009) 'The impermanent text in Catullus and other Roman poets,' in *Ancient Literacies: The Culture of Reading in Greece and Rome*, eds. W. A. Johnson and H. N. Parker. Oxford: 164–85.

Faulkner, R. O. (1969) *The Ancient Egyptian Pyramid Texts*. Oxford.

Fedeli, P. (1984) 'Sul prestito librario nell'antichità e sull'arte di sedurre i bibliotecari'. *StudUrb* 16: 165–8.

(1988) 'Biblioteche private e pubbliche a Roma e nel mondo romano', in *Le biblioteche nel mondo antico e medievale*, ed. G. Cavallo. Rome and Bari: 29–64.

Feeney, D. (2005) 'Review article. The beginnings of literature in Latin'. *JRS* 95: 226–40.

Fehrle, R. (1986) *Das Bibliothekswesen im Alten Rom. Voraussetzungen, Bedingungen, Anfänge.* Wiesbaden.

Fernández Uriel, P. and Rodríguez Valcárcel, J. A. (2006) 'Julio César y la idea de biblioteca pública en la Roma antica', in *Espacio y tiempo en la percepción de la antigüedad tardía. Antigüedad y Cristianismo* 23. Murcia: 965–79.

Ferrari, G. (1999) 'The geography of time: The Nile mosaic and the library at Praeneste'. *Ostraka* 8: 359–86.

Ferrary, J. L. (1976) 'L'empire de Rome et les hégémonies des cités grecques chez Polybe'. *BCH* 100: 283–9.

Fincke, J. (2004) 'The British Museum's Ashurbanipal Library Project'. *Iraq* 66: 55–60.

Flacelière, R. (1951) 'Le poète stoïcien Sarapion d'Athènes, ami de Plutarque'. *REG* 64: 325–7.

Flashar, H. (ed.) (2004) *Grundriss der Geschichte der Philosophie. Die Philosophie der Antike*, vol. III. Basle.

(2008) 'Commentary', in *The Cambridge Companion to Galen*, ed. R. J. Hankinson. Cambridge: 323–54.

Flemming, R. (2007) 'Galen's imperial order of knowledge', in *Ordering Knowledge in the Roman World*, eds. J. König and T. Whitmarsh. Cambridge: 241–77.

Fogagnolo, S. and Rossi, F. M. (2010a) 'Settore meridionale del Foro della Pace: l'impatto del cantiere di restauro severiano, corrispondenze e differenze rispetto al progetto originario', in *Arqueología de la construcción II. Los procesos constructivos en el mundo romano: Italia y Provincias Orientales (Anejos de AEspA 57)*, eds. S. Camporeale, H. Dessales, A. Pizzo. Madrid, Mérida: 93–104.

(2010b) 'Il *Templum Pacis* come esempio di trasformazione del paesaggio urbano e di mutamenti culturali dalla prima età imperiale ai primi del '900'. *Bollettino di Archeologia on line*, vol. speciale: 31–46 (www.archeologia.beniculturali.it/pages/pubblicazioni.html).

Ford, A. (2002) *The Origins of Criticism. Literary Culture and Poetic Theory in Classical Greece.* Princeton, NJ and Oxford.

Fortenbaugh, W. W. and Steinmetz, P. (1989) *Cicero's Knowledge of the Peripatos.* New Brunswick and London.

Fowler, D. (1999) *The Mathematics of Plato's Academy: A New Reconstruction.* 2nd edn. Oxford.

Fowler, H. W. and Fowler, F. G. (1905) *The Works of Lucian of Samosata* III. Oxford.

Fox, M. (1993) 'History and rhetoric in Dionysius of Halicarnassus'. *JRS* 83: 31–47.

(1996) *Roman Historical Myths.* Oxford.

Frahm, E. (2004) 'Royal hermeneutics: observations on the commentaries from Ashurbanipal's libraries at Nineveh'. *Iraq* 66: 45–50.

(2011a) 'Keeping company with men of learning: the king as scholar', in *The Oxford Handbook of Cuneiform Culture*, eds. K. Radner and E. Robson. Oxford: 508–32.

(2011b) *Babylonian and Assyrian Text Commentaries: Origins of Interpretation.* Guides to the Mesopotamian Textual Record 5. Münster.
Fränkel, E. (1957) 'Some notes on Cicero's letters to Trebatius'. *JRS* 47: 66–70.
Fraser, P. M. (1972) *Ptolemaic Alexandria*, 3 vols. Oxford.
Frede, M. (1981) 'On Galen's epistemology', in *Galen: Problems and Prospects*, ed. V. Nutton. London: 65–86.
Frier, B. W. (1985) *The Rise of the Jurists. Studies in Cicero's* Pro Caecina. Princeton.
Fromentin, V. (1989) 'La tradition directe des *Antiquités romaines* (livre i) et la question de la traduction latine de Lapus Biragus'. *MEFRA* 101: 37–62.
  (1993) 'À propos de la tradition manuscrite du livre IV des *Antiquités romaines* de Denys d'Halicarnasse'. *REG* 106: 102–19.
  (1998), *Les Antiquités romaines de Denys d'Halicarnasse.* Paris.
Frösén, J. (2009) 'Conservation of ancient papyrus materials', in *The Oxford Handbook of Papyrology*, ed. R. S. Bagnall. Oxford: 79–100.
Funaioli, G. (1907) *Grammaticae Romanae Fragmenta.* Leipzig.
Gabba, E. (1982) 'La "storia di Roma arcaica" di Dionigi d'Alicarnasso'. *ANWR* II.30.1: 799–816.
  (1991) *Dionysius of Halicarnassus and the History of Archaic Rome.* Berkeley, CA.
Galli, M. (2002) *Die Lebenswelt einer Sophisten. Untersuchungen zu den Bauten und Stiftungen des Herodes Atticus.* Mainz.
García Ballester, L. (1981) 'Galen as a medical practitioner: problems in diagnosis', in *Galen: Problems and Prospects*, ed. V. Nutton. London: 13–46.
  (1994) 'Galen as a clinician: his methods in diagnosis'. *ANRW* 2.37.2: 1636–71.
Gardiner, A. H. (1938) 'The house of life'. *JEA* 24: 157–79.
Garton, C. (1972) *Personal Aspects of the Roman Theatre.* Toronto.
Gastaldi, S. (1981) 'La retorica del IV secolo tra oralità e scrittura. Sugli scrittori di discorsi di Alcidamante'. *QS* 14: 189–225.
Gatti, G. (1960) 'Data, scopo e precedenti della pianta', in *La pianta marmorea di Roma antica: Forma Urbis Romae*, eds. G. Carettoni, A. Colini, L. Cozza and G. Gatti. Rome: 211–18.
Geagan, D. J. (1991) 'The Sarapion monument and the quest for status in Roman Athens'. *ZPE* 85: 145–65.
George, A. R. (2003) *The Babylonian Gilgamesh Epic: Introduction, Critical Edition and Cuneiform Texts.* Oxford.
Gigante, M. (1979) *Catalogo dei papiri ercolanesi.* Naples.
  (1985) 'La biblioteca di Filodemo'. *CErc.* 15: 5–30.
  (1990) *Filodemo in Italia.* Florence.
  (1995) *Philodemus in Italy: the Books from Herculaneum.* Transl. D. Obbink. Ann Arbor, MI.
  (1997) 'Atakta XVI'. *CErc.* 27: 151–6.
  (1999) *Kepos e Peripatos. Contributo alla storia dell'Aristotelismo antico.* Naples.

Gigon, O. (1953) *Kommentar zum ersten Buch von Xenophons Memorabilien*. Basel.
   (1956) *Kommentar zum Zweiten Buch von Xenophons Memorabilien*. Basel.
   (1959) 'Cicero und Aristoteles'. *Hermes* 87: 143–62.
Gill, C. (1995) *Making Men. Sophists and Self-Presentation in Ancient Rome*. Princeton.
Gill, C., Whitmarsh, T. and Wilkins, J. (eds.) (2009) *Galen and the World of Knowledge*. Cambridge.
Gleason, M. W. (2009) 'Shock and awe: the performance dimension of Galen's anatomy demonstrations', in *Galen and the World of Knowledge*, eds. C. Gill, T. Whitmarsh and J. Wilkins. Cambridge: 85–114.
Goldhill, S. (2008) 'The anecdote: exploring the boundaries between oral and literate performance in the Second Sophistic', in *Ancient Literacies: The Culture of Reading in Greece and Rome*, eds. W. A. Johnson and H. N. Parker. Oxford: 96–113.
Goldhill, S. and Osborne, R. (eds.) (1999) *Performance Culture and Athenian Democracy*. Cambridge.
Gottschalk, H. B. (1987) 'Aristotelian philosophy in the Roman world from the time of Cicero to the end of the second century AD'. *ANRW* 2.36.2: 1079–174.
Götze, B. (1937) 'Antike Bibliotheken'. *JDAI* 52: 223–47.
Goudriaan, K. (1989) *Over Classicisme: Dionysius van Halicarnassus en zijn Program van Welsprekendheid, Cultuur en Politik*, 2 vols. (PhD Diss. University of Amsterdam).
Grafton, A. and Williams, M. (2006) *Christianity and the Transformation of the Book. Origen, Eusebius and the Library of Caesarea*. Cambridge MA and London.
Grayeff, F. (1956) 'The problem of the genesis of Aristotle's text'. *Phronesis* 1 (2): 105–22.
Griffin, M. (1994) 'The intellectual developments of the Ciceronian age'. *CAH* 9 (2nd edn.). Cambridge: 689–728.
Gros, P. (1993) 'Apollo Palatinus'. *LTUR* 1: 54–7.
   (1995) 'Fortuna Huiusce Diei'. *LTUR* 2: 269–70.
   (2001a) *L'architettura romana dagli inizi del III secolo a.C. alla fine dell'alto impero*. Milan.
   (2001b) 'Les édifices de la bureaucratie impériale. Administration, archives et services publics dans le centre monumental de Rome'. *Pallas* 55: 107–26.
Gruen, E. S. (1984) *The Hellenistic World and the Coming of Rome*. Berkeley and Los Angeles.
   (1992) *Culture and National Identity in Republican Rome*. London.
Guarducci, M. (1974) *Epigrafia greca* 3. Rome.
Gudeman, A. (1912) 'Herennius Philo'. *RE* VIII.1: 650–61.
Gurney, O. R. (1952) 'The Sultantepe tablets: a preliminary note'. *AnSt* 2: 25–35.
   (1997) 'Scribes at Huzirina'. *NABU* 18.
Gurney, O. R. and Finkelstein, J. J. (1957) *The Sultantepe Tablets I*. London.
Gurney, O. R. and Hulin, P. (1964) *The Sultantepe Tablets II*. London.

Gutas, D. (1998) *Greek Thought, Arabic Culture. The Graeco-Arabic Translation Movement in Baghdad and Early 'Abbasid Society (2nd–4th/8th–10th centuries).* London and New York.

Gutzwiller, K. (2007) *A Guide to Hellenistic Literature.* Malden, MA and Oxford.

Habicht, C. (1969) *Die Inschriften des Asklepieions. Altertümer von Pergamon 8.3.* Berlin.

(1997) *Athens from Alexander to Antony.* Cambridge, MA.

Habinek, T. (1998) *The Politics of Latin Literature. Writing, Identity and Empire in Ancient Rome.* Cambridge.

(2005) *The World of Roman Song: From Ritualised Speech to Social Order.* Baltimore and London.

(2008) 'Situating literacy at Rome', in *Ancient Literacies: The Culture of Reading in Greece and Rome*, eds. W. A. Johnson and H. N. Parker. Oxford: 114–41.

Hadas, M. (ed. and transl.) (1951) *Aristeas to Philocrates (Letter of Aristeas).* New York.

Hagen, F. (forthcoming) 'Libraries in Ancient Egypt c. 1600–1000 BC', in *Libraries before Alexandria*, eds. K. Ryholt and G. Barjamovic. Oxford.

Halfmann, H. (1979) *Die Senatoren aus dem östlichen Teil des Imperium Romanum bis zum Ende des 2 Jh. n. Chr.* Göttingen.

(2004) *Éphèse et Pergame: urbanisme et commanditaires en Asie Mineure romaine.* Bordeaux and Paris.

Hankinson, R. J. (1992) 'Galen's philosophical eclecticism'. *ANRW* 2.36.5: 3505–22.

(1994) 'Usage and abusage: Galen on language', in *Language. Companions to Ancient Thought*, vol. III, ed. S. Everson. Cambridge: 166–87.

(2008a) 'The man and his work', in *The Cambridge Companion to Galen*, ed. R. J. Hankinson. Cambridge: 1–33.

(2008b) 'Epistemology', in *The Cambridge Companion to Galen*, ed. R. J. Hankinson. Cambridge: 157–83.

(ed.) (2008c) *The Cambridge Companion to Galen.* Cambridge.

(2009) 'Galen on the limitations of knowledge', in *Galen and the World of Knowledge*, ed. C. Gill, T. Whitmarsh and J. Wilkins. Cambridge: 206–42.

Hanslik, R. (1948) 'Tullius 47'. *RE* 7.A2: 1285–6.

Hanson, A. E. (1998) 'Galen: author and critic', in *Editing Texts. Texte edieren*, ed. G. Most. Göttingen: 22–53.

Harder, M. A. (1998) ' "Generic games" in Callimachus' *Aetia*', in *Genre in Hellenistic Poetry (Hellenistica Groningana 3)*, eds. M. A. Harder, R. F. Regtuit and G. C. Wakker. Groningen: 95–113.

(2002) 'Intertextuality in Callimachus' *Aetia*', in Fondation Hardt Entretiens 48: 189–233.

(2012) *Callimachus: Aetia. Introduction, Text, Translation and Commentary.* Oxford.

Harding, P. (2006) *Didymos on Demosthenes.* Oxford.

Harris, J. R. (1971) 'Medicine', in *The Legacy of Egypt*, ed. J. R. Harris, 2nd edn. Oxford: 118–37.
Harris, W. V. (1989) *Ancient Literacy*. Cambridge, MA.
Hatzimichali, M. (2011) *Potamo of Alexandria and the Emergence of Eclecticism in Late Hellenistic Philosophy*. Cambridge.
Havelock, E. A. (1963) *Preface to Plato*. Cambridge, MA.
Hayes, K. J. (2008) *The Road to Monticello: The Life and Mind of Thomas Jefferson*. Oxford.
Heessel, N.P. (2008) 'Astrological medicine in Babylonia', in *Astro-Medicine: Astrology and Medicine, East and West*, eds. A. Akasoy, C. Burnett and R. Yoeli Tlalim. Florence: 1–16.
Henderson, J. (2007a) 'The creation of Isidore's Etymologies or Origins', in *Ordering Knowledge in the Roman Empire*, eds. J. König and T. Whitmarsh. Cambridge: 150–74.
  (2007b) *The Medieval World of Isidore of Seville. Truth from Words*. Cambridge.
Henrichs, A. (1968) 'Vespasian's visit to Alexandria'. *ZPE* 3: 51–80.
Hidber, T. (1996) *Das Klassizistische Manifest des Dionys von Halicarnass*. Stuttgart and Leipzig.
Hill, H. (1961) 'Dionysius of Halicarnassus and the origins of Rome'. *JRS* 51: 88–93.
Hillscher, A. (1892) 'Hominum litteratorum Graecorum ante Tiberii mortem in urbe Roma commoratorum historia critica'. *JCP Suppl.* 18: 353–444.
Hinds, S. (1998) *Allusion and Intertext: Dynamics of Appropriation in Roman Poetry*. Cambridge.
Holford-Strevens, L. (1988) *Aulus Gellius*. (London. Rev. and exp. edn. (2003) *Aulus Gellius. An Antonine Scholar and his Achievement*. Oxford.)
Holmes, A. (1980) 'The Alexandrian library'. *Libri* 30.4: 283–94.
Höpfner, W. (1996) 'Zu griechischen Bibliotheken und Bücherschränken'. *AA*: 25–36.
  (2002a) 'Die Bibliothek Eumenes II. in Pergamon', in *Antike Bibliotheken*, ed. W. Höpfner. Mainz: 41–52.
  (2002b) 'Eine würdige Nachfolgerin. Die Erneuerung der Akademie in Athen unter Kaiser Hadrian im 2. Jh. n. Chr.', in *Antike Bibliotheken*, ed. W. Höpfner. Mainz: 63–6.
  (2002c) 'Pergamon – Rhodos – Nysa – Athen. Bibliotheken in Gymnasien und anderen Lehr- und Forschungsstatten', in *Antike Bibliotheken*, ed. W. Höpfner. Mainz: 67–80.
  (2002d) 'Bibliotheken in Wohnhäusern und Palästen', in *Antike Bibliotheken*, ed. W. Höpfner. Mainz: 86–96.
  (2002e) 'Die Celsus-Bibliothek in Ephesos', in *Antike Bibliotheken*, ed. W. Höpfner. Mainz: 123–6.
  (2002f) *Antike Bibliotheken*. Mainz.
Hornbostel-Hüttner, G. (1979) *Studien zur Römischen Nischenarchitektur*. Leiden.
Horsfall, N. M. (1976) 'The Collegium Poetarum'. *BICS* 23: 79–95.

(1993) 'Empty shelves on the Palatine'. *G&R* 2nd Ser. 40: 58–67.
(1996) *On Greek Libraries and Bookcases*. Berlin and New York.
(1998) 'Methods of writing, memorisation, and research'. *JRA* 11: 565–71.
Hose, M. (2007) ' "The silence of the lambs"? On Greek silence about Roman literature', in *De Grecia a Roma y de Roma a Grecia: un camino de ida y vuelta*, eds. Á. Sánchez-Ostiz, J. B. Torres Guerra and R. Martínez. Pamplona: 333–45.
Houston, G. W. (2001) Review of Casson 2001 in *Electronic Antiquity* 6 (1) http://scholar.lib.vt.edu/ejournals/ElAnt/V6N1/houston.html
(2002) 'The slave and freedman personnel of public libraries in ancient Rome'. *TAPA* 132: 139–76.
(2003) 'Galen, his books, and the *Horrea Piperataria* at Rome'. *MAAR* 48: 45–51.
(2004) 'How did you get hold of a book in a Roman library? Three second-century scenarios'. *CB* 80: 5–13.
(2007) 'Grenfell, Hunt, Breccia, and the book collections of Oxyrhynchus'. *GRBS* 47: 327–59.
(2008) 'Tiberius and the libraries: Public book collections and library buildings in the early Roman empire'. *L&CR* 43.3: 247–69.
(2009) 'Papyrological evidence for book collections and libraries in the Roman empire', in *Ancient Literacies: The Culture of Reading in Greece and Rome*, eds. W. A. Johnson and H. N. Parker. Oxford: 233–67.
Humfress, C. (2007) *Orthodoxy and the Courts in Late Antiquity*. Oxford.
Hunger, H. (1968) *Babylonische und Assyrische Kolophone*. Kevelaer and Neukirchen-Vluyn.
Hunter, R. (2006) *The Shadow of Callimachus. Studies in the Reception of Hellenistic Poetry at Rome*. Cambridge.
Hutchinson, G. (2008) *Talking Books: Readings in Hellenistic and Roman Books of Poetry*. Oxford.
Iacopi, I. (2007) *La casa di Augusto. Le pitture*. Milan.
Iacopi, I. and Tedone, G. (2005/2006) 'Bibliotheca e porticus ad Apollinis'. *MDAI(R)* 112: 351–78.
Iddeng, J. W. (2006) 'Publica aut peri! The releasing and distribution of Roman books'. *SO* 81: 58–84.
Indelli, G. (1978) *Polistrato: Sul disprezzo irrazionale delle opinioni popolari. Edizione, traduzione, e commento*. Naples.
Innes, M. (1997) 'The classical tradition in the Carolingian Renaissance. Ninth-century encounters with Suetonius'. *International Journal of the Classical Tradition* 3.3: 265–82.
Isager, J. (1976) 'Vespasiano e Augusto', in *Studia Romana in Honorem Petri Krarup Septuagenarii*, eds. K. Ascani, T. Fischer-Hansen, F. Johansen, S. S. Jensen and J. E. Skydsgaard. Odense: 64–71.
Jackson, E. B. (1994) 'Special libraries', in *Encyclopedia of Library History*, eds. W. A. Wiegand and D. G. Davis Jr. New York: 597–9.

Jacob, C. (1996) 'Lire pour écrire: navigations Alexandrines', in *Le pouvoir des bibliothèques. La mémoire des livres en Occident*, eds. M. Baratin and C. Jacob. Paris: 47–83.

(1998) 'Vers une histoire comparée des bibliothèques 1. Questions préliminaires, entre Grèce et Chine ancienne', *Quaderni di Storia* 48: 87–122.

(2000) 'Athenaeus the librarian', in *Athenaeus and his World: Reading Greek Culture in the Roman Empire*, eds. D. Braund and J. Wilkins. Exeter: 85–110.

(2001) 'Ateneo o il Dedalo delle parole', in L. Canfora (ed. and transl.) *Ateneo, I Deipnosofisti. I dotti a banchetto*. Rome: xi–cxvi.

(2004a) 'La citation comme performance dans les *Deipnosophistes* d'Athénée', in *La citation dans l'antiquité*, ed. C. Darbo-Peschanski. Grenoble: 147–74.

(2004b) 'La construction de l'auteur dans le savoir bibliographique antique: à propos des *Deipnosophistes* d'Athénée', in *Identités d'auteur dans l'antiquité et la tradition européenne*, eds. C. Calame and R. Chartier. Grenoble: 127–58.

(2010) 'Le bibliothécaire, le roi et les poètes'. *Athens Dialogues E-Journal*, Center for Hellenic Studies: http://athensdialogues.chs.harvard.edu/cgi-bin/WebObjects/athensdialogues.woa/wa/dist?dis=63

Jacoby, F. (1998) *Dionysii Halicarnasei Antiquitatum Romanarum quae supersunt: Supplementum Indices continens*. Stuttgart and Leipzig.

Jäger, W. (1936–55) *Paideia. Die Formung des Griechischen Menschen*. 3 vols. 2nd edn. Berlin.

Janko, R. (1995) 'Reconstructing Philodemus' *On Poems*', in *Philodemus and Poetry. Poetic Theory and Practice in Lucretius, Philodemus and Horace*, ed. D. Obbink. Oxford: 69–96.

(2000) *Philodemus On Poems. Book 1*. Oxford.

(2002) 'The Herculaneum library: Some recent developments'. *EClás* 44: 25–41.

(2008) 'New fragments of Epicurus, Metrodorus, Demetrius Laco, Philodemus, the *Carmen de Bello Actiaco* and other texts in Oxonian *Disegni* of 1788–1792'. *CErc.* 38: 5–95.

Johne, R. (1991) 'Zur Entstehung einer "Buchkultur" in der zweiten Hälfte des 5. Jahrhunderts v.*u.Z.*'. *Philologus* 135: 45–54.

Johnson, E. D. (1970) *History of Libraries in the Western World*, 2nd edn. Metuchen, NJ

Johnson, L. L. (1984) *The Hellenistic and Roman Library: Studies Pertaining to their Architectural Form* (PhD Diss. Brown University).

Johnson, W. A. (2000) 'Toward a sociology of reading in classical antiquity'. *AJPh* 121: 593–627.

(2006) 'The story of the papyri of the Villa dei Papiri'. *JRA* 19: 493–6.

(2010) *Readers and Reading Culture in the High Empire: A Study of Elite Reading Communities*. Oxford.

Johnson, W. A. and Parker, H.N. (eds.) (2009) *Ancient Literacies. The Culture of Reading in Greece and Rome*. Oxford.

Jolowicz, H. F. and Nicholas, B. (1972) *Historical Introduction to the Study of Roman Law*. Cambridge.
Jones, C. P. (1971) *Plutarch and Rome*. Oxford.
　(1978) 'Three foreigners in Attica'. *Phoenix*, 32: 222–34.
　(2009) 'Books and libraries in a newly-discovered treatise of Galen'. *JRA* 22: 390–7.
Jong, I. J. F. de (1987) *Narrators and Focalisers: The Presentation of the Story in the Iliad*. Amsterdam.
Jonge, C. C. de (2008) *Between Grammar and Rhetoric: Dionysius of Halicarnassus on Language, Linguistics and Literature*. Leiden.
Jory, E. J. (1970) 'Associations of actors in Rome'. *Hermes* 98 (2): 224–53.
Kannicht, R. (ed.) (2004) *Tragicorum Graecorum Fragmenta*, vol. V. Göttingen.
Kaster, R.A. (1995) *C. Suetonius Tranquillus, De Grammaticis et Rhetoribus. Edited with a Translation, Introduction and Commentary*. Oxford.
Kemp, A. (1991) 'The emergence of an autonomous Greek grammar', in *Sprachtheorien der Abenländische Antike*, ed. P. Schmitter. Tübingen: 302–33.
Kennedy, D. F. (1992) ' "Augustan" and "anti-Augustan": reflections on terms of reference', in *Roman Poetry and Propaganda in the Age of Augustus*, ed. A. Powell. Bristol: 26–58.
Kenyon, F. G. (1932) *Books and Readers in Ancient Greece and Rome*. Oxford.
Keulen, W. (2009) *Gellius the Satirist. Roman Cultural Authority in* Attic Nights. *Mnemosyne* Suppl. 297. Leiden and Boston.
Kleberg, T. (1973) 'Book auctions in ancient Rome?'. *Libri* 23: 1–5.
　(1975) 'Commercio librario ed editoria nel mondo antico', in *Libri, editori e pubblico nel mondo antico. Guida storica e critica*, ed. G. Cavallo (1984³ [1975¹>]). Rome and Bari: 25–80.
Klebs, E. (1894) 'Antistius 47'. *RE* 1.2: 2,558.
Kleiner, D. E. E. (1992) *Roman Sculpture*. New Haven, CT.
Kleve, K. (1989) 'Lucretius in Herculaneum'. *CErc.* 19: 5–27.
　(1990) 'Ennius in Herculaneum'. *CErc.* 20: 5–16.
　(1994) 'An approach to the Latin papyri from Herculaneum', in *Storia poesia e pensiero nel mondo antico. Studi in onore di Marcello Gigante*, ed. F. del Franco. Naples: 313–20.
　(1996) 'How to read an illegible papyrus. Towards an edition of *PHerc.* 78, Caecilius Statius, *Obolostates sive Faenerator*'. *CErc.* 26: 5–14.
　(2007) 'Lucretius' book II in *PHerc.* 395', in *Akten des 23. Internationalen Papyrologen-Kongresses. Wien, 22–28. Juli 2001*, ed. B. Palme. Vienna: 347–54.
Kleve, K. and Del Mastro, G. (2000) 'Il *PHerc.* 1533: Zenone Sidonio *A Cratero*'. *CErc.* 30: 149–56.
Klinghardt, M. (1999) 'Prayer formularies for public recitation: their use and function in ancient religion'. *Numen* 46 (1): 1–52.

Knight, V. H. (1995) *The Renewal of Epic: Responses to Homer in the Argonautica of Apollonius, Mnemosyne* Suppl. 152. Leiden, New York and Cologne.

Knox, B. M. W. (1985) 'Books and readers in the Greek world', in *The Cambridge History of Classical Literature*, eds. P. E. Easterling and B. M. W. Knox, vol. I. Cambridge: 1–41.

Knüvener, P. (2002) 'Private Bibliotheken in Pompeji und Herculaneum', in *Antike Bibliotheken*, ed. W. Höpfner. Mainz: 81–5.

Kohl, M. (2002) 'Das Nikephorion von Pergamon'. *RA*: 227–53.

Kollesch, J. (1981) 'Galen und die zweite Sophistik', in *Galen: Problems and Prospects*, ed. V. Nutton. London: 1–11.

Kondo, E. (1971) 'I *Caratteri* di Teofrasto nei papiri ercolanesi'. *CErc.* 1: 73–87.

König, A. (2007) 'Knowledge and power in Frontinus' *On Aqueducts*', in *Ordering Knowledge in the Roman Empire*, eds. J. König and T. Whitmarsh. Cambridge: 177–205.

König, J. P. (2001) 'Favorinus' *Corinthian Oration* in its Corinthian context'. *PCPS* 47: 141–71.

   (2009) 'Conventions of prefatory self-presentation in Galen's *On the Order of My Own Books*', in *Galen and the World of Knowledge*, eds. C. Gill, T. Whitmarsh and J. Wilkins. Cambridge: 35–58.

König, J. P. and Whitmarsh, T. (eds.) (2007) *Ordering Knowledge in the Roman Empire*. Cambridge.

König, J. and Woolf, G. (forthcoming a) 'Encyclopaedism in Classical Antiquity' in *Encyclopaedism from Antiquity to the Renaissance*, eds. J. König and G. Woolf. Cambridge.

König, J. and Woolf, G. (eds.) (forthcoming b) *Encyclopaedism from Antiquity to the Renaissance*. Cambridge.

König, R. and Winkler, G. (1975) *C. Plinius Secundus d. Ä, Naturkunde. Buch VII: Anthropologie*. Munich.

Korenjak, M. (2000) *Publikum und Redner. Ihre Interaktion in der sophistischen Rhetorik der Kaiserzeit*. Munich.

Kose, A. (1998) *Architektur, IV: Von der Seleukiden- bis zur Sasanidenzeit*. Mainz.

Kotzia, P. and Sotiroudis, P. (2010) 'Γαληνοῦ Περὶ Ἀλυπίας'. *Hellenika* 60: 63–150.

Krasser, H. (1995) 'Entwicklungen der römischen Lesekultur in trajanischer Zeit', in *Prinzipat und Kultur im 1. und 2. Jahrhundert. Wissenschaftliche Tagung Jena 1992*, ed. B. Kühnert. Bonn: 79–89.

   (1999) 'Lesekultur als Voraussetzung für die Rezeption von Geschichtsschreibung in der hohen Kaiserzeit', in *Geschichtsschreibung und Politischer Wandel im 3. Jh. n.Chr. Historia Einzelschrift 127*, ed. M. Zimmermann. Stuttgart: 57–69.

Krause, C. (1993) 'Bibliotheca Domus Tiberianae'. *LTUR* 1: 196.

Krevans, N. (2004) 'Callimachus and the pedestrian Muse', in *Callimachus II (Hellenistica Groningana 7)*, eds. M. A. Harder, R. F. Regtuit and G. C. Wakker. Leuven, Paris and Dudley, MA: 173–83.

Kroll, W. (1926) 'Libertatis atrium'. *RE* 13.1: 103–4.

Kumaniecki, C. (1962) 'Cicerone e Varrone'. *Athenaeum* N.S. 40: 228–9.

Kunihara, K. (1963) 'The history of the collegium poetarum'. *Annuario Instituto Giapponese di Cultura*, 1: 85–99.

Labriola, I. (2010) 'Il laboratorio di Aspasia'. *InvLuc* 32: 61–73.

Lanciani, R. (1900) *The Ruins and Excavations of Ancient Rome*. Boston and New York.

Lane Fox, R. (1994) 'Literacy and power in early Christianity', in *Literacy and Power in the Ancient World*, eds. A. K. Bowman and G. D. Woolf. Cambridge: 126–48.

La Rocca, E. (2001) 'La nuova immagine dei fori imperiali. Appunti in margine agli scavi'. *MDAI(R)* 108: 195–207.

Laursen, S. (1987) 'Epicurus, *On Nature* book XXV'. *CErc.* 17: 77–8.

(1995) 'The early parts of Epicurus, *On Nature*, 25th Book'. *CErc.* 25: 5–109.

(1997) 'The later parts of Epicurus, *On Nature*, 25th Book'. *CErc.* 27: 5–82.

Lehmann-Hartleben, K. (1932) 'Die Athena Parthenos des Phidias. Ein Beitrag zu ihrer Wiederherstellung'. *JdI*: 12–46.

Leone, G. (1984) 'Epicuro, *Della Natura*, libro XIV'. *CErc.* 14: 17–107.

(2002) 'Epicuro, *Della Natura*, libro XXXIV (*PHerc.* 1431)'. *CErc.* 32: 7–135.

(2005) 'Per la ricostruzione dei *PHerc.* 1149/993 e 1010 (Epicuro, *Della Natura*, libro II)'. *CErc.* 35: 15–25.

(2010) 'Il *PHerc.* 1010 (Epicuro, *Sulla Natura*, libro II): Anatomia del rotolo', in *Proceedings of the Twenty-Fifth International Congress of Papyrology, Ann Arbor 2007*. American Studies in Papyrology. Ann Arbor, MI: 409–26.

LiDonnici, L. R. (1995) *The Epidaurian Miracle Inscriptions. Text, Translation, and Commentary*. Atlanta.

Lightfoot, J. L. (2000) 'Romanized Greeks and Hellenized Romans: later Greek literature', in *Literature in the Greek and Roman Worlds. A New Perspective*, ed. O. Taplin. Oxford: 239–66.

Linderski, J. (1985) 'The Libri Reconditi'. *HSCPh* 89: 207–34.

Linssen, M. J. H. (2004) *The Cults of Uruk and Babylon: the Temple Ritual Texts as Evidence for Hellenistic Cult Practices*. Leiden.

Livingstone, A. (2007) 'Ashurbanipal: literate or not?'. *ZA* 97: 98–118.

Livingstone, N. (2001) *A Commentary on Isocrates' Busiris*. Leiden, Boston and Cologne.

Lloyd, S. (1954) 'Sultantepe, part II. Post-Assyrian pottery and small objects found by the Anglo-Turkish Joint Expedition in 1952'. *AnSt* 4: 101–10.

Lloyd, S. and Brice, W. (1951) 'Harran'. *AnSt* 1: 77–111.

Lloyd, S. and Göçke, N. (1953) 'Sultantepe: Anglo-Turkish joint excavations, 1952'. *AnSt* 3: 27–47.

Longo Auricchio, F. (2008) 'La biblioteca ercolanese'. *A&R* N.S. 2: 190–209.

Longo Auricchio, F., and Capasso, M. (1987) 'I rotoli della villa ercolanese: dislocazione e ritrovamento'. *CErc.* 17: 37–44.

López Férez, J. A. (1992) 'Galeno, lector y crítico de manuscritos', in *Tradizione e ecdotica dei testi medici tardoantichi e Bizantini*, ed. A. Garzya. Naples: 197–209.

Loraux, P. (1989) 'L'arte platonica di aver l'aria di scrivere', in *Sapere e scrittura in Grecia*, ed. M. Detienne. Rome and Bari: 229–62.

Luce, T. J. (1995) 'Livy and Dionysius'. *PLILS* 8: 225–39.

Lugli, G. (1946) *Roma antica. Il centro monumentale*. Rome.

(1960) *Fontes ad Topographiam Veteris Urbis Romae pertinentes. Regio Urbis Decima. Mons Palatinus*, vol. VIII. Rome.

Luraghi, N. (2003) 'Dionysios von Halicarnassos zwischen Griechen und Römern', in *Formen Römischer Geschichtsschreibung von den Anfängen bis Livius. Gattungen – Autoren – Kontexte*, eds. U. Eigler, U. Gotter, N. Luraghi and U. Walter. Darmstadt: 268–86.

Lyons, M. C. and Towers, B. (eds.) (1962) *Galen on Anatomical Procedures. The Later Books*. Cambridge.

Macfarlane, R. T. and Del Mastro, G. (2007) 'Il PHerc. 1491'. *CErc.* 37: 111–23.

MacLeod, R. (ed.) (2000a) *The Library of Alexandria: Centre of Learning in the Ancient World*. London and New York.

(2000b) 'Introduction: Alexandria in history and myth', in *The Library of Alexandria: Centre of Learning in the Ancient World*, ed. R. MacLeod. London and New York: 1–15.

Madvig, J. N. (ed.) (1965) *M. Tulli Ciceronis De Finibus Bonorum et Malorum Libri Quinque*. Hildesheim.

Maehler, H. (2004) 'Alexandria, the Museion, and cultural identity', in *Alexandria, Real and Imagined*, eds. A. Hirst and M. Silk. Aldershot and Burlington, VT: 1–14

Maiuri, A. (1925) *Nuove silloge epigrafica di Rodi e Cos*. Florence.

Maiuro, M. (2010) 'What was the Forum Iulium used for? The *fiscus* and its jurisdiction in first-century CE Rome', in *Spaces of Justice in the Roman World*, ed. F. De Angelis. Columbia Studies in the Classical Tradition 35. Leiden: 189–221.

Makowiecka, E. (1978) *The Origin and Evolution of Architectural Form of Roman Library*. Warsaw.

Mallowan, M. (1966) *Nimrud and Its Remains*. 2 vols. London.

Manetti, D. (2003) 'Galeno, la lingua di Ippocrate e il tempo', in *Galien et la Philosophie*, eds. J. Barnes and J. Jouanna. Fondation Hardt Entretiens 49: 171–220.

Manetti, D. and Roselli, A. (1994) 'Galeno commentatore di Ippocrate', *ANRW* 2.37.2: 1529–635.

Manganaro, G. (1976) 'Una biblioteca storica nel ginnasio a Tauromenion nel II sec. a.C.', in *Römische Frühgeschichte*, ed. A. Alföldi. Heidelberg: 83–96.

Mansfeld, J. (1994) *Prolegomena: Questions to be Settled before the Study of an Author, or a Text*. Leiden.

Mantovani, D. (2000) 'Aspetti documentali del processo criminale nella Repubblica'. *MEFRA* 112: 651–91.

Manuli, P. (1983) 'Lo stile del commento. Galeno e la tradizione ippocratica', in *Formes de pensée dans la collection Hippocratique*, eds. F. Lassere and P. Mudry. Geneva: 471–82.

Mar, R. (2009) 'La *Domus Flavia*, utilizzo e funzioni del palazzo di Domiziano', in *Divus Vespasianus. Il bimillenario dei Flavi*, ed. F. Coarelli. Milan: 250–63.

Marchese, R. R. (1998) *La morale e il singolo. Individualismo, modelli etici e poesia romana*. Palermo.

Marec, E. and Pflaum, H. G. (1952) 'Nouvelle inscription sur la carrière de Suétone, historien.' *CRAI* 96: 76–85.

Marinčič, M. (2007) 'Advertising one's own story. Text and speech in Achilles Tatius' Leucippe and Clitophon', in *Seeing Tongues, Hearing Scripts: Orality and Representation in the Ancient Novel*, ed. V. Rimell. Groningen: 168–200.

Marincola, J. M. (1997) *Authority and Tradition in Ancient Historiography*. Cambridge.

Mariss, R. (2002) *Alkidamas: Über diejenigen, die schriftliche Reden schreiben, oder über die Sophisten. Eine Sophistenrede aus dem 4. Jahrhundert v. Chr. eingeleitet und kommentiert*. Orbis Antiquus 36. Münster.

Marshall, A. J. (1976) 'Library resources and creative writing at Rome'. *Phoenix* 30: 252–64.

Martin, P. M. (1971) 'La propagande augustéenne dans les *Antiquités Romaines* de Denys d'Halicarnasse (Livre I)'. *REL* 49: 162–79.

(1972) 'Héraklès en Italie d'après Denys d'Halicarnasse (A.R. I, 34–44)'. *Athenaeum N.S.* 50: 252–75.

(1993) 'De l'universel à l'éternel: la liste des hégémonies (A.R. I, 2–3)'. *Pallas* 39: 193–214.

(2002) 'Rome, cité grecque dressée contre les barbares, d'après les *excerpta* de Denys d'Halicarnasse', in *Fragments des Historiens Grecs: Autour de Denys d'Halicarnasse*, ed. S. Pittia. Collection de L'Ecole française de Rome 298. Rome: 147–58.

Martini, W. (2004) 'Bemerkungen zur Statuenausstattung der hellenistischen Gymnasien', in *Das Hellenistische Gymnasion*, eds. D. Kah and P. Scholz. Berlin: 407–11.

Marvin, M. (1989) 'Copying in Roman sculpture: the replica series', in *Retaining the Original: Multiple Originals, Copies, and Reproductions*, ed. E. Preciado, Studies in the History of Art 20, National Gallery of Art. Washington: 29–45.

Mason, S. (2005) 'Figured speech and irony in T. Flavius Josephus', in *Flavius Josephus and Flavian Rome*, eds. J. Edmondson, S. Mason and J. Rives. Oxford: 243–88.

Mathieu, G. and Brémond, E. (eds.) (1928) *Isocrate. Discours*, vol. I. Paris.

Mattern, S. (2008) *Galen and the Rhetoric of Healing*. Baltimore.

Matthaios, S. (1999) *Untersuchungen zur Grammatik Aristarchs: Texte und Interpretation zur Wortartenlehre*. (Hypomnemata 126). Göttingen.

Mattingly, H. B. (1957) 'The date of Livius Andronicus'. *CQ* 7 (3/4): 159–63.

Maul, S.M. (2010) 'Die Tontafelbibliothek aus dem sogenannten "Haus des Beschwörungspriesters" ', in *Assur-Forschungen: Arbeiten aus der Forschungstelle 'Edition literarische Keilschrifttexte aus Assur' der Heidelberger Akademie der Wissenschaften*, eds. S. M. Maul and N. P. Heessel. Heidelberg: 189–228.

Mayhoff, K. (ed.) (1909) *C. Plini Secundi Naturalis Historiae Libri xxxvii*: vol. II, *Libri vii–xv*. 2nd edn. Leipzig.

McCracken, G. (1935) 'Cicero's Tusculan villa'. *CJ* 30 (5): 261–77.

McCrum, M. and Woodhead, A. G. (1961) *Select Documents of the Principates of the Flavian Emperors*. Cambridge.

McDonnell, M. (1996) 'Writing, copying, and autograph manuscripts in Ancient Rome'. *CQ* 46: 469–91.

McEwen, I. K. (2003) *Vitruvius: Writing the Body of Architecture*. Cambridge, MA.

McKenzie, J. S. (2003) 'Glimpsing Alexandria from archaeological evidence'. *JRA* 16: 35–64.

McKenzie, J. S., Gibson, S. and Reyes, A. T. (2004) 'Reconstructing the Serapeum in Alexandria from the archaeological evidence'. *JRS* 94: 73–121.

McKitterick, R. (1989) *The Carolingians and the Written Word*. Cambridge.

McNamee, K. (2007) *Annotations in Greek and Latin Texts from Egypt*. The American Society of Papyrologists. New Haven, CT.

Meadows, A. and Williams, J. (2001) 'Moneta and the monuments: coinage and politics in republican Rome'. *JRS* 91: 27–49.

Memelsdorff, M. (1890) *De Archivis Imperatorum Romanorum Qualia Fuerint usque ad Diocletiani Aetatem*. Halle.

Menci, G. (1988) 'Fabbricazione, uso e restauro antico del papiro: tre note in margine a Plinio, *NH* xiii 74–82', in *Proceedings of the XVIII International Congress of Papyrology, Athens 25–31 May 1986*, ed. B. Mandilaras, Greek Papyrological Society, vol. II. Athens: 497–504.

Meneghini, R. (2002a) 'Die Bibliotheca Ulpia. Neueste Ausgrabungen in der Bibliothek im Traiansforum in Rom', in *Antike Bibliotheken*, ed. W. Höpfner. Mainz: 117–22.

(2002b) 'Nuovi dati sulla funzione e le fasi costruttive delle "biblioteche" del Foro di Traiano'. *MEFRA* 114: 655–92.

(2007) 'La cartografia antica e il catasto di Roma imperiale', in *Res Bene Gestae. Ricerche di storia urbana su Roma antica in onore di Eva Maria Steinby*. Rome: 205–18.

(2009) *I fori imperiali e i mercati di Traiano. Storia e descrizione dei monumenti alla luce degli studi e degli scavi recenti*. Rome.

(2010) 'Le biblioteche pubbliche di Roma nell'alto impero', in *Neronia VIII: Bibliothèques, livres et culture écrite dans l'empire Romain de César à Hadrien*, ed. Y. Perrin. Collection Latomus 327. Brussels: 32–40.

Meneghini, R., Ballarin, A. and Berti, G. (2001) 'Il foro di Traiano. Ricostruzione architettonica e analisi strutturale'. *MDAI(R)* 108: 245–68.

Meneghini, R., Corsaro, A. and Caboni, B. P. (2009) 'Il Templum Pacis alla luce dei recenti scavi', in *Divus Vespasianus. Il bimillenario dei Flavi*, ed. F. Coarelli. Milan: 190–201.

Meneghini, R. and Santangeli Valenzani, R. (eds.) (2006) *Formae Urbis Romae. Nuovi frammenti di piante marmoree dallo scavo dei fori imperiali*. BCAR Suppl. 15. Rome.

Meneghini, R., Santangeli Valenzani, R. and Bianchi, E. (2007) *I fori imperiali. Gli scavi del comune di Roma 1991–2007*. Rome.

Mewaldt, J. (1909) 'Galen über echte und unechte Hippocratica'. *Hermes* 44: 111–34.

Meyer, E. (1960) 'Augusti. Ein Nachtrag'. *Mus. Helv.* 17: 118.

Meyer, E. A. (2004) *Legitimacy and Law in the Roman World. Tabulae in Roman Belief and Practice*. Cambridge.

Meyer, F. (1955) *Cicero und die Bücher*. Zurich.

Michel, J. H. (1998) 'Aulu-Gelle et la vie intellectuelle à Rome sous Hadrien et Antonin le Pieux', in *Synthèses romaines*, ed. J. H. Michel. Collection Latomus 240. Brussels: 1265–96.

Mielsch, H. (1995) 'Die Bibliothek und die Kunstsammlung der Könige von Pergamon'. *AA*: 765–79.

Militello, C. (1997) *Filodemo. Memorie Epicuree (PHerc. 1418 e 310). Edizione, traduzione e commento*. Naples.

Milkau, F. (1955) *Handbuch der Bibliothekswissenschaft*, vol. III (1). Leipzig.

Millar, F. G. B. (1977) *The Emperor in the Roman World*. London.

Millot, C. (1977) 'Epicure, *De la Nature*, livre XV'. *CErc.* 7: 9–39.

Minto, A. and Coli, U. (1947) 'Magliano'. *NSA* 1947: 49–68.

Moatti, C. (1991) 'La crise de la tradition à la fin de la république romaine à travers la littérature juridique et la science des antiquaires,' in *Continuità e trasformazione fra Repubblica e Principato*, ed. M. Pani. Bari: 30–45.

 (1993) *Archives et partage de la terre dans le monde romain. IIe siècle avant – Ier siècle après J.-C.* Rome.

 (ed.) (1998) *La mémoire perdue: recherches sur l'administration romaine*. Collection de l'École française de Rome. Rome.

 (2000) 'La mémoire perdue III. Recherches sur l'administration romaine: le cas des archives judiciaires pénales'. *MEFRA* 112 (2): 647–779.

 (2003) 'Les archives romaines. Réflexions méthodologiques', in *L'uso dei documenti nella storiografia antica*, ed. A. M. Biraschi. Naples: 27–43.

Momigliano, A. (1963) 'Pagan and Christian historiography in the fourth century A.D.', in *The Conflict between Paganism and Christianity in the Fourth Century*, ed. A. Momigliano. Oxford: 79–99.

 (1975) *Alien Wisdom. The Limits of Hellenisation*. Cambridge.

 (1990) *The Classical Foundations of Modern Historiography*. Sather Classical Lectures 54. Berkeley.

Mommsen, T. (1887) *Römisches Staatsrecht* 2, 1³. Leipzig.

Moraux, P. (1951) *Les listes anciennes des ouvrages d'Aristote*. Louvain.

(1973) *Der Aristotelismus bei den Griechen*. Berlin and New York.
Morgan, T. (1998) *Literate Education in the Hellenistic and Roman Worlds*. Cambridge.
  (1999) 'Literate education in classical Athens'. *CQ N.S.* 49: 46–61.
Morison, B. (2008) 'Language', in *The Cambridge Companion to Galen*, ed. R. J. Hankinson. Cambridge: 116–56.
Moroni, C. (ed.) (2009) '*Bibliotheca Flavia' ad Templum Pacis: i libri antichi delle biblioteche reatine ricostruiscono idealmente quella edificata dall'Imperatore Vespasiano nel Foro della Pace*. Catalog of the exhibition at Rieti, December 11, 2009–February 11, 2010. Rieti.
Mount, E. and Massoud, R. (1999) *Special Libraries and Information Centers. An Introductory Text*. Washington, DC.
Mülke, M. (2008) *Der Autor und sein Text. Die Verfälschung des Originals im Urteil antiker Autoren*. Berlin and New York.
Münzer, F. (1900a) 'Clodius 11'. *RE* 4.1: 65.
  (1900b) 'Cornelius 377'. *RE* 4.1: 1,516.
  (1900c) 'Faustus Cornelius Sulla'. *RE* 4.1: 1,515–17.
  (1930) 'Marcius 48'. *RE* 14.2: 1,554–5.
Murphy, T. (2004) *Pliny the Elder's Natural History. The Empire in the Encyclopedia*. Oxford.
Musurillo, H. (1961) *Acta Alexandrinorum: De Mortibus Alexandriae Nobilium Fragmenta Papyracea Graeca*. Leipzig.
Nagy, G. (1998) 'The library of Pergamon as a classical model', in *Pergamon, Citadel of the Gods. Archaeological Record, Literary Description, and Religious Development*, ed. H. Koester. Harrisburg, PA: 185–232.
  (2003) Review of West (2001) *Studies in the Text and Transmission of the Iliad* (Munich and Leipzig). *Gnomon* 75: 481–501.
Nesselrath, H.-G. (1990) *Die attische mittlere Komödie. Ihre Stellung in der antiken Literaturkritik und Literaturgeschichte*. Berlin and New York.
  (2006) *Platon. Kritias. Übersetzung und Kommentar*. Göttingen.
Neudecker, R. (2004) 'Aspekte öffentlicher Bibliotheken in der Kaiserzeit', in *Paideia. The World of the Second Sophistic*, ed. B. Borg. Berlin and New York: 293–313.
  (2010) 'The Forum of Augustus in Rome. Law and order in sacred spaces', in *Spaces of Justice in the Roman World*, ed. F. De Angelis. Columbia Studies in the Classical Tradition 35. Leiden: 293–313.
Nicholls, M. C. (2005) *Roman Public Libraries* (D.Phil. Thesis, University of Oxford).
  (2010a) '*Bibliotheca Latina Graecaque*: on the possible division of Roman public libraries by language' in *Neronia VIII: bibliothèques, livres et culture écrite dans l'empire romain de César à Hadrien*, ed. Y. Perrin. Collection Latomus 327. Brussels: 11–21.
  (2010b) 'Parchment codices in a new text of Galen'. *G&R* 57: 378–86.
  (2011) 'Galen and libraries in the *Peri Alupias*'. *JRS* 101: 123–42.

Nicolai, R. (2000) 'La biblioteca delle Muse. Osservazioni sulle più antiche raccolte librarie greche'. *GB* 23: 213–27.

(2004a) 'Isocrate e le nuove strategie della comunicazione letteraria: l'Antidosi come "antologia d'autore"', in *La cultura ellenistica. L'opera letteraria e l'esegesi antica*, eds. R. Pretagostini and E. Dettori. Rome: 187–97.

(2004b) *Studi su Isocrate. La comunicazione letteraria nel IV sec. a.C. e i nuovi generi della prosa*. Rome.

Nicolet, C. (1988) *L'inventaire du monde. Géographie et politique aux origines de l'empire romain*. Paris.

Nieddu, G. (1984) 'Testo, scrittura, libro nella Grecia arcaica e classica: note e osservazioni sulla prosa scientifico-filosofica', *S&C* 8: 213–61. Repr. in G. Nieddu (2004) *La scrittura 'madre delle muse': agli esordi di un nuovo modello di comunicazione culturale*. Amsterdam: 71–120.

(2003) 'Un poeta al lavoro: qualche riflessione sulla parodia dell'*Elena* nelle *Tesmoforiazuse*', in *Evento, racconto, scrittura nell'antichità classica*, eds. A. Casanova and P. Desideri. Florence: 55–90.

Ní Mheallaigh, K. (2007) 'Philosophical framing: the Phaedran setting of *Leucippe and Cleitophon*', in *Philosophical Presences in the Ancient Novel*, eds. J. R. Morgan and M. Jones. Groningen: 231–44.

Nissen, H. (1988) *The Early History of the Ancient Near East, 9000–2000 BC*. Chicago.

Nissen, H., Damerow, P. and Englund, R. K. (1993) *Archaic Bookkeeping: Early Writing and Techniques of Administration in the Ancient Near East*. Chicago.

Noè, E. (1979) 'Ricerche su Dionigi d'Alicarnasso: la prima stasis a Roma e l'episodio di Coriolano', in *Ricerche di storiografia greca di età romana*, ed. L. Troiani. Pisa: 21–116.

Norden, E. (1898) *Die antike Kunstprosa vom VI. Jahrhundert v. Chr. bis in die Zeit der Renaissance*, vol. I. Leipzig.

Nordh, A. (1949) *Libellus de Regionibus Urbis Romae*. Lund.

Norton, M.C. (2003) *Norton on Archives: The Writings of Margaret Cross Norton on Archival and Records Management*, ed. T.W. Mitchell. Chicago.

Noy, D. (2005) 'Rabbi Aqiba comes to Rome: a Jewish pilgrimage in reverse?', in *Pilgrimage in Graeco-Roman and Early Christian Antiquity: Seeing the Gods*, eds. J. Elsner and I. Rutherford. Oxford: 373–85.

Nutton, V. (1971) 'Two notes on immunities: Digest 27, 1, 6, 10 and 11'. *JRS* 61: 52–63.

(1972) 'Galen and medical autobiography'. *PCPS* 198: 50–62.

(1979) *Galen on Prognosis*. Berlin.

(1993) 'Galen and Egypt', in *Galen und das hellenistische Erbe*, eds. J. Kollesch and D. Nickel. Stuttgart: 11–31.

(2000) 'Medicine'. *CAH 11* (2nd edn.). Cambridge: 943–65.

(2004a) 'Review of Rocca, J. (2003) *Galen on the Brain* (Leiden and Boston)'. *MedHist* 48: 276–7.

(2004b) *Ancient Medicine*. London and New York.

(2009) 'Galen's library', in *Galen and the World of Knowledge*, eds. C. Gill, T. Whitmarsh and J. Wilkins. Cambridge: 19–34.

Oakley, S. P. (1997) *A Commentary on Livy, Books VI–X*. Oxford.

Oates, J. and Oates, D. (2001) *Nimrud: an Assyrian Imperial City Revealed*. London.

Obbink, D. (1996) *Philodemus On Piety Part 1. Critical Text with Commentary*. Oxford.

Ogilvie, R. M. (1958) 'Livy, Licinius Macer, and the libri lintei'. *JRS* 48 (1/2): 40–6.

Oliver, J. (1979) 'Flavius Pantaenus, priest of the philosophical Muses'. *HThR* 72: 157–60.

Oppenheim, A. L. (1960) 'Assyriology: why and how?' *Curr. Anthrop.* 1: 409–23.

(1964) *Ancient Mesopotamia: Portrait of a Dead Civilization*. 2nd edn. 1977. Chicago.

Osgood, J. (2006) *Caesar's Legacy*. Cambridge.

Osing, J. (2001) '"Onomastiká" e liste lessicali', in *Storia della scienza, I. La scienza antica (Enciclopedia Italiana)*. Rome: 161–3.

Otranto, R. (2000) *Antiche liste di libri su papiro*. Sussidi Eruditi 49. Rome.

(2010) 'Biblioteche antiche', in *Dizionario delle scienze e delle tecniche di Grecia e Roma*, ed. P. Radici Colace. Pisa and Rome: 244–50.

Outscher, U. R. (1995) 'Die Bibliothek', in *Ephesos: Der neue Führer*, ed. P. Scherrer. Vienna: 132–4.

Packer, J. E. (1995) 'Forum Traiani'. *LTUR* 2: 348–56.

(1997) *The Forum of Trajan in Rome: A Study of the Monuments*. Berkeley, CA.

Pahnke, E. (1962) *Studien über Ciceros Kenntnis und Benutzung des Aristoteles und die Herkunft der Staatsdefinition Rep. I, 39.* (PhD Diss. University of Freiburg).

Palmer, R. E. A. (1974) *Roman Religion and Roman Empire: Five Essays*. Philadelphia.

Palombi, D. (1993) 'Curia in Palatio'. *LTUR* 1: 134.

(1997) *Tra Palatino ed Esquilino. Velia, Carinae, Fagutal. Storia urbana di tre quartieri di Roma antica*. *RIA* Suppl. 1. Rome.

(1997–8) 'Compitum Acilium. La scoperta, il monumento e la tradizione medica del quartiere'. *RPAA* 70: 115–35.

(2007) 'Medici e medicina a Roma tra Carine, Velia e Sacra Via', in *Salute e guarigione nella tarda antichità*, eds. H. Brandenburg, S. Heid, and C. Markschies. Vatican City: 53–78.

Papachristodoulou, I. (1986) 'Νέα στοιχεία γιὰ βιβλιοθήκες στην αρχαία Ρόδο'. *Dodekanesiaka Chronika* 11: 265–71.

(1990) 'Das hellenistische Gymnasion von Rhodos. Neues zu seiner Bibliothek', in *Akten des XIII. Internationalen Kongresses für Klassische Archäologie*. Mainz: 500–1.

Papini, M. (2004) 'Ritratto di Crisippo', in *Forma. La città moderna e il suo passato*, ed. A. La Regina. Mostra Roma 2004–5. Milan: 50–5.

(2005) 'Filosofi "in miniatura". Il Crisippo dal *Templum Pacis*'. *BCAR* 106: 125–35.

Parker, H. N. (2008) 'Books and reading Latin poetry', in *Ancient Literacies: The Culture of Reading in Greece and Rome*, eds. W. A. Johnson and H. N. Parker. Oxford: 186–232.

Parkinson, R. (forthcoming) 'Libraries in Early Egypt, c. 2400–1600 BC', in *Libraries before Alexandria*, eds. K. Ryholt and G. Barjamovic. Oxford.

Parpola, S. (1983) 'Assyrian library records'. *JNES* 42: 1–29.

Pasquali, G. (1930) 'Biblioteca', in *Enciclopedia italiana* vol. VI. Rome: 942–7.

Payen, P. (2005) 'Les citations des historiens dans les traités rhétoriques de Denys d'Halicarnasse', in *La citation dans l'antiquité*, ed. C. Darbo-Pechanski. Grenoble: 111–33.

Pazzini, A. (1935) 'La *Schola Medicorum* ad Aesquilinas e l'origine di una falsa denominazione', in *Atti del III Congresso nazionale di Studi Romani I*, ed. C. Galassi Paluzzi. Bologna: 467–72.

Pearcy, L. T. (1993) 'Medicine and rhetoric in the period of the Second Sophistic'. *ANRW* 2.37.1: 445–56.

Pearson, L. (1987) *The Greek Historians of the West. Timaeus and his Predecessors*. Atlanta.

Pébarthe, C. (2006) *Cité, démocratie et écriture. Histoire de l'alphabétisation d'Athènes à l'époque classique*. Paris.

Pedersén, O. (1998) *Archives and Libraries in the Ancient Near East, 1500–300 BC*. Bethesda, MD.

Pelling, C. B. R. (2002) *Plutarch and History*. London.

(2007) 'Greek historians on Rome: Polybius, Posidonius and Dionysius of Halicarnassus', in *A Companion to Greek and Roman Historiography*, ed. J. M. Marincola. Oxford: 244–58.

Pendlebury, J. D. S. (1951) *The City of Akhenaten III*. Oxford.

Perilli, L. (2006) 'Il dio ha evidentemente studiato medicina. Libri e medicina nelle biblioteche antiche. Il caso dei santuari di Asclepio', in *Stranieri e non cittadini nei santuari greci. Atti del convegno internazionale (Udine, 20–22.11.2003)*, ed. A. Naso. Florence: 472–510.

(2007) 'Conservazione dei testi e circolazione della conoscenza in Grecia', in *Biblioteche del mondo antico. Dalla tradizione orale alla cultura dell'Impero*, ed. A. M. Andrisano. Rome: 36–71.

Perrin, Y. (ed.) (2010) *Neronia VIII: Bibliothèques, livres et culture écrite dans l'empire romain de César à Hadrien*. Collection Latomus 327. Brussels.

Petsalis-Diomidis, A. (2010) *'Truly Beyond Wonders'. Aelius Aristides and the Cult of Asklepios*. Oxford.

Pfeiffer, H. (1931) 'The Roman library at Timgad'. *MAAR* 9: 157–65.

Pfeiffer, R. (1949) *Callimachus Vol. I: Fragmenta*. Oxford.

(1968) *History of Classical Scholarship. From the Beginnings to the End of the Hellenistic Age*. Oxford.

Pflaum, H.-G. (1960–1961) *Les carrières procuratoriennes équestres sous le Haut-Empire romain*, 4 vols. Brussels.

Philippson, R. (1943) 'Papyrus Herculanensis 831'. *AJP* 64: 148–62.

Piacente, L. (1988) 'Utenti e prestito di libri nelle biblioteche dell'antica Roma'. *SL&I* 2: 49–64.

Picone, G. (1976) 'La polemica anticulturale nel discorso di Mario (*B. Iug.* 85)'. *Pan* 4: 51–8.

Piganiol, A. (1945) 'La propagande païenne à Rome sous le Bas-Empire'. *JS*: 19–28.

Pigeaud, J.-M. (1980) 'La physiologie de Lucrèce'. *REL* 58: 176–200.

Pintaudi, R. (2006) 'Un'etichetta di rotolo documentario'. *CdE* 81: 205–6.

Pinto, P. M. (2003) *Per la storia del testo di Isocrate. La testimonianza d'autore.* Bari.
  (2006) 'La biblioteca di Isocrate. Note sulla circolazione dei libri e sul lavoro intellettuale nel IV secolo a.C.'. *S&T* 4: 51–70.

Platthy, J. (1968) *Sources on the Earliest Greek Libraries with the Testimonia.* Amsterdam.

Porter, B. N. and Radner, K. (1998) 'Aššūr-aḫu-iddina [Esarhaddon]', in *The Prosopography of the Neo-Assyrian Empire, 1/I: A*, ed. K. Radner. Helsinki: 145–52.

Porter, J. I. (2007) 'Hearing voices: The Herculaneum papyri and classical scholarship', in *Antiquity Recovered: The Legacy of Pompeii and Herculaneum*, eds. V. C. G. Coates and J. L. Seydl. Los Angeles: 95–113.

Posener, G. (1936) *La première domination Perse en Egypte.* Cairo.

Posner, E. (1972) *Archives in the Ancient World.* Cambridge, MA.

Postgate, J. N. (1974) 'The *bīt akīti* in Assyrian Nabu temples'. *Sumer* 30: 51–74.

Pothecary, S. (2005) 'Kolossourgia. "A colossal statue of a work"', in *Strabo's Cultural Geography: The Making of a Kolossourgia*, eds. D. Dueck, H. Lindsay and S. Pothecary. Cambridge: 5–26.

Powell, J. G. F. (1995) 'Cicero's philosophical works and their background,' in *Cicero the Philosopher: Twelve Papers*, ed. J. G. F. Powell. Oxford: 1–36.

Puech, B. (1992) 'Prosopographie des amis de Plutarque'. *ANRW* 2.33.6: 4831–93.
  (2002) *Orateurs et sophistes grecs dans les inscriptions d'époque impériale. Avec préface de L. Pernot.* Paris.

Puglia, E. (1988a) *Aporie testuali ed esegetiche in Epicuro (PHerc. 1012). Edizione, traduzione e commento.* Naples.
  (1988b) '*PHerc.* 1039. Altro libro di Epicuro "Sulla Natura"?' *CErc.* 18: 19–26.
  (1993) 'Frammenti da *PHerc.* 1158'. *CErc.* 23: 29–65.
  (1995) 'Fra *glutinatores* e *scribi*,' in *Atti del V seminario internazionale di papirologia, Lecce 27–29 giugno 1994*, ed. M. Capasso. Galatina: 43–52.
  (1997) *La cura del libro nel mondo antico. Guasti e restauri del rotolo di papiro.* Naples.
  (1998) 'La soscrizione del libro XXVIII *Sulla Natura* di Epicuro (*PHerc.* 1479/1417)', in *Ricerche di papirologia letteraria e documentaria*, ed. M. Capasso. Papyrologica Lupiensia 6. Galatina: 101–6.

Purcell, N. (1988) 'The arts of government', in *The Oxford History of the Roman World*, eds. J. Boardman, O. Murray and J. Griffin. Oxford: 150–81.

(1993) 'Atrium Libertatis'. *PBSR* 61: 125–55.

(2001) 'The ordo scribarum. A study in the loss of memory'. *MEFRA* 113 (2): 633–74.

(2003) 'Becoming historical. The Roman case', in *Myth, History and Culture in Republican Rome. Studies in Honour of T. P. Wiseman*, eds. D. Braund and C. Gill. Exeter: 12–40.

Quack, J. F. (2006a) 'Zur Lesung und Deutung des Dramatischen Ramesseumpapyrus'. *ZÄS* 133: 72–89.

(2006b) 'Die hieratischen und hieroglyphischen Papyri aus Tebtynis – ein Überblick', in *The Carlsberg Papyri 7: Hieratic Texts from the Collection*, ed. K. Ryholt. CNI Publications 30. Copenhagen: 1–7.

Radiciotti, P. (1998) 'Osservazioni paleografiche sui papiri latini di Ercolano'. *S&C* 22: 354–70.

(2000) 'Della genuinità e delle opere tràdite da alcuni antichi papiri latini'. *S&C* 24: 359–73.

(2009) 'Ercolano: papyri latini in una biblioteca greca', in *Studi di egittologia e di papirologia* 6, ed. F. Serra. Pisa and Rome: 103–14.

Radner, K. (2006) 'Provinz. C. Assyrien'. *RlA* 11: 42–68.

(2009) 'The Assyrian king and his scholars: the Syro-Anatolian and the Egyptian schools', in *Of God(s), Trees, Kings, and Scholars: Neo-Assyrian and Related Studies in Honour of Simo Parpola*, eds. M. Luukko, S. Svärd and R. Mattila. Helsinki: 221–38.

(2011) 'Royal decision-making: kings, magnates and scholars', in *The Oxford Handbook of Cuneiform Culture*, eds. K. Radner and E. Robson. Oxford: 358–79.

Radner, K. and Robson, E. (eds.) (2011) *The Oxford Handbook of Cuneiform Culture*. Oxford.

Radt, W. (1998) 'Recent research in and about Pergamon: a survey (c. 1987–1997)', in *Pergamon, Citadel of the Gods. Archaeological Record, Literary Description, and Religious Development*, ed. H. Köster. Harrisburg, PA: 1–40.

(1999) *Pergamon. Geschichte und Bauten einer Antiken Metropole*. Darmstadt.

(2003) 'The library of Pergamon', in *Ancient Libraries in Anatolia. Libraries of Hattusha, Pergamon, Ephesus, Nysa (24th Annual Conference on Libraries and Education in the Networked Information Environment, June 2–5 2003)*, ed. A. Savaş, J. Seeher, W. Radt, V. M. Strocka and V. Idil. Ankara: 33–43.

Ranganathan, S. R. (1957) *The Five Laws of Library Science*. Madras.

Rawson, E. (1983) *Cicero, A Portrait*. 2nd edn. Ithaca, NY.

(1985) *Intellectual Life in the Late Roman Republic*. London.

Reade, J. E. (1986) 'Archaeology and the Kuyunjik archives', in *Cuneiform Archives and Libraries. Papers Read at the 30e Rencontre Assyriologique Internationale, Leiden, 4–8 July 1983*, ed. K. R. Veenhof. Leiden and Istanbul: 213–22.

(1998–2001) 'Ninive (Nineveh)'. *RIA* 9: 388–433.
Reinhardt, T. (ed. and transl.) (2003) *Marcus Tullius Cicero, Topica*. Oxford.
Rengakos, A. (2002) Review of West (2001) *Studies in the Text and Transmission of the Iliad* (Munich and Leipzig). *BMCR* 2002.11.15.
Reynolds, J. (1982) *Aphrodisias and Rome, JRS Monographs* 1. London.
Reynolds, L. D. (ed.) (1983) *Texts and Transmission. A Survey of the Latin Classics*. Oxford.
Reynolds, L. D. and Wilson, N. G. (1974) *Scribes and Scholars. A Guide to the Transmission of Greek and Latin Literature*, 2nd edn. Oxford.
Rice, E. E. (1983) *The Grand Procession of Ptolemy Philadelphus*. Oxford.
Richmond, O. L. (1914) 'The Augustan Palatium'. *JRS* 4: 193–216.
Rickman, G. (1971) *Roman Granaries and Store Buildings*. Cambridge.
Ritner, R. K. (1995) 'Egyptian magical practice under the Roman empire: the demotic spells and their religious context'. *ANRW* 2.18.5: 3333–79.
  (2000) 'Innovations and adaptations in ancient Egyptian medicine'. *JNES* 59: 107–17.
Rizzo, S. (2001) 'Indagini nei fori imperiali. Oroidrografia, Foro di Cesare, Foro di Augusto, Templum Pacis'. *MDAI(R)* 108: 215–44.
Roberts, C. H. and Skeat, T. C. (1983) *The Birth of the Codex*. London.
Roberts, L. G. (1918) 'The Gallic fire and Roman archives'. *MAAR* 2: 55–65.
Robson, E. (2007a) 'The clay tablet book in Sumer, Babylonia, and Assyria', in *A Companion to the History of the Book*, eds. S. Eliot and J. Rose. Oxford: 67–83.
  (2007b) 'Secrets de famille: prêtre et astronome à Uruk à l'époque hellénistique', in *Les lieux de savoir, I: lieux et communautés*, ed. C. M. Jacob. Paris: 440–61.
  (2008) *Mathematics in Ancient Iraq: a Social History*. Princeton.
  (2011a) 'Empirical scholarship in the Neo-Assyrian court', in *The Empirical Dimension of Ancient Near Eastern Studies*, eds. G. Selz and K. Wagensonner. Vienna: 603–30.
  (2011b) 'The production and dissemination of scholarly knowledge', in *The Oxford Handbook of Cuneiform Culture*, eds. K. Radner and E. Robson. Oxford: 557–76.
  (forthcoming) 'Tracing networks of cuneiform scholarship'.
Robson, E. and Stevens, K. R. (forthcoming) 'Scholarly tablet collections in first-millennium Assyria and Babylonia', in *Libraries before Alexandria: Ancient Near Eastern Traditions*, eds. G. Barjamovic and K. Ryholt. Oxford.
Rocca, S. (2003) *Animali (e uomini) in Cicerone (De Nat. Deor. 2, 121–161)*. Genoa.
Rochberg, F. (1998) *Babylonian Horoscopes*. Philadelphia.
Rodríguez Almeida, E. (1981) *Forma Urbis Marmorea. Aggiornamento generale 1980*. Rome.
Rodríguez Valcárcel, J.A. (2006–7) 'Bibliotecas y libros en la Roma del emperador Calígula'. *ETF(hist)* 19–20: 195–210.
Rogers, G. M. (1991) *The Sacred Identity of Ephesos: Foundation Myths of a Roman City*. London and New York.

Romano, E. (2005) 'Il difficile rapporto fra teoria e pratica nella cultura romana', in *Politica e cultura in Roma antica. Atti dell'incontro di studio in ricordo di I. Lana, Torino 16–17 Ottobre 2003*, eds. F. Bessone and E. Malaspina. Bologna: 81–99.

Romeo, C. (1979) 'Demetrio Lacone sulla grandezza del sole (*PHerc.* 1013)'. *CErc.* 9: 11–33.

(1988) *Demetrio Lacone, la poesia (PHerc. 188 e 1014). Edizione, traduzione e commento.* Naples.

Rondot, V. (2004) *Tebtynis II: Le temple de Soknebtynis et son dromos.* Cairo.

Rose, H. J. (1954) *A Handbook of Latin Literature.* London.

Roselli, A. (2002) 'ἐκ βιβλίου κυβερνήτης: i limiti dell'apprendimento dai libri nella formazione tecnica e filosofica (Galeno, Polibio, Filodemo)'. *Vichiana* ser. 4, 4: 35–50.

(2010) 'Libri e biblioteche a Roma al tempo di Galeno: la testimonianza del *de indolentia*'. *Galenos* 4: 127–48.

Roth, P. (2003) *Der Panathenaikos des Isokrates. Übersetzung und Kommentar.* Munich and Leipzig.

Rothschild, C. K. and Thompson, T. W. (2012) 'Galen's *On the Avoidance of Grief*: the question of the library at Antium', *Classical Philology* 107: 131–45.

Roueché, C. (1993) *Performers and Partisans at Aphrodisias in the Roman and Late Roman Periods. JRS* Monographs 6. London.

Roux, G. (1975) 'Salles de banquets à Délos'. *BCH* Suppl. 1: 525–54.

Rowell, H. T. (1952) 'Accius and the Faeneratrix of Plautus'. *AJPh* 73: 268–80.

Rüpke, J. (2004) 'Acta aut agenda: relations of script and performance', in *Rituals in Ink: A Conference on Religion and Literary Production in Ancient Rome, held at Stanford University in February 2002*, eds. A. Barchiesi et al. Stuttgart: 23–44.

(2006) 'Ennius's *Fasti* in Fulvius's temple: Greek rationality and Roman tradition'. *Arethusa* 39: 489–512.

Russell, D. A. (1973) *Plutarch.* London.

Russell, D. A. and Wilson, N. G. (eds.) (1981) *Menander Rhetor.* Oxford.

Ryholt, K. (1999) *The Carlsberg Papyri 4: The Story of Petese Son of Petetum and Seventy Other Good and Bad Stories.* CNI Publications 23. Copenhagen.

(2004) 'The Assyrian invasion of Egypt in Egyptian literary tradition', in *Assyria and Beyond: Studies Presented to Mogens Trolle Larsen*, ed. J. G. Dercksen. Leiden: 484–511.

(2005) 'On the contents and nature of the Tebtunis temple library. A status report', in *Tebtynis und Soknopaiu Nesos. Leben im römerzeitlichen Fajum*, eds. S. Lippert and M. Schentuleit. Wiesbaden: 141–70.

(2006) *The Carlsberg Papyri 6: The Petese Stories II.* CNI Publications 29. Copenhagen.

(2009) 'The life of Imhotep?', in *Actes du IXe congrès international des études démotiques*, eds. G. Widmer and D. Devauchelle. Bibliothèque d'étude 147. Cairo: 305–15.

(2010) 'Late period literature', in *The Blackwell Companion to Ancient Egypt*, vol. II, ed. A. B. Lloyd. Oxford: 709–31.

(2012) *The Carlsberg Papyri 10: Narratives from the Tebtunis Temple Library*. Copenhagen.

(forthcoming a) 'Libraries from Late Period and Greco-Roman Egypt, c. 700 BC–AD 300', in *Libraries before Alexandria*, ed. K. Ryholt and G. Barjamovic. Oxford.

(forthcoming b) 'The late Old Kingdom scribal archive at the pyramid of Netjerkhet'.

(forthcoming c) 'The excavation and early acquisition history of the Tebtunis temple library'.

Saller, R. S. (1982) *Personal Patronage under the Early Empire*. Cambridge.

Sanders, K. R. (1999) 'Toward a new edition of PHerc. 831'. *CErc.* 29: 17–30.

Sansone, D. (2004) 'Heracles at the Y'. *JHS* 124: 125–42.

Santoro, M. (2000) *[Demetrio Lacone] [La Forma di Dio] (PHerc. 1055). Edizione, traduzione e commento*. Naples.

Savaş, A. et al. (2003) *Ancient Libraries in Anatolia. Libraries of Hattusha, Pergamon, Ephesus, Nysa*. Ankara.

Sbordone, S. (1984) 'La biblioteca "Ulpia Traiana"'. *AAP* 33: 119–25.

Scappaticcio, M. C. (2008) 'Il PHerc. 817: spunti paleografici'. *CErc.* 38: 229–46.

Scheid, J. (2006) 'Oral tradition and written tradition in the formation of sacred law in Rome', in *Religion and Law in Classical and Christian Rome*, eds. C. Ando and J. Rüpke. Stuttgart: 14–33.

Schenkeveld, D. (1994) 'Scholarship and grammar', in *La philologie grecque à l'époque hellénistique et romaine*, ed. F. Montanari. Geneva: 263–98.

Schilling, R. (ed.) (1977) *Pline l'ancien: histoire naturelle, livre vii*. Paris.

Schironi, F. (2010) *ΤΟ ΜΕΓΑ ΒΙΒΛΙΟΝ: Book-Ends, End-Titles, and Coronides in Papyri with Hexametric Poetry*. Durham, NC.

Schlange-Schöningen, H. (2003) *Die römische Gesellschaft bei Galen. Biographie und Sozialgeschichte*. Berlin.

Schmakeit, I. A. (2003) *Apollonios und die Attische Tragödie. Gattungsüberschreitende Intertextualität in der Alexandrinischen Epik* (PhD Diss. University of Groningen).

Schmidt, O. (1899) 'Ciceros Villen'. *NJKAGLP* 3: 328–55, 466–97.

Schmidt, P. L. (2003) 'C. Poetarum'. *BNP* 3: 535.

Schnäbele, J. (1989) 'Les manuscrits anciens des *Antiquités Romaines* (livre II) et leur parenté'. *MEFRA* 101: 9–35.

Scholz, P. (2004) 'Elementarunterricht und intellektuelle Bildung im hellenistischen Gymnasion', in *Das Hellenistische Gymnasion*, eds. D. Kah and P. Scholz. Berlin: 103–28.

Schousboe, K. and Larsen, M.T. (eds.) (1989) *Literacy and Society*. Copenhagen.

Schrijvers, P. H. (1999) *Lucrèce et les sciences de la vie*. Leiden, Boston and Cologne.
Schubert, P. (2002) 'Strabon et le sort de la bibliothèque d'Aristote'. *LEC* 70: 225–37.
Schultze, C.E. (1980) *Dionysius of Halicarnassus as a Historian: an Investigation of his Aims and Methods in the 'Antiquitates Romanae'* (D. Phil. Thesis, University of Oxford).
   (1986) 'Dionysius of Halicarnassus and his audience', in *Past Perspectives: Studies in Greek and Roman Historical Writing*, eds. I. S. Moxon, J. D. Smart and A. J. Woodman. Cambridge: 121–41.
   (2000) 'Authority, originality and competence in the *Roman Archaeology* of Dionysius of Halicarnassus'. *HISTOS* 4 [www.dur.ac.uk/Classics/histos/2000/schultze1.html]
Schulz, F. (1946) *History of Roman Legal Science*. Oxford.
Schwartz, J. (1951) 'Pompeius Macer et la jeunesse d'Ovide'. *RPh* 77: 182–93.
Sedley, D. (1973) 'Epicurus, *On Nature* book XXVIII'. *CErc*. 3: 5–83.
   (1998) *Lucretius and the Transformation of Greek Wisdom*. Cambridge.
Sellers, E. (1896) *The Elder Pliny's Chapters on the History of Art*. London.
Sengelin, T. (1983) *Apollo Palatinus. Die Apollinische Präsenz auf dem Palatin in Augusteischer Zeit*. Vienna.
Sève, M. (1990) 'Sur la taille des rayonnages dans les bibliothèques antiques'. *RPh* 64: 173–9.
Severy, B. (2000) 'Family and state in the early imperial monarchy'. *CPh* 95: 318–37.
Shackleton Bailey, D. R. (ed.) (1965–70) *Cicero's Letters to Atticus*, 7 vols. Cambridge Classical Texts and Commentaries 3–9. Cambridge.
   (1976) 'Review of I. Shatzman, *Senatorial Wealth and Roman Politics*'. *Phoenix* 30: 209–10.
   (ed.) (1977) *Cicero: Epistulae ad Familiares*, 2 vols., Cambridge Classical Texts and Commentaries 16–17. Cambridge.
   (ed.) (1980) *Cicero: Epistulae ad Quintum Fratrem et M. Brutum*, Cambridge Classical Texts and Commentaries 22. Cambridge.
Shatzman, I. (1975) *Senatorial Wealth and Roman Politics*. Brussels.
Shear, T. L. (1981) 'Athens: from city-state to provincial town'. *Hesperia* 50: 356–77.
Shubert, S. B. (1993) 'The oriental origins of the Alexandrian library'. *Libri* 43: 142–72.
Sider, D. (2005) *The Library of the Villa dei Papiri at Herculaneum*. Los Angeles.
Sihler, E. G. (1905) 'The Collegium Poetarum at Rome'. *AJP* 26 (1): 1–21.
Simpson, W. K. (2003) *The Literature of Ancient Egypt*. 3rd edn. New Haven, CT.
Singer, P. N. (1997) *Galen. Selected Works*. Oxford.
Slater, W. J. (1976) 'Aristophanes of Byzantium on the *Pinakes* of Callimachus'. *Phoenix* 30 (3): 234–41.
   (1986) *Aristophanis Byzantii Fragmenta*. Berlin.
Sluiter, I. (1995) 'The embarrassment of imperfection. Galen's assessment of Hippocrates' linguistic merits', in *Ancient Medicine in its Socio-Cultural Context*, vol. II, eds. P. J. Van der Eijk, H. F. J. Horstmanshoff and P. H. Schrijvers. Amsterdam and Atlanta: 519–35.

Small, J. P. (1997) *Wax Tablets of the Mind. Cognitive Studies of Memory and Literacy in Classical Antiquity*. London.

Smith, R. R. R. (1993) *Aphrodisias I: The Monument of C. Julius Zoilos*. Mainz.

(1998) 'Cultural choice and political identity in honorific portrait statues in the Greek East', *JRS* 88: 56–93.

Smith, W. (1979) *The Hippocratic Tradition*. Ithaca, NY, and New York.

Snyder, H. G. (2000) *Teachers and Texts in the Ancient World: Philosophers, Jews, and Christians*. London and New York.

Soper, M. E. (1976) 'Characteristics and use of personal collections'. *Libr. Quart.* 46 (4): 397–415.

Spallone, M. (2008) *Giurisprudenza romana e storia del libro*. Rome.

Spetsieri-Choremi, A. (1995) 'Library of Hadrian at Athens: recent finds'. *Ostraka* 4: 137–47.

Speyer, W. (1971) *Die literarische Fälschung im heidnischen und christlichen Altertum: ein Versuch ihrer Deutung*. Munich.

Spinelli, E. (1986) 'Metrodoro contro i dialettici?'. *CErc.* 16: 29–43.

Stadter, P. A. (1972) 'The structure of Livy's *History*'. *Historia* 21: 287–307. Repr. in *Oxford Readings in Livy*, eds. M. Chaplin and C. Kraus (2009). Oxford: 91–117.

(2002) 'Plutarch's *Lives* and their Roman readers', in *Greek Romans and Roman Greeks: Studies in Cultural Interaction*, ed. E. N. Ostendfeld. Aarhus: 123–35.

Staikos, K. S. (2005) *The History of the Library in Western Civilization, 2: From Cicero to Hadrian*. New Castle, DE.

Stambaugh, J. E. (1978) 'The functions of Roman temples'. *ANRW* 2.16.1: 554–608.

Starr, R. J. (1987) 'Trimalchio's libraries'. *Hermes* 115: 252–3.

Steele, J. M. (2008) *A Brief Introduction to Astronomy in the Middle East*. London.

Stein, P. (1966) *Regulae Iuris: from Juristic Rules to Legal Maxims*. Edinburgh.

(1999) *Roman Law in European History*. Cambridge.

Steinby, T. (1956) *Romersk Publicistik. Skriftlig Nyhetstjänst och Opinion under Ciceros Tid*. Helsingfors.

Stephens, S. (2010) 'Ptolemaic Alexandria', in *A Companion to Hellenistic Literature*, eds. J. J. Clauss and M. Cuypers. Malden, MA and Oxford: 46–61.

Stephens, W. (2009) 'Ozymandias: Or, writing, lost libraries, and wonder'. *MLN* 124 (5: Suppl.): S155–S168.

Stern, W. O. and Thimme, D. H. (2007) *Kenchreai, Eastern Port of Corinth: VI. Ivory, Bone and Related Wood Finds*. Leiden.

Stock, B. (1983) *The Implications of Literacy. Written Language and Models of Interpretation in the Eleventh and Twelfth Centuries*. Princeton.

Stramaglia, A. (2011) 'Libri perduti per sempre: Galeno, *De Indolentia* 13; 16; 17–19', *Rivista di Filologia e di Istruzione Classica* 139: 118–47.

Strocka, V. M. (1978) 'Zur Datierung der Celsusbibliothek', in *Proceedings of the Xth International Congress of Classical Archaeology. Ankara-Izmir, 23–30/ IX/ 1973*, ed. E. Akrugal. Ankara: 893–9.

(1981) 'Römische Bibliotheken'. *Gymnasium* 88: 298–329.

(2000) 'Noch einmal zur Bibliothek von Pergamon'. *AA*: 155–65.

Strohmaier, G. (1976) 'Übersehenes zur Biographie Lukians', *Philologus* 120: 117–22.

(2004) 'Galen's not uncritical commentary on Hippocrates' *Airs, Waters, Places*', in *Philosophy, Science and Exegesis in Greek, Arabic and Latin Commentaries*, eds. P. Adamson, H. Baltussen, and M. W. F. Stone, vol. I. London: 1–9.

Strootman, R. (2010) 'Literature and the kings', in *A Companion to Hellenistic Literature*, eds. J. J. Clauss and M. Cuypers. Malden, MA and Oxford: 30–45.

Suerbaum, W. (1995) 'Der Pyrrhos-Krieg in Ennius' *Annales* VI im Lichte der ersten Ennius-Papyri aus Herculaneum'. *ZPE* 106: 31–52.

Suolahti, J. (1963) *The Roman Censors. A Study on Social Structure.* Helsinki.

Swain, S. (1989) 'Favorinus and Hadrian'. *ZPE* 79: 150–8.

(1990) 'Hellenic culture and the Roman heroes of Plutarch'. *JHS* 110: 126–45.

(1992) 'Plutarch's characterisation of Lucullus'. *RhM* 135: 307–16.

(1996) *Hellenism and Empire: Language, Classicism, and Power in the Greek World AD 50–250.* Oxford.

Swift Riginos, A. (1976) *Platonica. The Anecdotes concerning the Life and Writings of Plato.* Leiden.

Syme, R. (1958) *Tacitus*, 2 vols. Oxford.

(1978) *History in Ovid.* Oxford.

(1980) 'Biographers of the Caesars'. *Mus. Helv.* 37: 104–28, repr. in *Roman Papers* 3, ed. A. R. Birley (1994). Oxford: 1251–75.

(1988) 'Avidius Cassius. His rank, age and quality', in *Roman Papers* 5, ed. A. R. Birley. Oxford: 689–701.

Tamm, B. (1963) *Auditorium and Palatium.* Stockholm.

Tanner, R. G. (2000) 'Aristotle's works: the possible origins of the Alexandria collection', in *The Library of Alexandria: Centre of Learning in the Ancient World*, ed. R. MacLeod. London and New York: 79–91.

Taylor, J. (2011) 'Tablets as artefacts, scribes as artisans', in *The Oxford Handbook of Cuneiform Culture*, eds. K. Radner and E. Robson. Oxford: 5–31.

Taylor, L. R. (1949) 'On the chronology of Cicero's letters of 56–55 B.C.'. *CPh* 44: 217–21.

Teichmüller G. (1881–4) *Literarische Fehden im vierten Jahrhundert vor Chr.* 2 vols. Breslau.

Temperini, L. (1994) *Basilica Santi Cosma e Damiano.* Rome.

Tepedino Guerra, A. (1979) 'Il *PHerc.* 200: Metrodoro, sulla ricchezza', in *Actes du XVe congrès international de papyrologie, troisième partie. Problèmes généraux – papyrologie littéraire*, eds. J. Bingen and G. Nachtergael. Brussels: 191–7.

(1991) *Polieno, frammenti: edizione, traduzione e commento.* Naples.

(1992) 'Metrodoro "Contro i dialettici"?'. *CErc.* 22: 119–22.
Theodorides, C. (1976) *Die Fragmente des Grammatikers Philoxenos.* Berlin and New York.
Thomas, R. (1989) *Oral Tradition and Written Record in Classical Athens.* Cambridge.
 (1992) *Literacy and Orality in Ancient Greece.* Cambridge.
 (2003) 'Prose performance texts: *epideixis* and written publication in the late fifth and early fourth centuries', in *Written Texts and the Rise of Literate Culture in Ancient Greece*, ed. H. Yunis. Cambridge: 162–88.
 (2009) 'Writing, reading, public and private "literacies". Functional literacy and democratic literacy in Greece', in *Ancient Literacies. The Culture of Reading in Greece and Rome*, eds. W. A. Johnson and H. N. Parker. Oxford: 13–45.
Thompson, D. J. (2008) 'The Ptolemaic Library Project'. *AAntHung* 48: 67–72.
Thompson, D. L. (1981) 'The meetings of the Roman Senate on the Palatine'. *AJA* 85: 335–9.
Thompson, H. A. and Wycherley, R. E. (1957) *The Athenian Agora III.* Princeton, NJ.
Thompson, J. W. (1940) *Ancient Libraries.* Hamden, CT.
Tobin, J. (1997) *Herodes Atticus and the City of Athens: Patronage and Conflict under the Antonines.* Amsterdam.
Too, Y. L. (1998) *The Idea of Ancient Literary Criticism.* Oxford.
 (2000) 'The walking library of Athenaeus: The performance of cultural memories', in *Athenaeus and his World. Reading Greek Culture in the Roman Empire*, eds. D. Braund and J. Wilkins. Exeter: 111–23.
 (2010) *The Idea of the Library in the Ancient World.* Oxford.
Torelli, M. (1993) 'Bibliotheca templi Divi Augusti'. *LTUR* 1: 197.
Tortorici, E. (1993) 'La "Terrazza domizianea", *l'aqua Marcia* ed il taglio della sella tra Campidoglio e Quirinale'. *BCAR* 95: 7–24.
Touwaide, A. (1994) 'Galien et la toxicologie'. *ANRW* 2.37.2: 1887–986.
Trampedach, K. (1994) *Platon, die Akademie und die zeitgenössische Politik.* Stuttgart.
Trapp, M. (1995) 'Sense of place in the *Orations* of Dio Chrysostom', in *Ethics and Rhetoric. Classical Essays for Donald Russell on his Seventy-Fifth Birthday*, eds. D. Innes, H. Hine and C. Pelling. Oxford: 163–75.
 (2001) 'On tickling the ears: Apuleius' prologue and the anxieties of philosophers', in *A Companion to the Prologue of Apuleius' Metamorphoses*, eds. A. Kahane and A. Laird. Oxford: 39–46.
 (2004) 'Statesmanship in a minor key?', in *The Statesman in Plutarch's Works*, eds. L. De Blois, J. A. E. Bons, T. Kessels and D. M. Schenkeveld, vol. I. Leiden and Boston: 189–200.
Travlos, J. (1971) *Pictorial Dictionary of Ancient Athens.* London.
Trimble, J. (2007) 'Visibility and viewing on the Severan marble plan', in *Severan Culture*, eds. S. Swain, S. J. Harrison and J. Elsner. Cambridge: 368–84.

Tröster, M. (2005) 'Hellenism and truphē in Plutarch's Life of Lucullus', in *The Statesman in Plutarch's Works*, eds. L. De Blois, J. A. E. Bons, T. Kessels, D. M. Schenkeveld, vol. I. Leiden and Boston: 303–13.
  (2008) *Themes, Character, and Politics in Plutarch's Life of Lucullus*. Stuttgart.
Tucci, P. L. (2005) '"Where high Moneta leads her steps sublime": the Tabularium and the temple of Juno Moneta'. *JRA* 18 (1): 7–33.
  (2007) 'New fragments of ancient plans of Rome', a review of *Formae Urbis Romae. Nuovi frammenti di piante marmoree dallo scavo dei fori imperiali*, eds. R. Meneghini and R. Santangeli Valenzani. *BCAR* Suppl. 15, Rome 2006. *JRA* 20: 469–80.
  (2008) 'Galen's storeroom, Rome's libraries, and the fire of A.D. 192'. *JRA* 21 (1): 133–49.
  (2009a) 'Antium, the Palatium, and the Domus Tiberiana again'. *JRA* 22 (1): 398–401.
  (2009b) 'Nuove osservazioni sull'architettura del Templum Pacis', in *Divus Vespasianus. Il bimillenario dei Flavi*, ed. F. Coarelli. Milan: 158–67.
  (2011) 'Red-painted stones in Roman architecture'. *AJA* 116 (1): 589–610.
Tuori, K. (2010) 'A place for jurists in the spaces of justice?', in *Spaces of Justice in the Roman World*, ed. F. De Angelis. Columbia Studies in the Classical Tradition 35. Leiden: 43–65.
Turner, E. G. (1952) *Athenian Books in the Fifth and Fourth Centuries B.C. An Inaugural Lecture Delivered at University College London, 22 May 1951*. London. Rev. and updated transl. in *Libri, editori e pubblico nel mondo antico. Guida storica e critica*, ed. G. Cavallo (1984³ [1975¹]). Rome and Bari: 3–24.
  (1980) *Greek Papyri: An Introduction*. 2nd edn. Oxford.
  (1983) 'Sniffing glue'. *CErc*. 13: 7–14.
Turner, G. (1968) 'The palace and Bâtiment aux Ivoires at Arslan Tash: a reappraisal'. *Iraq* 30: 62–8.
Tutrone, F. (2006) 'Lucrezio e la biologia di Aristotele. Riflessioni sulla presenza dell'opera aristotelica nel *De rerum natura* e nella cultura greco-latina del I secolo a. C'. *Bollettino della fondazione nazionale Vito Fazio-Allmayer* 35 (1–2): 65–104.
  (2012) *Filosofi e animali in Roma antica. Modelli di animalità e umanità in Lucrezio e Seneca*. Pisa.
Ullmann, M. (1978) *Rufus von Ephesos. Krankenjournale*. Wiesbaden.
Usener, H. (1913–14) *Kleine Schriften*. Leipzig and Berlin.
Usener, S. (1994) *Isokrates, Platon und ihr Publikum. Hörer und Leser von Literatur im 4. Jahrhundert v. Chr*. Tübingen.
Vallance, J. (2000) 'Doctors in the library: the strange tale of Apollonius the bookworm and other stories', in *The Library of Alexandria: Centre of Learning in the Ancient World*, ed. R. MacLeod. London and New York: 95–113.
Van Buren, A. W. (1959) 'Newsletter from Rome', *AJA* 63: 383–99.

Van der Stockt, L. (1999) 'A Plutarchan hypomnema on self-love'. *AJP* 120: 575–99.
van Dijk, J. J. and Mayer, W. (1980) *Texte aus dem Rēš-Heiligtum in Uruk-Warka*. Berlin.
Van Elderen, B. (1998) 'Early Christian libraries', in *The Bible as Book: The Manuscript Tradition*, ed. J. L. Sharpe, III and K. van Kampen. London and New Castle, DE: 45–59.
Van Groningen, B. A. (1963) 'Ekdosis'. *Mnemosyne* XVI: 1–17.
van Heel, J. (1989) 'Un frammento perduto del *PHerc.* 831'. *CErc.* 19: 187–91.
van Minnen, P. (1998) 'Boorish or bookish?: literature in Egyptian villages in the Fayum in the Graeco-Roman period'. *JJP* 28: 89–194.
Van Rossum-Steenbeek, M. (1997) *Greek Readers' Digests? Studies on a Selection of Subliterary Papyri*. Leiden.
Van Straten, F. T. (1981) 'Gifts for the gods', in *Faith, Hope and Worship: Aspects of Religious Mentality in the Ancient World*, ed. H. S. Versnel. Studies in Greek and Roman Religion 2. Leiden: 65–151.
Vardi, A. (2001) 'Gellius against the professors'. *ZPE* 137: 41–54.
Vegetti, M. (1992) 'Aristotele, il Liceo e l'enciclopedia del sapere', in *Lo spazio letterario della Grecia antica*, vol. I, eds. G. Cambiano, L. Canfora and D. Lanza. Rome: 587–611.
Veldhuis, N. (2010) 'The theory of knowledge and the practice of celestial divination', in *Divination and Interpretation of Signs in the Ancient World*, ed. A. Annus. Chicago: 77–91.
Velsen, A. (1853) *Tryphonis Grammatici Alexandrini Fragmenta*. Berlin.
Verdin, H. (1974) 'La fonction de l'histoire selon Denys d'Halicarnasse'. *AncSoc* 5: 289–307.
Villard, P. (1997) 'L'éducation d'Assurbanipal'. *Ktema* 22: 135–49.
  (1998) 'Allusions littéraires et jeux de lettrés dans les rapports des devins d'époque néo-assyrienne', in *Intellectual Life of the Ancient Near East*, ed. J. Prosecký. Prague: 427–37.
von den Hoff, R. (2004) '*Ornamenta* γυμνασιώδη? Delos und Pergamon als Beispielfälle der Skulpturenausstattung hellenistischer Gymnasien', in *Das Hellenistische Gymnasion*, eds. D. Kah and P. Scholz. Berlin: 373–93.
von Lieven, A. (1999) 'Divination in Ägypten'. *AF* 26: 77–126.
  (2005) 'Religiöse Texte aus der Tempelbibliothek von Tebtynis – Gattungen und Funktionen', in *Tebtynis und Soknopaiu Nesos. Leben im römerzeitlichen Fajum*, eds. S. Lippert and M. Schentuleit. Wiesbaden: 57–70.
  (2007) *The Carlsberg Papyri 8: Grundriss des Laufes der Sterne. Das sogenannte Nutbuch*. CNI Publications 31. Copenhagen.
Von Staden, H. (1997) 'Galen and the "Second Sophistic" ', in *Aristotle and After*, ed. R. Sorabji. London: 33–54.
  (1998) 'Gattung und Gedächtnis: Galen über Wahrheit und Lehrdichtung', in *Gattungen Wissenschaftlicher Literatur in der Antike*, eds. W. Kullmann, J. Althoff and M. Asper. Tübingen: 65–94.

(2002) '"A woman does not become ambidextrous": Galen and the culture of scientific commentary', in *Classical Commentary: Histories, Practices, Theory*, eds. R. K. Gibson and C. S. Kraus. Leiden and Boston: 109–39.

(2004) 'Galen's Alexandria', in *Ancient Alexandria between Egypt and Greece*, eds. W. V. Harris and G. Ruffini. Leiden: 179–215.

(2006) 'Interpreting "Hippokrates" in the 3rd and 2nd centuries BC', in *Ärzte und ihre Interpreten. Medizinische Fachtexte der Antike als Forschungsgegenstand der Klassischen Philologie*, eds. C. W. Müller, C. Brockmann and C. W. Brunschön. Leipzig: 16–47.

(2009) 'Staging the past, staging oneself: Galen on Hellenistic exegetical traditions', in *Galen and the World of Knowledge*, eds. C. Gill, T. Whitmarsh and J. Wilkins. Cambridge: 132–56.

Wallace, R.W. (1995) 'Speech, song and text, public and private', in *Die athenische Demokratie im 4. Jahrhundert v. Chr.*, ed. W. Eder. Stuttgart: 199–224.

Wallace-Hadrill, A. F. (1983) *Suetonius: The Scholar and his Caesars*. London.

(1997) '*Mutatio morum*: the idea of a cultural revolution', in *The Roman Cultural Revolution*, eds. T. Habinek and A. Schiessaro. Cambridge: 3–22.

(2008) *Rome's Cultural Revolution*. Cambridge and New York.

Walter, U. (2004) *Memoria und Res Publica. Zur Geschichtskultur der Römischen Republik*. Frankfurt.

Ward, J. O. (2000) 'Alexandria and its medieval legacy: the book, the monk and the rose', in *The Library of Alexandria: Centre of Learning in the Ancient World*, ed. R. MacLeod. London and New York: 163–79.

Ward-Perkins, J. B. (1981) *Roman Imperial Architecture*. 3 vols. London.

Warmington, E. H. (1935) *Remains of Old Latin*. New Haven, CT and London.

Watt, W. (1963) 'Cicero, ad Atticum 4, 5'. *RhM* 106: 21–3.

Weaire, G. (2005) 'Dionysius of Halicarnassus' professional situation and the *De Thucydide*'. *Phoenix* 59: 246–66.

Weaver, P. (2004) '"*POxy*." 3312 and joining the household of Caesar'. *ZPE* 149: 196–204.

Webb, R. (2009) *Ekphrasis, Imagination and Persuasion in Ancient Rhetorical Theory and Practice*. Farnham.

Wegner, M. (1956) *Hadrian (Das Römische Herrscherbild 2, 3)*. Berlin.

Weitzmann, K. (1959) *Ancient Book Illumination*. Cambridge, MA.

Weinstock, S. (1957) 'The image and chair of Germanicus'. *JRS* 47: 144–54.

Weissert, E. and Radner, K. (1998) 'Aššūr-bāni-apli' [Assurbanipal], in *The Prosopography of the Neo-Assyrian Empire, I/1: A*, ed. K. Radner. Helsinki: 159–71.

Wendel, C. R. (1934) 'Telephus of Pergamon'. *RE* XIX: 369–71.

(1943) 'Die antike Bücherschrank'. *Nachrichten der Akademie der Wissenschaften in Göttingen, Phil.-Hist. Kl.* 7: 267–99.

(1949) 'Die bauliche Entwicklung der antiken Bibliothek'. *Zentralblatt für Bibliothekswesen* 63: 407–28.

(1952) *Handbuch der Bibliothekswissenschaft.* 3.1.2: *Das Griechisch-Römisch Altertum.* Wiesbaden.

(1954) 'Bibliothek'. *RAC* 2. Stuttgart: 230–74.

(1974) *Kleine Schriften zum Antiken Buch- und Bibliothekswesen,* ed. W. Krieg. Cologne.

West, M. L. (2001) *Studies in the Text and Transmission of the Iliad.* Munich.

Westbrook, R. (2005) 'Patronage in the ancient Near East'. *JESHO* 48: 210–33.

Westrup, C. W. (1929) 'On the antiquarian-historiographical activities of the Roman Pontifical College'. *Det Konegelige Danske Videnskabernes Selskab Hist.-filol. Meddelelser* 16 (3): 1–15.

White, P. (1992) '"Pompeius Macer" and Ovid'. *CQ* 42: 210–18.

(1993) *Promised Verse: Poets in the Society of Augustan Rome.* Cambridge, MA.

(2009) 'Bookshops in the literary culture of Rome,' in *Ancient Literacies: The Culture of Reading in Greece and Rome,* eds. W. A. Johnson and H. N. Parker. Oxford: 268–87.

Whitehead, D. (2004) 'Isokrates for hire. Some preliminaries to a commentary on Isokrates 16–21', in *Law, Rhetoric, and Comedy in Classical Athens. Essays in Honour of D. M. MacDowell,* eds. D. L. Cairns and R. A. Knox. Swansea: 151–85.

Whitmarsh, T. (2001) *Greek Literature and the Roman Empire: The Politics of Imitation.* Oxford.

Wilamowitz-Moellendorff, U. von (1889) *Euripides Herakles, I, Einleitung in die griechische Tragödie.* Berlin.

Wildberg, W., Theurer, M., Eichler, F., Keil, J. (1953) *Die Bibliothek (Forschungen in Ephesos V.1).* 2nd edn. Vienna.

Wilkins, J. (2007) 'Galen and Athenaeus in the Hellenistic library', in *Ordering Knowledge in the Roman World,* eds. J. König and T. Whitmarsh. Cambridge: 69–87.

Williams, R. V. (1997) 'The documentation and special libraries movement in the United States 1910–1960'. *JASIST* 48–9: 775–81.

Williamson, C. (1995) 'The display of law and archival practice in Rome', in *Acta Colloquii Epigraphici Latini Helsingiae 1991.* Helsinki: 239–51.

Wilson, A. (2007) 'Urban development in the Severan empire', in *Severan Culture,* eds. S. Swain, S. J. Harrison and J. Elsner. Cambridge: 290–326.

Winsbury, R. (2009) *The Roman Book: Books, Publishing and Performance in Classical Rome.* London.

Winter, F. (1908) *Altertümer von Pergamon 7: Die Skulpturen.* Berlin.

Wiseman, D. J. and Black, J. A. (1996) *Literary Texts from the Temple of Nabû*. London.

Wolter von dem Knesebeck, H. (1995) 'Zur Ausstattung und Funktion des Hauptsaales der Bibliothek von Pergamon'. *Boreas* 18: 45–56.

Woolf, G. (2000) 'Literacy', in *CAH* 11 (2nd edn.). Cambridge: 875–97.

Yarden, L. (1991) *The Spoils of Jerusalem on the Arch of Titus. A Re-investigation*. Stockholm.

Yount, L. (2010) *The Father of Anatomy: Galen and His Dissections*. Berkeley Heights, N.J.

Zadorojnyi, A.V. (2005) '"Stabbed with large pens": trajectories of literacy in Plutarch's *Lives*', in *The Statesman in Plutarch's Works, Vol. II: The Statesman in Plutarch's Greek and Roman* Lives, eds. L. De Blois, J. Bons, T. Kessels and D. Schenkeveld. Leiden and Boston: 113–37.

(2006a) 'Lords of the flies: literacy and tyranny in imperial biography', in *The Limits of Ancient Biography*, eds. J. Mossman and B. McGing. Swansea: 351–94.

(2006b) 'King of his castle: Plutarch, *Demosthenes* 1–2'. *CCJ (formerly PCPS)* 52: 102–27.

(2010) 'Transcribing Plato's voice: the Platonic intertext between writtenness and orality', in *Gods, Daimones, Rituals, Myths and History of Religions in Plutarch's Works. Studies Devoted to Professor Frederick E. Brenk by the International Plutarch Society*, eds. L. Van der Stockt, F. Titchener, H.-G. Ingenkamp and A. Pérez Jiménez. Malaga and Logan, UT: 369–90.

(2011) 'The ethico-politics of writing in Plutarch's *Life of Dion*'. *JHS* 131: 147–63.

Zamazálova, S. (2011) 'The education of Neo-Assyrian princes', in *The Oxford Handbook of Cuneiform Culture*, eds. K. Radner and E. Robson. Oxford: 313–30.

Zanker, P. (1983) 'Der Apollontempel auf dem Palatin', in *Città e architettura nella Roma imperiale. Atti del seminario. Analecta romana instituti danici* Suppl. 10. Odense: 21–40.

(1995) *Die Maske des Sokrates. Das Bild des Intellektuellen in der antiken Kunst.* Munich.

Zarmakoupi, M. (ed.) (2010) *The Villa of the Papyri at Herculaneum: Archaeology, Reception, and Digital Reconstruction*. Sozomena: Studies in the Recovery of Ancient Texts: Edited on Behalf of the Herculaneum Society, 1. Berlin and New York.

Zecchini, G. (1982) 'Asinio Pollione. Dall'attività politica alla riflessione storiografica'. *ANRW* 2.30.2: 1265–96.

(1987) *Il carmen de bello Actiaco: storiografia e lotta politica in età Augustea*. Stuttgart.

Zetzel, J. E. G. (1973) '*Emendavi ad tironem*: some notes on scholarship in the second century A.D'. *HSCPh* 77: 225–43.
  (1984) *Latin Textual Criticism in Antiquity*. Salem, NH.
Ziegenaus, O. and De Luca, G. (1968) *Das Asklepieion, 1 (Altertümer von Pergamon 11, 1)*. Berlin.
Ziegler, K. (1951) 'Ploutarchos von Chaironeia'. *RE* 21.1: 632–962.

General index

a studiis. See education
ab epistulis, 244, 249, 251, 253, 254, 255
ab epistulis graecis, 244, 249
Academy (of Plato), 86, 90
Aelius Largus, Titus. *See* librarians
Aelius Stilo Praeconinus, Lucius, 217, 218, 242, 288–9, 303, 304, 353
Aelius Tubero, Quintus, 142, 144
Aemilius Paullus, Lucius, 3, 124, 125, 128, 131, 132, 135, 136, 357
Aeschines, 92
Aeschylus, 89, 364, 367, 376
Akkadian
 books in libraries, 49
 language, 39, 44
akousterion, 304, 305
Alcidamas
 On those who write speeches, 91
Alexander the Great, 39, 68, 126, 368
Alexandria
 library at the Serapeum, 302
 library of Alexandria, 3–4, 6, 14, 31, 32, 75, 80, 126, 141, 185, 242, 298, 302, 307, 332, 339, 363, 366, 368, 369, 379, 385, 387, 392–4, 401, 402, 412
  and Egyptian culture, 23–5, 36
  destruction of, 16, 64–5, 167–72, 182, 295, 296, 373, 374, 387
  foundation of, 3, 14, 36, 75, 95, 365, 369–70
  impact of, 8, 12, 18, 37, 55, 64, 70, 73, 96–108, 109, 122, 123, 176–82, 364, 370–1, 373–6
  organisation of, 64, 65, 76–8, 117, 119, 126, 249, 260, 365, 371–3
 Museum of, 18, 65, 75, 76, 77, 79, 80, 117, 119, 121, 169, 172, 178, 253, 254, 303, 363, 368, 369, 370, 372, 373, 375, 388
 New Library of Alexandria, 16, 376
 Ptolemaic, 2, 11, 63–7, 71, 74–9, 80, 96–108, 109, 173–4, 302–3, 339, 364–76, 392–4

 Roman, 162, 167–82, 242, 246, 249, 252, 253, 254, 301, 303, 366, 367, 369, 381, 382, 385, 387, 391, 392
Alexis
 Linos, 88
Ammianus Marcellinus, 373, 379
Andronicus of Rhodes, 153, 155, 161, 215, 388
Annaeus Seneca, Lucius (Seneca the Younger), 154, 171, 359, 369, 379, 400
Annales Maximi, 130
Annius Postumus. *See* librarians
antiquarianism, 64, 80–1, 94, 97, 100–6, 144–8, 217, 351, 378
Antium, 298
 Cicero's house and library in, 215, 222–5, 227, 233, 338
 imperial villa at, 238, 249, 298, 310–11
Antoninus Pius, 256, 257, 258
Antony (Antonius, Marcus), 234, 371, 386
Anu-belšunu, 52, 53
Apellicon of Teos, 67, 68, 70, 71, 72, 73, 79, 155, 160, 161, 164, 165, 213, 214, 295, 371, 386
Apollonius of Rhodes
 Argonautica, 96–108, 177
Apollonius of Tyana, 238
apothekai (storerooms), 291–300, 307–9, 328, 395–6
Apuleius, 264, 274
Aquilius Regulus, Marcus, 140, 141
Aramaic, language and texts, 10, 11, 12, 39
archives
 augural, 126–31
 distinguished from libraries, 7–8, 13–14, 40–1, 131, 133, 294, 319, 329, 356, 380, 412–16
 legal, 410–12
 medical, 408–10
Aristarchus of Samothrace, 178–81, 354
Aristides, Aelius, 272, 380, 384
 Panathenaicus, 379
Aristo of Ceos, 155

463

Aristonicus, 178
  On Critical Signs, 178
  On the Alexandrian Museum, 178
Aristophanes
  Frogs, 89, 100
Aristophanes of Byzantium, 65, 78, 374
Aristotle, 13, 80, 91, 93, 95, 138, 169, 231, 304, 353, 357, 368
  library of, 8, 14, 18, 66–76, 77, 79, 80, 89–90, 152–66, 215, 216, 371, 388
  Rhetoric, 92
armaria (cabinets), 336–41, 344
Arpinum
  Cicero's library at, 30, 216, 229
Asinius Pollio, Gaius, 3, 36, 127, 130, 141, 234, 238–40, 241, 242, 261, 264, 277, 288–9, 290, 301, 303, 316–18, 339
Asklepieia
  libraries at, 192, 329, 331, 410
Assurbanipal, 10, 41, 42, 43, 44, 45, 54
  Assurbanipal's library. *See* Nineveh
Assyria, 38–57
  libraries. *See* libraries (by period/culture)
astrology, 7, 28, 31, 33–4, 36, 43, 44, 45, 53, 56
astronomy, 19, 31, 53–4, 56, 62, 186
Astura
  Cicero's villa at, 231
Athenaeum, 243, 244, 259, 275, 298
Athenaeus of Naucratis
  Deipnosophistae, 8, 63, 64, 65, 66, 77, 78, 79, 80, 88, 147, 169, 182, 373, 388, 399, 400
Athens
  Classical, 2, 58, 59–63, 66–7, 68–9, 72, 74, 78, 79, 80, 85–95, 121, 302, 368, 372, 388
    library of Aristotle. *See* Aristotle
  Hellenistic, 78, 79, 80, 121, 125, 174, 364, 368, 370
  libraries, 28, 274, 380, 384
    library of Hadrian, 19, 141, 272–3, 275, 281, 290, 380
    library of Pantainos, 273–4, 371
    library of Pisistratus, 2, 80, 368
  library of Hadrian, 385
  Roman, 19, 28, 73, 74, 141, 160, 161, 174, 192, 210, 213, 215, 222, 233, 237, 254, 272–4, 371, 379–80, 381, 384, 385, 386
Atrium Libertatis, 129, 238–9, 241, 242, 243, 266, 267, 288, 290, 314–20, 327, 329, 331, 339–40
Attalids, 67, 110, 120, 121, 240, 367, 374

Atticus (Pomponius Atticus, Titus), 74, 162, 163, 164, 165, 189, 209–13, 217, 218, 219, 220, 221, 222, 230, 231, 232, 233, 266, 318, 357, 358
  Liber Annalis, 231
augurs
  Syro-Anatolian, 44
Augustus, 7, 79, 189, 234, 239, 240, 241, 242, 245, 246, 248, 265, 266, 267, 272, 286, 290, 291, 320, 321, 322, 333, 335, 340, 341, 343, 344, 345, 361, 362, 371
Aulus Gellius
  Attic Nights, 2, 3, 8, 20, 39, 66, 78, 93, 147, 242, 243, 250, 263, 274, 285, 289, 312, 313, 314, 316, 322, 323, 328, 350, 353, 356, 358–9, 362, 373, 378, 399
Aurelius Victor, Sextus
  De Caesaribus, 243, 244

Babylonia, 38–57
  libraries. *See* libraries (by period/culture)
Balasî, 43, 54
benefactors, 6, 134, 135–6, 248, 255, 261, 264, 267–74, 378, 386
Berenice II, 100, 102
bilingual libraries, 10–12, 23, 57, 183, 239–42, 247, 269, 316–20, 333–6, 372
book collections
  distinguished from libraries, 7–8, 9–10, 58–63, 66–76, 85–95, 124–36, 141–4, 157–66, 291–300
Book of Nut, 31–2
book production, 3, 17, 61, 67, 71–2, 73–4, 137, 151, 171, 183, 193–5, 300–3, 328, 364–6, 394
book trade, 1, 14, 27, 61, 67, 70, 75, 78, 79, 80, 90, 109, 131, 137, 160, 161, 163, 189, 193, 196, 209, 213, 216, 227, 232, 348, 367
bookrolls. *See* papyri
books, circulation among the elite, 81, 85–95, 105, 108, 137, 155, 209–33, 314, 363, 377–400
booksellers (*bibliopolae*), 67, 73, 78, 89, 125, 131, 138, 151, 162, 163, 190, 214, 233, 303, 390, 406, 415
bookshops, 7, 74, 115, 303, 398

Caecilius of Caleacte
  On the Sublime, 144
Caecilius Statius, 188, 205
Caesar (Iulius Caesar, Gaius), 2, 16, 64, 65, 79, 125, 167, 168, 169, 171, 229, 230, 231,

238, 239, 240, 261, 272, 316, 318, 333, 334, 378, 387
De Analogia, 219
Caesarea Maritima
  library of Origen, 3, 4, 8
Caligula (Gaius), 291, 339, 377
Callimachus
  Aetia, 96–108
  Pinakes, 76–8, 96
Callixeinos
  On Alexandria, 64
Carthage
  libraries at, 15, 125, 274
catalogues (of ancient libraries), 9, 56, 57, 73, 76–8, 96, 117, 142, 237, 307
Cato the Elder (Porcius Cato, Marcus 'Censorius'), 134, 237, 312, 313, 315, 322, 350
  Origines, 19, 134, 135
Cato the Younger (Porcius Cato, Marcus 'Uticensis'), 157, 158, 160, 164, 318, 357
Chaeremon, 249
Chrysippus (Cicero's slave), 214
Chrysippus (Stoic philosopher), 186, 189, 191, 194, 198, 303, 304, 323, 391
classification (of books in libraries), 9, 58, 64, 75–6, 77
Claudius (Tiberius Claudius Caesar), 247, 249
Claudius Quadrigarius, Quintus, 312, 352, 353
Clearchus, 94
Cleopatra VII, 168, 371, 387
codex, 16, 140, 151, *See also* papyri (as material for ancient books)
Collegium Poetarum, 135
Collegium scribarum histrionumque, 133–4, 406, 407, 415
colophons (of cuneiform documents), 42, 46, 47, 49, 51–2, 53
commentaries, 7, 8, 32, 37, 40, 43, 46, 157, 158, 160, 175, 176, 177, 179, 180, 181, 182, 237, 243, 246, 292, 301, 322, 323, 353, 354, 364, 376, 390, 392, 411, 414, *See also* scholia
Commodus, Lucius Aurelius, 244, 291, 323
Comum
  Younger Pliny's library at, 8, 270, 274
copying (of ancient books). *See* book production
Cornelius Scipio Aemilianus Africanus, Publius, 125
Cornelius Scipio Africanus, Publius, 133, 357

Cornelius Sulla Felix, Lucius, 215
  library of, 67, 68, 73, 160–6, 189, 213, 215, 371, 386, 388
Cornelius Sulla, Faustus
  library of, 164, 165, 215–16, 232, 233
Crates of Mallos, 109
criticism. *See also* scholarship
  literary, 13, 20, 176
  textual, 31, 37, 92, 177, 178, 181, 186, 369
cultic texts, 28, 32, 126–8, 432
Cumae
  house and library of Cicero, 215, 216, 232
  villa and library of Faustus Sulla. *See* Cornelius Sulla, Faustus
cuneiform tablets (types of), 48–51
  Reš tablets, 53, 177
  Uruk tablets, 53–4

Daily Temple Ritual, 29
Delphi
  library at, 385
Demetrius Laco, 186, 189, 191, 194, 196, 199, 200, 201, *See also* Epicureans
Demetrius of Phalerum, 3, 75, 95, 370
Demosthenes, 92, 93, 179, 254
  On the crown, 93
  On the embassy, 93
dialects, dialectology, 39, 97, 99, 174–5, 176
Didymus (Chalcenterus), 178, 179–81, 182
  On the Aristarchean recension, 178, 180
Digest, 411
Dio Cassius, 12
  Roman History, 165, 170–1, 242, 244, 291, 295, 296
Dio of Prusa (Chrysostom), 264, 378
  Alexandrian Oration, 381, 382
Diocletian, 373
Diodorus of Sicily, 19
  Bibliotheca, 19, 34, 138, 147
Diogenes Laertius
  Lives of the Philosophers, 68, 72, 186, 187
Dionysius of Alexandria. *See* librarians
Dionysius of Halicarnassus
  Roman Antiquities, 19, 137–51
diorthôtes, 72
divination, 31, 34, 37, 43, 74
Djoser, 35, 36
doctors, 14, 33, 44, 50, 60, 90, 303, 304, 305, 306, 307, 354, 365, 366, 390, 392, 398, 406, 407, 408, 409, 410

Domitian, 241, 242, 243, 277, 278, 285, 286, 287, 288, 289, 290, 291, 298, 299, 301, 309, 320, 334, 369
drama, 94
  comedy, 9, 61, 76, 88, 131, 132, 188, 218
  tragedy, 9, 61, 76, 88, 93, 99, 131, 365, 366, 372
Drusus (Claudius Drusus Germanicus), 290, 320, 342, 343, 345
Dyrrachium
  library, 270, 271

education
  as culture (*paideia*), 11, 15, 60, 77, 80, 134, 149, 152, 154, 157, 158, 161, 170, 226, 227, 240, 241, 248, 257, 377–400
  literate, 6, 8, 9, 18, 50, 55, 56, 58, 61, 62, 88, 92, 94, 95, 124, 144, 174, 177, 181, 229, 240, 243, 249, 250, 273, 274, 276, 289, 322, 350, 352, 353, 380, 381, 382
  modern, 5, 402
  philosophical, 8, 63, 72, 73, 74, 75, 166, 187
  secretaries for (*a studiis*), 25, 251, 252, 253, 254, 255, 256, 257, 260
  specialist, 126, 360, 366, 398, 408, 411, 415
ekdosis. *See* publication
Ennius, 132, 135
  Annales, 17, 188, 205
  Iphigenia, 358
Enūma Anu Ellil, 54
Ephesus, 11, 252
  library of Celsus, 6, 28, 116, 141, 263, 268, 270, 271, 272, 273, 290, 328, 366, 372, 386
Epicureanism, 11, 152, 188, 194, 196, 359, 415
Epicureans, 166, 186, 187, 192, 194, 204, 388
Epicurus, 185, 186, 187, 189, 191, 193, 200, 203, 204
  On Nature, 186, 187, 189, 192, 193, 194, 196, 201, 202, 203
Epiphanius, 302
epitomes, 78, 154, 254
Eratosthenes of Byzantium, 65, 171–2, *See also* librarians
Esarhaddon, 35, 43, 44, 46, 47
Euclid, 87
euergetism. *See* benefactors
Euripides, 78, 79, 89, 93, 103, 106, 141, 364, 367, 376
  Heracles Furens, 100
  Medea, 99, 106

Euthydemus, 59–63, 90
excerpts, excerpting, 32, 39, 58, 64, 80, 94, 154, 182, 191, 221, 312, 313, 360
Ezida. *See* temples *and* libraries (as buildings/spaces)

Fabius Pictor, Quintus, 134
Favorinus, 314, 378, 385
festivals
  Egyptian, 29
  in Greek cities, 270
  Roman, 15, 127, 133
Flavians, 237, 250
Flavius, Gnaeus, 128, 129
forgeries, 89, 100, 364–7, 391–4, 400
Forma Urbis Romae (Marble Plan of Rome), 241, 265, 279, 281, 282, 283, 284, 285, 286, 326
Formiae
  Cicero's villa and book collection at, 222, 229, 230, 231
Forum of Augustus (*Forum Augustum*), 289, 320, 340, 343, 344
Forum of Caesar (*Forum Iulium*), 288, 290, 319, 320
Forum of Trajan, 288, 314, 315, 317, 319, 329, 330, 348, *See also* Rome: libraries
Fronto (Cornelius Fronto, Marcus), 237, 243, 322, 350, 351, 353, 356, 358, 362
Fulvius Nobilior, Marcus, 133, 135, 136
Fasti, 407

Galen, 8, 18, 263, 275, 282, 290, 292, 303, 307, 308, 309, 356, 362, 370, 375, 383, 389, 390, 400, 406
  Adversus Iulianum, 380–91, 410
  Anatomical procedures, 297
  Commentary on Hippocrates' Epidemics, 38, 292, 301, 354, 364–9, 376, 390, 392–4
  Commentary on Hippocrates' On the nature of man, 392
  De experientia medica, 127, 391
  Hygiene, 360, 408
  On anatomical procedures, 130, 292
  On antidotes, 391
  On composition of drugs according to kind, 292, 296, 396
  On his (my) own books, 302, 303, 307, 392, 415
  On the affected parts, 390

On the avoidance of grief, 4, 15, 16, 34, 45, 85, 111, 243, 278, 291, 292, 300, 301, 304, 307, 308–9, 311, 323, 329, 335, 354–5, 394–5, 396–7, 435
On the differences of pulses, 304
On the passions and errors of the soul, 359–60
On the usefulness of the parts of the body, 307, 415
Gavius Bassus
  De Origine Vocabulorum, 312
gerginakku, 41, 44, 45, 46, 49, 57
Germanicus (Iulius Caesar Germanicus), 241, 290, 320, 333, 341, 342, 343, 344, 345
Gilgamesh, 10, 49, 53
glutinatores, 224
grammar/grammarians, 8, 17, 61, 65, 67, 73, 74, 109, 173, 174, 175, 176, 177, 179, 214, 217, 240, 246, 249, 299, 303, 351, 352, 353, 354, 371, 372, 397
Great Tebtunis Onomasticon, 32
gymnasia
  book collections in, 15, 192, 212, 302, 332, 381
  Greek, 131, 302, 332, 336, 371, 380, 381
  libraries in. *See* libraries (as buildings/spaces)
  Roman, 15, 212, 267

Hadrian, 238, 243, 244, 251, 252, 253, 254, 255, 256, 258, 259, 260, 268, 272, 273, 275, 330, 331, *See also* Athens, library of Hadrian
Hadrian of Tyre, 237, 238, 244, 255, 258
handbooks, 6, 29, 30–2, 33, 54, 63, 73, 156, 210, 410, 413
Harran, 48, 49, 50, 55
Hecataeus of Abdera
  Aegyptiaca, 372
Herculaneum
  library at. *See* Villa of the Papyri
Herodes Atticus (Claudius Atticus Herodes Tiberius), 356, 358, 378
Herodotus
  Histories, 18, 29, 33, 34, 36, 104, 138
Hesiod, 24, 88, 93, 106, 109, 143
  Theogony, 99
Hipparchus, 65, 171, 172
Hippocrates and Hippocratic corpus, 33
  Epidemics, 76, 301, 353, 354, 364, 366, 392–4, 409

Historia Augusta, 243, 250, 251, 253, 309, 323, 329, 355
historiography, 12, 13, 18–19, 23, 28, 29, 33, 34, 35–6, 79, 93, 94, 97, 100–6, 110, 121, 124, 125, 127, 128, 130, 134, 135, 137–51, 165, 171, 173, 179, 188, 196, 206, 229, 237, 242, 243, 244, 245, 246, 250, 251, 253, 254, 296, 309, 317, 318, 319, 323, 329, 355, 360, 372, 384, *See also* narrative literature
Homer, 8, 9, 11, 24, 29, 32, 60, 63, 65, 76, 86, 88, 90, 93, 97, 98, 99, 100, 103, 109, 141, 143, 147, 173, 174, 175, 176, 178, 179, 180, 181, 312, 339, 354, 368
  Iliad, 374
Horace (Horatius Flaccus), 135, 144, 265, 310, 344
  Letter to Augustus, 15
Hortalus, Marcus, 341, 344
Hortensius, Quintus, 241, 320, 341
House of Life, 26, 33, 48
Huzirina
  cuneiform tablet collection at, 48–50
Hyginus, Gaius Iulius. *See* librarians

Imhotep, 10, 35, 36
Inaros, 35
inscriptions, 124, 135, 265, 317, 327
  cuneiform, 44
  dedicatory, 121, 264
  hieroglyphic, 32
  honorific, 33, 35, 173, 247, 248, 250, 251, 253, 254, 256, 257, 258
  in or about libraries, 4, 58, 134, 142, 250, 270, 273, 274, 308, 312, 314, 333, 334, 335, 336, 345, 409, 410
  monumental, 24, 32, 101, 130, 255, 268, 269, 272, 326, 385
  sepulchral, 248
  votive, 409
Isidore of Seville
  Etymologies, 1, 2–4, 7, 9, 11, 12, 20, 78, 125, 160
Isocrates, 89, 92, 93, 94, 254
  Ad Nicoclem, 91
  Aegineticus, 88
  Antidosis, 92, 93
  Busiris, 93
  Panathenaicus, 94
Iulius Africanus, Sextus. *See* librarians
Iulius Pappus, Tiberius. *See* librarians
Iulius Vestinus, Lucius. *See* librarians
Iulius Zoilus, Gaius, 248

Josephus, Flavius, 3, 372
  Jewish Antiquities, 13
  Jewish War, 12, 327
jurists, 14, 411

knowledge
  organisation of, 1, 17–20, 57, 61–3, 75–8, 105–6, 108, 137–51, 181–2, 313–14, 377, 416–17
  transmission of, 1, 16–20, 40, 57, 61–3, 66–75, 85, 108, 109, 181–2, 359–63, 364–76, 389–400

Larensis, 64, 78, 79, 80, 400
Latin
  books in libraries, 188, 196, 197, 213, 214, 218, 239, 240, 242, 247, 252, 259, 261, 286, 289, 297, 304, 316, 317, 320, 332, 333–6, 338, 342, 372
  language and literature, 1, 3, 4, 6, 9, 10, 11, 12, 13, 15, 16, 109, 124, 129, 130, 131–6, 154, 155, 174, 175, 243, 244, 328
  texts in libraries, 9
law, 408, 413, 415–16
  Jewish, 2, 302
  Roman, 128, 129, 134, 135, 257, 258, 314, 315, 316, 318, 320, 355, 410–12
laws
  of Greek cities, 85, 257, 258, 272, 364
Leandrius of Miletus
  Milesiaca, 101
Letter to Philocrates, 370, 372
lexicography, 32, 37, 179, 254, 323
librarians (*procuratores a bibliothecis/bibliothecarum, bibliothecarii, librarioli*), 173–4
  Aelius Largus, Titus, 248, 258
  Annius Postumus, 250–1
  Apollonius of Rhodes, 96
  Dionysius, 224, 225
  Dionysius of Alexandria, 250, 251, 252, 254, 260, 301
  Eratosthenes of Byzantium, 96, 171–2
  Eudaemon, 252–3, 255, 257, 260
  Hyginus, Gaius Iulius, 240, 246, 247, 249, 260
  Iulius Africanus, Sextus, 258–9
  Iulius Pappus, Tiberius, 247–8
  Iulius Vestinus, Lucius, 255, 257, 260, 456
  Maecenas Melissus, Gaius, 240, 242, 247, 260
  Menophilus, 224, 225
  Onesander of Paphos, 173
  Pompeius Macer, Gnaeus(?), 189, 240, 241, 242, 245–6, 247, 248, 260
  Scirtus, Tiberius Claudius, 248–9, 260
  Sextus, 250
  Suetonius Tranquillus, Gaius, 250, 251–2, 255, 257, 260
  Varro, Marcus Terentius, 2, 5, 80, 141, 234, 238, 239, 316–17
    De bibliothecis, 2, 16, 125
  Volusius Maecianus, Lucius, 238, 255–8, 260
  Zenodotus of Ephesus, 173
libraries
  as buildings/spaces
    architecture and decoration of, 6, 23, 25, 27, 28, 40, 47–8, 57, 58, 109–23, 239, 241, 261–71, 277, 346, 350, 380, 404
    location of, 26, 27, 48, 50, 64, 79, 80, 94, 116, 117, 119, 120, 121, 122, 123, 130, 169, 195, 228, 262, 263, 277, 346, 370, 373, 400, 407, 408, 412
    organisation of (*syntaxis*), 75–6, 79, 126, 189, 238, 293, 307, 316, 333, 338, 346, 370, 375, 399, 402, 403, 408, 410, 411, *See also* classification (of books in libraries)
  by period/culture, 85, 118
    Assyrian and Babylonian (cuneiform), 38–57
    Classical Greek, 59–63, 66–76, 85–95
    Egyptian, 10, 23–37
    Hellenistic, 63–6, 74–8, 167–82, 369–76
    Macedonian, 124–6
    medieval, 16, 17, 374
    modern, 19, 57, 76, 374, 375, 376, 401–5
    Roman, 78–81
    Roman imperial, 141–4, 183, 235, 369, 377–400
    Roman Republican, 124–36, 152–66, 209–34
  by type/function
    digital, 57
    private, 183, 209–34
    public, 120, 363
    special/specialist, 416–17
  definition of, 1, 5–9, 40–1, 57–62
  individual. *See* under place names, e.g. Alexandria, Rome, Timgad, etc.
library science, 416–17
libri lintei, 130, 329, 355
Licinius Crassus, Lucius, 164, 165, 210, 240

General index

Licinius Lucullus, Lucius, 164, 215
    library of, 3, 6, 19, 141, 157–60, 163, 166, 213, 221, 232, 240, 266, 356–7, 387–9
Licinius Murena, Lucius, 215
linen (as material for ancient books), 10
Livius Andronicus, Lucius, 130, 131, 132, 133, 134, 352
Livy (Titus Livius), 291, 339, 377
    Ab Urbe Condita, 127–8, 129, 133, 134, 139, 140, 141, 142, 145, 315
Longinus (pseudo-)
    On the Sublime, 144
Lucian of Samosata, 154
    Adversus Indoctum, 170, 296, 358, 379
Lucretius
    De Rerum Natura, 152, 154, 155, 166
Lyceum, 90, 94, 161, 169, 368, 381
Lycurgus, 364, 365, 372

Macedonian wars, 132, 135
Maecenas Melissus, Gaius. *See* librarians
magical literature, 25, 30
Manetho, 12, 372
    Aigyptiaka, 34
manuals. *See* handbooks
manuscripts, 16, 18, 40, 49, 50, 52, 74, 86, 178, 180, 183, 191–4, 206, 253, 254, 296, 303, 311, 328, 352, 354, 365, 367, 374, 375, 390, 393, 398, 405, 413, 438, *See also* book production
Marcus Atilius, 127
Marcus Aurelius, 312, 322, 350, 351, 353, 362
marginal notes of ancient books, 178, 190, 191–2, 196, 198, 199, 200, 201, 202, 204, 366, *See also* scholia
Martial (Marcus Valerius Martialis), 135, 244, 250, 303, 379
medicine/medical texts, 19, 20, 25, 28, 33, 37, 43, 46, 49, 53, 55, 56, 60, 62, 134, 275, 302, 304, 305, 306, 307, 328–9, 365, 366–7, 359, 365, 369, 383, 390, 391, 396, 398, 406, 407, 408–10, 412, *See also* doctors *and* scientific literature
memory/memorisation, 40, 45, 57, 62, 65, 69, 92, 130, 148, 269, 270, 285, 312, 322, 341, 343, 386, 391
Menander Rhetor, 380–2
meta-scholarship, 177–82
Metrodorus of Lampsacus, 184, 186, 187, 190, 194, 203, 205
Mithridates
    library of, 328

Mithridatic wars, 138, 174, 212, 240, 245
Mnemon of Side, 366, 367, 392, 393, 394, 398
mouseia (of Greek cities), 380–2
mythography
    Egyptian, 29, 30–1
    Greek, 96–108, 173, 336
    in cuneiform libraries, 40, 43

Nabû, 42, 44, 45, 47
Nabû-zuqup-kena, 46
narrative literature, 28, 31, 34–6, 99, 172, 336
Neleus of Scepsis, 66, 68, 69, 70, 71, 72, 73, 78, 79, 80, 371
Nero, 243, 249
networks
    of scholars, 19, 24, 189, 304, 307, 370
    social (of elite intellectuals), 19, 157–66, 361–3
Nicolaus of Damascus
    Universal History, 138, 140, 141
Nineveh, 39, 41, 42, 46, 47, 48, 50, 55
    Assurbanipal's library, 38, 41–5, 55
Numisianus, 366

Octavian. *See* Augustus
Octavius, Marcus, 192–3, 196, 201, 203
Offering Ritual, 29
oikemata, 293, *See also* *apothekai*
On the dialect of the Romans, 175
Onesander of Paphos. *See* librarians
opisthographs, 139, 190
ordo scribarum, 128
organisation (of libraries. *See* classification (of books in libraries)
Orosius
    History against the pagans, 130, 171
Ovid
    Fasti, 317
Ovid (Ovidius Naso), 15, 143, 246, 261, 265, 320, 322, 329
    Letters from Pontus, 245–6

paideia. *See* education
Papirius Paetus, Lucius, 217, 233
papyri (as testimonies for ancient libraries), 4, 142, 143
papyrus (as material for ancient books), 2, 10, 13, 16, 24, 25, 27, 28, 29, 32, 33, 35, 39, 61, 70, 71, 85, 87, 88, 90, 140, 141, 143, 151, 159, 173, 183, 224, 299, 303, 310, 333, 336, 338, 345, 371, 393, 407

parchment (as material for ancient books), 2, 10, 109, 159, 224, 371
Patrae
  library at, 352
Pausanias
  Description of Greece, 272, 380
pegmata, 225
pepaideumenoi. See education
Pergamum, 2, 79, 111–18, 174, 301, 367, 392
  Asklepieion, 331, 410
  library of Pergamon, 14, 67, 70, 72, 73, 77, 78, 80, 123, 126, 130, 169, 240, 307, 330, 332, 339, 370, 371, 372, 373, 374, 387, 412
Peripatos, 76, 81, 86, 152–66, 278, 323, 353, 370, 391
Petese Stories, 36, *See also* narrative literature
Pherecydes, 104, 105, 106, 147
Philodemus, 11, 141, 154, 155, 156, 166, 185, 187, 188, 189, 191, 192, 193, 196, 359, 415
Philostratus, 244
Philoxenus of Alexandria, 174, 175, 176
Photius
  Bibliotheca, 17, 94
Pindar, 103, 141, 176, 179
  Paeans, 100
  Pythian 4, 99, 106
Pisistratus, 2, 3, 10, 78, 79, 80, 368
Plato, 36, 37, 89, 90, 93, 143, 230, 354, 383, 389, 391
  Critias, 86
  Euthydemus, 194, 198
  Ion, 100
  Laws, 91
  Lysis, 194, 198
  Phaedrus, 400
  Theaetetus, 87
Plato (pseudo-)
  7th Letter, 230
Pliny the Elder (Plinius Secundus, Gaius)
  Natural History, 1, 9, 20, 142, 261, 290, 308, 317, 327, 334–6, 339–40, 345, 409
Pliny the Younger (Plinius Caecilius Secundus, Gaius)
  Letters, 4, 8, 140, 251, 270, 274, 340, 381
Plutarch of Chaeronea, 8, 12, 153, 383–9, 398, 399, 400
  Against Colotes, 388–9
  Life of Aemilius Paullus, 124, 128, 132

Life of Alcibiades, 88
Life of Caesar, 169
Life of Demosthenes, 143, 384
Life of Lucullus, 158, 266, 356, 387–9
Life of Sulla, 73, 74, 155, 161, 162, 165
On Isis and Osiris, 12
On the Delphic E, 384
On Tranquillity of Mind, 383, 386
Table Talks, 381
poetry, 60, 61, 85, 88, 91, 92, 94, 181, 354
  Archaic Greek, 28, 80, 99, 143
  Classical Greek, 99, 374
  Egyptian, 26
  Hellenistic, 96–108, 138, 143, 176, 177, 181, 291, 319
  Latin, 15, 135, 140, 196, 307, 360
  Middle Eastern, 10, 49, 51, 53
Polemo, Marcus Antonius, 254, 255
Polybius of Megalopolis, 18
  Histories, 124, 125, 135, 138
Pompeius Macer, Gnaeus (?). See librarians
Pompeius Theophanes, Gnaeus, 245
Pompey (Pompeius Magnus, Sextus), 164, 168, 230, 234, 240, 245, 328, 373
Porticus Metelli, 242
Porticus Octaviae
  library. See Rome: libraries
Postumius Albinus, Aulus, 135
Praefectura Urbi, 281, 326
praeiudicia, 411
priests, 7
  Babylonian, 40, 43, 49, 50, 52, 54, 55
  Chaldaean, 372
  Egyptian, 12, 25, 28, 29, 30, 31, 34, 37, 372
  Greek, 173, 273
  Jewish, 3
  of the Alexandrian Museum, 63, 172, 253, 254
  Roman, 126, 127, 131, 136, 251, 270, 406
    augurs, 128, 130, 135, 234, 315
    pontifices, 127–8, 129, 130, 135, 256, 411
  Syro-Anatolian
    augurs, 44
Proclus of Naucratis, 382
Procopius, 327
procurator a bibliothecis. See librarians
Psammetichus I, 24
Ptolemy I (Soter), 23, 25, 95, 173, 174, 370
Ptolemy II (Philadelphus), 3, 23, 64, 75, 77, 78, 79, 80, 302, 368, 370, 371, 372
Ptolemy III (Euergetes), 364, 365, 366, 371, 376, 393

Ptolemy IV (Philopator), 64
Ptolemy V (Epiphanes), 374
Ptolemy IX, 173
Ptolemy XIII, 168, 169
Public Libraries Movement, 402
publicatio/publicare (of a library), 261–5, 314, 318
publication (dissemination), 61, 67, 71, 72, 85, 92, 94, 128, 129, 138, 139–48, 162, 179, 217, 246, 292, 306, 307, 317, 328, 331, 360, 361, 392, 397, 398, 412, 413
Punic wars, 132, 133, 134, 145
Pyramid Texts, 25
Pyrrhic wars, 132

Quintius Flaminius, Titus, 135
Qumran community
  library of (Dead Sea scrolls), 11
quoting/quotations, 36, 44, 45, 78, 80, 92–4, 146, 147, 179, 180, 181, 182, 192, 204, 289, 312, 313, 315, 328, 351, 352, 388, *See also* excerpts, excerpting
Qurdi-Nergal, 49, 50

readers
  as users of ancient libraries, 7, 8, 20, 46, 57, 58, 80, 102, 103, 107, 136, 237, 241, 262, 263, 264, 267, 268, 269, 272, 276, 312–14, 322, 323, 341, 347–63, 382, 399
  modern, 87
  of ancient books, 10, 61–2, 72, 74, 81, 85, 99, 100, 101, 102, 103, 104, 105, 106, 107, 108, 226, 304, 307, 383, 387, 399, 400, 411, *See also* reading communities
reading communities, 12–13, 347–63
recitation, 40, 60, 63, 93, 137, 242, 265, 274, 276, 363
Regia, 130
Reš
  cuneiform library at, 50–4, 55, 56
rituals
  Babylonian, 40, 43, 45, 46, 47, 49, 52, 53, 54, 55, 56
  Egyptian, 29–31
  Greek, 97, 102, 103, 107
  Roman, 126–9, 280
Rome, 11
  imperial, 2, 6, 16, 18, 19, 51, 66, 67, 79, 80, 119, 137–51, 235, 369, 377–400
  libraries, 2, 3, 16, 18, 19, 28, 66, 67, 68, 73, 74, 75, 80, 119, 124–36, 137–51, 263, 267, 307, 308

Athenaeum, 244
  in the *Atrium Libertatis*, 238–9, 241, 266, 267, 275, 314, 320, 327, 329, 331
  in the *domus Tiberiana*, 243, 278, 295, 296, 297, 298, 335, 353
  in the palace of Tiberius, 297
  in the *Porticus Octaviae*, 241, 242, 266, 277, 296, 329
  in the *Templum Pacis*, 242–3, 275, 277, 278–85, 286–91, 293, 296, 297, 301, 302, 303, 304, 306, 312, 314, 323–9, 351, 353, 354, 367
  in Trajan's forum, 6, 243, 275, 313–14, 329, 330, 337, 347, 385; Ulpian library, 6, 7, 243, 250, 329, 355
  in Trajan's temple, 312, 314, 353
  library of Larensis, 78, 81
  library of Sulla. *See* Cornelius Sulla Felix, Lucius, library of
  of Tiberius, 320–2
  on the Palatine, 7, 240, 267, 296, 309, 330, 333–46, 354, 396; library of Apollo, 239–40, 241–2, 277, 286–91, 296, 297, 309, 314, 320–2, 329, 330
  Republican, 3, 5, 6, 8, 19, 58, 67, 68, 73, 74, 75, 80, 124–36

Sallust (Sallustius Crispus, Gaius), 147
  Bellum Iugurthinum, 163–4
sanctuaries. *See* temples
Satrap Stela, 25
scholars
  Assyrian and Babylonian, 42, 44, 45, 46, 47, 51–2, 55–6
  attached to libraries, 2–4, 6–7, 20, 58, 64, 76, 96–108, 109, 117, 119, 120, 167–8, 171–82, 240, 242, 246–7, 249–50, 251–2, 253–5, 260, 363, 369, 374, 375
  attached to royal courts, 14, 46, 47
  Christian, 16
  Hellenistic, 3, 18, 23, 31, 64, 65, 71, 76, 78, 79, 96–108, 167–8, 171–82, 369, 370, 374, 375
  Jewish, 3, 370
  Medieval, 16, 17, 94
  of the Classical era, 24, 37, 69, 70
  Roman, 19, 73, 74, 78, 80, 141, 148, 149, 161, 167–8, 171–82, 189, 214, 215, 218, 240, 241, 242, 246–7, 249–50, 251–2, 253–5, 260, 266, 267, 274, 301, 302, 304, 307, 354, 355, 387

scholarship, 1, 5, 7, 8, 10, 16, 18, 32, 37, 38–57, 65, 66, 73, 76, 77, 79, 80, 90, 94, 96, 124, 138, 147, 148, 312, 327, 374, 381, 411
scholia, 101, 103, 104, 105, 106, 178, 191, 202, 331, 344
science/scientific literature, 8, 17, 19, 20, 23, 24, 26, 28, 33–4, 37, 68, 72, 79, 134, 154, 313, 327, 377, 390, 391, 396, 397, 398
Scirtus, Tiberius Claudius. *See* librarians
scribes, 2, 7, 10, 26, 31, 32, 39, 43, 44, 46, 49, 50, 54, 73, 74, 186, 189, 190, 192, 193, 194, 195, 196, 197, 198, 199, 200, 201, 202, 203, 204, 205, 206, *See also* book production
scriptio continua, 61
scripts, variety of used in ancient documents, 10, 11, 28, 121, 133, 196, 200, 205, 206, 335, 394
  alphabetic, 10, 39
  Babylonian, 43, 46
  cuneiform, 39
  demotic, 10, 28, 30, 32, 33
  hieratic, 10, 28, 30, 32
  hieroglyphic, 10, 28, 30, 31, 32
Second Sophistic, 31, 137, 138, 147, 150, 274, 400
Septimius Severus, Lucius, 30, 282, 323
Septuagint, 3, 11, 12, 13, 65, 370, 372
Serenus Sammonicus, 185
Servius Claudius, 217–19, 228, 232
Severan dynasty and era, 279
Severus Alexander (Aurelius Severus Alexander, Marcus), 259
Sextus. *See* librarians
shrines. *See* temples
Sibylline Books, 265, 322
Sin-leqi-unninni, 52, 53, 55
Sinnius Capito, 303, 304, 312, 351
Socrates, 60, 61, 62, 63, 87, 90, 91, 92
Solon, 86, 93
sophists
  imperial, 6, 11, 237, 250, 254, 255, 378, 381, 382, 400
  of the Classical era, 60, 61, 62, 63
Sophocles, 93, 106, 147, 364, 367, 376
Special Libraries Movement, 404
SS. Cosma e Damiano, basilica and monastery, 277, 278, 279, 282, 284, 304, 323, 324
Statius
  Silvae, 285

statues in libraries, 47, 110, 113, 114, 116, 117, 118, 119, 120–1, 135, 239, 241, 264, 268, 269, 270, 273, 280, 284, 285, 290, 291, 327, 328, 330, 331, 336, 337, 338, 342, 343, 344, 356, 378, 380, 385, *See also* libraries: as buildings/spaces: architecture and decoration of
Strabo
  Geography, 37, 66–76, 79, 90, 104, 109, 119, 138, 153, 155, 161–3, 169, 171–2, 245, 303, 310, 370, 409
Strato of Lampsachus, 69, 75
Suda lexicon, 76, 77, 173–4, 175, 176, 177, 179, 215, 249, 254
Suetonius Tranquillus, Gaius. *See also* librarians
  De viris illustribus, 246, 247, 261, 290, 316, 344, 369
Sulpicius Apollinaris, Gaius, 243, 322, 353
Sulpicius Gallus, Gaius, 135
Sumerian, language and literature, 39, 44, 45

tabellae publicae, 315–16
tablets
  cuneiform, 10, 38–57
  pinakes in healing sanctuaries, 408–10
  Roman legal, 410–12
  Roman, for writing, 130
tabula dealbata, 130
Tabula Hebana, 320, 322, 342
Tabula Siarensis, 321, 343
Tabulae Publicae, 288, 321
tabularium, 130, 239
Tacitus
  Annales, 341, 342
  Dialogus, 378–9
  Histories, 13
Tašmetu, 45, 47
Tebtunis, 11
  temple library of, 10, 26–36
temples
  Babylonian
    Eanna, 51, 52
    Ezida, 45–8
    Reš, 38–54
  Egyptian
    of Heliopolis, 29, 36
    of Sais, 33
    of Seti I at Abydos, 29, 31, 33
    of Tebtunis, 10, 11, 26–9, 35
  Greek
    at Delphi, 265, 335, 336, 345, 385, 386, 388

Roman
    of Apollo on the Palatine, 239, 241, 259, 265, 277, 286, 289, 290, 291, 320–2, 329, 342, 344, 351, 371
    of Augustus (*templum divi Augusti*), 242, 248, 262, 289, 290
    of Castor and Pollux, 290
    of Ceres, 129
    of Hercules Musarum, 135
    of Juno Moneta, 130
    of Jupiter Capitolinus, 129
    of Minerva on the Aventine, 133, 134, 136
    Templum Pacis, 242, 259, 275, 277, 278–309, 312, 323–9, 351, 353, 354, 367, 378, 395, 396
Terence (Terentius Afer, Publius), 132, 133
Theocritus, 174, 177
Theodosian Code, 410
Theon of Alexandria, 177
Theophrastus of Eresus, 3, 76, 78, 79, 80, 90, 95, 155, 160, 164, 371, 391
    Characters, 155
Thucydides
    Histories, 18, 102, 148, 254
Tiberius, 242, 243, 245, 247, 248, 259, 290, 291, 310, 320, 330, 341, 342, 343, 345
Tibur
    library at, 353, 378
Timaeus of Tauromenium
    History, 18, 102, 104, 125, 134, 138
Timgad
    library of Rogatianus, 28, 263, 271–2, 273
Tiro, 216
Trajan, 6, 7, 249, 250, 251, 252, 268, 269, 270, 273, 276, 279, 284, 288, 290, 330
Treaty of Misenum, 233, 234
Tryphon of Alexandria, 176
Tullius Cicero, Marcus, 19, 74, 128, 135, 144, 154, 156, 164–6, 179, 189, 196, 209–33, 266, 312, 318, 338, 357, 379, 387
    Academica, 389
    De finibus, 157–60, 356–7
    De natura deorum, 154

Tullius Cicero, Marcus (2) [son of Cicero], 215, 231, 233
Tullius Cicero, Quintus, 215, 231, 233
Tusculum
    Cicero's villa and library at, 210, 211, 212, 216, 218, 222, 223, 224, 225, 227, 228, 232, 233, 356
    villa and library of Marcus Lucullus, 157, 166, 221, 266
Twelve Tablets, 410

Uruk. See Reš, cuneiform library at

Varro, Marcus Terentius, 2, 3, 9, 128, 139, 239, 289, 312, 326, 339, *See also* librarians,
    De lingua latina, 219, 289
    Hebdomades, 317
Vespasian, 242, 249, 277, 279, 280, 283, 285, 289, 301, 302, 323, 328
Via Sacra, 279, 280, 283, 290, 308, 316, *See also apothekai*,
    storerooms for books at, 277, 278, 292, 293, 296, 297, 299, 300, 328, 396
Vicus Sandaliarius, 303
Villa of the Papyri, 323
    book collection, 6, 11, 17, 141, 183–206, 264, 266, 300, 415
Vipsanius Agrippa, Marcus, 261, 272
Virgil, 246, 291, 339, 340, 377
    Aeneid, 16, 242, 352
Vitruvius Pol(l)io
    De architectura, 2, 6, 65, 266, 272
Volusius Maecianus, Lucius. *See* librarians

Xenophon, 93, 104, 147
    Cyropaideia, 93
    Memorabilia, 59–63, 90–1, 92

Zeno of Sidon, 186, 187, 204, *See also* Epicureans
Zenodotus of Ephesus, 76, 98, 173
Zeuxis, 365, 366
Zoilus (Gaius Iulius Zoilus?), 247

Index locorum

AE 1960, no. 26
    247–8
Aelius Aristides
  Orationes
    1.354 272,
      379–80
    18.6 380
    26.97 380
Alcidamas
  Contra sophistas
    4 91
Alexis
  Linos
    Fr. 140 K.-A 88
Ammianus Marcellinus
  Res Gestae
    14.6.28 379
    26.16.13 373
Aphthonius
  Progymnasmata
    12 302
Apollonius of Rhodes
  Argonautica
    1.23–7 103
    1.238 103
    1.648–9 105
    1.919–21 105
    1.941 103
    1.1220 105
    4.247–52 105
    4.282–93 106
    4.452–81 106
    4.1381–92 104–5
  Scholia on the *Argonautica*
    1.23–25a 104
    1.238 104
    1.648–9 105
    1.919–21 105
    1.1220 105
    4.303–6b 106
Apuleius
  Florida
    18 274

Aristophanes
  Ranae
    943 89
    1409 89
Aristotle
  Topica
    105b 91
Athenaeus
  Deipnosophistae
    1.3a–b 78–81
    4.139c 179
    5.187d 388
    5.203e 63, 64, 169–70, 373
    14.648c 389
Aulus Gellius
  Noctes Atticae
    1.2 358
    2.3.5 352
    5.21 312–13, 351, 378
    7.17 2, 373
    9.14.1 352
    11.17.1 243, 250, 312, 353
    13.20.1 243, 274, 322, 353
    13.25.2 312, 314
    14.3.3 93–4
    16.8.1–4 288–9, 353
    16.8.2 242–3, 323
    16.8.6 289
    17.16.1–4 328
    18.9.5 352
    19.5.4 353
    19.10 358
    19.14.3 353
Aurelius Victor
  De Caesaribus
    14.1.3 243–4

Callimachus
  Aetia
    Fr. 6 102
    Fr. 7.13–14 100
    Fr. 8 106
    Fr. 9 106

Fr. 24–5   105
Fr. 43.28–83   102
Fr. 54–60j [*Victoria Berenices*]
    100
Fr. 64   100
Fr. 67.1–14   97–8
Fr. 75.53–77   101
Fr. 92.2–3   101
Fr. 103   101
Fr. 110 [*Coma Berenices*]   100
SH 264.1 [*Victoria Berenices*]   102–3,
    105
Scholia Florentina
    30–5 (Pfeiffer 1, p.13)
    101–2
Cicero
  Ad Atticum
    1.4.3   210
    1.7   209, 210, 212
    1.10.4   209, 210
    1.11.3   209–10
    1.20.7   217–18
    2.1.12   218
    2.6.1   222
    4.4a.1, 2   222–4
    4.10   164–6
    4.10.1   215–16
  Ad familiares
    9.16.4   218
  Ad Quintum fratrem
    2.5.1   223
    3.4.5   213–14
  De finibus
    3.2.7–10   356–7
    3.7   157–8
    3.10   157, 160
  De legibus
    3.20.36   318
CIG
    3148   255
    5900   253–4
CIL
    3.431   252
    3.607   270–1
    8.20684   250–1
    10.1739   248–9
    10.7580   258
    14.2916   258
    14.5348   256
Cornelius Nepos
  Atticus
    2.4–5   213
    13.3   162–3

Dio Cassius
  Historia Romana
    40.50.2–3   165
    42.38   170
    53.1.3   296
    66.24.2   242
    73.17.4   244
Dio Chrysostom
  Orationes
    32.100   381
    37   274, 378
Diogenes Laertius
  Vitae philosophorum
    5. 51–7   68–9, 72
    10.27–8   186–7
Dionysius of Halicarnassus
  Antiquitates Romanae
    1.2   145
    1.5.1–2   146
    1.6.5   148
    1.8.3   148
    1.11.1   147
    1.13.1   147
    1.75.5   361
    1.90.2   146
    2.1–2   146
    7.66   150
    7.70.2   145–6
    14.5–6   150

Epiphanius of Salamis
  De mensuris et ponderibus
    11   302
Epistula ad Philocratem (Letter of Aristeas)   3,
    65, 370–2
    9   372
    10   372
Eunapius
  Vitae sophistarum
    456b   381

FgrH
    3 F 32   106
Fronto
  Epistulae ad Marcum Caesarem et invicem
    4.5   237–8, 243, 291, 322, 350–1

Galen
  Adversus Iulianum
    18A.247 K   390–1
    18A.260 K   391
  De alimentorum facultatibus
    6.480 K   397

Galen (*cont.*)
De anatomicis administrationibus
   2.216 K   395
   2.223–4 K   397
   11.12   291–2
De animi affectuum dignotione et curatione
   5.48 K   394
   5.48–50 K   359–60
De antidotis
   14.31 K   391
   14.66 K   395
De compositione medicamentorum per genera
   12.894 K   397
   13.362 K   296, 328
   13.362–3 K   396
   13.604–5 K   397
De diebus decretoriis
   9.794 K   389
De experientia medica
   7.1 = Deichgräber pp 102.18–104.20, 391
De indolentia
   8   293–4
   12   396
   12b   297
   13   303, 307, 354–5
   15   303, 307
   18   394, 396
   18–19   293, 295–300
   19   395
De libris propriis
   19.19 K   328, 395
   19.21 K   306
   19.21–2 K   275, 302, 304–6, 390
   19.33 K   397
   19.41 K   395
De locis affectis
   8.144 K   389
   8.148 K   389, 390, 398
De marcore
   7.690 K   397
De methodo medendi
   10.30–2 K   397
   10.457–8 K   397
De optima corporis constitutione
   4.738–9 K   397
De ordine librorum propriorum
   19.50–2 K   397
De pulsuum differentiis
   8.493–4 K   389, 397
   8.495 K   304
De sanitate tuenda
   6.347–8 K   360

De simplicium medicamentorum temperamentis ac facultatibus
   11.796–7 K   397
De tumoribus praeter naturam
   7.716 K   397
In Hippocratis De humoribus
   16.2–3 K   390
In Hippocratis De natura hominis commentaria
   15.24 K   395
   15.105 K   367, 392
In Hippocratis De officina medici commentariorum
   18B.630–1 K   390
   18B.778–9 K   390
In Hippocratis Epidemiarum lib. III commentaria
   17A.600–8 K   364–9, 392–6
In Hippocratis Epidemiarum lib. VI commentaria
   17B.194–5 K   301, 353–4, 390, 396
In Hippocratis Prognosticum commentarii
   18B.267 K   397
Granius Licinianus
   28.35–6   316

Hipparchus
   II.1.5 C 69   65
Horace
  Epistulae
   2.1.214   265
   2.2.92–105   265
  Scholia ad epistulam 1.3.17 (ps.-Acron)
   344

IGR
   3.107   252
Isidore of Seville
  Etymologiae
   6.1–7   1–4
   6.5   125–6, 160, 261, 317
Isocrates
  Ad Nicoclem
   41   91
   44   91
  Aegineticus
   5   88–9
  Busiris
   1   93
  Epistulae
   7   94–5
IvE
   5113   270

Josephus
  Antiquitates Judaicae
    12.2.1   372
  Bellum Judaicum
    7.5.7   327–8
Juvenal
  Saturae
    9.22–6   327

Livius Andronicus
  Fr. 30 (*Odyssea*)   130
Livy
  Ab urbe condita
    1.20.5–6   127
    9.46.5   128, 129
    25.1.12   127–8
    27.37.7   133–4
    43.16.13   315–16
Lucian
  Adversus indoctum
    5   296

Martial
  Epigrammata
    1.2.8   303
    5.5   250
    12.*Praef.*   379
Menander Rhetor
  2.392.15–18   381
  2.396.26–30   381
  2.426.26–31   381
  2.431.3–7   380

Orosius
  Adversus paganos
    5.18.27   130
Ovid
  Ex Ponto
    2.10.21–2   245–6
  Fasti
    4.623–4   317
  Tristia
    3.1.62–3   261, 265
    3.1.71–2   317–18, 329–30, 361
    3.15.5   361

Palatine Anthology
  15.23 (*Altar of Besantinus*)   254–5
Pausanias
  Descriptio Graeciae
    1.18.9   217, 380
    6.23.7   382
    10.4.1   380

Philostratus
  Vitae Apollonii
    8.20   238
  Vitae sophistarum
    589–90   244
    604   382
Philoxenus
  On the dialect of the Romans
    Fr. 323 Theodorides   175
    Fr. 328 Theodorides   175
Photius
  Bibliotheca
    224, 222b. 25–7   94
Plato
  Critias
    113b   86–7
  Leges
    811a   91
  Theaetetus
    142a–143c   87
Pliny the Elder
  Historia naturalis
    Praef. 17   308
    7.115   261, 316, 339
    7.210   334–6
    13.68–70   2
    29.2.4   409
    35.2.9–10   290–1
    35.6–10   339–40
    35.10   261
    36.33–4   317
    37.27   327
Pliny the Younger
  Epistulae
    1.4   274
    1.8   4, 8, 270, 360
    1.9.4–6   381
    2.17.8   228
    3.2   142
    3.5.17   360
    3.7.8   340
    9.11.2   142
    10.66   7
Plutarch
  Adversus Colotem
    1107E   388–9
  Aemilius Paullus
    3.2   128
    28.7   124
    28.11   388
  Caesar
    49.5–8   387
    49.6–7   169

Plutarch (*cont.*)
  Cicero
    27.6   165
  Demosthenes
    2.1   384
    2.2   384
  Lucullus
    42   266
    42.1   356
    42.1–4   387–9
    42.2   356
  De E apud Delphos
    384E   384
  De tranquillitate animi
    464F   383
    470C   386
  Quaestiones convivales
    675B   383
    705E   381
    718C   383
  Regum et imperatorum apophthegmata (Cicero)
    13.205C   165
Polybius
  Historiae
    3.26   129
    12.25d.1   138
    12.27.4   124–5
    39.1   109
POxy.
  10.1241   173
Procopius
  Bellum Gothicum
    4.21   327

Sallust
  Bellum Iugurthinum
    95   163–4
  Scholia in Homeri Iiadem
    1.423–4   180–1
    10.397–9a   180
    16.467c   181
Scriptores Historiae Augustae
  Divus Aurelianus
    1.5–10   355
    1.7–10   329
  Gordiani tres
    18.2–3   308
  Hadrianus
    11.3   251

  Tyranni triginta
    31.7–12   307
    31.10   323
Seneca
  De tranquillitate animi
    9.4–5   379
Statius
  Silvae
    4.3.16–17   285
Strabo
  Geographica
    2.1.5   171–2
    8.6.15   409
    13.1.54–5   66–76, 90, 95, 109, 153, 155, 161–2, 189, 213–15, 295, 303, 369–71, 400
    13.2.3.617–18   245
    17.1.8   63–5, 170, 172
Suda lexicon
  Δ 872   179
  Z 74   173–4
  K 227   76–8
  O 835   254
  T 1115   175–6
  Φ 394   174
Suetonius
  Caligula
    34.2   377
  Divus Augustus
    70   344
  Divus Iulius
    44   261, 316–17
    56.7   246
  Domitianus
    20   301

Tabula Hebana   320
  ll.1–4   342
Tabula Siarensis   321
  b.2.20–1   343
  b.2.22–3   343
Tacitus
  Annales
    2.37–8   341
    2.83   341–2
    3.58   128
  Dialogus
    21.6   378–9

Varro
  De lingua Latina
    5.98   128
  Venetus A, gr. 822   178

Vitruvius
- *De architectura*
    - 6.Praef. 4   2
    - 6.5   349–50
    - 6.5.2   266
    - 7. Praef. 4–7   65

Xenophon
- *Memorabilia*
    - 1.6.14   90–1
    - 2.1.21–34   92
    - 4.2   59–63
    - 4.2.8   90

Printed in Great Britain
by Amazon